Adult Development and Aging

Adult Development and Aging

JOHN C. CAVANAUGH

Bowling Green State University

Wadsworth Publishing Company • Belmont, California
A Division of Wadsworth, Inc.

Psychology Editor: Kenneth King
Editorial Assistant: Michelle Palacio
Production Editor: Jerilyn Emori
Managing Designer: Carolyn Deacy
Print Buyer: Randy Hurst
Designer: Wendy Calmenson
Copy Editor: William Waller
Photo Researcher: Stephen Forsling
Cover: Carolyn Deacy
Signing Representative: Art Minsberg

Acknowledgments are listed on page 568.

Cover Art: Robert Bechtle, *French Doors II*, 1966. Courtesy Crocker Art Museum, Sacramento, California. Gift of the Crocker Art Gallery Association.

Printed in the United States of America   34

2 3 4 5 6 7 8 9 10—94 93 92 91 90

Library of Congress Cataloging-in-Publication Data

ISBN 0-534-11640-X

To Bertha, Charles, Alma, and Julia
who were the pioneers I knew
To Barbara and Jack
who are my greatest teachers
To Patrice
who is my soul mate and best friend

C·O·N·T·E·N·T·S

My decision to write this textbook came not during a period of temporary insanity, nor from inspiration during my morning shower, but rather from a growing frustration with trying to find a text that meets multiple needs. The undergraduate course I teach is composed of a mix of students from several disciplines, especially from social sciences and health sciences. Many of these students are headed for occupations in social service agencies, corporations, or health care settings where they will interact with older adults on a daily basis.

The need for students to have an appreciation for the complex, multidisciplinary nature of gerontology is acute. Not only do students need to know the facts, but they also need to know how the facts interrelate and how to apply them. Meeting these student needs are the objectives of this book: (1) to provide a comprehensive account of adult development and aging; (2) to provide solid theoretical and empirical bases that enable students to become educated and critical consumers of gerontological information; (3) to provide a blend of basic and applied research—as well as current topics and controversies—that demonstrates the range and limitations of current knowledge; and (4) to present findings from multiple perspectives to show that adult development and aging is an emergent, vibrant, multidisciplinary field.

Coverage and Organization

Adult Development and Aging covers human development from young adulthood through old age. It is organized topically. Throughout the text, however, there are numerous cross-references to topics in other chapters, emphasizing that adult development and aging does not occur independently in different domains.

Coverage emphasizes psychological development, yet there are separate chapters that discuss health and social factors to provide a broader context. The text is firmly grounded in theory and research. Practical applications are interwoven throughout in order to tie research to everyday life. Several current topics and controversies are included to stimulate students' interest and to generate classroom discussion.

Although *Adult Development and Aging* frequently explores complex issues and difficult topics, key terms are defined when first used. Whenever possible, scientific terminology is used and, where appropriate, is supplemented with everyday usage (for example, cerebrovascular accident and stroke). The book is written for upper-division undergraduate students and should be easily understood by those with a minimal background in psychology.

Instructional Aids

Several instructional aids have been included in *Adult Development and Aging.*

Chapter Glossaries. Technical terms first appear in the text in **boldface** type and are usually defined at that point. These terms also appear in the Glossary at the end of each chapter. Chapter glossaries are included to assist the student in learning concepts and terms in context.

Box Material. Two types of boxes are used in each chapter. "How Do We Know?" boxes highlight a particular research study because of its representativeness or because it raises a particular issue about research design. "Something to Think About" boxes highlight a conceptual issue that could serve as the basis for further classroom or personal discussion.

Additional Readings. Each chapter includes a list of additional readings along with a short description of each. These readings have been selected carefully for readability and relevance to the chapter topic.

Test Bank. A test bank of multiple-choice items is available to assist the instructor in preparing exams. Items cover both factual and conceptual learning; each is marked with the correct answer.

Acknowledgments

No text ever gets far without a great deal of support from many people. I owe a considerable debt to Ken King, senior editor, for his belief in me and his dedication to the project. His comments were always helpful. He is the best editor around. I also would like to thank Jerilyn Emori, production editor, for her patience with a first-timer. Bill Waller did a great editing job and smoothed out the rough spots. The following individuals read all or parts of the manuscript and made numerous valuable suggestions: Fredda Blanchard-Fields, Louisiana State University; Steven W. Cornelius, Cornell University; Andrew C. Coyne, University of Medicine and Dentistry of New Jersey; Joseph M. Fitzgerald, Wayne State University; Charles E. Goldsmith, Mount Mary College; Ruth G. Lyell, San Jose State University; Dana J. Plude, University of Maryland, College Park; Jan Sinnott, Towson State University; Barbara F. Turner, University of Massachusetts, Boston; Nancy White, Youngstown State University; and Barbara W. Yee, University of Texas Medical Branch at Galveston.

Finally, I want to thank my wife Patrice. She put up with my long hours at the computer without complaint and gave me nothing but constant encouragement during the darkest hours when authors start to despair over meeting deadlines. She is truly remarkable.

Adult Development and Aging

Introduction to Adult
Development and Aging

Edward Hopper, *Cape Cod Evening*, 1939. National Gallery of Art, Washington, D.C.

"To be seventy years young is sometimes far more cheerful and hopeful than to be forty years old," wrote Oliver Wendell Holmes. In his day, about 100 years ago, being "seventy years young" was unusual. Since then, industrialized countries have experienced an unprecedented explosion in the number of older adults. Because of technological advances, disease, famine, and childbirth no longer take their high toll before we can reach old age. We are squarely in the midst of a monumental revolution that will have increasingly profound effects on our everyday lives.

This book summarizes what scholars have learned about traversing adulthood and growing old. Reading it gives you an advantage that the current population of older adults did not have: being able to study what growing old will be like. Never before have we had the chance to prepare as well for old age.

This opportunity is provided by scientists in many disciplines who are all interested in a common goal: understanding the aging process. The field of study that examines the aging process is **gerontology**. More formally, gerontology is the study of aging from maturity (young adulthood) through old age, as well as the study of the elderly as a special group. Gerontology is a fairly new scientific discipline, even though old people have been around throughout history. In the United States, for example, researchers conducted only a handful of studies involving older adults before the 1950s (Freeman, 1979). One reason that the study of older adults was so long in coming, as Freeman points out, is that authors and scientists throughout history conceptualized the aging process as one of inevitable, irreversible decline. Consequently, nothing was to be gained by studying aging, since it was already thought to be understood.

We now know that this picture of aging as nothing more than inevitable decline was an oversimplification. Aging involves both growth and decline. Still, many myths concerning old people survive: older adults are often pictured as incompetent, decrepit, and asexual. These myths of aging lead to negative stereotypes of older people, which may result in **ageism**, a form of discrimination against older adults simply because of their age (Butler & Lewis, 1982). This book will rebut these erroneous ideas. But it will not replace myths with idealized views of adulthood and old age. Rather, it will strive to paint an accurate picture of what it means to grow old today, recognizing that development across adulthood brings with it growth and opportunities as well as decline.

How much do you already know about aging? Take a few minutes to answer the questions in Table 1.1. The items provide an overview of the kinds of topics and research we will be encountering throughout this book. After you have read this book, you should be able to come back to this table

TABLE 1.1 · What is your aging IQ?

True or False?

1. Everyone becomes "senile" sooner or later, if he or she lives long enough.

2. American families have, by and large, abandoned their older members.

3. Depression is a serious problem for older people.

4. The numbers of older people are growing.

5. The vast majority of older people are self-sufficient.

6. Mental confusion is an inevitable, incurable consequence of old age.

7. Intelligence declines with age.

8. Sexual urges and activity normally cease around age 55 to 60.

9. If a person has been smoking for 30 or 40 years, it does no good to quit.

10. Older people should stop exercising, and rest.

11. As you grow older, you need more vitamins and minerals to stay healthy.

12. Only children need to be concerned about calcium for strong bones and teeth.

13. Extremes of heat and cold can be particularly dangerous to older people.

14. Many older people are hurt in accidents that could have been prevented.

15. More men than women survive to old age.

16. Deaths from stroke and heart disease are declining.

17. Older people on the average take more medications than younger people.

18. Snake-oil salesmen are as common today as they were on the frontier.

19. Personality changes with age, just as hair color and skin texture do.

20. Sight declines with age.

Answers

1. *False.* Even among those who live to be 80 or older, only 20% to 25% develop Alzheimer's disease or some other incurable form of brain disease. *Senility* is a meaningless term and should be discarded.

2. *False.* The American family is still the number-one caretaker of older Americans. Most older people live close to their children and see them often; many live with their spouses. In all, 8 out of 10 men and 6 out of 10 women live in family settings.

3. *True.* Depression, loss of self-esteem, loneliness, and anxiety can become more common as older people face retirement, the deaths of relatives and friends, and other such crises—often at the same time. Fortunately, depression is treatable.

4. *True.* Today, 12% of the U.S. population is 65 or older. By the year 2030, one in five people will be over 65.

5. *True.* Only 5% of older people live in nursing homes; the rest are basically healthy and self-sufficient.

6. *False.* Mental confusion and serious forgetfulness in old age can be caused by Alzheimer's disease or

(Source: National Institute on Aging)

other conditions that cause incurable damage to the brain, but about 100 other problems can cause the same symptoms. A minor head injury, a high fever, poor nutrition, adverse drug reactions, and depression can all be treated, and the confusion will be cured.

7. *False.* Intelligence per se does not decline without reason. Most people maintain their intellect or improve as they grow older.

8. *False.* Most older people can lead an active, satisfying sex life.

9. *False.* Stopping smoking at any age not only reduces the risk of cancer and heart disease but also leads to healthier lungs.

10. *False.* Many older people enjoy—and benefit from—exercises such as walking, swimming, and bicycle riding. Exercise at any age can help strengthen the heart and lungs and lower blood pressure. See your physician before beginning a new exercise program.

11. *False.* Although certain requirements, such as that for vitamin D, may increase slightly with age, older people need the same amounts of most vitamins and minerals as younger people. Older people should eat nutritious food and cut down on sweets, salty snack foods, high-calorie drinks, and alcohol.

12. *False.* Older people require fewer calories, but an adequate intake of calcium for strong bones can become more important as you grow older. This is particularly true for women, whose risk of osteoporosis increases after menopause. Milk and cheese are rich in calcium, as are cooked dried beans, collards, and broccoli. Some people need calcium supplements as well.

13. *True.* The body's thermostat tends to function less efficiently with age, and the older person's body may be less able to adapt to heat or cold.

14. *True.* Falls are the most common cause of injuries among the elderly. Good safety habits, including proper lighting, nonskid carpets, and keeping living areas free of obstacles, can help prevent serious accidents.

15. *False.* Women tend to outlive men by an average of 8 years. There are 150 women for every 100 men over age 65 and nearly 250 women for every 100 men over 85.

16. *True.* Fewer men and women are dying of stroke or heart disease. This has been a major factor in the increase in life expectancy.

17. *True.* The elderly consume 25% of all medications and, as a result, have many more problems with adverse drug reactions.

18. *True.* Medical quackery is a $10-billion business in the United States. People of all ages are commonly duped into "quick cures" for aging, arthritis, and cancer.

19. *False.* Personality doesn't change with age. Therefore, all old people can't be described as rigid and cantankerous. You are what you are for as long as you live. But you can change what you do to help yourself to good health.

20. *False.* Although changes in vision become more common with age, any change in vision, regardless of age, is related to a specific disease. If you are having problems with your vision, see your doctor.

and not only answer all of the items correctly but also understand why the statements are true or false.

To begin, we will consider the fundamental changes in U.S. demographics over the past several decades. We will take a look at what older adults are like, consider some issues of social policy that the United States will be facing in the future, and examine the number of elderly in other countries around the world. Following that, we will adopt a framework to guide our interpretation of research and theory in adult development and aging, the life-span developmental framework. We will consider some basic definitions of age and will see that age can be viewed in many different ways. Finally, by examining various research methods, we will see how the information presented in this book was obtained.

THE DEMOGRAPHICS OF AGING

Each year another group of adults reaches what society calls "old age." In 1989 over 2 million Americans reached this milestone, joining the more than 30 million already there. Who are these people? What are they like? What forces have shaped this much-heralded "graying of America"?

To answer these questions, we need to consider what we mean by *old age*. The most common definition of old age refers to crossing the arbitrary boundary of 65 years. There is nothing magical about that particular age, any more than there is about a legal drinking age of 21. But society uses 65 as a milestone. It was selected as the official marker of old age in the federal Social Security Act of 1935 and was subsequently adopted by virtually everyone. However, chronological age is a poor indicator of a person's physical, social, psychological, economic, or mental condition. Moreover, all people over age 65 are not the same.

Some researchers argue that we should discriminate between the "young-old" (aged 65 to 74) and the "old-old" (aged 75 and over). I will use the criterion of 65 in defining old age, keeping in mind the problems with using such an arbitrary index.

The population of older adults is constantly changing as new members enter the group and other members leave through death. With each new member comes a personal history reflecting a combination of many developmental influences. For example, the newest entrants into old age were born in the 1920s, meaning that they experienced the Depression and World War II and had more education, better medical care, and different occupational experiences than their predecessors. These experiential factors will be explored later in this chapter and will provide the basis for important discussions in other chapters. At this point it is important to recognize that the characteristics of older adults are changing rapidly. Approximately 60% of the current older population entered old age after 1975 (Uhlenberg, 1987). Clearly, this represents a substantial turnover in the older population.

How Many Older Adults Are There?

The number of older adults has grown steadily over the past century. First, between 1900 and 1985 there was a tenfold increase in the number of older adults (from 3 million to nearly 30 million). By 2010 nearly 10 million more are anticipated. Between 2010 and 2030 a major surge of growth is expected as the members of the "baby boom" generation reach old age, increasing the number by a whopping 25 million in just 20 years: Following the baby boom surge the rate of growth should slow and stabilize.

Older adults were only 4% of the total population in 1900 (see Figure 1.1). By 1985 this proportion had increased to 12%, and it will increase

Older adults differ among themselves. One way this is reflected is in the distinction between "old-old" and "young-old."

to roughly 17% by 2030. Another way of looking at the proportion of older adults is to look at how many there are for every 100 children under age 18 in the population. In 1900 the population was truly young: there were only 10 older adults for every 100 children. By 1985 the population had matured, with 46 old people for every 100 children. By 2030, the U.S. Census Bureau projects, the number of older adults will actually exceed the number of children.

Not only is the population as a whole aging, but the older population itself has aged. Over the last 60 years, for example, the percentage of older adults who are over age 75 (the "old-old") has increased from 29% in 1930 to nearly 50% in 1990. This trend reflects the fact that technological advances in health care are enabling people to live longer than ever before.

What accounts for the differing rates of growth in the number of older people? The number of people entering old age in any one year depends on three things: the number of people born 65 years earlier, the proportion of those born who survived to age 65, and the number of immigrants who joined this group over the years and are still living (Uhlenberg, 1987).

Clearly, these dramatic shifts in the composition of the population will have dramatic effects on daily life. From health care to city services and from wage scales to retirement benefits, the mechanisms of social support that all of us take for granted will undergo considerable stress as different groups vie for resources. Recognizing the problem and planning ahead for it are the only ways to avoid inevitably serious consequences.

What Are Older People Like?

If all that we know about a person is that he or she is old, we know virtually nothing other than how many years the person has survived. Older adults are not all alike, any more than all younger

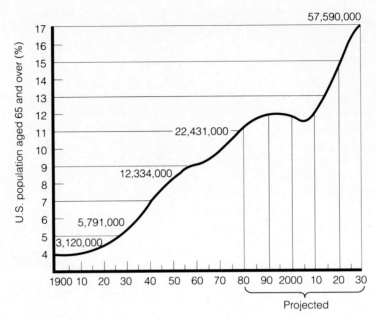

FIGURE 1.1 • Population of Americans aged 65 and over, 1900–2030 (projected)

(Source: U.S. Bureau of Census)

adults or all middle-aged adults are alike. In this section we will consider some of the main ways in which older adults are diverse. We will focus in particular on ethnicity, gender, marital status, employment and income, educational level, geographical distribution, and living arrangements.

Ethnicity. The elderly population is a very diverse group. One of the most important sources of this diversity is ethnicity. It is important to realize that the status and resources of many elderly members of minority groups reflect social and economic discrimination that they experienced earlier in life. As a result many such elderly people are needy and malnourished and have poor access to medical care, poor education, and substandard housing. This means that what may be true for white older adults may not be true for the aged who are from an ethnic or racial minority.

The elderly population in the United States has been growing faster among minorities than among whites (American Association of Retired Persons [AARP], 1988). In 1980 roughly 10% of the elderly population was nonwhite. This number is expected to increase to 15% by 2025 and to 20% by 2050. However, about 11% of Whites are 65 or over, whereas this percentage is 8 for Blacks, 6 for Asian/Pacific Islanders,* 5 for Hispanics, and 5 for Native Americans.

---

*An Asian/Pacific Islander is anyone who is a native of an Asian country or is a member of the native inhabitants of the Pacific Islands (e.g., Tahitians).

Examining the growth of the elderly population within minority groups reveals some interesting trends (AARP, 1988). The elderly are the fastest growing segment of the Black population. Between 1970 and 1980 elderly Blacks increased by 36% while the total Black population was growing by only 16%. Because Hispanics represent the fastest growing minority group, a substantial increase in their elderly is anticipated. The number of Asian/Pacific Islander elderly has grown dramatically over the last 20 years, showing a fourfold increase. Native-American elderly have increased faster than those of any other minority group. Between 1970 and 1980 alone the number of Native-American elderly increased by 65%, more than double the rate of White or Black elderly.

Gender Differences. Overall, elderly women outnumber elderly men (see Table 1.2), although the difference varies somewhat across racial and ethnic groups. As indicated in the table, these differences become more pronounced at higher age levels. For example, in the age group over 85 there are only about 43 White men for every 100 White women, and there are 61 Hispanic men for every 100 Hispanic women.

Differences favoring women were not always the case, however. Until 1930 the gender ratio among the older population actually favored men. This situation was due in part to the predominance of men among U.S. immigrants at the time. Additionally, many women died in young adulthood from complications of pregnancy and childbirth. Once mortality rates from childbearing began to decline, the gender ratio began to favor women (Uhlenberg, 1987).

Marital Status. Nearly 94% of U.S. adults reaching old age in this century have been married at least once. The current number of older adults who have been divorced is relatively small;

for example, roughly 15% of those turning 65 in 1980 had been divorced. Although the proportion of people who have ever been married will remain virtually unchanged into the foreseeable future, the number who have been divorced will not. Estimates are that 45% of those people turning 65 in the year 2020 will have been divorced (Cherlin, 1981). But because most people who get divorced eventually remarry, the typical older adult is either married or widowed. We will consider the topics of marriage, divorce, and widowhood in detail in Chapter 11.

As a reflection of the trends in gender differences in longevity, more elderly men are married than elderly women. This difference holds for all ethnic groups, as shown in Table 1.3. Not surprisingly, widows outnumber widowers. Divorce and separation rates among minority older adults are nearly double those of Whites.

Employment and Income. Only a few people continue to work full time after age 65; in fact, the trend over the past decade has been toward early retirement (see Chapter 12). With retirement comes a drop of nearly 45% in the typical person's income, which usually means a drop in standard of living.

The decline in income experienced by retirees is not felt equally across all groups. Although nearly one quarter of all older adults fall into the categories "poor" or "near poor," some segments of the older population are particularly disadvantaged. Cool (1987) estimates that the poverty rate for older women is 80% higher than that for males (18% versus 10%). More than half of the elderly poor are unmarried women. The poverty rate for Blacks is three times greater than that for Whites, and over one fourth of older Hispanics and one third of older Native Americans live below the official poverty level (Bengtson & Morgan, 1983; Cool, 1987).

TABLE 1.2 · Gender ratio for all races aged 65 and over in 1980

Race	Age					
Men per 100 Women	60–64	65–69	70–74	75–79	80–84	85 +
White	87	81	72	61	52	43
Black	80	73	69	63	60	50
Hispanic	86	76	77	76	73	61
Asian/Pacific Islander	84	93	109	89	67	60
Native American	87	77	82	74	66	59

(Source: American Association of Retired Persons. Reprinted with permission.)

Educational Level. The average educational level of older adults has changed dramatically over the last 3 decades. As recently as 1960 fewer than 20% of all older people had graduated from high school. By the year 2000 this proportion will have increased to nearly two thirds, with a substantial percentage having a college education as well. These generational differences in educational levels reflect the limited educational opportunities available to people born before World War I. Educational attainment is an important variable to consider in interpreting age-related differences. As will be discussed in detail in Chapter 6, differences in educational level account for some of the apparent age-related decline in intellectual abilities.

Geographical Distribution. Over the course of this century the proportion of older adults living in rural areas has declined. By 1985 over three fourths of all older adults were living in urban areas. Many of these urban dwellers live in clusters called **gerontic enclaves**, in which at least 20% of the residents are old. For the most part these urban dwellers are better off than their rural counterparts, who are more likely to be poor, to live in substandard housing, to exhibit more health problems, and to have less access to health care and other human services (Coward & Lee, 1985). The implications of these differences are explored more thoroughly in Chapter 14.

Elderly members of minority groups tend to be concentrated in certain regions of the United States. As indicated in the panels of Figure 1.2, they are more likely to live in large, industrialized, urban areas. Native-American elderly are the clear exception, largely because of government relocation to reservations over the last 2 centuries.

Living Arrangements. One widespread myth about older adults is that most of them live in institutions such as nursing homes. In fact, only 5% of all older adults live in institutions at any one time; the other 95% live in households (D. S. Smith, 1981). However, estimates are that between 20% and 25% of adults will spend at least some time in a long-term-care institution. For the 95% in households, though, two patterns are typical in all ethnic groups: First, married couples tend to live by themselves. Second, unmarried individuals tend to live alone. Of this group who live alone, 80% are women. This lopsided

TABLE 1.3 • Marital status of persons aged 65 and over in 1980

Race/Gender	Married	Widowed	Divorced/ Separated	Single (Never Married)
White				
Men	74.2%	13.9%	6.6%	5.4%
Women	36.1%	51.1%	6.0%	6.8%
Black				
Men	56.9%	22.1%	14.7%	6.3%
Women	25.0%	57.7%	11.6%	5.6%
Hispanic				
Men	65.0%	16.0%	12.8%	6.3%
Women	30.8%	49.9%	12.3%	7.1%
Asian/Pacific Islander				
Men	65.4%	12.9%	14.2%	7.5%
Women	30.2%	55.6%	10.1%	4.1%
Native American				
Men	59.7%	20.6%	13.6%	6.1%
Women	31.0%	55.1%	10.3%	3.6%

(Source: American Association of Retired Persons. Reprinted with permission.)

difference is produced by gender differences in longevity and age at marriage, which combine to produce a situation in which most women are widowed in later life (see Chapter 11).

Issues Related to Demographic Changes

We have noted several trends in the U.S. population during this century. Moreover, the trends are not likely to change in the foreseeable future. These changes in the composition of the older adult population contribute to potentially critical issues that will emerge over the next few decades.

One especially important area concerns the potential for intergenerational conflict.

Because the resources and roles in a society are never divided equally among different age groups, there is always a potential for conflict to erupt. One well-known intergenerational conflict is that between adolescents and their parents. Less well-known is the potential for conflict between the middle-aged and the old (Uhlenberg, 1987). This type of conflict has not been a source of serious problems in the past in American society because the elderly made up a small proportion of the population, family ties between adult children and their parents worked against conflict, and middle-aged people were hesitant to withdraw

States with concentrations
of Black elderly over 65 in 1980

States with concentrations of Native-
American elderly over 65 in 1980

States with concentrations of
Asian /Pacific Islander elderly
over 65 in 1980

States with concentrations of
Hispanic elderly over
65 in 1980

FIGURE 1.2 • Geographical distribution of elderly members of
minority groups in the United States

(Source: American Association of Retired Persons. Reprinted with permission.)

support from programs for the elderly. Despite these potent forces protecting against conflict, the situation is changing. To see this more clearly, let us project forward to the year 2030, when the baby boom generation will be old. Between now and 2030

1. The proportion of older adults will nearly double.

2. Older adults will be much more politically sophisticated and organized. They will be very well educated and will be familiar with life in a highly complex society in which one must learn to deal with bureaucracies.

3. Older adults will expect to keep their more affluent life-style, Social Security benefits, health care, and other benefits accrued through their adult life. A comfortable retirement will be viewed as something that everyone is entitled to.

4. The ratio of workers to retirees will fall from its current level of roughly 3.5:1 to 2:1. Thus, to maintain the same level of benefits, the working members of society will have to pay much higher taxes than workers do now.

5. The increase in divorce that has occurred over the past 2 decades may result in a lowered sense of obligation on the part of middle-aged adults toward their absent parents. For example, will adult children feel obliged to care for an elderly father who left the family when they were very young?

SOMETHING · TO · THINK · ABOUT

Implications of Changing Demographics

As described in this chapter, the number of older adults will be rising dramatically over the next several decades. It is important to stop and think about what impact this demographic change will have on our everyday lives.

Think for a moment about the services we all take for granted in a community. Many of these services are designed to serve people of all ages, such as garbage collection and street repair. Others are provided with a particular age group in mind. For example, schools and programs for abused and neglected children are targeted for younger people, whereas senior centers and Social Security are targeted primarily for older people. You can probably think of several more examples of each.

The important point in examining such services is that larger numbers of people in certain age groups may require a change in our priorities for which services are funded and which ones are not. In communities with large numbers of young families and few elderly, for example, most public money could be targeted for services for young adults and children, such as schools. Cities such as Rochester, Michigan, fall into this category. Rochester has seen rapid growth since the mid-1980s because of increased high-tech industry. This high growth means that many young families are now moving to the area. In communities with large concentrations of older adults, however, there may be little need for schools but an important need for transportation. This is especially true in places such as the retirement communities in Florida and elsewhere. Older adults have different needs in these communities than do younger adults in places such as Rochester.

These differences in needs mainly reflect differences in what issues are most salient for people of different ages. Such needs do not necessarily need to conflict. But in times of tight economic policies and finite amounts of money to spend, conflict is inevitable. This means that public debate between older and younger adults on how to spend public revenue will undoubtedly increase in the coming years. How can we meet the legitimate needs of adults of all ages? Can we avoid pitting schools for the children against transportation for older people who cannot drive? It's something to think about.

---

6. The more rapid increase in minority elderly will force a reconsideration of issues such as discrimination and access to goods and services.

No one knows for certain what society will be like by 2030. However, the changes we have noted in demographic trends suggest the need for taking action now. The information contained in the remainder of this book will provide a basis for this action. For the moment, reflect on some possible areas of conflict while reading "Something to Think About."

International Perspectives

The changing demographics in the United States are not unique, as displayed in Figure 1.3. Other industrialized nations such as France, Japan, and Sweden show similar trends. All of these countries have relatively low birthrates and death rates

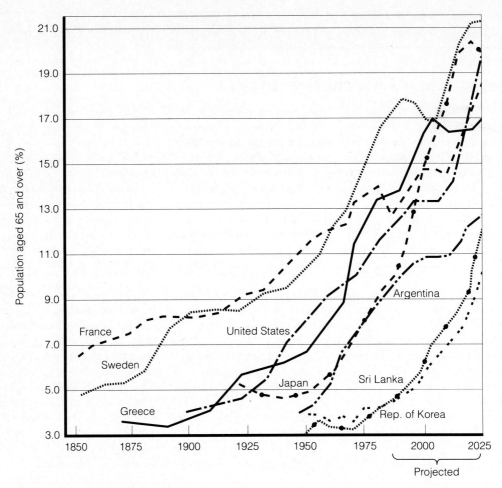

FIGURE 1.3 • Trends in percentage of the population aged 65 and over in selected countries, 1850–2025 (projected)

(Source: "Aging and Worldwide Population Change" by G. C. Myers, 1985, in R. H. Binstock and E. Shanas (Eds.), *Handbook of Aging and the Social Sciences* (2nd ed.) (pp. 173–198), New York: Van Nostrand Reinhold. Reprinted with permission of the Center of Demographic Studies, Duke University, and the author.)

and high standards of living. Although the developed countries account for only one fourth of the world's population, they contain nearly one half of the world's older adults (Meyers, 1985).

Third World countries, such as Sri Lanka, have relatively young populations. On the average

only 4% of the people living in the Third World are over age 65. However, these countries will also experience rapid growth in the elderly population over the next several decades (Meyers, 1985). Between 1980 and 2025, it is expected, the number of older adults living in less developed countries will quadruple; in developed countries the number will only double.

Just as there is potential for conflict between generations as a result of changing demographics, there is potential for conflict between nations. Dividing increasingly scarce resources across age groups in different countries will become a major issue in the decades ahead. How these issues are handled will have tremendous significance as we head into the 21st century.

We will have additional things to consider about aging in other societies and cultures in Chapter 10, where we view adult development from a social perspective. At that point we will take another look at how well the different generations get along and how older people are treated in various places around the world.

ADULT DEVELOPMENT AND AGING: A LIFE-SPAN PERSPECTIVE

The experience of being an adult and growing old can be approached from many perspectives: anthropological, sociological, biological, and medical, to name but a few. Each of these approaches offers a different perspective, and each makes its unique contribution to research and theory. The task of the psychological perspective on adult development and aging is to explain how behavior becomes organized and, in some cases, how it becomes disorganized (Birren & Cunningham, 1985). The psychological study of adult development and aging is considered part of the much broader field of **ontogenetic psychology**, the study of the organization of behavior from conception to death.

Ontogenetic psychology divides human development into an early phase, childhood and adolescence, and a later phase, consisting of young adulthood, middle age, and old age. The early phase is characterized by relatively rapid age-related increases in people's size and abilities. During the later phase changes in size are slow, but abilities continue to develop as people continue adapting to the environment (Birren & Cunningham, 1985).

Viewed from the point of view of ontogenetic psychology, adult development and aging cover only one part of the entire life span. However, the roots of many behaviors seen in adults date back to an earlier time. Recognizing that adulthood and aging are part of a much larger picture led to the **life-span perspective** (Baltes, Reese, & Lipsitt, 1980).

Viewed from the perspective of life-span development, adult development and aging are complex phenomena that are multiply determined and cannot be understood within the scope of a single disciplinary approach (Baltes et al., 1980). This means that understanding how adults change requires input from a wide variety of perspectives. Collectively, these different perspectives make up the life-span developmental framework, which is a blueprint for studying adulthood and aging. The major premises of this framework are as follows (Riley, 1979):

1. Aging is a lifelong process of growing up and growing old, starting with conception and ending with death. Thus, no single stage of a person's life (e.g., childhood, middle age, old age) can be understood apart from its origins and its consequences.

2. Aging consists of three processes, biological, psychological, and social. These processes are simultaneously interactive throughout life.

3. The life-course pattern of any individual is affected by social, environmental, and historical change.

4. New patterns of development across adulthood can cause social change. Thus, not only does social change influence people, but people, in turn, influence society.

The fact that aging is a lifelong process means that human development never stops (Brim & Kagan, 1980). Rather, there is a continuity of development, socialization, and adaptation (Clausen, 1986). Development involves the processes needed to reach an individual's potential in any domain (e.g., physical size, intellectual abilities, and social skills). **Socialization** refers to the ways in which people learn to function in society (see Chapter 10). Its focus is on the demands that members of society make on a person so that behavior, values, and feelings conform to society's expectations (Featherman, 1981). Finally, **adaptation** refers to modifying behavior in response to changing physical and social environments.

The lifelong interaction of the biological, psychological, and social forces of development points out the need for a holistic approach to the adult. If we want to understand what happens to a woman as she goes through menopause, for example, we must consider what occurs biologically and how those events interact with the social myths surrounding menopause and the psychological characteristics of the woman at the time. In this holistic approach human behaviors are **emergent**; that is, they cannot be understood or predicted by examining only their constituent parts. There is something that happens when the pieces of human behaviors are put together that goes beyond what one would expect from each piece alone. For example, you may have experienced the satisfaction of having the equation $E = mc^2$ finally come together and make sense when you learned what the letters and the concepts truly meant. This "aha phenomenon" changes your whole understanding of a topic but comes from

adding one bit of information. Your new perspective, however, emerges from the combination of information.

The final two premises in the life-span perspective relate to three concepts of time described by Neugarten and Datan (1973). **Life time** is the chronological age of the person, which is closely tied to biological changes (e.g., changes in the cardiovascular system and sensory systems). **Social time** is the system of age grading and age-related expectations closely related to socialization (e.g., the "proper" age at which to get married or retire). Finally, **historical time** refers to the succession of social, political, economic, and environmental events through which people live (e.g., the Depression, the Vietnam War, and "Reaganomics"). Neugarten and Datan's concept of historical time is most closely related to the third and fourth premises in the life-span developmental framework. Each of our lives is anchored in the major events of particular historical periods. These events affect people differently, depending on their age and position in society.

These different notions of time come together for each of us in our **social clock** (Hagestad & Neugarten, 1985; Neugarten & Hagestad, 1976). A social clock is our own personal timetable by which we mark our progress in terms of events in our lives. Our social clock is based on our incorporation of biological markers of time, such as menopause; social aspects of time, such as graduating from college; and historical time, such as a particular presidential election. As we will see in the next section, we use our social clock to check our progress against our timetable to see how we are doing.

What the life-span developmental framework offers is a way to organize the myriad changes that occur over a lifetime. But adopting this holistic perspective is hard, especially once we begin to realize just how many different events occur in our lives. One metaphor that may help is to think of the life span as made up of a huge number of rhythms (Bohannon, 1980). Our bodies and our communities create biological, psychological, and sociocultural rhythms, all of which are embedded in the larger environmental rhythm. Each of these rhythms varies; some change daily, others only monthly or even more slowly. Every culture has its unique rhythm, and what we learn about one may not hold for another. Moreover, different cultures will have problems trying to deal with one another, since each moves to its own rhythm. Bohannon extends this point to different age groups, arguing that dysrhythmias can affect social relations between them so that they do not mesh well. Only by studying adulthood and aging from a life-span developmental perspective both historically and cross-culturally can we understand the rhythmic and dysrhythmic patterns within and across societies.

THE MEANING OF AGE

One of the most important aspects of studying adult development and aging is understanding the concept of aging itself. Aging is not a single process. Rather, it consists of at least three distinct processes, primary, secondary, and tertiary aging (Birren & Cunningham, 1985). **Primary aging** refers to the normal, disease-free movement across adulthood. Changes in biological, social, or psychological processes in primary aging would be considered an inevitable part of the developmental process; examples include menopause, decline in reaction time, and experiencing the loss of family and friends. **Secondary aging** refers to developmental changes that are related to disease. The progressive loss of intellectual abilities in Alzheimer's disease is an example of secondary

aging. Finally, **tertiary aging** refers to the rapid losses that occur shortly before death. As described more fully in Chapter 6, tertiary aging is associated with a phenomenon known as terminal drop, in which intellectual abilities show a marked decline in the last few years preceding death.

Age as an Index

When most of us think about age, what comes to mind first is how long we have been around since our birth. This way of defining age is what is known as **chronological age**. Chronological age provides a shorthand way to index time and to organize events and data by using a commonly understood standard, calendar time. Chronological age is not the only shorthand index used in adult development and aging. Gender, ethnicity, and socioeconomic status are others.

No index variable itself actually causes behavior. In the case of socioeconomic status, for example, it is presumably not the size of the person's bank account per se that causes charitable behavior. But this point is often forgotten when age is the index variable, perhaps because it is so familiar to us and so widely used. However, age (or time) does not directly cause things to happen, either. Iron left out in the rain will rust, but rust is not caused simply by time. Rather, rust is a **time-dependent process** involving oxidation in which time is a measure of the rate by which rust is created. The important point here is that human behavior is affected by experiences that occur with the passage of time, not by time itself.

What do we need to do in order to know whether some behavior is actually time-dependent? Birren and Renner (1977) argue that we need to understand the underlying biological, social, and psychological processes that are all intertwined in an index such as chronological age. In short, what we need are better definitions of age.

Although chronologically older than most of his classmates, this man is psychologically younger than most of his same-age peers.

Definitions of Age

Age can be considered from several perspectives. Birren and Cunningham (1985) describe three of these: biological, social, and psychological.

Biological Age. **Biological age** represents the person's present position with respect to his or her potential life span. It is assessed by measuring the functioning of the various vital, or life-limiting, organ systems, such as the cardiovascular system. As individuals traverse adulthood, the vital organ systems lose their capacity for self-regulation and adaptation, resulting in an increased probability of dying.

Social Age. **Social age** refers to individuals' roles and habits in relation to other members of the society to which they belong. To the extent that a person shows the age-graded behavior expected by society, then that person is judged to be older or younger. For example, Loretta Lynn, who

married at 14, would be considered socially old in comparison with a norm of 22. In contrast, Bette Midler, who had her first child when she was middle-aged, would be considered socially young; most women have their first child during their 20s. Social age is judged on the basis of many behaviors and habits, such as style of dress, language, and interpersonal style.

Psychological Age. **Psychological age** refers to the behavioral capacities that people use to adapt to changing environmental demands. These abilities include memory, intelligence, feelings, motivation, and other skills that foster and maintain self-esteem and personal control. For example, a 15-year-old student named Michelle who attends MIT and majors in physics would be considered psychologically older in the intellectual domain, because the large majority of her classmates are 17 or over. On the other hand, Mildred, a 60-year-old English major, would be thought of as psychologically young in the intellectual area, because the vast majority of her classmates are between 17 and 25.

Issues in Studying Age

Most researchers in adult development and aging continue to use chronological age as a primary variable of interest. You may be wondering why, given the availability of more precise definitions of age. To answer this question, we need to examine how age is used in developmental research.

Developmental research can be categorized on the basis of how it uses the variable of age (Birren & Cunningham, 1985). In the **developmentally static approach** the major goal of the researcher is to describe individuals in particular age groups. For instance, a researcher may be interested in developing a theory about how 21-year-olds behave on dates and how 30-year-olds behave on dates. In this case age is used mainly to define the boundaries of the study. In contrast, the **developmentally dynamic approach** seeks to understand the processes of change. The focus here is to understand how people develop, what characterizes change, and how change happens. In the developmentally dynamic approach, for example, the researcher would be most interested in how 21-year-old daters evolve into 30-year-old daters.

The need for precision in defining the role of age is clearly more important in the developmentally dynamic approach. The ultimate interest of researchers in this approach is not in the passage of time per se but, rather, in the changes in behavior that emerge over time. These behavioral changes are only crudely indexed by chronological age. Once this fact is recognized, however, there are two courses that could be followed.

First, chronological age could be accepted as a **surrogate variable** (Birren & Cunningham, 1985) to represent the very complex, interrelated influences on people over time. Use of a surrogate variable such as age does not allow a researcher to state the cause of some behavior precisely, because the surrogate variable represents so many different things. If we say that memory for details shows an age-related decrease, for example, we do not know whether the difference stems from biological processes, psychological processes, social processes, or some combination of them. Even though chronological age is a crude index, however, it may provide useful information that can be used to guide future, more precise research that could narrow the number of explanations. The second option is to replace chronological age with one of the definitions described earlier that focus on some specific process, such as biological change.

To date, most researchers have chosen to use chronological age as a surrogate variable. However, the strategy adopted over the past decade is to combine this use of chronological age with the concepts of primary, secondary, and tertiary aging. In particular, most of the research reported in this book focuses on primary (disease-free) aging. Participants in most studies are described as "healthy, community-dwelling adults." Although this tie between surrogate variables and primary aging is often not stated explicitly, it nevertheless offers an important way to document and understand the processes of aging that are universal.

Relationships Between Age and Developmental Influences

Thus far, we have concentrated on how our interpretations of age data are clouded by a variety of influences. We come now to the issue of how the multiple determinants of adult development are related to age. Baltes (1979) identifies three sets of influences that interact to produce developmental change over the life span:

Experiencing major historical events such as the Great Depression has a profound influence on subsequent development.

Normative age-graded influences are those biological and environmental factors that are highly correlated with chronological age. Some of these, such as puberty, menarche, and menopause, are biological. Others involve socialization and cultural customs, such as the time when first marriage occurs and the age when one should retire.

Normative history-graded influences are events that most people in a culture experience at the same time. These events may be biological (such as epidemics), environmental (such as wars or economic depressions), or social (such as changing attitudes toward sexuality). Normative history-graded influences often serve to give a generation its unique identity, such as the Depression generation or the Vietnam War generation.

Nonnormative influences may be important for a specific individual but are not experienced by most people. These may be favorable events, such as winning the lottery or an election, or unfavorable ones, such as an accident or layoff.

The relative importance of these three influences depends on the specific behaviors examined and the particular point in the life span when they occur (Hultsch & Plemons, 1979). For example, history-graded influences may produce generational differences and conflict that could have important implications for understanding differences that are apparently age-related.

RESEARCH METHODS

As a part of psychology, the study of adult development and aging adheres to the principles of scientific inquiry that guide the parent discipline. It should also be clear by now that understanding how adults grow and change requires an extensive data base. Information concerning adult development and aging is gathered in the same ways as it is in other fields of psychology. Gerontologists also have the same problems as other psychologists: finding appropriate control groups, limiting generalizations to the groups included in the research, and finding adequate means of measurement (Kausler, 1982).

The usual approach to gathering data on adult development and aging has been to find ways to isolate the various factors that cause change over the life span (Maddox & Campbell, 1985; Nesselroade & Labouvie, 1985). However, some gerontologists advocate applied research on aging, and they are beginning to look for alternative methods that focus on the subjective experience of growing old. One alternative approach is naturalistic inquiry (Lincoln & Guba, 1985), which focuses on the problems of growing old in the "real world" rather than in the psychological laboratory. We will examine all of these approaches in this section. First, however, we must examine the three major effects that explain differences between and within people over time.

Age, Cohort, and Time of Measurement

Every study of adult development and aging is built on the combination of three fundamental effects: age, cohort, and time of measurement (Schaie, 1984).

Age effects reflect differences due to underlying processes, that is, biological, social, or psychological changes. Although usually represented in research by chronological age, age effects refer to inherent changes within the person and are not caused by the passage of time per se.

Cohort effects are differences due to experiences and circumstances unique to the particular generation one belongs to. An important issue in research is the definition of a cohort. Cohorts can be specific, as in all people born in one particular year, or general, such as the baby boom cohort. As described earlier, each generation is exposed to different sets of historical and personal events (e.g., World War II, home computers, educational opportunities). These experiences can affect behavior in profound ways, as we have already seen.

Time-of-measurement effects reflect differences stemming from social, environmental, historical, or other events at the time the data are obtained from the participants. For example, data concerning wage increases given in a particular year may be influenced by the economic conditions that year.

In conducting developmental research, investigators have attempted to identify and separate the three effects. This has not been easy, since they are interrelated. If one is interested in studying 40-year-olds, for instance, one must necessarily select the cohort that was born 40 years ago. In this case age and cohort are **confounded**, since one cannot know whether the behaviors observed are due to the fact that the participants are 40 years old or due to the specific life experiences they have had as a result of being born in a particular historical period.

Developmental Research Designs

What distinguishes developmental researchers most from their colleagues in other areas of psychology is a fundamental interest in understanding how people change. This means that developmental researchers must somehow look at the ways in which people differ across time. Doing so necessarily requires that they understand the distinction between age change and age difference. An **age change** occurs in an individual's behavior over time. For example, a person's reaction time may not be as short at age 70 as it was at age 40. An **age difference** is obtained when at least two persons of different ages are compared. For example, a person of 70 may have a longer reaction time than another person of age 40. Even though we may be able to document substantial age differences, we must not assume that they imply an age change. As we will see, in some cases age differences reflect age changes, and in some cases they do not.

If what we really want to understand in developmental research is age change (what happens as people grow older), we should strive to design our research with this goal in mind. Developmental researchers have not always found this to be easy, however. Moreover, different research questions require different research designs. We will consider the most common ways in which researchers gather data concerning age differences and age changes: cross-sectional, longitudinal, time-lag, and sequential. Figure 1.4 depicts a matrix containing each major effect (age, cohort, and time of measurement). Cohort is represented by the years down the left column. Time of measurement is represented by the years across the bottom. Age is represented by the numbers in the body of the table. We will see how this matrix can be used to construct the various developmental designs.

Cross-Sectional Designs. A **cross-sectional design** compares groups of people varying in age at one point in time. Any single vertical column in Figure 1.4 represents a cross-sectional design. Cross-sectional designs allow researchers to examine age differences but not age change. The reason has to do with how any observed differences are explained.

Because all participants are measured at the same time, differences between the groups cannot be due to time-of-measurement effects. That leaves two possibilities: age change and cohort differences. Unfortunately, we cannot distinguish between them, which means that we do not know whether the differences we observe between groups stem from inherent developmental processes or from experiences peculiar to their cohort. To see this more clearly, take a careful look at Figure 1.4. Notice that the different age groups are automatically formed when particular cohorts are selected, and vice versa. Thus, if the researcher wants to study people of a certain age at a particular time, he or she has no choice in choosing a cohort. This confounding of age and cohort is the major problem with cross-sectional studies.

Cross-sectional research tends to paint a bleak picture of aging. For example, early research on the development of intelligence across adulthood repeatedly showed large drops in performance with age (see Figure 1.5). The problem is that we have no way of knowing whether most people

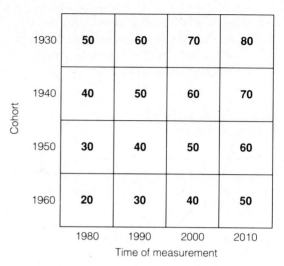

FIGURE 1.4 • Matrix of time of measurement, cohort, and age (the cells in the body of the matrix), from which research designs can be constructed as described in the text

show the same developmental progressions; that is, we cannot address the issue of individual differences over time.

Despite the confounding of age and cohort and the limitation of only being able to identify age differences, cross-sectional designs dominate the research literature in gerontology. The reason is a pragmatic one: because all of the measurements are obtained at one time, cross-sectional research can be conducted relatively quickly and inexpensively compared with other designs. As long as their limits are recognized, however, cross-sectional studies can provide a snapshot view of age differences that may provide insight into issues that could be followed up with other designs that are sensitive to age change.

Longitudinal Designs. A **longitudinal design** provides information about age changes; the strategy involves testing a single cohort over

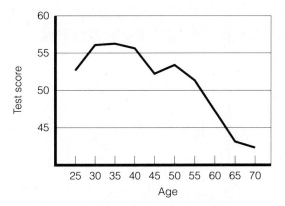

FIGURE 1.5 • Cross-sectional age differences in intelligence for a verbal meaning test

(Source: "A Cross-Sequential Study of Age Changes in Cognitive Behavior" by K. W. Schaie and C. R. Strother, 1968, *Psychological Bulletin, 70*, pp. 671–680. Copyright © 1968 by the American Psychological Association. Reprinted with permission.)

multiple times of measurement. A longitudinal design is represented by any horizontal row in Figure 1.4. A major advantage of longitudinal designs is that age changes are identified because we are studying the same people over time. But if age changes are found, can we say why they occurred?

Because only one cohort is studied, cohort effects are eliminated as an explanation of change. The other two potential explanations, age and time of measurement, are confounded, however. For example, suppose that we wanted to follow the 1930 cohort over time. If we wanted to test these individuals when they were 60 years old, we would have to do so in 1990. Consequently, any changes we identify could be due to changes in underlying processes or factors that are related to the time we choose to conduct our measurement. For instance, if we conducted a longitudinal study of salary growth, the amount of change in salary in any comparison could stem from real

change in skills and worth of the person to the company or from the economic conditions of the times. In a longitudinal study we cannot tell which of these factors is more important.

There are three additional potential problems with longitudinal studies. If the research measure requires some type of performance by the participants, one problem is **practice effects**. Practice effects refer to the fact that performance may improve over time simply because people are being tested over and over again with the same measures. Repeatedly using the same measure on the same people may have significant effects on their behavior, may make the measure invalid, and may have a negative impact on the participants' perceptions of the research (Baltes, Reese, & Nesselroade, 1977).

The second additional problem with longitudinal designs is **participant dropout**. Participant dropout refers to the fact that it is difficult to keep a group of research participants intact over the course of a longitudinal study. Participants may move, may lose interest, or may die. Suppose we want to examine the relationship between intelligence and health. Participant dropout can result in two different outcomes. We can end up with **positive selective survival** if the participants at the end of the study tend to be the ones who were initially higher on some variable; for example, the surviving participants are the ones who were the most healthy at the beginning of the study. In contrast, we could have **negative selective survival** if the participants at the conclusion of the study were initially lower on an important variable; for example, the surviving participants may have been those who initially weighed the least.

The extent to which the characteristics of the group change over time determines the degree of problem. We may not know exactly what differences there are between those who return for every session and those who do not. What we do know is that the people who always return, in general, are more outgoing, are healthier, have higher self-esteem, and are more likely to be married than those who drop out (Schaie & Hertzog, 1985).

In any case, the result may be an overly optimistic picture of aging. Compare some typical results from longitudinal studies of intelligence, shown in Figure 1.6, with those in Figure 1.5, which were gathered in cross-sectional studies. Clearly, the developmental trends represented are quite different, a point we will examine again in Chapter 6.

The third additional problem with longitudinal designs is that our ability to apply the results to other groups is limited. The difficulty is that only one cohort is followed. Whether the pattern of results that is observed in one cohort can be generalized to another cohort is questionable. Thus, researchers using longitudinal designs run the risk of uncovering a developmental process that is unique to that cohort.

Because longitudinal designs necessarily take more time and are usually fairly expensive, they have not been used very frequently in the past. However, there seems to be a recognition that following individuals over time is badly needed in order to further our understanding of the aging process. Thus, longitudinal studies are appearing more frequently in the literature.

Time-Lag Designs. **Time-lag designs** involve measuring people of the same age at different times. Time-lag designs are represented in Figure 1.4 by any top-left to bottom-right diagonal. Because only a single age is studied, there are no age-related differences. Because each cohort is associated with a unique time of measurement, however, these two effects are confounded. Time-lag designs are used to describe characteristics of people at a particular age. But they provide no

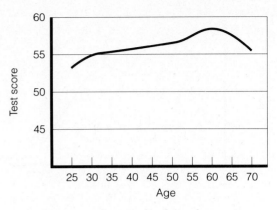

FIGURE 1.6 • Longitudinal age changes in intelligence for a verbal meaning test

(Source: "A Cross-Sequential Study of Age Changes in Cognitive Behavior" by K. W. Schaie and C. R. Strother, 1968, *Psychological Bulletin, 70*, pp. 671–680. Copyright © 1968 by the American Psychological Association. Reprinted with permission.)

information on either age differences or age change. For this reason time-lag designs are only rarely encountered.

Sequential Designs. Thus far, we have considered three developmental designs, each of which has problems involving the confounding of two effects. These effects are age and cohort in cross-sectional designs, age and time of measurement in longitudinal designs, and cohort and time of measurement in time-lag designs. These confoundings create difficulties in interpreting behavioral differences between and within individuals, as illustrated in "How Do We Know?" Some of these interpretive dilemmas can be alleviated by using more complex designs called sequential designs, which are shown in Figure 1.7 (Baltes et al., 1977; Schaie & Hertzog, 1982).

Sequential designs build on the designs we have already considered. As shown in the figure,

Conflicts Between Cross-Sectional and Longitudinal Data

As noted in the text, cross-sectional and longitudinal research designs have several limitations. What may not be clear, however, are the major implications that each has on drawing conclusions about age differences. Recall that in cross-sectional research we examine different groups of people of different ages at one point in time, thereby confounding age and cohort. In longitudinal research we examine one group of people at many points, thereby confounding age and time of measurement.

As an illustration of how using these two designs can result in opposite conclusions about age differences, let us examine the case of intellectual development. For many years a debate raged in the literature over whether intelligence increased, decreased, or remained the same across adulthood. This debate was fueled, in large part, by conflicting findings based on cross-sectional research and longitudinal research. As shown in Figure 1.5, cross-sectional data documented clear age differences in intelligence with age. In contrast, longitudinal data in Figure 1.6 showed no sig-

nificant age differences. What conclusions could be drawn about each type of data? Which data are "correct"?

In the case of cross-sectional data, the age differences could reflect either true differences that occur with age or differences that are due to cohort, or generational, effects. For example, the fact that older people never learned computer skills in school whereas younger people did may make a difference in how well one performs on current tests of intelligence. The problem is that we cannot differentiate between these two equally plausible explanations.

In the case of longitudinal data, the lack of age effects could be a reflection of a true lack of change with age. However, it is also possible that only the brightest and most healthy people survived to be tested at the end of the study. This would mean that the characteristics of the sample at the end were significantly different from those of the sample at the beginning. In short, we ended up with a very different group of people. Moreover, we also do not know whether the

lack of difference is due to other aspects of the environment that serve to support intellectual performance. Perhaps there are new discoveries about maintaining intellectual performance that assist older people. We cannot sort out all of these different explanations.

As will be described in Chapter 6, neither type of data is entirely correct. It turns out that the confounding of age and cohort in the cross-sectional data was misinterpreted as showing *age* differences, when actually most of what are seen are differences due to *cohort*. The longitudinal data are problematic because of differential survival; that is, by the end of the research only the healthiest individuals remained. These survivors were not representative of the group that began the study.

This example illustrates the need for extreme caution in comparing the results of cross-sectional and longitudinal studies. We need to avoid making the same mistakes as researchers in the past. Fortunately, we have a viable solution: the sequential designs.

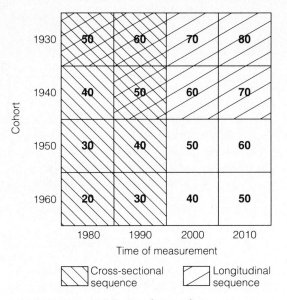

FIGURE 1.7 • Matrix of time of measurement, cohort, and age, demonstrating sequential research designs. The first and second vertical columns illustrate cross-sectional sequences described in the text. The top two horizontal rows, likewise, illustrate longitudinal sequences mentioned in the text. (The three squares with double cross-hatching are simply areas in the matrix where two sequences overlap.)

a *cross-sequential sequence* consists of two or more cross-sectional studies that are conducted at two or more points. These multiple cross-sectional designs each include the same age ranges; however, the participants are different in each wave of testing. For example, we might compare performances on intelligence tests for people between the ages of 20 and 50 in 1980 and then repeat the study in 1990 with a different group of people aged 30 to 60.

Figure 1.7 also depicts the *longitudinal sequence* design. A longitudinal sequence consists of two or more longitudinal designs that represent two or more cohorts. Each longitudinal design in

the sequence would begin with the same age range and follow people for the same length of time. For example, we may want to begin a longitudinal study of intellectual development with a group of 50-year-olds in 1980, using the 1930 cohort. We would then follow this cohort for a period of years. In 1990 we would begin a second longitudinal study on 50-year-olds, using the 1940 cohort, and follow them for the same length of time as we do the first cohort.

Schaie (1965, 1977) has argued that combining cross-sectional sequences and longitudinal sequences yields a "most efficient design." The combined design yields data that can be used to address most of the major questions that interest developmental researchers. As an example, let us consider Schaie's own research on intellectual development in adulthood. The research begins with a simple cross-sectional study in 1956 in which participants aged 22 to 67 years were given tests of intellectual abilities. In 1963 as many of these participants as possible were retested, providing longitudinal data on age changes in each of the four cohorts. At the same time, new groups of participants between 20 and 70 years old were recruited and tested. These new groups of participants formed a second cross-sectional study representing the same age groups that were tested in 1980. In 1970 both cross-sectional samples were retested, providing a second set of longitudinal measures for the 1956 sample and the first for the 1963 sample. Finally, the 1963 sample was tested a third time in 1977, providing comparable 14-year spans for each of the two groups.

Needless to say, sequential designs generate extremely large amounts of data that can be analyzed in many ways. One important analysis for gerontologists is to compare age effects with cohort effects (Schaie & Baltes, 1975). This analysis will tell whether observed age differences are due primarily to changes in underlying processes (age effects) or primarily to differences in experiential factors associated with growing older at a particular point in historical time (cohort effects). Traditional cross-sectional and longitudinal designs cannot address this issue. Because sequential designs include multiple repetitions of cross-sectional or longitudinal designs, they can separate the two effects. Understanding whether age differences are due to cohort differences is an extremely important issue. In Chapter 6 we will return to Schaie's research and see that cohort effects constitute an alternative explanation for age differences in adults' intellectual performance.

Although sequential designs are extremely powerful, few researchers use them. The biggest reasons are high cost and time. Following many people, generating new samples, and conducting complex analyses take considerable resources. In addition, sequential studies take a long time. In Schaie's research it took 21 years for all of the data to be collected and an additional 5 years or so for the analyses to be widely published. Clearly, this type of time commitment is not possible for most researchers, especially those who are trying to establish themselves in the field. Sequential designs may represent a lifetime effort.

Putting Research Designs Into Action

Research designs provide us with ways to structure the basic approach we take in gathering our data. Exactly how we gather the data involves making decisions about what we assume to be true about the behavior we plan on studying. In Chapter 2 we will consider some of these different assumptions when we discuss the world views of mechanism, organicism, and contextualism. For now, we will simply consider three approaches: experimentation, correlational techniques, and naturalistic inquiry.

Experimentation. The fundamental idea in **experimentation** is manipulation. That is, in an experiment the researcher is most interested in identifying differences between groups of people as a direct result of some variable that is present to different degrees across groups. The investigator exerts precise control over all aspects of the study, including the variable of interest, the setting, and the participants. For example, Kausler, Lichty, Hakami, and Freund (1986) wondered if memory for activities varied as a function of how long the activities were performed. To find out, they had younger and older adults perform 15 tasks; 5 were performed for 45 seconds, 5 for 90 seconds, and 5 for 180 seconds. Although they found no evidence of an effect due to duration, they did observe a significant age difference in performance. Because Kausler et al. systematically varied the duration of the activity for all participants, they met the criteria for experimentation, even though they did not find an effect.

Experimentation allows researchers to infer cause-and-effect relationships. In our example we can conclude that practice causes reaction time to improve. Moreover, one goal of experimentation is to identify relationships that generalize across different groups of people.

Correlational Techniques. Sometimes, the variables that researchers are interested in cannot be manipulated directly. For example, intelligence cannot be manipulated within a specific individual. When this is the case, investigators will usually examine how these variables are related to other variables of interest. **Correlational techniques** are the ways in which researchers identify how one developmental variable is related to, or covaries with, another developmental variable. For example, Cavanaugh and Murphy (1986) were interested in the relationship between anxiety and memory performance. They administered measures of anxiety and memory tests and calculated the correlations between the two. Their results showed that whether memory performance is related to anxiety depends on which measure of anxiety one chooses to use.

Correlational studies do not give definitive information concerning causal relationships; for example, a correlation between intelligence and problem-solving ability does not mean that one causes the other. However, correlational studies do provide important information about the strength of relationship between variables. Moreover, because developmental researchers are interested in how variables are related to factors that are very difficult, if not impossible, to manipulate, correlational techniques are used a great deal.

Naturalistic Inquiry. Since the late 1970s psychologists have become increasingly concerned that experimental and correlational approaches greatly oversimplify human behavior. In particular, both of these techniques rely on the assumption that the important factors that determine human behavior can be isolated and studied independently (Hesse, 1980). One approach that does not make this assumption is **naturalistic inquiry** (Lincoln & Guba, 1985).

Naturalistic inquiry assumes that human behavior is the result of complex, mutually dependent forces that cannot be studied in isolation. Human behavior must be studied in its natural environment and cannot be simulated in a laboratory. This approach relies on carefully conducted interactions between an inquirer (the researcher) and a participant. The information to be learned from the investigation may not be clear at the outset, but it will emerge as the study progresses. A common technique used in naturalistic inquiry is the in-depth interview, which provides a very rich set of data. Lincoln and Guba (1985) provide 14 principles that guide naturalistic in-quiry, covering everything from selecting the appropriate participants to conducting interviews to extracting the key information to reporting one's findings to others.

Naturalistic inquiry seems especially appropriate for research involving social interactions and such psychological issues as self-concept. Because topics such as these involve dynamic interchange, naturalistic inquiry provides a closer approximation of the "real world" than either the experimental or the correlational approach (Cavanaugh & Morton, 1989).

Research and the Bridge to Theory

How one decides to gather information about a topic in adult development and aging reflects how one conceptualizes the world. Moreover, the research approach chosen will have a major impact on the type of theory that is developed about the aging process. In turn, those theories will stimulate certain kinds of research and inhibit other kinds. This dynamic mutual relationship between research and theory provides the focus for Chapter 2.

SUMMARY

Gerontology is the field that examines the aging process from maturity to old age and studies older people in their own right. Older adults represent a rapidly increasing segment of the population. There has been a tenfold increase in elderly adults in the United States in this century. The characteristics of older adults vary to some extent across ethnic groups. Elderly members of minority groups are increasing more rapidly than white elderly. Differences are found primarily in the gender ratios and income levels across ethnic groups.

It is important to remember that individual differences among older adults are large.

Adulthood and aging can be approached from a life-span perspective, which has four basic tenets: (1) aging is a lifelong process, (2) aging is biological and psychosocial, (3) each person is influenced by a variety of factors, and (4) people and society influence each other. In this holistic approach, processes such as socialization and adaptation become especially important. The notions of life time, social time, and historical time represent the maturational and sociocultural influences on our lives.

Age can be viewed in several ways. Primary aging represents normal aging processes, secondary aging represents aging due to disease, and tertiary aging reflects rapid changes just before death. In addition, we can view age as biological age, social age, and psychological age. Age is also related to the determinants of development. Normative age-graded influences are those biological and environmental forces strongly correlated with age. Normative history-graded influences are events that are experienced by most people in a culture at a specific time. Nonnormative influences are those that are important for a specific person but not for most people.

Developmental research focuses on age, cohort, and time-of-measurement effects. Four major research designs are utilized. Cross-sectional research examines age differences across age groups and cohorts at one point in time. Longitudinal designs examine age changes in one cohort across multiple times of measurement. Time-lag designs examine trends in one age group across cohorts and times of measurement. Sequential designs are complex combinations of the simpler designs that provide possibilities for identifying the relative contributions of age, cohort, and time-of-measurement effects. Developmental researchers use experimentation, correlational techniques, and naturalistic inquiry to obtain their data. Each approach has advantages and disadvantages, and decisions about which to use should be made for the problem at hand.

GLOSSARY

adaptation • Modifying behavior in response to changing physical and social environments.

age change • A difference in an individual that is due to true time-dependent processes.

age difference • A difference in behavior among individuals that could be due to age, cohort, or time-of-measurement effects that may or may not be time dependent.

age effects • Differences in people due to underlying time-dependent processes.

ageism • A form of discrimination against adults simply because of their age.

biological age • A person's present position with respect to his or her potential biologically determined life span.

chronological age • How long a person has been alive in terms of calendar time.

cohort effects • Differences in people due to experiences and circumstances unique to their generation.

confound • To mingle two or more effects so that they cannot be separated.

correlational technique • A study in which a researcher examines the ways in which two or more behaviors are related to, or covary with, one another.

cross-sectional design • A comparison of people varying in age and cohort at a single point in time.

developmentally dynamic approach • Research in which the goal is to understand the processes of change.

developmentally static approach • Research in which the goal is to describe individuals in particular age groups.

emergent • A term used to describe new behaviors that are unpredictable from past behaviors or from their constituent parts.

experimentation • A study in which the investigator exerts precise control over the variable(s) thought to be responsible for a specific behavior.

gerontic enclaves • Clusters of urban dwellers in which at least 20% of the residents are elderly.

gerontology • The study of the aging process from young adulthood to old age, and the study of older adults as a separate group.

historical time • The succession of social, political, economic, and environmental events through which people live.

life-span perspective • The view that understanding development at any point in time requires knowing the past history of the organism and where it is headed, examined in a broad context of influences.

life time • The chronological age of a person.

longitudinal design • A study in which a single cohort is followed over a period of time.

naturalistic inquiry • A study in which the goal is a detailed description of behavior, which is examined in its natural setting.

negative selective survival • A problem in longitudinal designs in which people at the end of the study are those who scored the lowest at the beginning of the study.

nonnormative influences • Events that are experienced by a few people and are not correlated with chronological age.

normative age-graded influences • Biological and environmental factors that are highly correlated with chronological age.

normative history-graded influences • Events that are experienced by most people in a specific culture at a specific historical time.

ontogenetic psychology • The study of the organization of behavior from birth to death.

participant dropout • The failure of subjects in longitudinal designs to return for subsequent testings.

positive selective survival • A problem in longitudinal designs in which people at the end of the study are the ones scoring highest at the beginning of the study.

practice effect • The improvement over time of participants in longitudinal designs simply because the people are tested and retested with the same measures.

primary aging • Normal, disease-free movement across adulthood.

psychological age • A person's behavioral capacities available for adapting to changing environmental demands.

secondary aging • Developmental changes related to disease processes.

sequential design • A study in which two or more cross-sectional or longitudinal designs are implemented beginning at two or more different times.

social age • A person's standing in relation to the roles and behaviors he or she is expected to have in society.

social clock • The personal timetable by which we mark progress in life based on certain normative events.

social time • The system of age grading and age-related expectations closely related to socialization.

socialization • The ways in which people learn to function in society.

surrogate variable • A variable such as chronological age that stands for a complex set of interrelated processes.

tertiary aging • Rapid losses in functioning that occur shortly before death.

time-dependent processes • Processes that occur over the passage of time that are the causes of development.

time-lag design • A comparison of people of the same age from different cohorts tested at different times.

time-of-measurement effects • Differences in people due to the impact of social, environmental, historical, or other events at the time data are collected on the participants.

ADDITIONAL READING

A more thorough discussion of the demographics of aging can be found in

Uhlenberg, P. (1987). A demographic perspective on aging. In P. Silverman (Ed.), *The elderly as modern pioneers* (pp. 145–160). Bloomington: Indiana University.

An excellent discussion of the concepts of time and age, as well as how we use them, can be found in

Hagestad, G. O., & Neugarten, B. L. (1985). Age and the life course. In R. H. Binstock & E. Shanas (Eds.), *Handbook of aging and the social sciences* (2nd ed.) (pp. 35–81). New York: Van Nostrand Reinhold.

One of the best introductions to the issues involved in research designs is

Baltes, P. B., Reese, H. W., & Nesselroade, J. R. (1977). *Life-span developmental psychology: Introduction to research methods.* Pacific Grove, CA: Brooks/Cole.

Issues and Models of Adult Development

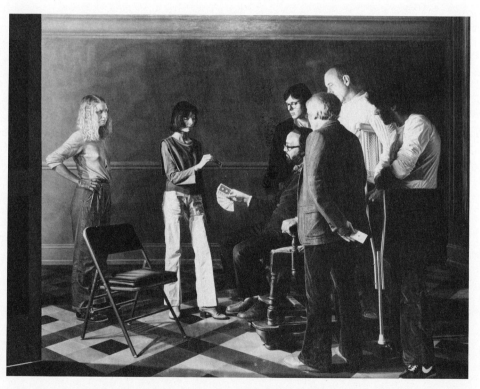

James Valerio, *Card Trick*, 1980. Courtesy Frumkin/Adams Gallery, New York.

At some point in your educational career you have probably said that you learned a lot of facts in a course but had little sense of what they meant. It is relatively easy to focus on separate pieces of information and to forget that they mean nothing unless there is some way to hold them all together in a coherent whole. The goal of this chapter is to provide the glue that will help you hold the facts in the rest of the book together.

The way in which we interpret developmental events and their interrelationships depends on the assumptions that underlie our point of view. If we believe that people are born to fulfill a certain destiny, for example, then we view a life event such as a job promotion quite differently than we would if we believed that people made their own lives. Thus, how a developmentalist interprets change or stability depends on his or her conception of human development. Our viewpoint is revealed in the positions we adopt on important issues and the models and theories we use to help make sense of events and their interrelationships across the life span. Thus, scientists do not conduct research without taking positions and making assumptions. These positions and assumptions may be stated explicitly at the outset, or they may be implicit and detectable only in the way the researcher interprets the data. The first part of the chapter will address the two major issues confronting developmental researchers: the interaction between nature and

nurture and the question of whether development is continuous.

In some cases scientists' underlying positions and assumptions form a coherent framework, or belief system. These sets of ideas are based on untestable assumptions that address important philosophical questions concerning development, including the issues of nature versus nurture and continuity. These general frameworks, termed **models**, shape researchers' views about biological maturation, environmental effects, developmental change, and the interventions that foster personal growth. In the second part of this chapter we will examine three models that have shaped the study of human development: mechanism, organicism, and contextualism. We will see how they differ in conceptualizing human development.

ISSUES IN ADULT DEVELOPMENT AND AGING

For roughly 2,200 years Western philosophers have wondered why and how people develop from birth to old age. The problem has been important enough that some of the greatest minds in history, such as Plato, Aristotle, René Descartes, John Locke, John Stuart Mill, and Charles Darwin, have provided fairly specific ideas concerning how development happens. Their ideas reflect the same two core issues that underlie the study of human development (Lerner, 1986): the **nature-nurture controversy** and the **continuity-discontinuity controversy**.

Given the importance of these two fundamental issues, researchers into adult development and aging have paid surprisingly little attention to them. For example, few books in the field even raise the topic of fundamental issues, although they may describe general models of development at length. The problem with this approach is that understanding developmental research and theory is facilitated by understanding the issues. Indeed, differences among developmentalists can often be traced to positions they take on these issues.

Having a firm grasp on the issues of development is important, for it provides a context for understanding why researchers and theorists believe certain things about aging or why some topics have been researched a great deal and others have been hardly studied at all. If one believes that a decline in intellectual ability is an innate and inevitable part of aging, for example, then research on intervention techniques to raise performance will not be done. Similarly, if one believes that personality characteristics do not remain fixed throughout adulthood, one is more likely to search for life transitions.

As we consider how each of the two fundamental issues fits into the study of adult development and aging, we will also see how positions on them can change. As we learn more about the ways in which adults develop, we may begin to question where we stand on a particular issue. Such reevaluation is good, because it means that the science of adult development and aging is not static. On the contrary, theoretical controversies abound in the field, as we will see clearly throughout this book.

THE NATURE-NURTURE CONTROVERSY AND ADULT DEVELOPMENT

"You are what you are, and that's that." "You are a product of your environment." These two statements summarize the two sides of the nature-nurture controversy. At issue here is the extent to which inborn, hereditary characteristics (nature) and experiential, or environmental, influences (nurture) determine who we are.

Historically, many people often adopted one position or the other. For example, John Calvin (1509–1564) and the American Puritans heavily stressed the inborn characteristics of humans; they adopted a strong "nature" position. In their belief system people were fundamentally evil because they had been born with original sin, which caused them to be depraved and to commit sinful acts. Behavior was explained in terms of these inborn tendencies; life experiences mattered little. Other thinkers, such as John Watson and B. F. Skinner, argued much later that how one raises a child could make considerable difference in the outcome, a very strong "nurture" position. Perhaps one of the most extreme positions has been taken by Skinner, who believes that given the proper environment and contingencies, any child can grow up to be a lawyer, politician, or anything else.

To be sure, much theorizing of this sort had to do with children. So, you ask, what about adults? It turns out that well into the second half of the 20th century, theorists simply adopted a "nature" position without really examining the issue carefully. The implicit belief in a "nature" view of adult development and aging is that certain changes will occur inevitably and that one can do nothing to alter their course. This approach to aging can be seen in the works of such divergent authors as Shakespeare, who described old age as second childishness, and David Wechsler, who believed that intellectual development in adulthood meant a loss of skills. Many of the myths that were discussed in Table 1.1 come from viewing adult development and aging from a predominantly "nature" position.

More recently, the pendulum seems to have shifted to the "nurture" side. For example, in Chapter 6 we will consider whether the decline in performance on intelligence tests is remediable. Several studies (see Willis, 1987) show that intellectual abilities that were thought to be part of the inevitable decline in old age turn out to be trainable; performance actually improves. These findings led to the idea that there is no inevitable loss of intellectual ability in normal aging, or at least very little. Perhaps it is simply a matter of skills getting rusty through disuse. This approach clearly suggests a "nurture" interpretation, since the explanation of developmental differences relies on life experiences rather than on inborn characteristics.

By actively pursuing the nature-nurture issue, theorists in child and adolescent development realized decades ago that to focus on which force, nature or nurture, was responsible for development was asking the wrong question. Rather, the more appropriate question is how do nature and nurture interact to produce development (Anastasi, 1958).

Patterns of Nature-Nurture Interactions: Focus on Nature

How do nature and nurture interact? Anastasi (1958) points out that heredity always relates to behavior in many ways. That is, any specific hereditary factor can be reflected in any of several possible behaviors. Which behavior is observed depends on the type of environment present at any give time. For example, children born with

Down's syndrome have a specific genetic defect, namely, an extra chromosome in the 21st pair. Although Down's syndrome results in mental retardation, the degree of retardation depends on the child's environment. Children placed in an unstimulating institutional environment are likely to be more severely retarded than children placed in a stimulating family environment with special education. Thus, how a given hereditary characteristic is manifested depends on the environment.

This same principle is being adapted in the study of some diseases associated with aging. For example, one theory of Alzheimer's disease holds that the illness has a genetic component (see Chapter 9). Whether one actually gets Alzheimer's disease, and possibly even the course of the disease itself, is influenced by the environment. Specifically, the genetic-predisposition hypothesis states that there has to be an environmental trigger in order for the disease to occur. Moreover, there is some evidence that providing a supportive environment for Alzheimer's patients improves their performance on cognitive tasks, at least for a while.

One difficulty in focusing on the "nature" side of things in studying adult development and aging is that it is difficult to determine whether a particular behavior or disease has a genetic component. Having lived for many years already, adults pose tough problems for geneticists. Documenting a genetic component in a behavior that may have been part of their repertoire for many years is very difficult. For this reason most work on genetics and aging tends to focus on disorders such as Alzheimer's disease and others discussed in Chapter 9. Here, the task is somewhat easier, because an abnormal gene can often be identified and linked to certain behavioral patterns.

Anastasi (1958) also points out that the effects of heredity on behavior vary from more to

The degree to which adults who have genetic diseases such as Down's syndrome are impaired depends on the quality of their environment.

less direct. This **continuum of influence** is shown in Figure 2.1. The left end represents hereditary effects that are the most direct, and the right end, those that are most indirect. The important point in this figure is that the type of effect influences our ability to intervene and alter behavior. When the effects of heredity are strong and direct, little effective intervention may be possible. For example, there currently is no way of effectively treating Huntington's disease, a genetic disorder that ultimately results in severe mental decline and death (see Chapter 9). In contrast, very indirect effects of heredity, such as social stereotypes, can be changed. Increased education about and experience with older adults, for instance, allows people to see that a stereotype such as inevitable intellectual decline is untrue.

Patterns of Nature-Nurture Interactions: Focus on Nurture

Just as the effects of heredity can be understood by considering the environment, so the effects of environment can be understood by considering heredity (Lerner, 1986). In this case the issue is the breadth of the influence of the environment (Anastasi, 1958). In some cases environmental effects are narrow, having a minimal impact on only a few specific aspects of behavior that last only a short time. Other environmental factors affect a wide range of behaviors, and their influence lasts a long time. This **continuum of breadth** is depicted in Figure 2.2.

Within this continuum of environmental effects, Anastasi suggests two general categories:

THE NATURE-NURTURE CONTROVERSY AND ADULT DEVELOPMENT

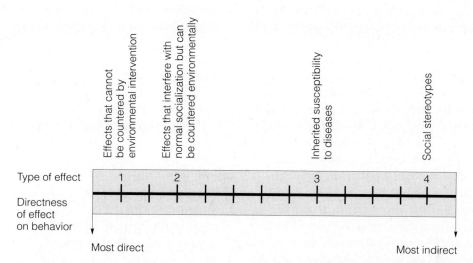

FIGURE 2.1 • Contributions of heredity to behavioral development vary along a continuum of directness. Numbers 1 through 4 refer to some points along this continuum.

(Source: *Concepts and Theories of Human Development* (2nd ed.) by R. M. Lerner, 1986, New York: Random House. Reprinted with permission of McGraw-Hill Book Company.)

organic effects and stimulating effects. **Organic environmental effects** are those that result in changes in the makeup of the person and affect what the person has and how he or she functions (Lerner, 1986). In short, they change a person's physical or physiological processes. Examples of organic environmental effects are losing a leg in an automobile accident or contracting a severe contagious disease such as polio; both would have clear effects on a person's physical makeup and have effects on behavior.

The second category of environmental effects on behavior is **stimulative environmental effects**. These effects open possibilities or otherwise stimulate individuals (Lerner, 1986). Two examples of stimulative environmental effects are social class and college education; both could lead to very different sets of life experiences that would promote the development of different skills. With

social class, for instance, a Hispanic older woman living in an inner-city ghetto is exposed to vastly different experiences than an elderly Black man living in a middle-class suburban area. Access to health care, proper nutrition, crime rate, and availability of supportive services are only a few of the differences that would have an impact on their lives.

The continuum of breadth is reflected in both organic and stimulative environmental effects. For example, diseases such as polio have a widespread and long-lasting effect, whereas a mild cold has a much narrower and short-lived effect. Likewise, the effects of social class are far more pervasive on behavior than a rude salesclerk.

As is the case with hereditary influences, environmental influences vary in how directly they influence behavior. In this case the outcome of a specific type of environmental effect, such as social class, depends on the inherited characteristics of the person. Given equally supportive and cognitively rich environments, for example, we would not expect a person in the late stages of Huntington's disease to profit as much as a normal middle-aged adult. Thus, even when we consider environmental influences, our genetic inheritance is important (Lerner, 1986). Assuming that all older adults should profit equally from cognitive training, for example, without taking into account their inborn characteristics is a mistake, as is assuming that a person cannot do a particular task simply because he or she is 70 years old.

We have seen that nature and nurture interact to influence behavior. To determine the form that behaviors will take, we must simultaneously consider the inborn, hereditary characteristics of an individual and the environment that the person is in. The key is the word *simultaneously*. Each of us is genetically unique and has unique interactions with a given environment. The two factors have to be considered together to yield an adequate

Environmental-effects continuum

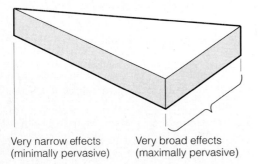

Very narrow effects   Very broad effects
(minimally pervasive)   (maximally pervasive)

FIGURE 2.2 • The contributions of environment to behavioral development vary along a continuum of breadth.

(Source: *Concepts and Theories of Human Development* (2nd ed.) by R. M. Lerner, 1986, New York: Random House. Reprinted with permission of McGraw-Hill Book Company.)

account of why we behave the way we do. Thus, looking primarily to the environment or primarily to the individual to find explanations of behavior and places to focus intervention is likely to end in frustration. Instead, we must focus on the unique interaction for that individual between nature and nurture. We will return to this point when we evaluate various models of development.

THE CONTINUITY-DISCONTINUITY CONTROVERSY AND ADULT DEVELOPMENT

The second major issue in developmental psychology actually is a derivative of the nature-nurture controversy. Given that people change over time, and given that rules govern these changes and that these rules describe nature-nurture interactions, how do these rules hold up across the life span? Can the same rules that describe an individual at one point be used to describe him or her at another point, or do we need to use different rules? If we can use the same rules to account for behavior at two different points, we have **continuity**. But if we need to use different rules at different times, we have **discontinuity** (Lerner, 1986).

The continuity-discontinuity controversy appears rather straightforward in these definitions. There is more to it, however, than establishing whether things are still the same or are different. The continuity-discontinuity debate is reflected in the competing views that adulthood is largely a matter of stability in behaviors and characteristics or that it is marked by significant and fundamental changes. The debate over the relative stability or change in behavior is especially heated in the areas of intellectual and personality

TABLE 2.1 · Hypothetical example of descriptive continuity and descriptive discontinuity for behavior when angry

	Behavior When Angry	
	Time 1	*Time 2*
Descriptive continuity	Hits others	Hits others
Descriptive discontinuity	Hits others	Yells at others

development. Our consideration of these areas in Chapters 6 and 8 will be colored by this controversy.

The continuity-discontinuity issue lies at the heart of accounting for change within individuals. As we will see, two additional aspects of the controversy have major implications for theory: description versus explanation and quantitative change versus qualitative change.

Description Versus Explanation

Within the general categories of continuity and discontinuity lies a distinction that refers to our ability to account for behavior: description versus explanation. This distinction is shown in Table 2.1. On the one hand, we may be able to provide descriptions of whether behaviors change. Suppose we wanted to know what a person did when he or she was angry at various points in life. If the behaviors were the same, such as always shouting regardless of age, then we would have **descriptive continuity**. But if the behaviors changed, such as hitting others when young but shouting when older, we would have **descriptive discontinuity**. In either case, what we have are simply descriptions of behavior; we do not know what may have caused them.

If we have a reason for behaviors, we may be able to provide explanations of them across the life span. If the same reason can be used for why

someone shouts at people at different points in life, we will have **explanatory continuity**. If we need different reasons, however, we will have **explanatory discontinuity**.

It is important to realize that descriptions and explanations of behavior can be combined in all possible ways (Lerner, 1986). For example, a person may change how he or she reacts when angry from young adulthood to old age, thereby displaying descriptive discontinuity. But the underlying reason for these different behaviors remains the same, thus producing explanatory continuity. The point is that we must not confuse *what* people do with *why* they do it.

Quantitative Versus Qualitative Changes

Consider the following situation: A person is presented with a dilemma concerning whether to stay with an alcoholic spouse. This person has given an ultimatum to the alcoholic. The alcoholic carries out the action anyway. What should the nonalcoholic spouse do?

This problem is typically solved differently depending on how old the respondent is (Labouvie-Vief, Adams, Hakim-Larson, Hayden, & Devoe, 1985; see Chapter 6). The explanation for these differences also varies, creating a situation of explanatory discontinuity. But explanatory discontinuity can result for two different reasons.

In our example the differences in solutions may have been a result of a **quantitative change**, that is, a change in how much (or how many) of something, perhaps intelligence, exists (Lerner, 1986). For example, perhaps the reason why the person gave different solutions was because he or she had learned more about marriages over the years and so was simply drawing on more experience.

In contrast, perhaps the difference reflects a **qualitative change**, in which the fundamental way in which the person thinks about the problem has changed. Qualitative change involves a difference in the essence of what exists. It is not a matter of "more of the same," which characterizes quantitative change. Rather, in qualitative change we are dealing with a brand new quality or person (Lerner, 1986). An example of the difference between quantitative and qualitative change is shown in Figure 2.3.

The notion of qualitative change has been adopted by many theorists in developmental psychology. Writers such as Jean Piaget, Erik Erikson, and Daniel Levinson have represented these qualitative changes by proposing sequences of stages that individuals pass through on their way to maturity. The concept of stages is explored in "How Do We Know?" and we will meet up with it again later in this chapter when we consider the organismic model.

Understanding Intraindividual Change

At this point we can combine the concepts of description, explanation, and quantitative and qualitative change. Any statement we make about intraindividual development forces us to take a position regarding (1) descriptive continuity-discontinuity, (2) explanatory continuity-discontinuity, and (3) the quantitative versus qualitative nature of the descriptions and expla-

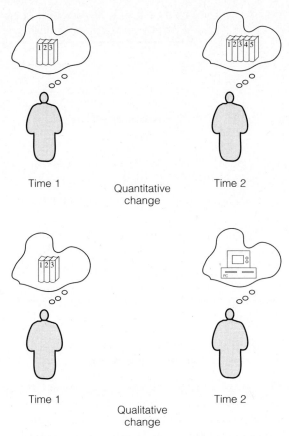

FIGURE 2.3 • Quantitative versus qualitative change. In quantitative change, differences are only in *amount*. In qualitative change, differences are in *kind*.

nations (Lerner, 1986). The combinations are represented in Figure 2.4. As can be seen, all combinations are possible. Which ones are most likely depends a great deal on what one is studying (e.g., motivation, personality, intelligence). The particular combination chosen also depends a great deal on one's model of development, as we will see.

The remainder of the chapter is devoted to a consideration of how adopting different positions

HOW · DO · WE · KNOW?

Stage Theories and Qualitative Change

Because some theories of human development view change as qualitative and adopt explanatory-discontinuity and descriptive-discontinuity positions as well, they use the concept of stages to represent these ideas. Each stage in the progression represents the emergence of new competencies that cannot be explained using the rules that governed earlier competencies. Within each stage these competencies are organized, forming **structures** that underlie and are responsible for all behavior. As the individual moves from one stage to another, the structures of interest, such as cognition or ego, are subject to a reorganization driven by internal forces, such as maturation. The role of the environment in this progression is to speed up or slow down the process; nurture does not play a role in starting or ending the reorganization itself.

Although stage theorists are interested in the underlying structure of psychological processes, this structure cannot be observed directly. To circumvent this problem, stage theorists examine behavior. However, they see behavioral change as reflecting changes in the underlying structure rather than merely a quantitative change in amount. But how are behaviors related to the underlying structure? To answer this question, stage theorists propose that a process connects behavior and the underlying structure. This connection is often believed to be invariant across the life span and serves as the interface between the individual and his or her structures and the external world.

For stage theorists, development of any psychological phenomenon (e.g., cognition or personality) is a goal-directed process aimed at achieving an ideal state (Pepper, 1942). For example, each stage in cognitive development is aimed at moving the person closer to the ideal state of thought. Thus, each reorganization of the person's underlying structure produces a closer approximation of the ideal end state.

Strict adherence to stage theory also implies that the progressive emergence of any specific ability occurs in a predetermined sequence that cannot vary from person to person. Cognitive development, for example, occurs in the same way in everyone, requiring the same number of stages that appear in the same order. Thus, strict stage theorists view development as consisting of stages that occur in the same invariant order across all people and that are not modifiable by manipulating the environment (Gottlieb, 1970, 1983; Reese & Overton, 1970).

In sum, stage theory is a way to represent changes in the rules that govern behavior across the life span. The stages serve as a shorthand way to summarize these rules, which are thought to describe everyone in that particular stage. We will encounter two important sets of stage theories, one in Chapter 6 concerning cognitive development and the other in Chapter 8 concerning personality and ego development.

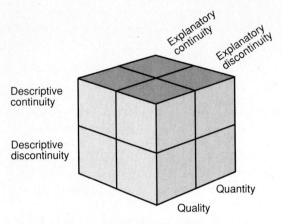

FIGURE 2.4 · The intraindividual change box. Intraindividual development involves change along three dimensions: descriptive continuity-discontinuity, explanatory continuity-discontinuity, and a quantitative-qualitative dimension.

(Source: *Concepts and Theories of Human Development* (2nd ed.) by R. M. Lerner, 1986, New York: Random House. Reprinted with permission of McGraw-Hill Book Company.)

on these issues has far-reaching effects on theory and research. As we explore the different models, notice how each one uniquely combines different positions.

Continuity-Discontinuity and Adult Development

We can understand most of the theoretical controversies in the study of adult development and aging by referring to the various combinations of factors in Figure 2.4. For example, there are hotly contested debates in the literature on intelligence and on personality development over the nature of development across adulthood. In intelligence, for instance, some argue for a position of descriptive discontinuity, explanatory continuity, and

quantitative change and maintain that the processes by which adults think do not change. Differences in performance on intelligence tests are thought to stem from increases or decreases in the amount of knowledge a person has. Others adopt a position of descriptive discontinuity, explanatory discontinuity, and qualitative change and argue that there are fundamental changes in the nature of thought. In this case differences in performance are said to reflect underlying changes in the ways we think.

The key to understanding theoretical debates in adult development and aging is to recognize that they stem from viewing the world in different ways. The behaviors under examination are often the same. It is the choice of positions on the issues that makes the difference. In the next section we will take a close look at where developmentalists stand on the major questions that confront them.

PHILOSOPHICAL MODELS OF DEVELOPMENT

Models play an extremely important role in the scientific study of human development. Different models represent different sets of philosophical assumptions about the nature of development. They also provide a way to understand why there are so many different theories of development. That is, just as different assumptions about the extent to which the government should become involved in people's lives result in very different ideas about how to solve social problems, so different assumptions about the nature of human development lead to different theories about how people change.

For developmentalists, one particular class of models is most important: world views. **World**

TABLE 2.2 · Summary of the major philosophical models of development

	Philosophical Model		
	Mechanism	*Organicism*	*Contextualism*
Metaphor	Machine	Organism	Historic event
Role of the individual	Passive	Active, interactive	Dynamic, interactive
Explanation of behavior	Reductionistic	Antireductionist	Antireductionist
	Additive	Emergent	Quantitative and qualitative
	Quantitative	Qualitative	Relativistic
	Efficient cause	Formal cause	
View of development	Continuous	Discontinuous	Dispersive

views are models that provide a way of looking at human development based on untestable assumptions about events and their interrelationships (Pepper, 1942). They embody the fundamental beliefs that scientists take for granted when they construct theories of human development, design research studies to learn about a specific aspect of development, or interpret information obtained by others. They specify the basic characteristics of people, and of reality itself, thereby defining what is important to study scientifically. In short, everything that a developmentalist does derives from a world view. One important aspect of world views is that they are not testable. This means that they cannot be proved right or wrong; they can only be either accepted or rejected. For most scientists, the criterion for accepting or rejecting a world view is the degree to which it is useful in helping them understand development.

Several world views have been offered over the years (Pepper, 1942). Three of them have heavily influenced the study of human development: **mechanism**, **organicism**, and **contextualism**. Each of these world views is associated with a particular **root metaphor**, or central idea, that captures the essence of the model. Each world view also has a unique way of viewing the important problems in human development, namely: individuals can be considered to play either a relatively passive, receptive role in their own development or to be active participants in constructing it; each model has its own way of explaining behavior; and, finally, whether developmental change is viewed in quantitative or qualitative terms has important implications, as we saw earlier. The assumptions made by each world view on these issues are summarized in Table 2.2.

The Mechanistic Model

In many respects, humans can be viewed as highly complex machines. We are composed of many separate parts, each of which has a specific role to play. These parts can be considered at several levels, from general (e.g., social, physiological, and psychological) to very specific and microscopic (e.g., individual brain cells).

The metaphor of the machine is the basis of the mechanistic model (Pepper, 1942; Reese &

Overton, 1970). Mechanists believe that all complex phenomena, such as chemical reactions, human behavior, or the movement of the planets, are machines that simply vary in complexity. The complex parts of these machines and their relationships are understood by breaking them down into simpler elements. This breaking down continues until the most basic elements are reached: simple chemical and physical processes identified in the natural sciences (chemistry and physics). Together, these processes form the most basic reality, to which all other more complex phenomena can be reduced. This means that the same set of basic laws from natural science can be used to explain all phenomena in any other science, because all organisms, including people, are subject to the same chemical and physical forces. This form of explanation is called **reductionism**, a reducing of the phenomena of a higher level to the elemental, fundamental units that compose it (Lerner, 1986). Thus, all we need to do to understand anything—biology, astronomy, or human behavior—is to bring it down to its most basic elements, the most fundamental level of analysis, the physical-chemical level. An example of reductionism is presented in Figure 2.5.

Think of it. Reductionism implies that there is nothing special about human behavior that makes it any different from the functioning of the heart or the movement of the planets. All of them are based on the same small set of natural laws. What this means is that if we knew what these fundamental laws were and understood them fully, we would understand everything.

Reductionism also implies a continuity of all things (Lerner, 1986). New laws are not needed to explain phenomena at different levels of complexity. Practically speaking, this means that we may not need to study humans in order to understand human behavior; any species may do, since all of them are subject to the same physical-chemical laws. Moving from one level of complexity to another, from rats to people, for example, simply involves adding more of whatever is present at the lower level. Differences between levels are purely quantitative.

Once we understand the components of the machine (person), we can ask the next logical question: how do you get the machine to work? The operation of mechanists' machines relies entirely on applying external forces, which produce a chainlike sequence of events. Individuals, as machines, are passive and cannot initiate action on their own. Thus, mechanism is squarely on the side of nurture. In the case of humans, external forces act on the person to cause behavior. These external forces are the only immediate causes, or **efficient causes**, of human behavior or anything else, for that matter. Thus, it is possible to predict what will happen to the machine (person) next if we fully understand what has happened up to this point. All we need to know are which forces operated in the past and what effect each of them had.

The Mechanistic Model and Adult Development. Human development from a mechanistic-behavioral perspective is viewed as a matter of accumulated experiences that are the product of both the environment and observational learning. To understand behavior at any point in the life span, one must understand the aspects of the environment that control the person's behavior at that point. Behavioral change ultimately comes only from changes in which environmental stimuli are in control. In a literal sense a person is the product of his or her environmental experiences. Development over the life span consists of continuous, quantitative additions to the individual's behavioral repertoire. Thus, older and younger adults differ only in terms of how many different behaviors they have.

As applied to adult development and aging, mechanism's major impact remains in the arena

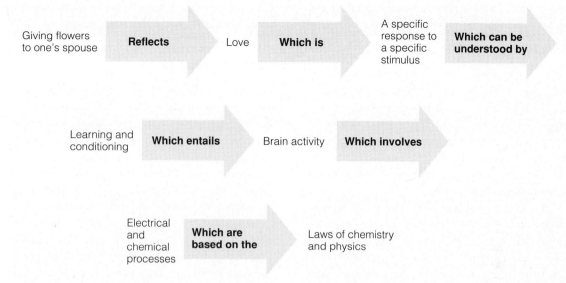

FIGURE 2.5 • Simplified example of a reductionist explanation of behavior

of intervention. For example, many intervention programs that are effective with incontinent older adults in nursing homes are grounded in mechanistic, behavioral principles (Burgio & Engel, 1987). These programs, based on **behavior modification**, are also highly effective in dealing with certain other problems. Likewise, many parents use mechanistic principles of reinforcement and punishment in raising their children. Clearly, under certain circumstances, mechanism provides a very useful world view.

Problems With the Mechanistic Model. The most important aspect of mechanism is reductionism, the belief that everything is made up of the same elements. This belief leads mechanistic theorists to assert that one needs only to study (understand) these basic components in order to know how everything else works. That is, reduce the most complex organism known in the universe, a human, to its physical and chemical com-

ponents, study those, and you will understand the human.

It all sounds so simple. The problem is that it does not work well all the time. In a very insightful article P. W. Anderson (1972) points out a serious logical flaw in the mechanists' logic. Just because you can reduce complex things down to simple elements does not imply that you can start with simple elements and reconstruct complex things. For example, it is fairly simple to reduce the human brain to its constituent chemicals. But it is no simple matter to start with these chemicals and build a human brain.

The problem that Anderson points out is that every time one moves from a lower to a higher level of complexity, things change. Something unexpected and new happens. New qualities and properties emerge that are unlike those found at the previous level. These unexpected properties cannot be understood by reducing them to the previous level; they require new understanding and research that is just as fundamental as the research done at the previous level. At each new stage we require new laws, concepts, and generalizations. In short, more is not just more; more is different (Anderson, 1972). And if more is different, the continuity assumption in mechanism must not be true, either. In other words, if new properties emerge as we move from lower to higher levels of complexity, then higher levels are not simply quantitatively greater than lower levels. Development must therefore involve an aspect of discontinuity.

A second problem with the mechanistic model concerns the definition of the environment. Wohlwill (1973) notes that mechanists have been extremely vague in specifying what constitutes the environment. He points out that depending on the needs of the theorist, environment could mean anything from the physical to the interpersonal, institutional, familial, social, or cultural context in which we live. This lack of precision makes it difficult to isolate the precise causal forces that shape development.

Finally, some mechanistic theories seem to violate the assumption of passivity. One of them, Bandura's (1986) social-learning theory, contains aspects such as self-monitoring that appear to argue for a more active role for the individual. Obviously, concepts implying an active organism cannot exist in mechanism. Because it is difficult to account for observational learning without these ideas, however, we could argue that they must be important nevertheless.

What if we were to acknowledge that emergent properties, discontinuities, heredity, and active organisms exist? Could these additions help save a mechanistic model? The answer, unfortunately, is no. As we will see in the next section, acknowledgement of emergence, discontinuity, heredity, and activity carries with it acceptance of several other beliefs that are antithetical to mechanism.

What we get is not a revised version of mechanism but an alternative world view, organicism.

The Organismic Model

The basic metaphor of the organismic model is the organism as a whole (Reese & Overton, 1970). This organism is an active participant, not a passive observer. The organism is not equal to the sum of the parts. Rather, the whole gives the parts a unique meaning that cannot be understood simply by looking at the parts. The same parts may be present in several different organisms, but because different organisms combine them differently, each organism has its own unique meanings. For example, all people are made up of the same facial elements (eyes, nose, etc.), but because these features are organized differently in individuals, each of us looks different. In short, a major point of organicism is that the whole is greater than the sum of the parts.

Organicism flatly rejects reductionism and holds that at each new level of organization new properties emerge that cannot be reduced to simpler elements (Anderson, 1972; Pepper, 1942; Schneirla, 1957; Tobach, 1981). Thus, a qualitative change occurs each time one moves from a lower to a higher level of organization. One cannot reduce a more complex phenomenon to a simpler one, because that would be like trying to explain watermelons by referring to grapes.

This inability to explain complex phenomena by reducing them to simpler ones is called the **epigenetic principle**. The epigenetic principle emphasizes that at each higher level of complexity some new characteristic emerges that was not present in, and cannot be predicted by, earlier stages of development (Gottlieb, 1970; Lerner, 1986). As depicted in Figure 2.6, behaviors that emerge later in development are not apparent during early developmental periods. Consequently,

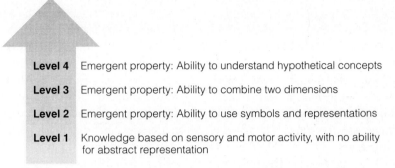

Level 4 Emergent property: Ability to understand hypothetical concepts

Level 3 Emergent property: Ability to combine two dimensions

Level 2 Emergent property: Ability to use symbols and representations

Level 1 Knowledge based on sensory and motor activity, with no ability
for abstract representation

FIGURE 2.6 • Example of the epigenetic principle in cognitive
development. This example is based loosely on Piaget's theory, which is
discussed in Chapter 6.

development is viewed as a series of qualitative changes that allow new behaviors to develop. Thus, there is an air of excitement, of the unexpected, of the new in the organismic model. At each new stage in development we get something that was not there in any form before.

Because something new emerges at each new stage of development, there is discontinuity from stage to stage. As noted earlier, this discontinuity reflects differences in *what* exists, not simply in *how much* exists. Discontinuity also implies that each level of complexity must be examined in its own right. Thus, the simple laws of natural science cannot be used to explain complex psychological phenomena such as human behavior.

How does discontinuity characterize development? The answer to this question lies in reconsidering the epigenetic principle. Recall that when we move from one level of organization to another, unpredicted properties emerge. Organicists believe that this discontinuity is due to the way the various components combine with one another. Unlike mechanists, who believe that the components simply add together, organicists believe that components have a **multiplicative, or interactional, relationship** with one another.

When components combine, they produce properties that can be understood only as a product of this interaction. For example, the cardiovascular system comprises the heart and circulatory system. To understand the concept of blood pressure, one cannot consider only the heart or only the circulatory system. Rather, one must consider them simultaneously, because blood pressure is determined by the dynamic interaction between the two components.

The multiplicative, or interactional, nature of the organismic model has an important implication: Nothing can be learned about an organism from the study of its parts in isolation. Rather, the organism must be studied as a whole, because it is not a machine that can be reduced to its simplest elements (von Bertalanffy, 1933). Just as the properties of water cannot be understood by studying the properties of hydrogen and oxygen, so humans cannot be understood by studying their underlying components (e.g., physiological processes) alone.

What causes development in the organismic model? Organicists believe that development stems from the internal reorganization process itself (Reese & Overton, 1970). The environment, although it may impede or facilitate change, does not play a direct role. More precisely, the organismic model rejects the efficient causes of the mechanist model in favor of **formal causes**.

The Organismic Model and Adult Development.

When the organismic model is translated into developmental theories, what results are views that emphasize the active role that people play in constructing their world (Reese & Overton, 1970). These views are in sharp contrast to those resulting from mechanism, which pictures individuals as passive responders to the environment. The active, constructivist view of organicism leads to an acceptance of change as a given, not as something that needs explaining in terms of simpler processes. More formally, organismic theories understand change by referring not to efficient causes but, rather, to formal causes inherent in the epigenetic principle (Reese & Overton, 1970).

Over the years the organismic model has emerged as the dominant one in the study of human development. Developmental theories based on this model are some of the best known in psychology. Piaget's theory of cognitive development and its extensions are examples that we will explore in detail in Chapter 6. Many of the theories of ego development in Chapter 8 are based on organicism as well. These and other organismic theories that we will encounter all emphasize that the parts making up the whole become reorganized at each new stage of development as a result of the person's active construction of his or her own functioning (Lerner, 1986).

Problems With the Organismic Model.

Although the organismic model fits better with most people's conception of development than does the mechanistic model, it is not perfect. Its problems stem from playing down the role of time-dependent processes as a cause of development and from largely ignoring individual differences (Gottlieb, 1970; Pepper, 1942; Scarr & McCartney, 1983; Tobach, 1981).

Because the organismic model proposes that each stage of development brings new competencies, time and past experience are deemphasized as determinants of current ability. The implications of this position are that past experience does not matter, that the timing of specific experiences does not matter, and that one cannot compare current competencies with past competencies. The problem is that past experiences certainly do matter, especially in terms of when they occur. For example, it is well known that language acquisition is much easier during early childhood than during adulthood, as anyone who has tried to learn another language in college can attest. In addition, it is also the case that newly acquired competencies are applied to problems we have already encountered but may not have been able to solve. We may well remember these earlier attempts and be aware that our current ability to deal with them is superior. This is the case in cognitive development (see Chapter 6) as well as in ego development (see Chapter 8). Note that the playing down of past experience by strict organicists is exactly opposite to the position of strict mechanists, who point to the past as the key to understanding the present. Can we really assume that growing up in a poverty-stricken area with little opportunity has no different consequences from growing up in relative wealth with the best of everything? No we cannot, as would follow from our earlier discussion on the nature-nurture controversy.

A second problem with organismic theories of development relates mainly to stage theory. The problem is that the sequence of developmental stages may not be either universal or inevitably directed toward a common ideal state. Recall that organicists assert that the cause of development is internal forces for reorganization (formal cause), leading them to believe in a universal sequence of unfolding stages (**predetermined epigenesis**). Predetermined epigenesis means that there are no differences across individuals in the developmental process, that is, that everyone passes through the same stages in the same order and ends up at the same point. Thus, development is context-free. Considerable research in cognitive, ego, and moral development has documented that predetermined epigenesis does not adequately describe what really occurs. There are substantial differences among people both within and across various cultural, socioeconomic, and ethnic groups, at least in terms of where the developmental progression apparently ends and perhaps even in the order in which developmental stages occur. We will take a close look at some of this work in later chapters. The important point here is that strict organicists assume that everyone is essentially the same. From personal experience and empirical research we know that to be false.

Thus, the organismic model is weak in the very areas in which the mechanistic model is strong: on the issues of the role of time, past experience, and individual differences. We may wonder, then, about combining mechanism and organicism into an integrated perspective. This perspective would include an emphasis on the environment, time, and incremental change from mechanism and an emphasis on emergence, qualitative change, and holism from organicism. There is a world view that includes these ideas, but it does so in ways that make it more than just a blend of mechanism and organicism. This third developmental model is contextualism.

The Contextual Model

Consider the following event: a person forgets a step in a routine. By itself this event has little meaning. But suppose we add that the forgotten step is omitting a semicolon at the end of a com-

puter command? In this case the act of forgetting is not serious, only frustrating, and it is something that could happen to anyone. If the forgotten step is how to get home from the store, however, the interpretation changes drastically. Thus, the same type of act, forgetting, has a different meaning depending on the time or context in which it occurs.

The key to understanding the third model, contextualism, is understanding the **historic event**. *Historic* is not meant to convey that something happened in the past but, rather, that whatever did happen occurred in a context. In short, contextualism argues that no act has meaning without a context, and no context has meaning without an act (Georgoudi & Rosnow, 1985; Pepper, 1942). Social reality is composed of ongoing, active, changing events that are the fundamental units of analysis. This distinguishes contextualism from both the reductionism of mechanism and the organismic and context-free emphases of organicism.

All events have three fundamental characteristics. First, the event is a concrete, particular, and individual occurrence (Dewey, 1908). Second, events unfold; they are set in time and have temporal duration. Taken one step further, this means that every event points both to past precedents and future consequences and possibilities (Hahn, 1942). Third, every event consists of a confluence of factors, relations, and activities that are all in a constant state of change. This point emphasizes that events are open-ended and constantly changing (Pepper, 1942). In this respect, contextualism agrees with organicism in accepting change as a given.

From a contextual perspective an experience such as forgetting bread at the store is a "dynamic, active, dramatic event [that] unfolds in time" (Pepper, 1942, p. 232). Everyday events become complex, dynamic patterns of relations that incorporate intentions, plans, or goals (Pepper,

1967) and the environmental conditions in which they occur. Events are not static phenomena that can be isolated and dissected into independent "personal" and "environmental" contributions. The environmental conditions may be necessary for the instigation of the event, but they are not sufficient to understand the meaning of the event. Moreover, whether the environment facilitates or hinders the individual may change across time.

Because the contextual model postulates inevitable change in all things, it is easy to think that we cannot learn anything through research. After all, what we learn today will be different tomorrow. But this idea misses an important point. The fact that events unfold over time does not preclude the possibility of continuity of certain environments or the recurrence of certain experiences. Contextualism does not stipulate the rate at which change happens, nor does it assume one standard rate of change for events. Change could proceed rapidly in some areas but be very slow in others. Depending on how frequently one makes observations, coupled with a slow rate of change, it becomes possible to discover what appear to be continuities over time. In such specific, circumscribed situations it may even be possible to consider linear causality. Thus, given the right set of circumstances, the world can appear mechanistic, even within the contextual model.

By emphasizing that change occurs in many ways and at many rates, contextualists accept the possibility of pure chance. This acceptance of chance distinguishes contextualism from mechanism and organicism, which are based on the assumption that the true order and unity of events can be determined (e.g., Hahn, 1942; Pepper, 1942; Thayer, 1968). Accepting the reality of chance does not mean that we can use chance as an explanation of everything, however. All that is meant is that all knowledge is **relative**, because

it is determined by the specific contexts in which events occur and because these contexts are themselves ultimately developing and impermanent realities. It also means a rejection of the search for universal laws. Instead, one must specify the limits, or contextual boundaries, of knowledge. This position is also very different from either mechanism or organicism, both of which hold that universal laws exist and that their identification must be the goal of scientific inquiry.

At a practical level the contextual model implies that the meanings and causes of events (e.g., human behavior) are likely to change over time and that some events happen purely by chance. For example, the cause of forgetting someone's name may change in real ways between age 20 and age 70. However, any one episode of forgetting could also be the result of random action in the brain. No universal, invariant law could explain these events so completely that we could always tell the difference between them.

Without question, contextualism emphasizes the intentional and purposive nature of human action (e.g., Georgoudi & Rosnow, 1985; Pepper, 1967). An important consideration in understanding humans as purposeful is that contexts can either facilitate or hinder the ability to reach the intended goal. Moreover, as was noted earlier, people both affect and are affected by their contexts. People come to know the world through action and the consequences of their actions, which in turn affect the future direction of development. Consequently, knowing becomes a process that occurs over time through dynamic, interactive shaping of the individual and the environment, rather than a static, passive, mechanistic "taking in" of the nature of things or the self-initiated knowing of an individual detached from the environment, as in organicism. In contextualism, thought is not subordinate to action; thought *is* action (Thayer, 1982). To a

These women exemplify the contextualist's belief that adult development involves growth and potential rather than decline.

contextualist, development is this active participation in the construction of contexts that, in turn, have a role in future action.

The assumption that development is an individual process of mutual shaping implies that there is no single ideal end point to development as there is in organicism. Moreover, there is no single set of basic laws that can predict development, as there is in mechanism. Thus, development in the contextual model is **dispersive**. That is, individual differences are the rule, and everyone has the potential to develop in his or her own unique ways (see Figure 2.7).

Contextualists recognize that development occurs both in small, quantitative increments and in large, qualitative steps (Pepper, 1942). The idea is that people change gradually, so that they appear the same if we look at them day to day. But if we compare how we are now to how we were years ago, we are likely to see very large, qualitative differences. Thus, contextualism combines the mechanistic and the organismic views of the nature of change.

The Contextual Model and Adult Development. The contextual model is the newest of the three we have considered, dating back only to the 19th century (Pepper, 1942; Rosnow & Georgoudi, 1986). Although anthropologists have developed several contextual theories (e.g., S. J. Gould, 1977; Johanson & Edey, 1981; Lovejoy, 1981; Masters, 1978), psychologists, in general, have been slow in adopting this model. Since the 1970s, however, an increasing number of developmental theorists have adopted a contextualist model. For example, Baltes, Dittmann-Kohli,

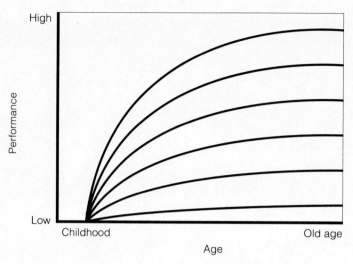

FIGURE 2.7 • Example of the contextualist principle of dispersive development, which highlights individual differences

and Dixon (1984) developed contextual approaches to intelligence, Thomae (1970) and Whitbourne (1986) proposed a contextual theory of personality, and Cavanaugh and Morton (1989) described a contextual theory of everyday memory and of sexual abuse. We will consider each in detail in later chapters.

Two characteristics of contextual theories of development are **embeddedness** (Lerner, Skinner, & Sorrell, 1980) and **dynamic interaction** (Lerner, 1984). Embeddedness refers to the fact that the most important aspects of human life exist at multiple levels of analysis: the inner-biological, individual-psychological, dyadic, social-network, community, societal, cultural, ecological, and historical. The important point about these levels is that they do not exist independently. Rather, aspects that exist at one level influence and, in turn, are influenced by aspects at other levels. Thus, each of these aspects is embedded in all others, and all exist in dynamic interaction with one another. Each level is both a producer and a

product of other levels. For example, our friends (social-network level) and ethnic group (cultural level) influence our attitudes (inner-psychological level); our personal attitudes, in turn, influence our friends.

How can we explain the role of embeddedness and dynamic interaction in human development? The answer lies in concepts discussed in Chapter 1: normative, age-graded influences; normative, history-graded influences; and nonnormative, life-event influences. These different influences point out that contextual theories are **multidimensional** (Baltes, Reese, & Lipsitt, 1980); in other words, aspects of many dimensions are involved in development. Viewed in this way, the life-span developmental approach outlined in Chapter 1 fits into the contextual model.

What the life-span approach and contextual theories have in common is a strong emphasis on the dynamic interdependence of the person and his or her context. They picture human behavior as an intricate web linking all of the various pieces. The human web links not only the different levels of aspects as they currently exist but also all of the aspects of the past. That is, just as changes at one level are linked to changes at another, changes at one time are linked to changes in the past. Thus, although there clearly is the potential for growth, this potential exists within the constraints of past experience (Brent, 1984; Lerner, 1984).

A second commonality is that contextualists focus on the individual rather than the group. This has led to the adaptation of the **ipsative approach** to fit the contextual model. The ipsative approach focuses on intraindividual change. The adaptation consists mainly of recognizing that attributes cannot be studied in isolation. The focus on the interrelationships among the attributes remains an important emphasis.

Because contextual theories of development are new, there has not been enough research based on them to draw any conclusions about additional similarities. With increasing popularity and demonstrated utility, however, these emerging theories could have a significant impact on the field during the 1990s.

Problems With the Contextual Model.
There are two major problems with the contextual model (Pepper, 1942). First, because each person has the potential to develop in a different way, identifying general trends may be impossible. That is, contextualism leaves open the possibility that there are no general principles of human development. This notion presents a problem for the traditional view that the goal of scientific inquiry is the identification of general laws (Lincoln & Guba, 1985). From the traditional view, contextualism may not be a model of science. As noted in Chapter 1, however, alternative views of science, such as naturalistic inquiry, do exist.

A second problem with the contextual model

is that it is very difficult to deal with the degree of complexity that contextualism demands. Because contextualists believe in the interconnectedness of everything, it is difficult to know how to conduct research. This view that "everything is related to everything else" often leads researchers to give up hope of ever being able to learn anything. After all, one cannot include all possible factors in one project. This problem also leads to the premature rejection of research on the ground that it ignored important factors.

Contextualists typically try to deal with complex interdependencies by arguing that one must determine whether theoretical interrelationships translate into practical, quantifiable interrelationships. For example, Lewontin (1981) notes that, in theory, every object in the universe has a gravitational interaction with every other object. In most everyday situations, however, this effect is trivial and safely ignored; we do not need to adjust our body positions each time someone in the room moves. The point is that in conducting contextual research we must establish whether we need to be concerned with every possible interrelationship or whether some can be safely ignored.

SCIENTIFIC IMPLICATIONS OF PHILOSOPHICAL MODELS

As I noted at the outset, philosophical models cannot be evaluated in terms of which one is right or wrong (Pepper, 1942; Reese & Overton, 1970). Rather, they are simply more or less useful in providing explanations of phenomena such as human behavior and development. The role that the world views of mechanism, organicism, and contextualism play is to shape the questions that researchers ask, the research designs that they use, and the ways in which they interpret their data. Thus, world views define the ballparks in which theories are posed and research is done. Each world view creates its own ballpark.

For example, a mechanist would be inclined to reduce behavior to a few principles of learning that hold true for all people, regardless of age. Thus, the mechanist would be most interested in identifying continuities across age in the environmental factors that cause behavior. Understanding adult development and aging would consist of searching for the environmental contingencies that govern behavior and uncovering the history of the person's experience with these contingencies. For example, understanding job satisfaction may consist of mapping the contingency between productivity and salary, on the assumption that salary would be viewed as a reinforcer for good work.

In contrast, an organicist would concentrate on those aspects of behavior that are unique to particular periods of life. The focus here would be on the discontinuities across the life span. Organicists would approach the job-satisfaction issue from the perspective of trying to identify the internal motivating factors for doing good work. For example, they might focus on a person's desire to achieve or the thought processes that underlie self-concept at a given point in the life span.

Finally, a contextualist would describe the relationship of current behavior to behaviors earlier in life, to current cultural and social influences, and to future potentials. The contextualist would also be interested in describing the reciprocal interactions among all of these factors. Job satisfaction in this case might be explored by trying to discern the congruity, or fit, between the personal needs of the individual and the opportunities provided by the environment.

The important point is that scientists working in different models ask fundamentally different questions about the nature of development. They collect different data and conclude very different things. As noted in "Something to Think About," they see the world through very different glasses.

The major implication for science is that some criterion other than "truth" must be used to evaluate theories based on different world views (Lerner, 1986). No one theory is intrinsically better than another. Consequently, Lerner suggests that theories be evaluated in terms of how well they *describe* and *explain* development, as well as their utility in developing ways to *optimize* human behavior. As we consider specific theories in later chapters, we will use these criteria to evaluate them.

PRACTICAL IMPLICATIONS OF PHILOSOPHICAL MODELS

Throughout the chapter we have focused on the theoretical and research implications of the various philosophical models. Before we end our discussion, however, it is important to note that these models have important applications in everyday life. These applications are most readily seen in the decisions we make about intervening, or helping others.

To facilitate our discussion, let us consider the Smith family. The Smiths live in the inner city of a large metropolitan area. Their income is barely above the poverty level, but it is enough to make them ineligible for most subsidy programs. Their outlook on life is not highly optimistic. If we decide to do something to help the Smiths, what will we do?

A mechanist will approach the situation believing that environmental factors need to be

SOMETHING · TO · THINK · ABOUT

World Views and Research

As we have seen, world views play a crucial role in determining how researchers and theorists view human development, ask questions, plan research, and interpret their data. In turn, each of us adopts a particular view in interpreting the information we obtain about development. Thus, world views are arguably the foundation on which everything else rests.

One of the problems that developmentalists encounter concerns the interpretation and evaluation of research. For example, suppose an investigator conducts a study of age-related differences in memory performance from a mechanistic perspective in which different aspects of memory are studied separately. What would an organicist or a contextualist say about this study? It is vital that we understand that one can evaluate the adequacy of research only from the perspective in which it was done. In our example the memory study could be evaluated only from a mechanistic viewpoint. Why is this so?

The reasons are relatively straightforward. As we saw, each world view takes a different combination of positions on the major issues of development. Consequently, we can know if a study is a good mechanistic investigation only if we evaluate how adequately it adopted the positions of the mechanistic model. To use another world view (organicism, for example) would be wrong, because the assumptions that underlie the research differ markedly. It would be equivalent to asking how good an apple tasted by using the criteria associated with grapefruit.

Unfortunately, many developmental researchers and theorists forget that using one world view to evaluate research based on another is inappropriate. Such mistakes lead to unnecessary controversy that diverts attention from the real issues. The point is not which research studies or theories are "right" but, rather, which ones provide adequate accounts of the phenomena they were intended to describe. We have three world views that have contributed to the study of human development. Clearly, the optimal strategy should be to use each of them to ask different questions about developmental processes. That way, we would have a much richer picture of what is really going on. Besides, our goal should be to obtain the broadest understanding of adult development and aging possible. It's something to think about.

---

changed. Consequently, the mechanist will suggest housing programs, income maintenance, and other approaches in which the Smiths are subjected to some externally driven change. Such an approach will ignore factors such as whether the Smiths want the programs in question and whether they like what is happening. In short, if you change the environment, everything will fall into place.

In contrast, an organicist will be likely to do little or nothing. From this perspective the Smiths are responsible for their own development, and no

How should we help the homeless? As noted in the text, what we believe about the nature of people and the causes of the problem determines our social policies.

outside intervention can change that. Attempts may be made to make the environment less of a hindrance, but the primary intervention will be to get them to become motivated to change. In other words, the family becomes responsible for its own behavior; the environment is innocent. This approach reflects a self-discovery, self-initiated, "you are what you are" philosophy.

Finally, the contextualist will argue that in order to help the Smiths it is necessary to change the social context in which they live. Not only will change have to occur in the environment, but the Smiths will need to realize that they have a role to play as well. For example, housing reform

will be ineffective unless the Smiths take advantage of the opportunity. The contextual perspective will play down the "quick fix" in favor of a more broad-based social policy.

We see these different perspectives every day. Politicians debate the relative merits of intervention programs from each point of view. In the United States we saw the failure of many mechanistic interventions instituted during the 1960s, and these programs underwent reform in the 1970s and 1980s. Perhaps in the future we will realize the vast complexity of the human condition and understand that complex problems require complex solutions.

SUMMARY

The nature-nurture controversy concerns the pattern of interaction between hereditary influences on behavior and environmental, or experiential, influences. When the focus is on the "nature" side, we see that behavioral expression of hereditary characteristics depends on the type of environment. Additionally, there is a continuum of influence of hereditary characteristics on behavior. When the focus is on nurture, we find a continuum of breadth of influence of the environment on behaviors. Within this continuum are organic environmental effects and stimulative environmental effects.

The continuity-discontinuity controversy concerns whether the behaviors and the rules that govern behaviors change over time. Three categories, or dimensions, can be identified: descriptive continuity versus discontinuity, explanatory continuity versus discontinuity, and quantitative versus qualitative.

Three world views have had considerable impact on the study of human development: the mechanistic model, the organismic model, and the contextual model.

Mechanism views people as passive and reactive. Explanations of complex phenomena are based on reduction to simpler systems; change occurs by continuous increments. Research and theory grounded in mechanism attempt to understand the environmental forces and contingencies that control behavior. Major problems are that its principle of reductionism does not work, it lacks precision about the definition of environment, and it violates the passivity assumption.

Organicism views people as active and views change as occurring in discontinuous, qualitative steps. A key principle is epigenesis, in which new properties emerge over time. Organicism underlies most stage theories of development. Research and theory grounded in organicism attempt to uncover the major steps, or stages, of developmental change in the organization of behavior. The main problems with the organismic world view are a tendency to play down past experience, a lack of universality in stages of development, and a lack of focus on individual differences.

Contextualism emphasizes that behavior only has meaning in a context. Change can be either continuous or discontinuous but occurs in multiple directions simultaneously. Developmental theories that are based in contextualism emphasize the embeddedness, dynamic interaction, and multidimensionality of human behavior. Problems with contextualism include a lack of ability to identify general laws and a lack of ability to deal with the level of complexity demanded by contextualism.

GLOSSARY

behavior modification • A technique of behavioral change, based on learning theories derived from mechanism, that uses the principles of reinforcement and punishment.

contextualism • A world view based on the notion of the event; sees individuals as dynamic and interactive, views change as both qualitative and quantitative, and is antireductionistic.

continuity • A situation in which the same rules can be used to account for behavior over time.

continuity-discontinuity controversy • The debate over whether development is marked by stability or by change and whether the rules that govern development remain the same or are different over time.

continuum of breadth • The degree to which environment affects behavior, ranging from narrow and temporary to pervasive and long lasting.

continuum of influence • The degree to which heredity influences behavior, ranging from direct to indirect.

descriptive continuity • A situation in which behaviors remain constant over time.

descriptive discontinuity • A situation in which behaviors change over time.

discontinuity • A situation in which different rules must be used to account for behavior over time.

dispersion • The belief of contextualism that no one set of laws can account for development; rather, each person may be a unique case that requires separate explanations.

dynamic interaction • In contextualism, the belief that the various levels of human life mutually shape one another.

efficient cause • In mechanism, an external force that results in development.

embeddedness • In contextualism, the belief that the most important aspects of human life exist at multiple levels, all of which are connected and intertwined with one another.

epigenetic principle • The idea that complex phenomena cannot be understood through reductionism, because at each new level of complexity some new characteristic emerges that was not present in and cannot be explained by earlier levels.

explanatory continuity • A situation in which we can give the same underlying reason for behaviors over time, whether or not the behaviors themselves change.

explanatory discontinuity • A situation in which we must give different reasons for behavior over time whether or not the behaviors themselves change.

formal cause • A force within the organism that is responsible for development.

historic event • Root metaphor of contextualism, holding that both context and behavior are necessary for meaning.

ipsative approach • A research strategy, focusing on intraindividual change, that can be used in the contextualist model.

mechanism • A world view based on the assumption that organisms are machinelike and passive; it views change as continuous, additive, and quantitative; based on reductionism.

models • General frameworks that shape researchers' views about the forces that cause development.

multidimensional • Occurring in many different ways and manifested at many levels; used to refer to development.

multiplicative, or interactional, relationship • The combining of components to produce properties that can be understood only as a product of this interaction.

nature-nurture controversy • The debate over the interaction between hereditary and environmental influences on behavior.

organic environmental effects • Influences that result in changes in the makeup of the person.

organicism • A world view based on the assumption that organisms are wholes and are active; it views change as discontinuous, emergent, and qualitative and is antireductionistic.

predetermined epigenesis • A belief of organicism that development is a universal process of unfolding of stages in a predetermined sequence.

qualitative change • Change in behavior that results from a fundamental reorganization and difference in the kind of characteristic that is present.

quantitative change • Change in behavior that results from a change in the amount of a characteristic that is present.

reductionism • A principle that allows a complex phenomenon to be understood by breaking it down into the elemental units that it is comprised of.

relativity • A belief in contextualism that knowledge or truth is not permanent but, rather, changes and evolves over time and contexts.

root metaphor • The central idea that captures the essence of a particular world view.

stimulative environmental effects • Influences that open up possibilities to individuals.

structure • In stage theories, an organized competency that underlies and is responsible for behavior.

world view • A philosophical model that provides a way of looking at human development; based on untestable assumptions about events and their interrelationships.

ADDITIONAL READING

An excellent source of more information on the nature-nurture and continuity-discontinuity controversies is

Lerner, R. M. (1986). *Concepts and theories of human development* (2nd ed.). New York: Random House.

The original source of the concept of world view and still the most comprehensive discussion of each of them is

Pepper, S. C. (1942). *World hypotheses*. Berkeley, CA: University of California Press.

The following is an edited book that consists of discussions on how the organismic and contextual world views have influenced theory and research on human development:

Kramer, D. A., & Bopp, M. (Eds.). (1989). *Transformation in clinical and developmental psychology*. New York: Springer.

The Aging Body

David Hockney, *My Parents*, 1977. Oil on canvas. © David Hockney, 1977.

ALL OF US HAVE SEEN PICTURES OF OUR relatives or friends that date from many years ago and have undoubtedly commented about how their appearances changed. Some signs of aging are obvious. As a rule we tend not to look favorably on the gray hair, the wrinkles, and the other changes that tell us we are growing older. Ah, we wish, if only we could *do* something. We are not alone. Juan Ponce de León, the Spanish explorer, spent a great deal of time and money wandering around Florida looking for the fountain of youth. He found a spring at St. Augustine, but, alas, it did not bring him eternal youth.

The truth is that we all must age. But that does not mean that every organ system in our bodies is over the hill by age 30. Or ever. On the contrary, there is considerable variability in how rapidly our bodies age. Our goal in this chapter is to identify normal patterns of aging and deviations from these norms due to disease or other causes. We will focus first on a basic question: how long will we live? Next, we will consider some of the normal changes that occur in several systems in the body. We will examine appearance and movement first, since those are the aspects of aging that we are most likely to notice. Then, we will consider the cardiovascular, respiratory, immune, and reproductive systems. Finally, we will conclude with a discussion of age changes in the brain.

This chapter is the first of two on biological and physiological development. In this chapter we focus on the major changes in body systems as well as on longevity. In Chapter 4 we will consider several specific diseases and many of the lifestyle factors that influence these physiological processes.

HOW LONG WILL WE LIVE?

How long we live depends on both intrinsic and extrinsic factors. **Intrinsic factors** are genetically programmed processes that are responsible for determining the maximum possible life span. **Extrinsic**, or environmental, **factors** encompass forces such as diseases or toxic chemicals that modify the intrinsic factors and shorten one's longevity, sometimes drastically. To understand intrinsic and extrinsic factors, though, we need to define longevity.

Longevity refers to the duration of an individual's life. It is expressed by two different concepts, **average longevity** and **maximum longevity**. Average longevity is commonly called "average life expectancy." It refers to the age at which half of the individuals who are born in a particular year will have died. Average longevity is affected by both intrinsic factors and extrinsic factors. For people in the United States average longevity has been increasing steadily over this century; recent estimates are presented in Figure 3.1. These increases in average longevity are due mostly to declines in infant mortality rates through the

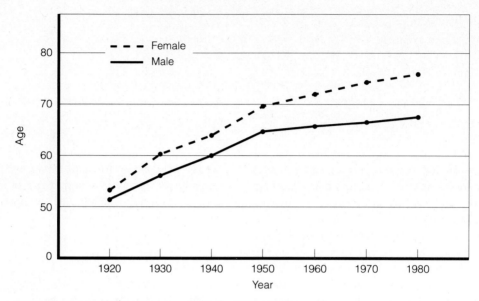

FIGURE 3.1 • Life expectancy at birth, 1920–1980
(Source: U.S. census data)

elimination of diseases such as smallpox and polio and through better long-term health care. Advances in medical technology and improvements in health care mean that more people will survive to old age, thereby increasing average longevity.

Maximum longevity refers to the oldest age to which any individual of a species lives. Although Methuselah is said to have lived to the ripe old age of 969 years, modern scientists are more conservative in their estimates of human's maximum longevity. Most estimates place the limit somewhere around 120 years (Fry, 1985).

Attempts have been made to predict the maximum longevity of different species, including humans, by considering important biological functions such as metabolic rate or relative brain size (Fry, 1985; Kirkwood, 1985). Unfortunately, none of these mathematical efforts has met with complete success, so the search for the underlying reasons for the differences in maximum longevity across species continues (Walford, 1983).

Intrinsic Factors in Longevity

The major intrinsic determinant of longevity is heredity (McClearn & Foch, 1985). Genealogical research over many years has determined that a good way to increase one's chances of a long life is to come from a family with a history of long-lived individuals (Dublin, Lotka, & Spiegelman, 1946). Tracing one's own family to test the hypothesis of inherited longevity can be enlightening. This is exactly what Alexander Graham Bell did in his genealogical study of William Hyde. Bell considered 8,797 of Hyde's descendants and found that children of parents who had lived beyond 80 survived about 20 years longer than children whose parents had both died before they were 60.

Evidence from research on twins also points toward the importance of genetics in determining longevity. Kallmann (1957) showed that even when identical twins lived in different

The fact that Bill is celebrating his 92nd birthday may reflect his genetic heritage. That he is surrounded by women reflects the substantial difference in average life expectancy between males and females.

environments, they died, on average, within about 3 years of each other, whereas fraternal twins died on the average of about 6 years apart.

Racial differences in longevity have also been noted. These differences are related mainly to socioeconomic factors—principally, lower access to quality health care—and not to genetic factors.

Extrinsic Factors in Longevity

Although heredity is a major determinant of longevity, extrinsic factors also affect the life span (Schneider & Reed, 1985). These include dis-

eases, smoking, exercise, and nutrition, as well as social class. The impacts of the first four factors are fairly well known, and they are described in Chapter 4. The impact of social class is reflected by the reduced access to goods and services, especially medical care, that characterizes most minority groups, the poor, and many of the elderly (American Association of Retired Persons, 1988).

But many environmental factors that affect how long we live are less obvious. For example, marriage has a beneficial effect, since married people tend to live as much as 5 years longer than unmarried people (Woodruff-Pak, 1988). Apparently, just having another person around to help take care of us, contribute to our financial stability, and help us regulate eating and sleeping habits can add years to our life.

The full impact of extrinsic factors is seen best when they are considered in combination. For instance, the American Cancer Society has estimated that a nonsmoking married person living in a rural area can expect to live 22 years longer than an unmarried smoker who lives alone in a large city.

Pulling It Together: How Long Will You Live?

By now, you may be a bit curious about how long you might expect to live. "Something to Think About" provides a forecast of what to expect, based on the combined influence of intrinsic and extrinsic factors. Although there are no absolute guarantees of accuracy, the estimate draws attention to the many, and sometimes surprising, influences on the length of one's life span. We will be examining some of the more important extrinsic influences in Chapter 4. Take a few minutes and answer the questions honestly. Can you live to be 100?

SOMETHING · TO · THINK · ABOUT

Can You Live to Be 100?

By keeping a running score based on your personal attributes, you will end up with a personalized life expectancy and an awareness of what you might do to live even longer. Begin by finding your life expectancy on Table 1. Take your present age, and find your starting life expectancy according to what sex and race you are. Now that you have your starting life expectancy, add and subtract years according to how you answer the questions on the life expectancy test.

TABLE 1 • Life expectancies*

Age	White Male	White Female	Black Male	Black Female	Age	White Male	White Female	Black Male	Black Female
10	72.7	79.6	67.2	75.2	25	73.5	79.9	68.1	75.6
11	72.7	79.6	67.2	75.2	26	73.6	80.0	68.2	75.7
12	72.7	79.6	67.2	75.2	27	73.7	80.0	68.3	75.7
13	72.8	79.6	67.3	75.2	28	73.7	80.0	68.4	75.8
14	72.8	79.6	67.3	75.2	29	73.8	80.0	68.6	75.8
15	72.8	79.6	67.3	75.3	30	73.9	80.1	68.7	75.9
16	72.9	79.7	67.4	75.3	31	73.9	80.1	68.8	76.0
17	72.9	79.7	67.4	75.3	32	74.0	80.1	69.0	76.0
18	73.0	79.7	67.5	75.3	33	74.1	80.2	69.1	76.1
19	73.1	79.7	67.5	75.4	34	74.1	80.2	69.3	76.2
20	73.1	79.8	67.6	75.4	35	74.2	80.2	69.4	76.2
21	73.2	79.8	67.7	75.4	36	74.3	80.3	69.6	76.3
22	73.3	79.8	67.8	75.5	37	74.3	80.3	69.7	76.4
23	73.4	79.9	67.9	75.5	38	74.4	80.3	69.9	76.5
24	73.4	79.9	68.0	75.6	39	74.5	80.4	70.0	76.6

*Life expectancies presented here are based on life tables computed by the National Center for Health Statistics for 1983 (National Center for Health Statistics, 1986).

Age	White Male	White Female	Black Male	Black Female	Age	White Male	White Female	Black Male	Black Female
40	74.6	80.4	70.2	76.7	65	79.5	83.7	78.4	82.3
41	74.6	80.5	70.4	76.8	66	79.9	84.0	78.9	82.6
42	74.7	80.5	70.6	76.9	67	80.3	84.2	79.4	83.0
43	74.8	80.6	70.8	77.0	68	80.7	84.5	79.9	83.3
44	74.9	80.7	71.0	77.1	69	81.1	84.8	80.4	83.7
45	75.0	80.7	71.2	77.2	70	81.5	85.1	80.9	84.1
46	75.1	80.8	71.4	77.4	71	82.0	85.4	81.5	84.6
47	75.2	80.9	71.7	77.5	72	82.5	85.7	82.1	85.0
48	75.4	81.0	71.9	77.7	73	82.9	86.1	82.7	85.5
49	75.5	81.1	72.2	77.9	74	83.4	86.4	83.3	86.0
50	75.7	81.2	72.5	78.1	75	84.0	86.8	84.0	86.5
51	75.8	81.3	72.8	78.3	76	84.5	87.2	84.6	87.0
52	76.0	81.4	73.1	78.5	77	85.1	87.6	81.2	87.4
53	76.2	81.5	73.4	78.7	78	85.7	88.0	81.8	87.9
54	76.4	81.7	73.7	78.9	79	86.2	88.4	82.4	88.5
55	76.6	81.8	74.1	79.1	80	86.9	88.8	87.1	89.0
56	76.8	81.9	74.4	79.4	81	87.5	89.3	87.8	89.6
57	77.1	82.1	74.8	79.7	82	88.2	89.8	88.5	90.2
58	77.3	82.3	75.2	79.9	83	88.8	90.3	89.3	90.9
59	77.6	82.4	75.6	80.2	84	89.5	90.9	90.1	91.6
60	77.9	82.6	76.0	80.5	85	90.2	91.5	91.0	92.4
61	78.2	82.8	76.5	80.9					
62	78.5	83.0	76.9	81.2					
63	78.8	83.3	77.4	81.6					
64	79.2	83.5	77.9	81.9					

(continued)

Heredity and Family

1. *Longevity of grandparents.* Have any of your grandparents lived to age 80 or beyond? If so, *add 1 year for each grandparent living beyond that age. Add one-half year for each grandparent surviving beyond the age of 70.*

————————

2. *Longevity of parents.* If your mother lived beyond the age of 80, *add 4 years. Add 2 years* if your father lived beyond 80. You benefit more if your mother lived a long time than if your father did.

————————

3. *Cardiovascular disease of close relatives.* If any parent, grandparent, sister, or brother died of a heart attack, stroke, or arteriosclerosis before the age of 50, *subtract 4 years for each incidence.* If any of those close relatives died of the above before the age of 60, *subtract 2 years for each incidence.*

————————

4. *Other heritable diseases of close relatives.* Have any parents, grandparents, sisters, or brothers died before the age of 60 of diabetes mellitus or peptic ulcer? *Subtract 3 years for each incidence.* If any of these close relatives died before 60 of stomach cancer, *subtract 2 years.* Women whose close female relatives have died before 60 of breast cancer should also *subtract 2 years.* Finally, if any close relatives have died before the age of 60 of any cause except accidents or homicide, *subtract 1 year for each incidence.*

————————

5. *Childbearing.* Women who have never had children are more likely to be in poor health, and they also are at a greater risk for breast cancer. Therefore, if you can't or don't plan to have children, or if you are over 40 and have never had children, *subtract one-half year.* Women who have a large number of children tax their bodies. If you've had over seven children, or plan to, *subtract 1 year.*

————————

6. *Mother's age at your birth.* Was your mother over the age of 35 or under the age of 18 when you were born? If so, *subtract 1 year.*

————————

7. *Birth order.* Are you the first born in your family? If so, *add 1 year.*

————————

8. *Intelligence.* How intelligent are you? Is your intelligence below average, average, above average, or superior? If you feel that your intelligence is superior, that is, if you feel that you are smarter than almost anyone you know, *add 2 years.*

————————

Health

9. *Weight.* Are you currently overweight? Find your ideal weight in Table 2. If you weigh more than the figure in Table 2, calculate the percentage by which you are overweight, and *subtract the appropriate number of years shown in Table 3.* If you have been overweight at any point in your life, or if your weight has periodically fluctuated by more than ten pounds since high school, *subtract 2 years.*

————————

10. *Dietary habits.* Do you prefer vegetables, fruits, and simple foods to foods high in fat and sugar, and do you *always* stop eating

before you feel really full? If the honest answer to both questions is yes, *add 1 year.*

_____

11. *Smoking.* How much do you smoke? If you smoke two or more packs of cigarettes a day, *subtract 12 years.* If you smoke between one and two packs a day, *subtract 7 years.* If you smoke less than a pack a day, *subtract 2 years.* If you have quit smoking, congratulations, you subtract no years at all!

_____

12. *Drinking.* If you are a moderate drinker, that is, if you never drink to the point of intoxication and have one or two drinks of whiskey, or half a liter of wine, or up to four glasses of beer per day, *add 3 years.* If you are a light drinker, that is, you have an occasional drink, but do not drink almost every day, *add 1½ years.* If you are an abstainer who never uses alcohol in any form, do not add or subtract any years. Finally, if you are a heavy drinker or an alcoholic, *subtract 8 years.* (Heavy drinkers are those who drink more than three ounces of whiskey or drink other intoxicating beverages excessively almost every day. They drink to the point of intoxication.)

_____

13. *Exercise.* How much do you exercise? If you exercise at least three times a week at one of the following: jogging, bike riding, swimming, taking long, brisk walks, dancing, or skating, *add 3 years.* Just exercising on weekends does not count.

_____

14. *Sleep.* If you generally fall asleep right away and get 6 to 8 hours of sleep per night, you're average and should neither add nor subtract

years. However, if you sleep excessively (10 or more hours per night), or if you sleep very little (5 or fewer hours per night), you probably have problems. *Subtract 2 years.*

_____

15. *Sexual activity.* If you enjoy regular sexual activity, having intimate sexual relations once or twice a week, *add 2 years.*

_____

16. *Regular physical examinations.* Do you have an annual physical examination by your physician which includes a breast examination and Pap smear for women, and a proctoscopic examination every other year for men? If so, *add 2 years.*

_____

17. *Health status.* Are you in poor health? Do you have a chronic health condition (for example, heart disease, high blood pressure, cancer, diabetes, ulcer) or are you frequently ill? If so, *subtract 5 years.*

_____

Education and Occupation

18. *Years of education.* How much education have you had? *Add or subtract the number of years shown in Table 4.*

_____

19. *Occupational level.* If you are working, what is the socioeconomic level of your occupation? If you do not work, what is your spouse's occupation? If you are retired, what is your former occupation? If you are a student, what is your parents' occupational level? *Add or subtract the number of years shown in Table 5.*

_____

(continued)

TABLE 2 · Ideal weight

To make an approximation of your frame size, extend your arm and bend the forearm upward at a 90-degree angle. Keep fingers straight and turn the inside of your wrist toward your body. If you have a caliper, use it to measure the space between the two prominent bones on *either* side of your elbow. Without a caliper, place thumb and index finger of your other hand on these two bones. Measure the space between your fingers against a ruler or tape measure. Compare it with these tables that list elbow measurements for *medium-framed* men and women. Measurements lower than those listed indicate you have a small frame. Higher measurements indicate a large frame.

Height in 1-in. heels	Elbow Breadth
Men	
5′2″–5′3″	2½″–2⅞″
5′4″–5′7″	2⅝″–2⅞″
5′8″–5′11″	2¾″–3″
6′0″–6′3″	2¾″–3⅛″
6′4″	2⅞″–3¼″
Women	
4′10″–4′11″	2¼″–2½″
5′0″–5′3″	2¼″–2½″
5′4″–5′7″	2⅜″–2⅝″
5′8″–5′11″	2⅜″–2⅝″
6′0″	2½″–2¾″

(Source: Metropolitan Life Insurance Company (Health and Safety Education Division))

Weights at ages 25–29 based on lowest mortality. Weight in pounds according to frame (in indoor clothing weighing 5 lbs for men and 3 lbs for women, shoes with 1-in. heels)

Height	Small Frame	Medium Frame	Large Frame
Men			
5′2″	128–134	131–141	138–150
5′3″	130–136	133–143	140–153
5′4″	132–138	135–145	142–156
5′5″	134–140	137–148	144–160
5′6″	136–142	139–151	146–164
5′7″	138–145	142–154	149–168
5′8″	140–148	145–157	152–172
5′9″	142–151	148–160	155–176
5′10″	144–154	151–163	158–180
5′11″	146–157	154–166	161–184
6′0″	149–160	157–170	164–188
6′1″	152–164	160–174	168–192
6′2″	155–168	164–178	172–197
6′3″	158–172	167–182	176–202
6′4″	162–176	171–187	181–207

Height	Small Frame	Medium Frame	Large Frame
Women			
4'10"	102–111	109–121	118–131
4'11"	103–113	111–123	120–134
5'0"	104–115	113–126	122–137
5'1"	106–118	115–129	125–140
5'2"	108–121	118–132	128–143
5'3"	111–124	121–135	131–147
5'4"	114–127	124–138	134–151
5'5"	117–130	127–141	137–155
5'6"	120–133	130–144	140–159
5'7"	123–136	133–147	143–163
5'8"	126–139	136–150	146–167
5'9"	129–142	139–153	149–170
5'10"	132–145	142–156	152–173
5'11"	135–148	145–159	155–176
6'0"	138–151	148–162	158–179

TABLE 3 • Risk to life of being overweight[*]

Age	Markedly Overweight (More Than 30%)		Moderately Overweight (10–30%)	
	Men	Women	Men	Women
20	−15.8	−7.2	−13.8	−4.8
25	−10.6	−6.1	−9.6	−4.9
30	−7.9	−5.5	−5.5	−3.6
35	−6.1	−4.9	−4.2	−4.0
40	−5.1	−4.6	−3.3	−3.5
45	−4.3	−5.1	−2.4	−3.8
50	−4.6	−4.1	−2.4	−2.8
55	−5.4	−3.2	−2.0	−2.2

[*]In years

(Source: Metropolitan Life Insurance Company (1976). Longevity patterns in the United States. *Statistical Bulletin, 57,* p. 2.)

20. *Family income.* If your family income is above average for your education and occupation, *add 1 year.* If it's below average for your education and occupation, *subtract 1 year.*

———————

21. *Activity on the job.* If your job involves a lot of physical activity, *add 2 years.* On the other hand, if you sit all day on the job, *subtract 2 years.*

———————

22. *Age and work.* If you are over the age of 60 and still on the job, *add 2 years.* If you are over the age of 65 and have not retired, *add 3 years.*

———————

Life-Style

23. *Rural versus urban dwelling.* If you live in an urban area and have lived in or near the city for most of your life, *subtract 1 year.* If you have spent most of your life in a rural area, *add 1 year.*

———————

(continued)

TABLE 4 · Education and life expectancy

Level of Education	Years of Life
Four or more years of college	+ 3.0
One to three years of college	+ 2.0
Four years of high school	+ 1.0
One to three years of high school	± 0.0
Elementary school (eight years)	− 0.5
Less than eighth grade	− 2.0

(Source: "Differential Mortality in the United States: A Study in Socioeconomic Epidemiology" (pp. 12, 18) by E. M. Kitagawa and P. M. Hauser, 1973, Cambridge, MA: Harvard University Press. And "Socioeconomic Mortality Differentials" by the Metropolitan Life Insurance Company, 1985, *Statistical Bulletin*, 56, 3–5.)

TABLE 5 · Occupation and life expectancy

Occupational Level	Years of Life
Class 1—Professional	+ 1.5
Class 2—Technical, administrative, and managerial. Also agricultural workers, as they live longer for their actual socioeconomic level	+ 1.0
Class 3—Proprietors, clerical, sales, and skilled workers	± 0.0
Class 4—Semiskilled workers	− 0.5
Class 5—Laborers	− 4.0

(Source: "Differential Mortality in the United States: A Study in Socioeconomic Epidemiology" (pp. 12, 18) by E. M. Kitagawa and P. M. Hauser, 1973, Cambridge, MA: Harvard University Press. And "Socioeconomic Mortality Differentials" by the Metropolitan Life Insurance Company, 1985, *Statistical Bulletin*, 56, 3–5.)

24. *Married versus divorced.* If you are married and living with your spouse, *add 1 year.*

A. *Formerly married men.* If you are a separated or divorced man living alone, *subtract 9 years*, and if you are a widowed man living alone, *subtract 7 years*. If as a separated, divorced, or widowed man you live with other people, such as family members, *subtract only half the years given above.* Living with others is beneficial for formerly married men.

B. *Formerly married women.* Women who are separated or divorced should *subtract 4 years*, and widowed women should subtract 3½ years. The loss of a spouse through divorce or death is not as life-shortening to a woman, and she lives about as long whether she lives alone or with family, unless she is the head of the household. Divorced or widowed women who live with family as the head of their household should *subtract only 2 years for the formerly married status.*

25. *Living status as single.* If you are a woman who has never married, *subtract 1 year for each unmarried decade past the age of 25.* If you live with a family or friends as a male single person, you should also *subtract 1 year for each unmarried decade past the age of 25.* However, if you are a man who has never married and are living alone, *subtract 2 years for each unmarried decade past the age of 25.*

_____

26. *Life changes.* Are you always changing things in your life: changing jobs, changing residences, changing friends or spouses, changing your appearance? If so, *subtract 2 years.* Too much change is stressful.

_____

27. *Friendship.* Do you generally like people and have at least two close friends in whom you can confide almost all the details of your life? If so, *add 1 year.*

_____

28. *Aggressive personality.* Do you always feel that you are under time pressure? Are you aggressive and sometimes hostile, paying little attention to the feelings of others? *Subtract 2 to 5 years depending on how well you fit this description.* The more pressured, aggressive, and hostile you are, the greater your risk for heart disease.

_____

29. *Flexible personality.* Are you a calm, reasonable, relaxed person? Are you easygoing and adaptable, taking life pretty much as it comes? *Depending on the degree to which you fit this description, add 1 to 3 years.* If you are rigid, dogmatic, and set in your ways, *subtract 2 years.*

_____

30. *Risk-taking personality.* Do you take a lot of risks, including driving without seat belts, exceeding the speed limit, and taking any dare that is made? Do you live in a high-crime neighborhood? If you are vulnerable to accidents and homicide in this way, *subtract 2 years.* If you use seat belts regularly, drive infrequently, and generally avoid risks and dangerous parts of town, *add 1 year.*

_____

31. *Depressive personality.*
Have you been depressed, tense, worried, or guilty for more than a period of a year or two? If so, *subtract 1 to 3 years depending on how well you fit this description.*

_____

32. *Happy personality.* Are you basically happy and content, and have you had a lot of fun in life? If so, *add 2 years.* People with feelings like this are the ones who live to be 100.

_____

Total _____

(Source: *Psychology of Aging* (pp. 145–154) by D. Woodruff-Pak, 1988, Englewood Cliffs, NJ: Prentice-Hall. Copyright © 1988 by Prentice-Hall. Reprinted with permission.)

APPEARANCE AND MOVEMENT

We see the signs of aging first in the mirror: gray hair, wrinkled skin, redistribution of fat, stooping posture. These changes occur gradually and at different rates. Some, such as in graying hair, begin by mid-life; others, such as postural changes, appear somewhat later. How we perceive that person staring back at us in the mirror says a great deal about how we feel about aging; positive feelings about the signs of aging are related to positive self-esteem (Berscheid, Walster, & Bohrnstedt, 1973).

How easily we move our bodies in negotiating the physical environment is also a major component of adaptation and well-being in adulthood (Lawton & Nahemow, 1973). Without mobility adults are forced to depend on others, which lowers their self-esteem and sense of competence. Having a body that moves effectively also allows us to enjoy physical activities such as walking, swimming, and skiing.

Age-related changes in appearance and movement are the most obvious signs of aging. In this section we will examine these changes and note their psychological impact.

Age Effects on Appearance

To get a complete picture of age-related changes in appearance, we will consider the skin, hair, voice, and body build separately.

Skin. The most visible changes in the skin in adulthood are the development of creases, furrows, and sagging (Whitbourne, 1985). These changes are universal and inevitable, affecting everyone at some point. They are due to a combination of changes in the structure of the skin and its connective and supportive tissue and to the cumulative effects of damage from exposure to sunlight (Klingman, Grove, & Balin, 1985).

Wrinkles are caused by four factors (Klingman et al., 1985). First, the outer, epidermal layer of skin becomes thinner through cell loss, causing the skin to become more fragile. Second, the collagen fibers that make up the connective tissue lose much of their flexibility, making the skin less able to regain its shape after a pinch, for example. Third, elastin fibers in the middle, or dermal, layer of skin lose their ability to keep the skin stretched out, resulting in sagging. Finally, the underlying layer of fat, which helps provide padding to smooth out the contours, diminishes.

It should be stressed that much of the facial wrinkling experienced by adults is preventable (Klingman et al., 1985). Facial wrinkles are not due solely to age but also to chemical, physical, or other traumas. For example, many features of the "old" face are sunshine-induced: precancers, cancers, benign growths, blotches, saggy or stretchable skin, wrinkles, coarse skin, and yellow skin. Proper use of sunscreens would slow the progress of these problems (Klingman, Aiken, & Klingman, 1982).

The coloring of light-skinned people undergoes some changes with age. The number of pigment-containing cells in the epidermal layer decreases, and those that remain have less pigment, resulting in somewhat lighter skin. In addition, "age spots," which are irregular areas of dark pigmentation that look like freckles, and moles, which are pigmented outgrowths, appear (Klingman et al., 1985). Some of the blood vessels in the skin may become dilated and create small, irregular red lines. **Varicose veins** may appear as knotty, bluish irregularities in blood vessels (Bierman, 1985).

Hair. Gradual thinning and graying of the hair of both men and women occurs inevitably with age, although there are large individual differences in the rate of these changes (Kenney,

1982). Hair loss is caused by destruction of the germ centers that produce the hair follicles, whereas graying results from a cessation of pigment production. Men usually do not lose facial hair as they age. However, women often develop patches of hair on their face, especially on their chin. This hair growth is related to the hormonal changes of menopause (Kenney, 1982).

Voice. How one's voice sounds is one way we judge the age of a person. Younger adults' voices are described as full and resonant, while older adults' voices are described as thinner or weaker. Some researchers (e.g., Benjamin, 1982) report that changes in the larynx, or voice box, the respiratory system, and the muscles controlling speech cause these changes. The changes include lowering of pitch, increased breathlessness and trembling, slower and less precise pronunciation, and decreased volume. However, other researchers contend that these changes result from poor health and are not normal aging (Ramig & Ringel, 1983). The question of whether changes in the voice are normative or mainly the product of disease processes remains unresolved.

Body Build. Two noticeable changes occur in body build during adulthood: a decrease in height and fluctuations in weight (Kenney, 1982). Height remains fairly stable until the 50s. Between the mid-50s and mid-70s men lose about half an inch, and women lose almost an inch (Adams, Davies, & Sweetname, 1970). Garn (1975) writes that this shortening is caused by compression of the spine from loss of bone strength, changes in the discs, and changes in posture. More details on changes in bone structure are provided below.

The experience of "middle-age bulge" is a common one. Shephard (1978) documented the typical pattern of weight gain from the 20s until the mid-50s, followed by weight loss throughout

old age. In old age the body loses muscle and bone, which weigh more than fat, in addition to some fat.

Psychological Consequences of Changes in Appearance. The appearance of wrinkles, gray hair, fat, and the like can have major implications for an individual's self-concept (Sontag, 1972). Middle-aged adults may still think of themselves as young and not take kindly others' references to them as "old." Because our society places high value on looking young and beautiful, middle-aged and older adults, especially women, may be regarded as less desirable on any number of dimensions, including intellectual capacity (Connor, Walsh, Lintzelman, & Alvarez, 1978).

An inevitable part of aging is changes in appearance that society does not highly value. Given this fact, the issue becomes whether to use any of the available means to compensate for these changes. Some age-related changes in facial appearance can be successfully disguised with cosmetics. Hair dyes can restore color. In more extreme steps, surgical procedures such as facelifts can tighten sagging and wrinkled skin. But even surgical procedures only delay the inevitable; at some point everyone takes on a distinctly "old" appearance (Klingman et al., 1985).

Not everyone tries to hide the fact that he or she is aging. Many older people have accepted changes in their appearance without a loss of self-esteem. These individuals compare their appearance with that of other people their age rather than with that of people much younger.

Movement

Smooth coordination of muscles, bones, and joints is essential for getting around in the environment. The ability to carry out desired actions has important psychological implications for the individual.

Muscles. As we grow older, the amount of muscle tissue in our bodies declines (Whitbourne, 1985). Despite this overall loss, there is little reduction in strength at least until the 40s, and even at age 70 the loss is no more than 20% (deVries, 1980). By age 80, however, the loss in strength is up to 40%, and it appears to be more severe in the legs than in the arms and hands (Grimby & Saltin, 1983; Shephard, 1981). Along with losses in strength in old age comes a reduction in endurance (Grimby & Saltin, 1983).

Losses in strength and endurance in old age have much the same psychological effect as changes in appearance (Whitbourne, 1985). In particular, these changes tell the person that he or she is not as capable of adapting effectively to the environment. Loss of muscle coordination (which may lead to walking more slowly, for example) may not be inevitable, but it can prove embarrassing and stressful.

Bones and Joints. Normal aging is accompanied by the loss of bone tissue from the skeleton (Exton-Smith, 1985). As noted earlier, these changes are also partly responsible for the loss of height with age. Bone loss begins in the late 30s, accelerates in the 50s, particularly in women, and slows by the 70s (Avioli, 1982). The sex difference in bone loss is important. Once the process begins, women lose bone mass approximately twice as fast as men (Garn, 1975). The difference is due to two factors: women have less bone than men in young adulthood, meaning that they start out with less ability to withstand bone loss before it causes problems; and the depletion of estrogen after menopause speeds up bone loss (Heaney, 1982). Figure 3.2 shows the changes that occur. Note that the process involves a loss of internal bone mass. This loss is coupled with the fact that bones become more porous, as described below. Note that there is also some age-related gain due

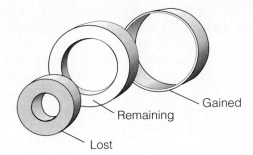

Gained

Remaining

Lost

FIGURE 3.2 • Age changes in the surface of a tubular bone in women between ages 30 and 80. Note that bone loss occurs in the central portion of bone, making it weaker, and that the gain in bone occurs on the outer surface.

(Source: "Bone Loss and Aging" (p. 45) by S. M. Garn, 1975, in R. Goldman and M. Rockstein (Eds.), *The Physiology and Pathology of Aging*, New York: Academic Press.)

to bone growth; however, this gain is limited to the outer surface of the bone.

All of these changes in bones result in an age-related increase in the likelihood of fractures (Currey, 1984) (see Figure 3.3). Moreover, when the bone of an older person breaks, it is more likely to snap and cause a "clean" fracture that is difficult to heal. Bones of younger adults fracture in such a way that there are many cracks and splinters that aid in healing. The change is analogous to the difference in breaking a young, green tree branch and an old, dry twig.

The normative changes that occur in bones sometimes become quite severe. Women are especially susceptible to severe bone degeneration, a disease called **osteoporosis**. The loss of bone mass and increased porosity create bones that resemble laced honeycombs (Meier, 1988). Osteoporosis appears more often in fair-skinned, white, thin, and small-framed women than in other groups (Avioli, 1982), and it is the leading cause

APPEARANCE AND MOVEMENT

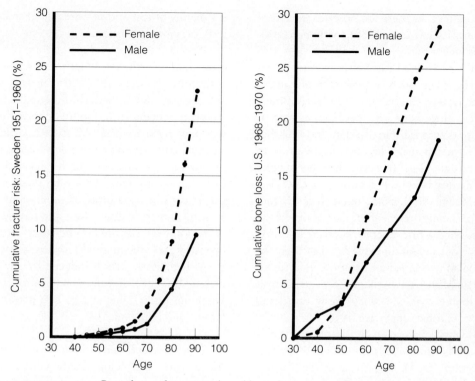

FIGURE 3.3 • Cumulative fracture-risk and bone-loss curves. The cumulative fracture figure is about 10 percentage points lower than the cumulative bone-loss figure.

(Source: "Bone Loss and Aging" (p. 43) by S. M. Garn, 1982, in R. Goldman and M. Rockstein (Eds.), *The Physiology and Pathology of Aging*, New York: Academic Press.)

of broken bones in women (Exton-Smith, 1985). Radiographic evidence suggests that at least 65% of all women over age 60 and virtually all women over age 90 are affected; in all, more than 20 million Americans are affected, with millions more at risk (Meier, 1988). For reasons not yet understood, the rate of osteoporosis is much greater in Whites than in Blacks (Meier, 1988). Osteoporosis is also related to low bone mass at skeletal maturity, deficiencies of calcium and vitamin D, estrogen depletion, and lack of exercise (Meier, 1988). The gender, age, and race factors are probably related to differences on the other

variables; for example, females tend to eat diets much lower in calcium than do males. Other risk factors include smoking, high-protein diets, and excessive alcohol, caffeine, and sodium intake (Exton-Smith, 1985).

The relationship of dietary calcium to osteoporosis is controversial (Meier, 1988). There is some evidence that dietary supplements of calcium after menopause do not slow the rate of bone loss; benefits appear to accrue when the supplements are provided before menopause. The reasons why estrogen depletion affects bone loss are also not understood, mainly because the effects must be indirect, as there are no estrogen receptors in bone tissue (Meier, 1988). Although estrogen-replacement therapy may slow bone loss, this approach must be used cautiously because of potential side effects such as endometrial cancer. Additionally, estrogen therapy must be continued indefinitely, since bone loss speeds up as soon as the therapy is stopped. Finally, data showing that vitamin D metabolism plays a causative role in osteoporosis are clear; however, whether supplementary dietary vitamin D retards bone loss is less certain (Meier, 1988). Some research shows that vitamin D administered after menopause slows the loss of bone, while other research does not. As in the case of calcium supplements, however, the U.S. Food and Drug Administration endorses vitamin D supplements as a therapy for osteoporosis on the grounds that side effects are minimal and that there are some supportive data.

Age-related changes in the joints occur as a result of a degeneration of the protective cartilage (Exton-Smith, 1985). Beginning in the 20s cartilage shows signs of deterioration, such as thinning and becoming cracked and frayed. Over time the bones underneath the cartilage become damaged. If this process occurs to a great extent, the disease **osteoarthritis** results. Osteoarthritis is marked by gradual onset and progression of pain and disability, with minor signs of inflammation (Rogers & Levitin, 1987). The disease usually becomes noticeable in late middle age or old age, and it is especially common in people whose joints are subjected to routine overuse and abuse, such as athletes and manual laborers. In a true sense osteoarthritis is a "wear-and-tear" disease. Pain is typically worse when the joint is used, but redness, heat, and swelling are minimal or absent. Osteoarthritis usually affects the hands, spine, hips, and knees, sparing the wrists, elbows, shoulders, and ankles. Drugs are typically ineffective in treating osteoarthritis; effective approaches consist mainly of rest and nonstressful exercises that focus on range of motion.

A second and more common form of arthritis is **rheumatoid arthritis**, a more destructive disease of the joints (Rogers, 1987). Rheumatoid arthritis also develops slowly, with the differences from osteoarthritis being in the joints involved and the type of pain experienced. Most often, a pattern of morning stiffness and aching develops in the fingers, wrists, and ankles on both sides of the body. Joints appear swollen. Therapy for rheumatoid arthritis consists of aspirin or other nonsteroidal anti-inflammatory drugs. Rest and passive range-of-motion exercises are also helpful. Contrary to popular belief, rheumatoid arthritis is not contagious, hereditary, or self-induced by any known diet, habit, job, or exposure. Interestingly, the symptoms often come and go in a pattern of relapsing and remitting.

Psychological Consequences of Changes in Movement. The changes in the joints, especially in osteoarthritis, have profound psychological effects (Whitbourne, 1985). These changes can severely limit movement, thereby reducing independence and the ability to complete normal daily routines. Moreover, joint pain is very difficult to ignore or disguise, unlike changes in appearance. Consequently, the adult who can use cosmetics to hide changes in appearance will not be able to use the same approach to deal with constant pain in the joints. Participation in an exercise program, however, appears to have some benefit (Folkins & Sime, 1980). Indeed, not only did participants in Munn's (1981) dance and movement training improve physically, they also reported significant increases in feelings of well-being.

Older adults who suffer bone fractures face, in addition to the usual discomfort, several other consequences. A serious fracture may force hospitalization or even a stay in a nursing home. In either case the recovery period is considerably longer than that for a younger adult. Seeing friends or relatives struggling during rehabilitation could result in a decrease in one's own activities as a precautionary measure (Costa & McCrae, 1980a).

THE CARDIOVASCULAR SYSTEM

Concern about heart disease and heart attacks is common in middle and old age. This concern is not new. The normative age-related decline in the heart and blood vessels has been known at least since the time of the ancient Greeks (Rockstein & Sussman, 1979). Cardiovascular disease, the leading cause of death today in industrialized countries, has been documented in autopsies of Egyptian mummies. Clearly, the cardiovascular system has heavily influenced conceptions of aging over the centuries. In this section we will consider age-related structural and functional changes in the heart and circulatory system. We will begin with the heart.

Cardiac Structure and Function

The heart is an amazing organ. In an average life span of 75 years, for example, the heart beats roughly 3 billion times, pumping the equivalent of about 900 million gallons of blood (Rockstein & Sussman, 1979).

The heart consists of four chambers: the right and left **atria** and the right and left **ventricles**. Between each chamber and at each entrance and exit are the heart valves. These valves ensure that the blood flows in only one direction as the heart contracts during a beat.

Blood pressure is the ratio of the systolic pressure, the pressure during the contraction phase of a heartbeat, to the diastolic pressure, the pressure during the relaxation phase. This pressure is created by the ventricles, which are literally pushing the blood through the circulatory system. The numbers associated with blood pressure, such as 120/80, are based on measures of the force that keeps blood moving through the blood vessels. Definitions of "normal" blood pressure are somewhat arbitrary (Kannel, 1985) and can vary depending on who is doing the defining and the age of the person who is having his or her blood pressure checked.

Structural Changes. Two age-related structural changes in the heart are the accumulation of fat (lipid) deposits and the stiffening of the heart muscle due to tissue changes (Lakatta, 1988).

Lipid deposits on the heart occur normally throughout the life span, but the effects are generally noticed only with advancing age (Lakatta, 1988). These deposits appear in the **pericardium**, the sac-like lining around the heart, on the **endocardium**, the internal muscle layer of the heart, and on the valves at the exits and entrances of the major blood vessels and between the atria and ventricles. By the late 40s and early 50s the lipid deposits in the pericardium may form a continuous sheet (Rockstein & Sussman, 1979).

With age the heart's ability to contract decreases because muscle tissue decomposes. Healthy muscle tissue of the endocardium and the heart valves is replaced by connective tissue, called collagen, which causes a thickening and stiffening of the affected area (Gerstenblith, 1980). This replacement is serious, because there is less functional muscle tissue to contract the heart; therefore, more effort must be exerted by the remaining muscle (Weisfeldt, 1980). These changes mean that the aging heart is less able to cope with physical stress (Lakatta, 1985).

Functional Changes. The age-related structural changes in the heart cause changes in cardiac functioning. **Cardiac output**, the volume of blood pumped by the heart every minute, decreases from about 5 liters per minute at age 20 to about 3.5 liters per minute by age 75. The pulse rate declines gradually over the entire life span from about 140 beats per minute in newborns to about 70 in young adults, and it continues decreasing slowly across adulthood. **Cardiac reserve**, the heart's ability to increase its output when confronted with sudden or prolonged stress, is diminished (Lakatta, 1985).

Heart Disease. The prevalence of heart disease increases exponentially with age (Lakatta, 1985). Overall, males have a higher rate of cardiovascular disease than women. Much of this difference is related to stress and poor diet (see Chapter 4). The most common heart disease in older adults is **ischemic heart disease**, which occurs in approximately 12% of women and 20% of men over 65 years of age (Lakatta, 1985). In this disorder the muscle cells of the heart receive insufficient oxygen because of partial blockages in the coronary arteries or poor circulation. This disease is a major contributing factor to another disease, heart failure, which is a severe reduction in the heart's functional abilities. In congestive heart failure cardiac output and the ability of the heart to contract decline. The heart enlarges, pressure in the veins increases, and there is swelling throughout the body.

Irregularities in the heartbeat, termed **cardiac arrhythmias**, are fairly common as people age (Lakatta, 1985). These disturbances include extra and uneven beats as well as fibrillation, in which the heart makes very rapid, irregular contractions. Why these changes occur is not entirely understood, but they may be related to the level of various salts (such as sodium and potassium) and minerals (such as calcium) in the bloodstream.

Cardiac arrhythmias can be very dangerous, because they may alter the normal functioning of the heart. For example, irregular contractions in the atria could cause improper filling of the ventricles, which together could seriously affect cardiac output. Additionally, ventricular arrhythmias may cause sudden death.

The Circulatory System

The circulatory system is composed of two major subsystems: the arteries, which carry oxygenated blood to the body, and the veins, which return oxygen-depleted blood back to the heart.

Structural Changes. A universal age-related change throughout the circulatory system is the calcification of the walls of the arteries, which causes them to dilate, lengthen, and lose elasticity (Bierman, 1985). This process occurs because with age calcium binds more readily to elastin, which is the connective tissue that keeps arteries elastic. Without elasticity to keep them in good tone, arteries tend to become stretched out, much as an overused rubber band loses its ability to regain its original length over time. Moreover, the calcium deposits make arteries stiffer, adding to the problem.

Arteriosclerosis is a very common disorder that is caused by degeneration and calcification of the arterial walls (Bierman, 1985). Arteriosclerosis does not refer to a particular disease but is a general term for these degenerative changes in the arteries resulting in their gradual thickening and loss of elasticity (Bierman, 1985). One common form of arteriosclerosis is atherosclerosis, which is responsible for the majority of deaths in Westernized society in people over age 65 (J. A. Brody & Brock, 1985).

Atherosclerosis involves the age-related buildup of atheromas and calcification along the inside of the arterial walls (Berkow, 1987).

THE CARDIOVASCULAR SYSTEM

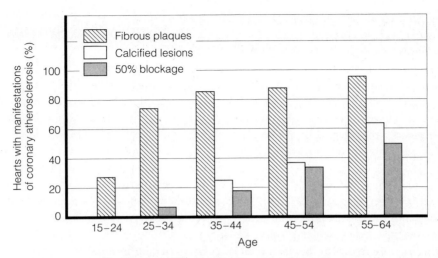

FIGURE 3.4 · Percentages of hearts showing sign of coronary atherosclerosis by age. Data for plaques and calcified lesions are derived from people who died from causes other than cardiovascular disease. Data for blockage include people who died of cardiovascular disease.

(Source: "Cardiovascular System Aging" by E. G. Lakatta, 1988, in B. Kent and R. N. Butler (Eds.), *Human Aging Research: Concepts and Techniques*, New York: Raven. Reprinted with permission.)

Atheromas are plaques that form from fat deposits. Much like sandbars in a river or mineral deposits inside pipes, atheromas interfere with the blood flow through the arteries. These deposits occur normally with age. However, excess deposits may occur through poor nutrition, smoking, and other aspects of an unhealthy life-style. Atheromas may cause arterial walls to balloon outward in an aneurysm, which may rupture. As shown in Figure 3.4, these deposits begin relatively early in life and increase with age.

Atheromas sometimes provide points where a blood clot or other mass becomes stuck, completely blocking the blood flow. If a complete blockage occurs in a major blood vessel of the heart, a myocardial infarction, or heart attack, results. The lack of blood kills the affected heart muscle, with the extent of the damage depending on the severity and extent of the blockage. A related and also painful condition is angina pectoris, which results when the heart's blood supply is partially restricted. Both of these conditions will be discussed in more detail in Chapter 4.

Atherosclerosis may become so severe in the coronary arteries (the arteries that supply blood to the heart itself) that it becomes life threatening. In some cases the blockage is nearly complete, and the arteries must be replaced surgically. This procedure, known as a coronary bypass, involves transplanting a blood vessel from another part of the body, usually the leg, to serve as a new coronary artery. Other techniques to treat atherosclerosis in the coronary arteries include inserting a tiny catheter or a balloonlike device into the arteries and clearing the blockage, scraping deposits off artery walls, and using lasers to clear the arteries (Bierman, 1985). For reasons not yet understood, blocked coronary arteries do not always produce noticeable symptoms, so that periodic checkups are very important.

Atherosclerosis can produce serious problems; heart attacks and hypertension (see below) are two examples. We have some control over the degree of atherosclerosis that occurs, as we will see in Chapter 4. However, because all humans develop fat deposits, some degree of atherosclerosis is considered a normal part of the aging process (Lakatta, 1988).

Functional Changes. As we grow older, the blood pressure tends to rise because of the structural changes in the cardiovascular system. In some cases this increase results in the disease **hypertension**. Estimates of the incidence of hypertension indicate that 18% of the population between 25 and 74 years of age have clinical hypertension, characterized by either systolic pressure over 160 or diastolic pressure over 95. Additionally, 17% of the people in this age range show borderline hypertension blood pressure between 140/80 and 160/95. It should be noted that because hypertension is largely a disease with no clear symptoms, most people with hypertension are not aware that they have a problem. However, hypertension is a major contributor to mortality (see Chapter 4). Compared with older adults with normal blood pressure, hypertensive elderly have three times the risk of dying from cardiovascular disease. Additionally, the long-term risk for a young hypertensive may even be greater (Kannel, 1985).

Psychological Consequences of Changes in the Cardiovascular System

The psychological consequences of cardiovascular disease have been the focus of hundreds of studies. Most of this research has emphasized the role of life-style and psychological factors. These variables will be considered in detail in Chapter 4.

THE RESPIRATORY SYSTEM

Many older adults complain about shortness of breath. This age-related problem is due to a decline in the effectiveness of the respiratory system. However, because air pollution, infections, smoking, and other factors all cause damage that could be mistaken for the effects of aging, it is difficult to determine what the strictly normative changes of aging are (Kenney, 1982). The changes described in this section are the combined effects of aging and living in a polluted environment.

Structural Changes

With increasing age irreversible changes occur in the rib cage, air passageways, and air sacs in the lungs. These changes all affect the functioning of the respiratory system. As we grow older, the rib cage becomes more rigid due to changes in the bones, and muscle tissue in the chest deteriorates. As a result the chest does not expand as far, decreasing the amount of air that can be taken in (Buskirk, 1985).

The lung itself changes in appearance over time (Rockstein & Sussman, 1979). Its youthful pinkish color gradually fades to gray. As the carbon particles that are breathed in the air stick to the lung, spots of black appear. The trachea and bronchial tubes become more calcified and increasingly rigid (Lebowitz, 1988).

The lungs contain thousands of air sacs, termed **alveoli**, which are separated from one another by the **septa**. Air that is breathed in fills the alveoli. Oxygen is passed into the bloodstream, and carbon dioxide is passed into the alveoli across the septa; this exchange of gases is the major function of the lungs. The more surface area that is available via the septa, the better the gas exchange. With increasing age, the alveoli become shallower, narrower, and stiffer, and the septa deteriorate and are destroyed (Reddan, 1981). These changes reduce the surface area available for the exchange of oxygen and carbon dioxide, resulting in a decrease in the efficiency of the system (Kenney, 1982).

Functional Changes

Changes in vital capacity (the maximum amount of air that can be taken into the lungs in a single breath) also occur over time due to the structural changes noted above. These changes begin in the 20s, and vital capacity decreases 40% by age 85 (Shephard, 1982). Structural changes also cause declines in reserve capacity (the amount of excess capacity the lungs have to deal with physical stress) and the maximum rate at which a person can breathe, adding to the shortness of breath encountered by older adults after exercise (Kenney, 1982). However, these changes in capacity can be moderated by regular exercise, even in old age (Buskirk, 1985). Exercise serves to increase lung capacity and slows the age-related declines in functioning (see Chapter 4).

Respiratory Disorders

Excluding upper-respiratory-tract infections, the most common and most incapacitating respiratory disorder is **chronic obstructive lung disease (COLD)**. Since the 1960s deaths directly attributed to COLD have tripled (Burdman, 1986). This increase appears to have several causes, including better diagnosis and increased long-term pollution.

Chronic obstructive lung disease is a family of disorders that includes emphysema, chronic asthmatic bronchitis, and chronic bronchitis. These conditions interfere with the passage of air in the bronchial tubes and cause abnormalities in the lungs. Smoking, air pollution, infection, heredity, allergies, and pollutants in some occupations, such as coal mining and textile factories, are but a few causes. COLD is a progressive disease in which the prognosis is usually very poor (Burdman, 1986).

Emphysema is a serious disease that is characterized by the destruction of the septa (Lebowitz, 1988). This irreversible destruction creates "holes" in the lung, effectively reducing the available surface area for the exchange of oxygen and carbon dioxide. To make matters worse, the bronchial tubes collapse prematurely when the person exhales, thereby preventing the lungs from emptying completely. In its later stages emphysema makes even the smallest physical exertion extremely difficult. In fact, a person with emphysema may have such poorly oxygenated blood that he or she becomes confused and disoriented. Once emphysema was thought to be an aspect of normal aging, but it now appears to be caused mainly by smoking. The disease is rare in nonsmokers, and such cases are probably caused by environmental pollutants, such as secondhand smoke and high levels of dust (Burdman, 1986).

Chronic bronchitis is characterized by an increase in the amount of mucous secretions in the bronchial tubes. This condition is also typically caused by smoking, and it may be present along with emphysema (Burdman, 1986).

Although upper-respiratory infections decrease in frequency with age, lower-respiratory infections such as pneumonia increase (Burdman, 1986). Consequently, pneumonia and related respiratory diseases are significant causes of death in older adults. It is thought that the increase in frequency of these infections may be due in part to a lack of exercise (Burdman, 1986).

Psychological Consequences of Changes in the Respiratory System

The effects of age-related changes in the respiratory system that people notice most are shortness of breath, termed **dyspnea**, and fatigue during physical exercise. The distress associated with dyspnea and fatigue is the major psychological consequence. It can be extremely frightening for a person to feel out of breath during moderate exercise.

The level of activity at which dyspnea is experienced declines across adulthood. Increased concern over especially serious episodes of shortness of breath is to be expected, and subsequent declines in physical activity may result. In some cases people may become overly cautious and withdraw from any form of exercise. Such withdrawal can have a detrimental effect on other aspects of physiological functioning (e.g., the cardiovascular system). Moreover, as we will see in Chapter 4, regular exercise has significant beneficial effects because it helps maintain higher levels of respiratory functioning.

Whitbourne (1985) hypothesizes that reduced respiratory functioning has negative effects on feelings of competence. Feelings that one is "out of shape" may follow experiences of dyspnea, which may ultimately lower a person's sense of well-being. This lowered sense of self-esteem may further reduce activity.

THE IMMUNE SYSTEM

Because we will consider several age-related diseases in Chapter 4, we need to have a basic understanding of the age-related changes occurring in the immune system, the body's main defense against invading organisms. The field of **immunology** has contributed to the understanding of aging in several ways, primarily by describing the mechanisms that underlie changes in the susceptibility to disease. In particular, the function of cells, the ability of cells to make antibodies, the control mechanisms in an immune response, and the influences on immune-system functioning are

a few of the discoveries related to aging that have been made in the last decade. Increased understanding of acquired immune deficiency syndrome (AIDS) in terms of how the immune system is destroyed and how AIDS relates to such age-related disorders such as dementia also advance our knowledge. In this section we will focus on the major changes seen with age that affect the ability to resist disease.

Lymphocytes

The human immune system is a highly developed defense against invasion. One of the components is responsible for the reactions in delayed skin tests, delayed hypersensitivity ("allergic reaction"), and graft rejection (for example, rejection of a transplanted organ). This component, the **lymphocytes**, provides defense against malignant (cancerous) cells, viral infection, fungal infection, and some bacteria (Berkow, 1987). There are three general families of lymphocytes: the **T-cells**, which originate in the thymus, **B-cells**, which originate in the bone marrow, and the **null cells**. Studies of these lymphocytes suggest that they do not show age-related changes in number but do show changes in function. For example, one of the functional changes involves a substance called **interleukin-2**, which is responsible for promoting T-cell proliferation. The ability of T-cells to produce interleukin-2 declines with age, resulting in a slowed response in producing T-cells (K. H. Jones & Ennist, 1985). In practical terms older adults' immune systems take longer to build up defenses against specific diseases after an immunization injection, for example. Of the various types of T-cells in the immune system, it appears that those involved with interleukin-2 show the most age-related change (Nagel & Adler, 1988). This could partially explain why older adults are more susceptible to infection and need to be immunized earlier against specific diseases such as influenza. One line of research in this area is investigating the possibility of administering interleukin-2 to older adults; results thus far seem to indicate that when this is done, T-cell functioning returns to normal (Nagel & Adler, 1988).

Considerable interest arose during the 1980s over one type of null cell, the **natural killer cell**. Natural killer cells provide a broad surveillance system to prevent tumor growth, although how this happens remains a mystery (Herberman & Callewaert, 1985). Natural killer cells have also been linked to resistance to infectious diseases and to a possible role in multiple sclerosis, a disease that typically manifests itself during young adulthood and early middle age (Nagel & Adler, 1988). However, age-related changes in the function of natural killer cells are not completely understood, leaving much to be learned in the coming years.

Antibodies and Autoimmunity

When lymphocytes are confronted with an invader, one of their responses is to produce an **antibody**, which protects the body from future invasions. Although longitudinal data on changes in the level of antibodies are lacking, cross-sectional research indicates that serum antibody levels for some specific antigens (invading organisms) differ across age. For example, levels of anti-tetanus toxoid antibody decrease with age, especially in women (Nagel & Adler, 1988).

In normal, healthy adults the immune system is able to recognize organisms that are native to the individual; that is, the immune system does not produce antibodies to organisms that occur naturally. One of the changes that occurs with age, however, is that this self-recognition ability begins to break down, and the immune system produces **autoantibodies** that attack the body

itself. This process, termed **autoimmunity**, is thought to be partially responsible for tissue breakdown and perhaps for aging itself (Nagel & Adler, 1988).

Psychological Consequences of Changes in the Immune System

At a practical level changes in the immune system are manifested as increased frequencies of illness. Psychologically, being ill more often could lead to lowered levels of self-esteem and the adoption of illness roles. Additionally, an important consequence is that many people believe that there is little that can be done; poor health is simply a product of aging.

Clearly, such beliefs are unwarranted. Chapter 4 provides considerable detail on health promotion and disease prevention, actions that are successful with adults of all ages. Moreover, immunizations are available for many diseases and should be part of an older adult's health program (Nagel & Adler, 1988). Immunizations against tetanus and diphtheria should be given about every 10 years as a booster. Vaccination against pneumococcal pneumonia can be accomplished in one dose; boosters are not recommended. Yearly immunization against influenza is also a good preventive measure.

THE REPRODUCTIVE SYSTEM

Human sexual behavior involves complex interactions among physiological and psychological factors. Age-related changes in these factors have important implications not only for sexual behavior but also for overall self-esteem and well-being. In this section we will consider what happens to the reproductive system as we age.

Reproductive Changes in Women

The major reproductive change in women is the loss of the ability to bear children. This change begins in the 40s, as menstrual cycles become irregular, and by the age of 50 to 55 it is complete in most women (Rykken, 1987). This transition during which a woman's reproductive capacity ends and ovulation stops is referred to as the **climacteric**. **Menopause** refers to the cessation of menstruation. This end of monthly periods results in decreases in the levels of estrogen and progesterone, changes in the reproductive organs, and changes in sexual functioning (Solnick & Corby, 1983).

A variety of physical and psychological symptoms may accompany menopause due to decreases in hormonal levels (Solnick & Corby, 1983). These include hot flashes, chills, headaches, depression, dizziness, nervousness, and a variety of aches and pains. Additionally, we noted earlier that sagging of the skin and osteoporosis have been associated with decreased estrogen. Although many women report no symptoms at all, most women do experience at least some physical problems due to their fluctuating hormones. The psychological consequences of menopause, which are often tied to the so-called "empty-nest syndrome," will be explored more fully in Chapter 11.

The genital organs undergo progressive change after menopause (O'Donohue, 1987). The vaginal walls shrink and become thinner, the size of the vagina is reduced, the production of vaginal lubricant is reduced and delayed, and some shrinkage of the external genitalia occurs. These changes have important effects on sexual activity, such as an increased possibility of painful intercourse and a longer time needed to reach orgasm. However, continued sexual activity throughout adulthood lowers the degree to which problems are encountered.

Despite the physical changes, the potential exists for continued sexual activity and enjoyment well into old age. Whether this occurs depends on the availability of a suitable partner. This is especially true for older women. The Duke Longitudinal Studies of Normal Aging (Busse & Maddox, 1985) found that older married women were far more likely to have an active sex life than unmarried women. Those married women whose sex life had ceased attributed their lack of activity to their husbands, who agreed with the judgment. In short, the primary reason for the decline in women's sexual activity with age is the lack of a willing or appropriate partner, not a lack of physical ability or desire (J. K. Robinson, 1983).

Reproductive Changes in Men

Just as women gradually lose the ability to bear children, men also experience a normative decline in the quantity of sperm (Rykken, 1987). The other changes that occur in the male reproductive system are not necessarily linked to the ability to father children. Men remain fertile well into old age. Sperm production declines by approximately 30% between age 25 and 60 and only by a further 20% by age 80 (Solnick & Corby, 1983). Thus, even at age 80 a man is still half as fertile as he was at age 25.

With increasing age the prostate enlarges, becomes stiffer, and may obstruct the urinary tract. The incidence of prostate cancer is especially high during middle age (Harman & Talbert, 1985). Some men also experience an abnormally quick decline in testosterone production during their late 60s. When this happens, men may report symptoms similar to those experienced by some menopausal women, such as hot flashes, chills, rapid heart rate, and nervousness (Harman & Talbert, 1985). Such rapid changes in hormone level are not normal. There is growing evidence that there is normally no reduction in the level of testosterone in men analogous to the hormone

Interest in sexuality and intimacy knows no age limits.

decline in women (Davidson et al., 1983). Testosterone level stays relatively constant in healthy community-dwelling men.

By old age men report less perceived demand to ejaculate, longer time to achieve erection and orgasm, and a much longer resolution phase during which erection is impossible (Rykken, 1987). One psychological component related to the decrease in men's sexual activity with age concerns their conceptions of masculinity, which are often linked to the ability to achieve erection and subsequently reach orgasm (Rykken, 1987). Sexual satisfaction for men in later life is directly related to the degree to which they believe myths of male sexuality, such as substantial declines in virility. Erectile failure can further damage confidence and self-esteem and support the mistaken idea that erection equals manhood. External factors such as career issues, alcohol consumption, poor health, and boredom can also lead to decreased activity.

As with women, as long as men enjoy sex and have a willing and appropriate partner, sexual activity can be a lifelong option. Mutual sharing derived from sexual activity can far outweigh any negative feelings that may accompany normal declines in performance (Weg, 1983).

Psychological Consequences of Changes in the Reproductive System

Engaging in sexual behavior is an important aspect of adult human relationships. As the discussion in this section clearly indicates, healthy adults at any age have the capacity to have and to enjoy sexual relationships. Moreover, the desire to do so normally does not diminish, either. Unfortunately, one of the myths in our society is that older adults cannot and should not be sexual. Many young adults find it difficult to think of their parents having a sexual relationship, and they find it even more difficult to think about their grandparents in this way.

Such stereotyping has important consequences. What comes to mind when you see an older couple being publicly affectionate? The reaction of many is that such behavior is "cute." But observers tend not to use the term *cute* to describe their own or their peers' relationships. Many nursing homes and other institutions actively dissuade their residents from having sexual relationships. Adult children may verbalize their opinion that their widowed parent does not have the right to establish a new sexual relationship. The message that we are sending is that sexual activity is fine for the young but is not permitted for the old. The major reason why older women do not engage in sexual relations is the lack of a socially sanctioned partner. It is not that they have lost interest; rather, they believe that they are simply not permitted to.

Clearly, being able to maintain sexual relationships into old age is important both for personal well-being and for the relationship itself. Societal pressure to cease sexual behavior could result in loss of self-worth and have serious consequences for the relationship.

THE BRAIN

Compared with changes in other organs, the specific changes that occur with age in the brain are difficult to see. There are few corollaries to the obvious signs that we have on our skin or the dyspnea we experience when we exercise. Evidence of brain changes is indirect—for example,

the forgetting of someone's name or difficulty in solving a complex math problem. Yet concern about brain aging is high during adulthood due to the mistaken idea that "senility" inevitably happens to us all.

In this section we will separate the myth from the reality of brain aging. Let us begin by taking a look at some key structures of the brain.

Brain Structures

In order to understand how the brain ages, we need to be familiar with its major structures. The building blocks of the brain are the **neurons**, an example of which is shown in Figure 3.5. Neurons have several specialized parts that play a role in receiving, conducting, and transmitting information. The **dendrites** act like an antenna, since their responsibility is to pick up the chemical signals coming in from other nearby neurons. The signal is brought into the **cell body**, where it is converted into an electrochemical impulse and sent down the axon to the **terminal branches**. The terminal branches act like transmitter stations. Chemicals called **neurotransmitters** are released at the terminal branches and carry the information signal to the next neuron's dendrites. The neurotransmitters are necessary for communication between neurons because neurons do not physically touch one another. The gap between neurons, across which neurotransmitters travel, is called the **synapse**.

We are born with roughly 1 trillion neurons of different sizes and shapes, which constitute all the neurons we will ever have. Neurons grow in size and complexity across the life span but, like heart-muscle cells, cannot regenerate (Bondareff, 1985). We will take a close look at age-related changes in neurons in the next several sections.

Numerous cross-sectional studies have documented a 5% to 10% drop in brain weight between the ages of 20 and 90, but the amount of

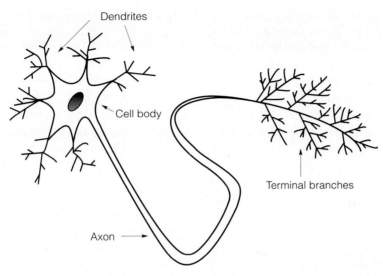

FIGURE 3.5 • Example of a neuron. Major structures are the cell body, dendrites, axon, and terminal branches.

loss is less in healthy adults and varies according to brain area (Bondareff, 1985). Most of the change occurs in the primary sensory and motor areas of the cortex (Whitbourne, 1985). Why changes should occur in these areas and not others is unclear.

Because the most important aspects of brain aging occur at the neuronal level, we will examine how neurons change with age. First, we will consider models of the aging brain based on different assumptions about neuronal decline or growth. Next, we will take a close look at specific structural changes in neurons. Third, we will consider changes in neural communication mechanisms. Finally, we will examine some of the psychological consequences of neural aging.

Models of the Aging Brain

Describing the effects of age on the brain is an enormous task. Individual experience and intrinsic physiological changes interact to produce an intricate set of changes in an already enormously complex system. Moreover, once a neuron dies, all the connections it made are lost, possibly along with the behaviors based on those connections.

Researchers differ in their views about the impact of developmental changes in the aging brain, but these views can be organized into two main perspectives (Whitbourne, 1985): the **neuronal fallout model** and the **plasticity model**.

Neuronal Fallout Model. The basis for the neuronal fallout model is the fact that neurons die and are not replaced (Hanley, 1974). Research questions in this model concern how the rate and extent of neuronal fallout varies across different areas of the brain and how much neuronal death must occur before it affects behavior. Although there is a great deal of redundancy in the human brain, with the same information being stored at several locations, it is still presumed that neuronal fallout reduces redundancy. That is, the neuronal fallout model assumes that there is a point at which neuronal death will seriously affect functioning (Henderson, Tomlinson, & Gibson, 1980). The effects of neuronal death will be more severe in those areas of the brain where there is little redundancy (Finch, 1982).

Neuronal fallout becomes critical if it includes "pacemaker" neurons (Brizzee, 1975). Pacemaker neurons control many other neurons and are not redundant. Their loss could cause a cascade of degeneration, in which neurons die when the neurons that stimulate them die (Greenough & Green, 1981). Thus, the loss of a few critical neurons may have serious harmful effects (Ordy, 1981).

Plasticity Model. The neuronal fallout model implies that the decline of sensory, motor, and other functions is an inevitable by-product of aging and that brain aging is primarily a matter of loss. An alternative viewpoint is presented in the plasticity model. According to this model, neurons that do not die take on the functions lost when other neurons are damaged or die. Neurons that are plastic grow new connections by adding new dendrites in response to novelty (Curcio, Buell, & Coleman, 1982). This growth not only may compensate for neuronal fallout but also may explain how new information comes to be processed (Greenough & Green, 1981). Certainly, not all neurons are plastic; neurons involved in spinal reflexes are not, for example. However, many neurons are able to grow new axons or longer dendrites when other neurons are damaged through trauma or degeneration (Greenough & Green, 1981).

This neurologically based plasticity model corresponds well to psychological models of intellectual development emphasizing that intellectual decline is not inevitable (Baltes, Dittmann-Kohli, & Dixon, 1984). The issue of intellectual plasticity will be discussed further in Chapter 6.

The plasticity model helps clarify the distinc-

tion between normal and abnormal aging (Buell & Coleman, 1981). Two populations of neurons are present in the aging brain, one that degenerates over time and one that continues to grow. It is hypothesized that the growing group predominates in normal aging, although there may be a point in very old age at which the degenerating group normally predominates. Buell and Coleman (1981) found a predominance of degenerating neurons only in individuals with organic brain disorders.

Synthesizing Models of the Aging Brain. At first glance the neuronal fallout and plasticity models seem incompatible. But this incompatibility is more apparent than real. Buell and Coleman's (1979) landmark research on neuronal plasticity documented the coexistence of dying and growing neurons. Both were present in the brains of all adults studied; ages ranged from 44 to 92 years. Consequently, it appears that a complete model of the aging brain requires an understanding of both why neurons die and why they grow. It may be that the pattern of losses and gains represents an adaptive function. That is, we may be programmed to generate neuronal connections almost indiscriminately while we are young, thereby allowing as much learning to occur as possible. The losses accompanying aging would then represent judicious pruning of unused, redundant, unnecessary connections that can be removed without seriously compromising the person's ability to function.

Structural Changes in the Neuron

According to both the neuronal fallout and the plasticity models, some neurons die as a matter of course, and a substantial amount of neuronal death is a primary indicator of abnormal aging. What kinds of changes do neurons undergo?

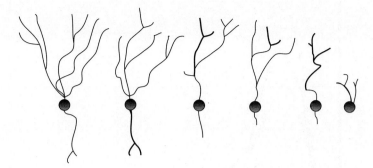

FIGURE 3.6 • Summary of progressive changes in dendrites with age

(Source: "Progressive Dendritic Changes in the Aging Human Limbic System" by M. E. Scheibel, R. D. Lindsay, U. Tomiyasu, and A. B. Scheibel, 1976, *Experimental Neurology*, 53, p. 426. Copyright © 1976 by Academic Press. Reprinted with permission.)

Cell Body. Aging neuronal cell bodies show distortions in the membrane around the nucleus and an accumulation of **lipofuscin**, a yellow pigment. Neurons in specific locations in the brain undergo other structural changes. For example, neurons in the hippocampus develop **neurofibrillary tangles**, in which fibers in the axon become twisted together to form paired helical, or spiral, filaments (Duara, London, & Rapoport, 1985). Large concentrations of neurofibrillary tangles are associated with behavioral abnormalities and are one defining characteristic of Alzheimer's disease, which is discussed in Chapter 9 (Bondareff, 1985).

Dendrites. Age-related structural changes in the dendrites have been observed. Recall that dendrites are the extensions of the cell bodies that receive information from other neurons. When dendrites deteriorate, a person's ability to process information is impaired (Duara et al., 1985).

Dendritic changes are complex. Scheibel (1982) maintains that dendrites are lost progressively from aging neurons. This process is shown in Figure 3.6. Dendritic branches are lost first from the outermost sections, but loss eventually spreads to include the entire structure. Ultimately, the neuron is reduced to a stump with no dendrites, at which point it dies. Scheibel's research has been used to provide support for the neuronal fallout model of brain aging (Whitbourne, 1985).

Buell and Coleman (1979) conducted a quantitative analysis in which they measured the length of the dendrites. Their results, shown in Figure 3.7, present a much different picture from Scheibel's. It is clear that in normal aging, dendritic length actually increases across adulthood. Only in abnormal aging such as in Alzheimer's disease do dendritic lengths decline. How Buell and Coleman drew this conclusion is examined in "How Do We Know?"

What should we conclude from this discussion? It appears that both descriptions may be correct (Duara et al., 1985). Curcio et al. (1982) point out that in normal aging some neurons die while others, perhaps most, are prospering and continuing to grow. Thus, Scheibel's (1982)

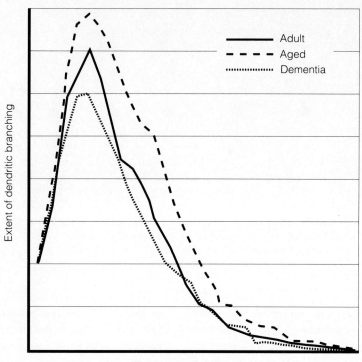

FIGURE 3.7 • Extent of dendritic branching according to the distance from the cell body. These data support the notion that dendritic growth still occurs in old age.

(Source: "Dendritic Growth in the Aged Human Brain and Failure of Growth in Senile Dementia" by S. J. Buell and P. D. Coleman, 1979, *Science, 206,* p. 855. Copyright 1979 by the American Association for the Advancement of Science. Reprinted with permission.)

research provides a description of the degradation process, and Buell and Coleman's (1979) research describes the growth.

Plaques. Damaged and dying neurons sometimes collect around a core of protein and produce **neuritic plaques**. Neuritic plaques have been found in samples taken at autopsy from both the hippocampus and the cerebral cortex (Kenney,

1982). Although the number of neuritic plaques increases with age, large numbers of them are not observed in normal brain aging until the age of 90 (Adams, 1980). Before that age high concentrations of neuritic plaques are characteristic of abnormal aging.

Because they are composed of degenerating neurons, neuritic plaques are believed to be a consequence rather than a cause of neural aging

Brain Aging Is Not All Decline: Evidence for Dendritic Growth

As noted in the text, one of the dominant views of brain aging is the neuronal fallout model, which pictures brain aging as characterized by loss and decline. Over the last decade, however, researchers have discovered strong evidence for neuronal growth across adulthood as well. This line of work was pioneered by Buell and Coleman (1979), who were among the first to describe this growth process. How did they find their evidence?

Buell and Coleman obtained samples of brain tissue from 15 individuals during autopsy. These individuals represented three groups: 5 were from neurologically normal middle-aged adults averaging 51.2 years; 5 were from

normal older adults, averaging 79.6 years; and 5 were from older adults who had brain diseases, averaging 76 years. The samples of brain tissue were from the area near the hippocampus.

The key measurement was the length of the average dendritic segment, which was obtained by dividing total length of the dendrite by the number of segments it contained. The researchers found that the average length of a dendritic segment was significantly longer in the normal elderly brains than in the normal middle-aged brains, and both were significantly longer than those in the demented brains.

The findings presented in Figure 3.7 demonstrated clear evi-

dence of continued growth of the dendrites in normal aging. Dementia represents a failure of this process and actually involves a shrinking of the dendrites. Buell and Coleman were the first to definitively document growth in the brain during adulthood and aging. They speculate that there are two different populations of neurons in the normal older adult. One group consists of dying neurons, represented by the fallout model. The other group consists of surviving and growing neurons. Buell and Coleman speculate that in normal aging the second group predominates until very late in life. How and when the shift from growth to decline occurs remains a mystery.

(Duara et al., 1985). As neuritic plaques become numerous, however, it is likely that they interfere with the normal functioning of healthy neurons (Bondareff, 1985).

Changes in Communication Among Neurons

Neurons do not work in isolation. Recall that because neurons do not physically touch one another, they communicate by releasing

neurotransmitters into the synapse. Changes with age occur in both the synapse and neurotransmitters (Bondareff, 1985).

Synapses. It is difficult to establish the pattern of age-related changes in synapses, because two complex processes are occurring (Cotman & Holets, 1985). First, synapses are lost through neuronal degeneration and death. Second, new synapses are formed as a result of new learning and the continued growth of neurons (Cotman &

Holets, 1985). These two opposing processes result in no net change in the number of synapses, but they do produce changes in the configuration of synapses (Hoff, Scheff, Bernardo, & Cotman, 1982; Hoff, Scheff, & Cotman, 1982). The way in which neurons are organized and interconnected changes with age, but what these changes mean for human behavior is unknown (Cotman & Holets, 1985).

Neurotransmitters. Changes in the level of neurotransmitters affect the efficiency of information transmission among neurons. Age-related changes occur along several neurotransmitter pathways, which are groups of neurons that use the same neurotransmitter (Rogers & Bloom, 1985).

One pathway in the brain is responsible for controlling motor movements. The main neurotransmitter in this pathway is **dopamine**. As we age, the level of dopamine decreases (McGeer & McGeer, 1980). If this decline is extreme, we develop Parkinson's disease. As described in Chapter 9, Parkinson's disease is mostly known for causing characteristic tremors and a shuffling walking style, as well as serious depression (P. S. Fry, 1986). Although there is no cure, the symptoms of Parkinson's disease can be alleviated by medications such as L-dopa, which crosses the blood-brain barrier and is converted to dopamine (Rogers & Bloom, 1985). The cause of the abnormal depletion of dopamine in Parkinson's disease is unknown (Dakof & Mendelsohn, 1986).

Age-related declines in the neurotransmitter **acetylcholine** are also well documented (Rogers & Bloom, 1985). Acetylcholine is one of the major neurotransmitters involved in memory processes (Drachman, 1977), and there is evidence that declines in it in the hippocampus are linked with memory problems in old age (Drachman, Noffsinger, Sahakian, Kurdziel, & Fleming, 1980). Much current interest in acetylcholine is

spurred by its link to Alzheimer's disease and Huntington's disease (see Chapter 9). Some researchers speculate that there are causal connections between these diseases and abnormally low levels of choline acetyltransferase, an enzyme responsible for synthesizing acetylcholine (see Rogers & Bloom, 1985).

Another neurotransmitter linked to memory and learning (Anlezark, Crow, & Greenway, 1973), as well as to the body's response to stress (Rogers & Bloom, 1985), is **norepinephrine**. The age-related decline of norepinephrine has been clearly established, but these changes appear to be specific to certain parts of the brain (Robinson et al., 1972). Significant declines in norepinephrine have been found in the cerebral cortex and brainstem, but not in midbrain areas. Bondareff (1985) suggests that the link between norepinephrine and memory could be explored further through norepinephrine replacement therapy for cognitively impaired elderly.

In contrast to the decline in norepinephrine in some areas of the brain, numerous studies have documented an age-related increase in blood levels of norepinephrine under a variety of conditions: lying down (e.g., Esler et al., 1981), standing up, (e.g., Saar & Gordon, 1979), during isometric exercise (e.g., Sowers, Rubenstein, & Stern, 1973), while being exposed to cold (e.g., Palmer, Ziegler, & Lake, 1978), and while being placed in an experimental learning situation (e.g., Barnes, Raskind, Gumbrecht, & Halter, 1982). This increase in blood levels of norepinephrine appears to be caused by an age-related decrease in the rate with which norepinephrine is absorbed throughout the body. For example, heart muscle becomes less sensitive to norepinephrine with age (Kendall, Woods, Wilkins, & Worthington, 1982).

Considerably less research has been conducted concerning age-related changes in levels of

serotonin, a neurotransmitter that is also involved in arousal and sleep (Rogers & Bloom, 1985). What little is known points to an age-related decline (Ponzio et al., 1982), which may underlie some of the age-related changes in sleep that are described in Chapter 4 (Frolkis & Bezrukov, 1979).

Finally, age-related declines in the level of the neurotransmitter **gamma-aminobutyric acid (GABA)** have been noted in the thalamus (McGeer & McGeer, 1975). Because the thalamus is the major relay station for incoming sensory information, declines in GABA may account for some of the sensory losses in old age (Kenney, 1982). We will consider sensory changes in detail in Chapter 5.

EEG Changes

Brain waves reflect the brain's activity. A record of brain-wave activity, called an **electroencephalogram (EEG)**, is one tool used in research. The most reliable age change in EEG activity involves a decline in alpha rhythm, which is the dominant frequency of brain waves (Woodruff, 1985). In one's teens and early 20s alpha rhythm is at its maximum of 10 to 10.5 cycles per second (cps) (Eeg-Olofsson, 1971). Adults in their 60s show an alpha rhythm of about 9 cps, and in adults over 80 it is reduced to between 8 and 8.5 cps. The reasons for this reduction are unknown (Woodruff, 1985).

Slower EEG frequencies are related to lower states of arousal. Consequently, older adults are, by this criterion, underaroused (Woodruff, 1985). Reaction time may be particularly affected by slowing of alpha waves, as described in more detail in Chapter 5. Extensive research over 3 decades on the relationship between this slowing and behavior has not produced conclusive findings (see Surwillo, 1975; Woodruff, 1985). However, the data do suggest a connection between low arousal, poor performance, and EEG. Brain-wave frequency itself may not be a biological timer, but it may well be a factor causing lower arousal, which, in turn, affects behavior (Woodruff, 1985).

Psychological Consequences of Neural Aging

A major concern that adults have about aging is that they will become "senile." The word *senile* conjures up images of mental incompetence, childlike dependency, and emotional instability. Older adults may consider an insignificant memory lapse as evidence of impending "senility," even though memory lapses occur throughout life (Cavanaugh, Grady, & Perlmutter, 1983).

In fact, the term *senility* has no valid medical or psychological meaning, and its continued use simply perpetuates the myth that drastic mental decline is a product of normal aging (Whitbourne, 1985). It is not. The diseases involving considerable loss of memory, emotional response, and bodily functions are **dementias**, which are described more fully in Chapter 9. But dementia is not a part of normal aging, because only 15% of people over age 65 have dementia (Katzman, 1987). People who develop dementia may show severe and progressive impairments of memory, judgment, comprehension, and motor functions (Huff, Growdon, Corkin, & Rosen, 1987). It is fear of developing dementia that makes people interpret the slightest mental or physical mistake as symptomatic.

Several aspects of psychological functioning are affected by normal brain aging, which may, in turn, affect adults' adaptation to the environment (Whitbourne, 1985). Changes in the sensory centers in the brain, notably, the thalamus and sensory cortex, reduce the quality of incoming information about the environment and the ability to integrate it (Bondareff, 1985). How these functional abilities change is the topic of Chapter 5. Age-related declines in recent memory, described in Chapter 7, may be caused by neural losses. These changes make it more difficult for older adults to complete daily routines that demand remembering information over time, and the elderly become less efficient at learning new facts and skills (Whitbourne, 1985).

The neuronal fallout model is used to explain this pattern of decline in sensory abilities and in some memory and learning abilities. The effect of neuronal plasticity may be found in areas of the cortex that involve abstract or higher-order thinking. Plasticity may be one reason why there is little evidence of age-related changes in experience-based problem solving, reasoning, and judgment (Horn, 1982). This dual pattern of neuronal fallout and plasticity may be the underlying mechanism that explains why some intellectual functions decline with age and others do not. These different patterns of change are considered in detail in Chapter 6.

SUMMARY

Longevity is divided into two categories: average longevity (affected by extrinsic, or environmental, factors and internal, or physiological, factors) and maximum longevity (the oldest age to which any individual of a species lives).

Changes in appearance are among the first and most obvious signs of aging. These changes include wrinkles, changes in skin pigment, gray hair, decreases in height, and changes in weight. Changes in movement include loss in muscle strength (mostly after age 70), loss of bone tissue, degeneration of joints, and increased susceptibility to broken bones. These conditions can be helped by diet and exercise.

Structural changes occur in both the heart and the arteries. Fat deposits accumulate throughout the cardiovascular system, and both the heart and the blood vessels become stiffer. The heart is less able to handle physical stress, the pulse rate declines, and the blood pressure increases. Atherosclerosis is the most common form of circulatory-system disease.

Changes in the respiratory system include declines in maximum breathing capacity and maximum breathing rate, destruction of the alveoli and the septa, and increased risk of COLD, emphysema, and lower-respiratory infections.

Changes in the immune system may underlie increased susceptibility to disease with age. The number of lymphocytes does not appear to change, but their functioning does. In particular, there are decreased levels of interleukin-2. Lower levels of some antibodies have been found, and autoimmunity becomes a problem in later life.

The main changes in the female reproductive system occur during menopause with the cessation of ovulation and menstruation and a decline in the production of female hormones. Changes in men occur more slowly across adulthood. Sexual activity typically continues in old age, but at a reduced rate. Older adults are sexually responsive, but the physiological changes they undergo during sexual activity occur more slowly.

Two theories have been proposed to account for changes in the brain. The neuronal fallout model holds that the brain ages because increasing numbers of neurons die. The plasticity model states that normal aging consists of selective pruning and dendritic growth, which compensates for localized loss. Changes have been documented in neuronal structure (primarily in diseases) and in general reductions in the level of several neurotransmitters. A decline in alpha rhythms has also been observed, although the reasons for the change are unclear.

GLOSSARY

acetylcholine • A neurotransmitter associated with memory and linked with Alzheimer's disease and Huntington's disease.

alveoli • Air sacs in the lungs.

antibody • A substance produced by lymphocytes to protect the body from invading organisms.

arteriosclerosis • So-called hardening of the arteries, caused by degeneration and calcification of the arterial walls.

atherosclerosis • A disease caused by the buildup of atheromas and calcification in the arteries.

atria • Upper chambers of the human heart.

autoantibodies • Antibodies that attack the body itself.

autoimmunity • The process by which the immune system begins attacking the body itself.

average longevity • The age at which half of the individuals born in a particular year have died.

B-cells • A category of lymphocytes that originates in the bone marrow.

cardiac arrhythmias • Irregular heartbeats.

cardiac output • The volume of blood pumped by the heart.

cardiac reserve • The amount of spare capacity the heart has to withstand physical stress.

cell body • The structure of the neuron that converts an incoming signal to an electrochemical impulse.

chronic obstructive lung disease (COLD) • A family of diseases, including emphysema and chronic asthmatic bronchitis, that interferes with the passage of air in the bronchial tubes and causes abnormalities in the lungs.

climacteric • The period during which women's reproductive capacity ends and ovulation stops.

dementia • A family of brain diseases characterized by progressively severe cognitive decline.

dendrites • Branchlike structures of neurons that receive incoming signals from other neurons.

dopamine • A neurotransmitter associated with Parkinson's disease.

dyspnea • Shortness of breath.

electroencephalogram (EEG) • Recording of the brain's electrical activity.

emphysema • A disease caused by destruction of the septa.

endocardium • The internal layer of muscles in the heart.

extrinsic factors • Environmental hazards or other forces that influence longevity.

gamma-aminobutyric acid (GABA) • A neurotransmitter associated with the thalamus and sensory functioning.

hypertension • High blood pressure.

immunology • The study of the immune system.

interleukin-2 • A substance responsible for promoting T-cell proliferation.

intrinsic factors • Internal biological processes that influence longevity.

ischemic heart disease • A disease in which the heart receives an insufficient blood supply.

lipofuscin • A yellowish pigment that accumulates in the brain with increasing age.

lymphocytes • A family of cells that provides defenses against invading organisms and tumors.

maximum longevity • The oldest age to which any individual of a species lives.

menopause • The cessation of menstruation.

natural killer cell • A type of null cell that provides broad protection against tumor growth.

neuritic plaques • A collection of dead or dying neurons around a core of protein.

neurofibrillary tangles • Abnormal fibers in the axon that become twisted together. High concentrations are associated with cognitive impairment.

neuronal fallout model • A model of brain aging based on the idea that the loss of neurons predominates.

neurons • Brain cells.

neurotransmitters • Chemicals that stimulate neurons across the synapse.

norepinephrine • A neurotransmitter associated with learning and memory.

null cell • A category of lymphocytes that includes natural killer cells.

osteoarthritis • A disease of the bones caused by wear and tear on cartilage in joints.

osteoporosis • Severe bone degeneration in which the loss of bone mass results in porous bones.

pericardium • Saclike lining around the heart.

plasticity model • A model of brain aging based on the idea that both loss and growth occur in the brain with age.

rheumatoid arthritis • A destructive form of arthritis accompanied by swelling and stiffness.

septa • Walls separating the alveoli.

serotonin • A neurotransmitter associated with arousal and sleep.

synapse • The gap between neurons.

T-cells • A category of lymphocytes, one of which produces interleukin-2, that originates in the thymus.

terminal branches • Branchlike structures that release neurotransmitters to pass a signal to other neurons.

varicose veins • Deteriorating blood vessels that usually occur in the legs.

ventricles • The lower chambers of the human heart.

ADDITIONAL READING

There are several excellent sources of more detailed information on age-related changes in the body. Basic overviews can be found in

Cart, C. S., Metress, E. K., & Metress, S. P. (1988). *Aging, health and society* (2nd ed.). Boston: Jones & Bartlett.

Whitbourne, S. K. (1985). *The aging body.* New York: Springer.

More-technical information is available. A continuing series of books, the *Aging Series*, published by Raven Press, provides up-to-date summaries of recent research. Multiple volumes appear each year with different editors. One of the most comprehensive books, with separate chapters on all of the topics covered in this chapter, is

Finch, C. E., & Schneider, E. L. (Eds.). (1985). *Handbook of the biology of aging* (2nd ed.). New York: Van Nostrand Reinhold.

Health and Aging

Fairfield Porter, *The Tennis Game*, 1972. Lauren Rogers Library and Museum of Art, Laurel, Mississippi.

ONE OF THE MOST DRAMATIC CHANGES over the last century is the virtual elimination of acute disease as a cause of death in Western societies (Fries & Crapo, 1986). **Acute diseases** have a relatively rapid onset and progress fairly quickly. **Chronic diseases**, which now account for the deaths of nearly everyone who does not die from an accident, have a much slower onset and course. Early in the 20th century acute diseases such as tuberculosis, polio, measles, diphtheria, and typhoid fever claimed tens of thousands of lives in the United States each year. Today, they have almost been eradicated in most Western countries. In fact, the risk of mortality from any of these diseases has been reduced by at least 99% in this century.

This change has fundamentally altered our concepts of health and illness. When we think of illness and its relationship to age, we focus on chronic disorders such as cardiovascular disease. Moreover, as we will see, many people have some chronic condition that affects their health. Health promotion programs have become the focus of much research, and they are primarily concerned with preventing chronic disease. Fries and Crapo (1986) comment that this change in the focus of prevention from acute to chronic diseases has gone largely unnoticed, even though its implications for health care are enormous. Caring for someone afflicted with a serious chronic disease is typically much more expensive than treating an acute disorder.

In this chapter we will consider several issues related to health and aging. All of these issues are at least partly under our control, and they all relate to our life-style. In examining them, we must take a critical attitude about some of the research, especially when only cross-sectional data are available. Before looking at specific diseases, let us first consider the general notion of health promotion and its relationship to aging.

HEALTH PROMOTION AND AGING

Health promotion refers to the notion that individuals can exert a significant influence over their health. This idea reflects a shift from the traditional biomedical view of health toward a broader biopsychosocial view that includes individual lifestyle, behavior, and the social and physical environment (Estes, Fox, & Mahoney, 1986). For example, L. W. Green (1980) called for a combination of health education and social policies to promote, improve, and protect health.

Over the past 2 decades numerous researchers have documented the connection between behavior and health (McGinnis, 1988). Their research shows that health involves much more than the action of bacteria and viruses. The environment in which we live, social factors, diet, exercise, personal habits, and even sleep have profound influences on our health. In fact, these influences are so powerful that Belloc and Breslow (1972)

SOMETHING · TO · THINK · ABOUT

Public Policy, Health Promotion, and Aging

Healthy life-styles pay off. But many of the elderly do not engage in behaviors that promote health and prevent disease, for the simple reason that they cannot afford to. Many older adults rely on Medicare and Medicaid as their sole sources of health insurance. Both of these programs were begun in the mid-1960s when equity and equal access to care were major social concerns. Both programs adhere tightly to the traditional biomedical model of disease; that is, illness and disease are covered, but health promotion is not. For example, treatment for pneumonia in the hospital or for a broken hip in a nursing home are usually covered. Going for a yearly physical examination that may prevent pneumonia often is not.

This situation has led to cries for reform by researchers and practitioners alike (Dychtwald,

1986). Among the recommendations for a new health care policy are these:

1. Health promotion policy must address not only physical needs but socioeconomic needs for adequate food, clothing, and housing as well. Changing life-styles will have little effect if people have inadequate resources.

2. Health promotion should be targeted at all adults, so that all may have the potential for a happy and healthy old age.

3. Medical insurance reimbursement must begin to reward the promotion of health, not just the treatment of disease. Moreover, we must provide incentives to stay healthy.

4. Community health services must begin to work in cooperation rather than in competition with one another.

This cooperative network would include a broad spectrum of services, from walk-in clinics to hospitals to nursing homes.

5. Public policy and private policy must work together. Corporate health care plans must take advantage of community resources, and public policy could incorporate ideas from the business world.

6. We must emphasize the need for training professionals in promoting health.

All of these goals are important. But a large hurdle needs to be overcome. To instill the value of health promotion means that the current concept of waiting until one is ill to seek a physician must change. How can we change this attitude? It's something to think about.

---

assert that it is tempting to conclude that a lifetime of good health practices not only produces good health but also extends the period of relatively good health by 30 years.

Despite the clear connections between lifestyle factors and health that gave rise to the health promotion movement, little emphasis has been placed on these connections in older adults.

Minkler & Pasick (1986) note that the elderly are often excluded from health promotion programs for four reasons: (1) the focus of such programs is on extending life, and the elderly are not perceived as having a future; (2) the goal is usually preventing premature death, and the elderly are considered to be beyond that point; (3) the programs often promote looking youthful and

TABLE 4.1 · Number of acute conditions per 100 people per year, by age and type of condition: United States, 1986

Type of Condition	Age Group			
	18–24	*25–44*	*45–64*	*65+*
All acute conditions	195.1	168.6	125.1	119.5
Infective and parasitic diseases	19.6	19.5	9.5	8.8
Common childhood diseases	—	0.4	—	—
Intestinal virus, unspecified	4.4	3.6	1.6	2.2
Viral infections, unspecified	6.0	8.9	5.8	3.8
Other	9.2	6.6	2.1	2.8
Respiratory conditions	98.5	86.8	66.7	48.2
Common cold	26.7	20.2	14.3	16.3
Other acute upper respiratory infections	11.1	6.8	6.0	3.2
Influenza	57.0	55.7	42.7	22.5
Acute bronchitis	1.6	1.9	1.8	3.9
Pneumonia	—	1.1	0.8	1.5
Other respiratory conditions	2.1	1.0	1.0	0.7
Digestive system conditions	7.2	5.1	4.5	7.3
Dental conditions	1.7	1.5	0.3	0.5
Indigestion, nausea, and vomiting	3.5	2.4	2.2	2.6
Other digestive conditions	1.9	1.2	2.0	4.2

(Source: National Health Interview Survey, U.S. Department of Health and Human Services, 1988)

preventing signs of aging; and (4) their focus is on avoidance of chronic disease, which is irrelevant for older adults since roughly 85% of them already have one chronic disease.

The view that health promotion comes "too late" for people over 65 is changing. It is now recognized that people of all ages benefit from changes in life-style. This point was emphasized by the federal government's publication in 1979 of two booklets, *Healthy People: The Surgeon General's Report on Health Promotion and Disease Pre-* *vention* and in 1980 of *Promoting Health/Preventing Disease: Objectives for the Nation*. One of the goals of these reports was to reduce the amount of time that older adults were restricted by acute or chronic disease. Moreover, the reports concluded that of the 10 leading causes of death in the United States, at least 7 could be substantially reduced if people changed just five habits: diet, smoking, lack of exercise, alcohol abuse, and stress.

A second aspect of health and disease that is

Type of Condition	Age Group			
	18–24	25–44	45–64	65 +
Injuries	32.9	27.9	20.4	21.3
Fractures and dislocations	2.0	3.8	3.8	1.3
Sprains and strains	8.3	6.0	5.5	3.4
Open wounds and lacerations	7.3	5.7	4.0	3.7
Contusions and superficial injuries	9.2	6.9	3.1	6.0
Other current injuries	6.2	5.4	4.1	6.9
Selected other acute conditions	26.8	21.5	12.7	17.6
Eye conditions	1.1	0.5	1.5	3.0
Acute ear infections	1.9	4.4	1.0	1.4
Other ear conditions	1.1	0.6	0.7	2.1
Acute urinary conditions	5.1	1.8	2.9	2.1
Disorders of menstruation	3.1	1.2	0.2	—
Other disorders of female genital tract	2.6	1.5	—	—
Delivery and other conditions of pregnancy and puerperium	5.7	3.8	—	—
Skin conditions	1.7	1.7	1.6	4.1
Acute musculoskeletal conditions	2.7	3.7	3.5	4.0
Headache, excluding migraine	1.1	2.0	1.3	1.0
Fever, unspecified	0.7	0.3	—	—

becoming better appreciated is the connection between age and certain acute and chronic diseases. Acute diseases normally last only a few days to a few weeks. Contrary to popular belief, people over age 65 have the lowest rate of acute disease of any adult age group; young adults have the highest. Rates for several common acute diseases are presented in Table 4.1.

The picture changes dramatically for chronic diseases, which may be difficult or impossible to treat effectively and may be debilitating or inca-pacitating. Although the elderly have the highest rates of any adult age group, there is a large increase in the number of chronic diseases between young adulthood and middle-age. Table 4.2 contains rates of some common chronic diseases.

In sum, the challenges confronting psychologists and health care professionals are to clarify the misconceptions about health and age, emphasize the relationship between life-style and health, and instill good habits in people of all ages. As we will see, in many cases changing one factor, such

TABLE 4.2 · Number of selected chronic conditions per 1,000 people, by age: United States, 1986

Type of Condition	Age Group			
	18–44	45–64	65–74	75+
Selected conditions of the genitourinary, nervous, endocrine, metabolic, and blood and blood-forming systems				
Goiter or other disorders of the thyroid	10.3	29.1	23.8	29.1
Diabetes	8.7	63.7	91.9	108.5
Anemias	15.2	12.9	24.4	18.9
Epilepsy	7.3	6.3	1.4	8.3
Migraine headache	49.4	45.5	21.3	20.1
Neuralgia or neuritis, unspecified	1.0	4.7	9.7	10.0
Kidney trouble	17.3	23.3	28.8	39.3
Bladder disorders	15.5	22.2	29.5	53.0
Diseases of prostate	1.4	12.5	26.7	22.6
Disease of female genital organs	30.2	20.8	8.5	—
Selected circulatory conditions				
Rheumatic fever with or without heart disease	6.8	13.4	16.0	7.6
Heart disease	39.3	123.2	250.0	319.4
Ischemic heart disease	5.7	59.1	120.9	154.4
Heart rhythm disorders	25.3	36.2	74.7	60.7
Tachycardia or rapid heart	5.5	11.7	30.9	23.2
Heart murmurs	18.3	13.6	18.7	19.5
Other and unspecified heart rhythm disorders	1.5	11.0	25.1	17.9
Other selected diseases of heart, excluding hypertension	8.3	27.9	54.4	104.3
High blood pressure (hypertension)	67.2	250.6	385.2	409.2
Cerebrovascular disease	1.3	18.1	46.7	96.7
Hardening of the arteries	0.7	21.7	38.0	91.7
Varicose veins of lower extremities	22.6	56.3	76.2	71.9
Hemorrhoids	46.7	73.2	70.2	64.1
Selected respiratory conditions				
Chronic bronchitis	36.5	45.8	62.9	55.4
Asthma	36.4	36.3	46.4	36.3

(Source: National Health Interview Survey, U.S. Department of Health and Human Services, 1988)

Type of Condition	Age Group			
	18–44	45–64	65–74	75+
Selected respiratory conditions				
Hay fever or allergic rhinitis without asthma	113.1	95.8	72.4	67.2
Chronic sinusitis	170.4	187.0	168.6	170.7
Deviated nasal septum	6.0	7.9	13.8	—
Chronic disease of tonsils or adenoids	10.6	2.3	4.2	2.0
Emphysema	0.7	18.4	44.5	32.7
Selected skin and musculoskeletal conditions				
Arthritis	47.9	284.6	443.3	540.1
Gout, including gouty arthritis	2.5	24.0	28.5	39.6
Intervertebral disc disorders	21.4	35.5	14.5	16.2
Bone spur or tendinitis, unspecified	6.3	16.6	12.1	9.3
Disorders of bone or cartilage	4.9	6.9	19.5	20.5
Trouble with bunions	8.3	21.4	32.9	46.7
Bursitis, unclassified	13.5	36.7	43.0	29.6
Sebaceous skin cyst	7.7	12.0	4.6	7.2
Trouble with acne	27.2	4.2	1.5	—
Psoriasis	10.0	13.8	17.7	25.7
Dermatitis	44.3	35.4	33.6	25.2
Trouble with dry (itching) skin, unclassified	21.9	21.0	27.7	38.4
Trouble with ingrown nails	20.0	32.9	39.6	57.8
Trouble with corns and calluses	19.4	34.0	39.7	54.4
Impairments				
Visual impairment	28.7	46.3	69.3	136.3
Color blindness	15.2	16.3	18.5	3.9
Cataracts	1.5	21.1	84.3	233.2
Glaucoma	0.9	10.3	29.1	58.5
Hearing impairment	51.8	136.2	244.2	378.4

(continued)

Type of Condition	Age Group			
	18–44	45–64	65–74	75 +
Impairments				
Tinnitus	15.3	49.2	83.2	88.3
Speech impairment	9.3	8.3	9.6	16.4
Absence of extremities (excludes tips of fingers or toes only)	5.0	13.1	22.8	17.3
Paralysis of extremities, complete or partial	4.9	10.0	11.6	22.9
Deformity or orthopedic impairment	132.2	161.6	158.4	195.7
Back	82.4	92.0	93.0	115.1
Upper extremities	14.8	23.2	13.8	18.1
Lower extremities	50.7	69.8	76.5	107.4
Selected digestive conditions				
Ulcer	21.3	28.2	42.9	30.0
Hernia of abdominal cavity	9.5	36.9	46.5	84.8
Gastritis or duodenitis	11.8	20.9	21.4	21.4
Frequent indigestion	25.4	31.3	43.3	35.6
Enteritis or colitis	10.3	11.1	11.2	46.2
Spastic colon	9.2	10.7	7.8	5.0
Diverticula of intestines	1.7	12.8	41.9	42.7
Frequent constipation	14.3	22.1	51.2	83.9

as lowering stress, can have a significant impact on other aspects, such as the risk of cardiovascular disease.

NUTRITION

You are what you eat. Despite this truism, nutrition and aging is a controversial topic. The controversy is not over whether diet is important. Everyone agrees about that. Rather, the issue is what type of diet is most beneficial and how food intake should be balanced across food groups. Nutritional status directly affects one's mental, emotional, and physical functioning (Guigoz & Munro, 1985; Steen, 1987). With increasing age this relationship becomes even more important, as health is determined in part by the cumulative effects of dietary habits over the years.

It is commonly believed that older adults as a group have poorer dietary habits than younger or middle-aged people and need to use vitamin and mineral supplements. This belief appears to be unfounded, at least until very old age (Lundgren, Steen, & Isaksson, 1987). This is not to say, of course, that older adults do not have nutritional problems. The institutionalized elderly, for example, often suffer various nutritional deficiencies, such as thiamine, vitamin B_{12}, and folic acid (Baker, Frank, Thind, Jaslow, & Louria, 1979). Economic factors often force the aged poor to eat inadequate diets. Loss of one's partner, which causes one to eat alone, removes the important social component of sharing a meal. Obtaining adequate nutrition is one of the most basic requirements for an adequate health maintenance program; the poorer nutrition of many needy older people clearly contributes to their overall higher rate of chronic disease.

Establishing Dietary Requirements

Nutritional requirements, food and drink preferences, and eating habits change across the life span. You have probably noticed that adolescents and young adults seemingly require huge quantities of "junk food," whereas middle-aged adults require more meats and vegetables. Seriously, though, there are important developmental differences in some dietary requirements.

One of the major problems confronting nutritionists is a lack of guidelines for older adults. The national committee that created the 1980 edition of the **recommended dietary allowances (RDAs)** distinguished only two age groups of adults: those between ages 25 and 50 and those 51 and over. By 1985 it was clear that considering everyone for over age 50 as a single group was a mistake. Moreover, the recommendations for the over-50 group were largely derived by simply extrapolating from younger age groups. In 1985 the committee proposed changes that make differential recommendations for nutrients involved in energy and protein metabolism for adults between 51 and 69 and for those over 70. However, the committee

decided that there were insufficient data to make recommendations for other nutrients (Guthrie, 1988). In particular, it noted that a decrease in the need for many nutrients due to loss of body mass with aging was offset by a need for increased nutrients due to less effective absorption and retention of nutrients.

In addition to changes in body metabolism that affect the need for nutrients, other important age-related factors affect nutrition. Age-related changes in vision may hinder older adults' ability to read food labels, recipes, stove settings, or menus. Changes in taste and acuity diminish the potential enjoyment of food. Poor teeth may interfere with the ability to chew, thereby limiting the foods a person can eat. All of these factors need to be considered when planning meals and making recommendations for older adults. Table 4.3 contains a summary of age-related changes that affect nutrition.

We will consider several major requirements briefly. At this point it is important to note that the role of various nutrients in maintaining good health must be emphasized across the life span. A diet that provides adequate vitamins, minerals, protein, and complex carbohydrates needs to be maintained. Such a diet should be rich in fresh vegetables, fresh fruits, low-fat dairy products, legumes, fish, poultry, and whole grains. Table 4.4 summarizes the daily dietary allowances of the National Academy of Sciences, based on both the 1980 and 1985 committees.

Proteins

Practically speaking, the protein needs of older adults are no different from those of younger adults (Steen, 1987). However, there is some evidence that protein metabolism in very old adults may be less efficient; if this is true, these individuals need more dietary protein (Munro & Young, 1978). One thing to keep in mind is that people

TABLE 4.3 · Factors affecting nutrient needs and food intake with age

A. Nutrient Needs

Decreased gastrointestinal motility, which contributes to constipation and gastrointestinal distress

Decreased hydrochloric acid secretion, which reduces absorption of iron and calcium

Decreased intrinsic factor, which limits vitamin B_{12} absorption

Decreased gastric and pancreatic secretion, which inhibits fat and protein digestion due to decreased insulin secretion and tissue response

Decreased glucose tolerance

Decreased cardiovascular adaption to stress

Decreased muscle mass and muscle cell metabolism

Increased body fat leading to decreased basal metabolic energy needs

Inability to concentrate urine and decreased thirst

Increased fluid needs due to diminished renal ability to conserve sodium

B. Food Intake

Decreased visual acuity, which limits food shopping, preparation, and menu reading

Diminished hearing, which reduces enjoyment of meal; conversation

Decreased taste and smell acuity, which depresses enjoyment of food

Poor dentition, which inhibits mastication

(Source: "Nutrient Requirements of the Elderly" by H. A. Guthrie, 1988, in R. Chernoff and D. A. Lipschitz (Eds.), *Health Promotion and Disease Prevention in the Elderly* (pp. 33–43), New York: Raven. Reprinted with permission.)

suffering from disease have greater protein needs at all ages (Isaksson, 1973). Because older adults suffer more diseases, on average, the elderly need to supplement their normal protein intake.

Carbohydrates

Carbohydrates provide the energy necessary to maintain metabolic, physical, and mental activity. Although energy needs decrease across adulthood, the recommended sources of carbohydrates remain the same, namely, whole grains, fruits,

vegetables, and naturally occurring sugars. It should be noted that the refining process for wheat flour and sugar decreases the amount of B vitamins (only three of which are restored by enriched flour), vitamin E, and trace minerals.

Vitamins and Minerals

As noted earlier, the recommended intakes of vitamins and minerals are very similar for young and old. Herbert (1988) reports little evidence that adjustments in vitamin intake should be made

TABLE 4.4 · Recommended dietary allowances, by age: 1980 and 1985 (proposed)

	Male				Female			
	1980		1985 (proposed)		1980		1985 (proposed)	
	23–50	51+	51–69	70+	23–50	51+	51–69	70+
Protein (gm)	56	56	64	62	44	44	54	53
Calcium (mg)	800	800	800	800	800	800	1000	1000
Phosphorus (mg)	800	800	800	800	800	800	1000	1000
Magnesium (mg)	350	350	350	350	300	300		
Iron (mg)	10	10	10	10	18	10	10	10
Zinc (mg)	15	15	15	15	15	15	12	12
Iodine (μg)	150	150	160	160	150	150	160	160
Selenium (μg)	—	—	70	70	—	—	55	55
Vitamin A (RE)	1000	1000	700	700	1000	800	600	600
Vitamin D (μg)	5	5	5	5	5	5	5	5
Vitamin E (mg)	10	10	10	10	8	8	8	8
Vitamin C (mg)	60	60	40	40	60	60	30	30
Thiamin (mg)	1.4	1.2	1.3	1.1	1.0	1.0	1.1	0.9
Riboflavin (mg)	1.6	1.4	1.4	1.3	1.2	1.2	1.2	1.2
Niacin (mg)	18	16	16	14	13	13	13	13
Pyridoxine (mg)	2.2	2.2	2.0	2.0	2.0	2.0	1.7	1.7
Folic acid (μg)	400	400	230	220	400	400	190	190
Vitamin B_{12} (μg)	3.0	3.0	2.0	2.0	3.0	3.0	2.0	2.0

(Sources: *Recommended Dietary Allowances* (9th ed.), 1980, Washington, D.C.: National Academy Press. Reprinted with permission. Also "Nutrient Requirements of the Elderly" by H. A. Guthrie, 1988, in R. Chernoff and D. A. Lipschitz (Eds.), *Health Promotion and Disease Prevention in the Elderly* (pp. 33–43), New York: Raven. Reprinted with permission.)

with age or that vitamin supplements are needed if one eats a well-balanced diet. Fads such as mega-vitamins should be avoided; the best advice is to get nutrition from food, not pills. The controversy surrounding relationships between nutrients and osteoporosis was discussed in Chapter 3. Additional relationships between specific nutrients and health will be noted throughout this chapter.

Diet and Health

Does what you eat affect how well you feel? The answer is a resounding yes. Considerable evidence has been gathered to show beyond doubt that dietary habits strongly influence physical health. Links have been established between serum cholesterol and cardiovascular disease and between various aspects of diet and cancer. For example, the American Heart Association is quite clear in its recommendations concerning the amount of fat in our diet: Foods that are high in saturated fats, such as whole milk, butter, and processed foods containing coconut or palm oil, should be replaced with low-fat milk, margarine, and unsaturated fats from vegetable oils. Eggs and red meat should be limited and replaced by fish, white-meat poultry (without the skin), and legumes. Additionally, the association recommends limiting sodium intake; high levels of sodium have been linked to hypertension.

The American Cancer Society has also issued extensive guidelines concerning diet. These recommendations include eating less fat and fewer salt-cured, smoked, and nitrite-cured foods; drinking less alcohol; and eating more fresh vegetables. The society points out that obesity greatly increases the risk for cancer. Excessive fat intake alone increases the chances of breast, colon, and prostate cancers. A high intake of commercially smoked meats (which contain nitrites and nitrates) is linked with stomach and esophageal cancers. Diets containing adequate levels of vitamin A may lower the risk of cancers of the larynx, esophagus, and lung. Similarly, high-fiber diets may reduce the risk of stomach and colon cancers.

As noted in Chapter 3, some researchers believe that diet can be used to prevent osteoporosis if it is begun in young adulthood. Because one of the causes of osteoporosis is a deficiency in calcium, diets should include foods that are high in calcium, for example, yogurt, broccoli, collards, turnip greens, salmon, sardines, oysters, and tofu. Interestingly, although protein is a daily requirement, too much protein can lead to loss of calcium through the urine.

In short, it is a good idea to become more aware of the things we eat and what effects they have. Eating should be an enjoyable activity. Why not make it a healthy one, too?

EXERCISE

One of the major ways of remaining youthful is to exercise. As far back as Hippocrates, physicians and researchers have known that exercise significantly retards the aging process. Recent evidence suggests that we can slow the process down by a decade or more (G. S. Thomas & Rutledge, 1986). Bortz (1982) and deVries (1983) report that the changes resulting from aging resemble those seen in people of any age during a prolonged period of bed rest. For example, confining young, healthy men in bed for 3 weeks will decrease cardiac output by 25% and maximum breathing capacity and oxygen consumption by nearly one third (Bortz, 1982). To understand how exercise has these effects, we must first understand what we mean by exercise.

Types of Exercise

Exercise done by people at any age can be grouped into two categories (Thomas & Rutledge, 1986): aerobic and low-intensity. **Aerobic exercise** places a moderate stress on the heart that is achieved by maintaining a pulse rate between 60% and 90% of the maximum. Maximum heart rate can be estimated by subtracting one's age from 220. Thus, for a 40-year-old person, the target range would be 108 to 162 beats per minute. The minimum time necessary to benefit from aerobic exercise depends on the intensity with which it is performed. For heart rates near the low end of the range, sessions should last roughly 60 minutes, whereas for high heart rates, 15 minutes may suffice. Examples of aerobic exercise include jogging at a moderate to fast pace, rapid walking, "jazzercise," swimming, and bicycling.

Low-intensity exercise occurs when the heart rate does not exceed 60% of maximum for

Older adults who engage in aerobic exercise are physiologically superior to many younger adults who are sedentary.

sure, better endurance, increased joint flexibility, and better neuromuscular coordination (E. L. Smith & Serfass, 1981). Psychologically, people who exercise regularly claim lower levels of stress (J. A. Blumenthal et al., 1988), better moods (Simons, McGowan, Epstein, Kupfer, & Robertson, 1985), and better cognitive functioning. Interestingly, the general effects of exercise appear to be fairly consistent across age; older adults benefit from exercise and show patterns of improvement similar to those of younger and middle-aged adults.

The lack of significant age-related differences in the pattern of benefits from aerobic exercise is important. Recall from Chapter 3 that there are normative age changes in the cardiovascular, respiratory, skeletal, and muscular systems that reduce the efficiency with which they work. Available evidence supports the idea that aerobic exercise tends to slow these changes (see Smith & Serfass, 1981). In physiological terms, then, an elderly individual who exercises regularly could be in better condition than a younger adult who is sedentary.

The optimal way to accrue the benefits of exercise, of course, is to maintain physical fitness across the life span. In planning an exercise program, however, two points must be remembered. First, one should always check with a physician before beginning a program of aerobic exercise. Second, moderation is extremely important; more is not better. Paffenbarger, Hyde, Wing, and Hsieh (1986) made this point clearly in their study of 16,936 middle-aged and elderly male Harvard graduates. They found that men who exercised moderately (walked 9 miles per week) had a 21% lower risk of mortality, while men who exercised strenuously (cycled for 6 to 8 hours per week) had a 50% lower mortality risk. However, men who engaged in extremely high levels of exercise (burning more than 3,500 calories per week) had a higher mortality rate than the other two groups.

sustained periods. Such exercise is sometimes called anaerobic. Examples of low-intensity exercise are stretching and range-of-motion exercises.

Aerobic Exercise and Aging

Research on the effects of aerobic exercise on young, middle-aged, and elderly adults reveals a range of benefits. Physiologically, adults of all ages show improved cardiovascular functioning and maximum oxygen consumption, lower blood pres-

In a sense, men in this latter group literally exercised themselves to death.

Despite the many benefits of fitness and the increasing popularity of health spas, many adults simply do not exercise. For older adults, at least, the reason seems to be that they do not think they need to (U.S. Department of Health and Human Services [DHHS], 1988). Women become less active earlier than men, and people with lower education become inactive sooner than college graduates (Ostrow, 1980). Still, role models exist. Wiswell (1980) notes that the late King Gustav of Sweden still played tennis regularly at 80 and that older Olympic champions functioned better than 25-year-olds who had sedentary jobs.

SMOKING

If everyone who smoked would stop today, that would do more to improve national health than any other single step. In the United States alone roughly 320,000 deaths each year are related to smoking, and 10 million more people have smoking-related chronic diseases (DHHS, 1988). In a study of Scandinavians, Scholl (1980) estimated that one third of all deaths in 50- to 60-year-old men could be avoided if all of the smokers had stopped at age 50.

These are sobering statistics. Despite age-related decreases in the rate of cigarette smoking, shown in Table 4.5, the chronic diseases caused by smoking often are at their worst in old age. As we will see, the problem with cigarette smoking is that the dangers are indirectly tied to age, in that it usually takes years before the devastating effects become apparent to the smoker.

The rates of smoking vary not only with age but also with sex and ethnic status. As noted in Table 4.5, adult men tend to smoke more than adult women, although this difference is negligi-

TABLE 4.5 • Percentage of adults over age 18 who smoke cigarettes: United States, 1985

Age Group	Males	Females
18–29	32.3%	31.7%
30–44	38.0	31.2
45–64	33.4	29.9
65+	19.6	13.5

(Source: National Health Survey, U.S. Department of Health and Human Services, 1988)

ble in young adults. Among ethnic groups Native Americans tend to smoke much less than Whites, Blacks tend to smoke more, and Hispanics and Asian Americans smoke about the same as Whites (DHHS, 1988). These differences in smoking rates result in different rates of smoking-related disease later in life; for example, lung cancer is relatively rare among elderly Native Americans.

The Hazards of Cigarette Smoking

The connection between cigarette smoking and lung cancer has been well documented for over 25 years by the U.S. surgeon general. The U.S. Public Health Service notes that smokers have 10 times as much lung cancer, 3 to 10 times as much cancer of the mouth and tongue, 3 to 18 times as much cancer of the larynx, and 7 to 10 times as much bladder cancer as nonsmokers. Smoking plays at least an indirect role in over half of all cancer deaths, and it is directly responsible for 75% of all lung cancer. Nine out of every ten people who develop lung cancer are dead within 5 years.

Clearly, smoking takes a frightening toll. But the prospect of lung cancer or other smoking-related disease has significantly lowered smoking rates only among men. For women, the number of smokers, especially among adolescents and young adults, is higher than ever. The American Cancer Society estimates that at current smoking rates lung cancer will become the most common form of cancer among both men and women. Lung cancer among older women is the only major cause of death to show an increase during the 1980s (DHHS, 1988).

Cancer is not the only disease caused by smoking. Emphysema, discussed in Chapter 3, and heart disease are two others. The carbon monoxide and nicotine inhaled in cigarette smoke foster the development of atherosclerosis and angina (Wantz & Gay, 1981). Women who smoke and take contraceptive pills for at least 5 years have an increased risk of heart attacks until menopause, even if they stop taking the pill (Layde, Ory, & Schlesselman, 1982). Smoking after the fourth month of pregnancy is linked with an increased risk of stillbirths, low birth weight, and perinatal death.

The Hazards of Secondhand Smoke

The hazards of cigarette smoke do not stop with the smoker. Nonsmokers who breathe the smoke of others are also at higher risk for smoking-related diseases, including chronic lung disease (DHHS, 1984), lung cancer (Pershagen, Hrubec, & Svensson, 1987; Sandler, Everson, & Wilcox, 1985), and heart disease (Garland, Barrett-Connor, Suarez, Criqui, & Wingard, 1985). Additionally, pregnant women who breathe secondhand smoke for as little as 2 hours a day at home or at work are more likely to give birth to infants who are below average in weight (T. R. Martin & Bracken, 1986). For these reasons many states and communities have passed stringent legislation severely restricting smoking. For example, beginning in April 1988 smoking was not allowed at all on airplane flights of 2 hours or less within the United States.

Quitting Smoking

If you smoke and want to quit, how should you proceed? Many people successfully quit on their own, but others have found assistance through formal therapy. Whether a particular approach is effective depends on the individual; no one approach works with everyone.

Most stop-smoking programs are multimodal, in that they combine a number of aspects from different therapeutic approaches. For example, Lando (1977) used several behavior modification techniques as well as "booster sessions" after therapy was over. Lando reported a success rate of 76%, which is much higher than the more typical 20% or 30% abstinence at 6- to 12-month follow-ups. It appears that the use of booster sessions is the key difference. Otherwise, the potential for relapse is quite high.

Because 70% to 80% of smokers who try to quit eventually relapse, Marlatt and Gordon (1980) investigated the relapse process itself. They concluded that for most people who have successfully quit smoking one cigarette is enough to create a full-blown relapse complete with feelings of utter failure. Marlatt and Gordon suggest that treatment programs take this into account and incorporate strategies to deal with these feelings caused by a "slip."

Although some people may find formal programs helpful in their battle to stop smoking, as many as 95% of those who quit do so on their own, according to a survey by the U.S. Surgeon General's Office. Schachter (1982) speculates that people tend to go to clinics only after they have tried to quit on their own and failed. Thus, those who attend a clinic may not be a representative sample of smokers who try to quit; success rates at clinics of 20% to 30% reflect success with difficult cases.

To date, however, no one has convincingly demonstrated that one method of quitting

TABLE 4.6 · Increased risk of cancer from smoking, and period of continued increased risk after quitting

	Increased Risk	Period of Increased Risk After Quitting
Lung cancer	10 times	10–15 years
Larynx cancer	3–18 times	10 years
Mouth cancer	3–10 times	10–15 years
Cancer of esophagus	2–9 times	Uncertain
Bladder cancer	7–10 times	7 years
Cancer of pancreas	2–5 times	Uncertain

(Source: *Adult Development and Aging* by M. Perlmutter and E. Hall, 1985, New York: Wiley. Reprinted with permission.)

smoking is more effective or less effective than another. It appears that what may matter most is the person's commitment to quitting and being in an environment that fosters not smoking.

If you smoke, the statistics about the effects of smoking on health and the availability of effective therapies may have convinced you to stop. You may wonder, then, whether your health would ever return to normal. It takes considerable time, but eventually people who quit smoking return to a normal risk of disease (see Table 4.6). For example, within 10 to 15 years the risk of lung cancer has dropped to normal. In the long run it is certainly worth everyone's while to quit.

DRINKING ALCOHOL

The majority of Americans drink alcohol; roughly 10% abuse it (National Institute of Alcoholism and Alcohol Abuse [NIAAA], 1983). In fact, nearly half of all of the alcohol consumed in the United States is drunk by only 10% of the drinkers. It is virtually impossible to escape being confronted with alcohol, either in person or through advertisements. By the time he or she reaches 18 years of age, for example, the average high school senior has seen 100,000 television commercials for beer alone!

Clearly, alcohol presents a serious health problem when consumed in excess, especially over a long period. In this section we will examine some of the effects of alcohol and alcohol abuse and their relationship with age.

Alcoholism and Aging

Nearly 18 million Americans are heavy drinkers, with roughly 11 million of them being alcoholics. Surveys conducted in the 1980s show that the incidence of problem drinking remains at a fairly constant rate of nearly 10% across adulthood (NIAAA, 1983; Post, 1987). Alcohol consumption tends to decrease with age, with drinking peaking between ages 30 and 44 and declining steadily thereafter (DHHS, 1988). Likewise, identification of individuals as alcoholics tends to peak by middle age. Two thirds of older alcoholics began drinking excessively earlier in life and persisted; only one third began abusing alcohol in old age (Scott & Mitchell, 1988).

Alcoholism is considered a **substance abuse disorder** by the American Psychiatric Association (1987). It is important to note that alcoholism is a form of **addiction**. That is, alcoholics demonstrate dependence and withdrawal. Dependence occurs when a drug becomes so incorporated into the functioning of the body's cells that it becomes necessary for "normal" functioning. If the drug is discontinued, the body's attempt to readjust to functioning without the drug is manifested in ways that are opposite of the effects of the drug. Since alcohol is a depressant, withdrawal symptoms include restlessness and irritability. Alcoholism results when the person becomes so dependent on the drug that it interferes with personal relationships, health, occupation, and social functioning.

Men are more likely to be diagnosed as alcoholics than women. However, the extent to which this finding reflects a true difference between the sexes or, rather, a diagnostic bias is unclear. For example, many alcoholics are depressed, which has led some authors to speculate that women who are heavy drinkers are more likely to be labeled as "depressed" rather than "alcoholic" (Kaplan, 1983).

Until the mid to late 1970s scientists and health care professionals appeared unaware that alcohol abuse was a serious problem beyond middle age. Surveys still show that the average level of consumption of alcohol declines beyond midlife (NIAAA, 1983). A closer look at the data reveals that more recent cohorts are drinking more, perhaps because the current older generation was influenced by the ideas that led to Prohibition. This means that alcohol-related problems in older adults are likely to become more serious in future years as these heavier-drinking cohorts age (Wattis, 1983). In any case, professionals are taking a closer look at drinking and aging and are realizing that alcoholism is a serious problem for all age groups.

Negative Effects of Alcohol

Alcohol affects health directly and indirectly. The main health problem for the long-term heavy drinker is liver damage (Eckhardt et al., 1981). Drinking more than five or six drinks per day causes fat to accumulate in the liver, which, over time, will restrict blood flow, kill liver cells, and result in a form of hepatitis. Continued heavy drinking will continue this process until cirrhosis develops, in which nonfunctional scar tissue accumulates. Cirrhosis is the leading cause of death in alcoholics.

Another serious result of long-term heavy drinking is the effect on brain chemistry. **Wernicke-Korsakoff syndrome** is found among these individuals (Eckhardt et al., 1981). Symptoms of this syndrome include severe loss of memory of recent events, severe disorientation, confusion, and visual problems. Although Wernicke-Korsakoff syndrome is actually caused by thiamine deficiency, alcohol is known to interfere with thiamine absorption (Thompson, 1978), and chronic alcoholics typically do not obtain all the nutrients they need.

Heavy drinking has also been linked with heart disease, although the nature of the connection is unknown (Eckhardt et al., 1981). It appears that alcohol affects the constriction of the heart muscle, thereby lowering its efficiency.

Alcohol abuse has serious implications that specifically affect women. Heavy alcohol consumption reduces fertility (Greenwood, Love, & Pratt, 1983) by producing amenorrhea, or no menstrual period, by direct effects on the pituitary and hypothalamus, and by thiamine deficiency. Drinking during pregnancy increases the risk of **fetal alcohol syndrome**, which includes specific facial abnormalities, growth deficiencies, central nervous system disorders, and mental retardation (Pratt, 1980, 1982).

Aging and the Negative Effects of Alcohol. The effect of alcohol on the brain, its effect on liver metabolism, and the level of blood alcohol following ingestion of a specific quantity of alcohol appear to change with age (Scott & Mitchell, 1988). Older adults' cognitive functioning seems to decrease more after a single drink than does that of younger adults (M. K. Jones & Jones, 1980). Some research comparing young and old alcoholics and nonalcoholics suggests that early heavy drinking may result in premature aging of the brain (Ryan & Butters, 1980). However, the issue of whether alcohol abuse causes premature aging is highly controversial (Ryan, 1982; Scott & Mitchell, 1988).

Little research has been conducted on changes with age in the way in which the liver metabolizes alcohol. What is known suggests that the effects depend on the amount of alcohol consumed. Small amounts of alcohol in older adults slow the process by which other drugs may be cleared from the system; in contrast, high quantities of alcohol speed up this process (Scott & Mitchell, 1988). Another important difference between young and old drinkers concerns the level of alcohol in the blood. If the two groups are given equal doses of alcohol, older adults will have a higher blood-alcohol concentration (Scott & Mitchell, 1988). This age difference has important implications, since blood-alcohol levels provide an index of relative impairment; for example, an older adult has to drink less alcohol to be declared legally intoxicated than a younger adult does.

Benefits of Alcohol

Not all of the effects of alcohol reported in the literature are negative. Results from several longitudinal studies have also demonstrated some positive effects on health of moderate drinking (roughly two to four drinks per day). Findings from the Kaiser-Permanente study (Klatsky, Friedman, & Siegelaub, 1981), the Alameda County study (Berkman, Breslow, & Wingard, 1983), the Framingham study (L. A. Friedman & Kimball, 1986; T. Gordon & Kannel, 1984), and the Albany study (T. Gordon & Doyle, 1987) documented lower mortality rates among light and moderate drinkers. Additionally, light drinkers may have a much lower risk of stroke than abstainers or heavy drinkers even after controlling for hypertension, cigarette smoking, and medication (Gill, Zezulka, Shipley, Gill, & Beevers, 1986).

Overall, the results reveal a U-shaped relationship between the amount of alcohol consumed and the mortality rate, with moderate drinkers having a lower death rate than either abstainers or heavy drinkers. The relationship seems to be stronger for men than for women, especially for men under 60.

Why does light or moderate drinking appear to have benefits? No one knows for sure. Apparently, the findings are unrelated to such things as group differences in personality, such as impatience and aggressiveness (Kaufman, Rosenberg, Helmrich, & Shapiro, 1985), protection against the effects of lipoproteins (Haskell et al., 1984), or poor experimental designs (T. Myers, 1983).

Quitting Drinking

Several approaches have been used to help problem drinkers achieve abstinence. The most widely known of these is Alcoholics Anonymous (AA).

Founded in 1935 by two former alcoholics, AA follows a strict disease model of alcoholism. The program itself is based on personal and spiritual growth, with the goal being total abstinence. Part of the AA philosophy is the notion that problem drinkers are addicted to alcohol and have no power to resist it. Moreover, abstaining alcoholics are in the process of recovering for the rest of their lives.

Even though AA has a long history, very little research has been done to document its effectiveness (Peele, 1984). The major reason is that AA is an anonymous fellowship, making it difficult to follow people over time. What little has been done suggests that AA, while helping many different kinds of people, may be especially effective for people with lower educational levels or higher needs for authoritarianism, dependency, and sociability (W. R. Miller & Hester, 1980).

Some form of psychotherapy is widely used in a variety of treatment settings, including Veterans Administration hospitals, care units in other hospitals, private treatment centers, and private counseling. These approaches include psychoanalysis (Blum, 1966), behavior modification (Wallace, 1985), psychodrama (Blume, 1985), assertiveness training (Materi, 1977), and group therapy (Zimberg, 1985). The primary goal of any of these approaches, in order to be effective, should be sobriety (Zimberg, 1985). Moreover, long-term sobriety may require combining psychotherapy with other programs such as AA. No research has been done specifically examining success rates as a function of age. In general, however, it appears that long-term sobriety of at least 3 years is achieved by no more than 30% of individuals seeking treatment (Armor, Polich, & Stambul, 1976; Wiens & Menustik, 1983). These data clearly indicate that the relapse potential for recovering alcoholics is very high.

CARDIOVASCULAR DISEASE

In Chapter 3 we noted several age-related changes in the cardiovascular system. Several diseases, such as ischemic heart disease, atherosclerosis, and hypertension, are more prevalent with increasing age. In this section we will consider additional types of cardiovascular disease. Throughout the chapter there are discussions of other aspects of health that influence the risk of cardiovascular disease, including nutrition, smoking, and stress.

As noted in Table 4.7, incidence rates of cardiovascular disease increase dramatically with age. For all the diseases listed except for angina, men outnumber women. Although the U.S. death rate from cardiovascular disease declined by more than one third from the early 1960s to the mid-1980s due to better prevention (Kannel & Thom, 1984), the rate of death for blacks remains nearly double that for whites (DHHS, 1988).

Coronary Disease

Recall that one of the changes in the heart with age is a gradual reduction in coronary blood flow. When this reduction becomes severe, the supply of oxygen to the heart muscle becomes insufficient, resulting in chest pain. Such pain, called **angina**, is described by some patients as a chest pressure, a burning pain, or a squeezing that radiates from the chest to the back, neck, and arms (Berkow, 1987). In most cases the pain is induced by physical exertion and is relieved within 5 to 10 minutes by rest. Treatment of angina in older adults is similar to that used with younger and middle-aged adults; depending on when the angina occurs, patients are given nitroglycerine, beta-blocking agents, or calcium-blocking agents.

Age-related increases in chronic diseases mean that many older adults take several different kinds of medications. Knowing about the proper use and potential adverse interactions of these drugs is an important part of health maintenance.

Another major age-related coronary disease is **myocardial infarction**, or heart attack. Myocardial infarction is especially serious for older adults; mortality following a heart attack is much higher for them (DHHS, 1988). Myocardial infarction occurs when the coronary blood flow drops below the level needed to sustain the heart muscle (Berkow, 1987). If it is sustained, the infarction effectively kills the heart muscle. The interruption in blood flow may result from a spasm, a progressive buildup of fatty plaques, or some combination of factors. The initial symptoms of myocardial infarction are identical to those of angina but are more severe and prolonged. Additionally, there may be general symptoms such as nausea, vomit-ing, sweating, and severe weakness. In as many as 25% of patients, however, chest pain may be absent. Such "silent" myocardial infarctions are more common in older adults, especially those with diabetes (Berkow, 1987). As with angina, treatment of older heart attack victims is the same as that for victims at other ages: careful evaluation and a prescribed rehabilitation program consisting of life-style changes in diet and exercise.

Cerebrovascular Disease

Atherosclerotic changes in blood vessels that supply the brain can reduce the supply of nourishment it receives and result in the malfunction or

TABLE 4.7 · Incidence of major cardiovascular diseases per 10,000 people, as a function of age: United States, 1988

Age	Coronary Disease		Cerebrovascular Accident		Angina		Myocardial Infarction	
	Men	Women	Men	Women	Men	Women	Men	Women
35–44	42	7	2	4	8	5	21	2
45–54	108	33	20	12	30	21	54	9
55–64	202	99	40	26	74	54	91	25
65–74	227	136	92	80	52	51	119	51
75–84	247	236	196	112	25	94	168	90

(Source: U.S. Department of Health and Human Services, 1988)

death of brain cells. This situation is termed **cerebrovascular disease**. When the blood flow to a portion of the brain is completely blocked, a **cerebrovascular accident (CVA)**, or stroke, results (Berkow, 1987). Causes of CVAs include a thrombus, which forms in a blood vessel in the brain already damaged by atherosclerosis; an **embolus**, which forms elsewhere and travels to obstruct a blood vessel in the brain; or a **cerebral hemorrhage**, in which a blood vessel bursts. The severity of a CVA and likelihood of recovery depend on the specific area of the brain involved, the extent of disruption in the blood flow, and the duration of the disruption. Consequently, a CVA may affect such a small area that it goes virtually unnoticed, or it may be so severe as to cause death.

The risk of a CVA increases with age; in fact, CVAs are the third leading cause of death among the elderly in the United States (DHHS, 1988). In addition to age, other risk factors include being male, being Black, and having high blood pressure, heart disease, or diabetes. The higher risk among Blacks appears to be due to a greater prevalence of hypertension in this population.

Rehabilitation following a CVA must take into account not only the physical effects but also the psychological ones. For example, the sudden loss of the ability to move or speak can have profound effects on a person's self-esteem and sense of independence. Both health care professionals and family members must provide a supportive context for recovery.

CANCER

Cancer is the second leading cause of death in the United States, behind cardiovascular disease. Every year nearly 950,000 people are diagnosed as having cancer, and roughly 475,000 die. Over the life span, nearly one in every three Americans will eventually develop cancer (DHHS, 1988).

One truly unfortunate aspect of these statistics is that many deaths due to cancer are preventable. Many forms of cancer, such as lung and colorectal cancer, are caused in large part by unhealthy life-

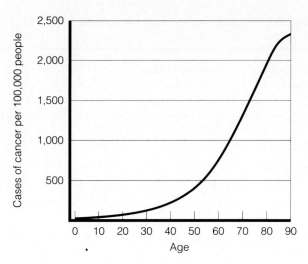

FIGURE 4.1 · Age-related incidence of cancer
(Source: National Cancer Institute)

styles. Others, including breast and prostate cancer, have high probabilities for cure if they are detected early. In this section we will consider some of the issues pertaining to cancer and age.

Cancer Risk and Age

The risk of getting cancer increases markedly with age (Young, Percy, & Asire, 1981). Figure 4.1 depicts the incidence rates for all forms of cancer as a function of age. As can be seen, the largest number of cases occurs in the age group 60–70. Notice that after age 40 the incidence rate increases sharply. For example, the incidence of cancer at age 50 is only about 400 cases per 100,000 people; by age 70, however, it has increased nearly fourfold to over 1,500 cases. Overall, half of all cancer occurs in individuals over age 65.

Table 4.8 contains estimates of the annual age-specific incidence rates of the most frequent types of cancer in older adults. For cancers that

occur in both sexes, rates are generally higher in men. For example, cancers of the lung, colon, rectum, pancreas, bladder, and stomach all occur more often in men in all age groups. Overall, cancers of the lung, colon, prostate, and breast are the most common.

Why the incidence of cancer should be much higher in the elderly remains a mystery. Part of the reason is poor health habits over a long period of time, such as cigarette smoking. As noted in Chapter 3, some researchers also believe that changes in the immune system, resulting in a decreased ability to inhibit the growth of tumors, may also be partly to blame. Clearly, much research still needs to be done.

Screening and Prevention

The most effective way to address the problem of cancer is through increased use of screening techniques and making life-style changes as a preventive measure. The American Cancer Society

TABLE 4.8 • Average annual age-specific incidence rates of cancers per 100,000 population: United States, 1978–1981

Cancer	Sex	Ages 65–69	70–74	75–79	80–84	85 +
Lung and bronchus	M	429.9	512.8	538.4	505.8	394.1
	F	133.6	134.5	117.1	96.3	80.8
Prostate	M	358.0	584.6	825.0	1035.4	1130.3
Breast	F	292.0	319.6	338.7	340.6	378.4
Corpus uteri	F	109.7	100.2	92.7	74.9	59.4
Colon	M	169.2	248.1	324.4	421.7	487.2
	F	131.7	192.9	260.4	334.4	367.1
Urinary bladder	M	113.2	166.4	213.4	255.1	282.6
	F	29.1	37.8	49.9	62.0	79.9
Rectum	M	88.7	122.7	140.8	164.4	181.8
	F	49.2	67.7	86.1	98.5	107.1
Buccal cavity and pharynx	M	78.4	77.6	83.3	84.6	89.9
	F	27.4	28.0	27.8	28.2	29.2
Stomach	M	57.0	76.0	105.3	133.2	157.9
	F	21.7	32.5	48.0	65.8	80.1
Pancreas	M	52.1	70.4	87.3	87.7	106.7
	F	35.9	45.2	55.9	72.8	84.4
Larynx	M	46.9	42.4	36.9	35.4	28.8
	F	6.5	5.0	5.5	3.6	2.6
Ovary	F	46.1	46.7	54.8	47.4	42.4
Non-Hodgkin's lymphomas	M	42.3	54.5	73.4	83.5	84.3
	F	35.8	45.0	57.3	59.7	55.2
Leukemias	M	40.5	63.6	81.7	115.8	147.5
	F	21.2	33.4	40.5	62.8	70.9
Kidney and renal pelvis	M	40.6	49.3	55.6	65.2	59.2
	F	18.0	19.6	24.2	23.1	22.1
Cervix uteri	F	24.7	25.0	23.9	24.1	27.6
Melanoma of skin	M	23.2	26.9	30.9	26.1	32.8
	F	14.4	14.6	13.8	17.1	21.2

(Source: Data taken from the SEER program of the National Cancer Institute)

TABLE 4.9 · Suggested screening steps for cancer

Test	Sex	Age	Frequency
Health counseling and cancer checkup	M & F	>20 >40	Every 3 years Every year
Breast self-examination	F	>20	Once a month
Physical examination		20–40 >40	Every 3 years Once a year
Mammography		35–40 40–50 >50	Baseline Every 1–2 years Once a year
Pelvic examination	F	20–40 >40	Every 3 years Once a year
Pap test	F	At onset of sexual activity to age 65	Yearly for 2 exams, then every 3 years
Endometrial biopsy	F	At menopause in women at high risk	
Prostate check	M	>40	Once a year
Rectal examination	M & F	>40	Once a year
Stool guaiac test	M & F	>40	Once a year

(Source: Summarized from recommendations of the American Cancer Society, 1980)

strongly recommends these steps for people of all ages, but older adults need to be especially aware of what to do. Table 4.9 contains guidelines for the early detection of some common forms of cancer.

One problem in cancer screening and prevention in the elderly is a reluctance on the part of some physicians to tackle the problem aggressively (List, 1987, 1988; Samet, Hunt, & Key, 1986). Whether this failure stems from a belief in the myth that older patients have substantially lower survival rates (actually, the survival rates are quite similar) or from some other set of reasons is unclear. For their part, many older adults are reluc-

tant to request the necessary tests (List, 1988). In any event, regular cancer screening should be part of all older adults' program of health promotion and disease prevention.

STRESS AND HEALTH

Stress is harmful to your health. Although this statement does not appear on packages or jobs, it is one that nearly everyone believes. It is also a widespread belief that stress-related health problems are the province of upper-level business executives, because of the large responsibilities they have. Lower-level employees are viewed as "safe," because they have little control over their working environment. Unfortunately, the relationships among job, stress, and health are not that simple. In fact, a carefully conducted study found that business executives had fewer stress-related health problems than waitresses, construction workers, secretaries, laboratory technicians, machine operators, farm workers, and painters (M. Smith, Colligan, Horning, & Hurrell, 1978). It appears that stress occurs most when people must be extremely vigilant, do complex work, and meet time demands placed on them by others. Responsibility and decision making alone seem not to matter.

Just as the belief that executives are more prone to stress-related illnesses than laborers is more myth than fact, many other aspects of stress and its relationship to health are not understood very well. Indeed, the nature of the relationship of stress to age remains underresearched and poorly understood. For example, it may surprise you to learn that more women than men reported that stress had had a significant impact on their health in the previous year and that the people between the ages of 30 and 44 reported the highest levels of stress (see Table 4.10). In this section we will examine the relationship between stress and illness and will look at some ways in which we can manage the stress in our lives. First, however, we must understand what we mean by stress.

The Meaning of Stress

Despite literally thousands of scientific studies on stress and its effects on health, we still cannot agree on a definition. To some, stress refers to something in the environment, as in "I am in a stressful relationship." Others see stress as a response to the environment, as in "I feel stress whenever I have to discipline the children." Fi-

TABLE 4.10 · Percentage of people 18 years of age or older who felt that stress had at least some effect on their health in the previous year: United States, 1985

	Males	Females
18–29 years	39.5	50.3
30–44 years	44.7	54.3
45–64 years	36.2	51.0
65 and over	22.1	38.7

(Source: National Health Survey, U.S. Department of Health and Human Services, 1988)

nally, still others define stress as an interaction between environmental conditions and a response to them.

All three positions have been adopted by various theorists over the years. We will focus on two theories that have had the most impact on the investigation of stress: the general adaptation syndrome and the stress and coping paradigm.

Selye's General Adaptation Syndrome

The single most influential person in the field of stress theory and research was Hans Selye (1956, 1979, 1982). More than anyone else, Selye was almost single-handedly responsible for popularizing the notion that stress has physical effects. He was one of the first to conceptualize stress as a response to things in the environment. He used the term *stressor* to represent the environmental stimulus that caused the person to react and the term *stress* to represent the response to the stressor.

Selye described stress as a nonspecific response; that is, it is a precise response that can be triggered by any number of stressors (Selye, 1956,

1979). Most of his work involved carefully describing this response, which became known as the general adaptation syndrome.

The **general adaptation syndrome** is the body's attempt to defend itself against stressors. The syndrome consists of three stages. During the **alarm stage** the body's defenses against stressors are mobilized. The sympathetic nervous system, responsible for the "fight or flight" response, quickly goes into action. Epinephrine (adrenaline) is released; the pulse, blood pressure, and respiration increase; more blood is diverted to the skeletal muscles; the sweat glands are activated; and the gastrointestinal tract is deactivated.

If the stressor continues, the organism enters the second phase, termed the **resistance stage**. During this stage the organism adapts to the stressor. The length of this stage depends on the potency of the stressor and how adaptable the organism is. Providing that adaptation is possible, the resistance stage can continue for a relatively long period. Outwardly, the organism looks normal during this stage. However, all is not well physiologically. Neurological and hormonal changes occur that Selye believed were related to stress illnesses such as peptic ulcers, hypertension, hyperthyroidism, ulcerative colitis, and some forms of asthma. Additionally, Selye believed that continual adaptation to stressors weakened the immune system, making infections more likely. Later in this section we will examine research evidence for these stress-illness links.

Organisms cannot resist stress indefinitely. At some point the **exhaustion stage** is reached. The ability to resist is gone, and the body begins to break-down. Depression is quite likely, and even death is a real possibility.

Combining the age-related changes described throughout this chapter with those in Chapter 3, we would predict that older adults are more likely to suffer the physiological consequences of stress more rapidly than younger adults. That is, older adults cannot withstand stress as long as their younger counterparts before their bodies begin to break down. This situation makes older adults more susceptible to stress-related illness.

The Stress and Coping Paradigm

An alternative and also very influential approach to stress is the **stress and coping paradigm**, developed by Richard Lazarus and his colleagues (Lazarus, 1984; Lazarus, DeLongis, Folkman, & Gruen, 1985; Lazarus & Folkman, 1984). As depicted in Table 4.11, Lazarus views stress not as an environmental stimulus or as a response but, rather, as the interaction of a thinking person and the event. How the person interprets the event is what matters, not the event itself or the person's response. Put more formally, stress is "a particular relationship between the person and the environment that is appraised by the person as taxing or exceeding his or her resources and endangering his or her well-being" (Lazarus & Folkman, 1984, p. 19). Note that this definition states that stress refers to a transactional process between a person and the environment, that the person's appraisal of the situation is key, and that unless the situation is considered to be threatening, challenging, or harmful, stress does not result.

Appraisal. Lazarus and Folkman (1984) describe three types of appraisals of stress (Table 4.11). **Primary appraisal** serves to categorize events into three groups based on the significance they have for the person's well-being: irrelevant, benign-positive, and stressful. Irrelevant events have no bearing on the individual; hearing about a typhoon nowhere near land in the South Pacific while sitting in your living room in Boston is an example. Benign-positive appraisals mean that the event has good effects; a job promotion is a

TABLE 4.11 • A theoretical schematization of stress, coping, and adaptation. Causal antecedents of stress are aspects of the person or environment that place demands on resources. Mediating processes determine whether particular demands are stressful and, if so, what should be done. Immediate and long-term effects are the outcomes of dealing with stress.

Causal Antecedents of Stress	Mediating Processes Time 1 . . . T2 . . . T3 . . . Tn Encounter 1 . . . 2 . . . 3 . . . n	Immediate Effects	Long-Term Effects
Person variables:	Primary appraisal	Physiological changes	Somatic health or illness
values or commitments beliefs: existential sense of control	Secondary appraisal	Positive or negative feelings	Morale (well-being)
	Reappraisal	Quality of encounter outcome	Social functioning
Environment:	Coping:		
(situational) demands, constraints	problem-focused		
resources (e.g., social network)	emotion-focused		
ambiguity of harm	seeking, obtaining and using social		
imminence of harm	support		
	Resolutions of each stressful encounter		

(Source: *Stress, Appraisal, and Coping* by R. J. Lazarus and S. Folkman, 1984, New York: Springer. Reprinted with permission.)

common example. Finally, stressful appraisals mean that an event, such as failing a course, has been perceived as harmful, threatening, or challenging.

Secondary appraisal refers to one's perceived ability to cope with harm, threat, or challenge. Secondary appraisal is the equivalent of asking three questions: "What can I do?" "How likely is it that I can use one of my options successfully?" "Will this option reduce my stress?" If a person

believes that there is something that he or she can do that will make a difference, stress is reduced and coping is successful.

Reappraisal involves being sensitive to changes in the situation. New information may become available that needs to be incorporated into one's appraisal. For example, you may come to discover that the person you are dating is already married, a fact that may lead you to make a new appraisal of your relationship. Reappraisal can both increase stress (as in this example) or can lower stress (if, perhaps, it was only a nasty rumor).

Coping. During secondary appraisal we may realize that we can do something effective to deal with the stress. Lazarus and Folkman define **coping** as "constantly changing cognitive and behavioral efforts to manage specific external and/or internal demands that are appraised as taxing or exceeding the resources of the person" (1984, p. 141). This definition points out several important aspects about coping. First, coping is an evolving process that is fine-tuned over time. Second, it is learned, not automatic. Third, it takes effort; it is something we work at. Finally, coping requires only that we manage the situation; we are not required to overcome or control it. Thus, we can cope with extreme weather even though we cannot control it.

How well we cope depends on several factors. Healthy, energetic people are better able to cope than frail, sick people. A positive attitude about oneself and one's abilities is also important. Good problem-solving skills put one at an advantage in having several options with which to manage the stress. Social skills and social support are important in helping us solicit suggestions and assistance from others. Finally, financial resources are important; having the money to purchase services makes it easier to cope with many problems.

Aging and the Stress and Coping Paradigm. Two important areas of age differences in the stress and coping paradigm that have been investigated are the sources of stress and coping strategies.

Age differences have been described for the kinds of things that people report as everyday stresses (Folkman, Lazarus, Pimley, & Novacek, 1987). Younger adults experienced more stress in the domains of finances, work, home mainte-

nance, personal life, family, and friends than did older adults. These differences were probably due to the fact that the young adults were parents of small children and were employed; parenting and work roles are less salient to retired older adults. The stresses reported frequently by older adults, coming mainly from the environment and social issues, may be more age-related than role-related. That is, environmental stress may be due to a decreased ability to get around in the environment rather than to a specific role.

Age differences in coping strategies are striking and consistent (Felton & Revenson, 1987; Folkman et al., 1987). For example, Blanchard-Fields and her colleagues have shown that younger adults tend to use defensive coping styles much of the time, whereas older adults choose coping strategies on the basis of whether they feel in control of the situation (Blanchard-Fields & Irion, 1988; Blanchard-Fields & Robinson, 1987; Irion & Blanchard-Fields, 1987). Even when people are faced with similar problems, age differences in coping style are apparent. For example, Felton and Revenson (1987) report that when trying to cope with their chronic illnesses, middle-aged adults were more likely to use interpersonal strategies such as information seeking than were older adults.

These age-related differences in coping strategies fit with developmental trends reported in the personality literature, reviewed in Chapter 8. In particular, there appears to be an age-related turning inward that is reflected in increased passivity and more self-reflective behavior. It may be that these changes in personality are also reflected in one's choice of a coping strategy.

Stress and Physical Illness

Considerable research has examined how stress causes physical illness. Zegans (1982) reviewed this literature and proposed numerous hypotheses about this connection. One of the most important of these involves the effects of stress on the immune system. Recall that Selye proposed that stress suppresses the activity of the immune system. V. Riley (1981) reports that increased levels of hormones called **corticoids** occur after prolonged stress and that they increase animals' vulnerability to viruses and possibly even cancer. However, the possibility of effective coping may alleviate these effects in animals (Laudenslager, Ryan, Drugan, Hyson, & Maier, 1983).

Research on humans has documented similar effects. Lower antibody levels and poorer functioning of B-cell lymphocytes (see Chapter 3) have been demonstrated in students who were under stress during examination periods (Jemmott et al., 1983; Kiecolt-Glaser, Speicher, Holliday, & Glaser, 1984). Interestingly, personality differences influenced the degree to which the immune system was affected. People who were motivated by power rather than friendship (Jemmott et al., 1983) and people who were lonely (Kiecolt-Glaser et al., 1984) were affected most.

This line of research suggests that stress lowers the ability of the immune system to fight infection. Given that immune function declines with age (see Chapter 3), it is reasonable to conclude that older adults are even more susceptible to these effects of stress. Although the relationship between stress and the immune system may help explain one mechanism of the stress-illness connection, it is not the only one. Additional connections between stress and illness can be seen in examining specific diseases.

Headaches. Nearly everyone gets an occasional headache ascribed to stress. For most of us, headaches are relatively minor problems. For the 10% to 12% of people who must seek medical attention, however, headaches present major difficulties (Holyroyd, Appel, & Andrasik, 1983). Those who seek physicians do not do so because

they have different kinds of headaches. Rather, they suffer from more serious or frequent headaches than the rest of us.

Holyroyd et al. (1983) describe the two types of headache: tension headache and vascular headache. Migraine headache is a severe version of vascular headache caused by restriction followed by dilation of the cerebral arteries, causing intense, throbbing pain. Research dating to the 1960s has demonstrated that stress is associated with tension headaches and that this relationship is strongest with events that are most like Lazarus's daily stresses. Vascular headaches are also associated with stress, but to a lesser extent.

Ulcers. That stress causes ulcers is accepted by virtually everyone. Many years of research on both animals and people have confirmed this belief. It appears that ulcers are most likely when the stressful situation has strongly negative aspects that cannot be avoided, presents unexpected annoyances, and requires difficult decisions with little personal control (M. Smith et al., 1978). We will discuss the issue of personal control in more detail in Chapter 8.

Cardiovascular Disease. Cardiovascular disease has several behavioral risk factors. One of the most provocative of these connections is between cardiovascular disease and self-imposed stress. Due to the work of M. Friedman and Rosenman (1974) we know that both personality and situational stress are related to cardiovascular disease. They identified two behavior patterns, which differ dramatically in terms of the risk of cardiovascular disease. A style termed **Type A behavior pattern** is associated with high rates of cardiovascular disease. An opposite style, **Type B behavior pattern**, is not associated with cardiovascular disease.

Type A people are intensely competitive, angry, hostile, restless, aggressive, and impatient.

They are also at least twice as likely as Type B people to develop cardiovascular disease, even when other risk factors such as smoking, diabetes, hypertension, and high serum cholesterol are taken into account. Furthermore, serious heart disease rarely occurs before age 70 except among Type A people. It does not seem to matter how much junk food Type B people eat, how many cigarettes they smoke, or how little exercise they get. They will probably not die prematurely from cardiovascular disease (Eisdorfer & Wilkie, 1977).

These findings led researchers and those involved in rehabilitating cardiac patients to advocate major changes in life-style following heart attacks or other serious cardiovascular disease. The thinking was that if Type A behavior predisposed people to cardiovascular disease, then eliminating Type A traits would serve as a protective function. It appears, however, that the relationship between Type A behavior and cardiovascular disease is more complex.

Beginning in 1981, researchers began reporting a reversal in the relationship when the risk for secondary cardiovascular disease was examined. That is, researchers began studying individuals who had already had serious cardiovascular disease and investigated whether Type A or Type B people had a higher risk of developing additional heart diseases (e.g., having a second heart attack). A series of investigations suggested that, contrary to the finding concerning risk of initial heart disease, Type A people actually recovered from their first heart attack better and had lower morbidity than Type B individuals (Case, Heller, Case, & Moss, 1985; Dimsdale, Gilbert, Hutter, Hackett, & Block, 1981; Shekelle, Gale, & Norusis, 1985). The strongest evidence for the reversal was reported by Ragland and Brand (1988), who examined 22-year follow-up data from the original Friedman and Rosenman study. Ragland and Brand (1988) also found lower morbidity following the first episode of serious cardiovas-

cular disease in Type A people (see "How Do We Know?").

Why do Type A people have a higher risk of heart attack but a better chance to survive than Type B people? The answers are unclear. It may be that some of the characteristics of Type A people that make them "movers and shakers" also make them feel that they need to overcome their disease. Indeed, researchers have noted that Type A people were much more likely to stick to diet and exercise regimens after heart attacks (Ragland & Brand, 1988) and had a more positive attitude about recovery (Ivancevich & Matteson, 1988). The laid-back approach of Type B people may work to their detriment during recovery.

Clearly, there is a need for caution in interpreting these findings. Type A and Type B patterns are just that—patterns. Only approximately 10% of the population is classified as a "pure" Type A or B. The rest of the people fall somewhere in between. Additionally, the relationship between Type A behavior and cardiovascular functioning is obviously complex and varies between men and women of different ages (Harbin & Blumenthal, 1985). It is beginning to look as if it is the hostility and anger component of Type A behavior that is the risk factor, rather than the entire behavioral cluster (Ivancevich & Matteson, 1988). Moreover, virtually nothing is known about how the relationship between Type A and cardiovascular disease is affected by increasing age, if at all. These issues need to be more thoroughly researched before we can have a firm understanding of the relationship between behavior and cardiovascular disease.

Stress and Psychological Illness

It is commonly believed that stress causes psychological problems. Despite years of research, there is little empirical support that even an accumulation of stressful life events causes depression,

HOW · DO · WE · KNOW?

The Type A Controversy: It's Not Always Bad to Be Intense

As noted in the text, the controversy over whether Type A behavior is seriously detrimental to one's health has profound implications for treatment. It is a good idea, then, to take a closer look at one study that found an unexpected result.

Ragland and Brand (1988) examined the 22-year mortality of 257 men with heart disease. These men were part of the Western Collaborative Group Study, which uncovered the connection between Type A behavior pattern and coronary disease. Of these 257 men, 135 had symptomatic myocardial infarctions, 71 had silent myocardial infarctions, and 51 had angina; of those who had symptomatic myocardial infarctions, 26 died suddenly or within 24 hours of the onset of symptoms. A follow-up through 1983 showed that 128 of the men had died, and their cause of death was coded from death certificates by two independent raters; 91 died of heart disease and 37 from unrelated causes. For the 91 men who died of heart disease, whether they died within 24 hours of symptom onset was noted. The key analyses examined whether short-term and long-term outcomes were related differently to Type A and Type B patterns.

Results showed an almost identical mortality rate for Type A and Type B men who died within 24 hours of symptom onset. For long-term mortality, the fatality rate was 19.1 per 1,000 person-years for Type A and 31.7 per 1,000 person-years for Type B. Even when the data were examined in more detail, the Type A advantage never disappeared.

Although the results of the study point toward the conclusion that Type A men who survive their initial bout with heart disease are more likely to survive in the long run, Ragland and Brand suggest several caveats. First, we do not know how Type A and Type B people actually respond to coronary disease. For example, one group may change their life-style more completely than the other. Second, Type A men may be more likely to seek medical help for suspected heart disease. Finally, behavior patterns identified years before coronary disease is diagnosed may be meaningless; behavior patterns may have changed in the intervening years.

Still, the Ragland and Brand study points out that Type A and Type B behavior patterns have complex relationships with heart disease. The study also points out that we must be cautious in interpreting longitudinal data involving predictions over long periods.

schizophrenia, or anxiety disorders. Dohrenwend (1979, p. 5) concluded that except for the death of a loved one or a very serious physical illness or injury, "it is difficult to find consistent evidence that other types of single life events can produce psychopathology in previously normal adults in societies free from war and other natural disasters." In order for stress to have a major influence on psychological functioning, Dohrenwend argues, three things must be present: (1) vulnerability from physical illness or injury, (2) undesirable life events, and (3) loss of social support. When all three factors occur simultaneously, psychopathology may result.

These freight car repairwomen work in a relatively dangerous and stressful occupation that could affect their health.

Managing Stress

The treatment of stress has been approached in many ways, based mainly on the various definitions of stress. Thus, if stress is seen as coming from environmental stimuli, treatment involves modifying, escaping, or ignoring these stimuli. Unfortunately, this approach is often impossible; for example, it may be very difficult to quit a job that is stressful. Thus, most therapeutic efforts have focused on teaching people new ways to deal with the physical responses involved with stress or new ways to appraise the situation cognitively.

Managing the Response. Three methods have proven effective in dealing with the body's response to stress. Relaxation training is effective, particularly in controlling hypertension, in-

somnia, and tension headaches (Lavey & Taylor, 1985). Meditation or focusing attention so as not to dwell on negative thoughts is also effective. Shapiro (1985) concluded that meditation is as effective at reducing anxiety, phobias, and hypertension as relaxation training. Finally, biofeedback training also appears to be as effective as relaxation training at lowering muscle tension and skin temperature (Andrasik, Blanchard, & Edlund, 1985). At this point, no one technique is superior to another.

Changing the Cognitive Component. The best-researched cognitive approach to stress management is stress inoculation (Cameron & Meichenbaum, 1982; Meichenbaum, 1985; Meichenbaum & Cameron, 1983). The notion of stress inoculation is similar to vaccination against disease. The process proceeds by training clients to identify the source of the problem, termed conceptualization; learning new and practicing old coping skills, called skills-acquisition rehearsal; and putting these skills into practice, termed application and follow-through. Several problems have been successfully treated with stress inoculation (Hamberger & Lohr, 1984), including test anxiety, public speaking anxiety, and social anxiety (Jaremko, 1983).

SLEEP AND AGING

One of the most common complaints as people grow older is sleep disturbance (Bootzin & Engle-Friedman, 1987). These complaints most often concern difficulty in falling asleep, frequent or prolonged awakenings during the night, early-morning awakenings, and the subjective experience of poor sleep quality. Effects of poor sleep are felt the next day, as everyone knows. Moodiness, poorer performance on tasks involving sustained concentration, fatigue, and lack of motivation are some of the telltale signs. In this section we will consider the extent of sleep-related problems across adulthood and examine some of the reasons for them.

How Widespread Are Sleep Disturbances?

Results from national surveys and drug-use studies confirm that sleep disturbances increase with age. Mellinger, Balter, and Uhlenhuth (1985) considered "serious" insomnia, defined as considerable difficulty in falling asleep or staying awake within the previous year. They reported that the prevalence of serious insomnia increased from 14% for the 18–34 age group to 25% for the 65–79 age group. Less severe insomnia showed similar age-

related trends. Together, 45% of those between the ages of 65 and 79 had had some difficulty with insomnia during the previous year. Thus, sleep disturbances affect many people, with the numbers increasing with age.

As we will see, many aspects of sleep decline with age. Interestingly, total sleep time over a 24-hour period does not change across adulthood (Webb & Swinburne, 1971), despite a significant drop with age in total sleep at night (Hauri, 1982). The explanation is that nap taking significantly increases with age (Zepelin, 1973).

Age-Related Changes in Sleep

The most reliable and valid measure of sleep is **polysomnography** (Bootzin & Engle-Friedman, 1981). Polysomnography consists of all-night recording of the electroencephalogram (EEG), the electrooculogram (EOG), and the electromyogram (EMG). The EEG measures electrical activity in the brain, the EOG registers eye movements, and the EMG measures muscle activity. Other physiological measures taken during sleep may include temperature, respiration, heart rate, and galvanic skin response.

Polysomnography has helped researchers identify five stages of sleep (Bootzin & Engle-Friedman, 1987). The brain activity of these stages is depicted in Figure 4.2. As we grow tired and relaxed, brain waves take on an irregular pattern of light sleep, marking Stage 1. Stage 1 sleep lasts about 5 minutes, during which time you are easily awakened if spoken to. With more relaxation, you enter Stage 2 sleep, which is characterized by a particular type of brain-wave activity called **sleep spindles**. Sleep spindles are bursts of brain electrical activity. You can still be awakened without too much difficulty, but by now you are clearly asleep. Stage 3 sleep is a short transition from the lighter sleep of Stage 2 to the deep sleep of Stage 4. In Stage 4 the brain emits large, slow **delta waves**,

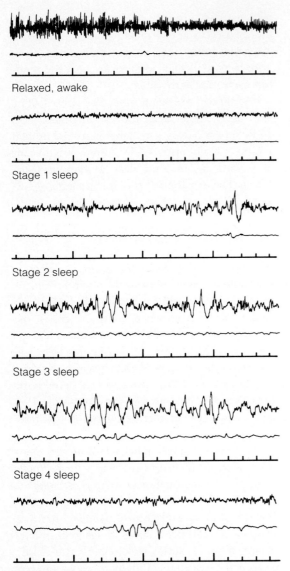

Relaxed, awake

Stage 1 sleep

Stage 2 sleep

Stage 3 sleep

Stage 4 sleep

REM, or paradoxical, sleep

FIGURE 4.2 • EEG recordings indicating wakefulness, Stages 1–4 of sleep, and REM sleep. Each record has three lines. The top line is the EEG from an electrode on the scalp. The middle line is a record of eye movements. The bottom line shows time in seconds.

(Source: *Biological Psychology* (3rd ed.) by J. W. Kalat, 1988, Belmont, CA: Wadsworth. Reprinted with permission.)

and you are hard to awaken. From Stage 4, you go back up the sleep ladder through Stages 3 and 2 and enter the most interesting phase of all, rapid-eye-movement sleep, or **REM sleep**. The body shows many signs of arousal, such as increased heart rate and respiration as well as eye movements, but the muscles are deeply relaxed, and you are very difficult to awaken. It is in REM sleep that dreaming occurs. Sleep continues in a cyclic fashion all night, progressing from REM to Stages 2, 3, and 4, unless you wake up. If that happens, then the cycles are disrupted, and sleep becomes abnormal.

Research based on examining the five stages of sleep has confirmed that sleep is not as good in the elderly as it is in the young. The most consistent age-related difference in sleep is an increase in the frequency of awakenings as morning approaches (e.g., Webb, 1982). Older adults have more difficulty falling back to sleep once they have awakened than younger adults. Webb and Campbell (1980) found that 50- to 60-year-olds took longer to fall back to sleep after being awakened after the first 80 minutes of sleep than did 21- to 23-year-olds. Webb and Campbell argue that this increased time to fall back asleep may be partly responsible for increased early morning awakenings among older adults. Older adults also have more trouble falling to sleep in the first place. Webb (1982) documented that it took women aged 50 to 60 twice as long to fall asleep initially as women aged 20 to 30.

Several age-related differences have been found concerning the stages of sleep as well. The most pronounced of these is a substantial reduction in deep, or slow-wave, sleep (Stages 3 and 4) (Miles & Dement, 1980; Reynolds et al., 1985). However, this reduction appears to be due to a lowering of the amplitude of EEG waves to such an extent that they no longer meet the scoring criteria for slow-wave sleep (Miles & Dement, 1980; Webb & Dreblow, 1982). Thus, slow-EEG sleep still occurs in older adults, but the scoring practices most widely used do not take the age-related reduction of EEG amplitude into account. However, when the scoring criteria are modified appropriately, the age difference disappears, and adults of all ages look alike (Feinberg, Fein, Floyd, & Aminoff, 1982; Webb, 1982). This issue highlights the need for age-relevant criteria not only in sleep but also, by extension, in other areas.

Slight differences in REM sleep have been noted between younger and older adults (Reynolds et al., 1985). Rather than increasing in duration over the course of the night as they do in younger adults, REM periods in older adults apparently remain constant or decrease in length.

We have all experienced the negative effects of "all-nighters" on next-day mood and performance. We tend to lose our temper more quickly, tire more easily, and have more problems paying attention. These negative effects increase with age. For example, Webb and Levy (1982) found that middle-aged adults (40 to 49 years old) showed significantly poorer performance on auditory vigilance, addition, and mood scales after two nights of sleep deprivation.

Although the data clearly show differences in sleep with age, these differences do not always result in complaints of sleep disturbance (Bootzin & Engle-Friedman, 1987). Differences in REM sleep, for example, may go unnoticed, whereas increased awakenings during the night will not. Thus, we need to be sensitive to the different levels of awareness that adults have of underlying changes in sleep.

Causes of Sleep Disturbance

Sleep is affected by numerous factors that operate across adulthood (Bootzin & Engle-Friedman, 1987): physical disorders, medication, alcohol, caffeine and nicotine, stress, and sleep habits and naps.

Physical Disorders. The most common physical disorders that affect sleep are sleep-related respiratory problems (Bootzin & Engle-Friedman, 1987). Among these are **sleep apnea**, a cessation of air flow for 10 seconds or longer occurring at least five times per night, and **hypopnea**, a 50% or greater reduction of air flow for 10 seconds or longer. Sleep apnea is the more common disorder, and it increases with age (Coleman et al., 1981).

Physical illnesses can also disrupt sleep because of discomfort or pain. Pain associated with arthritis is one of the most frequent causes of sleep disturbance in the elderly (Prinz & Raskind, 1978).

Medication. Both prescription and over-the-counter medications can disrupt sleep regardless of age (Karacen & Williams, 1983). For example, asthma medication may contain epinephrine, which may interfere with sleep if taken at night. Tricyclic antidepressants suppress REM sleep and can cause involuntary leg twitches. Several medications used to treat seizures, Parkinson's disease, and hypertension can increase nighttime awakenings.

One serious source of drug-induced sleep disturbances is sleeping pills, or **hypnotics**, and tranquilizers. Hypnotics have two dangers. First, they lose their effectiveness within two weeks of continued use (Kales, Allen, Scharf, & Kales, 1970). Second, tolerance to them develops rapidly, so larger and larger doses are needed to produce an effect.

Hypnotics and tranquilizers have several negative influences on sleep (Kales, Scharf, & Kales, 1978). Overall, they lower the amount of deep sleep and increase light, fragmented sleep. Hypnotics and tranquilizers decrease REM sleep on the night they are taken and produce large **REM rebound** on subsequent nights. REM rebound is characterized by restless dreaming, nightmares, and fragmented sleep. Finally, they produce drug hangover effects and impaired motor and intellectual functioning as well as moodiness the next day. The carryover effects are probably due to the fact that many of these drugs remain in the bloodstream for days, resulting in the possibility that side effects could be observed for a relatively long period after the person has stopped taking the drug (Bootzin & Engle-Friedman, 1987).

Alcohol. The effects of alcohol on sleep are similar to those produced by hypnotics and tranquilizers. Alcohol reduces REM sleep. Habitual heavy drinking produces fragmented sleep and several awakenings. Because alcohol is a depressant, it increases the effects of hypnotics and tranquilizers, with the potential for fatal outcomes.

Caffeine and Nicotine. Most people know that drinking a cup of coffee before bedtime is not usually a good idea. Not so well known is that smoking may have the same effect. The caffeine in the coffee and the nicotine in the cigarette produce insomnia or lighter and more fragmented sleep (Soldatos, Kales, Scharf, Bixler, & Kales, 1980). Reducing or eliminating excessive caffeine and nicotine can result in considerable improvement in sleep.

Stress. It should come as no surprise that stress impairs sleep. Even for people with no history of insomnia, worrying about exams, presentations, the kids, and one's spouse can cause sleep disturbances (Healey et al., 1981).

Sleep Habits and Naps. What do you do in your bedroom besides sleeping? Do you read, talk on the telephone, watch television, snack, listen to music, or, worst of all, worry? All of these behaviors can be incompatible with falling asleep and are very common in insomniacs (Bootzin,

1977). The bed no longer becomes a cue for sleeping; rather it becomes associated with arousal. The situation may become so bad that many insomniacs can seemingly sleep anywhere except in their own bed. In contrast, normal sleepers often have problems falling asleep anywhere else (Bootzin & Engle-Friedman, 1987). The solution to the problem is relatively easy. At the first sign of insomnia get out of bed and go somewhere else. By maintaining the bed as a cue to go to sleep, many insomniacs overcome their problem (Bootzin, 1977).

Another bad sleep habit is afternoon or evening naps (Webb, 1975). Such naps contain more deep sleep and less REM sleep. The night's sleep following one of these naps continues as if the nap were part of the night's sleep. That is, the entire night's sleep looks similar to the latter half of a normal night's sleep, containing more light and REM sleep and more awakenings (Webb, 1975). In contrast, morning naps have little effect on the subsequent night's sleep.

Taking naps whenever one feels tired has another, more serious effect. Individuals who adopt this strategy may develop disturbances in their **circadian rhythm**, or sleep-wake cycle. If such disturbances develop, an optimal sleeping time may never exist (Hauri, 1982), leading to chronic moodiness and fatigue. Disruptions of circadian rhythm are particularly common in hospital patients and the institutionalized elderly (Wessler, Rubin, & Sollberger, 1976). Additionally, excessive daytime sleepiness in the elderly may be indicative of an underlying disease and should be evaluated (Morewitz, 1988).

Treatment of Sleep Disorders

When most people have trouble sleeping, the first treatment they think of is medication. As we have seen, however, hypnotics have little long-term

Taking an afternoon nap could negatively affect the normal sleep cycle.

effectiveness and several potentially serious side effects. Consequently, treatments other than medication have been the focus of considerable work for 2 decades (e.g., Bootzin & Engle-Friedman, 1987; Borkovec, 1982). Two techniques that work well are stimulus control instructions and progressive relaxation.

Stimulus-Control Instructions. The goals of stimulus-control instructions (summarized in Table 4.12) are to help the insomniac acquire consistent sleeping rhythms, to ensure that the bed is a cue for sleeping, and to dissociate the bed from other competing activities (Bootzin, Engle-Friedman, & Hazelwood, 1983). In short, stimulus-control instructions seek to instill good sleeping habits.

Instructions for controlling stimuli are the most effective treatment for insomniacs of various ages (Bootzin, 1977; Borkovec, 1982; Lacks, Bertelson, Gans, & Kunkel, 1983; Puder, Lacks, Bertelson, & Storandt, 1983; Turner & Ascher, 1982). Combining this approach with support and sleep-hygiene information appears to be even better (Bootzin et al., 1983).

Progressive Relaxation. Progressive relaxation includes several types of techniques, such as transcendental meditation, yoga, hypnosis, and biofeedback as well as traditional relaxation methods. The goal of all these approaches when used to treat sleep disturbances is to get people to relax at bedtime so that they will fall asleep faster. One widely used version of progressive relaxation involves the successive tightening and relaxing of the various muscle groups in the body. Since its

TABLE 4.12 · Typical stimulus-control instructions

1. Lie down intending to go to sleep only when you are sleepy.

2. Do not use your bed for anything except sleep; that is, do not read, watch television, worry, or eat in bed. Sexual activity is the only exception to this rule.

3. If you find yourself unable to fall asleep, get up and go into another room. Stay up as long as you wish, and then return to the bedroom to sleep. Although you should not watch the clock, get out of bed immediately if you still cannot fall asleep. The goal is to associate the bed with falling asleep *quickly*. If you are in bed more than 10 minutes without falling asleep and have not gotten up, you are not following instructions.

4. If you still cannot fall asleep, repeat Step 3. Do this as often as necessary throughout the night.

5. Set your alarm and get up at the same time every morning irrespective of how much sleep you got during the night. This will help your body acquire a constant sleep rhythm.

6. Do not nap during the day.

(Source: "Sleep Disturbances" by R. R. Bootzin and M. Engle-Friedman, 1987, in L. L. Carstensen and B. A. Edelstein (Eds.), *Handbook of Clinical Gerontology* (pp. 238–251). New York: Pergamon Press. Reprinted with permission.)

development in the 1930s by Jacobson (1938), progressive relaxation has been the most widely prescribed and researched nonmedical therapy for sleep disturbances. There is now considerable evidence that it is effective in significantly shortening the time needed to get to sleep (Borkovec, 1982).

SUMMARY

Health promotion involves exerting influence over one's health through life-style. Changes in five habits would greatly improve health: diet, smoking, lack of exercise, misuse of alcohol, and stress.

Although there are known differences in metabolism, body composition, and the ability to use nutrients as we age, we do not fully understand how these changes affect nutritional needs. Protein and energy needs appear to change, but needs for vitamins and minerals do not. High-fat and high-sodium foods should be avoided.

Aerobic exercise has several benefits, including weight control, lower blood pressure, protection against cardiovascular disease, and improvement of muscle elasticity. Older adults appear to benefit from exercise much as do younger and middle-aged adults.

Quitting smoking would do more to improve health than any other single behavior. Smoking causes several pulmonary diseases, including lung cancer and emphysema, as well as cardiovascular disease and other cancers. Secondhand smoke is also connected with these diseases. Although older adults smoke less than younger adults, their rate of smoking-related disease is much greater.

A growing problem is alcoholism in older adults. Alcohol abuse has been linked to liver disease, brain damage, heart disease, and reduced fertility in women. Excessive drinking has been hypothesized to speed the aging process in the brain, but this idea remains controversial. Older adults show higher blood-alcohol levels than younger adults following ingestion of equal amounts. Moderate drinking has been shown to improve health and longevity, but the reasons are unknown. Treatment for alcohol abuse is carried out through Alcoholics Anonymous and various forms of psychotherapy, with sobriety as the goal.

Cardiovascular disease is the leading cause of death in the United States. The risk of cardiovascular disease increases dramatically with age. Angina and myocardial infarction are both caused by blockages of the blood flow to the heart muscle. Cerebrovascular diseases, including cerebrovascular accidents, are caused by blocking or bursting of blood vessels in the brain.

Cancer is the second leading cause of death in the United States and is also age-related. The most common forms of cancer in older adults are lung, colorectal, breast, and prostate. Many forms of cancer can be prevented by leading a healthy life-style and are more treatable with routine screening.

The primary ways to conceptualize stress are as something in the environment, as a bodily reaction, or as a cognitive process. Selye's general adaptation syndrome views stress in physiological terms and posits that the body cannot deal with continued stress over the long run. Lazarus considers stress to be the outcome of a cognitive appraisal in which the person decides which events are stressful and which are not. Older adults tend to use intrapersonal coping strategies, while younger and middle-aged adults use more interpersonal coping strategies. Stress has been linked with several diseases, such as ulcers, cardiovascular problems, and headaches.

Several age differences in sleep have been documented. These include increased frequency of awakening, time needed to go to sleep, and changes in brain wave activity. Sleep apnea increases with age. Several factors affect how well people sleep, including hypnotics and tranquilizers, alcohol, stress, and nap taking. Treatment for sleep disorders is accomplished through stimulus control or progressive relaxation.

GLOSSARY

acute diseases • Disorders with rapid onset and relatively short duration.

addiction • A disorder in which a person becomes physically dependent on a substance and suffers withdrawal symptoms when it is removed.

aerobic exercise • Exertion that places a moderate stress on the heart by maintaining a pulse rate between 60% and 90% of the maximum.

alarm stage • The first phase of the general adaptation syndrome, during which the body's defenses against stress are mobilized.

angina • Pain resulting from an insufficient supply of blood to the heart.

cerebral hemorrhage • The rupture of a blood vessel in the brain; one of the causes of a cerebrovascular accident.

cerebrovascular accident (CVA) • The medical term for a stroke, which is caused by a disruption in the blood supply to the brain.

cerebrovascular disease • A disorder in the blood vessels in the brain, sometimes marked by a cerebrovascular accident or cerebral hemorrhage.

chronic diseases • Disorders that develop slowly, persist over a long period, and are usually difficult to treat.

circadian rhythm • The sleep-wake cycle.

coping • In the stress and coping paradigm, cognitive or behavioral efforts aimed at managing the demands of stressful events.

corticoids • Hormones that are released after prolonged stress.

delta waves • Large, slow patterns of brain waves; used to define Stage 4 sleep.

embolus • A clot that forms in one location in a blood vessel and travels to another location, where it blocks blood flow.

exhaustion stage • The third phase in the general adaptation syndrome, in which continued stress makes the body break down, and death becomes a possibility if the stress is not stopped.

fetal alcohol syndrome • A disorder in which infants born of chronic alcoholic mothers display facial abnormalities, growth problems, and mental retardation.

general adaptation syndrome • Selye's theory of how the body reacts to stress.

health promotion • The effort to exert a significant influence over health through life-style.

hypnotics • Drugs that induce sleep.

hypopnea • A 50% or greater reduction in air-flow for 10 seconds or longer during sleep.

low-intensity exercise • Exertion during which the heart rate does not exceed 60% of the maximum.

myocardial infarction • The medical term for a heart attack, caused by a disruption of the blood supply to the heart muscle.

polysomnography • All-night recording of the electroencephalogram, electrooculogram, and electromyogram during sleep.

primary appraisal • The point in the stress and coping paradigm during which the person categorizes events into three groups based on their significance for well-being: irrelevant, benign-positive, and stressful.

reappraisal • The process in the stress and coping paradigm whereby the person incorporates changes in the situation into subsequent appraisals.

recommended dietary allowances (RDAs) • Guidelines published by the U.S. government that provide suggested levels of nutrient intake per day.

REM rebound • Sleep that is characterized by restless dreaming, nightmares, and fragmented sleep, often following the use of hypnotics.

REM sleep • A stage of sleep characterized by rapid brain activity and rapid eye movements.

resistance stage • The second phase in the general adaptation syndrome, during which the organism adapts to the stressor and stress-related illnesses begin to occur.

secondary appraisal • In the stress and coping paradigm, the process by which a person evaluates whether he or she is capable of dealing with the perceived stressful event.

sleep apnea • A sleep disorder in which a person stops breathing for 10 seconds or more at least five times per night.

sleep spindles • Short bursts of brain electrical activity; used to define Stage 2 sleep.

stress and coping paradigm • The theory of Lazarus and his colleagues that stress results from a process of appraisal that leads to the selection of coping strategies.

substance abuse disorder • One of a family of conditions characterized by misuse of a chemical or drug.

thrombus • A clot that blocks the flow of blood in a blood vessel; one of the causes of a cerebrovascular accident.

Type A behavior pattern • A cluster of behaviors marked by hostility, impatience, restlessness, and competitiveness that is related to a higher risk of cardiovascular disease.

Type B behavior pattern • A cluster of behaviors marked by calm, patience, and lack of competitiveness that is related to a relatively low risk of cardiovascular disease.

Wernicke-Korsakoff syndrome • A disease related to long-term chronic alcoholism and caused by vitamin deficiency; severe cognitive losses result.

ADDITIONAL READING

The field of health psychology is expanding rapidly, and there are several good introductions to the research literature. Although it is not developmental in focus, the following is an excellent overview:

Feist, J., & Brannon, L. (1988). *Health psychology.* Belmont, CA: Wadsworth.

One of the best sources of easy-to-understand statistics on health, including discussions on aging and minority groups, is

Office of Disease Prevention and Health Promotion, U.S. Public Health Service. (1988). *Disease prevention/health promotion: The facts.* Palo Alto, CA: Bull Publishing Co.

A good overview chapter of the specific relationships between health and behavior in the elderly is

Siegler, I. C., & Costa, P. T., Jr. (1985). Health behavior relationships. In J. E. Birren & K. W. Schaie (Eds.), *Handbook of the psychology of aging* (2nd ed.) (pp. 144–166). New York: Van Nostrand Reinhold.

A more technical summary of the research literature can be found in

Chernoff, R., & Lipschitz, D. A. (Eds.). (1988). *Health promotion and disease prevention in the elderly.* New York: Raven.

Sensation and Perception

M. C. Escher, *Hand with Reflecting Sphere*, 1935. © 1989
M. C. Escher Heirs/Cordon Art, Baarn, Holland.

THE FOCUS OF THIS CHAPTER IS DEVELopmental trends in sensation and perception. **Sensation** is defined as the reception of physical stimulation and its translation into neural impulses; **perception** is the interpretation of this sensory information (Plude, 1987). Imagine, for instance, that you are sitting in your living room when you see a form appear at the doorway. On closer examination you realize that it is your mother. From this example we can see the distinction between sensation (your reception of a form by your visual system) and perception (your interpretation of this form as your mother).

Sensation and perception have been studied widely in people of all ages, for two main reasons. First, our ability to cope with and adapt successfully to our environment is due in large part to our ability to detect, interpret, and respond to sensory information (Kline & Schieber, 1985). Second, the interpretive processes involved in perception have been linked with many different types of behavior, such as personality, learning style, and driving ability (Sterns, Barrett, & Alexander, 1985).

Because sensory and perceptual processes depend heavily on physiological structures, agerelated decrements are difficult to deny. No other area of research in adult development and aging is as clear-cut and consistent: the efficiency of sensory and perceptual processes declines as people age (Plude, 1987). However, the magnitude of decline varies across individuals and sensory systems. Moreover, many of the decrements commonly associated with advancing age can be offset by devices such as corrective lenses and hearing aids. Age-related declines can also be compensated for by relying on knowledge that has been accumulated over the life span. But not all decrements can be compensated for, and even compensation has its price in terms of reducing the capacity to perform well.

Thus, although the main theme of this chapter is age-related decline, we must remember that the majority of older adults are able to function adequately in everyday life. The key to this ability seems to be the gradual onset of change across adulthood, which allows people to make small adjustments in activities and behavior, such as turning up the volume on the television set.

In this chapter we will examine the extent of age-related changes in sensory and perceptual systems from the point of view that each has important effects on even the most basic activities of everyday life. To begin, we will consider the human information-processing framework, which serves as the underlying theme of this chapter (D. V. Howard, 1983; Lachman, Lachman, & Butterfield, 1979; Lindsay & Norman, 1977). Following this introduction, the age-related changes in the various sensory systems will be summarized. Age-related changes in perceptual processes will also be described, followed by a consideration of some applied problems, such as accident prevention and environmental design.

One note of caution before we begin. Most of the research we will encounter is based on cross-sectional designs. As pointed out in Chapter 1, we must not confuse age differences with age changes.

HUMAN INFORMATION PROCESSING

Simply put, people can be viewed as very sophisticated information processors who take in environmental stimulation, transform it into a code that can be analyzed and elaborated, and prepare and execute complex behavioral responses (Howard, 1983). As indicated in Figure 5.1, once information has been picked up by the individual, it must pass through four types of processing in order for a behavioral response to occur. A breakdown at any one of these points affects the entire system, resulting in a lowered ability to adapt.

Let us consider each of the five components in Figure 5.1. Information from the environment consists of all the things that impinge on us daily: music, pictures, touches, conversations, and so forth. The first interaction we have with the environment involves allowing these experiences to come in via the **sensory store**. The sensory store receives and registers all sensory experiences and notifies the person that something has happened. As noted at the beginning of the chapter, we call this process sensation. The processes of seeing, hearing, smelling, touching, tasting, and hurting involve sensation. Limitations at this level affect the amount and quality of information available for later processes.

The job at the second step, **perceptual encoding and analysis**, is to incorporate, interpret, and classify the information passed on by the sensory store. These processes are what we mean by perception. It is at this step that we attach meaning to information, store it for later use, and incorporate it into our knowledge base. How the ability to store and remember information develops across adulthood will be considered in Chapter 7. Decrements at this step also have important effects. For example, incorrectly identifying incoming information may result in executing the wrong response later on.

Once information has been cataloged and interpreted, it is passed on to the step responsible for **decision and response selection**. The major functions at this step are to decide if any action is necessary and, if so, to choose the appropriate response. At this point many abilities, traits, and personal experiences come into play. In life-span psychology these are typically referred to as intelligence and personality, which are considered in detail in Chapter 6 and Chapter 8. Faulty processing at this step has its most direct effect on the probability of making a correct decision and response.

If a decision to respond is made, the final step in the information processing framework is reached, **response execution**. This step is typically reflected by observable behavior: answering a question, turning the corner, and so forth. The way in which a response is executed is a product of both the previous processing steps and several additional factors, such as situational context, health, and experience.

Although the flow of information in Figure 5.1 is unidirectional, it is probably more accurately conceived of as a completely interactive process whereby processes later, or "higher," in the sequence feed back into earlier, or "lower," processes. Consequently, there are more interconnections in the system than are suggested in this diagram. What this means in practical terms is that one's perception of and response to a close

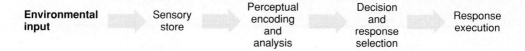

FIGURE 5.1 • A general model of human information processing

(Source: "A Review of Age Changes in Perceptual Information Processing Ability With Regard to Driving" by Panek et al., 1977, *Experimental Aging Research*, p. 388. Copyright © 1977 by EAR, Inc. Reprinted with permission.)

friend involve beholding a familiar person rather than an array of environmental energy comprising colors, shadows, and so on. Furthermore, the perceived object is embedded in a context of other objects that influences its interpretation. Thus, sensation and perception are clearly interactive and cannot be cleanly distinguished in actual practice (Howard, 1983).

An important distinction within the information-processing framework is that between peripheral and central processing. **Peripheral processing** involves processing information at the points of sensory store and response execution (Howard, 1983). Limitations in peripheral processing at input reduce the integrity of the sensory signal, and limitations at output restrict the range of possible responses. **Central processing** involves processing information in the brain (Howard, 1983). Limitations in central processing reduce the speed, efficiency, and allocation of processing resources available to support performance. Sensation is typically viewed as a peripheral process, whereas perception is considered a central process. In one sense limitations in peripheral processing are less severe than limitations in central processing, because the former are less pervasive and are more amenable to correction by prostheses of some sort. This issue will be highlighted as we consider the different sensory and perceptual systems.

SENSORY AND PERCEPTUAL FUNCTIONING

Sensation

As noted earlier, sensation refers to the registration of environmental information by the sensory receptors. Each of the primary senses (vision, hearing, taste, smell, touch, kinesthesis, and the vestibular system) responds to only one particular kind of stimulus. These associations are listed in Table 5.1.

When researchers describe the changes in sensory systems across the life span, they typically refer to the **absolute threshold**. An absolute threshold is the smallest amount of stimulus energy required for someone to detect the stimulation (Corso, 1981). Examples of absolute thresholds for the various senses are listed in Table 5.2. Related to the notion of absolute threshold is **difference threshold**, which is the smallest amount that a stimulus must be changed in order for a person to notice the difference (Corso, 1981).

Measuring sensory functioning and thresholds across the life span is difficult, for three reasons. First, the differences that are found across adulthood are probably not due simply to changes in processing ability. Structural-physiological

TABLE 5.1 • Summary of sensory systems and the stimuli to which they respond

Sensory System	Stimulus
Vision	Electromagnetic energy
Hearing	Sound waves
Taste	Chemicals in saliva
Smell	Molecules in the air
Touch, temperature, and pain	Pressure on the skin; heat and cold
Kinesthesis	Movement of the joints
Vestibular system	Gravity or acceleration

(Source: From *Psychology: The Frontiers of Behavior* by Ronald E. Smith, Irwin G. Sarason, and Barbara R. Sarason. Copyright © 1982 by Ronald E. Smith, Irwin G. Sarason and Barbara R. Sarason. Reprinted by permission of Harper & Row, Publishers, Inc.)

changes in neural pathways and in the brain that are involved in sensation contribute to behavior as well. How much of the observed declines is due to each source is unclear.

Second, researchers have difficulties in quantifying not only the physical stimuli but also, and more importantly, the variable of age. As noted in Chapter 1, chronological age is a rather imprecise measure. In the absence of a good alternative measure of functional age, however, chronological age is all we have (Nuttall, 1972).

Third, measuring sensory sensitivity is not as easy as it sounds. Regardless of how sensitive their equipment is or how precisely they control the stimuli, researchers must rely on the ability of individuals to report their sensory experiences (Gescheider, 1985). Adults of different ages may have different criteria for deciding when to respond. For example, some people may respond as soon as they think they detect something, whereas others may wait until they are absolutely certain. Consequently, in interpreting age-related differences in sensory functioning we must keep in mind that the differences could be due to either a change in sensory ability, the criteria for responding, or both.

Perception

The information that is received by sensory systems is organized into meaningful or recognizable units. This organizational aspect of information processing is what is meant by perception. More formally, perception refers to the interpretation of sensory information on the basis of previous experience (Plude, 1987).

Although sensation and perception can be differentiated theoretically, in everyday life they are completely interactive; we do not experience one without the other (Plude, 1987). As Plude points

TABLE 5.2 · Absolute thresholds of selected stimuli, expressed in everyday terms

Sensory System	Stimulus
Vision	Candle flame seen at 30 mi on a clear, dark night
Hearing	Tick of a watch under quiet conditions at 20 ft
Taste	1 teaspoon of sugar in 2 gal of water
Smell	1 drop of perfume diffused in the entire volume of a large apartment
Touch	Wing of a fly falling on your cheek from a distance of 1 cm

(Source: From *Psychology: The Frontiers of Behavior* by Ronald E. Smith, Irwin G. Sarason, and Barbara R. Sarason. Copyright © 1982 by Ronald E. Smith, Irwin G. Sarason, and Barbara R. Sarason. Reprinted by permission of Harper & Row, Publishers, Inc.)

out, perception itself is heavily influenced by experience or skill. For example, skilled radiologists can detect tumors on photographic plates that appear to the untrained eye to be random smudges.

VISION

Ours is a predominantly visual world. We rely extensively on sight in virtually every aspect of our waking life, from checking the time to combing our hair in the mirror. Perhaps because of our strong dependence on this sensory system, the age-related changes that occur in it have profound and pervasive effects. Loss of vision is second only to cancer as the most feared consequence of aging (Verrillo & Verrillo, 1985). Although the extent of visual impairment varies across people, it is likely that you will eventually encounter some form of visual impairment that requires treatment or that interferes with everyday life (Kline & Schieber, 1985).

In general, the major age differences in visual functioning can be grouped into two classes: changes in the structures of the eye and changes in the retina (Kline & Schieber, 1985). Structural changes begin to affect visual functioning during middle adulthood (around the 4th decade of life). Retinal changes occur later, usually around the 6th decade.

Structural Changes

As people age, several structures of the eye undergo change. From a peak in late adolescence and early adulthood, the visual system begins a slow, steady decline that starts in the 30s and continues for the remainder of the life span (Kline

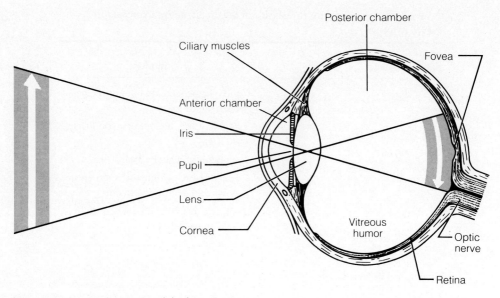

FIGURE 5.2 • Structure of the human eye

(Source: *Biological Psychology* (3rd ed.) by J. W. Kalat, 1988, Belmont, CA: Wadsworth. Reprinted with permission.)

& Schieber, 1985). An illustration of the major structures of the eye is presented in Figure 5.2. Changes in these structures affect the eye's **transmissiveness**, or the degree to which light can pass through it, and the eye's ability to adjust, or focus, termed its **accommodative power**. Changes in transmissiveness and in accommodative power manifest themselves as problems involving distance vision, binocular depth perception, sensitivity to glare, and color sensitivity. Four specific optical structures are particularly important.

The *cornea* is the major refracting structure of the eye and also serves a protective function. It undergoes three important age-related changes: (1) loss of luster, probably reflecting changes in refractive power and in the amount of fluid bathing its surface; (2) development of an opaque gray ring around its outer edge from an accumulation of fatty particles; and (3) decreased curvature and increased thickness, resulting in

increased astigmatism and blurred vision (Corso, 1981).

The *ciliary muscles* attach to the lens, contorting it to focus vision at different viewing distances. The major change in the ciliary muscles is increased atrophy, or loss of muscle tone (Corso, 1981). Atrophy reduces accommodative power, making it difficult to see nearby objects. We will consider accommodative changes in more detail later.

The *lens* is responsible for focusing light onto the retina. With age the amount of light reaching the lens is reduced because of a decrease in the diameter of the pupil (Kline & Schieber, 1985). The lens also becomes less flexible due to a variety of physical changes (Weale, 1982). These changes result in declines in both accommodative power and transmissiveness. Even the composition of light transmitted changes, largely due to increased yellowing of the lens (Kline &

Schieber, 1985). In addition, the lens is the site of serious pathology in the form of **cataracts**, which are opaque and interfere further with transmissiveness.

Finally, the *anterior and posterior chambers* are the fluid-filled spaces surrounding the lens. The fluid in the anterior, or front, chamber bathes the lens with nutrients obtained from the blood vessels of the eye. An obstruction of the fluid flow results in abnormally high pressure and the disease **glaucoma**, one of the most prevalent visual disorders in middle and late adulthood. The posterior, or rear, chamber is filled with a gelatinous fluid, the vitreous humor. With age, the vitreous humor becomes thinner, resulting in increased susceptibility to glare (Kline & Schieber, 1985).

Retinal Changes

The retina lines approximately two-thirds of the interior of the eye. The specialized receptor cells in vision, the rods and the cones, are contained in the retina. They are most densely packed toward the rear and especially at the focal point of vision, a region called the macula. At the center of the macula is the fovea, where incoming light is focused for detailed acuity, as when one is reading.

With increasing age the probability of degeneration of the macula increases (Kline & Schieber, 1985). **Macular degeneration** involves the progressive and irreversible destruction of receptors from any of a number of causes. This disease results in the loss of the ability to see details; for example, reading is extremely difficult, and television is often reduced to a blur.

A second retinal disease that is related to age is actually a byproduct of diabetes. Diabetes is accompanied by accelerated aging of the arteries, with blindness being one of the more serious side effects. **Diabetic retinopathy**, as this condition is called, can involve fluid retention in the macula,

detachment of the retina, hemorrhage, and aneurysms. Because it takes many years to develop, diabetic retinopathy is more common among people who developed diabetes relatively early in life, and it has been known to be the leading cause of blindness in the United States for several years (Lewis, 1979).

Age-Related Changes in Visual Abilities

The changes in the visual system produce important changes in visual abilities. We will consider several: those in absolute and difference thresholds, sensitivity to glare, accommodation, color sensitivity, acuity, adaptation, visual field, visual search, and critical flicker frequency.

Absolute and Difference Thresholds. The quality and quantity of the visual information extracted from the environment are determined mainly by the amount of light transmitted through the eye. Research consistently demonstrates that older adults require a greater intensity of light than young adults to detect the presence of a visual stimulus (Kline & Schieber, 1985). The most important practical consequence of this change is that as we grow older, we tend to require higher levels of illumination to perform daily tasks. Older adults do not see as well in the dark, which may account for their reluctance to go places at night.

Difference thresholds also increase with age (Corso, 1981). This means that older adults have more difficulty discriminating different levels of illumination, such as telling the difference between a 60-watt and a 75-watt light bulb.

Sensitivity to Glare. One possible intervention to correct for rising thresholds would be to increase illumination levels. However, this solution may not work, because we also become

Age-related decline in visual acuity results in difficulty reading small print.

aged people to hold reading material at increasing distances, and, once their arms become too short, in acquiring either reading glasses or bifocals.

An additional accommodative change involves the time required for refocusing from near to far or vice versa. As we age, the time we need to refocus increases (Corso, 1981). A major implication of this change is in driving. Because drivers are constantly alternating their focus from the instrument panel to other autos and signs on the highway, older drivers may miss important information because of their slower refocusing time (Panek & Rearden, 1986).

Color Sensitivity. Although the registration and detection of color are carried out by special color receptors in the retina, color sensitivity depends primarily on the composition of light, which is affected by changes in the structures of the eye. What little research there is suggests that with increased age there is greater difficulty in discriminating among blues, blue-greens, and violets (Kline & Schieber, 1985). The everyday consequences of these changes appear to be minor, especially when compared with changes in other visual functions.

Acuity. **Acuity** refers to the ability to resolve detail and discriminate among visual patterns. The most common way of testing visual acuity is the Snellen test, the familiar "eye chart," consisting of a standardized series of letters or symbols in different sizes that must be read at a distance of 20 ft. Investigations of visual acuity show a slight but steady decline between the ages of 20 and 60, with a more rapid decline thereafter (Richards, 1977). Figure 5.3 shows these changes. Decreases in visual acuity are manifested in many ways, with the consequences ranging from annoying to potentially serious, such as difficulty in reading medicine bottle labels.

increasingly sensitive to glare beginning around age 40 (Kline & Schieber, 1985). This change is especially important for older drivers, because reflected sunlight can pose a more serious problem for them. Consequently, the need for more illumination must be balanced with the need to avoid glare (Fozard & Popkin, 1978).

Accommodation. As noted earlier, accommodation is the process by which the lens adjusts to attain the best resolution possible, thereby allowing us to see nearby and faraway objects clearly. Considerable research demonstrates an age-related decrease in the ability of the eye to focus on nearby objects, a condition termed **presbyopia** (Kline & Schieber, 1985). Presbyopia is typically manifested first by the need of middle-

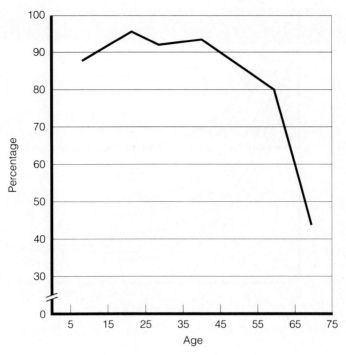

FIGURE 5.3 • Percentage of U.S. population with 20/20 vision, as a function of age

(Source: U.S. Department of Health, Education, and Welfare, 1977)

Adaptation. Adaptation is the change in sensitivity of the eye as a function of changes in illumination. There are two types of adaptation: **dark adaptation**, the increase in sensitivity to light in dark environments, and **light adaptation**, the adjustment of the eye to seeing in bright environments. Going from outside into a movie theater involves dark adaptation; going back outside involves light adaptation. Research indicates that the time it takes for both types of adaptation increases with age (Kline & Schieber, 1985); the data for dark adaptation are depicted in Figure 5.4. In addition, the final level of dark adaptation is less in older adults (Wolf, 1960). This means that as we age, it takes us longer to adapt to extreme changes in illumination, making us more susceptible to environmental hazards for the first few minutes following the change. Thus, older adults will take longer to visually recover from the bright lights of an oncoming car, making them less able to pick up critical information from the highway in the meantime.

Visual Field. The size of the **visual field** is found by having a person stare at a fixed point and noting when he or she can first see a target light moved in the periphery. Age changes in the retina affect the size of the visual field. Our peripheral

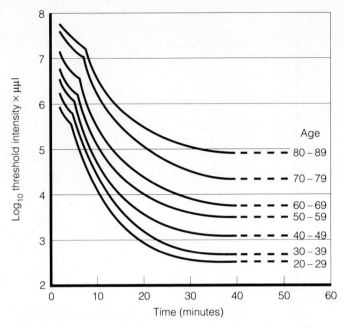

FIGURE 5.4 • Dark adaptation as a function of age and time in the dark

(Source: "Dark Adaptation as a Function of Age: I. A Statistical Analysis" by McFarland et al., 1960, *Journal of Gerontology, 15,* 149–154. Copyright © 1960 The Gerontological Society of America. Reprinted with permission.)

field decreases several degrees each decade after age 45 (Kline & Schieber, 1985). For example, the overall visual field for a young adult is about 170 degrees; by age 50 it has decreased to about 140 degrees. The result is that our ability to see things "out of the corner of our eye" decreases substantially as we age (Scialfa, Kline, & Lyman, 1987).

Critical Flicker Frequency. A classic and frequently used measure of visual ability is **critical flicker frequency (CFF)**. To test CFF, an individual is presented a flashing light, and the frequency of flashes is increased until they appear to fuse as a steady light. One of the most replicated findings

in aging research is that the fusing point occurs at a lower frequency for older adults (Botwinick, 1984).

One explanation of the lowering of CFF threshold with age is **stimulus persistence**. Stimulus persistence is the continued sensation that follows the termination of a stimulus (DiLollo, Arnett, & Kruk, 1982). Although there is considerable evidence that it increases with age, this does not provide a complete explanation of changes in CFF. The problem is that other visual-processing tasks involving afterimages do not show consistent age-related differences, despite the fact that stimulus persistence occurs (see Kline & Schieber [1985] for a more detailed discussion).

Visual Information Processing

As indicated earlier, the transition from sensation to perception involves some transformation of the incoming information. In vision, this transformation initially involves extracting contours and forms and storing them in a short-lived visual sensory buffer, called **iconic storage** (Kline & Schieber, 1985). The ability to extract information is measured by tests involving backward masking, encoding speed, and visual search.

Backward Masking. Backward masking has been the most commonly used way of investigating the time course of visual information processing. **Backward masking** involves presenting a target stimulus very briefly, followed by presenting a masking stimulus that diminishes the visual effectiveness of the target. The subject's job in the task is to identify the target. By varying the interval between the target and the mask, the tester can obtain an estimate of the speed of information processing.

Numerous researchers have documented that susceptibility to the mask increases only slightly with age (Kline & Schieber, 1985). That is, the interval between the target and the mask needed for people to still be able to identify the target stimulus is longer for older adults. The results of backward masking studies have been interpreted primarily as supporting the notion of age-related declines in the speed of information processing (DiLollo et al., 1982).

Encoding Speed. As noted earlier, incoming visual information is transferred to iconic storage for subsequent processing. **Encoding speed** refers to how rapidly this storage occurs. Encoding speed has been studied extensively, with the evidence clearly favoring an age-related difference. For example, Cerella, Poon, and Fozard (1982) documented age-related slowing of encoding speed in processing letters. They also noted that these results supported the notion that "perceptual span," or the amount of visual information that one can handle at one time, declines with age.

Visual Search. **Visual search** refers to how a person scans a visual scene and looks for important information or cues. Researchers have documented that visual-search strategies become less efficient, less systematic, and less complete with age (Kline & Schieber, 1985). These changes appear to begin around age 30 and continue throughout the life span. The most important practical implications of changes in visual search involve selective attention, a topic that we will consider in a later section.

Perceptual Organization and Flexibility

Once visual information has been encoded, the next step involves making sense of it. How well this is done is investigated most commonly by asking people to identify objects, reorganize their perceptions, discriminate target from nontarget stimuli, and view illusions.

Incomplete Stimuli. One way to examine how well people organize visual information is to ask them to identify objects from incomplete representations of them. All of the research findings based on this task document some degree of age-related decline (Kline & Schieber, 1985). This decline appears to be due primarily to a decreased ability to use partial information (Danziger & Salthouse, 1978).

Perceptual Flexibility. In addition to showing increased difficulty in organizing partial stimuli into coherent wholes, older adults also appear less likely to change their perception once it has been established. For example, when presented with the ambiguous "young woman/old woman" picture, older adults are less likely to see both images (Botwinick, Robbin, & Brinley, 1959). If they are told that a perceptual shift will be needed, however, older adults are capable of making it (Botwinick, 1962). Thus, perceptual flexibility appears to depend on providing appropriate structure and direction to the older adult.

Context Effects. A long line of research has documented that older adults show an increased sensitivity to the interfering effects of extraneous or irrelevant stimuli. Examples of this effect include the Stroop color-word task, in which, for example, the word *red* is printed in green ink and the subject is asked to state the color of the ink (Comalli, Wapner, & Werner, 1962); identifying embedded figures (Eisner, 1972); and positioning a rod vertically when it is placed inside a rotated frame (the rod-and-frame task) (Panek, 1982).

Susceptibility to context effects is considered a reflection of selective attention. **Selective attention** is the control of information processing so that a particular source of information is processed more fully than any other simultaneous sources of information (Plude et al., 1983). That is, selective attention enables us to pick out the key, or target, information from a background full of extraneous, or irrelevant, information. The research evidence showing increased context effects with age argues that selective attention shows an age-related decline across adulthood.

Illusions. Age-related differences in the magnitude of the effect of visual illusions depends on the particular illusion being examined. Susceptibility to the Müller-Lyer illusion tends to increase with age (Comalli, 1970; Leibowitz & Gwozdecki, 1967). In contrast, the effects of the Ponzo illusion appear to decrease with age (Leibowitz & Judisch, 1967; Wapner, Werner, & Comalli, 1960). Pollack and Atkeson (1978) in-

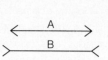

a. The Müller-Lyer illusion: which horizontal line segment is longer, A or B?

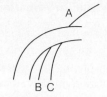

b. Which line is part of the same circular arc as A?

c. Are the horizontal lines straight or bowed?

d. The Ponzo illusion: which horizontal line is longer?

FIGURE 5.5 • Examples of illusions. In (a) and (d) both horizontal lines are of equal length. In (b) line A is the extension of line B. In (c) the horizontal lines are straight.

(Source for (a), (b), (c): *Biological Psychology* (3rd ed.) by J. W. Kalat, 1988, Belmont, CA: Wadsworth. Reprinted with permission.)

terpreted these patterns as primarily reflecting declines in sensory processes, in the former case, and declines in central processes, in the latter. Examples of some common illusions can be seen in Figure 5.5.

Psychological Effects of Visual Changes

Throughout this discussion we have noted some of the important consequences of age-related changes in the visual system. Taken together, they represent a set of changes that has the potential for disrupting everyday life. Evidence of visual changes in everyday life has been documented through surveys of over 400 adults ranging in age from 18 to 100 (Kosnik, Winslow, Kline, Rasinski, & Sekular, 1988). The responses indicated a two- to sixfold decline in visual ability in everyday situations, depending on the skill required.

One can readily comprehend the problems experienced by people performing tasks that most of us take for granted, such as reading a book, watching television, reading grocery labels, driving a car, and so on. But simply making things brighter for them is not the answer. For increased illumination to work, surrounding surfaces must not increase glare. Use of flat paint rather than glossy enamel and avoiding highly polished floors are two steps that could be taken in designing environments. Details on dials, such as on stoves and radios, may be difficult to distinguish, as are some subtle facial features. As Whitbourne (1985) notes, these experiences may be especially difficult for people who always had good vision when young. Such people may simply avoid cooking or listening to their favorite music and become homebodies out of fear that they may not recognize a face.

There is another aspect to environmental design and perception that may be overlooked. One problem that occurs commonly in nursing homes is wandering, especially among residents who have dementia. Researchers found that two-dimensional grid patterns are perceived as barriers by demented individuals (Hussian & Brown, 1987; Hussian & Davis, 1985). Use of these grids near exit doors has been effective in limiting wandering behavior, as described in "How Do We Know?"

People often do not recognize the extent of visual changes, because these occur slowly over many years. Lack of awareness of these changes usually results in a failure to seek ways to compensate or correct for the problems. Most unfortunate are those individuals who believe that these decrements are simply a sign of aging and are untreatable.

In any event, many of the normal age-related changes in vision can be remediated. Periodic vi-

sion examinations can detect changes early, and correction of visual problems may help avert the internalization of these changes as potential threats to self-esteem.

HEARING

We rely a great deal on hearing. Consider the difficulty we would face without being able to hear the alarm clock, the telephone, someone calling our name, or the knock at the door. One of the most well-known changes in normal aging is the decline in hearing ability, which is quite dramatic across the life span (Olsho, Harkins, & Lenhardt, 1985). Age-related declines in hearing can be characterized as progressive and may interfere with adaptation in later life.

Significant hearing loss is widespread in older adults. Anyone who has visited a housing complex for the elderly has probably noticed that television sets and radios are turned up in most of the apartments. Research indicates that nearly half of normal older adults have a relatively serious hearing impairment (P. D. Thomas et al., 1983). Hearing loss with age is greatest for high-pitched tones, a condition called **presbycusis**. Presbycusis is caused by several changes in the structure and functioning of the ear. The following discussion highlights age-related changes in the major structures of the ear, which are illustrated in Figure 5.6.

Structural Changes

The human auditory system can be divided into three major sections. The outer ear consists of the pinna and external auditory canal. With age, the pinna becomes stiffer, longer, and wider, and thicker, stiffer hairs develop. Wax buildup

HOW · DO · WE · KNOW?

Using Perceptual Stimuli to Limit Wandering in Demented Residents

Many residents of nursing homes are severely cognitively impaired, which means that they may not fully understand the consequences of their actions. One common problem in these individuals is wandering. Normally, wandering is not harmful if the demented resident stays within the building. But demented residents often wander through exit doors that are unlocked for safety reasons. Designing a way to get cognitively impaired residents to stay inside is a high priority.

Hussian and Brown (1987) tackled this problem experimentally. They studied eight male residents in a public mental hospital who had severe dementia. All eight men were active wanderers. Hussian and Brown observed 40 trips down a hallway during the baseline period before they intervened. The measure was how close the residents came to a door at the end of the hallway. Because

wandering was not prompted, the number of trips varied across residents.

The experimental manipulation consisted of placing strips of masking tape on the floor near the end of the hallway. The configurations used were 3, 4, 6, or 8 strips horizontally or 10 strips vertically, all with the grid beginning 3 ft from the end of the hallway, or 8 horizontal strips with the grid beginning flush with the end of the hallway. The measure was whether residents crossed the grid. Over a 2-month period 139 trips were observed.

At the end of the manipulation phase the strips were removed, and residents were observed again; 27 trips were noted.

The results showed that during baseline, 98% of all trips ended with residents reaching the door. During the manipulation phase, in contrast, as few as 30%

of the trips ended at the door. The most effective configuration was 8 horizontal strips placed 3 ft from the door, and the least effective was the vertical strip configuration. After the strips were removed, residents reached the door 67% of the time. In seven of the eight residents, crossings were eliminated in at least 60% of the trips. One resident never stopped.

Although the results documented a safe, economic, and unobtrusive way to limit potentially harmful wandering, there are several limitations to the study. These include individual differences among residents, recording only solitary wandering trips, potential misuse of grids, the fact that observers were not blind to experimental condition, and limits in the type of material and patterns used. Can you identify reasons why these limitations need to be addressed?

becomes greater in the external auditory canal (R. G. Anderson & Meyerhoff, 1982).

The second major section is the middle ear. Major structures in the middle ear are the tympanic membrane (eardrum), the ossicular chain (a series of three bones: hammer, anvil, and stirrup),

the round window, and the Eustachian tube. As a group these structures show some age-related change, but this change has little effect on hearing loss. The most-noted changes are a loss of resiliency in the tympanic membrane and a stiffening of the ossicular chain (Schow, Christensen,

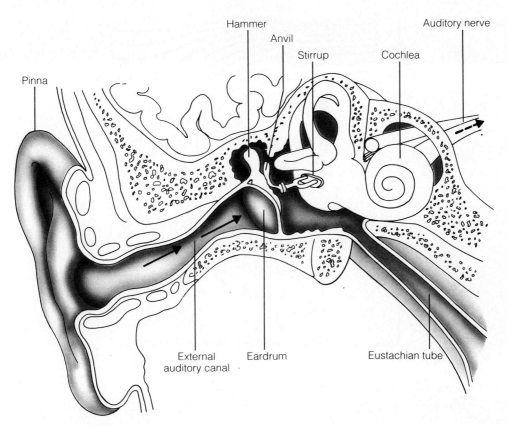

FIGURE 5.6 • Structures in the human ear
(Source: *Biological Psychology* (3rd ed.) by J. W. Kalat, 1988,
Belmont, CA: Wadsworth. Reprinted with permission.)

Hutchinson, & Nerbonne, 1978). Sound-transmission difficulties caused by structural defects in the middle ear cause a form of hearing loss called **conduction deafness**. However, conduction deafness is not age related, and it is not common among older adults (Schow et al., 1978).

The third major section of the ear, the inner ear, contains the receptor cells for hearing as well as the vestibular system, which is responsible for maintaining a sense of balance. The receptor cells for hearing are housed in the cochlea, on the or-

gan of Corti. The receptor cells are actually minute hair cells, which sit along a structure called the basilar membrane. When sound waves are transmitted to the inner ear, fluid motion stimulates the hair cells. Damage to the hair cells results in permanent hearing loss (Whitbourne, 1985). As we will see, this damage is caused by a combination of factors.

Types of Presbycusis. As noted earlier, presbycusis is the major age-related form of hearing

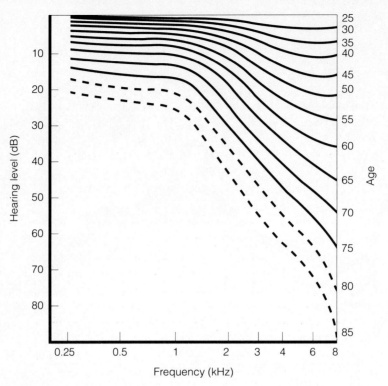

FIGURE 5.7 • Ability to detect pure tones, as a function of age and frequency (data for men only)

(Source: U.S. Department of Health and Human Services.)

loss. The extent of age-related changes in the ability to hear pure tones is shown in Figure 5.7. Presbycusis results from four types of change in the inner ear (Olsho et al., 1985): (1) sensory, consisting of atrophy and degeneration of hair cells; (2) neural, consisting of a loss of neurons in the auditory pathway; (3) metabolic, consisting of a diminished supply of nutrients to the cells in the cochlea; and (4) mechanical, consisting of atrophy and stiffening of the vibrating structures in the cochlea. Although the four types occur at different rates (12%, 31%, 35%, and 23%, respec-

tively), only rarely does an individual have only one of them (Schuknecht, 1974).

All of these types of presbycusis affect the ability to hear high-pitched tones. However, they differ in their effects on other aspects of hearing (Whitbourne, 1985). Sensory presbycusis has little effect on other hearing abilities. Neural presbycusis affects the ability to understand speech. Metabolic presbycusis produces severe loss of sensitivity to all pitches. Finally, mechanical presbycusis produces loss across all pitches, but the loss is greatest for high pitches.

Age-Related Changes in Auditory Abilities

Age-related changes in the auditory system affect several abilities: absolute threshold, pitch discrimination, and speech understanding. But all of these effects are moderated by the individual's history of exposure to noise. We will consider each of these in turn.

Hearing and Exposure to Noise. There is no doubt that lifelong exposure to noise has significant negative effects on hearing ability (Corso, 1981). Much of the research that established this relationship was conducted in industrial settings, but we now know that any source of sustained loud noise, whether from machinery or stereo headphones, produces damage.

An important question for developmentalists is whether the effects of noise are compounded by age. The results of several experiments demonstrate convincingly that the answer is no. It turns out that the effects of noise alone on hearing are actually greater than the effects of age alone (Corso, 1981). Cross-cultural evidence suggests that hearing loss is less in cultures that have lower exposure to noise. Corso (1981) refers to the damaging effect of repeated, sustained noise on adults' hearing as "premature presbycusis." Because of these effects workers in many industries are required to wear protective earplugs in order to guard against prolonged exposure. However, the use of stereo headphones, especially at high volume, can have the same serious effects and should be avoided.

The deleterious effects of repeated exposure to sustained loud noise makes it difficult to separate true age-related effects from noise-exposure effects. Consequently, caution is needed in interpreting developmental research reported in the following sections.

Absolute Threshold. Auditory sensitivity is typically assessed with pure tones, such as those used in standard hearing tests. With increasing age there is a decline in pure-tone sensitivity that is gradual at first but that accelerates during the 40s (Corso, 1984). The magnitude of hearing loss is typically greater for men than for women, but this may be due to differential exposure to noisy environments (Olsho et al., 1985).

Pitch Discrimination. The ability to discriminate small changes in pitch is important in many everyday activities, such as understanding speech and listening to music. After reviewing the literature on the ability to discriminate tones of different frequencies and intensities, Olsho et al. (1985) concluded that there was no clear-cut evidence of an age-related decline.

Speech Understanding. Hearing plays an obvious and ubiquitous role in understanding speech. Hearing loss may result in declines in the ability to understand speech, which may, in turn, affect one's ability to interact with others. People may not want to adjust their speech patterns or intensity to meet the needs of older adults, which may result in lower levels of social interactions.

Because most forms of presbycusis do not affect the frequencies used in most speech sounds until around age 80, presbycusis does not play a major role in speech understanding until then. However, a few consonant sounds such as *s, ch,* and *sh* do involve very high frequencies that are affected by presbycusis. Consequently, middle-aged and older adults may have trouble understanding words containing these sounds.

The most commonly used methods for measuring how well a person can hear speech sounds are speech recognition and speech discrimination, tested under ideal listening conditions. **Speech recognition** is measured by presenting the listener with a list of spondee words, two-syllable words with equal emphasis on both syllables (e.g., *airplane, baseball, birthday,* and *headlight*). **Speech discrimination** is tested with monosyllabic words that are termed "phonetically balanced" because the sounds in them are representative of their frequency of occurrence in English.

Several studies have documented an age-related decrease in both speech-recognition and speech-discrimination abilities, particularly after age 50 (Corso, 1981; Marshall, 1981; Olsho et al., 1985). These age differences are depicted in Figure 5.8. Age differences across adulthood become especially pronounced when the listening situation is made more difficult, such as when the rate of speech is increased or competing messages are presented (Bergman, 1971; Bergman et al., 1976; Marshall, 1981; Stine, Wingfield, & Poon, 1986).

Auditory Selective Attention. We often find ourselves in situations in which many people are talking but we need to pay attention to the individual speaking to us. This situation involves auditory selective attention, which is analogous to the visual selective attention described earlier.

One of the most widely used measures of auditory selective attention is the **dichotic-listening task**, also known as the divided-attention or controlled-attention task. In a dichotic-listening task the individual is asked to listen to two sets of auditory information presented simultaneously over a set of headphones. The person is then asked to recall one or both of the sets. The degree to which the competing message is filtered out is the measure of the level of auditory selective attention.

Research based on the dichotic-listening task consistently shows that auditory selective attention decreases with age. Older adults show a deficit relative to young adults on reporting the second set of information, the one held in memory while the first set of information is being re-

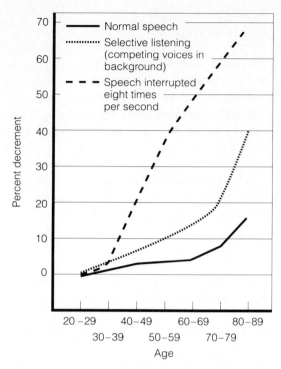

FIGURE 5.8 • Ability to perceive speech under different listening conditions: percent decrement from age 20

(Source: "Age-Related Decrements in Hearing for Speech: Sampling and Longitudinal Studies" by Bergman et al., 1976, *Journal of Gerontology, 31*, pp. 533–538. © 1976 by The Gerontological Society of America. Reprinted with permission.)

ported, but they are just as good as the young in reporting the first set (Craik, 1977). Additionally, as task difficulty increases, age differences become even greater (Madden, 1982; Wright, 1981).

Remediation of Hearing Loss

How does one treat hearing loss? The approach one chooses will depend largely on the type and extent of the problem. Fortunately, some of the known declines associated with presbycusis can be compensated for by hearing aids, especially if two are worn and balanced for each ear separately (Welford, 1980).

If hearing loss has significantly affected speech understanding, then two of the more widely used rehabilitation programs are speechreading, or lip-reading, and auditory training. Both procedures are based on integrating visual and auditory information. Speechreading involves watching a speaker's lips move in order to facilitate speech understanding. Speechreading is widely practiced among adults without their awareness. We all tend to use this technique when we have problems deciphering what is being said, for instance, in a noisy room. Auditory training involves attending to certain key sounds, words, and so forth while also watching the speaker's lips move.

Although these techniques are effective for most people, they tend to be underutilized. For one thing, many individuals with hearing problems simply are unaware of the extent of the loss. Consequently, they may be unlikely to seek hearing tests. Moreover, individuals on fixed incomes may not be able to afford these programs. As a result, many people who could benefit from these effective interventions are unable to obtain them.

Psychological Effects of Hearing Loss

Because hearing plays an almost irreplaceable role in social communication, its progressive loss could have an equally important effect on individuals' adjustment. It is often argued that loss of hearing in later life causes numerous adverse emotional reactions, such as feelings of loss of independence, social isolation, irritation, paranoia, and depression. Substantial research indicates that older people with hearing loss are generally not socially maladjusted or emotionally disturbed as a result of hearing loss per se (Norris & Cunningham, 1981). However, there is often a strain on the quality of interpersonal relationships due

to friends' and relatives' tendency to attribute emotional changes to hearing loss and their failure to communicate properly with a hearing-impaired person (P. D. Thomas et al., 1983).

Even though hearing loss does not directly affect overall adjustment, the fear of making an inappropriate response to a request, for example, may be present. Older adults tend to be more cautious in responding to verbal requests (Potash & Jones, 1977), perhaps as a result of prior embarrassing errors made in response to oral requests in social situations. Waiting until one is absolutely certain of what was said is one way to avoid such embarrassment. However, such caution may actually exacerbate difficulties in interpersonal communication by making others irritated at having to repeat requests or wait for responses.

Thus, hearing loss does not have a direct effect on older adults' self-concept or emotions, but it may negatively affect how one feels about interpersonal communication. Knowledge of hearing-loss problems and of ways to overcome them on the part of non-hearing-impaired individuals can play a large part in minimizing the effects of hearing loss.

TASTE

Have you ever heard the expression "too old to cut the mustard"? It dates back to when people made mustard at home by grinding mustard seed and adding just the right amount of vinegar ("cutting the mustard") to balance the taste. If too much vinegar was added, the whole concoction tasted terrible, so the balance was critical. Many families found that elderly members tended to add too much vinegar, resulting in the old saying.

Despite the everyday recognition that taste ability changes with age, we know very little about what actually happens across adulthood.

Whatever age differences we observe are not due to a decline in the sheer number of taste buds, however. Unlike other neural cells, the number of taste cells does not change appreciably across the life span (Engen, 1982).

Taste Sensitivity

Taste is one of our two chemical senses (smell is the other), because the receptors for taste, the taste buds, respond to particular chemical structures. Humans are sensitive to four tastes: salty, sweet, bitter, and sour. Taste sensitivity is measured in two ways. One is by the detection threshold, which is the concentration of a substance at which the taster can tell that it is different from water. The second is called the recognition threshold, the concentration of a substance needed so that the taster can identify the substance. Both thresholds increase with age (Moore, Nielsen, & Mistretta, 1982). Decreased sensitivity seems to hold across all four tastes, although there is some evidence that the changes are not uniform (Spitzer, 1988; Weiffenbach, Baum, & Burghauser, 1982). For example, Spitzer found that salty, bitter, and sour taste thresholds increased with age but that the sweet taste threshold did not. These decreases in sensitivity are slight, however, and many adults over age 60 have no apparent loss of sensitivity to detecting tastes.

Although there is some decrease in absolute sensitivity with age, additional evidence suggests that once threshold levels are reached, there are no differences between young and old. Bartoshuk, Rifkin, Marks, and Bars (1986) presented older and younger adults with substances representing all four different tastes at concentrations above absolute threshold. They found no evidence of significant age differences in the ratings of how intense the tastes were, indicating that all adults experience taste in roughly the same way.

Research on the density of taste buds on different parts of the tongue also shows no age differences (I. J. Miller, 1988). In fact, the evidence points to very large individual differences within age groups that are consistent across age groups.

Taste Preference

Given modest decreases in sensitivity with age, the question arises whether there are also age-related changes in people's taste preferences. The results of this line of research are conflicting. Some research has demonstrated a lower preference for sweetness among women and older adults (Enns, Van Itallie, & Grinker, 1979; Laird & Breen, 1939), whereas some researchers have found a greater preference for sweetness among the elderly (Dye & Koziatek, 1981).

C. Murphy and Withee (1987) helped clarify the issue. They found that preference differences depended on several factors, such as the type of substance and whether the substance was dissolved in water or another beverage. They discovered that older adults found salt and sugar more pleasant at higher concentrations than did young and middle-aged adults. These researchers point out, however, that the reasons for these different preferences are unclear. They may result from cultural experiences, the context in which the substances are consumed, or changes in the sensory system at more central (brain) levels. At present, however, it is impossible to decide among these possibilities.

Food Identification

As every cook knows, identifying which food one is eating involves not only taste but also smell and even cognitive components. That is, we identify foods on the basis of tasting them, smelling them, and being aware that certain things (e.g., spices) are present in the mixture. To examine the role played by taste alone, therefore, it is necessary to rule out other sources of information. This is usually done by pinching off the nose and blindfold-ing the tasters.

Early research examining age differences in the ability to identify foods indicated a decline across adulthood (Schiffman, 1977). When more careful methods are used to eliminate the smell and cognitive components of food identification, however, no age differences are found (C. Murphy, 1985). Murphy's research clearly shows that the often-heard comment that food becomes a less pleasurable experience with age has more to do with olfactory and cognitive cues than with taste.

Psychological Effects of Changes in Taste

There is little question that older adults complain more about boring food (Schiffman & Covey, 1984; Whitbourne, 1985). The source of these complaints, however, cannot be predominantly physiological changes in taste. We have seen that age differences in taste per se, although present, are minimal. Thus, the high incidence of food complaints among older adults is not based on sensory impairment.

The explanation appears to be that changes in the enjoyment of food are due to psychosocial issues, such as personal adjustment, or to disease (Whitbourne, 1985). For instance, we are much more likely to eat a balanced diet and enjoy our food when we eat with someone rather than alone. As noted in Chapter 4, such isolation may result in poor nutrition.

SMELL

As noted in the previous section, much of our enjoyment of food comes from the way it smells. Smell, or olfaction, has many other functions in people's everyday lives apart from enhancing taste. How something smells can warn of a gas leak or a fire, can be a sign of cleanliness, or can even be sexually arousing. A great many of our social interactions involve smell (or the lack of it). Billions of dollars are spent on making our bodies smell different. Consequently, any age-related change in sense of smell would have far-reaching consequences.

Olfactory Sensitivity

As with taste, it appears that there are very few changes in the receptors for smell (Whitbourne, 1985). However, age-related changes have been reported for central neural processes involved with olfaction. Thus, age differences in olfactory sensitivity are probably due to central, rather than peripheral, changes.

Measuring odor sensitivity is difficult, because we do not fully understand how odors are trans-formed into neural signals (Murphy, 1987). As a result the usual approach is to examine odor qual-ity rather than odor intensity. Researchers agree that the ability to detect odors remains fairly in-tact until the 60s, when it begins to decline fairly rapidly (Doty et al., 1984; Murphy, 1987; Schiff-man & Pasternak, 1979). But there is consider-able variability in the amount of change, both across and within individuals. That is, people vary widely in the degree to which their abilities to detect odors are affected by age. Even within the same individual, moreover, the degree of change depends on the odors being tested (Ste-vens & Cain, 1987).

These variations could have important prac-tical implications. A large survey conducted by the National Geographic Society indicated that older adults were not as able to identify particular odors as younger people. One of the odors tested was the substance added to natural gas that en-ables people to detect leaks.

Finally, a series of studies by Stevens and his colleagues demonstrates that the degree of change in olfaction is greater than the degree of change in taste (Stevens, Bartoshuk, & Cain, 1984; Stevens & Cain, 1985, 1986; Stevens, Plantinga, & Cain, 1982). As noted in the discussion of taste, much of the experience of eating comes from the odor of food. Thus, the increase in food complaints with age appears to result more from olfactory problems rather than from taste problems.

Psychological Effects of Olfactory Changes

The major psychological consequences of changes in olfactory ability concern eating, safety, and overall pleasurable experiences. As noted earlier, olfactory cues play an important role in enjoying food and in protecting us from harm. On the more general social level, decreases in our ability to detect unpleasant odors may lead to embarrassing situations in which we are unaware that we have body odors or may need to brush our teeth. Social interactions could suffer as a result of these problems.

Smells also play a key role in remembering past life experiences: the nose knows. Who can forget the smell of cookies baking in grandma's oven when we were little? Loss of olfactory cues may mean that our sense of the past suffers as well. Given evidence that exercising olfactory-discrimination abilities helps us preserve them (Engen, 1982), we may want to use our noses as much as possible.

THE SOMASTHETIC AND VESTIBULAR SYSTEMS

The somasthetic system conveys information about touch, pressure, pain, kinesthesis, and outside temperature. Without somasthesis we would not be able to sense the position or orientations of our limbs, the sensual movement of our lover's hand, the poke of a needle, or the nastiness of the wind-chill factor. Unlike the other sensory systems we have considered, the somasthetic system has multiple types of receptors and neural pathways, most of which convey specific information about bodily stimulation.

Information about balance is provided by the vestibular system. The vestibular system is designed to respond to the forces of gravity as they act on the head and then to provide this information to the parts of the brain that initiate the appropriate movements so that we can maintain our balance.

We know very little about how our somasthetic and vestibular systems change with age. Although the practical issues are obvious (avoiding falls, burns, and other injuries), researchers have been reluctant to focus on the underlying mechanisms. Perhaps this is because researchers formerly assumed that aging was associated with increases in "aches and pains," instability, and related deficits. However, the extent to which these stereotypes are real remains to be seen.

Touch Sensitivity

Various receptors in the skin respond to pressure. The distribution of these receptors is not consistent throughout the body, with greatest concentrations in the lips, tongue, and fingertips. Touch sensitivity is measured in two ways. One, the absolute threshold, is the least amount of pressure needed for a person to report feeling touched. The second, the **two-point difference threshold**, is the smallest distance between two sources of pressure applied to the skin that can be detected.

More is known about age effects on touch than about any other aspect of somasthesis. It has been known for many years that both absolute thresholds and two-point difference thresholds increase with age in the smooth (nonhairy) skin on the hand (Axelrod & Cohen, 1961; Cauna, 1965). Touch sensitivity in the hair-covered parts of the body is maintained into later life (Cauna, 1965; Kenshalo, 1977). Sensitivity to vibratory stimulation decreases in the lower but not the upper part of the body beginning around age 50 (Kenshalo, 1977).

Temperature Sensitivity

Is it warm or cold outside? Are you hot or cold? Anyone can answer these questions. We take steps to help our temperature regulation system by dressing for the season or by drinking hot or cold beverages. Despite these everyday steps that depend on our ability to sense hot and cold, we still have no idea what enables us to do it. All we know is that there may be separate receptors for warm and cold and that cold receptors may be more numerous (Whitbourne, 1985).

Temperature sensitivity is usually measured relative to **physiological zero**, which is the skin temperature at which neither warmth nor cold is felt. Temperatures slightly above or below physiological zero are not sensed as different. Because of the relative insensitivity of thermal receptors to skin temperatures near physiological zero, discomfort for warmth and cold is experienced only when the temperature of the skin reflects outside conditions that can be potentially harmful. The protective nature of the thermal receptor system is apparent from the fact that temperature changes away from physiological zero in either direction are sensed as more intense than changes toward it. In addition, our bodies adapt to constant temperatures. In other words, if we are placed in a very warm room, we will initially feel hot. But if the room temperature remains constant, we will eventually adapt to it. Temperature changes that affect large areas of the body are sensed more readily than those affecting small areas, which also provides a protective function.

Finally, at extremely high or low temperatures pain receptors are also triggered as an additional alert that steps must be taken for self-protection.

The complex way in which our thermal regulation and sensing system works makes it difficult to research. The few studies on aging and temperature sensitivity suggest a meaningful increase in the threshold for warmth (W. C. Clark & Mehl, 1971). Although there is a slight increase in the cold threshold, this change appears minimal (Hensel, 1981; Kenshalo, 1979). These data appear to conflict with lowered tolerance of cold by older adults, who often take few precautions when their core body temperature is lowered. However, the discrepancy may be due to different age effects between temperature sensitivity and temperature regulation (Whitbourne, 1985).

Pain Sensitivity

Age-related differences in sensitivity to pain are one of the most researched areas in somasthesis, yet we still do not have a clear picture of age trends (Harkins & Kwentus, in press). A major problem confronting researchers interested in pain threshold and pain tolerance (the highest level of pain that can be withstood) is that pain sensitivity varies across different locations on the body and with different types of stimulation. Moreover, experiencing pain is more than just a sensory experience; it involves cognitive, motivational, personality, and cultural factors as well.

Although clinical evidence abounds that there is an increase in pain complaints among the elderly, the research evidence is conflicting. Data showing everything from decreased sensitivity to increased sensitivity can be found (Harkins & Kwentus, in press). Corso (1987) notes that part of the problem is a lack of an appropriate operational definition for pain and related difficulties in understanding its various components. Overall, it appears that there are more similarities than differences across adulthood in the sensory response to pain (Harkins, Price, & Martelli, 1986).

Kinesthesis

Do you know how your arms are positioned right now? If so, you have experienced your sense of body position, kinesthesis. Kinesthesis involves sensory feedback concerning two kinds of movements. **Passive movements** are instigated by something (or someone) else, as, for example, in riding quietly in a car. **Active movement** is voluntary, as in walking.

Age-related changes in passive movements depend on the part of the body in question. For example, differences are not observed for passive movement of the big toe but are found for several joints, including the knees and the hips (Ochs, Newberry, Lenhardt, & Harkins, 1985). However, age differences in active movements are not found. For example, judgments of muscle or tendon strain produced by picking up different weights do not differ with age (Ochs et al., 1985).

The importance of kinesthesis in everyday life becomes most apparent when this sense is considered together with balance, which involves the vestibular system. Together, they provide crucial information that helps individuals avoid falls, which have additional risks for older adults (e.g., hip fractures). In the next section we will examine age-related changes in the vestibular system and consider age differences in falls.

Vestibular System

The vestibular system is responsible for keeping track of the body's orientation in space. This function is performed by structures called the semicircular canals, which are housed in the inner ear. Hair cells in the semicircular canals are stimulated by the movement of fluid, which is set in motion by the forces of gravity and acceleration when we move.

Age-related processes similar to the sensory and neural forms of presbycusis occur in the vestibular system. These vestibular changes are termed **presbystasis** (Krympotic-Nemanic, 1969). Neural degeneration of the hair cells may begin as early as age 40 (Bergström, 1978), increasing steadily to age 70 and more rapidly in late life (Ochs et al., 1985). These changes in the vestibular system, coupled with changes in kinesthesis, are important contributors to balance.

Vertigo, Dizziness, Falls, and Body Sway. Dizziness and vertigo caused by vestibular malfunction are common experiences for older adults, and they increase in frequency with age (Ochs et al., 1985). Dizziness is the vague feeling of being unsteady, floating, and lightheaded. Vertigo is the sensation that one or one's surroundings are spinning. These feelings are unpleasant by themselves, but they can also lead to serious injury from falls resulting from loss of balance.

The likelihood of falling increases with age, and falls are life-threatening events, especially for those 75 and older (Ochs et al., 1985). Environmental hazards such as loose rugs and slippery floors are more likely to be a factor for healthy, community-dwelling older adults, whereas disease is more likely to play a role in institutionalized individuals. Increases in body sway, the natural movement of the body to maintain balance, occur with increasing age. Connections between the degree of body sway and likelihood of falling have been shown, with people who fall often having more body sway (Fernie, Gryfe, Holliday, & Llewellyn, 1982; Overstall, Johnson, & Exton-Smith, 1978).

Orientation in space involves many cues besides kinesthetic and vestibular; visual and cognitive cues are also important. Consequently, a complete understanding of what causes older adults to fall more often must await future research that attempts to integrate age-related changes in these other systems with those that occur in the kinesthetic and vestibular systems.

Psychological Effects of Somasthetic and Vestibular Changes

Sensations from the skin, internal organs, and joints serve critical functions. They keep us in contact with our environment, help us avoid falling, serve communication functions, and keep us safe. In terms of self-esteem, how well our body is functioning tells us something about how well we are doing. Losing bodily sensations could have major implications: increased joint stiffness, loss of sexual sensitivity, and problems maintaining balance could result in increased cautiousness, loss of mobility, and decreased social interaction. How the individual views these changes is critical for the maintenance of self-esteem. Providing supportive environments that lead to successful compensatory behaviors can ameliorate the physical and social risks of lack of motor coordination.

REACTION TIME, ATTENTION, AND PROCESSING RESOURCES

One of the best-documented age-related changes is a slowing in performance and behavior (Salthouse, 1985). In fact, the slowing-with-age phenomenon is so well accepted that many gerontologists accept it as the only universal behavioral change yet discovered. In this section we will examine some of the evidence for psychomotor slowing. The research we will consider has important practical applications, as will be described in the following section, dealing with accidents.

Reaction Time

How rapidly could you hit the brakes if another car suddenly pulled out into your path? Rapid responses to events are studied in reaction-time tasks. Successful performance in such tasks involves many factors, including sensation, perception, attention, short-term memory, intelligence, decision making, and personality (Salthouse, 1985). Simply put, in reaction-time tasks people must (1) perceive that an event has occurred, (2) decide what to do about it, and (3) carry out the decision (Welford, 1977). Consequently, poor performance could be the result of a breakdown of any step in the process. Researchers have investigated how well adults of different ages perform in tasks involving simple reaction time, choice reaction time, and complex reaction time. We will consider each briefly.

Simple Reaction Time. **Simple reaction time** involves responding to one stimulus, such as pressing a button as fast as possible whenever a light comes on. Simple reaction time is usually broken down into two components: decision time and motor time. Decision time is the time it takes from the onset of the stimulus until the person begins to initiate a response. Motor time is the time needed to complete the response.

Consistent age differences in overall simple reaction time and in each of its components have been reported (Borkan & Norris, 1980; Salthouse, 1985). Interestingly, the most noticeable difference between young and old is in the decision time component.

Choice Reaction Time. In tasks involving **choice reaction time**, individuals are presented with more than one stimulus and are required to respond to each in a different way. For example, imagine being presented with two lights, one red and one blue. Your job is to press the left button every time the red light comes on and the right button when the blue light comes on. Age-related differences have been reported for such tasks, with older adults being significantly slower (Fozard, Thomas, & Waugh, 1976; J. C. Thomas, Waugh, & Fozard, 1978).

Complex Reaction Time. The most difficult reaction-time task is one involving **complex reaction time**, which requires making many decisions about when and how to respond. A good example of such a task is driving a car: the number of stimuli is extremely large, and the range of possible responses is huge. Cerella, Poon, & Williams (1980) report that the magnitude of age differences in complex-reaction-time tasks increases as the task becomes more difficult. Thus, older adults become increasingly disadvantaged as situations demanding rapid responding become more complex.

Experience and Reaction Time. The clear conclusion is that there are substantial age differences in speed of responding. But what would happen to these age differences if the individuals were allowed to gain experience with the laboratory reaction-time tasks through practice? Several studies have examined this question (e.g., Berg, Hertzog, & Hunt, 1982; Leonard & Newman, 1965; Madden & Nebes, 1980; Plude & Hoyer, 1981; Salthouse & Somberg, 1982). The dominant finding has been that practice results in considerable improvement among all age groups. However, age differences in overall level of performance are seldom eliminated completely with practice.

But what would happen if we examined the role of experience on a reaction-time task much closer to one performed in everyday life? That is what Salthouse (1984) decided to do. He examined performance in adults aged 19 to 72 on transcription typing. The typists in his study ranged

in speed from 17 to 104 words per minute, with ability and age being unrelated. Salthouse examined several components of reaction time, including choice reaction time, speed of repetitive tapping, and the rate at which people can substitute specific digits for letters (e.g., *3* for *d*). All of these tasks revealed the typical age-related decrement. However, one measure showed a difference favoring older adults: span of anticipation. This measure was derived from a manipulation of the number of simultaneously visible to-be-typed characters, and it was interpreted as an indication of how far ahead of the currently typed character the typist was focusing his or her attention. Because a greater span of anticipation minimizes the importance of the speed of perceptual-motor processes as a major factor in skilled typing, the larger span on the part of the older typists can be considered an extremely effective compensatory mechanism. A summary of Salthouse's findings are presented in Figure 5.9.

Exercise and Reaction Time. As we noted in Chapter 4, one of the benefits that some researchers claim for aerobic exercise is improved cognitive performance. Most of this work has focused on the effects of exercise on the speed of reaction time. Several studies of both simple and choice reaction times document significant improvement in performance in older adults as a function of sustained exercise (Baylor & Spirduso, 1988; Rikli & Busch, 1986; Spirduso, 1980; Tomporowski & Ellis, 1986). That is, older adults who exercised regularly had significantly faster reaction times than sedentary older adults. Moreover, these findings appear to hold up even when reaction time is decomposed into its components (Baylor & Spirduso, 1988).

These results do not mean that exercise affects all aspects of a reaction-time task equally, however. Blumenthal and Madden (1988) demon-

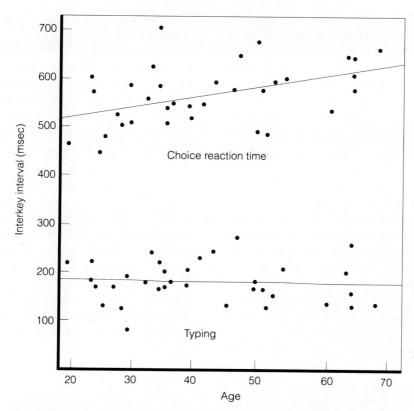

FIGURE 5.9 • Median interkey interval in milliseconds for the normal typing and choice-reaction-time tasks as a function of typist age. (Each point represents a single typist, and the solid lines illustrate the regression equations relating interkey interval to age.)

strated that the effects of exercise may be limited to the encoding and response components of a memory-search task. In contrast, age appears to account for slower rates of memory search. Thus, the benefits of exercise for older adults' reaction-time performance appear to stem from an enhancement of getting information in and getting the response out. What happens in between may be relatively unchanged.

Attention and Processing Resources

Earlier in this chapter I briefly introduced the notion of visual and auditory attention and the question of whether these were related to age. As a reminder and extension of that discussion let us note here that two major types of attention have been studied: sustained attention and selective attention.

Sustained attention refers to the ability to maintain vigilance over time (Giambra & Quilter, 1988). Research until the late 1980s appeared to support an age-related decline in sustained attention (Quilter, Giambra, & Benson, 1983; Surwillo & Quilter, 1964). However, Giambra and Quilter (1988) subsequently reported equivalent performance between young and old in a longitudinal study spanning 18 years. The discrepancy apparently was due to sampling problems; it turned out that the two earlier studies had had participants who were not representative of the elderly population as a whole. These data emphasize the points made in Chapter 1 about the need for careful consideration of participants in research; the results of one's study may change if care is not exercised.

As noted earlier, selective attention refers to the ability to filter out relevant from irrelevant information. Most of the research on selective attention has used the divided-attention paradigm, in which the person is asked either to screen out competing information or to perform two tasks at once. In general, research points to a decrement in older adults' ability to perform two tasks simultaneously (e.g., Madden, 1986, 1987).

The Processing-Resource Debate. One of the most popular theoretical constructs used to explain age differences in performance on divided-attention tasks is **processing resources** (Salthouse, 1988). Much as a computer has a fixed amount of memory to devote to problem solving, people have a certain amount of processing resources to allocate among the various tasks they are doing. Tasks vary in the amount of resources they require, from none at all (so-called automatic tasks) to a great deal (so-called effortful tasks). Many theorists and researchers believe that with increasing age comes a decline in the amount of available processing resources that accounts for poorer performance not only on attention tasks (Plude & Hoyer, 1985) but also on a

host of others (see Salthouse [1988] for a review of these).

On the surface the notion of processing resources offers a concise explanation of a wide range of age-related performance differences. But there is a nagging problem about the processing-resource construct: it has never been clearly defined (Baddeley, 1981; Salthouse, 1982, 1988). In a carefully designed series of investigations, Salthouse and his colleagues set out to see what could be done (Salthouse, 1988; Salthouse, Kausler, & Saults, 1988). Their goal was to provide an empirical test of the processing-resource explanation of age-related performance declines. The results demonstrate that complete reliance on this idea is probably a mistake. Salthouse was able to show that although some kind of processing-resource notion is the most parsimonious explanation, the strong version of the resource decline idea that marks much current research has little empirical support. In other words, something besides a decline in processing resources is responsible for performance decrements with age.

For the moment the role played by processing resources in age-related changes in performance on cognitive tasks remains to be determined. Salthouse's efforts have opened the door to some exciting theoretical developments in the next few years.

ACCIDENTS ACROSS ADULTHOOD

One of the most important applications of research described in this chapter, in conjunction with the information on health and physiological changes described in Chapters 3 and 4, is understanding how accidents occur and how to prevent them. Each year millions of adults are injured in accidents occurring on highways, at home, and in the workplace. Accidents are considered nonnor-

Age-related changes in sensory, motor, and physiological systems increase the likelihood that this woman may have an accident getting on or off the bus.

mative life events (Baltes, Reese, & Lipsett, 1980; Hultsch & Plemons, 1979); that is, they are not related to natural maturational processes. As we will see, however, the likelihood of accidents increases with age as the dynamic interaction between the person and the environment changes (Sterns, Barrett, & Alexander, 1985). Table 5.3 offers some suggestions about how to avoid some of the more common accidents.

The Highway

The relationship between age and automobile accidents depends on how one examines the data. If simply the number of accidents is considered, then accident rates drop across the adult life span beyond age 20. If the number of miles driven is factored in, however, older adults and teenagers are the two age groups most at risk for accidents (National Safety Council, 1981).

Psychologists approach the study of age and highway accidents by focusing on the role of skills known to be relevant to driving. Age, per se, does not lead to accidents; rather, it is decreased skills that can cause them (Panek, Barrett, Sterns, & Alexander, 1977). Barrett, Alexander, and Forbes (1977) identified three information-processing variables that are especially important in understanding accidents: perceptual strategies, selective attention, and reaction time.

TABLE 5.3 · Accidents and the elderly

Accidents seldom "just happen," and many can be prevented. Accidental injuries become more frequent and serious in later life. Thus, attention to safety is especially important for older people.

Several factors make people in this age group prone to accidents. Poor eyesight and hearing can decrease awareness of hazards. Arthritis, neurological diseases, and impaired coordination and balance can make older people unsteady.

Various diseases, medications, alcohol, and preoccupation with personal problems can result in drowsiness or distraction. Often mishaps are expressions of mental depression or of poor physical conditioning.

When accidents occur, older people are especially vulnerable to severe injury and tend to heal slowly. Particularly in women, the bones often become thin and brittle with age, causing seemingly minor falls to result in broken hips.

Many accidents can be prevented by maintaining mental and physical health and conditioning and by cultivating good safety habits. For example:

Falls are the most common cause of fatal injury in the aged. Proper lighting can help prevent them. Here's what you can do:

- Illuminate all stairways and provide light switches at both the bottom and the top.
- Provide night lights or bedside remote-control light switches.
- Be sure *both* sides of stairways have sturdy handrails.
- Tack down carpeting on stairs, and use nonskid treads.
- Remove throw rugs that tend to slide.
- Arrange furniture and other objects so they are not obstacles.
- Use grab bars on bathroom walls and nonskid mats or strips in the bathtub.
- Keep outdoor steps and walkways in good repair.

Personal health practices are also important in preventing falls. Because older people tend to become faint or dizzy after standing too quickly, experts recommend arising slowly from sitting or lying positions. Both illness and the side effects of drugs increase the risk of falls.

Burns are especially disabling in the aged, who recover from such injuries more slowly.

(Source: National Institute on Aging)

The relationship between measures of basic skills and on-the-road behavior has been studied by several researchers. Rackoff and Mourant (1979) found that older drivers (aged 60–70) who scored more poorly than younger drivers (aged 21–29) on tests of visual search, embedded figures, and reaction time also took longer to extract important information while driving. Shinar, McDowell, Rackhoff, and Rockwell (1978) reported that older drivers who were not as able to filter irrelevant information were less effective in their visual-search behavior on the road. Problems in selective attention are evident in accident victims' statements; "I never saw the other car" is a common example of a failure to detect important information.

Considerable evidence shows that older drivers are especially disadvantaged at night. For example, Sivak, Olson, and Pastalan (1981) found that older drivers needed to be considerably closer to signs at night in order to read them, despite the fact that they had been equated with the younger

- Never smoke in bed or when drowsy.
- When cooking, don't wear loosely fitting flammable clothing. Bathrobes, nightgowns, and pajamas catch fire.
- Set water heater thermostats or faucets so that water does not scald the skin.
- Plan which emergency exits to use in case of fire.

Many older people trap themselves behind multiple door locks that are hard to open during an emergency. Install one good lock that can be opened from the inside quickly, rather than many inexpensive locks.

Motor vehicle accidents are the most common cause of accidental death among the 65–74 age group and the second most common cause among older people in general. Your ability to drive may be impaired by such age-related changes as increased sensitivity to glare, poorer adaptation to dark, diminished coordination, and slower reaction time. You can compensate for these changes by driving fewer miles; driving less often and more slowly; and driving less at night, during rush hours, and in the winter.

If you ride on public transportation:

- Remain alert and brace yourself when a bus is slowing down or turning.
- Watch for slippery pavement and other hazards when entering or leaving a vehicle.
- Have fare ready to prevent losing your balance while fumbling for change.
- Do not carry too many packages, and leave one hand free to grasp railings.
- Allow extra time to cross streets, especially in bad weather.
- At night wear light-colored or fluorescent clothing and carry a flashlight.

Old people constitute about 11% of the population and suffer 23% of all accidental deaths. The National Safety Council reports that each year about 24,000 people over age 65 die from accidental injuries and at least 800,000 others sustain injuries severe enough to disable them for at least 1 day. Thus, attention to safety, especially in later life, can prevent much untimely death and disability.

drivers for daytime vision. A follow-up study in which older and younger drivers were equated for both daytime and nighttime vision revealed no performance differences, emphasizing that visual defects, not age, cause the problem (Sivak & Olson, 1982).

An additional problem facing older drivers is one that most people do not think about. As noted in Chapter 4, older adults tend to be taking more prescription and nonprescription medications than younger adults. Since many medica-

tions have side effects that could impair sensory, perceptual, and reaction-time processes, all adults, but especially the elderly, need to be aware of these effects.

The Home

Accidents in the home, such as falls, poisonings, and burns, are most common among children and the elderly (Sterns et al., 1985). Several age-related factors are associated with the increase in

---

SOMETHING · TO · THINK · ABOUT

Sensory-Perceptual Changes, Psychomotor Changes, and Intervention

We have reviewed a great deal of research documenting age differences in sensory, perceptual, and psychomotor abilities across adulthood. We have also considered appropriate interventions within each of these areas, such as eyeglasses, hearing aids, and environmental design. However, we have not really addressed the question of how these differences can be approached in an integrative way and translated into intervention or public policy.

Take a few minutes today and look carefully at your everyday surroundings. Notice how your apartment, your car, public buildings, and shopping centers are designed. Imagine that you are an older adult, and look again. What problems would you have? Are the aisles in the grocery store too shiny to see what items are down at the other end? Are sidewalks in good repair, with no hidden cracks that could be missed? Are controls on the stove easy to read? Are high-

way signs readable from a distance, even at night?

Jot down your impressions from your observations. What changes would you suggest making, based on your knowledge of developmental differences? Do the problems you have identified change your attitude about older people who complain that the world is stacked against them? Would you be willing to pay for these environmental changes? It's something to think about.

---

home accidents in later life. Among the most important of these are vestibular and kinesthetic changes and decrements in visual ability. In the earlier discussion of these problems it was noted that vestibular and kinesthetic cues help us keep our balance and that disruption of them may lead to falls. Accidental poisonings may result from a decreased ability to see warnings on labels due to loss of visual acuity or poor lighting levels. Visual-discrimination difficulties could result in older people's not being able to tell where the top step is in a stairway, perhaps resulting in a fall.

The Workplace

Injury from accidents in the workplace is related to age, but this relationship is complex. Overall, the pattern for both men and women is a decrease

with age in injury frequency but an increase with age in injury severity (Dillingham, 1981; Root, 1981). The relationship between age and injury frequency is attributable to younger workers' high injury rate, probably due to inexperience (Siskind, 1982). In terms of the increase with age in injury severity, older workers tend to take longer to recover from injuries because of changes in biological and physiological processes (see Chapters 3 and 4).

Accident Prevention

We are exposed to environmental risks every day. Maintaining a safe environment, then, cannot be obtained through eliminating risk entirely. Rather, it must be based on a balanced approach to minimizing risk wherever possible, instituting better assessment and screening procedures, and educating people about hazards (Singleton, 1979).

A good example of this approach is the work done by Sterns and his colleagues pertaining to driving (Sterns et al., 1978; Sterns, Barrett, Alexander, Valasek, and McIlvried, 1984; Sterns & Sanders, 1980). They developed an assessment and training program based on the sensory, perceptual, and reaction-time processes involved in driving. Intensive and extensive retraining on deficient skills (e.g., looking down the road) was found to hold up 2 years after training. Importantly, short-term training was not effective.

It appears that the key to addressing the problem of accidents is to remember that age alone does not cause accidents. Rather, it is the decline in skills that sometimes accompanies age that is responsible. As pointed out in this chapter, however, differences across (and even within) individuals in the rate and extent of such changes are quite large. Consequently, any accident-prevention strategies must be sensitive to individual differences rather than simply focusing on age. As pointed out in "Something to Think About," incorporating this knowledge is a desirable goal but may be difficult to accomplish.

SUMMARY

Sensation is the reception of physical stimulation and the translation of this stimulation into neural impulses. Perception is the interpretation of sensory information. Human information processing involves four main steps: sensory storage, perceptual encoding and analysis, decision and response selection, and response execution.

Most of the major structures of the eye undergo change with age. Particularly important are changes involving transmissiveness and accommodative power. With age, absolute and difference thresholds increase; we are more sensitive to glare; and color sensitivity, visual field, acuity, and CFF decline. Measures of visual information processing and perceptual organization and flexibility also document age-related decrements. Older adults are more susceptible to backward masking, are slower at visual encoding, and have poorer visual search. They are also affected more by illusions and context effects.

The most important change in hearing is presbycusis, a loss in sensitivity for high-pitched tones. In general, hearing thresholds increase with age, as do problems in understanding some elements of speech. Auditory information-processing abilities also show age-related decrements. Older adults show declines in dichotic listening and have poorer auditory selective attention.

Although taste thresholds increase with age, there is no evidence of age differences above threshold. No differences are found for food identification, but the evidence concerning taste preferences is conflicting.

There are few age-related changes in the receptors for smell, but there may be significant age changes in neural pathways. Some support for age differences in sensitivity to odors is reported, and the degree of change in olfaction may be greater than that in taste.

Evidence concerning age differences in the somasthetic and vestibular systems is limited. Touch sensitivity declines. Temperature sensitivity decreases for warmth but not for cold. The picture for age differences in pain sensitivity is very unclear. No differences in awareness of passive movements are reported, but differences are reported for active movement. Changes in the vestibular system may explain why older adults fall more often.

Considerable evidence shows that older adults have longer reaction times, with most of this difference accounted for in the decision-time component. However, older adults may be able to compensate through experience. Evidence concerning improvement following exercise suggests improved encoding and response times but no change in memory-search times.

Older adults may be as good as young adults in their ability to sustain attention. However, older adults perform much worse on selective-attention tasks. Although there is some merit to a processing-resource hypothesis about these differences, age-related declines in resources are only part of the story.

Older adults are more likely to have accidents than are young adults. The role of sensory changes in accidents is probably substantial, particularly in automobile accidents.

GLOSSARY

absolute threshold • The minimum amount of stimulus energy required for someone to detect the stimulation.

accommodative power • The ability of the eye to adjust, or focus.

active movement • Voluntary movement of the body.

acuity • The ability to resolve detail and discriminate among sensory patterns.

backward masking • A phenomenon in which a second stimulus blocks, or masks, the ability to identify the first stimulus.

cataract • An opaque spot on the lens of the eye.

central processing • All information processing done in the brain.

choice reaction time • The delay in making different responses to different stimuli.

complex reaction time • The delay in making many decisions about when and how to respond.

conduction deafness • Hearing loss caused by an inability to transmit sound in the ear.

critical flicker frequency (CFF) • The point at which a flashing light appears to fuse and become steady.

dark adaptation • The increase in sensitivity to light in dark environments.

decision and response selection • The step in information processing at which a decision to act is made and a behavior is selected.

diabetic retinopathy • Destruction of the retina that results from chronic diabetes.

dichotic-listening task • A situation in which two messages are presented simultaneously, and the person must either attend to both or block one out.

difference threshold • The smallest amount of stimulation that must be changed in order for someone to detect the change.

encoding speed • The rate at which incoming information is placed in iconic storage.

glaucoma • Abnormally high pressure in the front chamber of the eye.

iconic storage • A short-lived visual sensory buffer.

light adaptation • The adjustment in sensitivity of the eye in bright environments.

macular degeneration • Progressive and irreversible destruction of receptors in the eye.

passive movement • Body movement by something or someone else.

perception • The interpretation of sensory information.

perceptual encoding and analysis • The step in information processing involving interpretation and classification of incoming sensory information.

peripheral processing • Processing of sensory information at the point of sensory input or behavioral output.

physiological zero • The skin temperature at which neither warmth nor cold is felt.

presbycusis • Loss of hearing for high-pitched tones.

presbyopia • Loss in the ability to see nearby objects clearly.

presbystasis • Loss of the ability to maintain balance.

processing resources • Means that people bring to bear in performing a task.

response execution • The step in information processing at which behavior is produced.

selective attention • Control of information processing so that some information is attended to while other information is ignored.

sensation • The reception of physical stimulation and its translation into neural impulses.

sensory store • The step in information processing at which all incoming sensory experiences are received and registered.

simple reaction time • The delay in making a response to one stimulus.

speech discrimination • The ability to discriminate similar sounds.

speech recognition • The ability to recognize spoken words.

stimulus persistence • The continued sensation that follows termination of a stimulus.

sustained attention • The ability to maintain vigilance over time.

transmissiveness • The degree to which the eye allows light to pass through.

two-point difference threshold • The smallest distance between two sources of pressure on the skin that can be detected.

visual field • The area that a person can see when keeping the head still.

visual search • The scanning of a scene for important information.

ADDITIONAL READING

An excellent summary of most of the topics described in this chapter can be found in

Plude, D. J. (1987). Sensory, perceptual, and motor function in human aging. In P. Silverman (Ed.), *The elderly as modern pioneers* (pp. 73–87). Bloomington: Indiana University Press.

Additional, somewhat more technical reviews of research on the topics of vision, hearing, the vestibular system, reaction time and processing resources, and accidents can be found in

Birren, J. E., & Schaie, K. W. (Eds.). (1985). *Handbook of the psychology of aging* (2nd ed.). New York: Van Nostrand Reinhold.

Intellectual Development

Jack Beal, *Sydney and Frances Lewis*, 1975. Washington and Lee University, Lexington, Virginia.

WHAT HAPPENS TO INTELLIGENCE WITH age? At one time researchers and theorists were convinced that all intellectual abilities inevitably declined as people aged, due to biological deterioration. For instance, Wechsler (1958) writes that "nearly all studies . . . have shown that most human abilities . . . decline progressively after reaching a peak somewhere between ages 18 and 25" (p. 135).

In the decades since Wechsler's pessimistic view, extensive research has been conducted on the question of whether intellectual abilities decline. As we examine this research, it will become evident that we can no longer draw simple yes or no conclusions. We are moving further away from simple answers, rather than closer to them. Controversy is now quite common. For instance, Baltes and Schaie (1974) conclude that "general intellectual decline is largely a myth" (p. 35). Botwinick (1977) counters that "decline in intellectual ability is clearly a part of the aging picture" (p. 580).

Who is right? Does intelligence decline, or is that a myth? Answering these questions will be our goal in this chapter. Such widely divergent conclusions about age-related changes in intelligence reflect different sets of assumptions about the nature of intelligence, which are then translated into different theoretical and methodological approaches. These assumptions are firmly grounded in the positions and issues described in Chapter 2. We will examine three avenues of re-search on intelligence and age: the psychometric approach, the neofunctionalist approach, and the cognitive-process approaches. Along the way we will take a look at some attempts to modify intellectual abilities through training programs. But first, we need to consider the question of what intelligence is.

DEFINING INTELLIGENCE

What do we mean by intelligence? Is it being able to learn new things very quickly? Is it knowing a great deal of information? Is it the ability to adapt to new situations or to create new things or ideas? Or is it the ability to make the most of what we have and to enjoy life? Intelligence is all of these abilities and more. It is all of them in the sense that people who stand out on these dimensions are often considered smart, or intelligent. It is more than just these abilities because intelligence also involves the qualitative aspects of thinking style, or how one approaches and conceptualizes problems.

The point that intelligence seems to involve more than just a particular fixed set of characteristics has been demonstrated in some intriguing work by Sternberg and his colleagues (Sternberg, Conway, Ketron, & Bernstein, 1981). They compiled a list of behaviors that laypeople at a train station, supermarket, or college library reported to be distinctly characteristic of either exceptionally intelligent, academically intelligent, everyday intelligent, or unintelligent people. This list of behaviors was then given to experts in the field of intelligence and to a new set of laypeople, who were asked to rate either how distinctively characteristic each behavior was of an ideally intelligent, academically intelligent, or everyday intelligent individual or how important each behavior was in defining these types of intelligent individuals. Ratings were analyzed separately for the experts and the laypeople.

Sternberg and his colleagues found extremely high agreement between experts and laypeople on ratings of the importance of particular behaviors in defining intelligence. The two groups agreed that intelligence consisted of three major factors, or clusters of related abilities: problem-solving ability, verbal ability, and social competence. Problem-solving ability consists of behaviors such as reasoning logically and well, identifying connections among ideas, seeing all aspects of a problem, and making good decisions. Verbal ability includes such things as speaking articulately, reading with a high comprehension rate, and having a good vocabulary. Social competence includes behaviors such as accepting others for what they are, admitting mistakes, displaying interest in the world at large, and being on time for appointments.

Sternberg also wanted to know how these conceptions of intelligence differed across the adult life span. To find out, individuals from age 25 to 75 were asked to list behaviors that they viewed as characteristic of exceptionally intelligent 30-, 50-, or 70-year-olds. Behaviors such as motivation, how much intellectual effort people exert, and reading were said to be important indicators of intelligence for people of all ages. But other behaviors were specific to particular points in the life span. For example, planning for the future and being open-minded were listed most often for a 30-year-old. The intelligent 50-year-old was described as being willing to learn, having a well-established career, and being authoritative. At age 70, intelligent people were thought to be socially active, keeping up with current events, and accepting of change.

Sternberg's work points out that many different skills are involved in intelligence, depending on one's point of view. Interestingly, the behaviors listed by Sternberg's participants fit nicely with the more formal attempts at defining intelligence that we will encounter in this chapter. For example, the aspects of intelligence captured by problem-solving and verbal abilities coincides with the notions of "fluid" and "crystallized" intelligence, and the differences with age in the abilities thought to be important correspond to the qualitative changes discussed by cognitive theorists.

In summary, the various perspectives on everyday meanings of intelligence have connections with the different approaches to defining intelligence that we will examine in this chapter. Some psychologists, such as Schaie and Horn, have concentrated on measuring intelligence as performance on standardized tests; this camp represents the **psychometric approach**. Other psychologists have reinterpreted the data obtained in the psychometric approach and have postulated the **neofunctionalist view**, which emphasizes individual differences and plasticity. Still others have been more concerned with the thought processes that are involved rather than in performance on tests; they take a **cognitive-process approach** to intelligence. In this chapter we will consider these theories and the research they have stimulated into intellectual development across adulthood. We will discover that age-related changes in intelligence depend on how it is defined and measured.

THE PSYCHOMETRIC APPROACH

One way to define intellectual functioning is to examine how individuals' scores on various tests of intellectual abilities are interrelated. This psychometric approach to intelligence has a long history; attempts to interrelate performance measures date back to ancient civilizations, including the Chinese and the Greek (Doyle, 1974; Du Bois, 1968).

Because the psychometric approach focuses on the interrelationships among intellectual abilities, one major goal is to describe the ways in which these relationships are organized (Sternberg, 1985). This organization of interrelated intellectual abilities is termed the **structure** of intelligence. The most common way to describe the structure of intelligence is to picture it as a hierarchy (Cunningham, 1987). As shown in Figure 6.1, this hierarchy consists of individual test questions at the base, individual tests at the second level, primary abilities at the third level, followed by second- and third-order abilities, with general intelligence at the top. We will be focusing our discussion on the primary and secondary abilities.

The structure of intelligence is uncovered through sophisticated statistical detective work. First, researchers obtain people's performances on many types of problems. Next, the results are examined to determine whether performance on one type of problem—for example, filling in missing letters in a word—predicts performance on another type of problem—for example, unscrambling letters to form a word. If the performance on one test is highly related to the performance on another, the abilities measured by the two tests are said to be interrelated. In the psychometric approach large numbers of abilities that interrelate in this way are called a **factor**.

Most psychometric theorists believe that intelligence consists of several factors. Although estimates of the exact number of factors vary from a few to over 100, most researchers and theorists believe the number to be relatively small. We will examine two types of factors: primary mental abilities and second-order mental abilities.

Primary Mental Abilities

Early in this century researchers discovered the existence of several independent intellectual abilities, each indicated by different combinations of intelligence tests. The abilities identified in this way led Thurstone (1938) to propose that intelligence actually comprises several independent abilities, which he labeled **primary mental abilities**. Thurstone initially examined seven primary mental abilities: number, word fluency, verbal meaning, associative memory, reasoning, spatial orientation, and perceptual speed. Over the years this list has been refined and expanded, resulting in a current list of 25 primary mental abilities that have been documented across many studies (Ekstrom, French, & Harman, 1979). Short descriptions of each ability are presented in Table 6.1. Because it is difficult to measure all 25 primary abilities in the same study, researchers following in Thurstone's tradition concentrate on measuring only a subset. Typically, this subset consists of 5 primary mental abilities: number, word fluency, verbal meaning, inductive reasoning, and space. How these 5 abilities fare with age will be considered next.

Age-Related Changes in Primary Abilities. The most comprehensive investigation of age-related changes in primary mental abilities is a study by Schaie that began in Seattle in 1956 (Schaie, 1983). Seven cohorts, representing people born between 1889 and 1938, were included;

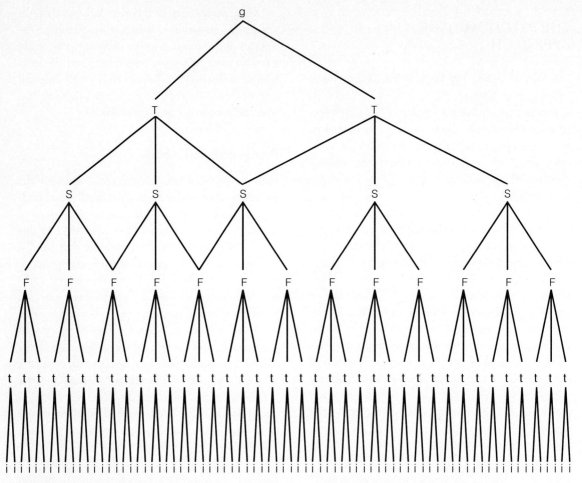

FIGURE 6.1 • A hierarchical structure of ability factors: i, items or questions; t, individual tests; F, primary ability factors; S, second-order factors; T, third-order factors; g, general factor

(Source: "Intellectual Abilities and Age" by W. R. Cunningham, 1987, in K. W. Schaie (Ed.), *Annual Review of Gerontology and Geriatrics* (Vol. 7) (pp. 117–134), © 1987 Springer Publishing Company, Inc. Reprinted with permission.)

162 people were tested in 1956, 1963, and 1970, and 250 others were initially tested in 1963 and retested in 1970 and 1977. Thus, it is possible to compare developmental trends on the five primary mental abilities listed earlier for two separate 14-year periods (1956–1970 and 1963–1977). This is exactly what Schaie and Hertzog (1983) did.

Schaie and Hertzog reported some complicated but interesting results. First, they found declines in performance on all five primary mental abilities after age 60 that were large enough to be of practical importance. That is, the amount of change in ability was likely to lead to decrements in everyday functioning. Second, there were also

TABLE 6.1 · Primary mental abilities indicated by repeated research

Factor	Factor Label	Examples of Tests That Define the Factor
V	Verbal comprehension	Vocabulary, reading comprehension, understanding grammar and syntax
CV	Verbal closure	Scrambled words, hidden words, incomplete words
FW	Word fluency	Word endings, word beginnings, rhymes
FA	Associational fluency	Controlled associations, inventive opposites, figures of speech
FE	Expressional fluency	Making sentences, rewriting, simile interpretations
O	Object flexibility	Substantive uses, improving things, combining objects
SP	Sensitivity to problems	Improvements for common objects, listing problems, finding deficiencies
CA	Concept formation	Picture-group naming, word grouping, verbal relations
RL	Logical reasoning	Nonsense syllogisms, diagramming relationships, deciphering languages
I	Inductive reasoning	Letter sets, locating marks, classifications
RG	General reasoning	Word problems, ship destination, language rules
ES	Estimation	Width determination, spatial judgment, quantitative estimation
N	Number facility	Addition, division, mixed numerical operations
S	Spatial orientation	Card rotations, cube comparisons, boat positions
CS	Speed (Gestalt) closure	Gestalt completion, incomplete pictures, concealed objects
CF	Flexibility of closure	Hidden figures, embedded figures, copying figures
VZ	Visualization	Form board, paper folding, surface development
P	Perceptual speed	Finding a's, number comparisons, identical pictures
FF	Figural flexibility	Toothpicks, planning patterns, storage
FL	Figural fluency	Decorations, alternate signs, make a figure
IT	Integration	Following directions, internalizing rules, manipulating numbers
MV	Visual memory	System-shape recognition, monogram recall, orientation memory
MS	Span memory	Digit span-visual, letter span-auditory, tone reproduction
MA	Associative memory	Picture-number pairs, first-last names, serial recall
MM	Meaningful memory	Recalling limericks, sentence completion, sentence recall

(Source: "Cognitive Factors: Their Identification and Replication," by Eckstrom et al., 1979, *Multivariate Behavior Research Monographs*, No. 79.2.) Reprinted by permission.

small drops in performance during the 50s; however, the impact that these changes had in a person's everyday life might be minimal. Schaie and Hertzog noted that the declines noted between ages 60 and 67 were greater than those observed between 53 and 60. Nevertheless, there was evidence that the decline in primary abilities that became more pronounced after age 60 might have begun earlier. Finally, estimates of the size of the age effects differed when the data were analyzed cross-sectionally and longitudinally. Schaie and Hertzog were able to show conclusively that cross-sectional data gave a much more pessimistic view of intellectual decline than did longitudinal data. Moreover, individual differences were often found to be quite large, making it difficult to draw general conclusions about individuals.

In sum, Schaie and Hertzog's data show reliable declines in primary mental abilities after age 60 that may affect people's everyday lives. However, the limits of their research must be kept in mind. Only a small subset of the primary abilities have been investigated systematically. This is especially important because many other related abilities may show different developmental patterns. Also, the amount of variance accounted for by age never exceeded 9%, meaning that most of the differences were due to something else. For these reasons, a complex theory may be needed to account more completely for age differences in primary abilities (Horn, 1982).

Second-Order Mental Abilities

Because the primary mental abilities are all aspects of intelligence, there are complex relationships among them that are best understood by moving to a higher level of abstraction. Careful consideration of the relationships among the primary mental abilities has resulted in the identification of **second-order mental abilities**, broad-ranging skills that each have several primary abil-

ities as their components (Horn, 1982). At present, at least six second-order abilities have been found, and they are described in Table 6.2. However, most of the research and discussion of these abilities has been focused on two: fluid intelligence and crystallized intelligence.

Fluid and Crystallized Intelligence. Horn (1978, 1982) points out that crystallized and fluid intelligence include many of the basic abilities that we associate with intelligence, such as verbal comprehension, reasoning, integration, and concept formation. Yet they are associated with age differently, are influenced by different underlying variables, and are measured differently.

Fluid intelligence refers to an individual's innate ability independent of acquired knowledge and experience, that is, basic information-processing skills. Fluid intelligence is reflected on tests of incidental learning and inductive reasoning, for example. **Crystallized intelligence** reflects knowledge that is acquired through experience and education; it represents intelligence as cultural knowledge. Crystallized intelligence is reflected on tests of intentional learning, vocabulary, information, and comprehension, to name a few.

It should be recognized that any given test can reflect both fluid and crystallized intelligence, and the examples indicate only some of the best, relatively pure, measures. No single test of either ability exists, because each represents a cluster of underlying primary abilities. As a general rule tests that minimize the role of acquired, cultural knowledge involve mainly fluid intelligence; those that maximize the role of such knowledge involve mainly crystallized intelligence.

Developmentally, fluid and crystallized intelligence follow two very different paths, as depicted in Figure 6.2. Performance on tests of fluid intelligence declines significantly as we grow older. Although our understanding of why this

Intellectual and creative abilities do not show across-the-board decline in adulthood. Like Henri Matisse many individuals make great contributions in old age.

drop occurs is not yet complete, it may be related to changes in the underlying neurophysiological processes such as neuronal fallout. In particular, decline in fluid intelligence is associated mainly with decrements in the ability to organize information, the ability to ignore irrelevant information, the ability to focus or to divide attention, and the ability to keep information in working memory (Horn, Donaldson, & Engstrom, 1981).

In contrast, crystallized intelligence is not thought to decline with age; indeed, it may even increase as a result of continued experience and lifelong learning. This makes sense because an individual is continually adding to his or her knowledge base by learning new words, acquiring new skills at home or work, and compiling information by reading, for example (Horn, 1982; Horn & Donaldson, 1980).

Considering intellectual development in terms of fluid and crystallized intelligence has proved useful for three reasons. First, it helps explain how older adults may be less able to perform tasks that are novel but may be as proficient as ever when it comes to situations that demand experience or practical knowledge. Second, the discovery that fluid and crystallized intelligence follow different developmental paths emphasizes that intellectual development is a complex process. Finally, research on fluid and crystallized intelligence has generated renewed interest in the interrelationships among intellectual abilities.

Although the concepts of fluid and crystallized intelligence are popular, they are not universally accepted. For example, they have been criticized as being nothing more than statistical artifacts (Guilford, 1980). Additionally, there are alternative ways to interpret age differences that involve considering several personal and

TABLE 6.2 • Descriptions of major second-order mental abilities

Crystallized Intelligence (Gc)

This form of intelligence is indicated by a very large number of performances indicating breadth of knowledge and experience, sophistication, comprehension of communications, judgment, understanding conventions, and reasonable thinking. The factor that provides evidence of Gc is defined by primary abilities such as verbal comprehension, concept formation, logical reasoning, and general reasoning. Tests used to measure the ability include vocabulary (What is a word near in meaning to temerity?), esoteric analogies (Socrates is to Aristotle as Sophocles is to _____?), remote associations (What word is associated with *bathtub, prizefighting,* and *wedding?*), and judgment (Determine why a foreman is not getting the best results from workers). As measured, the factor is a fallible representation of the extent to which an individual has incorporated, through the systematic influences of acculturation, the knowledge and sophistication that constitutes the intelligence of a culture.

Fluid Intelligence (Gf)

The broad set of abilities of this intelligence include those of seeing relationships among stimulus patterns, drawing inferences from relationships, and comprehending implications. The primary abilities that best represent the factor, as identified in completed research, include induction, figural flexibility, integration, and, cooperatively with Gc, logical reasoning and general reasoning. Tasks that measure the factor include letter series (What letter comes next in the following series d̲ f̲ i̲ m̲ r̲ x̲ e̲ ?), matrices (Discern the relationships among elements of 3-by-3 matrices), and topology (From among a set of figures in which circles, squares, and triangles overlap in different ways, select a figure that will enable one to put a dot within a circle and square but outside a triangle). The factor is a fallible representation of such fundamental features of mature human intelligence as reasoning, abstracting, and problem solving. In Gf these features are not imparted through the systematic influences of acculturation but instead are obtained through learning that is unique to an individual or is in other ways not organized by the culture.

Visual Organization (Gv)

This dimension is indicated by primary mental abilities such as visualization, spatial orientation, speed of closure, and flexibility of closure, measured by tests such as Gestalt closure (Identify a figure in

(Source: "The Aging of Human Abilities" by J. L. Horn, 1982, in B. B. Wolman (Ed.), *Handbook of Developmental Psychology* (pp. 847–870). © 1982 Reprinted with permission of Prentice-Hall, Inc., Englewood Cliffs, NJ.)

contextual variables (e.g., Labouvie-Vief, 1977); this criticism is taken up in the next section, on moderators of intellectual change.

Moderators of Intellectual Change

Based on the research we have considered thus far, two different developmental trends emerge: gains occur in experience-based processes, but losses are seen in our innate abilities. These losses are viewed as an inevitable result of the decline of physiological processes with age.

A growing number of researchers, though, disagree with the notion that intellectual aging necessarily involves an inevitable decline in fluid abilities (Labouvie-Vief, 1977, 1981; Schaie, 1979). These researchers do not deny that some adults show intellectual decline. Rather, they which parts have been omitted), form board (Show how cut-out parts fit together to depict a particular figure), and embedded figures (Find a geometric figure within a set of intersecting lines). To distinguish this factor from Gf, it is important that relationships among visual patterns be clearly manifest so performances reflect primarily fluency in perception of these patterns, not reasoning in inferring the patterns.

Auditory Organization (Ga)

This factor has been identified on the basis of several studies in which primary mental abilities of temporal tracking, auditory cognition of relations, and speech perception under distraction-distortion were first defined among other primary abilities and then found to indicate a broad dimension at the second order. Tasks that measure Ga include repeated tones (Identify the first occurrence of a tone when it occurs several times), tonal series (Indicate which tone comes next in an orderly series of tones), and cafeteria noise (Identify a word amid a din of surrounding noise). As in the case of Gv, this ability is best indicated when the relationships among stimuli are not such that one needs to reason for understanding but instead are such that one can fluently perceive patterns among the stimuli.

Short-Term Acquisition and Retrieval

This ability comprises processes of becoming aware and processes of retaining information long enough to do something with it. Almost all tasks that involve short-term memory have variance in this factor. Span-memory, associative-memory, and meaningful-memory primary abilities define the factor, but measures of primary and secondary memory can also be used to indicate the dimension.

Long-Term Storage and Retrieval

Formerly this dimension was regarded as a broad factor among fluency tasks, such as those of the primary abilities labeled associational fluency, expressional fluency, and object flexibility. In recent work, however, these performances have been found to align with others indicating facility in storing information and retrieving information that was acquired in the distant past. It seems, therefore, that the dimension mainly represents processes for forming encoding associations for long-term storage and using these associations, or forming new ones, at the time of retrieval. These associations are not so much correct as they are possible and useful; to associate *tea kettle* with *mother* is not to arrive at a truth so much as it is to regard both concepts as sharing common attributes (e.g., warmth).

simply suggest that these decrements may not happen to everyone to the same extent. There seem to be many reasons why performance differences occur; age alone does not fully explain why people vary in intelligence. In this section we will explore some of the social and biological factors that have been proposed as modifiers of intellectual development. These include cohort differences, educational level, occupation, personality,

health and life-style, mindlessness, and relevancy and appropriateness of tasks.

Cohort Differences. Do the differences in intellectual performance obtained in some situations reflect true age-related change or mainly cohort, or generational, differences? This question gets right to the heart of the debate over interpreting developmental research on

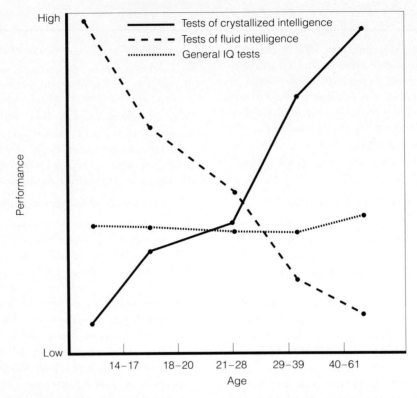

FIGURE 6.2 · Performances on tests used to define fluid, crystallized, and general intelligence, as a function of age

(Source: "Organization of Data on Life-Span Development of Human Abilities" (p. 463) by J. L. Horn, 1970, in L. R. Goulet & P. B. Baltes (Eds.), *Life-Span Developmental Psychology: Research and Theory*, New York: Academic Press. Reprinted with permission.)

intelligence. On the one hand, dozens of cross-sectional studies document significant differences in intellectual performance with age. On the other hand, several longitudinal investigations show either no decrement or even an increase in performance (Labouvie-Vief, 1985).

The way to resolve the discrepancy between the two approaches involves comparing data collected over long periods of time from several samples and analyzed simultaneously in both cross-sectional and longitudinal designs. When this has been done, it turns out that part of the apparent decline with age in performance on intelligence tests is due to generational differences rather than age differences (Schaie, 1979; Schaie & Hertzog, 1983; Schaie & Labouvie-Vief, 1974; Schaie & Parham, 1977).

As an example of what is meant by generational differences, let us consider a portion of the data reported by Schaie (1983), which is shown in Table 6.3. In analyzing data from his longitudinal study, he found significant cohort effects favoring the more recently born adults for the primary mental abilities of verbal meaning, space,

TABLE 6.3 · Average 21-year age changes estimated from independent samples, in *T*-score points[a]

Age Range	*n*[b]	Verbal Meaning	Space	Reasoning	Number	Word Fluency	Intellectual Ability	Educational Aptitude
25–46	76/79	−0.29	−1.64	−2.53	−0.64	−4.38*	−3.41	−0.73
32–53	70/77	−2.01	−3.93	−3.49	−0.31	−5.79*	−3.56	−2.47
39–60	71/72	−1.42	−4.81*	−2.86	−1.16	−4.47*	−3.52	−1.84
46–67	65/73	−6.91*	−2.76*	−6.56*	−3.59	−8.90*	−7.14*	−7.50*
53–74	70/70	−8.29*	−5.45*	−7.36*	−7.95*	−12.61*	−10.70*	−8.64*
60–81	72/58	−8.75*	−5.98*	−3.54*	−5.45*	−8.42*	−7.84*	−7.89*

[a]*T*-score is a statistical procedure for comparing test scores by normalizing and standardizing the raw scale scores.
[b]First number indicates frequency at first age; second number indicates frequency at second age.
*$p<.01$.

(Source: "The Seattle Longitudinal Study: A 21-Year Exploration of Psychometric Intelligence in Adulthood" by K. W. Schaie, 1983, in K. W. Schaie (Ed.), *Longitudinal Studies of Adult Psychological Development* (pp. 64–135). New York: Guilford. Reprinted with permission.)

number, inductive reasoning, and word fluency. In other words, scores on these primary abilities were related to when people had been born. There was a relatively constant gain in scores on reasoning from the 1889 cohort to the 1952 cohort, for example, even after other factors had been ruled out. Together, these data suggest that older cohorts may be at a significant disadvantage on tests of fluid abilities. It is important to note, however, that although cohort effects reduce the size of the age effects, they do not explain all of the age-related differences (Horn, 1982; Schaie & Hertzog, 1983).

Documenting cohort effects is one example of considering the context in which people develop. But cohort is a rather general concept, since there are many things that could differ from one generation to the next. We will now take a look at some of these more specific variables.

Educational Level. Even though researchers have known for many years that scores on in-

telligence tests are related to educational level (Miles & Miles, 1932), only since the late 1960s have investigators seriously considered the meaning of this relationship for intellectual development in adulthood. Several studies have now documented that differences in educational level can account for some of the age differences that emerge (Blum & Jarvik, 1974; Gonda, 1980; Granick & Friedman, 1973; R. F. Green, 1969; Schaie & Strother, 1968).

Granick and Friedman (1973) took into account the fact that older adults had less formal education, on the average, than younger adults. Once this relationship between age and education had been controlled for, the age-related decline in intelligence was significantly reduced. Other studies have compared people within a particular generation who differed in education. For example, Blum & Jarvik (1974) found better intellectual performance among older adult high school graduates than among older adults who had finished only elementary school.

The importance of education for intellectual development during adulthood may go beyond the absolute number of years spent in school (Gonda, 1980). For one thing, more highly educated individuals may adopt life-styles that foster the maintenance of cognitive abilities. Highly educated older adults are also the exception in their generation; opportunities to go to college were not as prevalent 50 years ago as they are now.

Taken together, these factors indicate that one source of the cohort effect may be differences in the type and amount of education. The evidence points to the maintenance of intellectual abilities in well-educated adults at least into old age. As more well-educated cohorts grow old, they may help change the stereotype of universal and inevitable intellectual decline with age.

Occupation. An interesting line of research concerns the role of occupation in intellectual development (Labouvie-Vief, 1981). Although it is sometimes hard to separate occupation and educational level, because certain jobs demand particular kinds or levels of education, the role of occupation can be examined in the following sense. Certain cognitive activities are demanded at work that may not be required at home. To the extent that a job requires a person to use these cognitive processes a great deal, that person may be less likely to show declines in them as he or she ages.

Indirect support for this assumption comes from research showing that when older people are familiar with the tasks used in intelligence tests, they perform much better (Labouvie-Vief & Gonda, 1976). To the extent that people become practiced at thinking in a certain way, they may be less likely to show declines in that kind of thinking as they grow older. More direct support comes from research conducted by Avolio and Waldman (1987), which is highlighted in "How Do We Know?"

Personality. Very little research has been conducted concerning the extent to which personality factors mediate intellectual functioning. Botwinick and Storandt (1974) found that as women's age increased, their effort and deliberation increased even though their performance on measures of brain function decreased. It was as if their effort and deliberation served as compensatory strategies in response to decrements in ability.

Lachman (1983) has studied the nature of change in personality and intellectual factors in later life from a different perspective. Based on data collected on two occasions about 2 years apart, she examined the causal relationship between perceptions of one's own cognitive abilities and performance on several measures of intelligence. Most important, she found that people changed in their perceptions of their abilities over time. Interestingly, the nature of this change was related to the subjects' initial level of fluid intelligence and sense of personal control over their own life. High initial levels of fluid abilities and internal control led to positive changes in people's perceptions of their abilities; low initial levels led to decreases in perceptions of ability. Thus, Lachman's results support the view that initial levels of cognitive ability affect changes in how abilities are perceived; no evidence for the reverse relationship was found.

Hayslip (1988) investigated relationships between personality and ability from an ego-development perspective (see Chapter 8). He was interested in establishing connections between how people view themselves and their level of intellectual ability. He found that anxiety over the adequacy of one's ideational ability and feelings about bodily integrity were related to crystallized intelligence, whereas using cognitive resources to deal with reality and organizational ability related to fluid intelligence. These relationships suggest that individual differences in the

HOW · DO · WE · KNOW?

Job as a Moderator of the Age-Aptitude Relationship

As noted in the text, there is a growing realization that people's everyday experience affects their performance on tests of intellectual abilities. This experience can range from formal education to work skills.

Avolio and Waldman (1987) examined performance on standard personnel aptitude tests and how it related to age, education, and job type. The tests, used widely in personnel departments, measured space visualization, numerical reasoning, verbal reasoning, symbolic reasoning, and mechanical reasoning. Participants were a random sample of 131 employees at a coal mine in the western United States; 82% of the employees were men. Of the participants, 69 were from the production department, representing unskilled workers, and 62 were from the machinery department, representing skilled workers.

The results showed very different patterns of correlations between performance on the aptitude tests and age as a function of job type. These differences remained even after corrections for level of education were made. Unskilled workers from the production department showed relatively high negative correlations between age and performance, ranging from $-.37$ between age and numerical reasoning to $-.57$ for age and verbal reasoning. In contrast, skilled workers in the machinery department showed little relationship between age and performance; the strongest relationship was $-.32$ between age and symbolic reasoning.

These results mean that there were very few differences between older and younger workers in the machinery department on aptitude tests, whereas such differences were common in production department workers. These findings support the idea that everyday experience affects the maintenance of intellectual abilities. In particular, certain job activities may provide workers with continued practice with various cognitive skills, thereby preventing marked decline. As we will see in our discussion of training primary abilities, this use-disuse hypothesis appears to explain much of the age differences in performance.

We must keep in mind, however, that Avolio and Waldman conducted a cross-sectional study, examined only a small number of aptitudes, and tested only coal-mine workers. Future research needs to include other occupations and skills and to examine performance from a longitudinal perspective.

maintenance of higher levels of intellectual functioning in later life may be motivated by the desire to protect oneself from feelings of worthlessness and loss of control over one's abilities.

Health and Life-Style. One of the most difficult problems in any study of aging is the separation of normal processes from abnormal ones. So far our discussion of intellectual development has ignored this distinction; we have been concerned only with normal changes. We know from our own experience, however, that not everyone is healthy and experiences only normal cognitive aging. Moreover, disease is a hit-or-miss proposition, affecting some people mainly physically, as in arthritis, and others mainly cognitively, as in the early stages of dementia. Thus, we need to consider how specific aspects of health influence intellectual ability.

The most obvious relationship between health and intelligence concerns *the functioning of the brain itself*. We noted in Chapter 3 that several normative changes in brain structure with age affect functioning. Disorders such as Alzheimer's disease and accidents involving head injuries may damage the brain and interfere with its functioning. In some cases these problems get worse as the individual ages. Obviously, the more extensive the damage, the more significant the impairment of intellectual ability.

The connection between disease and intelligence has been established fairly well in the case of *cardiovascular disease*. In particular, atherosclerosis, hypertension, and blood flow have been investigated most (Busse & Maddox, 1985). Wilkie and Eisdorfer (1971) found significant intellectual decline over a 10-year period in people with hypertension but no decline in people with normal or slightly elevated blood pressure. Hachinski (1980) argued that the effects of hypertension could be especially severe in the hippocampus, which in turn may be manifested behaviorally as declines in fluid intelligence (Horn, 1982).

Mindlessness. Langer (1985) offers an interesting explanation of the apparent decline in intellectual abilities in adulthood. She argues that cognitive processing occurs at two levels: a **mindful level**, at which we are aware of what we are doing and are actively involved with the environment, and a **mindless level**, at which we are unaware of what we are doing and are only passively involved with the environment. Mindlessness occurs when we allow the situation to dictate our behavior, rather than stepping back and critically evaluating what we should be doing. Many times

we go along with requests, for example, because everything seems to be correct: the con artist looks and acts like a bank executive, so we do not question his request to withdraw our savings. What we fail to do is ask ourselves whether the request is reasonable; we just go along because appearances say that we should.

Langer contends that mindlessness increases as we get older unless something is done to stop this rise. Moreover, older adults may engage in mindlessness at inappropriate times and appear incompetent. Unchecked increases in mindlessness may be part of the reason that institutionalized older adults seem less alert cognitively; that is, the institution may not foster mindfulness. In a provocative study Langer and Rodin (1976) demonstrated this point. When they increased mindfulness in nursing home residents by encouraging them to make decisions and by giving them responsibilities for plants, the residents became happier, healthier, and more alert and did better on memory tests.

Although Langer's notion of mindlessness is still controversial, it provides another alternative explanation for age-related changes in mental abilities. Her ideas also fit well with the widely held belief and research evidence that people who remain cognitively active—mindful, in Langer's terms—are those who show the least decline (Blum & Jarvik, 1974).

Relevancy and Appropriateness of Tasks. One serious problem with traditional psychometric measures of intelligence concerns their inadequacy at measuring adults' true abilities. The academic settings and skills that led to the development of these tests may not be equally important or relevant to adults. Consequently, it is argued that we need new tests for adults that are based on the problems they typically face.

Scheidt and Schaie (1978) made such an effort. Older adults were interviewed in parks, senior centers, and similar locations and were asked to name situations that involved using intelligence. In all, over 300 situations were described; looking for a place to live and figuring out how to pay a debt were two common examples; more of them are listed in Table 6.4. These responses provide a very different starting point for developing tasks for an intelligence test than trying to figure out how to measure classroom learning potential.

Willis, Schaie, and Lueers (1983) also looked at practical measures of intelligence, but from a different perspective. They examined the relationships between seven primary mental abilities, measured by traditional tests, and eight categories of everyday tasks, measured by the ETS Basic Skills Test. The categories of everyday tasks included understanding labels on medical or household articles, reading street maps, understanding charts or schedules, comprehending paragraphs, filling out forms, reading newspaper and phone directory ads, understanding technical documents, and comprehending news text. Three scores on the skills test were calculated; two scores reflected different levels of comprehension and information processing, literal and inference, and the third was the total score. Correlations between the scores for primary abilities and basic skills were very high for the older adults, indicating that the two tests were measuring similar things.

When Willis et al. examined their data to see which of the primary abilities best predicted each of the eight categories of everyday tasks, some interesting findings emerged. They had expected their measures of crystallized intelligence to be the best predictors, on the theory that these everyday skills should reflect cultural knowledge and should not decline with age. Much to their surprise, the measures of fluid intelligence, especially figural relations, were the best predictors most of the time. It was also true that older adults did not always perform as well as the younger adults on the skills test. In fact, the younger adults obtained near-perfect scores, whereas the older adults were significantly below ceiling, on average.

The Willis et al. study is important for two reasons. First, it shows that traditional tests of primary mental abilities may predict performance on real-life tasks. For supporters of the psychometric approach, these data show that a total rejection of traditional tests on the ground that they are inadequate may be unwarranted. Second, the findings also show that tests comprising what appear to be more relevant tasks may tap some of the same components of intelligence that the traditional tests are thought to measure. This opens the possibility of developing new tests that consist of familiar tasks but that still tap the components of intelligence identified in psychometric research.

The issue of task relevancy is still far from being settled, however. As we will see later, many researchers and theorists argue quite strongly that only by abandoning a purely psychometric approach and moving to a focus on everyday uses of intelligence will we advance our understanding of intellectual aging. As with most controversies, there is something to be said for both sides.

Modifying Primary Abilities

As we have seen, older adults do not perform as well on tests of some primary abilities as younger adults, even after taking the moderators of performance into account (Schaie & Hertzog, 1983). In considering these results, investigators began asking whether there was a way to slow down or even reverse the declines. Are the age-related differences that remain after cohort and other effects are removed permanent? Or might it be possible to reduce or even eliminate these differences if older adults were given appropriate training? Can we modify adults' intelligence?

TABLE 6.4 · Examples of ecologically valid indicators of intelligence in both social and solitary (nonsocial) settings

	Situational Attributes	Social Setting	Nonsocial Setting
High Activity	Common-supportive	Arguing with person about important point	Gardening in yard, planting seeds, weeding
		Being visited by son or daughter and their children	Doing weekly shopping in crowded supermarket
	Common-depriving	Pressured by salesperson to buy merchandise	Climbing several steps to building entrance
		Quarreling with relative	Cleaning apartment or household
	Uncommon-supportive	Having sexual intercourse	Preparing large meal for friends
		Traveling around city looking for new residence	Exercising for a few moments each day
	Uncommon-depriving	Waiting at end of long line for tickets to entertainment	Moving into new and unfamiliar residence
		Returning faulty or defective merchandise to store	Driving auto during rush-hour traffic
Low Activity	Common-supportive	Seeking aid or advice from friend or family member	Browsing through family photo album
		Offering money to son or daughter who needs it	Making plans for future
	Common-depriving	Hearing from friend that he or she is considering suicide	Eating meal alone in own home
		Hearing that close friend has recently died	Worrying about ability to pay a debt
	Uncommon-supportive	Entering darkened nightclub to have dinner	Recording day's events in diary
		Attending art exhibit	Wading in waist-high water in ocean
	Uncommon-depriving	Opening door to stranger selling product or soliciting opinion	Slipping on slick floor and falling
		While talking with someone, feeling that you have unintentionally hurt their feelings	Discovering you locked keys in car while shopping

(Source: "A Situational Taxonomy for the Elderly: Generating Situational Criteria" by R. J. Scheidt and K. W. Schaie, 1978, *Journal of Gerontology, 33*, pp. 848–857. Reprinted with permission. © 1978 The Gerontological Society of America.)

Attempts to answer these questions have appeared with increasing frequency since the mid-1970s. Several types of tasks have been examined, ranging from tests of primary mental abilities (Willis, 1987) to the information-processing skills necessary to drive a car (Sterns & Sanders, 1980). Of these, perhaps the most interesting and important research area is the attempt to modify primary abilities that show early and substantial declines.

Primary abilities that are known to begin to decline relatively early in adulthood, such as inductive reasoning, spatial orientation, memory abilities, and figural abilities (Baltes & Willis, 1982), have been examined most closely in intervention research. Labouvie-Vief and Gonda (1976) focused on inductive reasoning. They measured performance on the training task (the Letter Sets Test) and on a new transfer task that participants had not seen during training (Raven's Progressive Matrices). Training was given to three groups. Members of the first group were told to give themselves self-directional statements and feedback. The second group combined these practices with additional statements that were designed to help them cope with anxiety and to emphasize self-approval and success. Members of the third group received unspecific training; they simply practiced taking the Letter Sets Test with no instructions or feedback. Labouvie-Vief and Gonda found that inductive reasoning could be increased through training. They also found evidence for transfer of the training effects, since the performance of the trained groups was also better on the Raven's Progressive Matrices.

Project ADEPT. A much more comprehensive training study, involving a series of short longitudinal studies, was Pennsylvania State University's Adult Development and Enrichment Project (ADEPT) (Baltes & Willis, 1982). The training studies conducted as part of ADEPT provided for two levels of intervention in addition to a no-training control group. All groups were equivalent at the outset.

The first level of intervention involved minimal direct training and had test familiarity as its goal. The participants were given the same tests on several occasions to familiarize them with test taking, so that the researchers could learn about the effects of repeated testing alone.

The second type of training involved interventions tailored specifically for each of the primary abilities tested. Each training package was based on a thorough task analysis of the thinking processes involved in each ability. The resulting training programs varied a little in specific details, but in general they focused on teaching the relational rules associated with each test problem, over five sessions. Training on figural relations, for instance, involved practice with paper-and-pencil tests, oral feedback by the experimenter, group discussion, and review of the kinds of problems involving figural-relations ability.

Overall, the ability-specific training resulted in improvements in primary abilities. But the ability to maintain and to transfer the training effects varied. Evidence for long-term and broad transfer effects were strongest for figural relations. Training effects were found for inductive reasoning and attention/memory, but these effects did not transfer as well to new tasks.

These findings from the training studies become impressive when they are put in terms familiar to us. The size of Baltes and Willis's improvements in fluid abilities were equivalent to the average 21-year longitudinal decline in these abilities reported by Schaie (1983). The implication of this comparison is that the decline in primary abilities can be slowed or even reversed by proper intervention strategies. The results are even more exciting given that the training

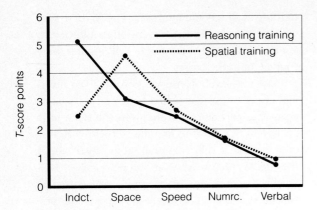

FIGURE 6.3 • Gains in *T*-score points, resulting from training for inductive reasoning or spatial orientation, on inductive reasoning (Indct), spatial orientation (Space), perceptual speed (Speed), numerical abilities (Numrc), and verbal abilities (Verbal)

(Source: "Training the Elderly on the Ability Factors of Spatial Orientation and Inductive Reasoning" by S. L. Willis and K. W. Schaie, 1986, *Psychology and Aging, 1*, pp. 239–247. Copyright 1986 by the American Psychological Association. Reprinted with permission of the author.)

packages in ADEPT were fairly short: an average of five 1-hour sessions. Although the reversal of age-related declines in all primary abilities and the duration of the effects of training remain to be seen, it is clear that we need to revise our view of pervasive, universal decline in primary abilities.

Other Attempts to Train Fluid Abilities.
Schaie and Willis have extended the findings from Project ADEPT (Schaie & Willis, 1986; Willis, 1987; Willis & Schaie, 1986). Their research involves the participants in Schaie's longitudinal study in Seattle, who were assigned to one of two groups based on their performance over a 14-year period (1970–1984). One group showed significant decline on either spatial ability or reasoning ability, and the other group remained sta-

ble on these measures. Schaie and Willis then provided a 5-hour training session on spatial ability and a similar session on reasoning ability for those who had declined. Training was also provided to the individuals who had remained stable, in order to examine the effects of training as a function of amount of decline.

Schaie and Willis found that the cognitive-training techniques could reverse declines that had been reliably documented over the 14-year period (see Figure 6.3). This reversal was noted for both spatial and reasoning abilities, and the gains essentially returned the individuals to earlier levels of functioning. In addition, the training procedures enhanced the performance of many older people who had remained stable. This finding demonstrates that training is not only effective in raising the performance of decliners but can even improve functioning in nondecliners beyond their initial levels. Schaie and Willis also reported that cognitive training appeared to be ability-specific. That is, training on spatial ability improved performance on tests of spatial ability but had little effect on reasoning ability.

Rather than simply training older adults on particular fluid abilities, Hayslip (1986) tried something different. He randomly assigned 414 community-dwelling older adults to one of four groups: inductive-reasoning training, anxiety reduction, no training at all, or posttest only. Several measures of inductive reasoning and other measures of intellectual abilities were given before training, 1 week after, and 1 month after training. Hayslip found that both training groups improved their performance, with the induction-training group having the highest level 1 month after training. However, he found little evidence of generalized training effects to other abilities. He concluded that at least part of the gain in performance was due to reductions in people's level of anxiety in taking tests of intellectual ability.

Considered together, the results from Project ADEPT, the data from Schaie and Willis's research, and Hayslip's work allow us to conclude that declines in fluid abilities are normative but that these declines may be somewhat reversible. We should still appreciate the fact that some degree of decrease in intellectual ability as defined by psychometricians is part of aging.

THE NEOFUNCTIONALIST APPROACH

In reaction to the traditional psychometric approach, particularly the research on moderators of intellectual abilities and training of fluid abilities, Baltes and his colleagues developed a second view of adult intellectual development, the neofunctionalist approach (see Baltes, Dittmann-Kohli, & Dixon, 1984; Dittmann-Kohli & Baltes, in press).

Basic Concepts

The neofunctionalist approach holds that there may be some intellectual decline with age but that there is also stability and growth in mental functioning across adulthood. It emphasizes the role of intelligence in human adaptation and daily activity. Four concepts are central to the neofunctionalist interpretation of existing research on adult intelligence: plasticity, multidimensionality, multidirectionality, and interindividual variability.

Plasticity. The first concept, **plasticity**, refers to the range of intraindividual functioning and the conditions under which a person's abilities can be modified within a specific age range. The research on training cognitive abilities de- scribed earlier (Project ADEPT, for example) indicates that there is considerable plasticity in intellectual functioning.

Multidimensionality. The second concept, **multidimensionality**, represents the idea that intelligence consists of a multitude of abilities with distinct structural relationships that may change with age (Horn, 1982; Sternberg, 1980). This idea was described earlier in our discussion of primary and secondary mental abilities. In short, intelligence consists of many abilities that are organized into several separate dimensions, which in turn are related to one another in complex ways.

Multidirectionality. The third concept, **multidirectionality**, refers to the distinct patterns of change in abilities over the life span, with these patterns being different for different abilities. For example, developmental functions for fluid and crystallized intelligence differ, meaning that the directional change in intelligence depends on the skills in question.

Interindividual Variability. The last concept, **interindividual variability**, acknowledges that adults differ in the direction of their intellectual development (Schaie, 1979). Schaie's sequential research indicates that within a given cohort some people show longitudinal decline in specific abilities, some show stability of functioning, and others show increments in performance (Schaie, 1979; Schaie & Hertzog, 1983). Interindividual variability is depicted in Figure 6.4.

The Dual-Process Model

Using these four concepts of plasticity, multidimensionality, multidirectionality, and interindividual variability, Baltes and his colleagues

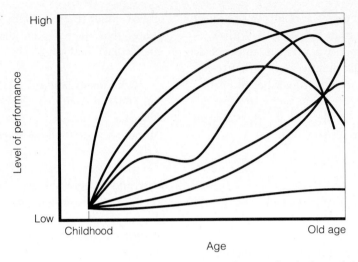

FIGURE 6.4 • Hypothetical examples of interindividual variability in the development of intelligence

proposed the neofunctionalist approach as a dual-process model. Two interrelated types of developmental processes are postulated. The first process, termed cognition as basic processes, concerns developmental changes in the basic forms of thinking associated with information processing and problem solving. Cognitive development in this first process is greatest during childhood and adolescence, as we acquire the requisite skills to handle complex cognitive tasks, such as those encountered in school. The second process, pragmatic intelligence, relates the basic cognitive skills in the first process to everyday cognitive performance and human adaptation. Pragmatic intellectual growth dominates adulthood. In the terminology of the psychometric approach, the neofunctionalists argue that adulthood is predominantly concerned with the growth of crystallized intelligence. But they expand the notion of crystallized intelligence that we considered earlier to include skills that are needed to function in adults' everyday lives.

The dual-process model proposed by the neofunctionalists makes an important step toward relating adult intelligence to successful functioning in one's environment. In this approach one must always be concerned with whether a prospective task is equally relevant for assessing adults' intelligence across the life span. Baltes et al. (1984) called for research aimed at examining what types of tasks are characteristic of adults' intellectual lives. As Scheidt and Schaie (1978) reported, these tasks are typically different from those found on traditional psychometric tests. Baltes and his colleagues argue that until more research like that of Scheidt and Schaie is done, we will learn little about how intelligence is applied to everyday life.

Denney's Model of Unexercised and Optimally Exercised Abilities

Although Denney does not explicitly characterize herself as a neofunctionalist, she has developed a model that also emphasizes the use of intellectual

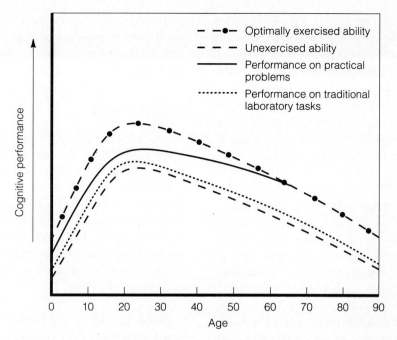

FIGURE 6.5 • Developmental curves showing performance on practical problems and traditional laboratory tasks plotted against unexercised and optimally exercised abilities.

(Source: "Aging and Cognitive Changes" (p. 820) by N. Denney, 1982, in B. B. Wolman, Ed., *Handbook of Developmental Psychology*, © 1982. Adapted by permission of Prentice-Hall, Inc., Englewood Cliffs, NJ.)

abilities in everyday life. Denney (1982) postulates two types of developmental functions. One of these functions represents untrained, or unpracticed, ability, and the other represents optimally trained, or optimally exercised, ability. **Unexercised ability** refers to the ability a normal healthy adult would exhibit without practice or training. Fluid intelligence is thought to be an example of untrained ability, since, by definition, it does not depend on experience and is unlikely to be formally trained (Horn, 1982). **Optimally exercised ability** refers to the ability a normal healthy adult would demonstrate under the best

conditions of training, or practice. Crystallized intelligence is an example of optimally exercised ability, since the component skills (such as vocabulary ability) are used daily.

Denney argues that the overall developmental course of both abilities is parallel: they tend to increase until late adolescence or early adulthood and slowly decline thereafter. As shown in Figure 6.5, performance on practical problems is always better than performance on traditional laboratory tasks even though all performances decline with age. Note that this difference is greatest in old age, where performance on practical problems intersects the curve for optimally exercised abilities. What this means is that the decline in optimally exercised ability limits the performance of the old even on problems involving practical or crystallized intelligence.

Denney's model seems to predict results reported in several studies of life-span differences in psychometrically measured intelligence (Labouvie-Vief, 1985) and the reported differential effects of training with age (Willis, Blieszner, & Baltes, 1981). What Denney has done is to pose yet another question concerning the measurement of adults' intelligence: are assessments of optimally exercised abilities better measures of intelligence when used across the life span than are assessments of untrained ability? In addition, Denney forces us to rethink what we mean by declines in abilities as measured by psychometric tests. Are the differences in performance due to true age-related change, or are they due to a lack of practice? Only additional research will help us figure out the answer.

COGNITIVE-PROCESS APPROACHES

Recall that the psychometric approach to intelligence is not concerned with the thinking processes that underlie intelligence; rather, psychometrics concentrates on interrelationships among performances on tests. In contrast, cognitive-process approaches focus mainly on the thinking processes that are believed to be the elements of intelligence; whether a particular answer is right or wrong is less important. We will consider two theories that are representative of this approach. First, we will examine Piaget's theory and the recent discussions concerning possible extensions of it. The second theory is Schaie's, which represents a very different way of theorizing about intelligence but still from a cognitive-process approach. Both theories postulate that intellectual changes are qualitative, even though they differ on many points. Let us see what each has to say.

Piaget's Theory

According to Piaget (1970), intellectual development is adaptation through activity that creates the very ways in which our knowledge is organized and, ultimately, how we think. Piaget believed that the development of intelligence stemmed from the evolution of increasingly complex cognitive structures. He organized his ideas into a theory of cognitive development that changed the way psychologists conceptualize the development of cognitive processes.

Basic Concepts. For Piaget, thought is governed by the principles of adaptation and organization. **Adaptation** refers to the process of adjusting to the environment. Just as animals living in a forest feed differently than animals living in a desert, how we think changes from one developmental context to another. Because all biological systems adapt, the principle of adaptation is fundamental to Piaget's theory. Adaptation occurs through **organization**, which is how the organism is put together. Each component part has its own specialized function, which is coordinated into the whole. In Piaget's theory the organization of thought is reflected in **cognitive structures** that change over the life span. Cognitive structures determine how we think. It is the change in cognitive structures, the change in the fundamental ways in which we think, that Piaget tries to describe.

What are the processes that underlie intellectual adaptation? Piaget defined two: assimilation and accommodation. **Assimilation** is the use of currently available knowledge to make sense out of incoming information. It is the application of

How people think about issues such as abortion is largely a function of their cognitive developmental level.

base. This is apparent in people's tendency to forget information about a person that violates a stereotype.

Accommodation involves changing one's thought to make it a better approximation of the world of experience. The child in our previous example who thought that cats were dogs eventually learns that cats are cats. When this happens, she has accommodated her knowledge to incorporate a new category of animal.

The processes of assimilation and accommodation serve to link the structure of thought to observable behavior. Piaget believed that most changes during development involved cognitive structures. His research led him to conclude that there were four structures that were reflected in the four stages in the development of mature thought: sensorimotor, preoperational, concrete operational, and formal operational. We will consider the major characteristics of each stage briefly. Since we are most interested in Piaget's description of adult thought, I will place more emphasis on it.

Sensorimotor Period. In this first stage of cognitive development intelligence is reflected in actions. Knowledge is gained through the use of sensory and motor skills, beginning with basic reflexes and moving to purposeful, planned sequences of behavior. A major acquisition in the sensorimotor stage is the object concept, in which the infant realizes that objects continue to exist even when they are out of sight.

Preoperational Period. Thinking in the preoperational period is best described as egocentric. Children at this stage believe that all people and inanimate objects experience the world, think, feel, and behave exactly as they do. There is evidence of rudimentary forms of reasoning, but it is not based on logical principles. For example, the mere co-occurrence of events will be

cognitive structures to the world of experience that makes the world understandable. For example, a child who only knows the word *dog* may use it for every animal she encounters. For example, when the child sees a cat and calls it a dog, she is using available knowledge, the word *dog*, to make sense out of the world, in this case the cat that is walking across the living room. The process of assimilation sometimes leads to considerable distortion of incoming information, since we may have to "force-fit" it into our knowledge interpreted as implying a causal relationship. For example, because the faucet is on when Daddy shaves, the faucet causes his shaving.

Concrete Operational Period. Logical reasoning emerges in the concrete operational period. Children at this stage are capable of classifying objects into groups based on a logical principle, such as fruits or vegetables; mentally reversing actions; realizing that when changes in one perceptual dimension are compensated for by changes in another, nothing happens to the amount of material (conservation); and understanding the concept of transitivity (e.g., if A > B, and B > C, then A > C). The ability to solve problems remains very concrete, and children do not have an understanding of abstract concepts in anything other than concrete terms.

Formal Operational Period. For Piaget, the acquisition of formal operational thought during adolescence marks the end of cognitive development. Because he argues that formal operational thinking characterizes adult thought, we will consider this stage in some detail. Several theorists have commented on the characteristics of formal operational thought (e.g., Basseches, 1984; Commons & Richards, 1984; Kramer, 1983, 1987; Labouvie-Vief, 1980, 1981, 1984; Sinnott, 1984b). On the basis of these commentaries, we will focus on four aspects of formal operational thought: (1) it takes a hypothesis-testing approach termed hypothetico-deductive; (2) thinking is done in one framework at a time; (3) the goal is to arrive at one correct solution; and (4) it is unconstrained.

Piaget (1970) describes the essence of formal operational thought to be a way of conceiving abstract concepts and thinking about them in a very systematic, step-by-step way. Formal operational thought is governed by a generalized logical structure that provides solutions to problems that

people have never and may never encounter. **Hypothetico-deductive** thought is similar to the scientific method, in that it involves forming a hypothesis and testing it until it is either confirmed or rejected. Just as scientists are very systematic in testing experimental hypotheses, formal operational thinkers approach problems in a logical, methodical way.

Consider the situation when your car breaks down. When you take it for repairs, the mechanic forms hypotheses about what may be wrong, based on your description. The mechanic then begins to test each hypothesis systematically. For example, the compression of each cylinder may be checked, one cylinder at a time. It is this ability to hold other factors constant while testing a particular component that marks formal operational thought. By isolating causes of the problem, the thinker arrives at a correct solution.

The application of hypothetico-deductive thought occurs in *one framework*, or viewpoint, at a time (e.g., Labouvie-Vief, 1980, 1981, 1984; Sinnott, 1984b). What this means is that formal operational thinkers tend to analyze hypothetical problems from only one perspective. When they consider political issues such as abortion or nuclear disarmament, for example, they tend to take one side and work through it without drawing from the opposite side. It is not that they cannot change sides. Rather, it is that they cannot integrate aspects from more than one side during their attempts at thinking about a problem. Two good examples of the single-framework characteristic are debates and legal proceedings. In a formal debate and in court, each side tries to make its own case by arguing logically from one point of view. A defense attorney, for example, is not going to adopt the prosecutor's viewpoint and argue that the defendant is guilty as charged. Rather, the case will be presented from one perspective, the defense's.

When we use hypothetico-deductive thought,

we do so in order to arrive at *one unambiguous solution* to the problem (e.g., Labouvie-Vief, 1980, 1981, 1984; Labouvie-Vief, Adams, Hakim-Larson, Hayden, & Devoe, 1985). Formal operational thought is aimed at resolving ambiguity; one and only one answer is the goal. When more than one solution occurs, there is a feeling of uneasiness, and a search for clarification is begun. This situation can be observed in high school classes when students press their teacher to identify the "right" theory or the "right" way to view a social issue. Moreover, when an answer is obtained, there is a great deal of certainty over it, because it was arrived at through the use of logic. When answers are checked, the same logic and assumptions are typically used, which sometimes means that the same mistake is made several times in a row. For example, a simple subtraction error may be repeated time after time in trying to figure out why one's checkbook failed to balance.

Formal operational thinking knows no *constraints* (e.g., Labouvie-Vief, 1984; Piaget, 1970). It can be applied to real or imaginary situations. It is not bound by the limits of reality (Labouvie-Vief, 1980). Whether it is possible to carry out a solution is irrelevant; what matters is that one can think about it. This is how people arrive at solutions to disarmament, for example, such as getting rid of all nuclear warheads tomorrow. To the formal operational thinker, the fact that this solution is logistically impossible is no excuse. The lack of reality constraints is not all bad, however. Reasoning from a "why not" perspective may lead to the discovery of completely new ways to approach a problem or even to the invention of new solutions.

Developmental Trends in Piagetian Thought. Considerable research has been conducted examining the developmental course of Piagetian abilities (Reese & Rodeheaver, 1985). Overall, the results are quite mixed and difficult to interpret, largely because the majority of studies are cross-sectional, the procedures used have strayed considerably from those described by Piaget, and the scoring criteria for performance are not systematized (Reese & Rodeheaver, 1985). Nevertheless, some general conclusions can be drawn (Papalia & Bielby, 1974; Rabbitt, 1977; Reese & Rodeheaver, 1985). We will consider the findings from research on formal operations and on concrete operations.

One serious problem for Piaget's theory is that many adults apparently do not attain formal operations. Several studies report that only 60% to 75% of American adolescents can solve any formal operational problems (Neimark, 1975), and some estimate that no more than 30% of adults ever complete the transition to the highest levels of formal operational thought (Kuhn, Langer, Kohlberg, & Haan, 1977; Tomlinson-Keasey, 1972). Piaget (1972) himself admitted that formal operations were probably not universal but, rather, tended to appear only in those areas in which individuals were highly trained or specialized.

Research examining age differences on formal operational tasks has shown that older adults do not perform as well as younger adults (Clayton & Overton, 1973). Clayton and Overton also found that performance on the formal operations tasks was correlated with measures of fluid intelligence.

Extreme pessimism at these results may be unwarranted, however. Kuhn and her colleagues showed that as many as 94% percent of the adolescents in her research demonstrated formal operational thought after being given appropriate background and practice (Kuhn & Angelev, 1976; Kuhn, Ho, & Adams, 1979). Chandler notes that the lack of evidence for formal operations in the elderly may be more indicative of their lack of interest in doing formal operational problems than a lack of ability; older adults "generally dislike bookish, abstract, or childish tasks of low meaningfulness'' (1980, p. 82). Tomlinson-Keasey (1972) points out that attainment of the highest levels of formal operations may even depend on preference, as well as personal experience and the cognitive structures that are available. These results imply that the estimates of how many people attain formal operations may be misleading, that formal operational thought is used only in specialized situations, and that adults' thinking is not described very well by Piaget. We will develop this last alternative in more detail later.

Because cross-sectional studies of formal operations showed a general lack of these abilities in adults, much of the research has focused on the development of concrete operations. Two types of tasks have been used most frequently: classification tasks and conservation tasks. In general, the results from these investigations support Papalia and Bielby's (1974) conclusion that cognitive operations decline in the reverse order of their acquisition. That is, the highest, most complex abilities are the last to be acquired but the first to be lost. However, investigations of concrete operations are all cross-sectional and involve highly specialized tasks. Thus, conclusions about age differences must be made with these facts in mind.

Some studies have documented significant age differences between older adults and middle-aged adults in performance on classification tasks, with older adults being worse (e.g., Denney & Cornelius, 1975; Storck, Looft, & Hooper, 1972).

A much larger number of investigators have examined conservation abilities. Papalia (1972) found that conservation of substance, weight, and volume increased during childhood and declined in old age in the reverse order that they were acquired in childhood. Although her results have been confirmed by some (e.g., Papalia, Salverson, & True, 1973; Storck et al., 1972), other researchers have found little evidence for a regression in conservation abilities (e.g., Chance,

Overcast, & Dollinger, 1978; Eisner, 1973; Papalia-Finlay, Blackburn, Davis, Dellmann, & Roberts, 1980). Still other researchers have obtained very inconsistent results, with the age differences not mirroring any particular pattern (Hornblum & Overton, 1976; Hughston & Protinsky, 1978; Protinsky & Hughston, 1978).

Clearly, whether conservation abilities change across adulthood remains an open question. Attempts to explain the results by sex differences, educational level, intelligence, and even institutionalization have not succeeded (Reese & Rodeheaver, 1985). It may be that traditional concrete operations tasks, like traditional formal operations tasks, may not be interesting or challenging to older adults (Chandler, 1980).

Going Beyond Piaget: Postformal Thought

Consider the following problem (Labouvie-Vief et al., 1985, p. 13):

> John is known to be a heavy drinker, especially when he goes to parties. Mary, John's wife, warns him that if he gets drunk one more time, she will leave him and take the children. Tonight John is out late at an office party. John comes home drunk.
>
> Does Mary leave John? How certain are you of your answer?

When this and similar problems are presented to people of different ages, interesting differences emerge. Formal operational adolescents' responses clearly showed the ambiguity of the situation but also clearly reflected the need to search for the right answer. The ambiguity was considered a problem rather than an acceptable state of affairs. This is evident in the following answer:

> It's a good chance that she would leave him because she warns him that she will leave him and

take the children, but warning isn't an absolute thing. . . . And, I'd be absolutely sure that, well let's see . . . I'm trying to go all the way. I'm trying to think of putting everything [together] so I can be absolutely certain of an answer. . . . It's hard to be absolutely certain. "If he gets drunk, then she'll leave and take the children." I want to say yes 'cause everything's in that favor, in that direction, but I don't know how I can conclude that she does leave John. (Labouvie-Vief et al., 1985, pp. 17–18)

When adults were given the same problem, they handled it differently, for the most part. Their responses showed a combination of logic, emotion, and tolerance for ambiguity, as can be seen in the following example:

There was no right or wrong answer. You could get logically to both answers [yes or no]. . . . It depends on the steps they take to their answer. If they base it on what they feel, what they know, and they have certain steps to get an answer, it can be logical. (Labouvie-Vief et al., 1985, p. 41)

Based on a strict interpretation of formal operational thought, the adults who made responses like the second example showed little evidence of formal operational thinking. Thus, it could be argued that Labouvie-Vief et al.'s research supports the data described earlier that point to declines in formal operational thought across adulthood. But not everyone agrees that the research examining formal operational thinking across adulthood points to loss. Rather than concluding that differences in performance reflect declines in ability, the results are seen as indicative of another, qualitatively different, style of thinking. This latter interpretation implies that Piaget's theory may need modification. Specifically, it has been proposed that these performance differences on Piagetian tasks reflect cognitive development beyond formal operations.

Developmental Progressions in Adult Thought. According to several authors, Piaget's theory is limited in its ability to explain adult thinking (Basseches, 1984; Cavanaugh, Kramer, Sinnott, Camp, & Markley, 1985; Commons, Richards, & Kuhn, 1982; Labouvie-Vief, 1980, 1981; Riegel, 1973; Sinnott, 1984b). These writers point out that Piaget is concerned with describing logical, hypothetico-deductive thinking in his stage of formal operations but that this is not the only kind of thinking that adults do. In addition, they argue that Piaget's stage of formal operations is primarily limited to explaining how people arrive at one "correct" solution. How adults discover or generate new problems and how they sometimes appear to accept several possible solutions are not explained. Finally, the fact that adults often limit their thinking in response to social or other realistic constraints appears to be in conflict with the unconstrained generation of ideas characteristic of formal operations.

For these reasons it has been proposed that there is continued cognitive growth beyond formal operations (Commons, Richards, & Armon, 1984; Commons, Sinnott, Richards, & Armon, 1989). **Postformal thought**, as it is called, is characterized by a recognition that "truth" (the correct answer) varies from situation to situation, that solutions must be realistic in order to be reasonable, that ambiguity and contradiction are the rule rather than the exception, and that emotion and subjective factors usually play a role in thinking.

In one of the first investigations of cognitive growth beyond adolescence, Perry (1968) traced the development of thinking across the undergraduate years. He found that adolescents relied heavily on the expertise of authorities to determine what was right and wrong. At this point thinking is tightly bound by the rules of logic, and the only legitimate conclusions are those that are logically derived. For Perry, the continued development of thinking involves the development of increased cognitive flexibility. The first step in the process is a shift toward relativism. Relativism in thought refers to realizing that more than one explanation of a set of facts could be right, depending on one's point of view. Although relativism frees the individual from the constraints of a single framework, it also leads to skepticism. Because one can never be sure if one is right or wrong, the skeptic may not try to develop knowledge further, which may lead to feeling confused or adrift. Perry points out that the price of freeing oneself from the influence of authority is the loss of the certainty that came from relying on logic for all the answers.

In order to develop beyond skepticism, Perry showed, adults develop commitments to particular viewpoints. In Perry's later stages adults recognize that they are their own source of authority, that they must make a commitment to a position, and that others may hold different positions to which they will be equally committed. In other words mature thinkers are able to understand many perspectives on an issue, choose one, and still allow others the right to hold differing viewpoints. Thinking in this mature way is different from thinking in formal operational terms.

Several people have expanded on Perry's work. Arlin (1975) describes a type of thinking that she labels **problem finding**, to emphasize that for many adults finding and defining problems is a more accurate description of what they are doing. Sinnott (1984b) takes a slightly different approach. She concentrates on elaborating **relativistic thinking**, which is characterized by the realization that neither knowledge nor problem solutions are absolute or permanent. Rather, what is truth changes depending on the circumstances. Sinnott has shown that relativistic thinking occurs commonly in adulthood and is used on both hypothetical and everyday kinds of problems. Commons et al. (1982) identified a develop-

mental progression based on increasingly complex ways of integrating information. They found that adults improved with age in their ability to integrate information first within one system, then across multiple systems, and ultimately across more global systems.

Labouvie-Vief proposes that adult thinking is characterized not only by the acquisition of relativism but also by the integration of emotion with logic (Labouvie-Vief, 1980, 1981; Labouvie-Vief et al., 1985). She sees the main goal of adult thought as effectiveness in handling everyday life, rather than as the generation of all possible solutions. To her, adults make choices not so much on logical grounds but on pragmatic, emotional, and social grounds. Mature thinkers realize that thinking is a social phenomenon that demands making compromises and tolerating ambiguity and contradiction.

Consider what happens when two persons on opposite sides of an issue try to influence a neutral party. Each person argues that he or she arrived at a conclusion on the basis of a careful, logical analysis. But each debater will view the other's argument as irrational and wrong, despite the fact that neither position is actually "logically" wrong. Arguments tend to appear rational only to those who agree with the conclusion (Kitchener & King, 1989).

Labouvie-Vief (1980) argues that individuals understand this type of debate differently at different points in development. The formal operational thinker recognizes the conflict but insists that there is a logic-based way to prove which side is right. A young adult may be skeptical about both sides, since both make reasonable points (Perry, 1970). The mature thinker, however, not only recognizes the conflict but also sees that each position is based on an approach considered to be valid. The mature thinker then decides which side he or she believes to be more valid and adopts that view. When deciding what to do concerns the future, such as whether one should marry right now, then the position one takes is based on an abstract vision of what is possible (Labouvie-Vief & Lawrence, 1985). Because one may not be able to know for certain what to do, the mature thinker creates likely scenarios of what may happen and then decides what to do on that basis.

Research evidence for continued cognitive growth in adulthood is based mostly on interviews or verbal explanations of performance that are analyzed for evidence of postformal thinking. Evidence is accumulating that at least some adults engage in thinking that is characteristic of that described in the theoretical writings (e.g., Basseches, 1984; Commons et al., 1982; Labouvie-Vief et al., 1985; Sinnott, 1984b). For example, Blanchard-Fields (1986) presented stories about events by two participants holding different views about the events. Participants were asked about the contradictory viewpoints and how they would resolve them. Nearly all adults showed relativistic thinking, because they recognized that both viewpoints could be right, depending on one's perspective, and many of them also demonstrated commitment to one position. Adolescents, however, showed little evidence for either relativistic thought or commitment.

Whether the findings from research examining relativistic or other forms of postformal thought document qualitative cognitive growth is a topic of debate. For example, Kramer (1983) argues that it is possible to interpret relativistic and related thinking within Piaget's original framework. Her main point is that formal operations include the kinds of thinking described in the postformal literature. For instance, constraining possible solutions to only those that are realistic is simply a subset of generating all possible solutions, a defining characteristic of formal operational thought. Consequently, adult thinking may be different from adolescent thinking, but arguing for additional stages is not necessary.

Cavanaugh and Stafford (1989) point out that because the roles of experience and education are not understood and because the measures of postformal thought vary considerably from study to study, firm conclusions on the nature of adult cognitive development may be premature.

Perhaps the best conclusion is that the notion of possible stages of cognitive development beyond formal operations is intriguing and has focused our attention on the existence of different styles of thinking across adulthood. However, the evidence supporting a separate stage is limited and is open to different interpretations, emphasizing the need for caution. As pointed out in "Something to Think About," however, the resolution of this debate may have important practical implications.

Schaie's Theory

Although Piaget's theory is the best known and most researched cognitive-process approach to intellectual development, it is not the only one. Moreover, Piaget's theory does not appeal to many psychologists who focus on adult development, because the theory is strongly child-oriented. They want to modify it, as we have seen, to reflect the kinds of thinking that adults really do. Another approach is to not use Piaget at all; it is an example of this kind of stage theory to which we now turn.

Schaie (1977–1978) offers one alternative based on his research on adult intellectual development. His stages describe changes across the life span (see Figure 6.6). He suggests that during childhood and adolescence the focus is on the acquisition of information and problem-solving skills. He contends that Piaget's theory is an example of a theory that explains this process. He also feels that it is unlikely that we continue to develop more sophisticated ways to learn beyond those described by Piaget. Therefore, if we are to

---

SOMETHING · TO · THINK · ABOUT

Practical Implications of Cognitive Stages

One of the most important questions we can ask about stage theories of cognitive development is whether the stages make a difference in human interaction. The answer to this question appears to be yes. When two persons who think at different levels try to interact, there may be a greater possibility for misunderstanding than when they operate at the same cognitive level.

Let us consider a situation in which a parent is dealing with an adolescent. Here we have the possibility of postformal thought coming into conflict with formal operational thought. Due to the nature of each mode of thinking, it is unlikely that the formal operational individual would concede to the wishes of the other if there was a sharp difference of opinion. It may be up to the postformal individual to capitalize on his or her ability to see situations from multiple perspectives and frame the situation in a way compatible with the formal thinker. Moreover, the formal thinker would be less persuaded by an emotional argument than by a logical argument.

Think of other situations in your own life when you have had sharp disagreements with others. Was one reason for the disagreement a result of the way in which you both thought about the problem? How could you get around the limitations in thinking? How could you develop a strategy that would work with people of different levels of cognitive development? It's something to think about.

---

understand what happens during adulthood, Schaie believes, we must shift our focus from how knowledge is acquired to how it is used.

As individuals pass into young adulthood, they are no longer in a position to concentrate primarily on acquiring skills. As people begin careers and families, they concentrate more on achieving their goals. But to do so means that they must apply their knowledge to real-world problems, which involve social as well as abstract cognitive skills that are not measured well by most standardized intelligence tests. Schaie suggests that cognitive and social functioning begin to merge even more than in the past. Intellectual performance is likely to be best when tasks have, in his terms, "role-related achievement potential"; in other words, we do better on tasks when

we are committed to them. Finally, a key theme in young adulthood is learning how to monitor oneself, keeping track of how things are going and how much progress is being made toward goals that may be years away.

During middle age, Schaie believes, the emphasis shifts again. Once the person has become competent and independent, he or she is in a position to assume responsibility for others. Covering the time from the late 30s to the early 60s, this stage involves learning to appreciate the effects that one's own problem solutions have on one's family and friends. Part of this realization comes from the need for many people to develop what Neugarten (1969) calls "executive abilities." These involve understanding how an organization works. When you are responsible for developing a

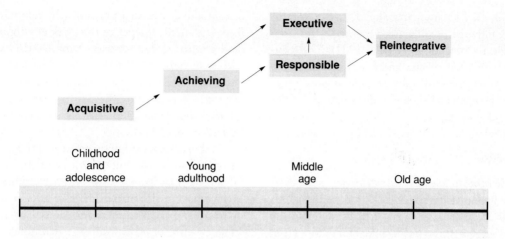

FIGURE 6.6 • Schaie's stages of cognitive development
(Source: "Toward a Stage Theory of Adult Cognitive Development" by K. W. Shaie, 1977–1978, *Journal of Aging and Human Development, 8*, pp. 129–138. Copyright 1977 by Baywood Publishing Co., Inc. Reprinted with permission of the author.)

solution to a marketing problem, for example, both subordinates and superiors need to be kept informed of the progress, because they are affected by the decisions. Finally, it is often during middle age that people become involved in socially responsible organizations at work (e.g., unions) and the community (e.g., the PTA).

Later in life the need to acquire new skills or to monitor the effects of decisions decreases. The future seems shorter, and retirement eliminates the need to deal with these effects. What happens now is a reintegration of intellectual abilities into a simpler form. The emphasis is on remaining intellectually involved in meaningful situations. In Schaie's words this stage "completes the transition from 'what should I know?' through the 'how should I use what I know?' to the 'why should I know?' phase of life" (1977–1978, p. 135). Intellectual endeavors in later life are influenced by motivational and attitudinal considerations more than at any other time.

In sum, Schaie's model is a competency-based

approach to adult intellectual development. Standardized intelligence tests do not measure his stages very well. Consequently, little research has been done on his framework (Schaie, 1979). Still, his approach makes intuitive sense and stands as one of the few attempts to describe intellectual development from a life-span perspective. Once new assessment instruments are developed, it is likely that more work will be done on this framework.

ADAPTING TO INTELLECTUAL CHANGE

Throughout this chapter we have focused on major theories of intellectual development. An emerging theme in research on cognitive development in adulthood and old age is an emphasis on special forms of intellectual growth in adulthood: expertise and wisdom. This research is not formally tied to any particular theory of intelligence; rather, it is influenced mainly by research in cognitive psychology (Hoyer, 1984). The focus is on both what people know and how they use their knowledge to solve problems—in other words, how adults become more adaptive in their day-to-day world.

Expertise

An idea that underlies such disparate notions as crystallized intelligence and postformal thought is that in some sense what one knows increases the older one gets. It is typically taken for granted that how much one knows about fixing automobile engines, for example, depends on how much experience one has had in doing it. This simple idea has been picked up by several researchers and translated into the general question of how experience, and the expertise that results, influences adult intellectual development.

Cognitive psychologists interested in **expertise** focus on the development of the knowledge system (e.g., J. R. Anderson, 1982). Our knowledge in a specific domain, such as chess, consists of both what pieces move in what ways, termed **declarative knowledge**, and of strategies that typically lead to victory, termed **procedural knowledge**. Declarative knowledge, knowing what, and procedural knowledge, knowing how, both increase with practice and experience in most situations.

A particularly interesting area of research on expertise is professional knowledge and productivity (e.g., Birren, 1969; Featherman, 1980; Kohn & Schooler, 1978, 1982). Research on expertise demonstrates that older adults in good health and in supportive environments have the capacity to maintain or increase high levels of functioning in select areas, usually their areas of specialization (Dixon, Kramer, & Baltes, 1985).

Longitudinal investigations into the relationship between characteristics of the work environment and cognitive functioning support this view (Kohn & Schooler, 1978, 1982). The level and rate of intellectual development during adulthood appear to vary as a function of the cognitive complexity and demands of the work environment (Dixon et al., 1985).

Perhaps the most important aspect of research on expertise is that knowing a great deal about something may help compensate for declines in some underlying cognitive processes. As we noted in Chapter 4 concerning typing, as well as in this chapter with regard to training, maintenance of skills appears to be partly a matter of keeping knowledge, and intellectual abilities, current.

Wisdom

The idea that old people are wise has been around for a very long time. It is also an idea that appears in many different societies and cultures (see Chapter 10). Kekes (1983) notes that **wisdom** is a kind of interpretive knowledge that combines breadth and depth. The wise person is one who understands the significance of what is commonly known. Subsumed by wisdom is good judgment regarding how to conduct one's life and a thorough understanding of one's potentials and limitations. There is also a belief that wisdom can be acquired only through life experience; it cannot be taught.

Dittmann-Kohli and Baltes (in press) draw on earlier work on the development of wisdom across adulthood (Clayton, 1975, 1982; Clayton & Birren, 1980; Meacham, 1982b) and define it as "good judgment about important but uncertain matters in life." Dittmann-Kohli and Baltes offer several signs that can be used to identify and assess wisdom: (1) an expertise in the pragmatic aspects of daily living; (2) understanding of the significance of a

Young people have much to gain from taking advantage of the wisdom of the old.

content domain; (3) breadth of ability to define and solve problems; (4) recognition of the complexity, difficulty, and uncertainty in problems; and (5) good, practical judgment.

Approaching wisdom as being an expert in living necessarily implies that it takes years of life experiences to become wise. Living into old age may be the best way to achieve it.

SUMMARY

Three ways to understand intellectual development were discussed: the psychometric approach, the neofunctionalist approach, and cognitive-process approaches.

The psychometric approach is mainly concerned with understanding the interrelationships among performances on intelligence tests. Pri-

mary mental abilities are those that have been identified by interrelating performances on tests. It appears that the primary mental abilities decline noticeably after age 60; however, there is evidence that the decline may begin earlier. Second-order mental abilities represent relationships among the primary abilities. Two second-order abilities have been heavily researched. Crystallized intelligence represents experiential knowledge and does not normally decline with age. Fluid intelligence represents innate abilities and appears to decline normally with age. Several mediators of intellectual development have been identified. Among these are cohort differences, educational level, occupation, personality, health and life-style, mindlessness, and the relevancy and appropriateness of tasks. Several studies have documented that adults' intelligence is not fixed. Most important is the evidence that primary abilities can be increased through training. These results offer the possibility of slowing or perhaps eliminating the decline in some primary abilities.

The neofunctionalist approach grew out of a reaction to the psychometric approach based on a reinterpretation of its research. Four concepts are central to the neofunctionalist approach: plasticity, multidimensionality, multidirectionality, and interindividual variability. Two interrelated types of developmental processes are postulated: cognition as basic processes and pragmatic intelligence. The emphasis in the neofunctionalist approach is that intelligence theory must relate to people's everyday lives. Related to this idea is the notion that some abilities are untrained, or unpracticed, and show decline with age, whereas others are optimally exercised and show more stability until old age.

The cognitive approaches include Piaget's theory and its extensions as well as Schaie's theory. Piaget argues that one's cognitive structures develop in a stagelike fashion based on the principles of adaptation and organization. He contends that cognitive structure does not change qualitatively in adulthood, meaning that formal operations is the end point of development. Evidence on the theory is mixed. Some theorists have interpreted the different kinds of thinking that are sometimes seen in adults as evidence for postformal cognitive development. Postformal thought is characterized by an increasing realization of the relative nature of truth and an increasing tolerance of ambiguity. Schaie's theory is based on what he thinks are the main ways in which intelligence is used across the life span. He maintains that we go from acquisition (in childhood) to achieving and responsibility (in adulthood) to reintegration (in old age).

Research on expertise and wisdom has emphasized two adaptive dimensions of intellectual growth. Expertise appears to increase across adulthood and may depend on the cognitive complexity and demands of the work environment. Wisdom is viewed as expertise in living, making it something that is acquired through life experience.

GLOSSARY

accommodation • For Piaget, adjustments made to cognitive structures to make them correspond better to the external world.

adaptation • For Piaget, the process of adjusting to the environment.

assimilation • For Piaget, the use of existing cognitive structures to understand incoming information.

cognitive-process approach • A view of intelligence that emphasizes thought processes rather than performance.

cognitive structures • For Piaget, the fundamental ways in which we think.

crystallized intelligence • A second-order mental ability reflecting a person's knowledge acquired through experience.

declarative knowledge • Knowing facts.

expertise • State in which a high level of domain-specific knowledge is available.

factor • In the psychometric approach, abilities that are related to one another.

fluid intelligence • A second-order mental ability reflecting a person's innate learning skill.

hypothetico-deductive • In formal operations, the property of thought involving the logical testing of hypotheses.

interindividual variability • In the neofunctionalist approach, differences in people in the direction of their development.

mindful level • Cognitive processing that we are aware of.

mindless level • Cognitive processing occurring below conscious awareness.

multidimensionality • In the neofunctionalist approach, the notion that intelligence consists of many abilities with distinct structures.

multidirectionality • In the neofunctionalist approach, the distinct patterns of change in abilities over time.

neofunctionalist approach • A view of intelligence that emphasizes individual differences and plasticity.

optimally exercised ability • A skill that an adult would exhibit under the best conditions of practice, or learning.

organization • For Piaget, how the organism's mental processes are grouped together.

plasticity • In the neofunctionalist approach, the range of intraindividual functioning and the degree to which abilities can be modified.

postformal thought • Thinking that goes beyond the limits of formal operations.

primary mental abilities • In the psychometric approach, first-order abilities that are based on relationships among test performances.

problem finding • A type of thinking characteristic of postformal thought.

procedural knowledge • Knowing how to do things.

psychometric approach • A view of intelligence that emphasizes performance on standardized tests.

relativistic thinking • A type of postformal thought in which knowledge and solutions are viewed as depending on the situation.

second-order mental abilities • In the psychometric approach, broad-range abilities based on interrelationships among primary mental abilities.

structure • In the psychometric approach, the organization of intellectual abilities.

untrained ability • A skill that an adult would exhibit under conditions of no learning or practice.

wisdom • Knowledge about life that is broad and deep.

ADDITIONAL READING

An excellent review of the psychometric approach and a discussion of developmental trends in psychometric intelligence can be found in

Horn, J. L. (1982). The aging of human abilities. In B. B. Wolman (Ed.), *Handbook of developmental psychology* (pp. 847–870). Englewood Cliffs, NJ: Prentice-Hall.

Schaie, K. W. (1983). The Seattle Longitudinal Study: A twenty-one year exploration of psychometric intelligence in adulthood. In K. W. Schaie (Ed.), *Longitudinal studies of adult psychological development* (pp. 64–135). New York: Guilford.

A summary of the neofunctionalist perspective can be found in

Baltes, P. B., Dittmann-Kohli, & Dixon, R. A. (1984). New perspectives on the development of intelligence in adulthood: Toward a dual-process conception and a model of selective optimization with compensation. In P. B. Baltes & O. G. Brim, Jr. (Eds.), *Life-span development and behavior: Vol. 6* (pp. 33–76). New York: Academic Press.

Two excellent sources for descriptions of postformal thought are

Commons, M. L., Richards, F. A., & Armon, C. (Eds.). (1984). *Beyond formal operations: Vol. 1. Late adolescent and adult cognitive development.* New York: Praeger.

Commons, M. L., Sinnott, J. D., Richards, F. A., & Armon, C. (Eds.). (1989). *Beyond formal operations: Vol. 2. Comparisons and applications of adolescent and adult developmental models.* New York: Praeger.

Memory

Andrew Wyeth, *Children's Doctor*, 1949. Brandywine River Museum, Chadds Ford, Pennsylvania.

MEMORY IS SUCH A PERVASIVE ASPECT OF our daily lives that we take it for granted. From remembering where you keep your toothbrush to tying your shoes to timing soft-boiled eggs, memory is always with you. Moreover, it even gives you a sense of identity. Imagine how frightening it would be to wake up and have no memory whatsoever. No recollection of your name, address, who your parents were, or anything else. As pointed out in "Something to Think About," memory is indispensable.

Perhaps that is why we put so much value on maintaining a good memory in old age. Society views memory as the yardstick with which to measure whether a person's mind is intact. It stereotypes older adults as people whose memory is on the decline, people for whom forgetting is not to be taken lightly. Forgetting a loaf of bread when one is 25 is all right. Forgetting it when one is 65 is cause for concern ("Do I have Alzheimer's disease?"). Thus, we have more at stake here than just another cognitive process. We may be dealing with something that intimately involves our sense of self (Cavanaugh, Morton, & Tilse, 1989).

It is difficult to get an overview of the research on aging and memory, as we could for intellectual aging. The main problem is a lack of clearly defined theories to guide research. Although many researchers have adopted an information-processing framework, this approach does not make explicit predictions about the development of memory. Consequently, much of the research on aging and memory is conducted outside of theory. Additionally, some researchers focus on how underlying memory processes differ across age groups, whereas others are more concerned with age differences in the ways in which people use memory in everyday life.

In this chapter we will take a close look at memory from several vantage points. First, we will adopt an information-processing model of memory and consider evidence about age-related differences in each aspect of the model. Next, we will examine more closely the research on age differences in people's ability to get information into memory and subsequently get it back out. Then, we will consider two important domains in which people use memory: discourse and everyday life. From there we will move to how adults evaluate their memory abilities and will consider such topics as metamemory and memory attributions. Finally, we will survey the literature on clinical applications of memory research, with special emphasis on assessment of memory problems.

STRUCTURAL ASPECTS OF MEMORY

Theorists agree that memory is a process that consists of several different ways of bringing information in, transforming it, and getting it back out. Beyond agreement at this general level, however,

SOMETHING · TO · THINK · ABOUT

What Is Memory For?

As noted in the text, memory plays a pervasive role in our everyday lives. We take for granted all of the things we use memory for and seldom pause to marvel at how well it works most of the time. One of the things that we often fail to ask is what functions memory serves.

Most of the research described in this chapter views memory as an end in itself. That is, people are given the task of learning and remembering some material, and that is it. Doing well on the memory test is the name of the game. Indeed, there are many situations in life that present similar demands. We may need to have considerable information at our fingertips in order to answer questions after a presentation, for example.

But many situations in everyday life call for the use of memory to serve some other function. That is, we use memory as a means to an end. For example, we use memory when we summarize the most recent episode of our favorite soap opera, tell other people about ourselves, or reminisce about our high school days. In these situations we are using memory, for sure, but the point is not just how much we remember. More often, the idea is to facilitate social exchange, to allow other people to get to know us, or to give ourselves a shared past with others.

These different uses of memory raise some intriguing questions about adult development and aging. Is it possible that there may be differences in the ways in which adults of different ages use memory? How would these differences affect performance on traditional memory tests? What should our criteria be for good versus poor memory? These questions are something to think about as we explore what has been discovered about aging and memory.

---

they differ considerably in how they conceptualize the structure of memory. Most adopt an information-processing approach that builds on the ideas presented in Chapter 5. That is, they view memory as consisting of several discrete components, much as a computer does. Others adopt viewpoints that represent memory as consisting of different levels, propositional networks, schemata, and other related ideas. Because the information-processing view has had the biggest impact on memory research, we will focus on it.

The information-processing approach to memory is based on three assumptions (Neisser, 1976): (1) the individual is an active participant in the process, (2) both quantitative and qualitative aspects of memory performance can be examined, and (3) information is processed through a series of hypothetical stages, or stores. These memory stores are a sensory memory for each sensory modality, a short-term primary memory, a working memory, a longer-term secondary memory, and a relatively permanent tertiary memory.

Using an information-processing model of memory raises two fundamental questions for adult development and aging: (1) Is there evidence of age-related differences in the structural components, or stores? (2) Are the differences observed in the components due to changes in

Using external memory aids such as recipe cards is an effective and efficient way to help oneself remember.

how people bring information in, how they get information out, or both? In this section we will briefly consider the first question and look at the evidence for age differences in each of the components. We will take up the second question a bit later.

Sensory Memory

The earliest step in memory processing is **sensory memory**, where new, incoming information is registered. How this information gets picked up from the environment by the different sensory systems and the pattern of age differences in these abilities were described in Chapter 5. The data suggest a small decrement in ability with age, which appears to be attributable to a slowing of information processing. Although these small decrements cannot explain the much larger age-related declines observed in other aspects of memory, they may be part of a cumulative influence that does significantly affect performance. That is, the small changes in sensory memory may combine with small changes in other early aspects of memory to ultimately create a large difference in later stages. However, we need more research on sensory memory before we can conclude that a cumulative process is, indeed, occurring.

Primary Memory

Imagine yourself standing in a phone booth in a distant airport. You look up the number of an old friend you want to meet for lunch. Once you find it, you say it a few times, insert the money, and dial it before it slips out of your mind. This scenario describes one of the more common experiences of primary memory. Stated more formally,

primary memory is a short-lived, limited-capacity store in which information is still "in mind" while it is being used (Poon, 1985).

Because primary memory is a temporary, small-capacity store, most developmental research has examined possible changes with age in capacity and retention rate. Considerable evidence has shown little if any change in primary memory (Craik, 1977; Fozard, 1980; Poon, 1985). In terms of capacity, most studies find no differences in digit span (e.g., Craik, 1968), and even those that do (e.g., Botwinick & Storandt, 1974) find only a minimal difference. How efficiently information can be retrieved from sensory memory also shows no difference with age (e.g., Poon & Fozard, 1980; A. D. Smith, 1975). The only age difference consistently reported is in how fast information is retrieved from primary memory. Older adults tend to take slightly longer to recall the most recently presented items on a list (e.g., Waugh, Thomas, & Fozard, 1978).

These findings for primary memory again raise the possibility that a cumulative process is occurring. The small decrements in primary memory may compound small decrements in sensory memory, resulting in a relatively more important influence on subsequent processing than that for each one separately. Again, we need more research examining these compound effects before we will be able to draw firm conclusions.

Working Memory

A theoretical construct that is growing in popularity is working memory. **Working memory** is viewed as a small-capacity store in which the items that are currently being processed reside (Kausler, 1985). In working memory information may be subjected to some manipulation, as in mentally reversing a string of digits and stating them backwards. The most important way in which information is held in working memory is through **rehearsal**, involving either rote repetition or making more extensive connections between the information in working memory and information already contained in memory (Craik & Lockhart, 1972; Kausler, 1985).

There is growing evidence that the capacity of working memory declines somewhat with age (Light, Zelinski, & Moore, 1982; Parkinson, Lindholm, & Inman, 1982; Wright, 1981), although the extent of the decline is still in doubt. More important, perhaps, is the age-related decline in rehearsal that results in poorer quality information being passed along the system (Kausler, 1985). That is, older adults' ability to keep information in working memory may decline, as may their ability to pass incoming information from working memory to later steps in the process. Although working memory per se has not been the focus of as much adult developmental research as other aspects of memory, it is likely that it will become an important explanatory concept in the future.

Secondary Memory

Secondary memory refers to what many people regard as the "bread and butter" of memory, the ability to remember rather extensive amounts of information over relatively long periods. Everyday life is full of examples: remembering routines, performing on an exam, summarizing a book or movie, and remembering an appointment. Memory researchers have adapted these examples and created a wide variety of tasks requiring individuals to remember long lists of information. These everyday and research-based examples are indications that secondary memory represents a very-large-capacity store in which information can be kept for long periods.

Because secondary memory includes so many of the day-to-day activities we adults perform, it has been the focus of more research than any other

Activities such as spinning involve retrieving elaborate memory representations for each aspect of the activity as well as accurately monitoring what one is doing.

single topic in memory development (Poon, 1985). In this section we will briefly survey the evidence concerning age differences in secondary-memory performance. We will reconsider many of these points when we examine age differences in storage and retrieval.

Typically, secondary memory is studied by having people learn a list of items and then asking them to recall or recognize the items. **Recall** is obtained by asking the person to remember as much of the to-be-learned material as possible. Everyday examples of recall include telling everything that you can remember about a movie or taking an essay exam. **Recognition** is tested by asking the person to pick out items that were learned from a longer list that includes both the target items and distractor items. Experimental manipulation is done to examine the variables

that influence secondary-memory performance. Researchers vary in how the to-be-learned items are presented (e.g., in organized groups, with cues, or randomly); the speed at which they are presented; the familiarity of the material; and the conditions for remembering the items (e.g., presenting recall cues or making a recognition test easy or hard).

The results from hundreds of studies that have examined age differences in secondary memory point to several conclusions. Overall, older adults perform worse than younger adults on tests of recall, but these differences are less apparent or may be eliminated on tests of recognition (Poon, 1985). Older adults also tend to be less efficient at spontaneously using strategies such as elaboration and putting items into categories to organize information during study. When older adults are instructed to use organizational strategies, however, they not only can do so but also show significant improvement in performance (Smith, 1980). These findings suggest that older adults are not as good in situations requiring them to devise an efficient way to acquire disorganized information, especially when they will be expected to recall it later. When environmental supports are provided during initial learning or at recall or when memory is tested through recognition, older adults benefit considerably.

Smaller age differences between younger and older adults have also been noted when the pacing of the experiment is slower (Canestrari, 1963). Older adults perform better when they, rather than the experimenter, pace the task. This finding fits well with the notion that aging brings a slowing in information processing (Salthouse, 1985; see also Chapter 5). Additionally, practice on the memory task results in a substantial improvement in older adults' performance (Treat, Poon, & Fozard, 1981), as does having people engage in a related task before learning the list of items (Hultsch, 1971). Better memory performance after practice parallels similar improvements following practice on tests of skills related to fluid intelligence (see Chapter 6). Finally, using material that is more familiar to older adults also improves their performance (Barrett & Wright, 1981; Hanley-Dunn & McIntosh, 1984).

Not all of the factors that influence secondary-memory performance are due to experimental manipulations. It also appears that at least one personal-ability factor plays a role: vocabulary level. In a study of recognition Bowles and Poon (1982) found no age difference between young and old groups who had a high vocabulary level, but there was a significant difference in favor of younger adults in groups with a low vocabulary level. Although it is still unclear why older adults with high vocabulary levels perform better, it may be

that they use memory skills to build extensive vocabularies. In any event, we will return to this intriguing finding later when we consider similar results in memory for discourse.

What, then, can we conclude about secondary memory? It appears that older adults are disadvantaged when left on their own to face relatively rapid-paced, disorganized information. However, secondary-memory performance appears to be quite flexible and manipulable, with improvements coming from a variety of sources. In later sections we will consider some attempts to explain why age differences occur and several ways in which secondary-memory problems can be corrected.

Tertiary Memory

Information for very-long-term storage is housed in **tertiary memory**. Such information includes facts learned earlier, the meaning of words, past life experiences, and the like. Very little research has been conducted on age differences in tertiary memory, for a variety of reasons. For one thing it is difficult to design an adequate test of very-long-term memory so that we know how to interpret performance. For example, we often cannot know whether an incident that someone recalls from the past is what actually happened, because we cannot verify the facts. Additionally, if a person does not remember a fact from years past, it may be due to an inability to retrieve the information or to a failure to have learned the information in the first place.

One way that tertiary memory is tested is with questionnaires asking about events of public knowledge assumed to be available to everyone. A typical question would be to ask for the name of the spacecraft that exploded after launching in January 1986. Researchers who have examined adults' performance on tests of knowledge about the Challenger disaster and other events find little difference in performance across age groups (e.g., Botwinick & Storandt, 1974; J. L. Lachman & Lachman, 1980; Perlmutter, Metzger, Miller, & Nezworski, 1980; Poon, Fozard, Paulshock, & Thomas, 1979; Warrington & Sanders, 1971). Camp (1989) has conducted considerable research on people's ability to combine pieces of tertiary memory and answer inference questions. He has participants answer inference questions such as what horror movie character would want to avoid the Lone Ranger. Camp finds that older adults respond with the werewolf (who can be killed only with silver bullets, the Lone Ranger's trademark) as well as, and often better than, young adults.

One demonstration of how good tertiary memory can be is a study by Bahrick, Bahrick, and Wittlinger (1975). They tested high school graduates aged 17 to 74 for recall of their classmates' names and recognition of their faces in yearbook pictures. Recognition of faces was consistently over 90% up to 15 years after graduation. Amazingly, adults in their 70s could still recognize 70% of their classmates' names 48 years after graduation! Clearly, tertiary memory remains fairly good. The study also demonstrates that in some areas it is possible to assess the accuracy of very-long-term memory. Being able to verify what individuals remember with some record of the "true" event is extremely important in evaluating our ability to remember over long periods of time.

The lack of age differences in tertiary memory is not really surprising. The information we keep in tertiary memory is very similar to the information that relates to crystallized intelligence, such as world knowledge and vocabulary. As pointed out in Chapter 6, crystallized intelligence undergoes little if any decrement with age. Thus, it may be that tertiary memory is also related to this set of abilities.

SOURCES OF AGE DIFFERENCES: STORAGE AND RETRIEVAL PROCESSES

Thus far, we have established that at least in some aspects of memory there are substantial differences between older and younger adults. For the most part these differences favor the young. But an important question that we have ignored concerns how these differences come about. Are older adults poorer at getting information into memory? Or do they get the information in just as well but have more difficulty getting it back out? Or is the problem a combination of the two?

Traditionally, memory researchers have tried to answer these questions by proposing three processes: encoding (the act of bringing information in and transforming it), storage (the act of putting and keeping information in one of the memory stores), and retrieval (the act of finding and reporting information that has been stored). These processes, combined with the components of the information-processing model, were thought to describe the entire memory system.

In the past few years, however, memory researchers have learned that a two-stage model does as good a job (Howe, 1988). In the two-stage model the concepts of encoding and storage are not considered separately but as one process, called **storage**. The second process is termed **retrieval**. In this view storage entails getting information in, while retrieval entails getting information out. In the two-stage model performance passes through three states (Howe, 1988): (1) an "unmemorized" state, in which information has not yet been learned; (2) a "partially memorized" state, in which the information is sometimes remembered and sometimes forgotten; and (3) a "memorized" state, in which the information is always remembered. Additionally, two general retrieval processes are distinguished. **Heuristic retrieval** is any recovery process that produces both successes and failures; retracing one's steps to find lost keys produces several failures (looking in the wrong spot) but may produce the keys as well. Heuristic retrieval is used when information has been only partly learned. **Algorithmic retrieval** is any recovery process that produces error-free performance; using a distinctive tag or cue to remember information is an example. Algorithmic retrieval is used when information has been learned very well.

For many years memory researchers have tried to identify whether age differences are due primarily to storage problems, retrieval problems, or both. In the following sections we will briefly consider the evidence.

Age Differences in Storage

Results from several lines of research point to a clear age-related decrement in storage processes (Craik, 1977; Kausler, 1982; Poon, 1985). One major line of work has focused on the use of memory strategies to improve the efficiency of storage, and another has examined how deeply incoming information is processed. A third approach focuses on a different issue and attempts to separate various aspects of storage.

The Use of Strategies. When confronted with large amounts of information that we need to remember, we tend to use various techniques that reduce the difficulty of the task and increase the efficiency of storage. These techniques that make getting information in easier are collectively referred to as **strategies**.

One extremely effective strategy for learning new information is to organize it. For example, consider your efforts to learn the information in courses in college. It is much easier to learn the necessary facts of chemistry, psychology, literature, and so forth if you keep separate notebooks for each class. Imagine the potential for confusion if you simply mixed all of the class notes together. There is substantial evidence that older adults do not spontaneously organize incoming information as often or as well as younger adults (Craik, 1977; Craik & Rabinowitz, 1984; Kausler, 1982). For example, older adults are less likely to take advantage of similarities in meaning (e.g., between *river* and *lake*) among words presented randomly in a list as a way to organize the items for more efficient learning (Denney, 1974). Because the number of items remembered from such a list is highly related to the use of organization, younger adults outperform older adults on such tasks. Interestingly, older adults can use organization if they are told to do so (Schmitt, Murphy, & Sanders, 1981) or are experienced with sorting words into categories (Hultsch, 1971); see Figure 7.1. However, the results of these manipulations are often short lived; older adults tend not to continue using organization over the long run.

The frequency of spontaneous use of other strategies also appears to decrease with age. For example, older adults are less likely to use imagery (forming pictures of items in one's mind) and other mnemonics (e.g., using the first letters of items to form a word, such as *NASA*) (Kausler, 1982). When explicitly instructed to do so, however, older adults can use many types of strategies. Moreover, their performance improves significantly compared with that of older adults who are not instructed.

Specific Components of Storage. Based on these findings, it is clear that there is an age-related decrement in storage processes. However, is it the case that all aspects of storage processes show this decrement, or is it more apparent in some than in others?

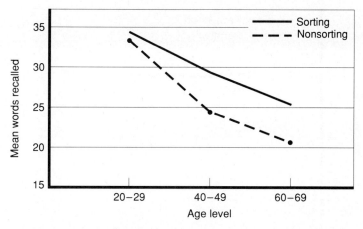

FIGURE 7.1 • Mean number of words correctly recalled, as a function of age and sorting condition

(Source: "Adult Age Differences in Free Classification and Free Recall" by D. F. Hultsch, 1971, *Developmental Psychology, 4,* pp. 338–342. Copyright 1971 by the American Psychological Association. Reprinted with permission of the author.)

In a series of studies Howe (1988) showed that the age-related decrement in storage processes is localized in making connections between incoming information and information that was previously stored in memory. Older adults have more difficulty making these connections than do younger adults. Once these connections have been made, however, older and younger adults are equivalent in maintaining them.

Howe's results may relate to differences we noted earlier concerning working memory. Recall that some researchers point to working memory as the step where rehearsal processes allow links to be made between incoming and previously stored information. In any event we must be careful not to conclude that the entire storage process deteriorates with age. Rather, some aspects are probably more sensitive to age-related alterations than others.

Age Differences in Retrieval

Once we get information stored, we may at some point need to find it again. Many researchers have shown that older adults have more difficulty retrieving information than do younger adults (Burke & Light, 1981; Craik, 1977; Kausler, 1982; Poon, 1985). Most of this research comes from two areas: (1) comparisons of recall and recognition performances and (2) studies of enhanced retrieval conditions. Additionally, some evidence localizing the retrieval decrement is available.

Recall Versus Recognition. As noted earlier, in the discussion of secondary memory, two types of retrieval tests are typically used in research. In free-recall tests no cues are given; a person is simply asked to remember all of the items on a list,

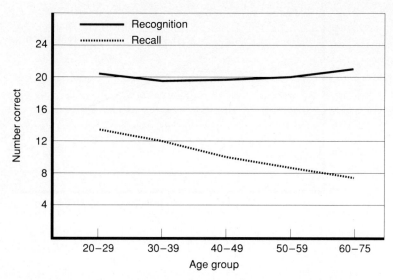

FIGURE 7.2 • Recall and recognition scores, as a function of age

(Source: "Memory Storage and Aging" by D. Schonfield and B. A. Robertson, 1966, *Canadian Journal of Psychology, 20,* pp. 228–236. Copyright 1966 by the Canadian Psychological Association. Reprinted with permission.)

for example. Recall tests are thought to place heavy demands on the retrieval process, because all of the guidance for finding the correct information must be self-generated. In contrast, recognition involves picking the newly learned item from a list of both newly learned and distractor items. Because the environment provides considerable help, recognition tests are thought to place fewer demands on retrieval processes.

Studies consistently show substantial age differences on recall tests but small or nonexistent differences on recognition tests (Poon, 1985) (see Figure 7.2). These performance differences are interpreted as evidence that older adults have less effective retrieval processes when they must generate their own retrieval cues. When help is provided, such as in recognition tests, older adults' performance improves.

Enhanced Retrieval Conditions. In addition to recall and recognition tests, there are other ways to get at the ways in which retrieval cues help people remember. For example, it is possible to provide cues in a recall task. **Cued recall** involves providing some hint, or aid, within the general constraints of a recall test. Asking a person to remember all of the fruits in a word list or to recall that the capital of Nepal begins with the letter *K* are examples. Older adults benefit relative to younger adults in cued recall compared with free recall; overall, age differences are reduced but not eliminated (A. D. Smith, 1977).

Specific Components of Retrieval. As noted in the discussion of storage, an important issue is whether age differences are equivalent for all aspects of retrieval. Apparently, they are not. Howe

(1988) has documented that age differences are substantially greater for algorithmic retrieval than for heuristic retrieval. This indicates that younger adults may be better than older adults at retrieving a specific piece of information correctly, but both age groups are just as good at using general retrieval strategies that do not guarantee success.

Relative Contributions of Storage and Retrieval Differences

It should be clear from this discussion that younger adults find it easier than older adults to store incoming information and to retrieve it later. But this difference still leaves two questions unresolved: Are changes in memory with age primarily the result of decrements in storage, in retrieval, or in both? If both processes are responsible, then do both decline at the same rate? Based on the available evidence, the answers are that (1) changes in memory with aging are a consequence of decrements in both storage and retrieval, (2) these decrements are more substantial for retrieval, and (3) these decrements occur in specific subcomponents of storage and retrieval and do not generalize to all aspects of them (Howe, 1988).

The research on storage and retrieval processes is important, for several reasons. First, it emphasizes that age-related decrements in memory are complex; they are not due to changes in a single process. Second, intervention programs must consider both storage and retrieval. Training people to use storage strategies without also training them how to use retrieval strategies will not work. Third, theories of how memory changes with aging must take individual differences into account, especially differential rates of change in component processes. General theories must consider both those components of processes that change and those that do not.

The picture that emerges is very similar to the one we encountered in our consideration of intelligence in Chapter 6. Specifically, the question of how memory changes with age cannot be answered unless one is willing to look at different aspects of memory. As we consider memory in different contexts in the rest of this chapter, we will see additional evidence why this is true.

MEMORY FOR PROSE

Adults of all ages spend a great deal of time reading books, magazines, and newspapers, listening to conversations, and watching television programs and movies. Collectively, such material is termed **discourse** in the memory literature. Within discourse research the study of whether there are age differences in how well adults remember **prose**, or text passages, is one of the fastest growing areas in memory research. As recently as 1975 there was virtually no research on the topic. By the late 1980s, however, the field had mushroomed to such an extent that several literature reviews had appeared, and many important issues had been identified (G. Cohen, 1989; Hartley, 1989; Hultsch & Dixon, 1984; B. J. F. Meyer, 1987; Meyer & Rice, 1989; Spilich, 1985; Zelinski & Gilewski, 1988). This rapid growth probably reflects prose retention's closer relation to everyday life than memory for word lists.

To preview a bit, we will see that age differences are minimized when tasks are made more naturalistic by providing unlimited study time and long reading passages and requiring only a verbal summary. However, younger adults appear to have a clear advantage in learning short passages. These differences may become more important as we continue to move toward a society in which

Research on memory for text indicates that older adults usually remember the gist of the passage as well as do younger adults.

computerization makes rapid acquisition of large amounts of information mandatory (Meyer, 1987).

In this section we will focus on adults' ability to remember information they have read. Most of the research on discourse processing has been concerned with reading; however, relevant related data on other tasks will be noted where appropriate. Our primary concern will be to understand the **person**, **task**, and **text variables** that affect learning and memory.

Person Variables

One of the most researched issues in the literature is whether the presence or absence of age differences in memory for text depends on how the investigator equates the age groups on education and verbal ability (Meyer & Rice, 1983). There is general agreement that average- and low-verbal older adults with mainly a high school education perform significantly poorer than younger adults (e.g., G. Cohen, 1979; Dixon & von Eye, 1984; Spilich, 1983; Taub, 1979). The picture is less clear with high-verbal, college-educated older adults. Some researchers obtain age differences (e.g., Cohen, 1979; Light & Anderson, 1975) while others do not (e.g., Mandel & Johnson, 1984; Meyer & Rice, 1981). In related research examining memory for television programs, Cavanaugh (1983, 1984) also found no differences in high-verbal groups but significant differences in low-verbal groups. A representative set of results showing this differential connection between age and verbal ability is shown in Table 7.1.

Why is there such consistency regarding poor-verbal, lower-educated groups and such disagreement concerning high-verbal, higher-educated groups? Meyer (1987) provides an insightful discussion of this question. She points out that the pattern of results may be due to the use of tests of

TABLE 7.1 · Proportion of statements correct for comprehension, probe recall, and recognition, as a function of age, vocabulary, and level of information

Measure*	Young		Old	
	High Verbal	Low Verbal	High Verbal	Low Verbal
Comprehension				
Central (21)	.98	.77	.99	.70
Plot-relevant (21)	.81	.57	.79	.44
Plot-irrelevant (21)	.61	.39	.59	.23
Probe recall				
Central (14)	.95	.71	.92	.59
Plot-relevant (14)	.74	.51	.80	.34
Plot-irrelevant (15)	.29	.20	.26	.08
Recognition				
Central (14)	.90	.81	1.00	.71
Plot-relevant (14)	.77	.56	.89	.37
Plot-irrelevant (14)	.38	.23	.34	.11

*Numbers in parentheses refer to the total numbers of rated statements at each level summed across programs (free recall) or the total numbers of questions at each level summed across programs (probe recall and recognition).

(Source: "Comprehension and Retention of Television Programs by 20- and 60-year-olds" by J. C. Cavanaugh, 1983, *Journal of Gerontology, 38*, pp. 190–196. Reprinted by permission. © 1983 The Gerontological Society of America.)

verbal ability that are differentially sensitive to high ability levels. That is, some tests, such as the Vocabulary Subtest of the Wechsler Adult Intelligence Scale-Revised (WAIS-R), are poorer at discriminating people with high ability than other tests, such as the Quick Test (Borgatta & Corsini, 1964), which is a very difficult, 100-word vocabulary test. For example, adults who score in the 75th percentile on the Vocabulary Subtest of the WAIS-R score only at the 25th percentile of the Quick Test. Consequently, adults who score high on the vocabulary subtest may not be truly high on verbal ability. Meyer (1987) argues that many of the studies that found age differences in so-called "high-verbal" groups did not use sufficiently sensitive tests of verbal ability. Studies that included truly high-verbal adults found no age differences.

A second reason for the different patterns of age differences concerns the strategies that readers use. Rice and Meyer (1985) asked young and older adults of both average and high verbal ability about the strategies they used while reading. Reading behaviors that foster good comprehension were reported least often by older, low-verbal adults. Meyer (1987) argues that these data support the view that the lack of age differences between younger and older high-verbal adults is due to the older group's continued use of effective reading strategies. Meyer, Young, and Bartlett (1986) tested this hypothesis by training older average-verbal adults to use more effective reading strategies. Following five 90-minute training sessions, use of effective strategies and text recall were substantially better.

Besides verbal ability, another person variable that affects performance is the amount of prior knowledge. Hartley (1989) found that text recall varied in relation to how much people knew about the topic beforehand. Older adults appear especially likely to intrude pieces of prior knowledge into their recall of new information (Hultsch & Dixon, 1983). Interestingly, how prior knowledge affects text recall also appears to vary with age (S. W. Smith, Rebok, Smith, Hall, & Alvin, 1983). Smith et al. found that young adults added prior knowledge to make unorganized stories more coherent, whereas older adults added prior knowledge to make well-organized stories more interesting.

Task Variables

Just as the way in which tasks are presented affects secondary-memory performance, as we saw, these variables also affect text memory. One of the most important task variables affecting text memory is speed of presentation. Some studies show that older adults are differentially adversely affected by rapid presentation (Cohen, 1979; Stine, Wingfield, & Poon, 1986). Specifically, between 100 and 120 words per minute (wpm) appears to be the critical speed for exceeding older adults' processing capability. Meyer and Rice (1989) report that the average reading speed for older adults is

121 wpm, compared with 144 wpm for younger adults. They note, however, that nearly half of their older adults read more slowly than 120 wpm; few younger adults read as slowly. Thus, older adults may be at a disadvantage when presented with text at speeds geared to younger adults. Indeed, when the speed-of-presentation variable is removed and participants can pace themselves, age differences are eliminated (e.g., Harker, Hartley, & Walsh, 1982; Meyer & Rice, 1981; Meyer et al., 1986).

Text Variables

In your personal experience you have undoubtedly found that all text material is not created equal. Some books or passages are very easy to read, comprehend, and remember, and others are not. Texts differ considerably in how they are structured, that is, in how all of the information they contain is organized. One way to think about text organization is to compare it to an outline that is taught in composition classes. Some information is basic and is given prominence in the outline; other information simply expands the main points by providing details and is embedded in the outline. In a well-organized text the main ideas are all interrelated, and the passage is like a tightly woven tapestry. Such texts are more memorable, especially if you follow the built-in organizational structure.

Researchers have spent considerable effort examining whether there are age differences in memory for different kinds of information in texts. There appear to be no age differences in adults' memory for the major organizational elements of texts, such as the sequence of events or causal connections between events (e.g., Meyer & Rice, 1989; Meyer, Rice, Knight, & Jessen, 1979). However, remembering this kind of information does seem to be related to verbal ability; low- and average-ability adults are less able to use these organizational elements and remember fewer of them than high-ability adults (Meyer, 1983).

Because texts are constructed with information at different hierarchical levels of importance, a key question is whether there are age differences in memory for these different levels. Answering this question amounts to looking for age differences between memory for main ideas and memory for details. The literature on this issue is large and complex (Hultsch & Dixon, 1984; Meyer, 1987). In general, the data indicate that when text is clearly organized, with emphasis on structure and the main ideas, no age differences are observed concerning sensitivity to the organizational structure of the passage. Average-verbal older adults do not benefit from "signaling" of important ideas, do not use the organizational structure to facilitate learning or retrieval as efficiently, and make fewer inferences about what they read. As a result, average-verbal older adults show a performance deficit compared with their younger average-verbal counterparts. In contrast, high-verbal older adults are very sensitive to the emphasis given to different pieces of information and to the overall structure of the text. In fact, they may be oversensitive to emphasis, since they tend to allocate more of their processing capacity to emphasized details than to the main ideas. Once again, it appears that verbal ability is more important than age in understanding the patterns of performance.

Text Memory and Secondary Memory

The research we have considered in this section is actually another way to examine secondary memory, since it involves learning large amounts of information and remembering it over time (Poon, 1985). Thus, it is useful to draw parallels between the two literatures and compare the important influences on memory for word lists and memory for text.

The most striking aspect about this comparison is that both are affected by a similar set of variables. Performance on word-list tasks and text-memory tasks are influenced by pacing, prior knowledge or familiarity, and verbal ability. Note that age is not one of these influential variables. Being old does not necessarily mean that you cannot remember, especially if the situation provides an optimal opportunity to do so.

Spilich (1985) notes that age differences are obtained for steps leading up to the understanding of text. In particular, older and younger adults may have different definitions of words and use different classifications for words. This may mean that the associations formed in secondary memory for verbal material may differ for young and old. At a practical level this means that we should not assume that people of all ages understand the same meaning for a word or sentence. Additionally, older adults appear to have difficulty in carrying forward the relevant information extracted from sentences. Such difficulties may interfere with subsequent comprehension of the text as a whole.

MEMORY IN EVERYDAY LIFE

As we noted at the beginning of this chapter, memory is such a part of our everyday life that we take it for granted. Strange as it may seem, only recently has there been substantial interest in examining the uses of memory in everyday life for age differences (West, 1986a). This research is extremely important, however, for several reasons. First, it may shed some light on the generalizability of findings based on laboratory tasks such as word-list recall. Second, new or alternative variables that affect performance could be uncovered. Third, research on everyday memory may force us to reconceptualize memory itself. In this section we will focus on two aspects of everyday memory that have received the most attention: spatial memory and memory for activities.

Spatial Memory

Practical **spatial memory** involves remembering the location of objects; remembering landmarks; remembering routes through cities, countrysides, or buildings; and mentally rotating locations (Kirasic & Allen, 1985). We will consider the developmental trends in each of these abilities.

Memory for Location. People's memory for location is tested in three ways (Kirasic & Allen, 1985). One way is based on the psychometric approach described in Chapter 6, in which relevant primary mental abilities such as spatial ability are tested. Results from this approach indicate that performance reaches a maximum during the 2nd or 3rd decade of life and decreases steadily thereafter.

The most common way to test people's memory for location, termed the experimental approach, is to present them with an array of objects, remove the objects, and ask the participants to reconstruct the array. Older adults do not perform this task as well as younger adults, regardless of whether the objects are household items (Attig, 1983; Pezdek, 1983; Waddell & Rogoff, 1981) or building locations on a map (Light & Zelinski, 1983; Ohta & Kirasic, 1983; M. Perlmutter, Metzger, Nezworski, & Miller, 1981; Thomas, 1985). Charness (1981) found that younger chess players could reconstruct chess boards more accurately than older players, even though the two groups were matched for chess-playing ability. In contrast to this consistent picture of age decrement, West and Walton (1985) found no decline when they conducted interviews of young and old participants about the exact location in their home of common personal items such as keys. West and Walton argue that familiarity and the fact that household locations are unlikely to change are the most likely reasons for the lack of age differences.

The third way to test spatial memory is termed the ecological approach. In this technique spatial memory consists of actually carrying out tasks in real physical space. For example, Kirasic (1981) had older and younger adults plan and execute the most efficient route possible in picking up items on a designated shopping list. The manipulation was the shopper's familiarity with the supermarket; some shoppers were tested in their usual supermarket, and others were tested in a different one. Younger adults performed equivalently in the two settings, whereas older adults performed better in the familiar environment.

Recall of Landmarks. Most studies of landmark recall involve the ability to place landmarks correctly on a map or other representation of a large-scale space. Young adults are more likely to organize their recall of a familiar downtown area based on spatial cues, which gives them an advantage in recalling correct location (Evans, Brennan, Skorpanich, & Held, 1984). Older adults' recall is influenced by frequency of usage, symbolic significance, natural landscaping, ease of finding the landmark, and uniqueness of architectural style. In addition, there is some evidence that older adults are less accurate at learning locations when the information is presented sequentially, as is often done in a travelogue or tour (Walsh, Krauss, & Regnier, 1981), and at locating landmarks on a scale model (Ohta & Kirasic, 1983).

These studies suggest that older and younger adults use different strategies to learn and remember spatial locations. Older adults may be more likely to use experiential or personal relevance as a way to remember location, whereas young adults may be more spatially based.

Route Learning. How people remember the way from one place to another has only been investigated in a handful of studies. Sinnott (1984a) asked participants to describe routes to and around the hospital where they were undergoing a battery of tests and to recognize specific pathways that occurred en route from one area of the hospital to another. She found no differences with age on any of these tasks. Ohta (1981) also found no age differences in adults' ability to find unknown routes to a specific room when the known route was blocked. However, he did report that older adults were less accurate in drawing sketch maps of routes inside buildings.

Configurational Learning. **Configurational learning** requires people to combine spatial and temporal information so that they can recognize a location when they view it from a different perspective. When configurational learning is tested with unfamiliar locations, young adults outperform older adults (Herman & Coyne, 1980; Ohta, Walsh, & Krauss, 1981; Walsh et al., 1981). In contrast, no age differences were found in distance and directional judgments or in efficient route planning when familiar locations were used, such as one's hometown or a familiar grocery store (Kirasic, 1980; Kirasic & Allen, 1985) (see Figure 7.3).

Memory for Activities

Research on memory for activities has involved a wide variety of tasks, including following instructions, recalling activities performed in a research laboratory, and remembering to perform actions.

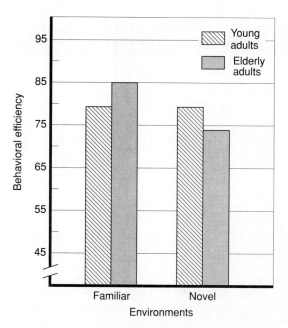

FIGURE 7.3 • Differences in the behavioral efficiency of young and old adults while shopping in familiar and novel supermarkets

(Source: "Aging, Spatial Performance, and Spatial Competence" by K. C. Kirasic and G. L. Allen, 1985, in N. Charness (Ed.), *Aging in Human Performance* (pp. 191–223). Chichester, England: Wiley. © 1985 John Wiley & Sons, Inc. Reprinted with permission of the publisher.)

Kausler (1985) notes that encoding of activities and actions that one performs in a laboratory is probably automatic, requiring no cognitive effort or resources. His view is supported by evidence that rehearsing the names of activities that participants perform does not affect performance. However, he argues that actually remembering the activities one has performed involves cognitive effort, since reliable age decrements are observed. Indeed, organization, an effortful process, facilitates recall (Bäckman, 1985; Bäckman & Nilsson, 1984, 1985). In essence, Kausler is contending that the recall of activities performed

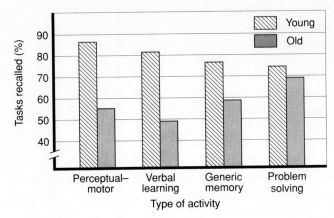

FIGURE 7.4 • Age differences in recall of perceptual-motor, verbal learning, generic memory, and problem-solving activities

(Source: "Memory for Activities: Rehearsal Independence and Aging" by D. H. Kausler and W. Lichty, 1988, in M. L. Howe & C. J. Brainerd (Eds.), *Cognitive Development in Adulthood* (pp. 93–132). New York: Springer-Verlag. © 1988 Reprinted with permission of the publisher.)

in a laboratory is a direct analogue to everyday life, since many everyday memory situations involve the intentional, effortful retrieval of information learned incidentally or automatically (such as trying to remember the weather forecast broadcast during the news the night before in order to know how to dress).

Whether actions are actually performed by the participants or are merely watched also affects how many activities will be correctly remembered. Bäckman (1985) and Cohen and Faulkner (1989) both found that performed actions were remembered more accurately than activities that had only been watched. Moreover, Cohen and Faulkner report that older adults are more likely to say that they actually performed tasks that they in reality only observed. Although more research on this issue is clearly needed, these findings have important implications. In situations where accuracy is crucial, such as in reporting one's recent activities to a physician or police officer, older

adults may be more likely to confuse what they saw with what they did.

The type of task performed may have an effect on the likelihood that it will be remembered later. Kausler and Hakami (1983) found that older adults remembered problem-solving tests better than perceptual-motor, generic memory, and learning word lists (see Figure 7.4). The reason for such differences remains to be uncovered. West (1986a) suggests that better-remembered tasks may be more familiar and, thereby, more memorable.

There is one area where older adults are consistently superior: remembering to perform an action. This form of memory is termed **prospective memory** (Meacham, 1982a) and involves remembering to remember (J. E. Harris, 1984b). When younger and older adults were asked to call in on either a fixed or a variable schedule, older adults were consistently better at remembering to do so (Moscovitch, 1982; Poon & Schaffer, 1982;

West, 1984). Their secret was simple: they wrote down the number and message to be given. Younger adults relied on their own internal remembering strategies, which turned out to be a serious mistake.

Everyday Memory Versus List-Learning Performance

Because much of the research on everyday memory has involved analogues to everyday life that are simulated in the laboratory, there is a natural tendency to compare performances on these tasks with performance on more traditional list-learning tasks. Overall, age decrements in performance are less prevalent on everyday-memory tasks than on list-learning tasks (West, 1986a). Why this is the case remains open to speculation. One thing is clear, however. Older adults perform consistently better when they are confronted with information that is familiar, which in turn enhances the motivation to perform the task in the first place (L. C. Perlmuter, 1989).

One of the few areas in which list-learning tasks and tasks closer to everyday life can be compared is memory for pictures. A series of studies conducted by Park and her colleagues examined many of the traditional issues in laboratory research, including context effects, retention intervals, and stimulus complexity (Park, Puglisi, & Smith, 1986; Park, Puglisi, & Sovacool, 1983, 1984; Park, Royal, Dudley, & Morrell, 1988). Whereas older adults show decrements in their ability to remember words, Park and her colleagues showed that immediate memory for pictures was relatively unaffected by age. Age differences are observed only when delayed tests are given, and then only at certain intervals, as shown in Figure 7.5. This research shows that we need to be cautious in generalizing the findings from laboratory list-learning tasks using words even to list-learning tasks using pictures.

Overall, the direct comparison between everyday memory and list learning is hampered by the lack of data establishing equivalent everyday tasks and list-learning tasks. What is needed is a comprehensive analysis in which the memory demands of many everyday tasks and list-learning tasks are described. This analysis, similar to one conducted by Scheidt and Schaie (1978) for tasks involving intelligent behavior (see Chapter 6), would provide a way to address the reasons for the presence or absence of age differences across different task domains.

SELF-EVALUATIONS OF MEMORY ABILITIES

We are our own harshest critics when it comes to memory performance. We analyze, scrutinize, nit-pick, and castigate ourselves for the times we forget, rarely praise ourselves for remembering, and continue to be on guard for more memory slips. The self-evaluations we make about memory form a crucial part of our daily life and may affect it in ways that traditionally were unrecognized.

The self-evaluations we make about memory are complex (Cavanaugh, 1989; Cavanaugh et al., 1989). They are based not only on memory and performance per se but also on our attributions and judgments of our effectiveness. These latter two ideas, borrowed from the social cognition literature, will be explored in detail in Chapter 9. In this section we will focus on the ways in which we are aware of our memory.

Types of Memory Awareness

Interest in what people know about or are aware of concerning memory is an old topic in both philosophy and psychology (Cavanaugh & Perlmutter, 1982). Psychologists have dabbled with

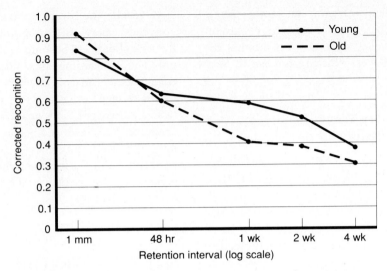

FIGURE 7.5 • Corrected picture-recognition scores (proportion correct minus proportion incorrect guesses) for young and older adults across five retention intervals (Imm = immediate)

(Source: "Forgetting of Pictures Over a Long Retention Interval in Young and Old Adults" by D. C. Park, D. Royal, W. Dudley, & R. Morrell, 1988, *Psychology and Aging, 3*, pp. 94–95. Copyright © 1988 by the American Psychological Association. Reprinted with permission of the author.)

the topic for almost a century, studying everything from reports of children's awareness of problem-solving skills (Binet, 1903) to computer simulation of self-monitoring systems (Bobrow & Collins, 1975). In recent decades work on memory awareness has taken on a more developmental flavor. This work focuses on the experience that one knows something (**feeling-of-knowing**); the awareness of monitoring, or keeping track (**executive processes**); and the knowledge that certain person factors or task factors make a memory task easier or harder (**metamemory**).

Cavanaugh (1989) adapted some ideas first developed by Klatzky (1984) and proposed that each of these emphases corresponds to a different type of awareness: systemic awareness, epistemic awareness, and on-line awareness.

Systemic awareness is consciousness of facts about memory, that is, awareness of the memory system and how it works. It involves information that can be put into the form "I know that . . ." For instance, most people know that recall is typically harder than recognition, that memory strategies are often helpful, and that primary memory is not limitless. Cavanaugh and Perlmutter (1982) argue that these facts about memory are what constitute metamemory. Systemic awareness is typically assessed in questionnaires and interviews.

Epistemic awareness refers to the ability to know about the extent and soundness of one's general knowledge base. In other words epistemic awareness is knowledge about our own knowledge base. The notion is that at times we must make judgments about whether we know something, how well we know it, or how sure we are that we know it is correct. Examples of epistemic awareness include feeling-of-knowing (e.g., "Haven't we met before?"), eyewitness testimony (e.g., being sure that the person you saw was the defendant), awareness of the sources of memory (e.g., distinguishing between actual experience and observation [Cohen & Faulkner, 1989]), awareness of the reliability of memory (e.g., knowing whether something that is remembered today will be remembered next week), and awareness of changes in knowledge states (e.g., knowing when something new has been learned or when old knowledge has been shown to be invalid). Epistemic awareness occurs during retrieval, when the judgments about our knowledge occur (Klatzky, 1984).

On-line awareness refers to the consciousness of ongoing memory processes, and it involves the monitoring aspect of executive processes. We can be aware of the *process* of remembering in many ways. At times it is the awareness of how we are studying, how we are searching for some particular fact, or how we are keeping track of time for an appointment. At other times on-line awareness is reflected in the questions we ask ourselves while doing a memory task. For example, when faced with having to remember an important appointment later in the day, we may consciously ask ourselves whether the steps we have taken (writing a note) are sufficient.

The following sections provide closer looks at age differences in systemic awareness and on-line awareness. Little research has examined epistemic awareness across adulthood. We will begin by considering the results obtained through questionnaires.

Questionnaire Data on Systemic Awareness

Several questionnaire studies of systemic awareness have been conducted in the last 2 decades (see Dixon, 1989, for a review). In general, older adults report more memory problems and have more negative views of current memory functioning than young adults (e.g., Cavanaugh, 1986–1987; Cavanaugh & Poon, 1989; Chaffin & Herrmann, 1983; Dixon & Hultsch, 1983b; M. Perlmutter, 1978; Roberts, 1983; Zelinski, Gilewski, & Thompson, 1980).

The pattern of age differences in systemic awareness is interesting. Older adults seem to know less than younger adults about the internal workings of memory and its capacity, view memory as less stable, expect that memory will deteriorate with age, and perceive that they have less control over memory (Cavanaugh & Poon, 1989; Chaffin & Herrmann, 1983; Dixon & Hultsch, 1983b; Zelinski et al., 1980). The belief in inevitable decline with age appears to be especially reliable. Williams, Denney, and Schadler (1983) found that none of their participants over age 65 expected memory to improve over time. Their participants also said that decline was related to expectations, less use of memory, lower levels of memory demands, and inactivity.

The belief in inevitable decline is not thought to involve all aspects of memory equally, however. Older adults view memory capacity as declining more rapidly than memory strategies (Dixon & Hultsch, 1983b), and name retrieval is particularly problematic (Cavanaugh & Poon, 1989; Chaffin & Herrmann, 1983; Zarit, 1982). In contrast, remembering errands, appointments, and places appears to remain unchanged (White & Cunningham, 1984).

Although questionnaire studies of systemic awareness provide important information, they must be interpreted carefully (Cavanaugh & Perlmutter, 1982). The need for caution is highlighted by the fact that it was not until the late 1980s that researchers began asking what the questionnaires were actually measuring and whether this changed with age. Cavanaugh (1986–1987) discovered that how questions are worded makes a difference in how older adults respond. When questions request a general, or overall, rating of memory, for example, older adults give more negative ratings than younger adults. But when the question pertains to a specific aspect of memory, such as memory for dates or errands, older adults' ratings are equivalent to those of younger adults.

Related work by Hertzog and his colleagues shows that the structure of systemic awareness changes across adulthood (Hertzog, Dixon, Schulenberg, & Hultsch, 1987; Hertzog, Hultsch, & Dixon, in press). That is, the kinds of things people know about memory tend to form groups, or domains, of knowledge. As we age, the makeup of these domains changes, so that by old age we incorporate some personality factors into memory knowledge. We will return to this issue of changes in structure in a later section, which outlines the possible course of development in the self-evaluation of memory.

Predicting Performance and On-Line Awareness

Recall that on-line awareness involves knowing what we are doing with memory right now. On-line monitoring has been examined from a limited number of perspectives in adult developmental research. Two of them are variations on predicting how well one will do on a memory task. One technique requires that people predict how well they will do before they have had any experience with the task. For example, a person is asked to predict how many words he or she will remember from a 20-item list without being able to see the list. The second major technique requires people to make performance predictions after they have seen the task. This time, the person sees the list first and then is asked to predict how many words

he or she will remember. The third approach involves the prospective memory research discussed earlier, in the section on everyday memory. All three approaches assume that prediction involves monitoring current memory processing. Results from each technique lead to different developmental trends.

Predictions Without Experience. In general, studies examining the accuracy of predictions made before actually performing the task have documented a tendency for older adults to overestimate how well they will do (e.g., Bruce, Coyne, & Botwinick, 1982; Coyne, 1983; Mason, 1981; Murphy, Sanders, Gabriesheski, & Schmitt, 1981). That is, older adults typically predict that they will be able to remember more items than they actually can.

Overestimation is not universal, however. Camp, Markley, & Kramer (1983) asked older adults to predict recall of 15 words that were high in imagery, frequency, concreteness, and meaningfulness. Older adults underestimated their performance when they were told to think about the strategies they might use before predicting. Similarly, Berry, West, & Scogin (1983) found that older adults underestimated performance for both laboratory and everyday memory tasks. They also found that the best memorizers might be the ones with the best on-line awareness; the correlation between prediction accuracy and performance was .60.

Predictions After Experience. A much different picture emerges when participants have a chance to experience the task before making a performance prediction. One way this is done is by asking people to rate their confidence that they will be able to remember each item. Results from several studies using this approach demonstrate that older adults are just as accurate in predicting their recall and recognition performances as younger adults (e.g., Lovelace, Marsh, & Oster, 1982; Perlmutter, 1978; Rabinowitz, Ackerman, Craik, & Hinchley, 1982). The usual finding is that, regardless of age, adults overestimate performance on recall tasks but underestimate performance on recognition tasks.

The results of the Camp et al. (1983) and Berry et al. (1983) studies, plus the findings from research on prediction following task experience and the findings from the prospective-memory research described earlier, lead to the following conclusions: Older adults are at a disadvantage when asked to predict performance if they are given no information about the task. But when this information is forthcoming, either from direct experience, from instructions pertaining to important things to think about, or from a request for predictions on familiar everyday tasks, older adults do as well as younger adults.

Developmental Trends in Systemic and On-Line Awareness

How does memory awareness change with age? Do people become more aware of memory processes? less aware? It appears that the answer is not as easy as that. In a series of papers, Cavanaugh proposes a model of memory self-evaluation that incorporates the variables that are thought to be involved in this process (Cavanaugh, 1989; Cavanaugh, Kramer, Sinnott, Camp, & Markley, 1985; Cavanaugh & Morton, 1989; Cavanaugh, Morton, & Tilse, 1989).

Developmentally, Cavanaugh (1989) argues that there is a shift during adulthood from an emphasis on systemic awareness to an emphasis on on-line awareness. That is, younger adults are most concerned with acquiring knowledge about how memory works in various situations. In contrast, older adults are more concerned with keeping track of ongoing processes. This shift leads to two hypotheses. First, younger adults should be sensitive to and be able to demonstrate a great number of memory facts, whereas older adults may not show such knowledge to the same degree. Second, younger adults should be less sensitive to memory failures, since they are not monitoring themselves as closely. Older adults, however, should be very sensitive to episodes of forgetting. Additionally, older adults should tend to take more personal responsibility for forgetting because of their tendency to believe that their memory failures are due to their age or to actions under their control.

What Cavanaugh's model emphasizes is that memory performance at any age is heavily influenced by our own perceptions of our memory abilities. For example, self-evaluations of our abilities lie at the heart of important memory decisions such as how much effort to exert and which strategy to use. The important implication is that personal evaluations of memory performance may not be objectively accurate but, rather, the result of what we subjectively believe to be true. What we think our performance means may not match what others think about the same performance. Evidence supporting this point presented earlier, along with data from the clinical realm to be discussed later, is in line with the model.

Although Cavanaugh's entire model has not been tested, it does account for a considerable amount of the research findings we have encountered. For example, older adults do seem to be more sensitive to memory failures, appear to know less about strategies, and give different reasons for forgetting than young adults (e.g., Cavanaugh et al., 1983; Cavanaugh & Morton, 1989; Dixon & Hultsch, 1984). This point is emphasized in "How Do We Know?" Moreover, this model is

HOW · DO · WE · KNOW?

Older Adults' Attributions About Everyday Memory

As noted in the text, we evaluate our memory abilities in a variety of ways. One way involves making decisions concerning who or what is responsible for our performance. These decisions, called attributions, are thought to play an important role in memory performance.

To examine this question, Cavanaugh and Morton (1988) examined older adults' attributions about their everyday memory experiences. In particular, they focused on three dimensions: causality, or who is responsible; stability, or the degree to which the situation will recur; and controllability, or the degree to which something can be done

to change the outcome. They interviewed 20 older adult volunteers in their homes. All of these individuals completed the Metamemory in Adulthood scale and a semistructured interview which assessed attributions.

The results showed some very interesting patterns. Over three fourths of the respondents had a clearly internal locus, which meant that they felt responsible for their memory performance. Also, the majority of the subjects said that their performance was stable and under their own control. Eighty-five percent said that memory was very important to them. However, 80% also said that they were not worried about

their memory abilities; of these, 81% said that they could change their memory functioning if they wanted. Interestingly, only a few people thought that memory performance was completely uncontrollable. The vast majority of people who thought that their memory abilities had changed since they were younger attributed this change to health.

The results indicate that older adults have complex sets of attributions about memory and that people vary in how they explain performance. However, there are several problems with this investigation. How many can you identify?

---

similar to Schaie's (1977–1978) model of styles of intellectual behavior, described in Chapter 6. Both models emphasize that age differences in performance could be the result of different processing styles and could have little to do with true decrements.

The whole issue of the interface between memory and reasons for success or failure is a good example of the interdisciplinary nature of gerontology. This interface brings together researchers in memory and social cognition, a topic that will be discussed in Chapter 8.

CLINICAL ISSUES AND MEMORY TESTING

To this point we have been trying to understand the changes that occur in normal memory with aging. Although there still is much to learn in that regard, it is fair to say that we know a great deal. Clinicians face an additional need. They are often confronted with clients who complain of memory difficulties. They must somehow differentiate those individuals who have no real reason to be concerned from those with measurable deficits. At issue here is the differentiation of normal and abnormal changes in memory with aging. What criteria should be used? What diagnostic tests would be appropriate to evaluate adults of various ages?

Unfortunately, there are no easy answers to these questions (Erickson, Poon, & Walsh-Sweeney, 1980; Poon, 1986). As we have seen, the exact nature of normal changes in memory with aging is far from understood. This means that we have no norms, or standards, by which to compare people who may have problems. Second, we also do not have a comprehensive battery of memory tests that taps a wide variety of memory functions. Clinicians are left with hit-or-miss approaches and often have little choice but to piece together their own assessment battery (Poon et al., 1986).

Fortunately, the situation is changing. Since the mid-1980s experimental researchers and clinicians have begun to work closely to devise a comprehensive battery. This collaboration is producing results that will help address the key questions in memory assessment: Has something gone wrong with memory? Is the loss normal? What is the prognosis? What can be done to help the client compensate or recover?

In this section we will consider some of the efforts being made to bridge the gap between laboratory and life. We will begin with a brief synopsis of the link between memory and mental health. After that, we will consider some of the ways in which memory can be assessed in the clinical setting.

Memory and Mental Health

Several psychological disorders involve distorted thought processes, which result in less-than-optimal memory performance. The two disorders that have been the main focus of research are depression and dementia (see Poon, 1986); but other disorders, such as amnesia following a head injury or brain disease, are also important. Depression is characterized by feelings of helplessness and hopelessness (American Psychiatric Association, 1987; see Chapter 9). Dementia involves substantial declines in cognitive performance that may be irreversible and untreatable (American Psychiatric Association, 1987; see Chapter 9). Alzheimer's disease is the most common form of dementia. Much of the research on clinical memory testing is on differentiating the changes in memory due to depression from those involved in Alzheimer's disease.

The influence of serious depression on memory has been well-documented. For example, depressed people show a decreased ability to learn and recall new information (e.g., Breslow, Kocsis, & Belkin, 1981; R. M. Cohen, Weingartner, Smallberg, Pickar, & Murphy, 1982); a tendency to leave out more information (e.g., McAllister, 1981); a decreased ability to organize (e.g., Breslow et al., 1981); less effective memory strategies (e.g., Weingartner, Cohen, & Bunney, 1982); an increased sensitivity to sad memories (Kelley, 1986); and decreased attention and reaction time (Breslow et al., 1981; Cohen et al., 1982). Additionally, clinical models of depression emphasize its effects on cognition in everyday life (Beck, 1967, 1976; Garber & Seligman, 1980). In general, seriously depressed individuals develop negative expectations, decreased concentration, and attentional deficits that result in poorer memory. In contrast, mildly depressed individuals show little decrement. Unfortunately, few researchers have asked whether the effects of depression on memory vary with age. What data there are suggest that once normative age differences in secondary memory are eliminated statistically, few differences remain. However, much more research needs to be done before we have a clear answer. Additionally, we need to know more about the possible effects of mild and moderate levels of depression. Because many older people report some symptoms of depression (see Chapter 9), it is important to know whether these symptoms are at all related to the pattern of age-related differences in memory reported throughout this chapter.

Alzheimer's disease is characterized by severe and pervasive memory impairment that is progressive and irreversible. As described in Chapter 9, the memory decrements in Alzheimer's disease involve the entire memory system, from sensory to tertiary memory. The important point for this discussion is that the changes that occur early in Alzheimer's disease are very similar to those that occur in depression. However, since depression is treatable and Alzheimer's disease is not, it is important to differentiate the two. This differentiation is the underlying reason for the major effort to develop sensitive and comprehensive batteries of memory tests.

Memory, Nutrition, and Drugs

An area that may be often overlooked as a cause of memory failures in later life is nutrition (M. Perlmutter et al., 1987). Unfortunately, we know very little about how specific nutrient deficiencies relate to memory. The available evidence links thiamine deficiency to memory problems in humans (Cherkin, 1984), and it links niacin and B_{12} deficiencies to diseases in which memory failure is a major symptom (Rosenthal & Goodwin, 1985).

Likewise, many drugs have been associated with memory problems. The most widely known of these is alcohol, which if abused over a long period creates severe memory loss (see Chapter 4). Less well known are the effects of other prescription and over-the-counter medications. For ex-

ample, sedatives and tranquilizers have been found to impair memory performance (Block, DeVoe, Stanley, Stanley, & Pomara, 1985).

These data indicate that it is important to consider older adults' diets and medications when assessing their memory performance. What may appear to be serious decrements in functioning may, in fact, be induced by poor nutrition or specific medications. Adequate assessment is essential in order to avoid diagnostic errors.

Questionnaire Assessments

One behavior that is clearly related to affective status is memory complaint, the concerns that people express about their abilities and failures to remember. There is some evidence that memory complaints correlate with performance (Zelinski et al., 1980), but their relationship is much stronger with depressed mood (Zarit, Cole, & Guider, 1981). Roughly 12 questionnaires assess memory complaints (Gilewski & Zelinski, 1986). These questionnaires assess a variety of memory situations, such as remembering people's names or remembering the time of year it is. Unfortunately, only a few of these questionnaires are sufficiently reliable and valid for diagnostic use across a wide age range of adults (Gilewski & Zelinski, 1986).

Still, Gilewski and Zelinski strongly advocate the use of memory questionnaires in clinical practice, as long as they are multidimensional. For example, comprehensive questionnaires should tap such things as frequency of forgetting, change in memory over time, seriousness of memory failures, use of strategies, daily memory demands, memory for past events, and what efforts are made when forgetting occurs. Table 7.2 contains sample items from several questionnaire assessments.

TABLE 7.2 • Sample items from memory questionnaires that assess forgetting of names

	Questionnaire	Item
Younger Target Population	Everyday Memory Questionnaire	1. Forgetting the names of friends or relatives or calling them by the wrong names.
	Inventory of Memory Experiences	7. How often do you find that just when you want to introduce someone you know to someone else, you can't think of his or her name?
Older Target Population	Metamemory in Adulthood	2. I am good at remembering names.
	Wadsworth Memory Questionnaire	Do you forget names of new people you meet, even after being introduced several times?
	Metamemory Questionnaire (Niederehe et al.)	12. How often do you have difficulty remembering any of the following things . . . (a) names?
	Memory Questionnaire	11. How often do you forget names?
	Memory Complaints Questionnaire	8. Do you have trouble remembering any of the following . . . someone's name?
	Metamemory Questionnaire (Zelinski et al.)	4. How often do these present a memory problem to you . . . (a) names?

(Source: "Questionnaire Assessments of Memory Complaints" by M. J. Gilewski and E. M. Zelinski, 1986, in L. W. Poon (Ed.), *Handbook for the Clinical Memory Assessment of Older Adults* (pp. 93–107). © 1986 American Psychological Association. Reprinted with permission of the author and publisher.)

Behavior Rating Scales

Behavior rating scales are instruments designed to assess memory status as evaluated by an observer, usually a mental health professional (McDonald, 1986). The most common rating scales that tap memory are structured interviews. These interviews vary in length from very short to extensive, which means that they also vary in how sensitive they are at picking up abnormal memory performance.

Most structured interviews were developed with an eye toward diagnosing Alzheimer's disease (see also Chapter 9). The most common of these are the various mental status examinations (Blessed, Tomlinson, & Roth, 1968; Folstein,

Folstein, & McHugh, 1975; Kahn, Goldfarb, Pollack, & Peck, 1960). These rating scales are short and easy to administer and serve as screening devices for severe memory impairment. Items on these scales focus on orientation to time and place and contain simple memory tests such as spelling *world* backwards. A more extensive mental status exam, developed by Mattis (1976), provides a more complete view of cognitive processes. Mattis's scale examines primary memory and secondary memory more thoroughly than the other mental status exams.

A very important source of diagnostic information is a person who is close to the client. This person, typically a spouse or adult child, provides a different, more objective perspective. For example, the diagnosis of Alzheimer's disease is often furthered by examining the discrepancy between the client's assessment of memory functioning and the significant other's assessment of the client's memory functioning (Reisberg et al., 1986). In the middle stages of the disease the clients' reports of memory problems drop, but significant others' reports continue to increase.

Recommendations

Although questionnaires and rating scales are important in clinical diagnosis, they are not enough. Increasingly, clinicians are advocating the use of tasks developed in the laboratory as part of research on basic memory processes in the clinic (e.g., Ferris, Crook, Flicker, Reisberg, & Bartus, 1986).

Ferris and Crook (1983) propose nine criteria for a comprehensive cognitive battery, such as that it samples a variety of cognitive functions, is sensitive to deficits, takes less than 1 hour to administer, has high reliability and validity, and is of appropriate difficulty for the population being studied. They recommend that all aspects of memory (primary, secondary, and tertiary) as well as attention and perceptual-motor speed be included in this battery. These suggestions have been supported and adopted by many of the leading clinicians involved in research on abnormal memory changes (e.g., Corkin, Growdon, Sullivan, Nissen, & Huff, 1986; Mohs, Kim, Johns, Dunn, & Davis, 1986).

REMEDIATING MEMORY PROBLEMS

The large number of memory complaints by older adults, as well as the substantial number of older adults who experience memory loss due to physi-

cal or psychological disorders, has resulted in the growth of memory training programs (Wilson & Moffat, 1984). In this section we will examine some of the attempts to remediate memory problems with training in memory skills. Then we will consider some of the individual differences that affect how successful these programs are.

Training Memory Skills

The notion that memory can be improved through acquiring skills that are practiced is very old, dating back to prehistory (Yates, 1966). Books that outline how to improve memory have also been around for a very long time (Grey, 1756), and the older versions do not differ in most respects from those published more recently (e.g., Lorayne & Lucas, 1974; West, 1986b). J. E. Harris (1984a) lists four major methods of improving memory: internal strategies (e.g., forming an image of the information to be remembered in one's mind), repetitive practice (rehearsing the information over and over), physical treatments (e.g., drugs), and external aids (e.g., writing the information to be remembered on a notepad).

Most research on memory training concerns internal strategies (Bellezza, 1981), which supply meaning and help organize incoming information (P. E. Morris, 1979). Examples of internal strategies include a locus method (remembering items by mentally placing them in locations in a familiar environment), mental retracing (thinking about all the places you may have left your keys), turning letters into numbers, and forming acronyms out of initial letters (e.g., NATO). Most memory courses train people to become proficient at using one of these internal strategies. For example, Yesavage (1983) trained older adults to use images to help themselves remember people's names. As shown in Figure 7.6, this training was effective. Older adults have also been successfully trained to use the locus method as a way to help

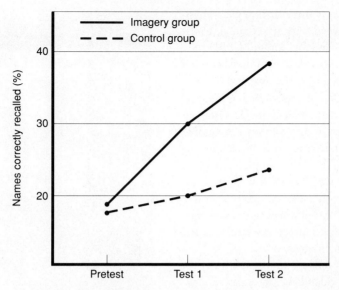

FIGURE 7.6 • Proportion of names recalled at three points in the study. Pretest occurred in first session. Test 1 was after imagery training (in the imagery group) and after attitude training (in the control group). Test 2 was after both groups had received training in the face-name mnemonic.

(Source: "Imagery Pretraining and Memory Training in the Elderly" by J. A. Yesavage, 1983, *Gerontology, 29*, pp. 271–275. Copyright 1983 by S. Karger. Reprinted with permission.)

them remember items to be purchased at the grocery store (Anschutz, Camp, Markley, & Kramer, 1985). Similar research has shown that training on most internal strategies improves memory significantly. Unfortunately, these training programs have rarely been assessed over long intervals, so the degree of improvement after the course ends and how long this improvement lasts is largely unknown. One of the few exceptions was a 3-year follow-up to the grocery shopping study (Anschutz, Camp, Markley, & Kramer, 1987). Although Anschutz and her colleagues found that loci were readily available, older adults had abandoned their use of the locus method as a memory aid. Clearly, more research needs to be conducted in order to understand why adults stop using internal memory strategies that are effective in improving recall.

A second approach to memory training is repetitive practice, which involves viewing memory as a kind of "mental muscle." Exercising memory on one type of task strengthens it, setting the stage for better memory in a variety of other tasks (J. E. Harris & Sunderland, 1981). Exercising memory may have important benefits to a person during the rehabilitation process. For one thing, the person knows that something is being done about his or her memory problems. This may result in the belief that improvement is possible and that it is worth the effort. Second, there is suggestive evidence from both animal research (Wall, 1975) and human research (Black, Markowitz, &

Cianci, 1975) that early intervention with physical exercise promotes recovery after damage to the motor cortex. Harris and Sunderland (1981) raise the possibility that the same benefit may accrue if memory practice is begun at the first sign of loss.

Although considerable research has focused on the underlying neurological mechanisms in memory, little definitive information is available that can be easily translated into treatment approaches (Cooper, 1984). For example, we still do not know for certain which neurotransmitters are primarily involved with memory, since attempts to improve memory by administering drugs that act on certain neurotransmitters has largely failed to produce long-term changes.

External memory aids are objects such as diaries, address books, calendars, notepads, microcomputers, and other devices commonly used to support memory in everyday situations (Cavanaugh et al., 1983; J. E. Harris, 1980). Some external aids involve the use of external storage of information, while others involve the use of external aids to cue action (M. Perlmutter et al., 1987). External storage can range from writing down intermediate results during mental calculations to building large computer data bases. Examples of external cuing aids include notes to remind one of a lunch date or to get bread from the store. Advocating the use of external aids in memory rehabilitation is becoming increasingly popular. For example, Zgola (1987) recommends external aids in working with Alzheimer's patients. J. E. Harris (1984) suggests that for external cues to be most effective, they should (1) be given close to the time that action is required, (2) be active rather than passive, (3) be specific to the particular action, (4) be portable, (5) fit a wide range of situations, (6) store many cues for long periods, (7) be easy to use, and (8) not require a pen or pencil.

West (1986b) cautions that overreliance on external aids can be a problem. She argues that

A remedial program that emphasizes using external memory aids such as calendars is an effective intervention with cognitively impaired people.

memory is much like a muscle, which needs to be exercised in order to be kept sharp. Consequently, we need to use internal strategies as much as possible, because they strengthen memory more than external strategies do. In practice, the best course is probably to use a mixture of both.

Individual-Difference Variables in Memory Training

As we have seen throughout this chapter, adults are a very heterogenous group when it comes to memory performance. For example, research reviewed earlier shows that verbal ability, prior knowledge, cognitive style, and affective status influence how well one performs on memory tasks. Treat, Poon, Fozard, & Popkin (1978) argued that these variables should be considered when designing memory training programs, especially for older adults. Moreover, training may be more effective when changes in affective status (Popkin, Gallagher, Thompson, & Moore, 1982) and feelings of self-efficacy (Berry, 1986; Cavanaugh et al., 1989) are major goals of the program. Yesavage (1984) found that the benefits of memory training were greatest when participants were also provided relaxation training; in fact, the memory improvement shown by people who had received only relaxation training roughly matched the decrements observed in studies of secondary memory.

The important point to keep in mind in designing memory training programs is that it is very unlikely that everyone will benefit equally from the same program. Some people may benefit most from training in the locus method, whereas others need training in the use of external aids. Only by tailoring programs to individual needs will long-term benefits be observed (Yesavage & Rose, 1983).

SUMMARY

From an information-processing perspective memory can be divided into sensory memory, primary memory, working memory, secondary memory, and tertiary memory. Few age differences are observed for either sensory memory or primary memory; these differences tend to be related to speed of processing. Evidence is emerging that working-memory capacity declines with age. Most research on age differences in memory have focused on secondary memory. In general, word-list tasks show marked age differences in recall but not in recognition. Older adults also devise and use fewer strategies and appear less able to mentally manipulate information. But they do appear to benefit from practice and instruction. Tertiary memory tends to remain intact well into old age.

Research on storage and retrieval processes indicates that both decline with age. Older adults are less efficient at getting information into memory, but they are as good as young adults at keeping it there once it gets in. Older adults also show retrieval problems that are more substantial than their storage problems. However, the decline in retrieval appears to be confined to algorithmic retrieval of specific information.

Age differences in memory for discourse tend to vary with several factors. High-verbal individuals appear not to differ with age, whereas low-verbal people do. Amount of prior knowledge is also positively correlated with performance. Organization of text materials is important; older adults are less able to reorganize text if necessary. Older adults also recall fewer details from text than do younger adults.

Memory performance in everyday life also varies across situations. Laboratory-based tasks tend to pick up age differences. Depending on the situation, however, older and younger adults perform comparably on a wide range of real-world tasks. Memory for location declines unless older adults are tested in everyday environments in familiar settings. Older adults also tend not to remember activities that they have performed, but this difference disappears on some tasks. For prospective memory, older adults are often superior.

Self-evaluations of memory ability have been studied in questionnaires and prediction paradigms. On questionnaires, older adults report more problems and give lower overall ratings than younger adults. On specific questions, however, no age differences are found. Prediction accuracy appears to depend largely on experience with the task. Without experience younger adults are more accurate, but with experience age groups tend not to differ. Self-perceived ability has been hypothesized to play a major role in memory performance. Older adults may evaluate themselves overly negatively.

Memory performance is affected by mental disorders such as severe depression and Alzheimer's disease. In the clinical setting memory is assessed by questionnaires and rating scales. These scales serve as screening devices for primary and secondary memory. Memory problems are usually remediable. Training typically involves skills, such as internal and external strategies.

GLOSSARY

algorithmic retrieval • Any recovery process that produces error-free performance.

behavior rating scale • An assessment of memory ability through observation of the person's behavior.

configurational learning • The process of combining spatial and temporal information so that a place can be recognized from a different vantage point.

cued recall • Providing some hint, or aid, within the general constraints of a memory test.

discourse • Material that is meaningful and is spoken or written.

epistemic awareness • Consciousness of the "correctness" of one's knowledge.

executive processes • Cognitive processes that keep track of thinking.

feeling-of-knowing • Believing that one knows something that is temporarily not retrievable.

heuristic retrieval • Any recovery process that produces both success and failures.

metamemory • knowledge of one's own memory ability.

on-line awareness • Consciousness of one's ongoing cognitive processing.

person variables • Characteristics of the learner that influence performance.

primary memory • A short-lived and limited-capacity store.

prose • Text passages used in discourse memory research.

prospective memory • Preparation for remembering future events.

recall • A type of memory tested by asking a person to remember as much as possible with no cues.

recognition • A type of memory tested by asking a person to choose the correct answer from among alternatives.

rehearsal • A process involving either rote rehearsal or making more extensive connections between information in working memory and information already in memory.

retrieval • A process of recovering stored information.

secondary memory • A relatively large-capacity store that holds information for long periods.

sensory memory • The earliest step in memory processing, at which information from the sensory system is handled.

spatial memory • Remembering the locations of things.

storage • A process by which information is encoded and housed in memory.

strategies • Techniques that make information storage or retrieval easier.

systemic awareness • Consciousness of facts about memory.

task variables • Characteristics of the learning situation that influence performance.

tertiary memory • Very large and long-term storage.

text variables • Characteristics of the material to be learned that influence performance.

working memory • A small-capacity store in which items currently being used reside.

ADDITIONAL READING

General overviews of memory research can be found in

Howe, M. L., & Brainerd, C. J. (Eds.), *Cognitive development in adulthood*. New York: Springer-Verlag.

Poon, L. W. (1985). Differences in human memory with aging: Nature, causes, and clinical implications. In J. E. Birren & K. W. Schaie (Eds.), *Handbook of the psychology of aging* (2nd ed.) (pp. 427–462). New York: Van Nostrand Reinhold.

Poon, L. W., Rubin, D. C., & Wilson, B. (Eds.). (1989). *Everyday cognition in adult and late life*. New York: Cambridge University Press.

An excellent source of information about how memory is assessed in clinical settings is

Poon, L. W. (Ed.). (1986). *Handbook for the clinical memory assessment of older adults*. Washington, DC: American Psychological Association.

Personality

Alex Katz, *Supper*, 1974. Hood Museum of Art, Dartmouth College, Hanover, New Hampshire. Gift of Joachim Jean Aberbach.

MOST OF US WILL EVENTUALLY ATTEND A high school reunion. It is amusing, so it is said, to see how our classmates have changed over the years. In addition to gray or missing hair and a few wrinkles, one possible area of change is in their personality. Will Jackie be the same outgoing person she was as captain of the cheerleaders? Will Shawn still be as shy at 48 as he was at 18? In order to learn as much about our friends as possible, suppose we make careful observations of our classmates' personalities over the course of several reunions. Now, at the gathering marking 60 years since graduation, the group wants to examine the trends we observed. Did our classmates' personalities change substantially? Or did they remain essentially the same as they were 60 years earlier?

How we think these questions will be answered provides clues to our personal biases concerning personality stability or change across adulthood. As we will see, opposing views of descriptive continuity and descriptive discontinuity (see Chapter 2) are more obvious in personality research than in any other area of adult development.

Why should the area of personality be so controversial? The answer lies in the paradoxical beliefs we hold about personality itself. At one level we all believe that people have complex personalities that remain relatively constant over time. A stable personality makes it easier to deal with a person in different situations; indeed, when a person behaves in ways that violate our expectations, we act surprised. Imagine the chaos that would result if every week or so everyone woke up with a brand new personality: the once easygoing husband is now a real tyrant, trusted friends are now completely unpredictable, and our patterns of social interaction are in a shambles. Clearly, we must rely on consistency of personality in order to survive in day-to-day life.

Still, we like to believe that we can change undesirable aspects of our personalities. Imagine what it would be like if, for example, there were no way to overcome shyness, if anxiety were a lifelong, incurable curse, or if our idiosyncratic tendencies that cause others to tear their hair out could not be eliminated. Our assumption of the modifiability of personality is very strong indeed. The field of psychotherapy is a formal verification of that.

This chapter deals with stability and change in personality across adulthood. To begin, we will consider personality development from one of the oldest theoretical positions, psychoanalytic theory, and focus on ego development. Next, we will examine some of the popular views that grew from theories of ego development and see whether adult personality develops in stages. Third, we will shift our focus to theories that emphasize traits or other components as the building blocks of personality. Fourth, we will consider the increasingly popular and emerging cognitive theories, which emphasize the role of choice and life events in understanding personality development. Finally, we will examine a few particular aspects of personality: self-concept, attributional style, life satisfaction, and sex roles.

EGO DEVELOPMENT ACROSS ADULTHOOD

One way to view personality is as the organization of needs, motives, dispositions, habits, and abilities that are used to reach certain higher-order goals. These goals are, in turn, set by biological instincts, cultural forces, or personal experience, depending on the specific theory. The way in which individuals think about and combine these various influences is thought to be crucial. Viewing personality in this way has its roots in Freud's psychoanalytic theory. Over the years his work was extended and modified by many theorists, including his daughter Anna and several of his own students, such as Carl Jung. These theorists were concerned with **ego development** and the idea that we are constantly seeking ways in which to define our personal identity in everyday life. Ego development entails increasingly complex, more integrated, and more effective ways of dealing with reality and handling anxiety, and it is thought to be the basis for personality development across the life span.

Jung's Theory

Jung represents a turning point in the history of psychoanalytic thought. Initially allied with Freud, he soon severed the tie and developed his own ideas, which have elements of both Freudian theory and humanistic psychology. He was one of the very first theorists to believe in personality development in adulthood; this marked a major break with Freudian thought, which argued that personality development ended in adolescence.

Jung's theory emphasizes that each aspect of a person's personality must be in balance with all of the others. This means that each part of the personality will be expressed in some way, whether through normal means or through neurotic symptoms or in dreams. Jung asserts that the parts of the personality are organized in such a way as to produce two basic orientations of the ego. One of these orientations is concerned with the external world; Jung labels it extraversion. The opposite orientation, toward the inner world of subjective experiences, is labeled introversion. In order to be psychologically healthy, both of these orientations must be present, and they must be balanced. Individuals must be able to deal with the external world effectively and also be able to evaluate their inner feelings and values. It is when people overemphasize one orientation or the other that they are classified as "extraverts" or "introverts."

According to Jung, there are two important age-related trends in personality development. The first relates to the introversion-extraversion distinction. Young adults are more extraverted than older adults, perhaps because of the needs that younger people have in finding a mate, having a career, and so forth. With increasing age, however, the need for balance creates a need to focus inward and explore personal feelings about aging and mortality. Thus, Jung argued that with age comes an increase in introversion.

The second age-related trend in Jung's theory involves the feminine and masculine aspects of our personalities. Each of us has elements of both masculinity and femininity. In young adulthood, however, most of us express only one of them while usually working hard to suppress the other. In other words young adults most often act in accordance with sex-role stereotypes appropriate to their culture. As they grow older, people begin to allow the suppressed parts of their personality out. This means that men begin to behave in ways that earlier in life they would have considered feminine, and women behave in ways that they formerly would have thought to be masculine. These changes achieve a better balance that allows men and women to deal more effectively with their individual needs rather than being driven by socially defined stereotypes. This balance, however, does not mean that there is a reversal of sex roles. On the contrary, it represents the expression of aspects of ourselves that had been there all along but that we had simply not allowed to be shown. We will return to this issue at the end of the chapter when we consider sex-role development.

Jung stretched traditional psychoanalytic theory to new limits by postulating continued development across adulthood. Other theorists took Jung's lead and argued not only that personality development occurred in adulthood but also that it did so in an orderly sequential fashion. We will consider the sequences developed by two theorists, Erik Erikson and Jane Loevinger.

This actor is portraying King Lear, a Shakespearean character who experienced Erikson's struggle of integrity versus despair when he divided his kingdom among his children, who then fought among themselves and rejected him.

Erikson's Stages of Psychosocial Development

The best known theorist of life-span ego development is Erikson (1982). According to him, personality is determined by the interaction between an inner maturational plan and external societal demands. He proposes that the life cycle comprises eight stages of ego development, summarized in Table 8.1. The sequence of stages is thought to be biologically fixed.

Each stage in Erikson's theory is marked by a struggle between two opposing tendencies, both of which are experienced by the person. The names of the stages reflect the issues that form the struggles. The struggles are resolved through an interactive process involving both the inner psychological and the outer social influences. Successful resolutions establish the basic areas of psychosocial strength; unsuccessful resolutions impair ego development in a particular area and adversely affect the resolution of future struggles. Thus, each stage in Erikson's theory represents a kind of crisis.

The sequence of stages in Erikson's theory is based on the **epigenetic principle** (see Chapter 2), which means that each psychosocial strength has its own special time of ascendancy, or period of particular importance. The eight stages represent

TABLE 8.1 · Summary of Erikson's theory of psychosocial development, with important relationships and psychosocial strengths acquired at each stage

Stage	Psychosocial Crisis	Significant Relations	Basic Strengths
1 Infancy	Basic trust versus basic mistrust	Maternal person	Hope
2 Early childhood	Autonomy versus shame and doubt	Parental persons	Will
3 Play age	Initiative versus guilt	Basic family	Purpose
4 School age	Industry versus inferiority	"Neighborhood," school	Competence
5 Adolescence	Identity versus identity confusion	Peer groups and outgroups; models of leadership	Fidelity
6 Young adulthood	Intimacy versus isolation	Partners in friendship, sex, competition, cooperation	Love
7 Adulthood	Generativity versus stagnation	Divided labor and shared household	Care
8 Old age	Integrity versus despair	"Mankind," "my kind"	Wisdom

(Source: *The Life Cycle Completed: A Review* by E. H. Erikson, 1982, New York: Norton. Reprinted with permission of W. W. Norton & Company, Inc. © 1982 by Rikan Enterprises Ltd.)

the order of this ascendancy. Because the stages extend across the whole life span, it takes a lifetime to acquire all of the psychosocial strengths. Moreover, Erikson realizes that present and future behavior must have its roots in the past, since later stages build on the foundation laid in previous ones.

Erikson argues that the basic aspect of a healthy personality is a sense of trust toward oneself and others. Thus, the first stage in his theory involves trust versus mistrust, representing the conflict that an infant faces in developing trust in a world it knows little about. With trust come feelings of security and comfort.

The second stage, autonomy versus shame and doubt, reflects children's budding understanding that they are in charge of their own actions. This understanding changes them from totally reactive beings to ones who can act on the world intentionally. Their autonomy is threatened, however, by their inclinations to avoid responsibility for their actions and to go back to the security of the first stage.

In the third stage the conflict is initiative versus guilt. Once children realize that they can act on the world and are somebody, they begin to discover who they are. They take advantage of wider experience to explore the environment on their own, to ask many questions about the world, and to imagine possibilities about themselves.

The fourth stage is marked by children's increasing interest in interacting with peers, their need for acceptance, and their need to develop competencies. Erikson views these needs as representing industry versus inferiority, which is manifested behaviorally in children's desire to accomplish tasks by working hard. Failure to succeed in developing self-perceived competencies results in feelings of inferiority.

During adolescence, Erikson believes, we deal with the issue of identity versus identity confusion. The choice we make, that is, the identity we form, is not so much who we are but, rather, whom we can become. The struggle in adolescence is choosing from among a multitude of possible selves the one we will become. Identity confusion results when we are torn over the possibilities. The struggle involves trying to balance our need to choose a possible self and the desire to try out many possible selves.

During young adulthood the major developmental task involves establishing a fully intimate relationship with another. Erikson (1968) argues that intimacy means the sharing of all aspects of oneself without fearing the loss of identity. If intimacy is not achieved, isolation results. One way to assist the development of intimacy is to choose a mate who represents the ideal of all one's past experiences. The psychosocial strength that emerges from the intimacy-isolation struggle is love.

With the advent of middle age the focus shifts from intimacy to concern for the next generation. The struggle occurs between a sense of generativity (the feeling that people must maintain and perpetuate society) and a sense of stagnation (the feeling of self-absorption). Generativity is seen in such things as parenthood, teaching, or providing goods and services for the benefit of society. If the challenge of generativity is accepted, the development of trust in the next generation is facilitated, and the psychosocial strength of care is obtained.

In old age individuals must resolve the struggle between a sense of ego integrity and a sense of despair. This last stage begins with a growing awareness of the nearness of the end of life, but it is actually completed by only a small number of people (Erikson, 1982). The task is to examine and evaluate one's life and accomplishments and to verify that it has meaning. This process often involves reminiscing with others and actively seeking reassurance that one has accomplished something in life. People who have progressed successfully through earlier stages of life face old age enthusiastically and feel that their life has been full. Those feeling a sense of meaninglessness do not anxiously anticipate old age, and they experience despair. The psychosocial strength achieved from a successful resolution of this struggle is wisdom. Integrity is not the only issue facing older adults; Erikson points out that they have many opportunities for generativity as well. Many older people play an active role as grandparents, for example, and many maintain part-time jobs.

Extensions and Interpretations of Erikson's Theory. Erikson's theory has had a major impact on thinking about life-span development. However, some aspects of his theory are unclear, poorly defined, or unspecified. Traditionally, these problems have led critics to dismiss the theory as untestable and incomplete. The situation is changing, however. Other theorists have tried to address these problems by identifying common themes, specifying underlying mental processes, and reinterpreting and integrating the theory with other ideas. These ideas are leading researchers to reassess the utility of Erikson's theory as a guide for research on adult personality development.

Logan (1986) points out that Erikson's theory can be considered as a cycle that repeats: from basic trust to identity and from identity to integrity. In this approach the developmental progression is trust ⟶ achievement ⟶ wholeness. Throughout life we first establish that we can trust ourselves and other people. Initially, trust involves learning about ourselves and others, represented by the first two stages (trust versus mistrust and autonomy versus shame and doubt). The recapitulation of this idea in the second cycle is seen in our struggle to find a person with whom we form a very close relationship yet not to lose our own sense of self (intimacy versus isolation). Additionally, Logan shows how achievement, our need to accomplish and to be recognized for it, is a theme throughout Erikson's theory. During childhood this idea is reflected in the two stages initiative versus guilt and industry versus inferiority, whereas in adulthood it is represented by generativity versus stagnation. Finally, Logan points out that the issue of understanding ourselves as worthwhile and whole is first encountered during adolescence (identity versus identity diffusion) and is reexperienced during old age (integrity versus despair). Logan's analysis emphasizes that psychosocial development, although complicated on the surface, may actually reflect only a small number of issues. Moreover, he points out that we do not come to a single resolution of these issues of trust, achievement, and wholeness. Rather, they are issues that we struggle with our entire lives.

One aspect of Erikson's theory that is not specified is the rules that govern the sequence in which issues are faced. That is, Erikson does not make clear why certain issues are dealt with early in development and others are delayed. Moreover, how transitions from one stage to the next happen is also not fully explained. Van Geert (1987) proposes a set of rules that fills in these gaps. He argues that the sequence of stages is guided by three developmental trends. First, an inward orientation to the self gradually replaces an outward orientation to the world. This trend is similar to Jung's increase in introversion with age. Second, we move from using very general categories in understanding the world to using more specific

ones. This trend is reflected in cognitive development, in that our earliest categories do not allow the separation of individual differences (for example, we use *dog* to mean all sorts of animals). Third, we move from operating with limited ideas of social and emotional experiences to more inclusive ideas. During childhood we may love only those people we believe are deserving, for example, whereas in adulthood we may love all people as representatives of humanity. By combining these three developmental trends, van Geert constructs rules for moving from one stage to another.

Although van Geert's approach has not been tested completely, his ideas fit with Erikson's theory and with other related data. For example, Neugarten (1977) points to an increase in interiority with age across adulthood, an idea very similar to van Geert's inward orientation. Cognitive developmental research (see Chapter 6) supports the development of more refined conceptual categories. Thus, van Geert's approach may be quite useful in understanding psychosocial development as well as in providing a way to identify the cyclic progression described by Logan.

Viney (1987) shows how other approaches to human development can add to Erikson's theory. As an example, she points to the sociophenomenological approach, which emphasizes that people change in how they interpret and reinterpret events. That is, the meaning of major life events changes from earlier to later in the life span. In a study that examined individuals between the ages of 6 and 86, she documented that the positive and negative descriptors that people used to characterize their lives changed considerably. Interestingly, these shifts in descriptors appear to parallel Erikson's stages. For example, adults over age 65 are more likely to talk about trying to get their lives in order or that they feel completely alone than are adults under age 65. Although Viney's research was not intended to be a direct test of

Erikson's theory, her results indicate that we may be able to document his stages in research based on different approaches to development. Additionally, Viney's research may indicate that the themes identified by Erikson are applicable to many situations, including the way in which we view events.

Finally, some critics argue that Erikson's stage of generativity is much too broad to capture the essence of adulthood. For example, Kotre (1984) contends that adults experience many opportunities to express generativity that are not equivalent and do not lead to a general state. Rather, he sees generativity more as a set of impulses felt at different times in different settings, such as at work or in grandparenting. Only rarely, Kotre contends, is there a continuous state of generativity in adulthood. He asserts that the struggles identified by Erikson are not fought constantly; rather, they probably come and go.

Loevinger's Theory

Loevinger (1976) saw a need to extend the groundwork laid by Erikson both theoretically and empirically. For her, the ego is the chief organizer, the integrator of our morals, values, goals, and thought processes. Because this integration performed by the ego is so complex and is influenced by personal experiences, it is the primary source of individual differences at all ages beyond infancy. Ego development is the result of dynamic interaction between the person and the environment. Consequently, it consists of fundamental changes in the ways in which our thoughts, values, morals, and goals are organized. Transitions from one stage to another depend on both internal biological changes and external social changes to which the person must adapt.

Although Loevinger proposes eight stages of ego development, beginning in infancy, we will

focus on the six that are observed in adults (see Table 8.2). An important aspect of her theory is that most people never go through all of them; indeed, the last level is achieved by only a handful of individuals. There is growing cross-sectional and longitudinal evidence that these stages are age-related (Cook-Greuter, 1989; Redmore & Loevinger, 1979). At each stage Loevinger identifies four areas that she considers important to the developmental progression: character development, reflecting a person's standards and goals; interpersonal style, representing the person's pattern of relations with others; conscious preoccupations, reflecting the most important things on the person's mind; and cognitive style, reflecting the characteristic way in which the person thinks. As we consider the ego levels important for adults, we will examine them in terms of these four areas.

A few adults operate at the *conformist* level. Character development at this stage is marked by absolute conformity to social rules. If these rules are broken, feelings of shame and guilt result. Interpersonally, conformists need to belong and show a superficial niceness. Of central importance is appearance and social acceptability. Conformists see the world only in terms of external tangibles, such as how one looks and if one behaves according to group standards. Thinking is dominated by stereotypes and clichés and is relatively simplistic.

Most adults in American society operate at the *conscientious-conformist* level. At this stage character development is marked by a differentiation of norms and goals; in other words, people learn to separate what they want for themselves from what social norms may dictate. They deal with others by recognizing that they have an impact on them and on the group as a whole. They begin to have some preoccupation with issues of personal adjustment and coping with problems, needing reasons for actions, and recognizing that

TABLE 8.2 · Summary of Loevinger's stages of ego development in adulthood

Stage	Description
Conformist	Obedience to external social rules
Conscientious-conformist	Separation of norms and goals; realization that acts affect others
Conscientious	Beginning of self-evaluated standards
Individualistic	Recognition that the process of acting is more important than the outcome
Autonomous	Respect for each person's individuality; tolerance for ambiguity
Integrated	Resolution of inner conflicts

there are many opportunities in life from which they may choose. There is still concern with group standards, and the desire for personal adjustment is sometimes suppressed if it conflicts with the needs of the group.

The next level, the *conscientious* stage, is marked by a cognitive style in which individuals have a beginning understanding of the true complexity of the world. Their focus becomes understanding the role that the self plays; character development involves self-evaluated standards, self-critical thinking, self-determined ideals, and self-set goals. This level represents a move away from letting other people or society set their goals and standards for them. Interpersonal relations are characterized by intensity, responsibility, and mutual sharing. People evaluate behavior using internalized standards developed over the years. They come to realize that they control their own future. Although more complex, conscientious people still think in terms of polarities, such as love versus lust or inner life versus outer appearance. But they recognize responsibility and obligation in addition to rights and privileges.

Loevinger postulates that the *individualistic*

level builds on the previous (conscientious) level. A major acquisition at the individualistic level is a respect for individuality. Immature dependency is seen as an emotional problem, rather than as something to be expected. Concern for broad social problems and differentiating one's inner life from one's outer life become the main preoccupations. People begin to differentiate process, the *way* things are done, from outcome, the answer; for example, people realize that sometimes the solution to a problem is "right" but the way of getting there involves hurting someone. The flavor of the individualistic person is an increased tolerance for oneself and others. Key conflicts are recognized as complex problems: dependence as constraining versus dependence as emotionally rewarding, and morality and responsibility versus achievement for oneself. The way of resolving these conflicts, however, usually involves projecting the cause onto the environment rather than acknowledging their internal sources.

At Loevinger's *autonomous* level comes a high tolerance for ambiguity with conflicting needs both within oneself and others. Autonomous individuals' interpersonal style is characterized by a

Being committed to broad social concerns is the essence of Loevinger's individualistic phase of ego development.

respect for each person's independence but also by an understanding that people are interdependent. The preoccupations at this level are vividly conveyed feelings, self-fulfillment, and understanding of the self in a social context. Autonomous people have the courage to acknowledge and face conflict head on rather than projecting it onto the environment. They see reality as complex and multifaceted and no longer view it in the polarities of the conscientious stage. Autonomous individuals recognize that there are multiple ways to view a problem and are comfortable with the fact that other people's viewpoints may differ from their own. They recognize the need for others' self-sufficiency and take a broad view of life.

The final level in Loevinger's theory is termed the *integrated* stage. Inner conflicts are not only faced but also reconciled and laid to rest. There is a renunciation of goals that are recognized to be unattainable. People at the integrated level cherish an individuality that comes from a consolidated sense of identity. They are very much like Maslow's (1968) self-actualized person; that is, they are at peace with themselves and have realized their maximum potential. They recognize that they could have chosen other paths in life but are content with and make the most out of the one that they picked. Such people are always open to further growth-enhancing opportunities and make the most out of integrating new experiences into their lives.

Loevinger's theory is having an increasing impact on adult developmental research. One of its advantages is that it is more empirically based than Erikson's theory, so that researchers can document the stages more precisely. Loevinger's theory is the major framework for research examining relationships between cognitive development and ego development (King, Kitchener, Wood, & Davison, 1989). For example, Blanchard-Fields (1986) found the ego level, as measured by Loevinger's sentence-completion task, was the best predictor of young and middle-aged adults' reasoning on social-dilemmas tasks, such as what to do about an unwanted pregnancy. Likewise, Labouvie-Vief, Hakim-Larson, and Hobart (1987) reported that ego level, based on Loevinger's task, was a strong predictor of the coping strategies used across the life span from childhood to old age. Both studies documented an age-related increase in ego level that was associated with higher levels of problem-solving ability or with more mature coping styles.

Research Relating to Ego Development

In addition to the research underlying Erikson's and Loevinger's theories, several investigators have examined ego development empirically. In this section we will consider some of this work briefly.

The Kansas City Studies. One of the earliest series of studies on adult personality development was begun in the 1950s by Neugarten and her colleagues (Neugarten & Associates, 1964). Large representative samples of people aged 40 to 80 living in Kansas City were asked to take projective tests of personality, to fill out questionnaires, and to be interviewed. Three sets of findings are important; the first two address Jung's proposals concerning the moves toward introversion and androgyny with age, and the third concerns patterns of personality types.

Older adults showed a rising preoccupation with self along with an increasingly passive and fatalistic orientation toward the external world; in short, they became more introverted. For example, the 40-year-olds thought that they could influence the environment by acting boldly, whereas the 60-year-olds were more likely to think that the environment controlled them. Introspection increased with age, typically manifested as contemplation, reflection, and self-evaluation.

Jung's belief that men allow their femininity to show and that women allow their masculinity to come out also received support. In response to projective personality tests in which participants were asked to tell stories about men and women, those over 55 were much more likely to describe people as having characteristics of both sexes. Thus, the older respondents described men as being both strong and nurturant and depicted women as being both supportive and assertive.

The findings from the Kansas City research have been supported by several more-recent studies (Brown, 1982; Feldman, Biringen, & Nash, 1981; Gutmann, 1977). The same patterns have been noted cross-culturally (Gutmann, 1977), adding strength to the conclusion that the results reflect a basic developmental process rather than something that is a result of particular social pressures.

The third set of findings from the Kansas City studies provides insight into the relationship between personality types and adaptation. Neugarten, Havighurst, and Tobin (1968) describe four personality types that are unrelated to age but are related to life-style. Additionally, aspects of personality related to social adaptation do not vary with age; these include goal-directed behavior, coping styles, and life satisfaction. Taken together, these results mean that the fundamental ways in which we interact with other people tend to remain constant as we age.

In sum, Neugarten's research demonstrated no age difference in those aspects of personality involved directly with interpersonal and environmental interactions. However, age and sex differences were both obtained for intrapsychic dimensions involved with how we see ourselves in relation to others.

Ryff's Implementation-Culmination Sequence. Ryff has conducted several multidimensional cross-sectional studies that complement Neugarten's work (Ryff, 1984; Ryff & Heincke, 1981). Ryff's research focuses on what she labels the **implementation-culmination sequence**. Implementation means an emphasis on being active, achievement-oriented, and concerned with establishing oneself in the occupational, familial, and sociocultural spheres. Culmination refers to a more inward-oriented emphasis in late adulthood on completing, contemplating, and accepting earlier life endeavors (Ryff, 1984). Ryff asked people of different ages to answer questions about their values and personalities as if they were younger than, older than, or at their real age. Her results for women point toward the conclusion that middle age is viewed as a time for implementing and old age is seen as a time for culminating. Her data for women complement ideas that we encountered in previous sections. Jung's notion of increased introversion, Neugarten's work, and Erikson's concepts of generativity and ego integrity provide conceptual explanatory frameworks.

Results for men were inconsistent; in some cases the shift was obtained, but in others it was not. Why these sex differences occur is not clear. In part, they may be due to men's and women's different life experiences. These findings point out that complex multidimensional patterns of adult personality development may be the rule; no general trends held for all participants.

Lowenthal's Research. One of the most ambitious and interesting cross-sectional multidimensional studies was conducted by Lowenthal and her colleagues (Lowenthal, Thurnher, & Chiriboga, 1975). They chose to examine four age groups of people who were in transitional phases of life: high school seniors, newlyweds, middle-aged parents, and preretirees. Each participant underwent an 8-hour interview that included both open-ended questions and a battery of personality tests. These measures yielded dozens of indexes, including degree of preoccupation with stress, perceptions of change, life-style configurations, self-image, and personal views on one's life.

Several themes emerged from the work of Lowenthal and her associates. Family-centeredness was a major theme in every group, but it was manifested in different ways. For example, parenthood was a major goal for the two younger groups, whereas older women tended to refocus this child-centered theme to their husbands. A second major theme was that the participants varied on measures of life-style, self-concept, social horizons, life-course perspectives, values and goals, emotional experience, and psychological resources from those individuals having limited role involvement and few social activities, termed **simplistic** people, to those having many roles and behaviors involving a wide variety of activities, termed **complex** people. An interesting trend was observed when levels of happiness were compared with where individuals fell on the simplistic-complex dimension. The happiest young adults were those judged most complex. Among older adults, however, complex people were the least happy, perhaps because they had fewer opportunities for participation and self-expression. In late middle age, people who reported the fewest emotional experiences, the lowest levels of stress, and the fewest life transitions—the simplest types—were the happiest.

Several consistent sex differences also emerged. Lowenthal et al. found that men moved from insecurity and discontent through buoyancy and almost uncontrolled energy to order, control, and industry and, finally, to a mellow, satisfying relationship with themselves that arose out of making fewer demands either on themselves or on the environment. Women progressed from dependency and helplessness to a more assertive, aggressive, and energetic style similar to that of middle-aged men. These differences reflect alternative developmental courses for men and women. The extent to which at least part of the age-related differences are due to cohort effects remains to be seen. It would be interesting to repeat Lowenthal's study in a few years to see whether the women's movement has had any impact on developmental sequences. In any case Lowenthal and her colleagues have shown that contrary to what most ego-development theories propose, it may not be possible to talk about developmental sequences that ignore sex.

STAGE THEORIES BASED ON PERSONAL MYTHS AND TRANSITIONS

Erikson's belief that personality development proceeds in stages laid the foundation for many later theorists' efforts. As we have seen, some of these efforts were designed to refine the notion of ego development. In this section we will consider other attempts to describe stages of personality development based on the central ideas of personal myths and alternating periods of stability and transition. Before we start, though, take a moment to think about your own life, as suggested in "Something to Think About."

When Gail Sheehy published her books *Passages* (1976) and *Pathfinders* (1981), they were met with instant acceptance. For many people the idea that adults go through an orderly sequence of stages that includes both crises and stability reflected their own experience. Belief in the midlife crisis was especially strong. Actually, Sheehy based much of her writing on the findings of two studies, one by Roger Gould and the other by Daniel Levinson. In this section we will briefly examine these two studies and each researcher's accompanying theory, as well as other evidence concerning the existence of personal crises.

Roger Gould and the Rejection of Myths

Gould (1978) strongly believes that psychoanalytic theory has much to offer the study of adult personality. In particular, he believes that a person's primary developmental task is to grow out of basic biological helplessness and immaturity and to shed major false assumptions, or myths, in order to achieve adult maturity. Based on this belief, Gould organizes adult development into six major periods between the ages of 16 and 60. Each period is characterized by a particular myth. Age per se plays a major role in Gould's theory, because he believes that an internal clock defines the tasks to be accomplished at each period. (This clock is similar to the social clock hypothesized by Neugarten and Hagestad [1976] and described in Chapter 1.) Gould's six stages are summarized in Table 8.3.

Between the ages of 16 and 22 the major developmental task is to leave our parents' world, and the assumption to be rejected is that "I'll always belong to my parents and believe in their world." Young people at this stage are struggling between their need for autonomy and their need to feel safe and secure.

The period between the ages of 22 and 28 is marked by the myth that "doing things my parents' way will bring results. If I become too frustrated, confused, or tired or am simply unable to cope, they will step in and show me the right way." Young adults in this period must deal with strong ties to their parents along with the growing realization that they are now on their own. Gould argues that they tend to choose partners who allow them to recreate their parent-child relationship in some way. In short, the independence that young adults like to believe they have from their parents is an illusion. Along with this illusion of independence is an illusion of optimism concerning what they can accomplish. This myth, that "if I do what I'm supposed to, I will be rewarded," means that careers are often chosen after very little reflection and that simply working harder is viewed as the answer to most problems.

Gould's third stage, between ages 28 and 34, is a time of soul searching and disillusionment. We believe that we are not accomplishing our dreams and that life is going downhill. The major myths that trigger this questioning are that "life is simple and controllable" and that "there are no significant contradictory forces within me." A major trigger of this distress, according to Gould,

The Personal Side of Stage Theories

Studying stage theories generally makes us wonder how we stand. Evaluating our own ego development and other aspects of personality can be both fun and humbling. It can be fun in the sense that learning something about oneself is enjoyable and enlightening; it can be humbling in the sense that we may have overestimated how advanced we really are. There is another side to this personal evaluation, though, that is equally important.

Take a few moments and think back perhaps 5 or 10 years. What things were important to you? How well did you know yourself? What were your priorities? What did you see yourself becoming in the future? What were your relationships with other people based on? Now answer these questions from your perspective today.

If you are like most people, answering these questions will make you see the ways in which you have changed. Many times we are in the worst position to see this change, because we are embedded in it. We also find ourselves reinterpreting the past based on the experiences we have had in the meantime.

It is change in the ways that we see ourselves that is the focus of the stage theories we have considered. We do look at the world differently as we grow older. Our priorities do change. Take a few moments now and jot down how you have changed over the years since high school. Then write down how you see yourself now. Finally, write down how you would like to see your life go in the future. These ideas will give you something to think about now and again later when we consider Whitbourne's ideas about scenarios and life stories.

---

is parenthood; as we pass values down to children, we are forced to examine them in ourselves.

Problems and challenges increase during the fourth stage, which occurs between ages 34 and 45. Here the major false assumption is the "there is no evil or death in the world; the sinister has been destroyed." Gould sees the early 40s as an especially uncomfortable time, constituting the mid-life crisis. We are forced to see our negative side, our own mortality, and many other unpleasant issues.

Gould has less to say about his final two stages. Things get better from ages 43 to 53, the fifth stage. We feel that we are whoever we are going to be, and we become less competitive and more inner directed. During the sixth stage, from age 53 to age 60, the negative feelings of the 40s diminish even further.

Gould's theory is based on a cross-sectional study of 524 white, middle-class men and women ranging in age from 16 to 60. His participants indicated how applicable to their present lives various statements about feelings were. These statements had been made by people who were outpatients in therapy. Gould based his conclusions on comparisons of relative frequencies indicated by each age group; no statistical tests comparing group averages were conducted. Thus, we do not know whether the differences he reports represent true differences between age

TABLE 8.3 • Summary of Gould's theory

Ages 16–22	Characteristic myth: I'll always belong to my parents and believe in their world.
Ages 22–28	Characteristic myth: Doing things my parents' way will bring results. If I become too frustrated or tired or am simply unable to cope, they will step in and show me the right way.
Ages 28–34	Characteristic myth: Life is simple and controllable. There are no contradictory forces within me.
Ages 34–45	Characteristic myth: There is no evil or death in the world. The sinister has been destroyed.
Ages 45–53	Characteristics: We are whoever we are going to be. We become less competitive and are more inner directed.
Ages 53–60	Characteristics: We continue on the path begun in the previous stage.

groups. Moreover, as noted in Chapter 1, the use of cross-sectional research presents additional interpretive problems. Even if the differences are real, for example, we cannot know whether they reflect age change or cohort effects. Although Gould's ideas are provocative, raise some interesting questions, and are intuitively appealing, it is better to view them as hypotheses worth pursuing than as explanations of development.

Daniel Levinson and Stability-Transition Cycles

Levinson's theory, which appeared at about the same time as Gould's, is based on a different set of assumptions. Levinson believes that adult development consists of alternating periods of **stability** and **transition** (Levinson, Darrow, Kline, Levinson, & McKee, 1978). That is, we experience times when we are changing and other times when we are not. Figure 8.1 depicts the major periods that Levinson identifies.

Central to Levinson's theory is his belief that adults engage in the formation of **life structures**, the values, beliefs, and priorities we live by. Dur-

ing periods of stability we build the structure; during periods of transition we change the structure. Indeed, Levinson himself does not view his theory as describing personality development (Levinson, 1979). But several aspects of personality development are included in his theory, and many people view it in that way.

For Levinson, transitions involve shifts in life structures, requiring that different aspects of one's life become central issues. Transitions do not necessarily entail turmoil or conscious questioning, but they are universal. Levinson's emphasis on transitions is similar to Erikson's belief that crisis is the basis for developmental change.

Levinson puts special emphasis on the midlife transition, which he believes occurs in men during their early 40s. This period is typically tumultuous and involves resolving discrepancies in one's self-image and competing needs. In particular, he points to four issues, or "polarities," that face a man at mid-life. First, men struggle between attachment and separateness, reflecting the push to have intimate relationships with others versus the pull to look inside themselves. Second, they confront the issue of destruction and crea-

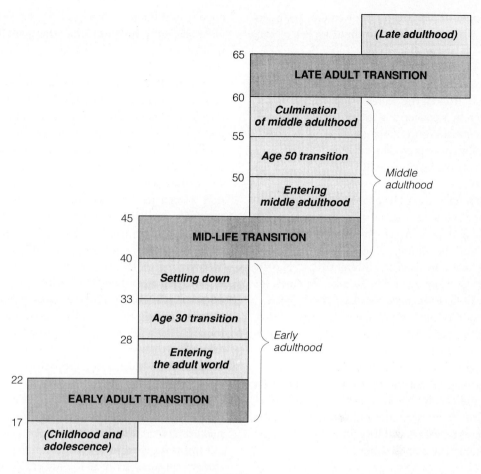

FIGURE 8.1 • Levinson's theory of adult development. The numbers on the left correspond to the ages at which periods begin and end.

(Source: *The Seasons of a Man's Life* by D. J. Levinson, C. Darrow, E. Kline, M. Levinson, & B. McKee. © 1978 by Daniel J. Levinson, New York: Knopf. Reprinted with permission of Alfred A. Knopf, Inc.)

tion, in which they realize that they have the capacity to destroy and to build new aspects of life. Third, facing masculinity and femininity entails allowing both traditionally masculine and traditionally feminine traits to emerge. Finally, dealing with the issue of youth and age means coming to grips with one's own aging.

Finally, Levinson's ideas have had a consider-

able impact on the career-development literature. As will be discussed in Chapter 12, an important contribution of his theory is the concept of "mentoring," in which older, more experienced employees provide guidance for younger, less experienced ones.

Levinson's initial research was a short-term longitudinal study of 40 men from a variety of occupations who were interviewed and tested in depth. Although the longitudinal aspect of this study is an improvement over Gould's research, Levinson's findings can be criticized on many of the same grounds. For example, he provides no information about the degree of agreement among his researchers concerning the coding of data, the sample consisted only of men, and the conclusions are not always supported by data. Still, Levinson's work has had considerable influence on other researchers.

Much of this additional work focuses on whether Levinson's stages can be documented in women. Women's development does occur in stages, but the timing of important transitions and the issues involved are different (R.L. Harris, Ellicott, & Holmes, 1986; Reinke, Holmes, & Harris, 1985; Roberts & Newton, 1987). For example, women appear to have a major transition around age 30 rather than at mid-life, and they tend to be influenced to a greater extent by family issues. Why these differences occur is unclear. Women may be responding to conflicts between career and family, but the evidence is inconsistent. Overall, however, these data suggest that the concept of periods of stability and transition may hold for both men and women.

In Search of the Mid-Life Crisis

One of the most important ideas in both Gould's and Levinson's theories is that middle-aged adults experience a personal crisis that results in major changes in life structure. This belief in a mid-life crisis is not universally shared, however. Many theorists simply do not think that it exists.

Some research seems to document the crisis. Jaques (1965) reported that male artists went through a crisis precipitated by the recognition of their own mortality. Time since birth was replaced by time left to live in the minds of these middle-aged men. Chew (1976) suggests that marriages grow stale and that the quest for lost youth leads men to intensified sexual yearnings. Among women, Chew found that the combination of menopause and the empty nest resulted in depression and crisis. Levinson (1978) writes that middle-aged men in his study reported intense internal struggles that were much like depression.

Baruch (1984) summarizes a series of retrospective interview studies of American women between the ages of 35 and 55. The results showed that women in their 20s were more likely to be uncertain and dissatisfied than were women at mid-life. Middle-aged women only rarely mentioned normative developmental milestones such as marriage, childbirth, or menopause as major turning points in their lives. Rather, unexpected events such as divorce and job transfers were more likely to cause crises. Studies extending Levinson's theory to women have not found strong evidence of a traumatic mid-life crisis either (Harris et al., 1986; Reinke et al., 1985; Roberts & Newton, 1987).

The mid-life crisis was also missing in data obtained as part of the Berkeley studies. Most middle-aged men said that their careers were satisfying (Clausen, 1981), and both men and women appeared more self-confident, insightful, introspective, open, and better equipped to handle stressful situations (Haan, 1985; Haan, Milsap, & Hartka, 1986). Even direct attempts to find the mid-life crisis failed. In two studies Costa and McCrae (1978) could identify only a handful of men who fit the profile, and even then the crisis came anytime between 30 and 60. A replication and extension of this work, conducted by Farrell and Rosenberg (1981), confirmed the initial results.

McCrae and Costa (1984) point out that the idea of a mid-life crisis has become widely accepted as fact in the mass media. People take it for granted that they will go through a period of intense psychological turmoil in their 40s. The problem is that there is little hard scientific evidence of it. The data suggest that mid-life is no more or no less traumatic for most people than any other period in life. Perhaps the most convincing support for this conclusion comes from the research of Farrell and Rosenberg (1981). These investigators initially set out to prove the existence of a mid-life crisis, since they were firm believers in it. After extensive testing and interviewing, however, they emerged as nonbelievers.

Conclusions Concerning Stage Theories

What should we conclude about stage theories? At this point it is fair to say that the evidence for Gould's stagelike progressions in personality development or for Levinson's life structures is weak. Neither theory deals adequately with individual differences in timing or crises or transitions, which appear to be the rule rather than the exception. The safest position is that Gould's and Levinson's theories are beginning steps in understanding how people view themselves and the changes that they perceive. The issue that must be resolved in future research is whether these perceived changes are normative and age-related or whether they may occur at any point in adulthood.

PERSONALITY TRAITS ACROSS ADULTHOOD

Consider the following anecdote:

Over the course of numerous meetings it becomes apparent that Michelle is always surrounded by a group of people. On closer observation you see

why this is so. She walks up to people and initiates conversations, is at east with strangers, is pleasant, and is often described as the life of the party.

What can we say about Michelle? One conclusion could be that she is an outgoing, or extroverted, person. How did we arrive at this judgment? We probably combined several aspects of her behavior into a concept that describes her rather concisely. What we have done is to use the notion of a personality **trait**.

Extending this same reasoning to many areas of behavior is the basis for trait theories of personality. More formally, people's behavior is said to be understood best in terms of attributes that reflect underlying traits. We use the basic tenets of trait theory when we describe ourselves and others with terms like *calm, aggressive, independent, friendly,* and so on.

Three assumptions are made about traits (McCrae & Costa, 1984). First, traits are based on comparisons of individuals, because there are no absolute quantitative standards for concepts such as friendliness. Second, the qualities or behaviors making up a particular trait must be distinctive enough to avoid confusion. Imagine the chaos that would result if friendliness and aggressiveness had many behaviors in common yet some that were vastly different. Finally, the traits attributed to a specific person are assumed to be stable characteristics. We normally assume that people who are friendly in several situations are going to be friendly the next time we see them. These three assumptions are all captured in the definition of a trait: a trait is any distinguishable, relatively enduring way in which one individual differs from others (Guilford, 1959, p. 6).

Most trait theories have several guiding principles in common. An important one for our present discussion concerns the structure of traits. Structure refers to the way in which traits are thought to be organized within the individual. This organization is usually inferred from the pattern of related and unrelated traits and is generally expressed in terms of **dimensions**. Personality structures can be examined over time to see whether they change with age.

Costa and McCrae's Model

Although many different trait theories of personality have been proposed over the years, few have been concerned with or have been based on adults of different ages. A major exception to this is the model proposed by Costa and McCrae (1988; McCrae & Costa, 1984, 1987; McCrae, Costa, & Busch, 1986). Their model is strongly grounded in cross-sectional, longitudinal, and sequential research. It consists of five independent dimensions of personality: neuroticism, extroversion, openness to experience, agreeableness-antagonism, and conscientiousness-undirectedness.

The first three dimensions of Costa and McCrae's model, neuroticism, extroversion, and openness to experience, have been the ones most heavily researched. Each of these dimensions is represented by six facets that reflect the main characteristics associated with it. The remaining two dimensions were added to the original three in the late 1980s in order to account for more data and to bring the theory closer to other trait theories. In the following sections we will consider each of the five dimensions briefly.

Neuroticism. The six facets of neuroticism are anxiety, hostility, self-consciousness, depression, impulsiveness, and vulnerability. Anxiety and hostility form underlying traits for two fundamental emotions: fear and anger. Although we all experience these emotions at times, the frequency and intensity with which they are felt vary from one person to another. People who are high in trait anxiety are nervous, high-strung, tense, worried, and pessimistic. Besides being prone to anger, hostile people are irritable and tend to be hard to get along with.

The traits of self-consciousness and depression relate to the emotions shame and sorrow. Being high in self-consciousness is associated with being sensitive to criticism and teasing and to feelings of inferiority. Trait depression refers to feelings of sadness, hopelessness, loneliness, guilt, and low self-worth.

The final two facets of neuroticism, impulsiveness and vulnerability, are most often manifested as behaviors rather than as emotions. Impulsiveness is the tendency to give in to temptation and desires due to a lack of willpower and self-control. Consequently, impulsive people often do things in excess, such as overeating and overspending, and they are more likely to smoke, gamble, and use drugs. Vulnerability refers to a lowered ability to deal effectively with stress. Vulnerable people tend to panic in a crisis or emergency and to be highly dependent on others for help.

McCrae and Costa (1984) note that, in general, people who are high in neuroticism tend to be high in each of the traits. High neuroticism typically results in violent and negative emotions that interfere with people's ability to handle problems or get along with other people. We can see how this cluster of traits would operate: a person gets anxious and embarrassed in a social situation such as our class reunion, the frustration in dealing with others makes the person hostile, which may lead to excessive drinking at the party, which may result in subsequent depression for making a fool of oneself, and so on.

Extraversion. The six facets of extraversion can be grouped into three interpersonal traits (warmth, gregariousness, and assertiveness) and three temperamental traits (activity, excitement seeking, and positive emotions). Warmth, or attachment, refers to a friendly, compassionate, intimately involved style of interacting with other people. Warmth and gregariousness (a desire to be with other people) make up what is sometimes called sociability. Gregarious people thrive on crowds; the more social interaction, the better. Assertive people make natural leaders, take charge easily, make up their own minds, and readily express their thoughts and feelings.

Temperamentally, extraverts like to keep busy; they are the people who seem to have endless energy, talk fast, and want to be on the go. They prefer to be in stimulating, exciting environments and will often go searching for a challenging situation. This active, exciting life-style is evident in the extrovert's positive emotion; these people are walking examples of zest, delight, and fun.

An interesting aspect of extraversion is that this dimension relates well to occupational interests and values. People high in extraversion tend to be social workers, business administrators, and salespeople or to have other people-oriented jobs. They value humanitarian goals and a person-oriented use of power. Individuals low in extraversion tend to prefer task-oriented jobs, such as architecture or accounting.

Openness to Experience. The six facets of openness to experience represent six different areas. In the area of fantasy, openness means having a vivid imagination and active dream life. In aesthetics, openness is seen in the appreciation of art and beauty, a sensitivity to pure experience for its own sake. Openness to action refers to a willingness to try something new, whether it be a new kind of cuisine, a new movie, or a new travel destination. People who are open to ideas and values are curious and value knowledge for the sake of knowing. Open people also tend to be liberal in their values, often admitting that what may be right for one person may not be right for everyone. This outlook is a direct outgrowth of open individuals' willingness to think of different possibilities and their tendency to empathize with others in different circumstances. Open people also experience their own feelings strongly and see them as a major source of meaning in life.

Not surprisingly, openness to experience is also related to occupational choice. Open people are likely to be found in occupations that place a high value on thinking theoretically or philosophically and less emphasis on economic values. They are typically intelligent and tend to subject themselves to stressful situations. Occupations such as psychologist or minister, for example, appeal to open people.

Agreeableness-Antagonism. The easiest way to understand the agreeableness-antagonism dimension is to consider the traits that characterize antagonism. Antagonistic people tend to set themselves against others; they are skeptical, mistrustful, callous, unsympathetic, stubborn, and rude; and they have a defective sense of attachment. Antagonism may be manifested in ways other than overt hostility. For example, some antagonistic people are skillful manipulators or aggressive go-getters with little patience. In some respects these individuals have characteristics similar to the Type A behavior pattern (see Chapter 4).

Scoring high on agreeableness, the opposite of antagonism, may not always be adaptive either, however. These people may tend to be overly dependent and self-effacing, traits that often prove annoying to others.

Conscientiousness-Undirectedness. Scoring high on conscientiousness indicates that one is hardworking, ambitious, energetic, scrupulous, and persevering. Such people have the will to achieve (Digman and Takemoto-Chock, 1981), that is, to work hard and make something of oneself. Undirectedness is viewed primarily as meaning lazy, careless, late, unenergetic, and aimless.

Research Evidence. Costa and McCrae have investigated whether the traits that make up their model remain stable across adulthood (e.g., Costa & McCrae, 1980b, 1988; Costa, McCrae, & Arenberg, 1980). Because their results are very consistent from study to study, we will consider the findings from the Costa, McCrae, and Arenberg study as representative. The data came from the Baltimore Longitudinal Study of Aging for the 114 men who took the Guilford-Zimmerman Temperament Survey (GZTS) on three occasions, with each of the two follow-up testings about 6 years apart.

What Costa et al. found was astonishing. Even over a 12-year period, the 10 traits measured by the GZTS remained highly stable; the correlations ranged from .68 to .85. In much of personality research we might expect to find this degree of stability over a week or two, but to see it over 12 years is noteworthy. Even when the researchers looked at individual scores, it was apparent that people had changed very little.

We would normally be skeptical of such consistency over a long period. But similar findings were obtained in other studies conducted over a 10-year span by Costa and McCrae (1977) in Boston, an 8-year span by Siegler, George, and Okun (1979) at Duke University, and a 30-year span by Leon, Gillum, Gillum, and Gouze (1979) in Minnesota. Even more amazing was the finding that personality ratings by spouses of each other showed no systematic changes over a 6-year period (Costa & McCrae, 1988). Thus, it appears that individuals change very little in self-reported personality traits over periods of up to 30 years and over the age range of 20 to 90. As described in

"How Do We Know?" these stable traits also relate to such things as being happy.

This is a truly exciting and important conclusion. Clearly, lots of things will change in people's lives over 30 years. They will marry, divorce, have children, change jobs, face stressful situations, move, and maybe even retire. Social networks and friendships will come and go. Society will change, and economic ups and downs will have important effects. Personal changes in appearance and health will occur. People will read volumes, see dozens of movies, and watch thousands of hours of television. But their underlying personality dispositions will hardly change at all. Or will they?

Other Research on Personality Traits

Although Costa and McCrae provide one of the few theory-based models of personality traits in adulthood, several other researchers have collected longitudinal data about traits. Neugarten and her colleagues (1964) provided some of the earliest findings based on interviews, projective tests, and questionnaires administered to a large, representative sample of adults between the ages of 40 and 80 over a 10-year span. They found that adaptational processes such as coping styles, life satisfaction, and strength of goal-oriented behavior remained stable. However, they also discovered a shift from **active mastery** to **passive mastery** among the men in their sample. Men at age 40 felt in control of their lives; they viewed risk-taking positively and believed that they had considerable energy to tackle problems head-on. By age 60, however, men viewed their environment as harmful and threatening and themselves as accommodating.

The shift from active to passive mastery has been observed in several cultures, including the Navajo and the Lowland and Highland Mayans of Mexico. With increasing age there is a tendency to accommodate the self to outside influences

---

HOW · DO · WE · KNOW?

Personality Traits and Well-Being: Happy and Unhappy People

We all know what it feels like to be happy, and we also know what it feels like to be unhappy. But for researchers in personality, feelings are not enough. They want to identify the parts of our personalities that underlie being happy and being unhappy.

Costa and McCrae (1980b) examined the relationships between personality and happiness in three studies. Their participants were a subsample of 1,100 men who were members of the Normative Aging Study. The participants came from a variety of socioeconomic groups, and most were veterans. They were asked to complete a series of four questionnaires over a 3-month interval. These questionnaires measured personality traits and subjective well-being.

Results from the first investi-gation showed that similar relationships held between personality and well-being across a number of different scales. Moreover, different clusters of traits seemed to relate to happiness and unhappiness. Fear, anger, and poor impulse control were related to unhappiness, whereas sociability, tempo, and vigor related to happiness. Thus, it appears that happiness and unhappiness represent different aspects of personality; they are not two sides of the same coin.

In the second study Costa and McCrae tested this idea. Specifically, they examined whether neuroticism was differentially related to unhappiness and whether extraversion was differentially related to happiness. Their suspicions were confirmed.

Having documented that dif-ferent dimensions of personality influenced happiness and unhappiness, Costa and McCrae asked another question: does this relationship hold over long periods of time, or is it limited to short-term mood changes? In the third study they compared scores on the personality tests administered 10 years earlier to current measures of happiness. They found that scores on the earlier personality tests accurately predicted current happiness or unhappiness.

This series of studies is representative of the careful research done by Costa and McCrae, which shows that personality is relatively stable over very long periods of time. It also should serve as a model of carefully thought-out, programmatic scientific inquiry.

---

and a tendency for men and women to become more preoccupied with inner feelings, experiences, and cognitive processes. Gutmann (1978) argues that this increasing **interiority** reflects a normative shift in personality, and Neugarten (1973) points out that it is one of the best documented changes in personality across adulthood. Although interiority reflects many of the charac-teristics of introversion, it also indicates that older adults tend to decrease their attachments to the external world.

One of the largest longitudinal studies on personality development was conducted by researchers in Berkeley, California. In this investigation the parents of participants being studied in research on intellectual development were followed for roughly 30 years between ages 40 and 70 (Maas, 1985; Maas & Kuypers, 1974; Mussen, 1985). One of the major contributions of the Berkeley studies was the identification of life-style components and personality types (see Table 8.4). In the original report of the data Maas and Kuypers (1974) identified six distinct life-style clusters for mothers: husband-centered, uncentered, socializing, work-centered, disabled-disengaging, and group-centered. Four life-style clusters were found for fathers: family-centered, hobbyist, remotely sociable, and unwell-disengaged. Additionally, Maas and Kuypers found seven personality clusters, four for mothers and three for fathers.

The patterns of stability and change in the life-style and personality clusters differed for mothers and fathers. Overall, the evidence points to consistency over time in terms of the life-style one leads and the personality cluster one represents. Within particular life-style groups, however, there was change in how most people in that group behaved. Work-centered mothers showed the most change, moving from unsatisfying marriages and poor economic situations in their 30s to satisfying employment and new friendships by middle age. Group-centered mothers also showed positive changes. Uncentered mothers, who in young adulthood focused exclusively on their homes and families, had by their 70s experienced many losses such as the death of their spouse and declining health. These women had the lowest economic status and had little energy left for their children and grandchildren (Maas, 1985). Interestingly, personality factors later in life were not predicted well by personality predictors earlier in life. Apparently, the quality of a woman's marriage and other life circumstances (such as income and availability of leisure time) are overriding factors in personality development. In part, the powerful influence of life circumstances in this group of women may have been due to the lack of personal control these women had over their lives (Mussen, 1985).

For fathers, few changes in behavior patterns within life-style groups were found (Maas & Kuypers, 1974; Mussen, 1985). However, personality types did shift. The change was most apparent for the conservative-ordering fathers, who as young adults were shy, withdrawn, conflicted, and beset by marital problems. By age 70 these men had become controlling, conventional, and even more distant. Active-competent fathers went from being explosive, irritable, tense, and nervous as young adults to being charming and attractive in their later years. In sum, these data suggest that life-style during young adulthood is the better predictor of life satisfaction in old age for women but that personality is the better predictor for men.

Additional analyses of the Berkeley data provide other insights into personality development. Haan examined data from **Q-sorts**, a technique in which an individual arranges descriptors of personality into piles varying in the extent to which they reflect oneself (Haan, 1976, 1981, 1985; Haan et al., 1986). Six components of personality were derived from the Q-sort approach: self-confident-victimized (comfort with oneself and certainty of acceptance by others); assertive-submissive (degree of direct and aggressive style of living); cognitively committed (degree of intellectual and achievement orientation); outgoing-aloof (degree of social enjoyment of others); dependable (degree of controlled productivity); and warm-hostile (degree of interpersonal giving and support) (Haan et al., 1986).

Haan and her colleagues found that orderly, positive progressions over time were observed for all of the personality components except assertive-submissive. These trends are shown in Figure 8.2. When Haan tried to explain these developmental patterns, however, she ran into difficulty. Theories that predict stagelike progressions, such as Levinson's, could not account for the results.

TABLE 8.4 • Aspects of stability and change in Maas and Kuypers's personality styles for men and women

Personality Type	Features Common Early and Late in Adult Life	Differences Early and Late in Adult Life
Fearful-ordering mother	Depressed mood and activity level Low adaptive capacity Low sense of self-worth Health and economic disadvantage	More anxiety in old age More positive family life in early adult life
Anxious-asserting mother	Anxiety and tension Assertiveness and restlessness Low satisfaction High self-doubt Need to share Health disadvantage Interpersonal conflict	More ego disorganization in late life
Autonomous mother	Aloofness High mental capacity Positive sense of self Cheerfulness Criticalness Interpersonal distance	
Person-oriented mother	Warm, close, nonconflictual interpersonal relations	
Person-oriented father		More unrewarding career and financial strain in young adulthood
Active-competent father	High capacity Positive sense of self Interpersonal directness	More irritability and worry in young adulthood More charm and nonconformity in late life
Conservative-ordering father		Shyer and less demonstrative in young adulthood More relaxed and even-tempered in young adulthood More overcontrolled and conservative in late life

(Source: *From Thirty to Seventy* by H. J. Maas and J. A. Kuypers, 1974, San Francisco: Jossey-Bass. Reprinted by permission of the author and publisher.)

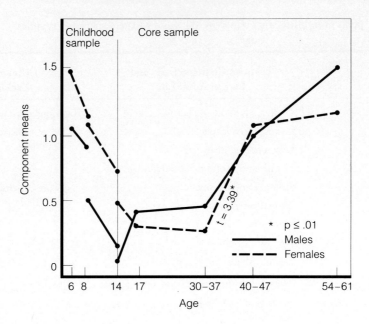

a. Average scores for self-confident-victimized

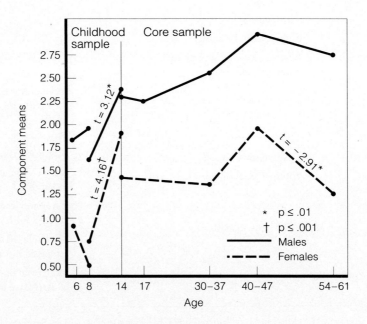

b. Average scores for assertive-submissive

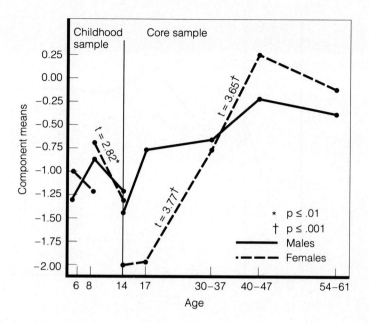

c. Average scores for cognitively committed

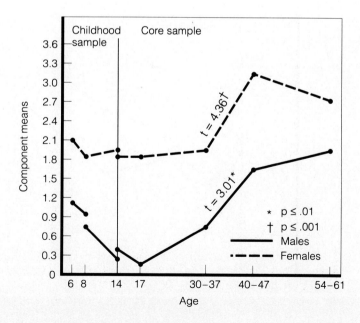

d. Average scores for outgoing–aloof

(continued)

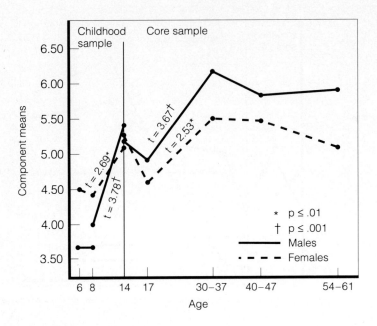

e. Average scores for dependable

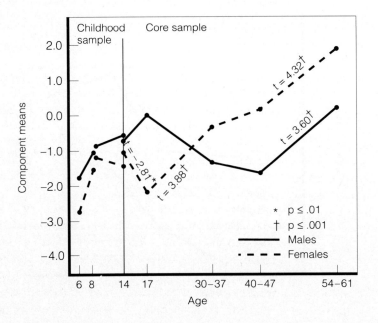

f. Average scores for warm–hostile

Contrary to these theories, personality did not change in all areas simultaneously, nor was there evidence of change only during stage transitions. In other words Haan's data suggest little support for the notion of general crisis followed by periods of stability. However, her data also cannot be explained by a smooth, orderly increase across adulthood. The observation of several sex differences, the nonlinear trends over time, and the lack of equal improvement in all components indicates that personality development is a complicated process. Haan et al. argue that changes in personality probably stem from life experiences that may "force" a person to change. We will consider a stronger version of this view later in the chapter when we examine cognitive theories of personality.

Chiriboga and his colleagues conducted an 11-year longitudinal study of the relationship between stressful life events and personality in people who were aged 16 to 65 at the beginning of the study (Chiriboga, 1984, 1985; Fiske & Chiriboga, 1985). They found that personality dimensions such as self-concept, life satisfaction, and interpersonal style were relatively stable over the 11 years. However, the degree of stability in these traits was directly related to the amount of stress experienced. Specifically, people who experienced the fewest stressful events were the least likely to change. These findings indicate that for personality traits to change, people must be confronted with a compelling reason such as stressful life events.

Conclusions: Personality Traits Across Adulthood

What can we conclude from the research on the development of personality traits across adulthood? On the surface it appears that we have conflicting evidence. Costa and McCrae, among others, argue strongly for stability, whereas Neugarten and the Berkeley group argue for change and stability. A partial resolution can be found if we consider how the research was done. Clearly, the overwhelming evidence supports the view that personality remains stable throughout adulthood when data are averaged across many different kinds of people. On the other hand, if we ask about specific aspects of personality in very specific kinds of people, we are more likely to find evidence of both change and stability.

The key factor in understanding when traits change and when they remain stable seems to be the role of life experiences. If a person experiences few events that induce him or her to change, then change is unlikely. In this view a person will be at 60 very much the same as he or she is at 30, all other factors being held constant. As we will see in the next section, on cognitive theories, this factor has been incorporated into formal theories of personality. Alternatively, the discrepancy could also be due in part to the kinds of tests being used. The data strongly supporting stability tend to be based on self-report questionnaires, and the data supporting change tend to be based on projective tests and Q-sorts. Future research will have

FIGURE 8.2 (pp. 268–270) • Overview of the results of a longitudinal study of personality. Notice the degree of variability across dimensions both in overall shapes of the curves and patterns of sex differences.

to clarify the extent to which a specific method influences the outcome.

Even in the research documenting changes, though, there is still considerable evidence that people do not change so much as to become unrecognizable. On the basis of personality traits, then, we should have little difficulty knowing our high school classmates many years later. Interestingly, one of the pioneers of psychology, William James, made the same observation a century ago:

> Already at the age of twenty-five you see the professional mannerism settling down on the young commercial traveller, on the young doctor, on the young minister, on the young counsellor-at-law. You see the little lines of cleavage running through the character, the treks of thought, the prejudices, the ways of the "shop" in a word, from which the man can by-and-by no more escape than his coat sleeve can suddenly fall into a new set of folds. On the whole, it is best he should not escape. It is well for the world that in most of us, by the age of thirty, the character has set like plaster, and will never soften again. (1890, p. 121)

COGNITIVE THEORIES

Implicit in theories of ego development and in some of the research on traits is the notion that how we perceive the world is important. These perceptions result from the explicit emphasis on the interaction between the person and the environment as the major force behind personality development. However, neither ego nor trait theories focus on how these perceptions are actually involved in personality development. Cognitive theories of personality development do.

The basis of cognitive theories is the individual's own conception of how his or her life should proceed. How a person thinks things are is more important for personality development than how

things really are. In other words it is how people perceive themselves that matters, not what the scores on personality tests indicate. Personality development in adulthood is related to one's awareness of changes in personal appearance, behavior, reactions of others, and an appreciation of the increasing closeness of death.

We will examine the work of two theorists whose research flows directly from a cognitive perspective. Hans Thomae developed a cognitive theory of personality based on his longitudinal research in Germany. Susan Krauss Whitbourne investigated people's own conceptions of the life course and how they differ from age norms and the expectations for society as a whole.

Thomae's Cognitive Theory of Personality

Thomae (1970, 1976, 1980) has offered a cognitive theory of personality that can also be viewed as a cognitive theory of aging. He lists three postulates that form the basis for explaining personality development, especially in terms of adjusting to one's own aging:

1. Perception of change, rather than objective change, is related to behavioral change. Only if we think we have changed over time will we act differently, regardless of whether other people think we have changed. This postulate, besides being fundamental to all cognitive theories of personality, also refers to people's belief in future change. Personality change is more or less likely depending on whether the individual thinks that change is normative.

2. People perceive and evaluate any change in their life situation in terms of their dominant concerns and expectations at that time. They view the same problem differently depending on what stage of life they are in. For example, the main source of people's identity changes as

they move from being a student to being a spouse, a worker, a parent, and so on. These different life stages motivate the person to perceive situations differently.

3. Adjustment to aging is determined by the balance between people's cognitive and motivational structures. If people perceive their life situation positively, believe that growth has occurred, and perceive change as complementing their interpretation of their current life stage, then adjustment to aging is possible.

Thomae's three postulates lead to the conclusion that personality change during adulthood cannot be reduced either to a "happens–does not happen" dichotomy or to a simple examination of scores on personality tests. Rather, personality change is in the personal eye of the beholder. Each of us has the potential to change, but whether it happens depends on our desire for change.

Thomae studied these processes of change in a longitudinal investigation that has come to be known as the Bonn Longitudinal Study of Aging. The purpose of the study was to identify the most important components in the many pathways to successful aging (Thomae, 1976). The Bonn study differed in important ways from the other longitudinal studies we have encountered. Structured personality tests based on trait theories were not used. Instead, data were gathered from open-ended interviews and from unstructured, projective personality tests. The focus was clearly on the individual's perceptions, not on objective criteria. In addition to these measures the Bonn study considered a wider range of topics than is usual in personality research: social conditions, life history, future plans, intelligence, attitudes, and health. These additional variables gave Thomae a more complete picture of his participants.

Much consistency and some change in personality were found. Thomae identified 10 subsystems based on interactions among biological, social, and perceptual-motivational processes. These interactions define the aging process in any specific person-environment interaction. More important, he found that adaptation in old age was not the result of one particular combination of the processes. Instead of one unique pattern of successful aging, Thomae found many.

Patterns of successful aging are the outcomes of complex interactions among the subsystems. There are many paths to successful personality growth and aging, because the number of interactions is very large. Despite the complexity of these interactions, however, Thomae noted that unless people's perceptions of themselves and of the situation require change, overall stability will be the most likely outcome.

Whitbourne's Life Story Approach

A second approach in the cognitive camp is based on Whitbourne's (1987) idea that people build their own conceptions of how their lives should proceed. The result of this process is the **life-span construct**, the person's unified sense of the past, present, and future.

There are many influences on the development of a life-span construct: identity, values, and social context are a few. Together, they shape the life-span construct and the ways in which it is manifested. The life-span construct has two structural components, which in turn are the ways in which it is manifested. The first of these components is the **scenario**, which consists of expectations about the future. The scenario translates aspects of our identity that are particularly important at a specific point into a plan for the future. The scenario is strongly influenced by age norms that define key transition points; for example, graduating from college is a transition that is normally associated with the early 20s. In short, a scenario is a game plan for how we want our lives to go.

Joan, a typical college sophomore, may have the following scenario: She expects that her course of study in nursing will be difficult but that she will finish on time. She hopes to meet a nice guy along the way whom she will marry shortly after graduation. She imagines that she will get a good job at a major medical center that will offer her good opportunities for advancement. She and her husband will probably have a child, but she expects to keep working. Because she feels that she will want to advance, she assumes that at some point she will obtain a master's degree. In the more distant future she hopes to be a department head and to be well-respected for her administrative skills.

Tagging certain expected events with a particular age or time by which we expect to complete them creates a social clock (see Chapter 1). Joan will use her scenario to evaluate her progress toward her goals. With each major transition she will check how she is doing against where her scenario says she should be. If it turns out that she has achieved her goals earlier than she expected, she will be proud of being ahead of the game. If things work out more slowly than she planned, she may chastise herself for being slow. If she begins to criticize herself a great deal, she may end up changing her scenario altogether; for example, if she does not get a good job and makes no progress, she may change her scenario to one that says she should stay home with her child.

As Joan starts moving into the positions laid out in her scenario, she begins to create the second component of her life-span construct, her **life story**. The life story is a personal narrative history that organizes past events into a coherent sequence. The life story gives events personal meaning and a sense of continuity; it becomes our autobiography. Because the life story is what we tell others when they ask about our past, it eventually becomes somewhat overrehearsed and stylized. An interesting aspect of the life story, and

According to Whitbourne, this new Ph.D. graduate already has constructed a scenario of what he expects to happen in the next few years of his life.

autobiographical memory in general, is that distortions will occur with time and retelling (Neisser & Winograd, 1988). In the case of life stories distortions allow the person to feel that he or she was "on time" rather than "off time" in terms of past events in the scenario. In this way people feel better about their plans and goals and are less likely to feel a sense of failure.

Whitbourne (1986) conducted a fascinating cross-sectional study of 94 adults ranging in age from 24 to 61. They came from all walks of life and represented a wide range of occupations and life situations. Using data from very detailed interviews, Whitbourne was able to identify what she believes is the process of adult identity development based on an equilibrium between identity and experience. Her model is presented in Figure 8.3.

FIGURE 8.3 • Whitbourne's model of adult identity processes
(Source: *The Me I Know: A Study of Adult Identity* by S. K. Whitbourne, © 1986, New York: Springer-Verlag. Reprinted with permission of the publisher.)

As can be seen, the processes of equilibrium are based on Piaget's concepts of assimilation and accommodation (see Chapter 6). Whitbourne has explicitly attempted to integrate concepts from cognitive development with identity development in order to understand how identity is formed and revised across adulthood. The assimilation process involves using already existing aspects of identity to handle present situations. Overreliance on assimilation makes the person resistant to change. Accommodation, on the other hand, reflects the willingness of the individual to let the situation determine what he or she will do. This often occurs when the person does not have a well-developed identity around a certain issue.

Not surprisingly, Whitbourne (1986) found that the vast majority of adults listed family as the most important aspect of their lives. It is clear that adults' identity as "loving" constitutes the major part of the answer to the question "Who am I?" Consequently, a major theme in adults' identity development is trying to refine their belief that "I am a loving person." Much of this development is in the area of acquiring and refining deep, emotional relationships.

A second major source of identity for Whitbourne's participants was work. In this case the key seemed to be keeping work interesting. As long as individuals had an interesting occupation that enabled them to become personally invested, their work identity was more central to their overall personal identity.

Although Whitbourne found evidence of life transitions, she found no evidence that these transitions occurred in stagelike fashion or were tied to specific ages. Rather, she found that people tended to experience transitions when they felt they needed to and to do so on their own time line.

Conclusions: Cognitive Theories

Although more research is needed, the cognitive theories have much to offer the study of adult personality development. Converging evidence from a variety of sources points to the conclusion that adults experience both change and stability and that the extent of each may be largely within their control. Adults appear to remain the same unless they perceive a need to change. Future research is likely to integrate the theoretical framework of cognitive theories with the research methods used in studying ego development and traits. This combination may provide an explanation for conflicting findings in those literatures and give us considerable insight into why some people seem to stay the same while others do not.

PARTICULAR ASPECTS OF PERSONALITY

Some aspects of personality are not tightly tied to a particular theoretical view but are studied separately. Among them are self-concept, attributional style, life satisfaction, and sex roles.

Self-Concept

Recall that in the cognitive view of personality it is the individual's subjective perception that matters, not objective reality. Self-perceptions and how they differ with age have been examined in a wide variety of studies and have been shown to be related to many behaviors. Changes in self-perceptions are often manifested in changed beliefs, concerns, and expectations. **Self-concept** is the organized, coherent, integrated pattern of self-perceptions (Thomae, 1980). It includes the notions of self-esteem and self-image.

Kegan (1982) attempted to integrate the development of self-concept and cognitive development. He postulated six stages of the development of self, corresponding to stages of cognitive development described in Chapter 6. Kegan's first three stages, which he calls incorporative, impulsive, and imperial, correspond to Piaget's sensorimotor, preoperational, and concrete operational stages (see Chapter 6). During this time, he believes, children move from knowing themselves on the basis of reflexes to knowing themselves through needs and interests. At the beginning of formal operational thought during early adolescence (see Chapter 6), he argues, a sense of interpersonal mutuality begins to develop; he terms this period the interpersonal stage. By late adolescence or young adulthood, individuals move to a mature sense of identity based on taking control of their own life and developing an ideology; Kegan calls this period the institutional stage. Finally, with the acquisition of postformal thought (see Chapter 6) comes an understanding that the self is a very complex system that takes into account other people; Kegan terms this period the interindividual stage. Kegan's (1982) work emphasizes the fact that personality development does not occur in a vacuum. Rather, we must not forget that the person is a complex integrated whole. Consequently, an understanding of the development of self-concept or any other aspect of personality is enhanced by an understanding of how it relates to other dimensions of development.

In one of the few longitudinal studies of self-concept, Mortimer, Finch, and Kumka (1982) followed a group of men for 14 years, beginning when the participants were college freshmen. They found that self-image consisted of four dimensions: well-being, interpersonal qualities, activity, and unconventionality. Well-being included self-perceptions concerning happiness, lack of tension, and confidence. Interpersonal qualities referred to self-perceptions concerning sociability, interest in others, openness, and warmth. The activity component consisted of self-perceptions of strength, competence, success, and activity. The unconventionality dimension indicated that men saw themselves as impulsive, unconventional, and dreamy. Clearly, what Mortimer et al. found concerning self-image is very closely related to Costa and McCrae's model of personality, described earlier in this chapter.

Over the 14-year period the men in the Mortimer et al. study showed little change as a group. The structure of self-concept remained stable. Some fluctuation at the level of self-image was noted, though. Both well-being and competence declined during college but rebounded after graduation. Self-perceptions of unconventionality declined after college. Sociability showed a steady decline across the entire study.

When the data were examined at the intraindividual level, it became clear that self-perceptions of confidence were related to life events. The course of a man's career, his satisfaction with career and marriage, his relationship with his parents, and his overall life satisfaction followed patterns that could be predicted by competence. For example, men whose competence scores remained above the group average experienced few problems related to their jobs and had higher marital and life satisfaction than men whose competence scores were below the group average.

Interestingly, a man's degree of confidence as a college senior influenced his later evaluation of life events, and it may have even set the stage for a self-fulfilling prophecy. Mortimer et al. suggest that these men may actively seek and create experiences that fit their personality structure. This hypothesis is supported by longitudinal research on gifted women, whose high self-confidence in early adulthood becomes manifested as a high life satisfaction during their 60s (Sears & Barbee, 1978).

The results from the Mortimer et al. (1982) study are strikingly similar to the data from the Berkeley studies described earlier in this chapter. Recall that data from these studies also support the idea that life events are important influences on personality development. In the present case life events clearly influence one's self-concept. We will consider in the next section how adults explain why certain things or certain events happen to them.

Personal Control

Suppose you do not perform as well as you think you should have on an exam. Was it your own fault? Or was the exam too picky? How we answer such questions sheds light on how we tend to explain, or attribute, our behavior. The study of attributions is one of the major areas in social psychology and is the topic of numerous theories. Among the most important ways in which we analyze the cause of events is in terms of who or what is in control in a specific situation. **Personal control** is the degree to which you believe that your performance in a situation depends on something that you personally do. A high sense of personal control implies a belief that performance is up to you, whereas a low sense of personal control implies that your performance is under the influence of forces other than your own.

Personal control has become an extremely important idea in a wide variety of settings (Baltes & Baltes, 1986). For example, it is thought to play a role in cognitive development (see Chapter 6), in memory performance (see Chapter 7), in depression (see Chapter 9), and in adjustment to institutionalization (see Chapter 13). Despite this range of research we do not have a clear picture of developmental trends in people's sense of personal control.

Most of the research on personal control has been conducted using a locus-of-control framework. Locus of control refers to who or what one thinks is responsible for performance. Traditionally, researchers label people who take personal responsibility "internal" and people who believe that others (or chance) are responsible "external." Evidence from both cross-sectional studies (e.g., Gatz & Siegler, 1981; Ryckman & Malikioski, 1975) and longitudinal studies (e.g., Lachman, 1985; Siegler & Gatz, 1985) is contradictory. Some find that older adults are more likely to be internal than younger adults, whereas others find older adults more likely to be external than younger adults.

Lachman (1986) argues that a major reason for the conflicting findings is the multidimensionality of personal control. Specifically, she shows that one's sense of control depends on which domain, such as intelligence or health, is being assessed. Moreover, she demonstrates that older adults often acknowledge the importance of outside influences on their behavior but still believe that what they do matters.

It appears that one's sense of personal control is a complex, multidimensional aspect of personality. Consequently, general normative age-related trends may not be found. Rather, changes in personal control may well depend on one's experiences in different domains and may differ widely from one domain to another.

Life Satisfaction

One general way to examine the influence of personality is by assessing overall life satisfaction. There is little doubt that life satisfaction has been included in more research than any other aspect

The degree to which one is satisfied with aspects of life is not related to age.

of personality. Hundreds of studies have examined adults' feelings of well-being, morale, and happiness. In addition, many researchers have tried to discover the major ingredients in life satisfaction. In this section we will briefly consider this work.

In one of the most ambitious studies of its kind, Cameron (1975) examined the life satisfaction of over 6,000 people ranging in age from 4 to 99. He concluded that life satisfaction, expressed as happiness, sadness, or neutral moods, was equivalent across all age groups. Satisfaction was determined primarily by social class, sex, and the person's immediate life situation, not by age. Likewise, Kozma and Stones (1983) found no relationship between age and life satisfaction in an 18-month longitudinal investigation. A review of 30 years of similar research led Larson (1978) to conclude that age had little bearing on overall life satisfaction. In general, 3 decades of research pointed to health as the single most important determining factor. Larson also noted that money, housing, social class, social interaction, marital status, and transportation had significant influence.

Specific personality factors also seem to have important effects on overall life satisfaction. McCrae and Costa (1983) found that both neuroticism and extraversion were related to happiness. Men who were high in neuroticism were more likely to feel dissatisfied and unhappy, and men high in extraversion were more likely to feel satisfied and happy. These relationships held regardless of the psychological maturity of the participants.

Schulz (1972) raises an interesting issue concerning life satisfaction: Does its nature change with age? In other words, does feeling happy at 75 mean the same thing as feeling happy at 25? Schulz argues that people's feelings about life do not change in intensity with age but that the more qualitative aspects of feelings could be different. Life experiences during adulthood may have colored positive experiences during young adulthood with negative feelings, and negative experiences with positive feelings. The loss of a job in young adulthood may have been viewed very negatively at the time, for example, but the subsequent acquisition of a much better job in mid-life changed this view to a far more positive one.

Schulz goes on to say that older adults do not necessarily have more negative feelings and attitudes than younger adults. Increases in negative events such as poorer health, decreasing income, or death of one's spouse do not inevitably lead to increases in negative feelings. This lack of a relationship could be due in part to changing expectations about life, which may offset the negative consequences of loss.

In sum, whether life satisfaction changes with age is a complex issue that depends much more on life experiences and their associated feelings than it does on age.

Sex-Role Development Across Adulthood

One of the more hotly debated topics in personality research across adulthood is whether there is a sex-role reversal with age. The basic argument is that as men and women age, they begin to acquire aspects of the opposite gender's sex-role stereotype. For example, men may become more sensitive and nurturant, and women, more assertive.

There is considerable evidence that changes do occur but that these changes do not represent a reversal in sex roles. Data from the Berkeley studies document a move toward greater similarity between older men and women. For example, Haan (1985; Haan et al., 1986) and Livson (1981) found that both men and women became more nurturant, intimate, and tender with age. This acceptance of both male and female personality characteristics, termed **androgyny**, appears to be much more descriptive of older adults than sex-role reversal. Other researchers have also documented an increased tendency with age for men and women to describe themselves similarly (Sinnott, 1982; Turner, 1982).

The move toward androgyny may not always be apparent at the behavioral level. Although older men often indicate a greater willingness to develop close relationships, for example, few actually have the skills to do so (Turner, 1982). Troll and Bengtson (1982) argue that the change is more internal than external and tends to involve feelings about dependence and autonomy. Moreover, they point out that much of the change may be due to the failing health of elderly men. Because older wives tend to be healthier than their husbands, the balance of power may shift out of necessity to wives, and men may be forced to accept a more dependent role.

It will be interesting to see whether the trend toward androgyny continues over the next few generations. Changes in how younger men and women view themselves as a result of women's new roles in society may shift the trend downward in age or may make it disappear altogether. Only time will tell.

SUMMARY

Ego-development theories view personality as an organization of needs, motives, dispositions, habits, and abilities that are used to reach higher goals. Jung pioneered the field of adult ego development. He argues that there is an age-related increase in introversion and an increase in the manifestation of behaviors that are associated with the opposite sex. Erikson describes eight stages of ego development based on the idea that each stage involves the resolution of a struggle between competing forces. Three of his stages relate directly to adulthood: intimacy versus isolation, generativity versus stagnation, and ego integrity versus despair. Recent additions and modifications of Erikson's theory have addressed problems such as the cyclic nature of stages and how transitions between stages occur. Loevinger describes an alternative view of ego development that relates it to cognitive development and social development; six of her stages are observed across adulthood (conformist, conscientious-conformist, conscientious, individualistic, autonomous, and integrated). Research on ego development in the Kansas City studies, Ryff's research, and Lowenthal and her colleagues' work documents age-related changes in ego.

Other stage theories of personality base development on personal myths and alternating periods of stability and transition. Gould argues that development consists of breaking childhood bonds and giving up a series of personal myths. Levinson contends that life structures undergo change by alternating between periods of stability and transition. Neither theory has much empirical support, and they should be viewed as interesting hypotheses rather than explanations of development. Moreover, there is little evidence to support a belief in a mid-life crisis.

Trait theory assumes that personality consists of many stable, enduring characteristics (traits) that can be grouped into a few dimensions. Costa and McCrae postulate five dimensions of adult personality: neuroticism, extraversion, openness to experience, agreeableness-antagonism, and conscientiousness-undirectedness. Longitudinal research examining the traits that make up their model shows that the underlying trait dimensions do not change significantly across adulthood. However, additional research on combinations of personality and life-style as well as other traits reveals some evidence for change. A major explanatory variable for this discrepancy may be stressful life events.

Cognitive theories of personality emphasize the role of subjective perceptions in understanding developmental changes. Thomae argues that these subjective impressions are more important than objective reality, since it is the subjective perception that is related to changes in personality. That is, only if the person believes that change is needed will change be observed. Whitbourne examined people's conceptions of how their lives were organized. She found that people developed scenarios (life plans) and life stories (autobiographies).

Kegan proposes that self-concept develops in a stagelike manner that parallels cognitive development. However, research evidence points to stability unless one experiences life events that push for change. Age-related changes in sense of personal control remain unclear; apparently, personal control is a complex, multidimensional aspect of personality that is situationally determined. Life satisfaction seems to remain fairly constant across adulthood. A few individual-difference variables have been identified, including neuroticism and several demographic variables. Adults tend to develop more-androgynous sex roles with age; a sex-role reversal has little support.

GLOSSARY

active mastery • A person's attempts to overcome problems by dealing with them directly.

androgyny • The presence of characteristics of both traditional masculinity and femininity.

complex • Having many roles and activities.

dimensions • Related sets of personality traits.

ego development • The process by which we change in our personal identity.

epigenetic principle • The property of emergence in development (see Chapter 2).

implementation-culmination sequence • The shift in adulthood from being active and achievement-oriented to being more inward-oriented.

interiority • An inward focus thought to be characteristic of old age.

life-span construct • A person's unified sense of past, present, and future.

life story • A personal narrative history that organizes autobiographical events into a coherent sequence.

life structures • The values, beliefs, and priorities we live by, according to Levinson.

passive mastery • Attempts to deal with problems by either not taking action or letting events take their course.

personal control • The feeling that we are in charge of situations.

Q-sorts • A way of measuring personality by having the subject arrange descriptions into piles varying in the degree to which they are self-descriptive.

scenario • A person's expectations about the future.

self-concept • The organized, coherent, integrated pattern of self-perceptions.

simplistic • Having few roles or social activities.

stability • In Levinson's theory, a period in which we work to solidify goals set at a previous transition.

trait • A general attribute of behavior that is thought to remain stable across situations and time.

transition • In Levinson's theory, a period of inner struggle during which we question ourselves.

ADDITIONAL READING

General overviews of personality research and theories in adulthood can be found in

Wrightsman, L. S. (1988). *Personality development in adulthood.* Beverly Hills, CA: Sage Publications.

Bengtson, V. L., Reedy, M. N., & Gordon, C. E. (1985). Aging and self-conceptions: Personality processes and social contexts. In J. E. Birren & K. W. Schaie (Eds.), *Handbook of the psychology of aging* (2nd ed.) (pp. 544–593). New York: Van Nostrand Reinhold.

A good introduction to and summary of Erikson's theory is

Erikson, E. H. (1982). *The life cycle completed: Review.* New York: Norton.

An excellent example of the multidirectionality of personality development and an application of the interview method is

Whitbourne, S. K. (1986). *The me I know: A study of adult identity.* New York: Springer-Verlag.

Psychopathology and Intervention

Alberto Giacometti, *The Artist's Mother*, 1950. Oil on canvas, 35⅜ × 24″. Collection, The Museum of Modern Art, New York. Acquired through the Lillie P. Bliss Bequest.

MARY LIVED BY HERSELF FOR 30 YEARS after her husband died. * For all but the last 5 years or so of this period, she managed very well. Her children, who live in various parts of the country, visited her occasionally. Friends down the street looked in on her and cooked meals on occasion. Little by little, though, family members began noticing that Mary wasn't quite "right"; for example, her memory slipped, she sounded confused sometimes, and her moods swung without warning. Some family members attributed these changes to the fact that she was in her 80s. But when they discovered that she sometimes forgot about things in the refrigerator and then ate them even though they had molded and that she occasionally ate other strange things, they began to think differently. The family ultimately realized that she could no longer care for herself and that help had to be found. She moved to a type of group home but continued to deteriorate. She started having trouble remembering things from even a few minutes before. Names of family members became mixed up, at first, and later were forgotten. She began to wander. Finally, Mary had to leave the group home and be placed in a nursing home. The times when she was living in the present became fewer. Her physical abilities continued to deteriorate, until eventually she could not feed herself. Toward the end of her life she could not eat solid food and had to be force-fed. Mary died of Alzheimer's disease after more than 15 years of slow, agonizing decline.

Situations like this happen to families every day. Certainly, behavior like Mary's is not part of normal aging. But for families and even for professionals, it is not until something very strange happens that this realization occurs. When it does, it often results in tumultuous family upheaval. Depending on the particular problem, it may mean deciding whether to institutionalize a spouse or a parent, another very difficult process.

This chapter is about the people who do not make it through adulthood to old age in the normal way. This minority of adults develop disorders that cause them problems in their daily lives and that sometimes rob them of their dignity. The two ailments that present the most difficulty are depression and dementia, so those are the two that we will concentrate on. Other problems pose difficulties as well. Some, such as physical difficulties and stress, were dealt with in Chapter 4. Others, such as paranoid disorders, occur rather infrequently.

As we consider different types of psychopathology, we will note how each is diagnosed, what is known about cause and treatment, and what families do when caring for a victim. In the final section we will consider some therapeutic techniques used in community outpatient clinics, nursing homes, and other institutions to try to provide the most supportive environment possible.

*This case is true, but the names have been changed to maintain confidentiality.

PSYCHOPATHOLOGY AND THE ADULT LIFE COURSE

Problems like the ones just described are considered to be sufficiently abnormal to most people to warrant the label "mental illness" or "mental disorder." What distinguishes the study of mental disorders, or **psychopathology**, in adulthood and aging is not so much the content of the behavior as its context, that is, whether it interferes with daily functioning. In order to understand psychopathology as it is manifested in adults of different ages, we must see how it fits into the life-course perspective outlined in Chapter 1.

Defining Mental Health and Psychopathology

The first issue confronting us in understanding psychopathology is how to distinguish it from mental health. It turns out that this is not easy. Few scholars have written about what mental health is except to say what it is not. What constitutes normal or abnormal behavior is hard to define precisely, because expectations and standards for behavior change over time, over situations, and across age groups (Birren & Renner, 1980). Thus, what is considered mental health depends on the circumstances under consideration.

Birren and Renner (1980) summarize several arguments concerning the nature of mental health and argue that mentally healthy people have the following characteristics: (1) a positive attitude toward self, (2) an accurate perception of reality, (3) a mastery of the environment, (4) autonomy, (5) personality balance, and (6) growth and self-actualization.

In contrast, we could consider behaviors that are harmful to oneself or others, lower one's well-being, and are perceived as distressing or disrupt-

ing to be abnormal or maladaptive (Fry, 1986). Although this approach is used frequently with younger or middle-aged adults, it presents problems when applied to older adults. Some behaviors that would be considered abnormal under this definition may actually be adaptive under some circumstances for many older people (e.g., depression, isolation, passivity, aggressiveness) (Birren & Renner, 1979). Consequently, an approach to defining abnormal behavior that emphasizes the consideration of behaviors in isolation and from the perspective of younger or middle-aged adults is inadequate for defining abnormal behaviors in the elderly (Gurland, 1973). For example, because of physical, financial, social, health, or other reasons, some older adults do not have the opportunity to master their environment. Depression or hostility may be an appropriate and justified response to such limitations. Moreover, such responses may actually help them deal with their situation more effectively and adaptively.

The important point in differentiating normal from abnormal behavior (or mental health from mental illness) is that behaviors must be interpreted in context. In other words, we must consider what else is happening and how the behavior fits the situation in addition to such factors as the age and other personal characteristics of the individual.

Taking a Life-Course Perspective: The Biopsychosocial Approach

Suppose two persons, one young and one old, came into your clinic, each complaining about a lack of sleep, changes in appetite, a lack of energy, and feeling "down." What would you say to them?

If you proceeded to evaluate them in identical ways, you might be headed for trouble. Just as we have seen in other chapters that older and younger adults may think differently or view themselves differently, the meaning of their symptoms may also differ, even though the symptoms appear to be the same. This point is not always incorporated into views of psychopathology. For example, the medical model assumes that an underlying cause, or disease, is responsible for abnormal or maladaptive behavior and that the symptoms of the mental disease are fairly constant across age. Although the medical model provides the basis for most clinical diagnosis, it is inadequate for understanding psychopathology in old age.

One good alternative framework is the **biopsychosocial approach**, which holds that psychopathology results from a complex interaction of interpersonal factors, intrapersonal factors, biological and physical factors, and life-cycle factors (Fry, 1986; Lipowski, 1975). The biopsychosocial approach, depicted in Figure 9.1, makes it clear that we can identify and treat mental disorders only after taking all of these factors into account. Each factor focuses attention on normative developmental changes and helps the clinician determine if the client's behaviors are "normal" or "abnormal."

Interpersonal Factors. Interpersonal factors involve the nature of a person's relationships with other people, especially family members and friends. Important developmental differences occur in the interpersonal realm; for example, younger adults are more likely to be expanding their network of friends, whereas older adults are more likely to be experiencing losses. Thus, feelings of grief or sadness would be considered normal in older adults but might not be in younger adults (Parkes, 1972).

Intrapersonal Factors. Intrapersonal factors include variables such as age, sex, personality, and cognitive abilities. All of these variables influence the behaviors that people exhibit and affect our

interpretation of them. For example, an older Black female who lives in a high-crime area may be highly suspicious of other people. To label her behavior paranoid may be inappropriate. In short, we must ask whether the behavior we see is appropriate for a person of this age, sex, personality type, ability level, and so forth.

Biological and Physical Factors. Various chronic diseases, limitations on functioning, and other ailments can provide an explanation of behavior. Because health problems increase with age (see Chapters 3 and 4), we must be increasingly sensitive to them when dealing with older adults.

Life-Cycle Factors. How one behaves at any point is strongly affected by one's past experiences and the issues one is facing. These life-cycle factors must be taken into account in evaluating adults' behaviors. For example, a middle-aged woman who wants to go back to school may not have an adjustment disorder; she may simply want to develop a new aspect of herself. Likewise, an older man who provides vague answers to personal questions may not be resistant; he may simply be reflecting his generation's reluctance to disclose one's inner self to a stranger.

Implications of the Biopsychosocial Approach

Viewing adults' behavior from a multidisciplinary life-course perspective makes a big difference in how we approach psychopathology. One of the most important effects is on psychological assessments.

Issues in Clinical Assessment. Identification of mental disorders rests on accurate evaluation and assessment. Psychologists have a myriad of tests and measures at their disposal for assessing adults' functioning. Such assessment is a major

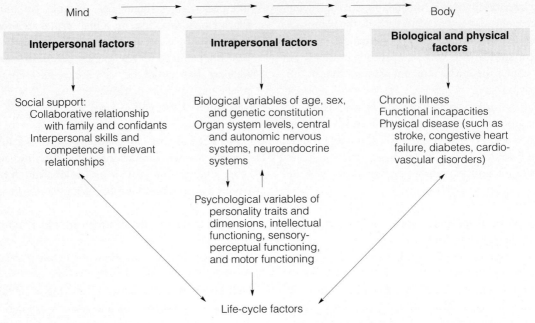

FIGURE 9.1 • The biopsychosocial model

(Source: *Depression, Stress, and Adaptations in the Elderly: Psychological Assessment and Intervention* (p. 4) by P. S. Fry, 1986, Rockville, MD: Aspen. Reprinted with permission of Aspen Publishers, Inc. © 1986.)

problem if the person is elderly, because virtually all of the tests and measures were developed for use with young and middle-aged adults (Fry, 1986; Zarit, Eiler, & Hassinger, 1985). Very few tests have been standardized with the elderly, which means that we have little idea what a "typical" older adult would score, let alone one who is experiencing some problem.

An additional problem is that the primary diagnostic guide, the *Diagnostic and Statistical Manual III-R* published by the American Psychiatric Association (1987), does not provide different lists of symptoms for disorders based on the age of the individual. This problem stems from the use of the medical model as the basis for the DSM III-R. As we will see in the discussion of depression, for example, the symptom pattern differs for young and old adults in important ways.

Allowances need to be made when assessing older adults. For example, they tend to report their problems in more global terms than younger adults, and they may tire more easily during the

TABLE 9.1 • An application of the biopsychosocial model to the clinical assessment of the elderly

Characteristics of the Model

The approach ensures that all important physical and psychosocial assets and liabilities of the client will be assessed and will receive concurrent attention.

The approach requires that the rigid distinctions between intellectual functioning, perceptual functioning, behavioral disorders, and physical dimensions be dropped and a more holistic picture of the elderly client be formulated.

The approach requires that mental health status of the client be assessed not merely in terms of the client's psychosocial characteristics but equally with respect to environmental and ecological resources and liabilities.

The approach stresses that a number of mini-interviews (structured or semistructured) and follow-up meetings structured over time are more appropriate to assessment of the elderly than is a comprehensive single interview.

The approach relies on interview technologies such as CARE or OARS methodology in which structured or semistructured interviews are designed to assess the functional status of the respondents, their perceptions of needed services, and their strengths and assets in physical and emotional health and activities of daily living.

Functions and Specific Assessment Objectives

Analysis of the elderly client's problem situation

Analysis of the antecedents and consequences of the elderly client's behavioral responses

Analysis of the elderly client's assets and deficits in functioning

Analysis of the elderly client's social relationships and social support networks

Motivational analysis

Analysis of the elderly client's social, cultural, and physical environment

Developmental analysis of the elderly client in terms of past and present adaptations and adjustments

Identification of specific targets for remediation and intervention

(Source: *Depression, Stress, and Adaptations in the Elderly: Psychological Assessment and Intervention* (p. 45) by P. S. Fry, 1986, Rockville, MD: Aspen. Reprinted with permission of Aspen Publishers, Inc. © 1986.)

assessment session (Fry, 1986). Consequently, adhering to rigid time schedules, limited standardized instructions, and specific wordings of questions may be inappropriate.

Integrating the Biopsychosocial Approach.
A way to avoid many of the difficulties in the assessing of older adults is to integrate the biopsychosocial approach into the assessment process (Fry, 1986). Table 9.1 describes the characteristics and functions of this integrated perspective.

As noted in the table, adopting this integrated model ensures that all relevant dimensions of functioning are assessed, that a more holistic approach is adopted, that mental health status is put into proper context, that assessment sessions are shorter and more flexible, and that the assessment addresses the person's ability to function in the natural environment. Additionally, an integrated approach attempts to document the client's problem, its antecedents and consequences, and the client's available resources and motivation and to identify appropriate treatment options. The use of this integrated framework will allow the clinician to learn as much as possible about the person's problem, make a more accurate diagnosis, and recommend the most effective treatment.

As we consider specific types of psychopathology, we will emphasize the need to conduct comprehensive, multifaceted assessments based on the biopsychosocial approach. We will see that only when such assessments are made will the diagnosis and recommendations for treatment be appropriate.

DEPRESSION

Depression is one of the most common mental disorders and the most treatable (La Rue, Dessonville, & Jarvik, 1985). Estimates are that at any one point between 2% and 5% of all adults have a clinical depressive disorder; the odds across adulthood of ever having a depressive disorder are between 15% and 20% (Nolen-Hoeksema, 1988).

It is difficult to imagine anyone who has not felt "down" or "blue" at some point. Indeed, most older adults admit to having some depressive symptoms (Gallagher & Thompson, 1983). This does *not* mean, however, that most older adults are clinically depressed; researchers estimate that fewer than 1% of adults over age 60 are severely depressed (Blazer, Hughes, & George, 1987). In fact, the rate of severe depression among older adults (1%) is lower than that in younger age groups (roughly 4%) (Nolen-Hoeksema, 1988).

Women who are diagnosed as having a severe depressive disorder outnumber men in young adulthood and old age, but men outnumber women during the latter part of mid-life (ages 55 to 64) (Leaf et al., 1988). This difference may reflect a sex bias on the part of clinicians, how-

ever, who may simply be more willing to diagnose depression in women (Feinson, 1987; Rodeheaver & Datan, 1988). For example, the much higher rate of diagnosed alcoholism in men during young adulthood and early middle age and a connection between alcoholism and depression suggest that depression in men is a common but undiagnosed problem (Turner, 1987). Other factors that reflect possible sex bias are also associated with the higher rates of clinical depression: being widowed (Vernon & Roberts, 1982); lower economic resources (Hirschfield & Cross, 1982); and being in poorer health (Salzman & Shader, 1979). These data argue strongly that we need to be cautious in interpreting differential rates of depression in men and women.

Diagnosis of Depression

The criteria for diagnosing depressive disorders are described in two classification systems: the DSM (American Psychiatric Association, 1987) and the Research Diagnostic Criteria (RDC) (Spitzer, Endicott, & Robins, 1978). Although these two sets of criteria, summarized in Table 9.2, differ somewhat in their specificity, they are similar in viewing depression as a multidimensional disturbance in biological, social, and psychological functioning (Gallagher & Thompson, 1983).

The most prominent feature of clinical depression is **dysphoria**, that is, feeling down, or blue. Importantly, older adults may not label their "down" feelings as depression but, rather, as "pessimistic" or "helpless" (Fry, 1986). Older adults are also more likely to show signs of apathy, subdued self-deprecation, expressionlessness, and changes in arousal than are younger people (Caird & Judge, 1974; Epstein, 1976). It is common for older depressed individuals to withdraw, not speak to anyone, confine themselves to bed, and not take care of bodily functions. Younger adults may

The stereotype that most elderly are depressed is not supported. In fact, there is evidence that the rate of severe depression may decrease in old age.

engage in some of these behaviors but to a much lesser extent.

The second major component of clinical depression is the accompanying physical symptoms. These include insomnia, changes in appetite, diffuse pain, troubled breathing, headaches, fatigue, and sensory loss (Lehmann, 1981). The presence of these physical symptoms in the elderly must be evaluated carefully. As noted in Chapter 4, some sleep disturbances may reflect normative changes that are unrelated to depression; however, regular early morning awakening is consistently related to depression, even in the elderly (Rodin, McAvay, & Timko, 1988). Alternatively, the physical symptoms may reflect an underlying physical disease that is manifested as depression. Indeed, many elderly people admitted to the hospital with depressive symptoms turn out to have previously undiagnosed medical problems that are uncovered only after thorough blood and

metabolic tests (Sweer, Martin, Ladd, Miller, & Karpf, 1988). Additionally, the incidence of **hypochondriasis** (being overly concerned with one's health) increases with age and must be diagnosed differentially from depression (Gallagher & Thompson, 1983). Thoughts about suicide are particularly important, especially in the elderly, and should be considered a serious symptom (Osgood, 1985). Note that feelings one might expect to be evaluated, such as excessive worry or self-pity, are not included. This is because they are not unique to depression and do not help clinicians discriminate depression from other disorders (Spitzer et al., 1978).

Third, the symptoms described must last at least 2 weeks. That is, the person must be experiencing a set of symptoms on a consistent basis for a reasonable length of time. This criterion is used to rule out the experience of transient symptoms that are commonly experienced by all adults, especially after a negative experience such as receiving a rejection letter from a potential employer or getting a speeding ticket.

Fourth, other causes for the observed symptoms must be ruled out. For example, other health problems, neurological disorders, alcoholism, or other forms of psychopathology can cause depressive symptoms. These must be considered in order to know how to treat the problem.

Finally, the clinician must determine the effect that the person's symptoms is having on his or her daily life. Is the ability to interact with other people impaired? Can he or she carry out domestic responsibilities? What about effects on work or school? Is the person taking any medication? Clinical depression involves significant impairment in daily living.

Assessing symptoms of depression is often done through the use of self-report scales, such as the Beck Depression Inventory (Beck, Ward, Mendelson, Mock, & Erbaugh, 1961), the Zung Self-Rating Depression Scale (Zung, 1965), the

TABLE 9.2 · Comparison of criteria for major depression: Research Diagnostic Criteria (RDC) and DSM III

	RDC for Major Depressive Disorder (MDD)	DSM III Criteria for Major Depressive Episode (MDE)
Mood disturbance	One or more distinct periods with dysphoric mood or pervasive loss of interest or pleasure	Dysphoric mood or loss of interest or pleasure in all or almost all usual activities and pastimes
	In both systems, mood disturbance is characterized by descriptors such as depressed, sad, downhearted and blue, hopeless, down in the dumps, don't care anymore, or irritable. While this disturbance does not need to be dominant, it must be prominent and persistent. Momentary shifts from dysphoric mood to another serious emotional state such as anxiety or anger would preclude a diagnosis of major depression.	
Related symptoms	At least five of the following are required as part of the episode and four for probable MDD:	At least four of the following must be present regularly:
	1. poor appetite or weight loss, or increased appetite or weight gain 2. sleep difficulty (insomnia) or sleeping too much (hypersomnia) 3. psychomotor agitation or retardation (but not merely subjective feelings of restlessness or being slowed down) 4. loss of energy, fatigability, or tiredness 5. loss of interest or pleasure in usual activities, or decrease in sexual drive not limited to a period of delusion or hallucinating 6. feelings of worthlessness, self-reproach, or excessive or inappropriate guilt 7. complaints or evidence of diminished ability to think or concentrate (e.g., slowed thinking or indecisiveness) 8. recurrent thoughts of death or suicide, or any suicidal behavior	
Duration	Dysphoric features: 2 weeks for definite; 1–2 weeks for probable. Related symptoms: not specified but presumed at least 2 weeks.	Dysphoric features: not specified but presumed at least 2 weeks. Related symptoms: must be present nearly every day for at least 2 weeks.

(Source: *Clinical Geropsychology: New Directions in Assessment and Treatment* (pp. 14–15) by P. M. Levinsohn and L. Teri (Eds.), 1983, Elmsford, NY: Pergamon Press. Copyright © 1983 by Pergamon Press, Inc. Reprinted with permission.)

Center for Epidemiological Studies Depression Scale (Radloff, 1977), or standard interviews, such as the Hamilton Rating Scale for Depression (M. Hamilton, 1967). Because these scales were all developed on younger and middle-aged adults, they are most appropriate for these age groups. The most important difficulty in using these scales with older adults is that they all include several items assessing physical symptoms. Although the presence of such symptoms is usually indicative of depression in younger adults, as we noted earlier such symptoms may not be related to depression at all in the elderly. For this reason Yesavage and his colleagues (1983) developed the Geriatric Depression Scale, which focuses exclusively on psychosocial aspects of depression.

	RDC for Major Depressive Disorder (MDD)	DSM III Criteria for Major Depressive Episode (MDE)
Exclusionary criteria	1. None of the following, which suggest schizophrenia, is present: delusions of being controlled, or of thought broadcasting, insertions, or withdrawal nonaffective hallucinations auditory hallucinations more than one month of *no* depressive symptoms but delusions or hallucinations preoccupation with a delusion or hallucination to relative exclusion of other symptoms or concerns definite marked, formal thought disorder 2. Does not meet criteria for schizophrenia, residual type.	1. Preoccupation with a mood-incongruent delusion or hallucination or bizarre behavior cannot be dominant in the clinical picture before or after the occurrence of an affective syndrome. 2. Mood disturbance cannot be superimposed on schizophrenia, schizophreniform disorder, or a paranoid disorder. 3. Organic mental disorder or uncomplicated bereavement is ruled out as a cause of mood disturbance.
Impairment of functioning	Sought or was referred for help during the dysphoric period, took medication, or had impairments in functioning with family, at home, at school, at work, or socially.	Not specified

An important point to keep in mind about these depression scales is that the diagnosis of depression should never be made on the basis of a test score alone. As we have seen, the symptoms observed in clinical depression could be indicative of other problems. Only by a thorough assessment of many aspects of functioning can a clinician make an accurate assessment.

Causes of Depression

Several theories about the causes of depression have been proposed. They can be grouped into two main categories: biological, or physiological, theories and psychosocial theories.

Biological and Physiological Theories. The most popular of the biological and physiological theories links depression to imbalances in or insufficient supplies of particular neurotransmitters such as the catecholamines (Maas, 1978; see Chapter 3). As we noted in Chapter 3, neurotransmitters are chemicals that provide the communication links between the neurons, or brain cells. Because most neurotransmitter levels decline with age, some researchers postulate that depression in the elderly is more likely to be a biochemical problem (Gerner, 1980; Gerner & Jarvick, 1984). However, the link between neurotransmitter levels and depression is still unclear. The problem is that response to drug therapies has not yet been shown to be directly related to changes in neurotransmitter levels.

Other researchers argue that depression may be due to abnormal functioning of the hemispheres in the brain (Weingartner & Silberman, 1982). Neuropsychological tests, that is, tests that measure brain function, and electroencephalograms (EEGs) document abnormalities and impairments in the right hemisphere (Davidson, Schwartz, Saron, Bennett, & Goleman, 1979).

Depression is also linked to physical illness, especially in the elderly. Salzman and Shader (1979) and Verwoerdt (1980, 1981) note that there is considerable evidence that worsening physical health in the elderly often goes hand in hand with worsening symptoms of depression; expressions of guilt, crying, irritability, anxiety, and dependency are common. Among the physical diseases that often include obvious symptoms of depression are dementia, brain tumors, cerebrovascular disease, hypothyroidism, and cardiovascular disease (Fry, 1986). Given the connection between physical diseases and depressive symptoms, it is clearly important for the diagnostic process to include a complete physical examination.

Psychosocial Theories. A major theme of psychosocial theories of depression is **loss** (Butler & Lewis, 1982). Bereavement has been the type of loss receiving the most attention, but the loss of anything considered personally important could also be a trigger. Gaylord and Zung (1987) identified eight types of loss that may result in dysphoria or depression: loss of a loved one; loss of health or physical attractiveness; loss of job or caretaking roles; loss of personal possessions; loss of life-style; failure of plans or ventures; loss of group membership or status; and loss of a pet. Moreover, these losses may be real and irrevocable, threatened and potential, or imaginary and fantasized. Moreover, the likelihood that these losses will occur varies with age. Middle-aged adults are more likely to experience the loss of physical attractiveness, for example, whereas older adults are more likely to experience the loss of a loved one.

The belief that negative life events cause depression is widely held. Indeed, major negative life events often trigger feelings of sadness and dysphoria. Additionally, some theorists view depression as resulting from a search for the self that uncovers negative or missing aspects of identity. These issues are especially important in understanding depression in mid-life. It may be that events surrounding changes in employment and family result in a questioning of self, which in turn may result in dysphoria.

However, the research evidence suggests that events probably do not cause cases of severe depression (Fry, 1986; Gaylord & Zung, 1987). The lack of evidence for an event trigger for severe depression despite popular belief to the contrary probably reflects a difference of perspective. That is, feeling "down" is extremely common after experiencing a traumatic event; as noted in Chapter 14, it is a universal experience during the grieving process. When people experience these feelings, they may have a tendency to label themselves as "depressed." But as we have seen, feelings alone are not enough to indicate severe clinical depression. What happens following a significant loss is a much milder form of depression, which may in fact be a normal response to the situation (Blazer & Williams, 1980).

An important and as yet unresolved question is whether the milder forms of depression are simply variants of severe depression or whether the two are completely different disorders. If they are different, their causes may not be the same, and they may not respond to the same treatments. Moreover, we also need to learn how psychosocial issues and biological or physiological factors are interrelated.

Freud viewed depression (or melancholia, in his terminology) as a profoundly painful dejection, cessation of interest in the outside world, loss of the capacity to love, and a lowering of self-regarding feelings that resulted in severe self-reproaches (Mendelson, 1982). For Freud, this loss becomes internalized, and the displeasure felt toward someone else becomes focused on oneself. Thus, in psychoanalytic terms, depression is hostility turned inward.

The loss of self-esteem is also an important part of psychoanalytic theories of depression. In general, this loss comes from faulty aspects of how one presents oneself, the superego, the ideal self, and self-critical ego functions (Mendelson, 1982).

Behavioral and cognitive theories of depression point to uncontrollable events and their interpretation and one's internal belief system as causes (Nolen-Hoeksema, 1988). The idea behind these theories is that experiencing unpredictable and uncontrollable events instills a feeling of helplessness, which results in depression. Additionally, perceiving the cause of negative events as some inherent aspect of the self that is permanent and pervasive also plays an important role in causing feelings of helplessness and hopelessness.

One explanation for lower rates of depression in the elderly is that they face fewer aversive and uncontrollable traumatic events than most stereotypes of aging suggest (Nolen-Hoeksema, 1988). It is also possible that there is a cohort difference operating (Klerman, 1986); older generations have better strategies for dealing with their own depression, such as engaging in activities designed to get their minds off the problem. In some cases, changing older adults' negative attitudes about the acceptability of seeking help from mental health professionals for depression may be necessary (Nolen-Hoeksema, 1988).

Treatment of Depression

As we have seen, depression is a complex problem that can result from a wide variety of causes. We have also noted that depression can vary in severity, from fairly normal responses to traumatic events to very serious, life-threatening lack of concern for oneself. Thompson and Gallagher (1986) note that all forms of depression benefit from therapy. For the severe forms, it may be necessary to administer medications. In some cases of severe, long-term depression, electroconvulsive therapy may be required. For the less severe forms of depression, and usually in conjunction with medication for severe depression, there are various forms of psychotherapy.

Drug Therapy. Two families of drugs are used to combat severe depression. The most commonly used medications are the **heterocyclic antidepressants (HCAs)**. HCAs were formerly known as tricyclic antidepressants, but the recent marketing of monocyclic, bicyclic, and tetracyclic antidepressants led to the change in terminology (Berkow, 1987). Although HCAs are effective in at least 70% of cases, they are most effective with younger and middle-aged individuals (Berkow, 1987; Epstein, 1978). The main problem with HCAs in older age groups is that the elderly are more likely to have medical conditions or to be taking other medications that inhibit their use. For example, people who are taking antihypertensive medication or who have any of a number of metabolic problems should not take the tricyclic HCAs (Baldessarini, 1978). Moreover, the risk for side effects beyond the typical one of dry mouth are much greater in the elderly (Epstein, 1978), although some of the newer HCAs have significantly lower risk. Because HCAs must be taken for roughly a week before the person feels relief, compliance with the therapy is sometimes difficult.

A second group of drugs that relieves depression is the **MAO inhibitors**, so named because they inhibit MAO, a substance that interferes with the transmission of signals between neurons. MAO inhibitors are generally less effective than the tricyclics and can produce deadly side effects (Walker & Brodie, 1980). Specifically, they interact with foods that contain tyramine or dopamine—mainly cheddar cheese but also others, such as wine and chicken liver—to create dangerously, and sometimes fatally, high blood pressure. MAO inhibitors are used with extreme caution in the United States, usually only after HCAs have proved ineffective. Research on other MAO inhibitors that have reduced risk is under way (Berkow, 1987).

If the periods of depression alternate with periods of mania or extremely high levels of activity, a diagnosis of **bipolar disorder** is made (American Psychiatric Association, 1987). Bipolar disorder is characterized by unpredictable, often explosive mood swings as the person cycles between extreme depression and extreme activity. The drug therapy of choice for bipolar disorder is **lithium** (Berkow, 1987), which came into widespread use in the early 1970s. Lithium is extremely effective in controlling the mood swings, although we do not completely understand why it works. The use of lithium must be monitored very closely, because the difference between an effective dose and a toxic dose is extremely small (Mahoney, 1980). Because lithium is a salt, it raises the blood pressure, making it dangerous to use with individuals who have hypertension or kidney disease. The effective dosage level for lithium decreases with age; physicians unaware of this change run the risk of inducing an overdose, especially in the elderly (Maletta, 1984). Compliance is also a problem, because no improvement is seen for between 4 and 10 days after the initial dose (Berkow, 1987) and because it turns out that many individuals with bipolar disorder do not like having their moods controlled by medication (Jamison, Gerner, & Goodwin, 1979).

Electroconvulsive Therapy. **Electroconvulsive therapy (ECT)** is viewed by many people as an extreme and even cruel form of therapy. This perspective was probably justified in the past, when ECT was used as depicted in books and movies such as *One Flew Over the Cuckoo's Nest.* The popular perception is that ECT is used only for the most severely mentally disturbed individuals; it was this view that forced Thomas Eagleton to withdraw his candidacy for the vice-presidency of the United States in 1972.

In fact, ECT is an extremely effective treatment for severe depression, especially in people whose depression has lasted a long time, who are suicidal, who have serious physical problems caused by their depression, and who do not respond to medications (Salzman, 1975; R. D. Weiner, 1979). ECT is now tightly regulated, and it can be used only after review of each individual case (Walker & Brodie, 1980). ECT involves passing a current of 70 to 150 volts from one of the person's temples to the other for less than 1 second (Weiner, 1979). This results in a seizure similar to that experienced in severe forms of epilepsy. To prevent the person from injury, he or she is given a strong muscle relaxant. The effective voltage appears to increase with age, which means that treatments need to be spaced further apart and the person monitored more closely (Weiner, 1979).

ECT has some advantages (Salzman, 1975). Unlike antidepressant medications, it has immediate effects. Usually, only a few treatments are required, compared with long-term maintenance schedules for drugs. But ECT also has some side effects. Memory of the ECT treatment itself is lost. Memory of other recent events is temporarily disrupted, but it usually returns within a week or two (Salzman, 1975).

The use of ECT with older adults was long thought to be very risky. However, research demonstrates that with careful monitoring the severely depressed elderly benefit considerably. Indeed, ECT may be safer for older adults with heart disease than HCA therapy (Salzman, 1975).

Psychotherapy. Psychotherapy is an approach to treatment based on the idea that talking about one's problems to a therapist can help. Often, psychotherapy can be very effective by itself in treating depression. In cases of severe depression, psychotherapy may be combined with drug or ECT therapy. Of the more than 100 different types of psychotherapy, two general approaches seem to work best with depressed people: behavior therapy and cognitive therapy.

The fundamental idea in **behavior therapy** is that depressed people receive too few rewards or reinforcements from their environment (Lewinsohn, 1975). Thus, the goal of behavior therapy is to get them to increase the "good things" that happen to them. Often, this can be accomplished by having people increase their activities; if they do more, the likelihood is that more good things will happen. Additionally, behavior therapy seeks to get people to decrease the number of negative thoughts they have, because depressed people tend to look at the world pessimistically. They get little pleasure out of activities that nondepressed people enjoy a great deal: seeing a funny movie, playing a friendly game of volleyball, or being with a lover.

To get activity levels up and negative thoughts down, behavior therapists usually assign "homework," tasks that force clients to practice the principles they are learning during the therapy sessions (Gallagher & Thompson, 1983; Lewinsohn, 1975). This may involve going out more to meet people, joining new clubs, or just learning how to enjoy life. Family members are instructed to ignore negative statements made by the depressed person and to reward positive self-statements with attention, praise, or even money.

An effective approach that incorporates Lewinsohn's (1975) behavioral approach but is presented in a less traditional therapeutic setting is the *Coping With Depression Course* (Lewinsohn, Steinmetz, Antonuccio, & Teri, 1984). The course adopts a **psychoeducational approach**, in that the principles of behavior therapy are embedded in an educational program. The advantage of a psychoeducational approach is that the stigma of receiving traditional psychotherapy is removed, since classes are held in a workshop setting. However, research indicates that the course is as effective as traditional behavior therapy for mildly and moderately depressed adults of all ages (Gallagher & Thompson, 1983).

Cognitive therapy for depression is based on the idea that depression results from maladaptive beliefs or cognitions about oneself. From this perspective, a depressed individual views the *self* as inadequate and unworthy, the *world* as insensitive and ungratifying, and the *future* as bleak and unpromising (Beck, Rush, Shaw, & Emery, 1979). In cognitive therapy the person is taught how to recognize these thoughts, which have become so automatic and ingrained that other perspectives are not seen. Once this awareness has been achieved, the person learns how to evaluate the self, world, and future more realistically. These goals may be accomplished through homework assignments similar to those used in behavior therapy. These often involve reattribution of the causes of events, examining the evidence before drawing conclusions, listing the pros and cons of maintaining an idea, and examining the consequences of that idea. Finally, individuals are taught to change the basic beliefs that are responsible for their negative thoughts. For example, people who believe that they have been failures all their lives or that they are unlovable are taught how to use their newfound knowledge to achieve more realistic appraisals of themselves (Gallagher & Thompson, 1983).

Cognitive therapy alone is also an effective treatment for mildly and moderately depressed adults of all ages. However, the process of change may take longer in older adults, who may also need more encouragement along the way. Despite the need for extra support, older adults are able to maintain the gains made during therapy as well as younger and middle-aged adults (Gallagher & Thompson, 1983).

The goal of *psychoanalytic therapy* is to alter the personality structure so that the individual can function more adaptively. Because the underlying cause of psychopathology is thought to lie in relationships earlier in life, much of psychoanalytic therapy deals with feelings about conflicts in past events and relationships. To achieve the goal of adaptive functioning, one of two approaches is used. In the first the therapist helps the client gain insight into the maladaptive defenses and character defects causing the problem. Feelings about events and relationships earlier in life are discussed, and potential solutions are explored. In the second approach the goal is not insight but, rather, support of existing coping mechanisms to better face current problems. In **supportive therapy** the strengthening of adaptive defenses and the replacement of maladaptive defenses is of pri-

mary concern. Both insight and supportive therapies are effective with adults of all ages.

Two versions of psychoanalytic therapy particularly useful with older adults are **life review therapy** and **reminiscence**. The goal of both therapies is to use the memories of previous events and relationships as ways to confront and resolve conflicts. Life review therapy and reminiscence can be done individually or in groups, and they can be unstructured or structured (by using particular topics as triggers). Although both approaches have become very popular and are claimed to be effective (Kaminsky, 1978; Lesser, Lazarus, Frankel, & Havasy, 1981), why they work and how remembering the past relates to specific cognitive and emotional processes are unknown (Merriam, 1980).

Suicide

Although one does not have to be depressed to commit suicide, depression is the most common reason (Osgood, 1985). Suicide in depressed people represents a logical extension of their belief that they are unworthy, that the future is bleak, and that the world no longer has a place for them.

Every year, roughly 25,000 people in the United States commit suicide. Researchers believe that the true rate is much higher, because most officials will rule that a death is accidental if at all possible to save the family from the stigma associated with suicide. Drug overdoses are often considered to be accidental, for example, as are most single-car accidents. Some researchers estimate the number of actual suicides to be much higher (Osgood, 1985), possibly as high as 100,000 per year (Stenback, 1980).

Suicide and Age. The relationship between suicide rates and age changed considerably between the early 1960s and the 1980s (see Figure

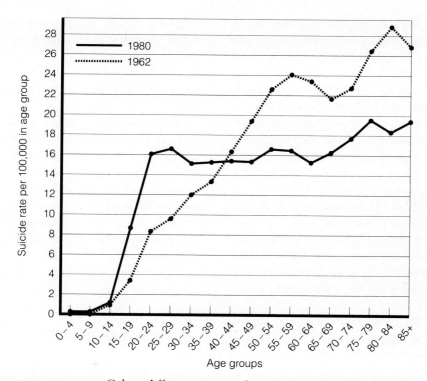

FIGURE 9.2 • Cohort differences in suicide rates. Note that the rates of adolescent and young adult suicide were much higher in 1980, but the rates for other adult age groups were much lower.

(Source: National Center on Health Statistics.)

9.2). Suicide rates for young adults (ages 20 to 35) showed a considerable increase, from between 8 and 12 per 100,000 people in 1962 to about 16 per 100,000 in 1980. However, suicide rates for middle-aged and elderly adults were much higher in 1962 (ranging from 20 to 29 per 100,000) than in 1980 (ranging from 15 to 19 per 100,000) (National Center for Health Statistics, 1988). Reasons for the changes are unclear, especially since some authors report contradictory data concerning the elderly (Osgood, 1985).

What is clear about the relationship between suicide and age is that older White males commit suicide at a much higher rate than any other group, perhaps as much as three times more than White males at age 20 (Sainsbury, 1986). Comparable statistics in other countries reveals an even wider gap: in Japan, the rate for those over 75 is five times higher than that for those aged 15 to 24, and in France the rate is six times higher (Palmore & Maeda, 1985).

In understanding these age differences, we must keep several important points in mind. Many more young people attempt suicide than actually succeed, with the ratio of unsuccessful attempts to successes about 7:1 (Stenback, 1980).

Around mid-life, however, the ratio switches, so that by old age successes outnumber unsuccessful attempts by nearly 8:1 (Sendbeuhler & Goldstein, 1977). This switch has led many theorists to believe that suicide attempts by younger people are more often cries for help or acts of hostility directed at others, such as parents or lovers. In contrast, older adults seldom attempt suicide as a means of getting attention; rather, they are clearly interested in killing themselves and are far more deadly in their methods (Osgood, 1985).

The older adults who commit suicide are also far more likely to be physically ill than are younger suicide victims. About half of the elderly men and about one third of elderly women who commit suicide are seriously ill, many with cancer or a disease that affects the brain (Whitlock, 1986).

Suicide, Race, and Sex. Overall, White males have the highest rate of successful suicide, followed by nonwhite males, White females, and nonwhite females. For White males, late adolescence and the first few years of adulthood show a relatively high rate, falling slightly through mid-life and rising dramatically in late life. Nonwhite males also show an early peak, but their rate drops throughout young adulthood and then levels off. Because White males have more power, the loss of it through retirement and other role loss in old age is more difficult to handle. White women show a slight increase in suicide rate in mid-life, followed by a decrease through old age. Finally, nonwhite women have a low rate of suicide throughout adulthood.

The large difference in suicide rates between White and nonwhite men in later life is thought by some researchers to be related to social power (Osgood, 1985). That is, the loss of power in old age is thought to be a precipitating factor in the high rate of suicide among White males. Also, the substantial difference in overall suicide rates between men and women may be misleading (Williams, 1977). That is, women actually outnumber men in suicide attempts, but men tend to use more lethal means, such as guns and jumping from high places, compared with women, who prefer less lethal means such as poison or sleeping pills.

No adequate explanation of women's suicide statistics has been offered. The notion that the peak in White women's rate during mid-life reflects the "empty nest syndrome" is inadequate, because it fails to explain why nonwhite women are able to experience the same event with no corresponding increase in suicide. Much more research needs to be done in order to understand these issues.

ANXIETY DISORDERS

Imagine that you are about to give a speech before an audience of 500 people. In the last few minutes before your address you begin to feel nervous, your heart starts to pound, and your palms get sweaty. These feelings, common even to veteran speakers, are similar to those experienced by individuals with **anxiety disorders**, a group of conditions that are based on fear or uneasiness. Anxiety disorders include anxiety states, in which feelings of severe anxiety occur with no specific trigger; phobic disorders, characterized by irrational fears of objects or circumstances; and obsessive-compulsive disorders, in which thoughts or actions are repeatedly performed for no apparent reason, in order to lower anxiety.

Symptoms of Anxiety Disorders

Common to all of the anxiety disorders are physical changes that interfere with social functioning, personal relationships, or work. These physical changes include dry mouth, sweating, dizziness, upset stomach, diarrhea, insomnia, hyperventilation, chest pain, choking, frequent urination, headaches, and a sensation of a lump in the throat (Fry, 1986). These symptoms occur in adults of all ages, but they are particularly common in older adults due to loss of health, relocation stress, isolation, fear of losing control over their lives, or guilt resulting from feelings of hostility toward family and friends (Fry, 1986). Himmelfarb (1984) demonstrated the importance of these factors in understanding anxiety disorders in the elderly. After Himmelfarb statistically controlled the relationship between age and anxiety for such factors as health, quality of housing, and social support, the relationship was substantially reduced. Thus, we must be cautious in interpreting reports that the frequency of anxiety disorders increases with age. Such reports may be indicative of other, more important, factors.

Another important issue concerning anxiety disorders in older adults is that anxiety may be an appropriate response to the situation. For example, helplessness anxiety is generated by a potential or actual loss of control or mastery (Verwoerdt, 1981). Additionally, a series of severe negative life experiences may result in a person's reaching the breaking point and appearing highly anxious. Many older adults who show symptoms of anxiety disorder have underlying health problems that may be responsible for the symptoms. In all cases the anxious behavior should be investigated first as an appropriate response that may not require intervention. The important point is to evaluate the older adult's behavior in context.

Treatment of Anxiety Disorders

Both drug therapy and psychotherapy are used to treat anxiety disorders. **Benzodiazepines** are the most widely prescribed medications for anxiety (Fry, 1986). They include such drugs as Valium, Librium, Serax, and Ativan. Although benzodiazepines are effective with adults of all ages, they must be used very carefully with older adults. Effective dosage levels are lower in the elderly, and the potential for side effects is much greater. Most important, these drugs can cause decreased cognitive functioning, which may be mistaken for early dementia. In general, the benzodiazepines may cause drowsiness, loss of coordination, headaches, and lower energy levels. Moreover, because of the potential for addiction, the long-term use of these drugs should be avoided.

In most cases the treatment of choice for anxiety disorders is psychotherapy. A broad range of approaches is effective with adults of all ages. Of particular note are the relaxation techniques described in Chapter 4. These procedures help the anxious person learn to relax and to control the feelings of anxiety before they get out of hand. Other behavioral techniques such as systematic desensitization are especially effective with phobias. The advantage of these psychotherapeutic techniques is that they usually involve a few sessions, have high rates of success, and offer clients procedures that they can take with them. Best of all, they have no long-term side effects, unlike their medical counterparts.

SCHIZOPHRENIC AND PARANOID DISORDERS

Some forms of psychopathology, referred to as psychoses, involve losing touch with reality and the disintegration of personality. Two behaviors that occur in some forms of these disorders are **delusions**, which are belief systems not based on reality, and **hallucinations**, distortions in perception. Two types of psychoses that occur in adulthood are schizophrenia and paranoid disorders.

Schizophrenia

Schizophrenia is characterized by the severe impairment of thought processes, including the content and style of thinking; distorted perceptions; loss of touch with reality; a distorted sense of self; and abnormal motor behavior (American Psychiatric Association, 1987). Individuals with schizophrenia show these abnormal behaviors in several ways: bizarre delusions (e.g., that they are Jesus or that they are being spied on); loose associations (e.g., saying that they have a secret meeting with the president of the United States in the local bowling alley); hearing voices that tell them what to do; believing that they can read other people's minds; or believing that their body is changing into something else. Additionally, schizophrenic individuals tend to show very little or highly inappropriate emotionality (e.g., laughing hysterically at the news of a major tragedy). They are often confused about their own identity, have difficulty working toward a goal, and tend to withdraw from social contact.

Most researchers believe that schizophrenia occurs most often before age 45 (Post, 1987). When schizophrenic symptoms occur in late life, there is some question about whether they represent true schizophrenia, a paranoid disorder, or a form of dementia. These researchers assert that older adults tend to show different symptoms than younger or middle-aged adults; older adults' delusions focus more on sex and personal possessions, whereas younger adults' delusions are more likely to involve mystical or religious themes. Some researchers disagree, however, maintaining that there are few differences with age in the numbers of individuals who experience schizophrenic symptoms and no differences in the nature of the symptoms (Blazer, George, & Hughes, 1988). More research is needed to clarify the issue.

What is clear is that over the long haul schizophrenics tend to show one of three outcomes. Some experience only one episode and are hospitalized for a brief period. Others show a gradual decrease in symptoms over time, perhaps as a result of living in institutions. Still others have symptoms that remain constant over their entire adult life span. In general, most older schizophrenic adults need some sort of structured care. The trend toward deinstitutionalization in the United States over the past few decades has resulted in many older schizophrenic adults ending up either in nursing homes, where the staff often has neither the training nor the time to respond effectively, or, unfortunately, as homeless street people.

Paranoid Disorders

The hallmark of **paranoid disorders** is a well-formed delusion. Most often, three delusions involve persecution ("People are out to get me"). The distinction between paranoid disorders and schizophrenia is fuzzy; indeed, one type of schizophrenia is termed "paranoid type." In general, it is believed that hallucinations, loose associations, and absent or inappropriate emotions do not occur in paranoid disorders (American Psychiatric Association, 1987).

Beliefs in delusions can result in anger, resentment, or even violent acts. Because paranoid individuals are extremely suspicious and rarely seek help on their own, such people tend to come to the attention of authorities after having repeated run-ins with the police or neighbors, starting legal proceedings against others on mysterious grounds, or registering complaints about fictitious or distorted events.

Paranoid disorders are relatively rare among adults of all ages (about 1%) but tend to increase slightly with age (Post, 1987). Paranoid symptoms are commonly associated with dementia, as discussed later, as well as with the use of amphetamines. Fry (1986) notes that three conditions are associated with the onset of paranoid disorders at all ages but are especially important in late life: social isolation, marginal life circumstances and financial losses, and sensory losses, especially hearing loss. Some researchers argue that paranoid disorders in the elderly should not be viewed as illnesses at all but, rather, as minor maladjustments that should be considered only for their nuisance value. Due to these factors the diagnosis of paranoid disorders needs to rule out other possible explanations for the behaviors.

Treatment of Schizophrenic and Paranoid Disorders

Traditionally, treatment of schizophrenic and paranoid disorders has emphasized medication. For schizophrenia, drug therapy consists of **antipsychotics**, medications that are believed to work on the dopamine system (see Chapter 3). Some of the more commonly used antipsychotics are Haldol, Thorazine, and Mellaril. These medications must be used with extreme caution in adults of all ages due to the risk of serious toxic side effects, especially the loss of motor control. Despite these risks antipsychotics are often used in nursing homes and other institutions as tranquilizing agents to control problem patients.

Drug treatment for paranoid disorders includes antipsychotics for the most severe cases and benzodiazepines for milder cases. Neither approach, however, is consistently effective.

In general, schizophrenic and paranoid individuals are difficult to treat in psychotherapy. The severe thought disturbances characteristic of schizophrenia make it difficult for therapists to work with clients. Because of their extreme suspiciousness, paranoid individuals may be reluctant to cooperate in psychotherapy. If these

barriers can be overcome, however, there is some evidence that supportive therapy may be effective (Fry, 1986). The goals of therapy for schizophrenic individuals tend to be adaptive rather than curative, that is, helping these people adapt to daily living rather than attempting to cure them. In contrast, the goal for paranoid individuals is more likely to be curative, that is, a significant reduction in delusionary thought, because the source of the delusions in many of these individuals is a lack of stimulation.

DEMENTIA

Probably no other condition associated with aging is more feared than **dementia**. In dementia people may literally "lose their mind," being reduced from complex, thinking, feeling human beings to confused, vegetative victims unable even to recognize their spouse and children. Approximately 4.4 million older Americans, or roughly 15% of people over age 65, have some type of dementing disorder (Davies, 1988). Estimates are that the number may double in the next 50 years due to the increase in very old adults (Crook, 1987). Fewer than 1% of the people are afflicted at age 65, but the incidence rises sharply to 20% of those over 80.

Although there is a real basis for fearing dementia, it is important to realize that the vast majority of older adults are *not* demented. For many people, it is the *fear* of dementia that is the most serious problem, leading them to label every time that they misplace their keys a symptom. It is hard to know how many older adults have unstated fears because they can no longer remember things in the same ways they did when they were younger. But as noted in Chapter 7, memory abilities show some normative changes with age. Consequently, it is important to realize that what many people believe are signs that they are "going senile" are actually quite normal.

The Family of Dementias

The term *dementia* does not refer to a specific disease but, rather, to a family of diseases that have similar symptoms. About a dozen forms of dementia have been identified. All are characterized by cognitive and behavioral deficits involving some form of permanent damage to the brain. Because dementia involves identifiable damage to the brain, it is also one of the diseases termed **organic mental disorders**. These criteria mean that dementia involves severe cognitive and behavioral decline and is not caused by a rapid onset of a toxic substance or by infection (American Psychiatric Association, 1987).

Dementias can be classified in several ways. For many years the age of the patient at diagnosis was used as the basis for classification. Dementias diagnosed in people younger than 60 to 65 years old were termed presenile, and those diagnosed in people older than 60 to 65 were termed senile dementia. Over the past 2 decades, however, this terminology has been declining in popularity and meaning, largely because new discoveries are revealing that age makes little difference in the types of underlying neurological changes (Crook, 1987). Thus, the trend is to refer to the various diseases by name rather than by the terms *presenile* and *senile*.

A second way to group dementias is more useful and important. Some dementias can be treated effectively, and a few can even be reversed. This distinction between reversible and irreversible dementias has profound implications for the patient. Reversible dementias, **delirium**, and pseudodementia stem from treatable causes.

Reversible dementia refers to a loosely defined set of disorders that are characterized by cognitive difficulties but are treatable (Zarit & Zarit, 1983). Delirium is characterized by impaired awareness of self and surroundings, attention deficits, tendencies toward hallucinations and delusions, disorientation, changes in alertness, disturbed sleep patterns, and rapid changes in symptoms and their severity; memory may be affected (Lipowski, 1980). The common underlying factor is a disruption of cerebral metabolism; susceptibility to such metabolic disruptions increases with age. Indeed, the National Institute of Aging (1980) emphasizes that almost any internal disturbance can lead to cognitive symptoms in older adults.

Common causes include the toxic effects of medications (see Table 9.3) or drug interactions, infections, electrolyte imbalances, malnutrition, and potassium deficits. Symptoms may also appear following surgery, fractures, head injuries, changes in the environment, or the death of a close relative. As noted earlier, depression may manifest itself as cognitive impairment (Wells, 1979). The important point is that cognitive symptoms, especially in an older adult, do not necessarily indicate an untreatable, irreversible disease; careful diagnosis is an absolute must. Unfortunately, such careful diagnoses are often unavailable because of the lack of physicians who specialize in geriatric medicine. As a result many older adults are misdiagnosed as having suspected Alzheimer's disease when they actually have a treatable disorder such as delirium or depression. Additionally, physicians who are not geriatric specialists often dismiss serious cognitive or behavioral symptoms as part of normal aging, which they clearly are not.

In this section we will focus on dementias that are irreversible and degenerative. The most common and widely known of these is Alzheimer's disease, but others are important as well: multi-

TABLE 9.3 · Drugs that may cause cognitive deficits as side effects

antidepressants (used to treat depression)

benzodiazepines (used to treat anxiety disorders)

bromocriptine (used to treat Parkinson's disease)

carbamazepine (used to treat seizure disorders)

cimetidine (used to treat ulcers)

digoxin (used to treat congestive heart failure and cardiac arrhythmias)

lithium (used to treat bipolar disorder)

meclizine (used to prevent dizziness or motion sickness)

neuroleptics (used to treat psychotic disorders or severe behavior problems)

phenobarbitol (used to treat seizure disorders)

phenytoin (used to treat seizure disorders)

ranitidine (used to treat ulcers)

scopolamine (often used before surgery)

---

infarct dementia, Parkinson's disease, Pick's disease, Creutzfeld-Jakob disease, Huntington's disease, and normal-pressure hydrocephalus.

Alzheimer's Disease

Alzheimer's disease is the most common form of progressive, degenerative dementia, accounting for perhaps as many as 70% of all cases of dementia (Davies, 1988). We have only recently realized how common Alzheimer's disease is, however. When Alois Alzheimer first described the sequence of changes in 1907, he was referring to a person 51 years old. For the next 60 years physicians believed that the disease was very rare and that it was a form of presenile dementia. It was not until Tomlinson, Blessed, and Roth (1970) showed that the same kinds of changes occurred in both early onset and late onset of the disease that physicians realized that age was not a factor. As a result virtually all that we know about Alzheimer's disease has been learned in the past 20 years, with discoveries coming almost daily.

The rapid growth in awareness that Alzheimer's disease is a major health problem resulted in the formation of the Alzheimer's Disease and Related Disorders Association (ADRDA) in 1980. The ADRDA serves as a national advocacy group, sponsors workshops and research into the causes and treatment of the disease, and provides support groups for family care givers. Nearly 200 chapters have been formed in communities throughout the United States, with roughly 1,000 family support groups (Lombardo, 1988). Another important function of the ADRDA is to provide information; its book *Understanding Alzheimer's Disease* (Aronson, 1988) provides a nontechnical summary of the disease and the complex family, ethical, and legal issues involved in it.

Underlying Changes in the Brain: Neuropathology and Neurochemistry. The changes in

The Alzheimer's Disease and Related Disorders Association is a nationwide group dedicated to providing information and support to family members of victims. For information on the association and the chapter nearest you, call the toll-free number.

the brain that characterize Alzheimer's disease are microscopic. This means that definitive diagnosis of the disease can be done only at autopsy; brain biopsies are an alternative, but the risks are so high that they are rarely performed (Crook, 1987). The microscopic changes that define Alzheimer's disease are **neurofibrillary tangles**, **senile plaques**, and **granulovacuolar degeneration**.

Neurofibrillary tangles are accumulations of pairs of filaments in the neuron that become wrapped around each other; when examined under a microscope, these paired filaments look like intertwined spirals. Neurofibrillary tangles occur throughout the cortex and hippocampus (see Chapter 3), and the number of tangles is directly related to the severity of symptoms (Farmer, Peck, & Terry, 1976). Senile plaques are spherical structures consisting of a core of **amyloid**, a protein, surrounded by degenerated fragments of dying or dead neurons. The plaques are also found throughout the cortex and hippocampus and are related to the severity of the disease (Blessed, Tomlinson, & Roth, 1968). Degeneration of neurons in the hippocampus results in the formation of "vacuoles," or spaces that become filled with fluid and granular material. Although granulovacuolar degeneration is a defining characteristic of Alzheimer's disease, its relationship to the severity of the disease is still unknown.

In addition to these three changes, atrophy of various parts of the brain has been found in Alzheimer's disease. However, brain atrophy is not a reliable indicator, since it is associated not only with Alzheimer's disease but also with many other diseases as well as normal aging (Crook, 1987).

Considerable research over the past decade has uncovered specific deficits in neurotransmitters. Most notable is a marked decrease in the enzyme **choline acetyltransferase**, a marker for acetylcholine, a neurotransmitter involved in learning and memory (Davies & Maloney, 1976). The decline in acetylcholine appears to be caused mainly by the degeneration of the **nucleus basalis of Meynert** and surrounding structures in the base of the brain (Whitehouse et al., 1982). These changes may be the cause of the drastic declines in cognitive functions associated with Alzheimer's disease. Other studies have revealed decreases in several neurotransmitters, including noradrenaline (Bondareff, Mountjoy, & Roth, 1982), serotonin (Gottfries, Roos, & Winblad, 1976), and dopamine (Gottfries, Gottfries, & Roos, 1969). Changes in these neurotransmitters may be related to other symptoms, such as agitation, sleep disturbances, and perceptual difficulties.

Although the changes occurring in the brains

of Alzheimer's victims are substantial, we must use caution in assuming that they represent qualitative differences from normal aging. They may not. Gottfries (1985) notes that all of the changes seen in Alzheimer's disease, from cognitive changes to the changes in neurotransmitters, are also found in normal elderly people. To be sure, the changes in Alzheimer's disease are much greater. But the important point is that Alzheimer's disease may be merely an exaggeration of normal aging and not something qualitatively different from it.

Symptoms and Diagnosis. The major symptoms of Alzheimer's disease are gradual changes in cognitive functioning: declines in memory, learning, attention, and judgment; disorientation in time and space; difficulties in word finding and communication; declines in personal hygiene and self-care skills; inappropriate social behavior; and changes in personality (Crystal, 1988; Davies, 1988). These symptoms tend to be vague in the beginning, and they mimic other psychological problems such as depression or stress reactions. For example, an executive may not be managing as well as she once did and may be missing deadlines more often. Slowly, the symptoms get worse. This executive, who once could easily handle millions of dollars, cannot now add two small numbers. A housewife cannot set the table. A person who was previously outgoing is now quiet and withdrawn; a gentle person is now hostile and aggressive. Emotional problems become increasingly apparent, including depression, paranoia, and agitation. As the disease progresses, the patient becomes incontinent and more and more dependent on others for care, eventually becoming completely incapable of even such simple tasks as dressing and eating. In general, the symptoms associated with Alzheimer's disease are worse in the evening than in the morning, a phenomenon that is referred to as **sundowning** among care givers.

The rate of deterioration in Alzheimer's disease is highly variable from one patient to the next, although progression is usually faster when onset occurs earlier in life (Bondareff, 1983). However, it is possible to identify a series of stages that the patient goes through (Reisberg, Ferris, de Leon, & Crook, 1982); these stages are summarized in Table 9.4. It is important to realize that many diseases cause the problems outlined in stages 1 and 2. In fact, fewer than 10% of those individuals at stage 2 will develop more serious cognitive impairment within several years of the clinical evaluation (Reisberg, Ferris, Anand, de Leon, Schneck, & Crook, 1985). Cognitive deficits such as those described in stage 3 typically indicate the presence of the serious decline characteristic of Alzheimer's disease (Reisberg et al., 1985).

Although a definitive diagnosis of Alzheimer's disease depends on an autopsy, the number and severity of behavioral changes allows physicians to make increasingly accurate early diagnosis (Crook, 1987). In order for this earlier diagnosis to be relatively accurate, however, it must be comprehensive and broad. Table 9.5 provides the set of guidelines developed by a work group convened by the National Institute of Neurological and Communicative Diseases and Stroke (McKhann et al., 1984). Note that a great deal of the diagnostic effort goes into ruling out other possible causes for the observed cognitive deficits. This point emphasizes the fact that all possible treatable causes for the symptoms must be eliminated before a physician makes a diagnosis of Alzheimer's disease. Unfortunately, many physicians do not conduct such thorough diagnoses.

As noted in Table 9.5, the clinical diagnosis of Alzheimer's disease consists of noting the history of the symptoms, documenting the cognitive

TABLE 9.4 • Stages of dementia as measured by the Global Deterioration Scale, with corresponding clinical phases and characteristics

GDS Stage	Clinical Phase	Clinical Characteristics
1. No cognitive decline	Normal	No subjective complaints of memory deficit. No memory deficit evident on clinical interview.
2. Very mild cognitive decline	Forgetfulness	Subjective complaints of memory deficit, most frequently in following areas: (a) forgetting where one has placed familiar objects and (b) forgetting names one formerly knew well. No objective evidence of memory deficit on clinical interview. No objective deficits in employment or social situations. Appropriate concern with respect to symptomatology.
3. Mild cognitive decline	Early confusional	Earliest clear-cut deficits. Manifestations in more than one of the following areas: (a) patient may have gotten lost when traveling to an unfamiliar location; (b) co-workers become aware of patient's relatively poor performance; (c) word- and name-finding deficits become evident to intimates; (d) patient may read a passage or a book and retain relatively little material; (e) patient may demonstrate decreased facility in remembering names upon introduction to new people; (f) patient may have lost or misplaced an object of value; (g) concentration deficit may be evident on clinical testing.
		Objective evidence of memory deficit obtained only with an intensive interview conducted by a trained geriatric psychiatrist. Decreased performance in demanding employment and social settings. Denial begins to become manifest in patient. Mild to moderate anxiety accompanies symptoms.
4. Moderate cognitive decline	Late confusional	Clear-cut deficit on careful interview. Deficit manifest in following areas: (a) decreased knowledge of current and recent events; (b) may exhibit some deficit in memory of one's personal history; (c) concentration deficit elicited on serial subtractions; (d) decreased ability to travel, handle finances, etc.
		Frequently no deficit in following areas: (a) orientation to time and person; (b) recognition of familiar persons and faces; (c) ability to travel to familiar locations.

(Source: "The Global Deterioration Scale for Assessment of Primary Degenerative Dementia" by B. Reisberg, S. H. Ferris, M. J. de Leon, and T. Crook, 1982, *American Journal of Psychiatry, 139*, pp. 1136–1139. Copyright 1982 by The American Psychiatric Association. Reprinted with permission.)

GDS Stage	Clinical Phase	Clinical Characteristics
		Inability to perform complex tasks. Denial is dominant defense mechanism. Flattening of affect and withdrawal from challenging situations occur.
5. Moderately severe cognitive decline	Early dementia	Patient can no longer survive without some assistance. Patients are unable during interview to recall a major relevant aspect of current lives, e.g., their address or telephone number of many years, the names of close members of their family (such as grandchildren), the name of the high school or college from which they graduated.
		Frequently some disorientation to time (date, day of week, season, etc.) or to place. An educated person may have difficulty counting back from 40 by 4s or from 20 by 2s.
		Persons at this stage retain knowledge of many major facts regarding themselves and others. They invariably know their own names and generally know their spouse's and children's names. They require no assistance with toileting or eating but may have some difficulty choosing the proper clothing to wear and may occasionally clothe themselves improperly (e.g., put shoes on the wrong feet, etc.).
6. Severe cognitive decline	Middle dementia	May occasionally forget the name of the spouse on whom they are entirely dependent for survival. Will be largely unaware of all recent events and experiences in their lives. Retain some knowledge of their past lives, but this is very sketchy. Generally unaware of their surroundings, the year, the season, etc. May have difficulty counting from 10, both backward and, sometimes, forward. Will require some assistance with activities of daily living, e.g., may become incontinent, will require travel assistance but occasionally will display ability to travel to familiar locations. Diurnal rhythm frequently disturbed. Almost always recall their own name. Frequently continue to be able to distinguish familiar from unfamiliar persons in their environment.
		Personality and emotional changes occur. These are quite variable and include (a) delusional behavior (e.g., patients

(continued)

GDS Stage	Clinical Phase	Clinical Characteristics
		may accuse their spouse of being an imposter; may talk to imaginary figures in the environment or to their own reflection in the mirror); (b) obsessive symptoms (e.g., person may continually repeat simple cleaning activities); (c) anxiety symptoms, agitation, and even previously nonexistent violent behavior may occur; (d) cognitive abulia (i.e., loss of willpower because an individual cannot carry a thought long enough to determine a purposeful course of action).
7. Very severe cognitive decline	Late dementia	All verbal abilities are lost. Frequently there is no speech at all—only grunting. Incontinent of urine; requires assistance toileting and feeding. Loses basic psychomotor skills (e.g., ability to walk). The brain appears to no longer be able to tell the body what to do. Generalized and cortical neurological signs and symptoms are frequently present.

impairments, conducting a general physical exam and neurological exam, performing laboratory tests to rule out other diseases, obtaining a psychiatric evaluation, performing neuropsychological tests, and assessing functional abilities (Crystal, 1988). The history or progress of the disease should be obtained from both the patient, if possible, and a family member. The questions asked *must* cover when the problems began, how they have changed, what the patient is capable of doing, and other medical problems.

The cognitive impairments are typically documented through a **mental status exam** (Blessed, Tomlinson, & Roth, 1968; Folstein, Folstein, & McHugh, 1975), which is a brief series of questions tapping orientation ("What day is this? Where are you?"), memory, arithmetic ability (counting backwards), ability to follow directions, motor skills (copying a design), and general

information ("Who is the president now?"). The general physical exam and neurological exam help rule out other causes such as cardiovascular disease, nutritional problems, or strokes.

A series of laboratory tests must be conducted to rule out additional causes of the observed behaviors. Blood tests look for evidence of chronic infections and for abnormal levels of vitamin B_{12}, folic acid, and thyroid hormone. An EEG should be performed to rule out subtle seizures and to verify that the characteristic "diffusely slow" EEG pattern in Alzheimer's disease is present. Computerized axial tomography, or **CT scans**, a computerized image of the brain based on X rays; magnetic resonance imaging, or **MRI scans**, in which magnetic beams are used instead of X rays; and positron emission tomography, or **PET scans**, in which radioactive isotopes are injected in the brain are all used in diagnosing Alzheimer's disease. However, none of these imaging techniques provides conclusive evidence; at best they can rule out the presence of tumors, strokes, or other abnormalities (Crystal, 1988).

A psychiatric evaluation must be done to rule out any serious emotional problems that may be causing the observed deficits. A battery of neuropsychological tests should be administered to document the extent of the cognitive deficits and to provide additional information concerning the possibility of tumors or strokes. The functional abilities of the patient must be evaluated as well; these include **instrumental daily activities**, such as cooking and cleaning, and personal self-care skills, such as dressing and bathing.

Searching for a Cause. We do not know what causes Alzheimer's disease. The most widely held notion is that a viral infection causes the changes in the brain (Davies, 1988). The viral idea is credible, because a virus appears to be involved in Creutzfeld-Jakob disease, another form of dementia. If a virus turns out to be responsible, it is probably slow-acting. Unfortunately, scientists have not yet been able to detect a specific virus in the brains of people with Alzheimer's disease.

A second idea about a cause that has been widely reported is aluminum toxicity (Thal, 1988). The idea here is that aluminum, which is deadly to brain cells, starts the chain of events leading to Alzheimer's disease. Although high concentrations of aluminum have been reported in Alzheimer's disease victims, there is no evidence that links the use of aluminum in daily life, such as in cookware or deodorant, to Alzheimer's disease.

One of the major concerns of families of Alzheimer's disease victims is the possibility that it is inherited. Breitner (1988) reviews the evidence to date and concludes that genetic factors may be a powerful determinant of Alzheimer's disease. Although there are several methodological difficulties in doing genetics research, it appears from family trees and studies of relatives and twins that Alzheimer's disease shows an **autosomal dominant** inheritance pattern. An autosomal dominant pattern is one in which only one gene from one parent is necessary to produce the disease; this means that there is a 50% chance that the child of an affected parent will have the disorder. An autosomal dominant pattern for Alzheimer's disease makes sense, since we know that at least two other forms of dementia, Pick's disease and Huntington's disease, are autosomal dominant.

Some research has linked Alzheimer's disease with Down's syndrome, a genetic form of mental retardation (Breitner, 1988). People with Down's syndrome develop severe cognitive impairments and brain changes like those in Alzheimer's disease during middle adulthood and old age. Some researchers thought that the gene for Alzheimer's disease might be on the same chromosome responsible for Down's syndrome, but the evidence appears to be against it.

Even if a specific gene is identified, many questions about the cause of Alzheimer's disease will remain. Why does it take so long for the genetic defect to appear? What mechanism starts it? Why is there so much variation when it appears? Answers to these questions will help considerably in understanding how Alzheimer's disease develops.

Supposing that an autosomal dominant pattern were responsible, what would this mean for the relatives of Alzheimer's disease victims? Actually, it would depend on the relative's age. Even though the risk would always be greater, even at age 65 this increased risk would have little practical significance, because the overall incidence of Alzheimer's disease at this age is low. But by age 80 the risk to first-degree relatives would be roughly 25%, compared with 6% in the general population (Breitner, 1988). Although these

TABLE 9.5 · Criteria for the diagnosis of probable Alzheimer's disease

1. Criteria for clinical diagnosis of *probable* Alzheimer's disease include

   Dementia established by clinical examination and documented by Mini-Mental State Test (Folstein, Folstein, & McHugh, 1975), Blessed Dementia Scale (Blessed, Tomlinson, Roth, 1968), or some similar examination and confirmed by neuropsychological tests

   Deficits in two or more areas of cognition

   Progressive worsening of memory and other cognitive functions

   No disturbance of consciousness

   Onset between ages 40 and 90, most often after age 65

   Absence of systemic disorders or other brain diseases that in and of themselves could account for progressive deficits in memory and cognition

2. Diagnosis of *probable* Alzheimer's disease is supported by

   Progressive deterioration of specific cognitive functions, such as language (aphasia), motor skills (apraxia), and perception (agnosia)

   Impaired activities of daily living and altered patterns of behavior

   Family history of similar disorders, particularly if confirmed neuropathologically

   Laboratory results of normal lumbar puncture as evaluated by standard techniques, normal pattern or nonspecific changes in EEG, such as increased slow-wave activity, and evidence of cerebral atrophy on CT with progression documented by serial observation

3. Other clinical features consistent with diagnosis of *probable* Alzheimer's disease, after exclusion of causes of dementia other than Alzheimer's disease, include

   Plateaus in course of progression of illness

   Associated symptoms of depression; insomnia; incontinence; delusions; illusions; hallucinations; catastrophic verbal, emotional, or physical outbursts; sexual disorders; and weight loss

   Other neurological abnormalities in some patients, especially with more advanced disease and including motor signs, such as increased muscle tone, myoclonus, or gait disorder

(Source: National Institute of Neurological and Communicative Diseases and Stroke)

numbers are not reassuring, they are considerably lower than the risk for many other autosomal dominant genetic diseases, such as Huntington's disease.

Tests can be developed to detect genes that transmit diseases via an autosomal dominant pattern. Such a test already exists for Huntington's disease. As discussed in "Something to Think About," however, the availability of a test is not always welcome, even when there is a high risk of passing the disease on to one's children.

Intervention Strategies. Alzheimer's disease is incurable. However, much research has been done looking for ways to alleviate the cognitive deficits. Most of this work has focused on various

Seizures in advance disease

CT normal for age

4. Features that make diagnosis of *probable* Alzheimer's disease uncertain or unlikely include

Sudden, apoplectic onset

Focal neurological findings such as hemiparesis, sensory loss, visual field deficits, and uncoordination early in the course of the illness

Seizures or gait disturbance at onset or very early in course of illness

5. Clinical diagnosis of *possible* Alzheimer's disease

May be made on basis of dementia syndrome, in absence of other neurological, psychiatric, or systemic disorders sufficient to cause dementia and in the presence of variations in onset, in presentation, or in clinical course

May be made in presence of second systemic or brain disorder sufficient to produce dementia, which is not considered to be cause of dementia

Should be used in research studies when single, gradually progressive severe cognitive deficit is identified in absence of other identifiable cause

6. Criteria for diagnosis of *definite* Alzheimer's disease are

Clinical criteria for probable Alzheimer's disease

Histopathological evidence obtained from biopsy or at autopsy

7. Classification of Alzheimer's disease for research purposes should specify features that may differentiate subtypes of the disorder, such as

Familial occurrence

Onset before age of 65

Presence of trisomy-21

Coexistence of other relevant conditions, such as Parkinson's disease

---

drugs that could improve memory (Bartus, Dean, & Fisher, 1986; Crook, 1987; Thal, 1988). These drugs have included a wide variety of compounds aimed at improving cerebral blood flow or levels of various neurotransmitters. Although some drugs have been reported to improve cognitive functioning, these successes have often been achieved with carefully selected patients on carefully selected tests (Crook, 1987). In terms of clinical application none of the drugs has shown reliable improvements in a wide variety of patients (Thal, 1988).

In contrast to the poor picture for improving cognitive performance, improving other behavioral problems is possible. Drugs that are used primarily in younger patients for the treatment of

S O M E T H I N G · T O · T H I N K · A B O U T

Genetic Tests for Dementia— Difficult Choices

When scientists discovered that they could tell whether someone was carrying the gene for Huntington's disease, they thought it would be a welcome relief to thousands of families. After all, Huntington's disease is a terrible scourge of adults in their 30s, 40s, or 50s, eventually institutionalizing most and killing them all. As noted in the text, those with one parent who has the disease run a 50-50 chance of having it themselves and, if they have children, of passing it on to them. So it seemed likely that the ability to determine in advance who would develop or escape the disease would be welcomed by affected families, allowing them to plan more practically about having children, choosing jobs, obtaining insurance, planning finances, and pursuing social and leisure interests.

But the scientists were wrong. Only a small fraction of those at risk and close enough to obtain the test have done so. Why?

The answer is not with the test, which involves a genetic analysis of blood samples taken from the person being tested and from six or so family members. At

present the test is administered at government expense on a trial basis at five medical centers: Columbia University, Johns Hopkins University, Massachusetts General Hospital, the University of Michigan, and the University of Minnesota.

Perhaps the answer lies in the fact that if the test comes back positive, there is a high probability that you will develop the disease yourself. In short, you learn that you face a long, terrible death. The test is 99% accurate.

Samuel L. Baily, former chairman of the National Huntington's Disease Association, chose not to have the test even though his mother died from Huntington's disease at age 58, 8 years after she was diagnosed. Baily, symptom-free at age 52, said that he would rather just take his chances with the disease, which had also killed his maternal grandfather. He prefers to live with the hope of not getting it than with the knowledge that he will.

Others choose a different course. Karen Sweeney, 28, who is married and has four children, told interviewers that she had to know (Brody, 1988). The stress of

knowing that her mother and grandfather both died from the disease had taken its toll on her and on her marriage. After moving to Baltimore to be eligible for the Johns Hopkins testing program, Karen and her husband went through extensive counseling before the test. For Karen, the news was good: no Huntington's.

Certainly, Huntington's disease and all other forms of dementia are terrible, killer diseases. With research rapidly advancing on Alzheimer's disease, it is likely that a test for a genetic marker for it will be developed in the next decade. It is also likely that a test will be available before there is a cure. If you had relatives who had died from Alzheimer's disease or Huntington's disease, if you were planning to have a family, and if a test were available, what would you do? It's something to think about.

Keeping persons with Alzheimer's disease involved in everyday activities is an important aspect of good caregiving.

schizophrenia, such as thioridazine and haloperi-dol, are effective in lowering the severe psychiatric symptoms that develop during the course of Alzheimer's disease (Salzman, 1984). Similarly, antidepressants are effective in alleviating the depressive symptoms that typically accompany the early stages of the disease (Crook & Cohen, 1983), and sedatives may be effective for sleep disturbances. However, these medications should be used with considerable caution, since dosage levels for older adults may be far lower than those for younger patients, and side effects may be much more serious (Salzman, 1984).

As will be described later, a number of interventions that do not involve drugs are also available. Cognitive problems can be addressed by creating a supportive environment, such as label-ing the contents of cupboards, and by using behavioral techniques to teach new strategies (Mace & Rabins, 1981). Depression, irritability, wandering, and emotional problems can also be effectively dealt with through behavioral techniques. Most important in this regard is the introduction of a straightforward daily schedule in which meals, medications, and naps always come at the same time. Environmental interventions such as control of lighting, noise, and temperature in bedrooms may also help alleviate sleep disturbances.

In the long run most Alzheimer's disease patients become completely dependent on others, leaving care givers few intervention options. We will consider the burden on the family members in a later section.

Multi-Infarct Dementia

Until Tomlinson et al.'s (1970) discovery that Alzheimer's disease was not rare, most physicians and researchers believed that most cases of dementia resulted from cerebral arteriosclerosis and its consequent restriction of oxygen to the brain. As described in Chapter 3, arteriosclerosis is a family of diseases that, if untreated, may result in heart attacks or strokes. For the present discussion it is the stroke, or **cerebral vascular accident (CVA)**, that concerns us. CVAs result from a disruption of the blood flow, termed an **infarct**, which may be caused by a blockage or hemorrhage.

A large CVA may produce severe cognitive decline, but this loss is almost always limited to specific abilities. This pattern is different from the classic, global deterioration seen in dementia. However, it is believed that a series of small CVAs can produce this global pattern. This condition is termed **multi-infarct dementia** (Hachinski, Lassen, & Marshall, 1974). Multi-infarct dementia accounts for 10% to 15% of all cases of dementia (Crook, 1987).

The course of multi-infarct dementia is very different from that seen in Alzheimer's disease (Crook, 1987). Multi-infarct dementia has a sudden onset, and its progression is described as stepwise, or stuttering. This is in contrast to the insidious onset and gradual progression of Alzheimer's disease. The symptom pattern in multi-infarct dementia is highly variable, especially early in the disease. Again, this is in contrast to the similar cluster of cognitive problems shown by Alzheimer's disease patients.

Blass and Barclay (1985) report that the median survival of multi-infarct dementia patients is only 2 to 3 years, much shorter than that of Alzheimer's disease patients. They argue that the diagnosis of multi-infarct dementia should be

reconsidered if the patient survives longer than 2 years without any evidence of additional CVAs.

The diagnosing of multi-infarct dementia is similar to that of Alzheimer's disease. Evidence of CVAs from diagnostic imaging (CT, MRI, or PET scans) and a history of cerebrovascular disease are usually the key factors (Davies, 1988). In a small percentage of cases, however, evidence of both Alzheimer's disease and multi-infarct dementia is found.

Multi-infarct dementia is especially tragic compared with Alzheimer's disease, in that there are known risk factors that can be controlled. Among these are hypertension and others noted in Chapters 3 and 4. Attention to these factors earlier in life may well lower the risk of multi-infarct dementia considerably.

Parkinson's Disease

Parkinson's disease is known primarily for its characteristic cluster of motor problems: very slow walking, stiffness, difficulty getting in and out of chairs, and a slow tremor. These behavioral symptoms are caused by a deterioration of the neurons in the midbrain that produce the neurotransmitter dopamine (Lieberman, 1974). Administration of the drug L-dopa greatly alleviates these behavioral problems.

The connection between Parkinson's disease and dementia was not generally recognized until the late 1970s. Researchers now estimate, however, that between 30% and 50% of people with Parkinson's disease will develop dementia (Boller, 1980). Interestingly, the changes occurring in the brain observed at autopsy, the symptoms, and the course of the dementia seen in Parkinson's disease are indistinguishable from those in Alzheimer's disease (Boller, Mizutani, & Roessmann, 1980).

Some researchers argue that the combination

of Parkinson's disease and Alzheimer's disease is a disorder distinct from Parkinson's disease without dementia. Support for this belief comes from the fact that Parkinson's disease patients with dementia tolerate all anti-Parkinsonian drugs such as L-dopa very poorly compared with patients with Parkinson's disease without dementia (Lieberman et al., 1979). Why some people with Parkinson's disease develop dementia and others do not remains a mystery.

Pick's Disease

Pick's disease is a very rare form of dementia that is clinically very hard to discriminate from Alzheimer's disease. Nevertheless, it is quite distinct neuropathologically, that is, in terms of the structural changes in the brain. Some researchers and clinicians note that patients in the early stages of Pick's disease show little memory impairment but marked behavioral changes, such as social inappropriateness, loss of modesty, and uninhibited sexual behavior (Lishman, 1978). Neuropathological changes include striking atrophy of the frontal and temporal lobes, the absence of both senile plaques and neurofibrillary tangles, but the presence of so-called "Pick's bodies" in neurons (Davies, 1988). An interesting research question is why the cognitive changes in Pick's disease so closely resemble those in Alzheimer's disease even though the structural changes in the neurons are quite different. Perhaps a partial explanation is that the nucleus basalis of Meynert, a major source of acetylcholine, is destroyed in both diseases (Price et al., 1982). An additional interesting parallel is that Pick's disease appears to be determined by a single autosomal dominant gene (Sjogren, Sjogren, & Lindgren, 1952), the same genetic mechanism being investigated as a factor in Alzheimer's disease.

Creutzfeld-Jakob Disease

Creutzfeld-Jakob disease is another very rare form of dementia that is characterized by a relatively early onset, very rapid course (rarely more than 2 years), and severe changes in EEG patterns (Siedler & Malamud, 1963). These changes appear to be caused by severe neuronal degeneration, a very marked proliferation of **astrocytes** (star-shaped cells in the brain), and a spongy appearance of the gray matter in the brain. There are no senile plaques or neurofibrillary tangles, as in Alzheimer's disease, no massive atrophy, as seen in Pick's disease, and no vascular damage, as in multi-infarct dementia (Lishman, 1978).

The most important aspect of Creutzfeld-Jakob disease is that it appears to be transmitted by a virus. It is known to be transmissible to chimpanzees (Gibbs et al., 1968) and other animals from humans. There are also at least three confirmed cases of accidental transmission of Creutzfeld-Jakob disease from animals to humans (Crook, 1987). Moreover, the disease is clinically and neuropathologically related to kuru, a transmissible form of dementia found in the Fore linguistic tribe in New Guinea (Gajdusek, 1977). Gajdusek's research shows that the virus responsible is transmitted through the practice of cannibalism and has an incubation of many years. The research documenting that these forms of dementia are communicable earned these investigators a Nobel Prize and opened research to the possibility that Alzheimer's disease may also be caused by a virus.

Huntington's Disease

Huntington's disease is an autosomal dominant disorder that usually begins between the ages of 35 and 50. The disease usually manifests itself through involuntary flicking movements of the arms and legs, the inability to sustain a motor act such as sticking out one's tongue, prominent psychiatric disturbances such as hallucinations, paranoia, and depression, and clear personality changes, such as swings from apathy to manic behavior (Berkow, 1987). Cognitive impairments typically do not appear until late in the disease. The onset of these symptoms is very gradual. The course of Huntington's disease is progressive; patients ultimately lose the ability to care for themselves physically and mentally. Walking becomes impossible, swallowing is difficult, and cognitive loss becomes profound (Berkow, 1987). Changes in the brain thought to underlie the behavioral losses include degeneration of the **caudate nucleus** and the small-cell population, as well as substantial decreases in the neurotransmitters GABA and substance P. Although antipsychotic medications are sometimes used to control the psychiatric disturbances and agitated behaviors, they are only partially effective (Berkow, 1987). As noted earlier, a test is available to determine whether one has the marker for the Huntington's disease gene.

Normal-Pressure Hydrocephalus

Normal-pressure hydrocephalus is another rare form of dementia that is characterized by enlarged **cerebral ventricles** but normal cerebrospinal fluid pressure (Crook, 1987). The ventricles are the chambers in the brain that contain cerebrospinal fluid. This condition is caused most often by a head injury or hemorrhage deep in the brain (Hakim & Adams, 1965). The early symptoms are usually general cognitive deficits, hesitancy or shuffling during walking, and urinary incontinence (Berkow, 1987). The diagnosis can be confirmed through CT scans, which document the enlarged ventricles, but clinical observation of these three problems is usually sufficient (Mulrow, Feussner, Williams, & Vokaty, 1987). Treatment

of the disease is usually through **shunting**, a procedure that helps drain the cerebrospinal fluid to lower the pressure. Many patients do not respond to this procedure, however, especially if the disease has been present a long time (Berkow, 1987).

Caring for Dementia Patients at Home

The changes that happen to a person who has a form of dementia are devastating, not only to the patient but also to the whole family. It is extremely difficult to watch a spouse, parent, or sibling go from being the independent, mature adult whom you knew to being a helpless shell who is oblivious to his or her surroundings.

Despite these formidable emotional issues, the vast majority of dementia patients are cared for by their family members at home. Until the mid-1970s little was known about their experience, and little information was available on effective home-care strategies. The appearance of Mace and Rabin's *The 36-Hour Day* in 1981 marked a major turning point; their book remains one of the best guides for families caring for a dementia patient. Throughout the 1980s researchers have focused on two main lines of investigation concerning caregiving: identifying effective strategies of care and documenting the stress and burden felt by the family.

Because the majority of people with dementia have Alzheimer's disease, most of the research focuses on caretakers of these patients. The advice offered, however, applies to caregivers of all dementia patients.

Effective Caregiving Strategies. Aronson (1988) provides an excellent summary of the interventions and decisions that caretakers can make that will make the care of Alzheimer's patients as successful as possible. Key steps to be taken once a diagnosis is made include obtaining accurate information about the disease; involving the patient as much as possible in decisions; identifying the primary caregiver; reassessing the patient's living situation; setting realistic goals; making realistic financial plans; identifying a source of regular medical care; maximizing the patient's opportunity to function at his or her optimal level; making realistic demands of the patient; and using outside services as needed. The goal of these early steps is to build a broad support network of relatives, medical personnel, and service providers that may be needed later. The new responsibilities of family members require changes in daily routines; people adjust to these roles at different rates.

Many behaviors and situations that we take for granted need to be rethought when we find ourselves caring for an Alzheimer's disease patient. Dressing, bathing, and grooming become more difficult or even aversive to the patient. Use of Velcro fasteners, joining the patient during a bath or shower, and other such changes may be necessary. Nutritional needs have to be monitored, because patients may forget that they have just eaten or may forget to eat. Medications must be used with considerable caution. Changes in personality and sexual behavior need to be viewed as part of the disease. Sleeplessness can be addressed by establishing consistent bedtimes, giving warm milk or tryptophan, and limiting caffeine intake. Wandering is an especially troublesome problem, because it is difficult to control; making sure that the patient has an identification bracelet with the nature of the problem on it and making the house accident-proof are two preventive steps; in severe cases of wandering it may be necessary to use restraints, but only under the direction of a health care professional. Incontinence, which usually occurs late in the disease, is a troubling and embarrassing issue for the patient; use of special undergarments or diapers or medications to treat the problem are two of the available options. It is important to realize that

incontinence is not necessarily related to Alzheimer's disease. For example, stress incontinence, which is fairly common among older women, is unrelated to dementia.

One of the most difficult issues faced by caregivers concerns taking things away from the patient and restricting activity. Relatively early in the disease the patient will experience problems handling finances. It is not uncommon for patients to spend hundreds or even thousands of dollars on strange items, to leave the checkbook unbalanced and bills unpaid, and to lose money. Although the patient can be given some money to keep, it is necessary for someone else to handle the day-to-day accounts. Traveling alone is another sticky issue. Families of dementia patients often wait until a major calamity occurs before recognizing their loved one's deteriorating condition. Instead, families should limit solo excursions to places within walking distance; all other trips should be made with at least one family member along. Driving is often another contentious issue, especially if the patient does not recognize his or her limitations. Once it is clear that the patient cannot drive, the family must take whatever steps are necessary. In some cases this entails simply taking the car keys, but in others it becomes necessary to disable the car. Suggesting that the patient could be "chauffeured" is another alternative.

Two rapidly growing options for caregivers are respite care and adult day care. **Respite care** is designed to allow family members to get away for a time. It can consist of in-home care provided by professionals or temporary placement in a residential facility. In-home care is usually used to allow caregivers to do errands or to have a few hours free, while temporary residential placement is typically reserved for a more extended respite, such as a weekend. Respite care is a tremendous help to caretakers. In one study there was marked improvement in family members' reports of problems after a 2-week respite (Burdz, Eaton, & Bond, 1988). **Adult day care** provides placement and programming for frail elderly people during the day. This option is used most often by adult children who are employed. The demand for respite and adult day care far exceeds their availability, making them limited options. An additional problem is that many insurance programs will not pay for these services, making them too expensive for caregivers with limited finances. Even when services are available, however, many families do not use them until their informal support system begins to break down (Caserta, Lund, Wright, & Redburn, 1987).

In general, family members must change their entire daily routines in order to care for a dementia patient. Such complete alterations in habits, coupled with watching the deterioration in their loved one, create an extremely stressful situation.

Family Stress and Burden. Taking care of a person with dementia is an extremely stressful, time-consuming job. For many caregivers it becomes a full-time job, going from a situation that they control to one that controls them. In her book *Another Name for Madness* Marion Roach (1985) vividly describes what the process is like. She relates the range of feelings she experienced caring for her mother (who was in her early 50s when she was diagnosed with Alzheimer's disease): anger, frustration, worry, pity, guilt, and a host of others.

Researchers have documented what Roach and all other caregivers go through. The most commonly used concept to describe the experience is **burden** (Zarit, Reever, & Bach-Peterson, 1980). Burden relates to the experience of psychological stress and distress as the result of caring for a frail elder. Most of the research on burden has been focused on caretakers of Alzheimer's disease patients, although some work has documented similar experiences in those caring for

stroke patients and head-injured patients as well (Schulz, Tompkins, & Rau, 1988).

Caregivers experience considerable negative effects. In general, they report chronic fatigue, anger, depression, loss of friends, loss of time to themselves, dissatisfaction with other family members, physical and mental strain, stress symptoms, less life satisfaction, and lower well-being (Chenoweth & Spencer, 1986; Colerick & George, 1986; George & Gwyther, 1986; Gilhooly, 1986; Haley, Levine, Brown, Berry, & Hughes, 1987; Kinney & Stephens, in press; Morycz, 1985; Quayhagen & Quayhagen, 1988; Zarit, Todd, & Zarit, 1986). Men tend to report higher levels of morale than women (Gilhooly, 1984; Zarit et al., 1986), perhaps because women become more emotionally involved in caregiving and care for more severely impaired patients. Married daughters caring for their parents often are forced to quit their jobs (Brody, Kleban, Johnsen, Hoffman, & Schoonover, 1987), whereas married sons often are not. Spouses who care for their partner report lower levels of physical health, mental health, and financial resources than spouses without such a burden (George & Gwyther, 1986; Gilhooly, 1984).

One important finding is that it is *far* more likely that daughters rather than sons will care for their parents (Brody, 1985). Moreover, daughters may have to deal not only with the problems of caregiving but also with resentments at having to assume a form of "child-rearing" responsibilities in mid-life. Compared with spouse caregivers, daughters have many more competing pressures such as career and family, adding to their burden (Brody, 1985; Quayhagen & Quayhagen, 1988).

Considerable research documents that it is not a specific aspect of Alzheimer's disease or related disorders, such as wandering or incontinence, that cause these problems (e.g., Gilhooly, 1986; Zarit et al., 1986). Rather, it is the caregiver's *perception* of the situation that matters. For example, the perception that one's social support system is gone is a powerful predictor of the decision to institutionalize the patient, whereas the actual physical condition of the patient is not (George & Gwyther, 1988).

Some investigators of caretaker burden (Haley et al., 1987; Kinney & Stephens, in press; Stephens, Norris, Kinney, Ritchie, & Grotz, 1988) have adopted a stress and coping approach based on Lazarus and Folkman's (1984) model, described in Chapter 4. In this approach it is the perception that one's resources are being taxed by the present situation that causes the burden, not the objective "real" situation. This approach, described in more detail in "How Do We Know?" fits well with the data and should provide a useful framework for future research.

FAMILY INTERVENTION AND FAMILY THERAPY

Although many problems encountered during adulthood are best resolved at an individual level, other problems involve family factors and home relationships. These latter difficulties are best handled by working with the family as a whole. If adults are able to receive adequate help from family members and have a positive, collaborative relationship with them, their whole mental outlook, behavioral functioning, and adaptation to life is enhanced (Fry, 1986). Because family ties remain important throughout adulthood (see Chapter 11), family intervention is an important topic for adults of all ages. As we will see, because family therapy is effective for families confronting Alzheimer's disease, it is likely that this approach will grow in popularity in the future.

This section looks at the goals of family intervention and family therapy and discusses some important aspects of evaluating family

dynamics. We will also consider some age-related issues pertaining to family dynamics that are important considerations in designing effective interventions.

What Is Family Therapy?

Family therapy, based on **general systems theory**, views the family as an independent system of members who mutually influence one another (Haley, 1971). Consequently, to change the behavior of one family member means changing the whole family system. In addition, we must understand what particular roles are played by each member (e.g., parent, child, nurturer, martyr, and so forth) and how these roles are interrelated. Families also have certain rules that govern the communication among their members; these must be identified as well.

An assumption in family therapy is that functional families work toward the growth and development of their members, whereas dysfunctional families produce the distress or destruction of their members. These ends are achieved by implementing the roles and rules of the family.

The role of the family therapist is to identify the roles played by each member and the rules by which they play. Although there are several different ways in which these identifications are made and the therapy is carried out, all agree on the importance of improving the communication skills among family members as the first step.

Common Issues in Family Therapy With Older Adults

Issues addressed in family therapy reflect the myriad of problems that occur in family relationships. When these problems involve older adults, however, they tend to focus on three themes (Fry, 1986): conflicts between spouses, conflicts

HOW · DO · WE · KNOW?

Caregiver Burden: A Stress and Coping Approach

As noted in the text, caring for a dementia patient is a highly demanding and stressful job. Some researchers have begun to study the effects of caregiving by turning to the model of stress and coping proposed by Lazarus and Folkman (1984). Briefly, this model postulates that stress is the perception that one's resources are being taxed and that one is being threatened. To measure stress in this way, Lazarus and his colleagues developed the Hassles Scale, which measures whether stressful events have happened recently, and, if so, to what extent they were perceived as troublesome.

Kinney and Stephens (in press) adapted this idea to the caregiving situation. They believed that the amount of burden experienced by caretakers of Alzheimer's disease patients could be understood in Lazarus and Folkman's framework. Kinney and Stephens developed the 42-item Caregiving Hassles Scale. Each item on the scale is a commonly encountered situation, such as giving the patient a bath. Respondents indicate whether each event has occurred in the previous week and to what extent it represents a difficulty (on a four-point scale).

Caretakers of Alzheimer's disease patients reported many hassles. The most common ones involved assisting the patient with daily living (bathing, dressing) and dealing with cognitive limitations and behavior problems. The severity of perceived problems correlated with poor caretaker-patient relations and higher levels of anxiety, hostility, and depression in caregivers. Hassles that were related to patients' behavior problems proved most troublesome; apparently, dealing with emotional outbursts and the like presented serious problems for coping.

A key aspect of the Kinney and Stephens data is that the specific behaviors that were perceived as hassles varied a great deal across caregivers. This finding is in keeping with Lazarus and Folkman's notion that it is not what happens that matters but how you perceive what happens that matters. Kinney and Stephens have provided a useful approach to the study of caregiving and have made use of a general model of stress and coping to do so. It demonstrates that the study of adult development and aging does involve the application of concepts and models developed in different contexts to many other settings.

between elderly parents and their adult children, and conflicts in communications and expectations.

Conflicts Between Spouses. One common problem confronting spouses of all ages is change in life circumstances. For middle-aged adults, these changes may include children's leaving home or a new job. For older spouses, these changes include retirement, loss of income, or physical incapacitation. In all of these cases such changes may reactivate earlier problems in the marriage. Despite feeling unhappy, many of these couples continue to live together out of fear of change or economic necessity. Conflict between the spouses may arise out of each party's resistance to change, inability to meet the other's needs, or feelings of being forced to adopt new and unwanted roles (e.g., as a caregiver).

Conflicts Between Adult Children and Their Elderly Parents. When adult children become caregivers to their parents, conflict may result from the stress. Assuming additional responsibility for the management of an elderly parent often takes a high toll, as discussed earlier in this chapter. Elderly parents may try to assume control of the household, the spouses of the adult children may resent the extra duties put on their partners, or the adult children may resent their parents for disrupting the household. Additionally, older parents may be unfairly blamed for marital problems between adult children and their spouses. The results of such conflicts can be devastating to the family.

Problems of Communications and Roles. Many families cannot maintain open communication with all of their members, especially during times of conflict. Such open communication is clearly needed between adult children and their parents. What is often overlooked is that adult children need to be able to openly discuss matters with their parents but may not feel comfortable in doing so. For example, middle-aged adults may feel the urge to talk about their feelings with their parents, who have experienced middle-age firsthand, but may be reluctant. Additionally, one generation may place excessive role demands on the other, such as the oldest generation expecting the middle generation to be perfect parents and perfect achievers in the workplace.

Techniques for Family Therapy

Herr and Weakland (1979) discuss several techniques for family intervention. Most important is **communication skills training**, in which family members learn how to listen to other family members and to express their own feelings more clearly. Early in the family therapy process it is important for the therapist to determine what the problems confronting the family really are and to uncover any hidden agendas a particular member has. Additionally, realistic goals for recovery must be set. It is also important for the therapist to ascertain how the family dealt with similar problems in the past and to determine which solution strategies worked and which ones failed. New alternatives are offered as needed. Also important is determining and explicitly stating the family rules for interaction and pointing out when these rules need to be changed. Finally, the family members must all agree on the nature and direction of change.

Several studies have documented that family therapy is effective in dealing with problems involving older adult family members (e.g., Cicirelli, 1986; Zarit & Anthony, 1986). Family therapy is often the approach of choice in addressing problems stemming from caregiving. For example, the increased ability to communicate feelings of guilt, anger, closeness, and love allow family members to deal with their feelings more adaptively.

WORKING WITH THE INSTITUTIONALIZED ELDERLY

Traditionally, one of the most underserved groups of older adults has been residents of nursing homes. However, these individuals can benefit significantly from a wide variety of intervention programs targeted for different levels of ability (Weiner, Brok, & Snadowsky, 1987). Indeed, nursing homes are one of the fastest growing areas of mental health intervention in developing strategies and programs. The ability of cognitively

Group activities such as coloring Easter eggs play an important role in fostering a sense of personal control and identity among the institutionalized elderly.

impaired individuals to benefit from such intervention has been sadly underestimated in the past; we now know that even people with moderately severe impairment can benefit. In this section we will consider some of the major techniques that are used with institutionalized elderly people to optimize their abilities.

A word of caution is needed before we begin our survey. These techniques have been widely adopted, but there is very little research evidence that they are effective. Although future research may demonstrate that these programs work, for the time being we must be careful not to assume that they will result in improvements in functioning.

Sensory Training

Sensory training is aimed at bringing a person back in touch with the environment (Weiner et al., 1987). This technique is effective in getting highly regressed residents who have psychomotor, sensory, verbal, or cognitive deficits to reexperience their surroundings and remake social contacts. Sensory training begins with social introductions among group members, followed by body-awareness exercises and sensory stimulation. These activities stimulate social participation and sensory experience through the use of common objects. Having participants talk or think about their experiences also enhances cognitive activity.

Sensory training works best when groups are not too large, five to seven persons, and when they are conducted every morning, 7 days a week. The meeting place and time should always be the same, to eliminate confusion. Any materials that can be used to stimulate the senses, from cotton balls to sandpaper to different colored objects, are appropriate.

The major advantage of sensory training is that individuals who are usually excluded from other groups because of the sensory or cognitive impairments can benefit. And because no special equipment needs to be purchased, sensory training is inexpensive as well.

Reality Orientation

Reality orientation is a technique based on repetition and relearning that was developed for the moderately confused resident (Stephens, 1975). The key to reality orientation is that it is a 24-hour program that is integrated in the entire environment. The goal is to keep the resident in touch with what is going on in the world in every way possible.

Implementing a reality orientation program involves several things. Residents are addressed by a title such as Mr. or Mrs. unless they specify otherwise. Plenty of clocks and bulletin boards with calendars are placed in prominent locations. Name cards are used at meals. Activities are interesting and diversified and are announced on the public address system. Birthdays are recognized individually, and special meals are served on holidays. Visiting hours are liberal, and volunteers are encouraged to visit. Color-coded rooms and hallways are used. Independence is encouraged as much as possible. In short, everything that occurs in the institution is geared to keeping residents in touch with reality.

Attitude therapy is usually used in conjunction with reality orientation. Basically, attitude therapy aims at identifying each resident's primary interactive style, which is then dealt with by the staff in certain specified and consistent ways. For example, active friendliness is used with apathetic, withdrawn residents; passive friendliness, with frightened, suspicious residents; matter-of-factness, with manipulative residents; kind firmness, with depressed residents; and a no-demands approach, with angry, hostile residents. Attitude therapy is designed to reinforce adaptive behaviors and not to reinforce maladaptive behaviors.

Remotivation Therapy

Remotivation therapy is a structured program based on a set of standard topics intended to reawaken the interest of apathetic residents (Weiner et al., 1987). The program works by getting a group of 10 to 15 residents to discuss a topic such as clothing or food in a five-step process: creating a climate of acceptance by welcoming each member, creating a bridge to reality by selecting a topic for discussion, sharing the world of reality by asking the group members about the topic, appreciating the world of reality by getting members to share their ideas or stimulating reminiscence, and creating a climate of appreciation by noting the good contributions made by each member. Remotivation therapy should be conducted once or twice a week for between 30 minutes to an hour. The structured program lasts 12 weeks. Group leaders for remotivation therapy should have completed a 30-hour course in the technique at a training center, primarily because the program adheres to a rigid, precise format and requires preparation.

Additional Therapeutic Approaches

In addition to sensory training, reality therapy, and remotivation therapy, a host of other interventions are used in institutions. Three of the more popular ones are activities-recreation therapy, milieu therapy, and supportive group therapy.

Activities and recreation therapy helps to optimize residents' functioning and improve their quality of life by getting them involved in physical and mental activities (Haun, 1965). A comprehensive program should include a wide variety of voluntary activities that can be performed individually, in small groups, and in large groups. The ability to choose activities is the key; whether it is playing solitaire or watching movies in a group, the benefits of participation are greater if it is the resident's choice (Weiner et al., 1987). Being able to make decisions fosters independence and self-esteem.

Milieu therapy takes a different approach. Rather than a staff member designing the program, the resident designs the environment so that it most closely reflects the kind of setting that he or she was used to before entering the nursing home (Weiner et al., 1987). This enables the resident to sustain social roles and puts responsibility for these roles on the resident rather than the staff. Residents in a milieu therapy program are placed together based on similarities in their primary needs, degree of independence, and degree of disability.

Many nursing homes and other residential facilities are beginning **supportive group therapy** for their residents. These groups serve many functions, but mainly they focus on promoting better human relationships, dealing with feelings of loneliness or inferiority, and encouraging coping (Hartford, 1980). These groups have been shown to increase residents' sense of personal control, life satisfaction, and trust (Moran & Gatz, 1987).

Pet therapy is one of the fastest growing techniques with institutionalized older adults (Brickel, 1984). Pets are used to enhance feelings of responsibility and control (see Chapter 13), trigger reminiscence, and promote social interaction. Short-term gains in positive feelings about oneself, well-being, and cognitive functioning have been reported, but few detailed studies of pet therapy have been conducted.

SUMMARY

Defining abnormal behavior is difficult and must take several factors into account. Many definitions are not appropriate for older adults, because what is abnormal or maladaptive varies with age.

The biopsychosocial approach allows consideration of psychopathology from a life-course perspective, focusing attention on the interpersonal, intrapersonal, biological and physical, and life-cycle factors that influence mental health. This approach also emphasizes that assessment of older adults must put their symptoms in a life-cycle context.

Depression is one of the most common and treatable psychopathologies. Diagnosis focuses on mood, physical symptoms, duration, and effect on daily life. Mistakes can be made if depressive symptoms are not differentially diagnosed from physical or other disorders. Neurotransmitter imbalance, abnormal hemisphere functioning, physical illness, loss, and uncontrollable events are the most commonly theorized causes. Treatment can be through drugs, such as heterocyclic antidepressants, MAO inhibitors, and lithium; through electroconvulsive therapy; or through psychotherapy, such as behavioral and cognitive therapy. Suicide rates have changed in different age groups over the past few decades, but elderly White males still have the highest rate.

Anxiety disorders involve fear or uneasiness about some aspect of the environment. Some of these disorders involve vague feelings, and others are focused on specific issues. Anxiety disorders can be treated with medication, although this approach must be used with caution because these drugs can be addictive. The treatment of choice is psychotherapy.

Schizophrenic and paranoid disorders are serious types of psychopathology that involve distorted thinking. Schizophrenia is marked by severe thought disturbances, hallucinations, and delusions. Paranoid disorders do not involve the severe thought disturbances of schizophrenia but do involve well-formed delusions. Treatment of schizophrenic and paranoid disorders is difficult: medication and psychotherapy are used.

Dementia is a family of diseases that affect the

brain. The irreversible forms include Alzheimer's disease, multi-infarct dementia, Parkinson's disease, Pick's disease, Creutzfeld-Jakob disease, Huntington's disease, and normal pressure hydrocephalus. Alzheimer's disease is the most common. Its characteristic neurological changes can be definitively identified only by autopsy or brain biopsy. These changes include neurofibrillary tangles, senile plaques, and granulovacuolar degeneration. Neurotransmitter levels also drop. Symptoms include severe cognitive impairment, personality changes, disorientation, and language problems. A diagnosis is tentatively made after comprehensive physical, neurological, and psychological examinations. Genetics may play a role, as may a virus. Other forms of dementia have characteristic behavioral and neuropathological changes that can be detected only after careful differential diagnosis. Caring for dementia patients is extremely stressful, and caregivers report a wide variety of symptoms.

Several therapeutic interventions are successful in nursing homes. These include sensory training, reality orientation, remotivation therapy, activities-recreation therapy, milieu therapy, supportive group therapy, and pet therapy.

GLOSSARY

activities and recreation therapy • An intervention that uses physical activity as the basis for getting people in touch with their environment.

adult day care • A program for adults with dementia or other incapacitating disorders that provides structured programming.

Alzheimer's disease • A type of dementia that involves progressive loss of all cognitive, emotional, and psychomotor abilities and that is eventually fatal.

amyloid • The protein base of senile plaques.

antipsychotics • Medications used in the treatment of schizophrenia that alter the functioning of the dopamine neurotransmitter system.

anxiety disorders • A group of conditions involving fear or uneasiness that results in the physical reaction of anxiety or panic.

astrocytes • Star-shaped cells in the brain that occur in Creutzfeld-Jakob disease.

attitude therapy • An intervention, often used in conjunction with reality orientation, that focuses on people's styles of interpersonal interaction.

autosomal dominant • A pattern of genetic inheritance in which only one gene is required for the trait or characteristic to emerge.

behavior therapy • An approach based on the idea that psychopathology results from learning abnormal patterns of behavior due to poor or inconsistent patterns of reinforcement.

benzodiazepines • The most common medications used to treat anxiety disorders; must be used with caution because of the possibility of addiction.

biopsychosocial approach • A model of psychopathology that emphasizes the interaction of interpersonal factors, intrapersonal factors, biological and physical factors, and life-cycle factors as the causes of abnormal behavior.

bipolar disorder • A type of affective disorder in which periods of depression alternate with periods of mania.

burden • The stress and strain experienced by caregivers.

caudate nucleus • A portion of the brain that deteriorates in Huntington's disease.

cerebral vascular accident (CVA) • Medical term for a stroke, caused by a disruption of blood flow in the brain.

cerebral ventricles • Spaces in the brain that are filled with cerebrospinal fluid.

choline acetyltransferase • An enzyme marker for the neurotransmitter acetylcholine, which declines significantly in Alzheimer's disease.

cognitive therapy • An approach based on the idea that abnormal behavior is caused by irrational beliefs about oneself.

communication skills training • A major intervention in family therapy in which family members are taught how to interact with one another more effectively.

Creutzfeld-Jakob disease • A type of dementia that is characterized by a relatively early onset, very rapid course (rarely more than 2 years), and severe changes in EEG patterns.

CT scan • A diagnostic imaging technique based on the use of X rays.

delirium • A form of treatable organic mental disorder that is marked by sudden and rapid onset, mental confusion, and other symptoms usually caused by a toxic substance or other disease.

delusions • Belief systems, not based on reality, that occur in paranoid and schizophrenic disorders.

dementia • A type of psychopathology involving the gradual, progressive loss of cognitive and motor functioning.

dysphoria • A symptom of depression involving feeling down, or blue.

electroconvulsive therapy (ECT) • The application of electrical currents to the head in order to treat severe depression.

family therapy • An approach based on the idea that the family system should be the focus of intervention because abnormal behavior results from dysfunctional interactions and communication among family members.

general systems theory • The theoretical framework that underlies family therapy.

granulovacuolar degeneration • A process by which neurons develop granular deposits in large numbers in Alzheimer's disease.

hallucinations • Misperceptions of reality that occur in schizophrenic disorders.

heterocyclic antidepressants (HCAs) • The most commonly used medications to treat depression.

Huntington's disease • A type of dementia that begins in mid-life and is characterized by motor deterioration and marked psychiatric problems.

hypochondriasis • The state of being overly concerned with one's health.

infarct • A disruption of blood flow.

instrumental daily activities • Daily chores such as cooking and cleaning.

life review therapy • An approach based on the use of events from one's past to deal with current issues or problems.

lithium • A medication used to treat bipolar disorder.

loss • One type of psychosocial cause of depression, triggered by the disruption of a significant relationship.

MAO inhibitors • A form of medication used to treat depression; must be used with extreme caution due to the possibility of toxic reactions.

mental status exam • A short screening measure of cognitive functioning used in the diagnosis of dementia and related disorders.

milieu therapy • An intervention that allows residents of institutions to design the type of environment they would like to have.

MRI scan • A diagnostic imaging technique based on the use of powerful magnetic fields.

multi-infarct dementia • A disorder caused by multiple small disruptions of brain blood flow over a period of time.

neurofibrillary tangles • Abnormal fibers in neurons that develop in very large numbers in Alzheimer's disease.

normal-pressure hydrocephalus • A type of dementia that is characterized by enlarged cerebral ventricles but normal cerebrospinal fluid pressure.

nucleus basalis of Meynert • A structure at the base of the brain that degenerates in Alzheimer's disease.

organic mental disorder • A family of psychopathologies that involve damage to the brain.

paranoid disorder • A type of psychopathology marked by well-developed delusions.

Parkinson's disease • A type of dementia characterized by a slow tremor.

PET scan • A diagnostic imaging technique based on the use of positrons.

pet therapy • An intervention based on the use of animals to foster well-being and the sense of personal control.

Pick's disease • A type of dementia characterized by marked deterioration of the frontal and temporal lobes.

psychoeducational approach • A type of psychotherapy for depression based on putting behavior therapy concepts into an educational program.

psychopathology • Abnormal behavior that interferes with the person's ability to cope.

reality orientation • An intervention based on repetition and relearning that brings individuals back into contact with their environment.

reminiscence • A type of therapy similar to life review therapy, using recollections from one's past to deal with current issues and problems.

remotivation therapy • An intervention used to reawaken the interest of apathetic individuals.

respite care • An intervention that allows caregivers to have time away from the patient.

schizophrenia • A type of psychopathology characterized by the severe impairment of thought processes, including the content and style of thinking, distorted perceptions, loss of touch with reality, distorted sense of self, and abnormal motor behavior.

senile plaques • Spherical structures that develop in large numbers in the brain in Alzheimer's disease; they consist of dead neurons surrounding a core of amyloid protein.

sensory training • An intervention used in institutions to bring residents back in touch with their surroundings through the use of their senses.

shunting • A treatment for normal-pressure hydrocephalus in which tubes are inserted to drain excess cerebrospinal fluid.

sundowning • A phenomenon in Alzheimer's disease in which patients' symptoms become much worse in the late afternoon and evening than in the morning.

supportive group therapy • An intervention aimed at promoting better human relationships.

supportive therapy • An approach that emphasizes strengthening of adaptive defenses and replacement of maladaptive defenses without requiring insight.

ADDITIONAL READING

Two good sources of general information about many types of psychopathology and therapies are

Fry, P. S. (1986). *Depression, stress, and adaptations in the elderly.* Rockville, MD: Aspen.

L. L. Carstensen, & B. A. Edelstein (Eds.), *Handbook of clinical gerontology.* New York: Pergamon Press.

A very readable and comprehensive resource on Alzheimer's disease is

Aronson, M. K. (Ed.) (1988). *Understanding Alzheimer's disease.* New York: Scribner's.

Stratification Systems, Ethnicity, and Culture

Laura Wheeler Waring, *Anna Washington Derry*, 1927. National Museum of American Art, Smithsonian Institution. Gift of the Harmon Foundation.

GROWING OLD IS NOT JUST A PRIVATE, personal experience. Rather, people grow old in the midst of a larger social context. Growing old is the experience of many people interacting in a myriad of ways.

This chapter sets the stage for considering adult development and aging from that broader social perspective. We will explore this perspective by moving from a more personal level of analysis to a more encompassing level. First, we will consider the notions of status and role, two of the central ideas in understanding adulthood from a social-psychological framework. Next, we will see how societies organize themselves based on age, creating age stratification systems that help to define the statuses and roles we are given. The various stratification systems in Western society bring up the issue of money; we will see how economic factors have an impact on status and role. Two other topics round out our survey. Ethnicity is an important consideration in the United States, which is populated by a wide variety of people with different backgrounds. Finally, we will consider how cultures differ in their views of age and the aging process.

Many of the issues in this chapter concerning personal relationships will be described more fully in Chapter 11, and those concerning work will be detailed in Chapter 12. Thus, the present chapter serves as a bridge between the personal side and the societal side of adult development and aging.

STATUSES AND ROLES

From a social-psychological perspective the most important things that happen in adulthood are the changes: new aspects of life are added, some aspects remain, and some are taken away. When students graduate from college and take a job, for example, they take on new responsibilities and give up some of the freedoms they enjoyed in school. They must go to work even if they do not feel very well, rather than simply rolling over and skipping class. Bosses are not as willing as professors to accept excuses when work is finished late. In short, moving into the adult world brings considerable changes. With these changes people are viewed differently by society and come to behave differently as a result. They assume more personal responsibility for their actions. Understanding these changes involves knowing one's place and function in society. The concepts of status and role assist us in this endeavor. Status and role are two basic elements that help define who we are and influence the development of self-concept and well-being. They underlie much of the research and theory in social-psychological approaches to adult development and aging.

Two major approaches are used to study the impact of status and role, the structural perspective and the interactionist perspective. They differ in several ways, most importantly in their view of the flexibility and activity of the individual.

The Structural Perspective

Classical sociological theory concentrates on social structures, and it uses the concepts of status and role to define particular positions in society as well as the behavioral expectations associated with these positions. Rosow (1985) applies the **structural perspective** from classical sociological theory to adult development and aging. To him, **status** refers to a formal position in society that can be clearly and unambiguously specified and that may denote particular rights, privileges, prestige, and duties for the person. For example, traditional labels of "masculine," "elderly," and "minority" connote clusters of rights and privileges, such as senior-citizen discounts or certain seats on the subway, that may be independent of individual effort. The statuses that people occupy define the social contexts for evaluating the behavior of others and serve to anchor people in the social structure. For example, a person having the status "elderly" who asks someone to give up his seat on the subway is evaluated differently from a person having the status "young adult" who makes the same request.

Rosow (1985) defines **role** as the behaviors appropriate for any set of rights or duties. For example, people with particular statuses are expected to behave in certain prescribed, or normative, ways. Those with the status of parent are expected to care for their children; parents who do not, violate the normal parental role. Rosow's approach emphasizes those roles that are essential to societal survival, such as parental roles and work roles. It should be noted, though, that people also engage in many personally meaningful roles that are not included in Rosow's system. For example, many people assume nonstatus roles as hobbyists, weekend athletes, church workers, and the like that are viewed as important but not vital to societal survival.

Rosow's definitions imply that status and role

TABLE 10.1 • Combinations of status and role to form role types essential to society in the structural perspective

Status	Role	
	Present	*Absent*
Present	Institutional	Tenuous
Absent	Informal	Nonrole

(Source: Based on "Status and Role Changes Through the Life Cycle" by I. Rosow, 1985, in R. Binstock and E. Shanas (Eds.), *Handbook of Aging and the Social Sciences.* © 1985 Van Nostrand Reinhold.)

can be considered as independent concepts. For example, society uses certain dimensions in certain situations (e.g., income) to define status, with no particular connection to roles. That is, status can be present or absent, and so can roles. Based on this view, he presents a four-part combination of statuses and roles: institutional, informal, tenuous, and nonrole (Table 10.1). Each role type shows a distinctive developmental pattern across adulthood, as depicted in Figure 10.1.

Institutional Roles. **Institutional roles** have clear normative behavioral expectations associated with formal statuses such as child, teacher, parent, and public official. Thus, this category reflects the presence of both status and role, but it still allows considerable flexibility in behavior. Institutional roles increase through young and middle adulthood and decline sharply during old age. The precipitous decline in institutional roles in late life is due mainly to the end of parenting and employment. However, individuals in some professions such as politics, college teaching, medicine, and law are able to keep some of their institutional roles by remaining actively involved or by assuming emeritus or ex-officio positions.

The typical developmental pattern in institutional roles (increasing until middle age and declining in later life) reflects a connection with the amount of power exerted by a particular age group at any particular time (Uhlenberg, 1988). Power, or the amount of influence one group has over another, is a major determinant of one's status in society. We will return to this idea later when we consider age stratification.

Informal Roles. **Informal roles** are specific expected behaviors that are unattached to status. Examples of those with informal roles include personal confidants, informal helpers, mentors, volunteers, and the like, all of whom are expected to do certain things but who do not accrue formal status for doing them. Informal roles increase through late adulthood and then level off. The increase in informal roles with age is, in part, the flip side of the decrease in institutional roles in old age. As individuals give up positions in society that have formal roles, they often look for and assume positions with considerable flexibility and personal importance. However, many of these positions have little status. Being a volunteer in the local soup kitchen, for example, may bring the admiration of acquaintances but is unlikely to bring a status.

Tenuous Roles. **Tenuous roles** are performed by individuals with a definite status but with no clearly defined role behaviors. Tenuous roles increase with age, reaching their peak in late life. Two subcategories of people with tenuous roles can be identified. **Titular positions** are held by those with honorary or nominal roles, such as Nobel Prize winners. The members of the British royal family are good examples of individuals who hold titular positions. Although they are greatly respected, they have no formal decision-making power and serve primarily a ceremonial function. **Amorphous positions** are held by those with a

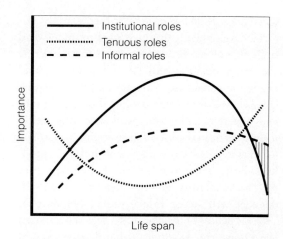

FIGURE 10.1 • Developmental course of the relative importance of role types across the life span

(Source: "Status and Role Change Through the Life Cycle" (p. 80), by I. Rosow, 1985, in R. Binstock and E. Shanas (Eds.), *Handbook of Aging and the Social Sciences,* ©1985 Van Nostrand Reinhold. Reprinted with permission of the publisher.)

clear status but few guidelines to direct behavior. Rosow places older adults in this category. The elderly have reached a clear status based on their age, but no formal role for them in American society has been defined.

Nonrole. Rosow includes the category of nonrole largely for completeness. The absence of status and role occurs only in highly idiosyncratic behavior that has no social importance.

The most important implication of Rosow's typology is that old age in the United States represents status without a role. In Rosow's view old age is a time of loss of social identity that cannot be prepared for.

The structural perspective is useful in describing the ways in which social structures influence the elderly through the predictable loss of certain social roles. Role loss is a major theme in psychosocial development, and it is used to understand such things as depression (see Chapter 9), changes in relationships (see Chapter 11), and changes in careers (see Chapter 12). For example, it is believed that some of the adjustment problems experienced by some workers during retirement stem from the loss of meaningful work roles.

However, Rosow's argument has two problems. First, simply because people lose aspects of their social identity does not mean that their self-concept will suffer (Hagestad & Neugarten, 1985). The loss of the parental role when children leave home, for example, is hardly ever accompanied by psychological turmoil. Moreover, the opportunity to develop new informal roles through friendships could even bolster personal identity and counteract the effects of losses in societally essential social roles. Second, Rosow's view of the elderly as victims of society does not fit well with the considerable evidence that most older people successfully meet their environmental demands.

In sum, Rosow concentrates on the influence of society, which is clearly important, but tends to ignore the active role of the individual in negotiating the developmental changes in statuses and roles. This latter point is the focus of the interactionist perspective.

The Interactionist Perspective

According to the structural perspective, status and role are bestowed on individuals by society; individuals have little if any influence on them (Passuth & Bengtson, 1988). In contrast, the **interactionist perspective** emphasizes the individual's active interpretations of social structure as the main determinants of status and role (George, 1980; Passuth & Bengtson, 1988). Interactionists maintain that people subjectively define their own relationships to social structures and are able to mold and alter those relationships if necessary.

The interactionist perspective is important for three reasons. First, we often choose the particular statuses we occupy and the specific roles we act out. If we do not like them, we may have the option to make changes. Second, not all roles have narrowly defined behavioral expectations but, rather, offer a range of optional behaviors. Parenting is an example of a role with a wide range of acceptable behaviors, because there is considerable flexibility in how one can rear children effectively. Third, people create many informal roles in areas of interest to them. For example, people who become mediators in a debate or dispute voluntarily assume the informal role of peacemaker; when a truce is declared, their "role" is over.

The most important idea proposed in the interactionist perspective of status and role is that people are able to create and modify social structures. The individual's interpretations and perceptions are necessary elements in any attempt to understand human behavior. The interactionist perspective has influenced a great deal of work in adult development and aging. As we saw in Chapter 2, the interactionist perspective is reflected in theorizing about the interplay of heredity and environment. Some cognitive-developmental theories emphasize the active interaction with and interpretation of the environment (Chapter 6), as well as perceptions of stress (Chapter 4). Additionally, the interactionist perspective has led to several theories of how people interact with their environment, the focus of Chapter 13.

Adopting the Best of Both Worlds

Certainly, neither the structural perspective nor the interactionist perspective is completely correct. Both have merit. Society does define some roles, as in Rosow's institutional category; however, society does not often specify the behaviors appropriate to that role in detail. In these more ambiguous situations it is more useful to adopt an interactionist perspective and consider how the person perceives his or her situation. Such a combined view helps us address the issue of how status is used to define a person's place in society. The most important way in which status and role have been examined is in stratification systems.

SOCIAL STRATIFICATION BASED ON AGE

As we noted earlier, status defines a person's position in society. **Stratification systems** are universal processes of dealing with the distribution of valued things, such as prestige, esteem, wealth, privilege, and power (Streib, 1985). They are based on a variable or set of variables comprising easily identifiable characteristics of people such as age, race, sex, and social class. Once people have been stratified, society creates shared belief systems about these differences in order to reinforce the basis for the stratification systems (Dowd, 1980). Psychologists acknowledge the importance of these variables by including them in research as "individual-difference variables."

Of the many characteristics of people that form the basis for stratification systems, age is the most important in the study of adult development and aging (Riley, 1985; Streib, 1985). However, stratification systems based on ethnicity, sex, and social class add to the various privileges or lack thereof at each age. Hence, we will also consider these systems later.

Every culture on earth makes distinctions based on age (Fry, 1988). Certain points in the life span, whether tied with ritual or not, mark the transition from one state, such as childhood, to another, adulthood. In the study of adult development and aging, consideration of how American and most other Western societies make such distinctions, and their importance in understanding behavior, led to the age stratification model (Riley, 1971, 1987; Riley, Johnson, & Foner, 1972).

The Age Stratification Model

The **age stratification model** grew from an attempt by social gerontologists to discover normative patterns of aging that provide a broad appreciation of individual situations and the constraints put on people by social institutions (Passuth & Bengtson, 1988). As described below, the age stratification model is a way of describing and understanding how society makes distinctions in behavior, rights, privileges, and so forth. The model has become one of the most influential perspectives in the social-psychological study of aging (Passuth & Bengtson, 1988). It has its basis in the fact that society holds different behavioral expectations through statuses and roles for people of different ages, thereby creating **age grades**, or age strata. Age grades place limits on the roles one has and the status one accrues. When you are told to "act your age," for example, you are really being told to behave in accordance with a particular set of age-graded behavioral norms.

The set of social roles that one is allowed to perform depends on personal characteristics, structural factors in society, and the composition of one's birth cohort. As defined in Chapter 1, a birth cohort is a group of people born at the same time in history who age together. Each cohort is unique because it has its own characteristics, such as size and social class distribution, and each experiences its own set of historical influences that shape attitudes and behavior. For example, Elder (1974) showed that the cohort of children who grew up during the Depression of the 1930s had different values as adults than other cohorts before or after. The members differed, for example, in expecting that their children's lives would be better than their own, among other things.

One goal of the age stratification model is to examine how successive birth cohorts move across time, a process termed **cohort flow** (Dowd, 1980). Cohort flow is important because as successive cohorts fill various statuses and roles, society changes as well. When a very large cohort such as the baby boom generation reached the labor market, for example, competition for jobs was far more intense than when the smaller Depression-era cohort entered. As this cohort ages, changes in advertising techniques (more middle-aged models), television programs (such as *thirtysomething*), and other aspects of daily life will continue. We will consider other aspects of cohort flow and the changing influence of cohorts a bit later.

Components of the Age Stratification Model

The age stratification of society is based on four components (Riley, 1987). The first component is a population of different people who can be grouped into age grades. Second, the ability of each of these strata to contribute to societal needs depends on a number of physical, social, or psychological factors. We will consider this point in detail when we discuss the concept of societal significance. Third, the patterning and distribution of social roles may be linked both directly to age, such as setting a voting age, or indirectly to age, such as setting wide age ranges for certain responsible jobs. Age-graded roles, those directly tied to age, usually appear as sets of roles available simultaneously to all members of a cohort. How a

Formal rituals such as bar mitzvahs and retirement parties are ways to mark transitions in age-stratification systems. This initiation rite among the Xavante in Brazil reflects the universal nature of such rituals.

society goes about setting age-graded roles provides a reliable guide to its priorities and values (Hendricks & Hendricks, 1986). The fourth component involves age-related expectations that guide the ways in which people behave in their roles. What is considered appropriate behavior depends on the age of the person occupying the role.

At any one time the age stratification of society is hierarchical, meaning that it can be studied much as social class can (Riley, 1971). Where one falls in the age hierarchy has a major influence on one's opportunities for societal power and rewards (Foner, 1986; Henretta, 1988). One important implication of the age stratification of society is that different strata have different levels of power. That is, different strata have more or less control over other people and the goods and services provided in society. For example, upper-level executives of the Ford Motor Company have much more power and control over the kinds of cars available to consumers, the prices of these cars, and their availability than do the people who put the cars together on the assembly line. Recall that power is associated with institutional roles in Rosow's system, thereby forming a relationship between age and power that peaks in middle age but declines in old age. At first blush it would be logical to conclude that age differences may provide an explanation for power differences. Despite this relationship, however, age alone is insufficient to explain power differences (Cain, 1987; Hendricks & Hendricks, 1986; Streib & Bourg, 1984). To understand power differences more fully, we need two other concepts, allocation and socialization.

Allocation refers to the process of assigning and reassigning people of various ages to different roles (Riley et al., 1972). Despite changes in the size and composition of successive cohorts, many basic needs of society remain constant. This means that certain roles in society must be performed, necessitating occasional redefinitions of age-appropriate roles to meet societal needs. For example, fast-food restaurants need employees in order to remain in business. With the declining number of teenagers in the late 1980s, many restaurants began recruiting older adults through television advertisements that depicted older employees. In general, the criteria used to allocate specific roles reflect a combination of social values and the aging process.

Socialization is the other concept needed to help explain differences between cohorts. Socialization is the process by which individuals learn and internalize the norms and values of society (Passuth & Bengtson, 1988), ensuring smooth transitions from one cohort to another (Riley et al., 1972). The age stratification model views socialization as a process that molds individuals and cohorts together. As we will see later when we consider socialization in detail, however, we are better prepared for some transitions than others.

The age stratification model provides a comprehensive framework for understanding aging in the broader social context. But it is not perfect. For one thing, it does not discuss how people's intentions concerning the roles they would like to occupy influence development (Hendricks & Hendricks, 1986). Attitudes are important (Riley et al., 1972), but how they operate is not fully explained. Although the model treats all people in a particular cohort alike, we must not overlook the individual differences within birth cohorts (Dannefer, 1988).

Still, the age stratification model has provided important insights, which we will examine. We will focus in particular on the relationship between where one falls in the age hierarchy and how much clout and access to rewards one has.

Age Stratification and Societal Significance

As noted earlier, the study of cohort flow is an important part of the age stratification model (Riley, 1985). Investigating how cohorts move from one age grade to another and how successive cohorts deal with the demands at a particular age stratum are the main ways in which cohort flow is examined. One key discovery from studies of cohort flow is that age plays an important role in determining the degree of control that members of one cohort exert over others. This point, referred to as a cohort's **societal significance**

(Uhlenberg, 1988), is best understood through the following example:

Suppose that all the members of a birth cohort (for example, those born within 5 years of one another) were suddenly removed from society. What would the consequences be? If the cohort were all people aged 25 to 29 or 45 to 49, major reorganizations would be required in families, to replace parents; in work settings, to fill numerous vacancies; in government, to occupy empty decision-making positions; in the news media, to report the changes, and so on. But what if the cohort were 75 to 79 years old? In contemporary American society not much would change. Few of these individuals are parents of dependent children, are employed, hold government positions, and so forth. In short, few hold roles that are essential for keeping society functioning, as described in the structural perspective (Rosow, 1985).

Uhlenberg (1988) creates this scenario to drive home a point about age stratification and societal significance. A cohort is viewed as important, that is, as having societal significance, to the extent that the lives of its members are connected in significant ways within families and organizations and to the extent that it has access to power and money. Because the connections of people to families and organizations are the topics of Chapters 11 and 12, I will not dwell on them here. However, you should note that other types of connections to society are important, too: political affiliations, volunteer groups, and friendships.

People in different layers of society have different degrees of impact on others. Individuals higher in the stratification system have much more influence on those below them than vice versa. For example, 100 voters have little impact on a senator or member of parliament, on the average, but 100 senators or members of parliament have considerable impact on the average

citizen. Such inequalities extend across many relationships, such as parents and children, executives and subordinates, "haves" and "have-nots." Inequalities also exist across age groups. These inequalities do not mean that those in subordinate positions have no influence at all; 100 voters can begin a process of removing an elected official from office. The point is that power and rewards are more easily obtained by some groups than by others.

Inequality of influence is affected by three factors (Uhlenberg, 1988). First, position and influence are strengthened to the extent that individuals make decisions that affect others. In some hospitals or nursing homes middle-aged and younger adults exert considerable power over the elderly by deciding everything from when they go to bed or take a bath to what and when they will eat. Second, the ability to control how money is spent is directly associated with the power in a relationship. Husbands who control their wives' access to money wield considerable power, often closing their access to employment or self-betterment. Third, differences in personal influence can be structured into relationships by giving them status differences. Job levels in corporations have different titles to reflect levels of influence.

To keep things relatively simple, we can analyze differences in degree of influence in different activities or relationships by considering three groups: those with strong positions, those with weak positions, and those who are uninvolved with that particular activity or relationship (Uhlenberg, 1988). Table 10.2 presents an overall picture of various combinations of social activity and position of influence (strong, weak, uninvolved). Examples of the roles that would be included with each combination are listed in the body of the table. Cohorts whose members fall mainly in the "strong" column are those with the greatest societal significance.

Cohorts move from one column to another as

TABLE 10.2 • The structure of social activities based on combinations of social activity and position in activity

Domain of Social Activity	Position in Activity		
	Strong	*Weak*	*Uninvolved*
Household or family	Head or spouse	Dependent child	Single or group living
Economic arena			
Production of goods and services	Employer, boss, professional	Other workers	Retired or unemployed
Consumption of goods and services	Consumer with discretionary income to spend	Poor or dependent person	————
Politics	Legislator, executive, judge	Active citizen	Inactive citizen
Mass media	Writer, producer, director, actor	Consumer	Nonparticipant
Volunteer group	Board member, leader	Volunteer	Uninvolved
Friendship and caregiving	Active friend or caregiver	Dependent	Loner

they traverse adulthood. This implies that **age norms** may be present within different activity-position combinations. Age norms focus attention on behaviors that are expected for a cohort as it moves through adulthood toward old age. As we will see in the following discussion, social activities vary in terms of whether age norms for behaviors are present.

Social Institutions and Age Norms. In considering the combinations of activity and position in Table 10.2, you may have realized that society builds in different participation rates for people of different ages for some activities and not others. For example, American society has no strong age norms for political activity, being a volunteer, and being a friend. People of all ages are equally welcome. Some norms exist for media

activities, but it is difficult to agree on them. Although there is evidence of a shift in marketing strategies to include more older groups, the dominant market remains younger adults (Powell & Williamson, 1985). This situation is likely to change over the next decade, however, as the baby boom cohort continues to age. Signs of change are already apparent: more products are being designed and marketed for middle-aged adults, and the growing political clout of this generation was exemplified in the selection of Senator Dan Quayle as a vice-presidential nominee. In short, there are no firm structural barriers in society to keep healthy older adults from being consumers of goods, services, and media products; active, voting citizens; friends; or members of clubs, churches, or other voluntary organizations (Uhlenberg, 1988).

In American society the strongest age norms lie in the domains of family and work. In the family domain two activities are guided by age norms: parenting children from birth through adolescence, and functioning as husband and wife. Both activities become much less likely with increasing age. Adults over 65 rarely have young children of their own, and becoming widowed is much more probable. Based on these two trends, Uhlenberg (1988) argues, the social institutions most necessary for societal functioning are structured in such a way as to reduce the involvement of people as they grow older.

Age norms in the workplace are well known. The advent of mandatory retirement during the middle part of this century institutionalized the notion that older adults should not work. As we will see in Chapter 12, retirement involves a great deal more than just quitting work; for many it means a loss of identity and loss of influence.

The declining opportunities for healthy older adults to participate in family and occupational activities means that the societal significance of cohorts diminishes in the later years of life. In part, this diminishing influence is related to cohort size, which also declines as members die. With present mortality rates, for example, the size of a cohort is reduced by half from age 75 to 85 (Uhlenberg, 1987). Furthermore, as members become incapacitated, they move from holding weak positions to becoming uninvolved; people with debilitating diseases are unable to attend church services, vote, or maintain even distant relationships with family members. This change also serves to reduce a cohort's societal significance.

Now that we have established that cohorts experience these changes in societal significance, we must turn to two important questions: How rapidly do the changes occur? What are the historical trends?

Developmental Trends in Societal Significance. We have seen that as cohorts age, they decline in influence, especially in the domains of family and work. Although it is impossible to know precisely how much of the decline is due to health factors or social factors, it is possible to estimate the effects of each. Figure 10.2 depicts the developmental progression in societal significance of the 1910–1914 birth cohort when the cohort members are from 55 to 99 years old (Uhlenberg, 1988). Three curves are shown, each representing a different pattern of societal significance. In each case the distance above the horizontal axis is the cohort's share of the total societal significance of the entire population.

The uppermost curve (B) is an approximation of the upper boundary for the societal significance for the 1910–1914 cohort in later life. The curve reflects the changing size of the cohort over time relative to the entire population, and it equates societal significance with sheer numbers of people. In 1970, for example, the cohort of 55- to 59-year-olds represented 7.9% of the population of the United States. This percentage, and hence the cohort's societal significance, declines steadily, so that by the time the members are between the ages of 95 and 99 (in the year 2010), they will represent 0.3% of the population. This curve represents primarily biological influences, since it is based entirely on mortality statistics. Thus, it represents what healthy, active older adults' societal significance would be in a society that was not age stratified.

The middle curve (C) represents the percentage of cohort members living in families. As noted earlier, being removed from a household that includes other family members means a loss of contact and social interaction. What this curve reflects is that older adults are less connected with others via family ties than are younger and middle-aged adults, thereby reducing societal

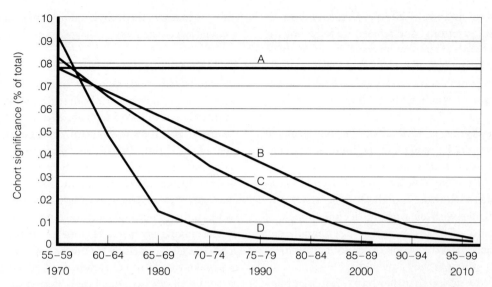

FIGURE 10.2 • Alternative curves of a cohort's societal significance. **A**, no change in societal significance with age; **B**, societal significance proportional to cohort's relative size; **C**, societal significance proportional to cohort's relative familial involvement; **D**, societal significance proportional to cohort's relative familial and work involvement.

(Source: "Aging and the Social Significance of Cohorts" (p. 416) by P. Uhlenberg, 1988, in J. E. Birren and V. L. Bengtson (Eds.), *Emergent Theories of Aging*, New York: Springer.)

significance below what would be expected based on biology alone.

The bottom curve (D) represents the further reduction in societal significance for a cohort based on retirement. More than any other change, separation from work removes older people from ties to others and reduces their influence. By the time the cohort is 65 to 69 years old, its societal significance is virtually negligible due to losses in family and work ties.

The importance of family and work ties in determining societal influence is also evident in Figure 10.2 in another way. Note that the middle and bottom curves actually begin higher than the top curve when the cohort is between the ages of 55 and 59. This implies that the family and work domains provide levels of societal significance

well above that which would be expected by the size of the cohort alone. In a mere decade this influential position is nearly completely lost.

The key point in Figure 10.2 is the size of the discrepancy between the top curve, based only on numbers of people, and the bottom curve, which reflects the actual state of affairs. In contemporary American society we have created an age stratification system that systematically eliminates a large number of people from influencing how that society operates. As bad as this situation appears, however, it will get worse. Recall from Chapter 1 that the number of older adults in the United States is increasing and will grow tremendously as the baby boom generation ages. By sheer numbers alone the top curve will be higher for the baby boomers, indicating that they could expect more societal significance. Unless current trends in retirement, parenting, and remarriage following the death of one's spouse are reversed, however, little change in the actual societal significance of old baby boomers will occur (Clark, Maddox, Schrimper, & Sumner, 1984; Uhlenberg & Chew, 1986).

The decline in societal significance depicted in Figure 10.2 helps explain the increase with age in tenuous roles, described earlier (Rosow, 1985). Recall that tenuous roles have no formal status associated with them. Combining the increase in tenuous roles with age with the decline in societal significance of cohorts points to a systematic disenfranchisement of people from formal connections to society as they grow old.

The realization that they have been disenfranchised from society may make some people decide to fight back. Indeed, the civil rights and women's movements began in part from such realizations. When it comes to age groups, however, the situation becomes complicated (Henretta, 1988). As we noted in Chapter 1, an increase in the number of elderly could result in competition for resources with the young. Whether a conflict will occur between elderly baby boomers and their children or grandchildren remains to be seen. It is true that conflict may result from cohort-specific issues such as sheer size and the institutionalized process of removing older adults from socially important roles. It is also true that because we have advance knowledge of pending intergenerational trouble, conflict need not be inevitable. We will come back to this issue later in this chapter and again in Chapter 15.

Age Stratification and Socialization

As noted earlier, socialization is the process by which we internalize social values and expectations and ensure the smooth transition of cohorts. Socialization is by nature an active, reciprocal process that ties the individual to society and one generation to the next.

The Socialization Process. For many years the study of socialization was limited to investigating how children learn from their parents to be adults. The idea that adults are also socialized for many of their roles was not fully recognized until the 1960s (Brim, 1968). Socialization in adulthood mostly entails learning how to become a responsible member, participant, and contributor to society as well as acquiring a sense of teamwork, unity of purpose, and cooperation and consensus among age peers (Dannefer, 1988). Brim (1968) argues forcefully that adult socialization is equivalent to adult education, in that the goal is to bring about an integrated, consensual, and smoothly operating social order.

Much of the work on adult socialization focuses on the interaction between the socializer and the one being socialized (Dannefer, 1988). This research is based on the interactionist perspective discussed earlier, and it emphasizes that socialization is actually a two-way street. The socializer transmits a set of expectations that define the norms, roles, and values that the other person is supposed to accept. The one being socialized responds to these expectations, accepting some and modifying others, thereby providing feedback to the socializer.

The active, reciprocal process of socialization occurs in a variety of settings: parent-child interactions, formal teaching settings, marriage, employer-employee relationships, and so on. The common element of socialization settings is that they involve some form of relationship, whether it is formal or informal, explicit or implicit (Dowd, 1980).

This traditional view of socialization as a reciprocal process has been severely criticized (Dannefer, 1988; Passuth, 1984). The critics argue that this perspective implies that the goal of socialization is to stifle innovation and preserve what is perceived to be normative behavior in each succeeding cohort. Socialization strives for a certain sameness across cohorts, labeling variability in behavior as aberrant. For example, parents try to socialize their children to hold the same standards for behavior as they do. When their children act very differently, such as by wearing "punk" hairstyles, they attempt to eliminate these expressions of variation and individuality.

Dannefer (1988) argues that imposing uniformity is not a requirement of socialization. Rather, he contends, values and behavioral norms can be transmitted in a way that still allows room for variability. Look around at society, Dannefer says: there is considerable variability among people who hold the same values. People who take a general stance against abortion, for example, differ markedly in whether they are willing to sanction abortion in a few narrowly defined situations, such as rape or incest. Adult socialization involves transmitting not only a common set of values but also room to personalize them.

The general process of socialization can be broken down into more specific components. Two of the most important are anticipatory socialization and resocialization.

Anticipatory socialization is the process whereby people are prepared for changes in role or status (George, 1980). It involves learning about new norms and expectations that will accompany a role or status change. For example, most adults are socialized to assume the role of parenthood by their own parents, through parenting classes, and through books on the topic. Anticipatory socialization is often aided by giving the person the opportunity to practice the new role without actually assuming it. For instance, considerable knowledge about child care is gained by baby-sitting before having children of one's own.

Being able to anticipate role and status changes is important. Unanticipated changes are usually more stressful and are more likely to result in poorer adjustment, at least in the short run (George, 1980). In Chapter 14 we will see that this is true concerning the death of a loved one. Moreover, preparing for role and status changes is related to our sense of identity. Imagine how hard it would be if, for instance, we had no advance knowledge of what it was like to be a parent. If nothing else, the odds in favor of success would be low. Perhaps the frequently reported disillusionment in young adulthood after starting work (see Chapter 12) is actually the result of facing failure after one's anticipatory socialization has led to the expectation of success.

Research on anticipatory socialization shows that young people tend to anticipate many events during adulthood and base their behavior on past successes (Lowenthal, Thurnher, & Chiriboga, 1975; Sheehy, 1981). Anticipatory socialization for events occurring in late life also occurs. For example, formal preretirement programs prepare workers by pointing out potential problems and raising important financial and psychological issues (Kamouri & Cavanaugh, 1986).

Resocialization involves a reorganization of one's expectations and occurs after a new role or status has been acquired. The degree of reorganization required depends on several factors, such as the amount of previous experience one has had and the amount of difference between one's previous and current role and status (George, 1980). In short, resocialization entails learning after the fact all the things that your mother never taught you.

When Does Adult Socialization Occur?

Brim (1968) provides the most complete assessment of the situations in adulthood that involve socialization. Two of the most common are role and status transitions, as we discovered earlier. We know from Rosow's (1985) work that most of these transitions occur during young and middle adulthood, because old age has little status and few formal roles. Young adults receive considerable socialization for role and status changes, ranging from preparation for careers to marriage and parenthood. One of the changes for which older adults are socialized is the transition from being employed to being retired.

A second major time of socialization involves occupational changes. Moving from one job to another, being laid off, being promoted, and other job-related changes are often accompanied by preparatory training or resocialization.

Changes in the family cycle are also targets for socialization. We have already noted that socialization for the transition to parenthood is common. The family provides a major setting for the job of socializing one's children. Resocialization typically accompanies divorce, children's moving out, and widowhood. Although these preparation experiences are seldom formal, they are often quite extensive and occur through interactions with family and acquaintances.

Moving from one place to another often involves considerable anticipatory socialization, as one prepares, and resocialization, after one arrives. As will be noted in Chapter 13, anticipatory socialization is especially helpful when the elderly move.

SOCIAL STRATIFICATION BASED ON GENDER

There is a Moroccan parable that goes something like this: At birth, each boy is surrounded by 100 devils and each girl by 100 angels. With each year of life 1 devil is exchanged for 1 angel, so that if people live to be 100 years old, men end up surrounded by angels and women by devils. The assumption in this parable is that it makes a great deal of difference whether you are growing old as

a male or as a female. (Whether men turn out as angels and women as devils, of course, is open to debate.)

Throughout this book differences between men and women are noted, from longevity to family and work roles. Later in this chapter we will see how differences between men and women are reflected in socioeconomic status and in cultures around the world. It can be argued that whether someone is male or female is the person's most important single attribute, because it relates to virtually every other aspect of the individual's life. Because I note many differences between men and women elsewhere, I will not repeat them here. Rather, I will focus on highlighting what we need to know about male-female differences in adult development and aging.

One of the problems confronting us in trying to understand differences between men and women as they develop is that most of the research has aimed at documenting rather than explaining these differences. For example, there are considerable data concerning male-female differences in longevity and health (see Chapters 3 and 4). But we still do not have more than a rudimentary understanding of why these differences exist. The same problem arises in other areas. Differences between men and women have been described in personality development (see Chapter 8), relationships (see Chapter 11), and work (see Chapter 12), but little has been done to explain them (B. F. Turner, 1982). In part, the lack of explanations reflects the tendency for psychological research in general to be descriptive. But it also reflects a tendency on the part of social scientists to overlook the differences that gender makes.

This tendency to overlook the importance of gender is apparent when we consider the typical subject in a study of adult development. A careful inspection of the research shows it is more likely to be a man (Rossi, 1985; Turner, 1982). This is especially true in the areas of personality and work, where many of the original theoretical frameworks are based solely on research conducted on men. For example, Levinson's original work on life transitions (described in Chapter 8) looked only at men. The problem, of course, is that generalizing from all-male samples to women is difficult and perhaps unwarranted and inaccurate. Moreover, Turner (1982) points out that even studies that include both men and women often rely on overall group differences by age or gender and disregard the myriad of life events and historical effects that influence behavior. Thus, group averages may obscure important individual differences.

The important point here is that although we know that men and women differ in many aspects of adult development, many issues remain to be resolved. We need to learn why these differences occur, how they vary from person to person, and how they reflect the interaction of biological and psychosocial influences on development. Moreover, because there are more older women than older men, the lack of sensitivity to gender differences becomes a political and social policy issue as well. For example, even though many more older women than men are poor, no systematic effort to address this gender gap has been proposed. It is clear that gender differences in the experience of adult development and aging must be addressed, and the reasons for these differences must be identified.

SOCIAL STRATIFICATION BASED ON ECONOMICS

We noted earlier that stratification systems result in differential access to the things that society has to offer. One result of stratification is the division of people based on their financial resources, usually referred to as their **socioeconomic status**

(SES) (Streib, 1985). Whether different classes are called the rich and the poor or the elite and the masses, various levels of socioeconomic status can be found in all societies (Fry, 1988). These divisions reflect a basic system of inequality; some people simply acquire more material goods than others. These inequalities are displayed in any number of ways, from whether people wear Ralph Lauren clothes or hand-me-downs, to whether they drive a BMW or are forced to walk, to whether they have health insurance and get high-quality care.

Differential access to the basic goods and services of society has a profound impact on adult development and aging (Chen, 1985). For example, people with lower SES are likely to be more unhealthy, which in turn lowers their life expectancy.

Defining Levels of Socioeconomic Status

What constitutes a particular SES level? A social class is generally thought to exist when individuals accept similar people as members and reject dissimilar others as not belonging (Streib, 1985). Membership consists of a willingness to associate with one another on informal occasions and a sense that other members make the most appropriate marriage partners. In short, members feel that they have a common bond reflecting similarities of values and behavior.

The specific criteria for membership in various social classes differ. In some cases, such as royalty or aristocracy, membership is exclusively by birth. In most cases, however, membership in a particular social class is defined by occupation, education, residence, and income (Streib, 1985). Most researchers use occupation and income to define class membership, especially in urban areas. By these criteria social class is highly visible in the ways one dresses, the car one drives, and the type of house in which one lives. Behavioral expectations are relatively clear, such as the use of colloquial speech and the importance of status symbols. Although the prevailing view in the United States is that social class mobility is possible, in many countries such mobility is not (Sokolovsky & Sokolovsky, 1982).

Mobility Between Social Classes

A great deal of class identification is acquired through socialization during childhood and adolescence, from both family and peer influences. Being educated in certain schools, interacting with adults in particular kinds of jobs, and differential access to goods, services, and power have a major impact on individuals' life-styles and values.

The belief that **upward mobility** between social classes is possible is deeply rooted in the American culture (Elder, 1974). "Pull yourself up by your own bootstraps," "get an education and get ahead," and "the American dream" all reflect the belief that hard work will pay off in increased status. It is almost a cliché to say that parents work hard so that their children will have it better than they did. Politicians use this belief as the basis for campaign rhetoric. Indeed, breaking the cycle of poverty means fostering upward mobility.

Although upward mobility is still possible in the United States, it is becoming much more difficult. The most important reason is economic; moving up is simply beyond the financial means of many people. With the average price of a new house nearing $150,000 at the end of the 1980s, many young families find themselves unable to afford the move. A second reason is that if one does not have ready access to educational and occupational options, it is difficult to obtain the skills necessary to become upwardly mobile. Desire is certainly important, but if one cannot obtain the education or training necessary, it is not

enough. Economic and educational barriers also intersect; the rapid rise in college tuition, coupled with lower levels of governmental support for financial aid, puts college out of the reach of many lower- and lower-middle-class individuals.

Upward mobility is a stressful event, because it involves considerable role change (George, 1980). People who successfully improve their social status may show behaviors that reflect both their class of origin and their newly acquired status. This mixture is a potential source of stress; for example, marriages involving people from different social classes are more likely to end in divorce (see Chapter 11). Deciding whether to sever ties with one's class of origin is difficult, and many people find that they must redefine old relationships.

Upward mobility is not the only movement through social classes. Although not part of the American dream, **downward mobility** occurs when a person moves to a lower social status. Downward mobility occurs for many reasons, but the most common ones are loss of one's job and, for women, divorce. Losing one's socioeconomic status is an important source of stress, especially in terms of feeling shame and worthlessness (Lazarus & Folkman, 1984). Downward mobility is especially hard on families with young children, who may not understand what is happening.

Socioeconomic Status and Women

The socioeconomic status of women was traditionally determined by their fathers and husbands. Women's occupational achievements were generally not considered if they were married. For example, women in many states had difficulty with credit ratings. The past few decades have seen enormous strides toward recognizing women's independent achievements. As will be noted in Chapter 12, most women are now employed outside the home, a major change from the 1950s.

Women are found in virtually every career, meaning that they can establish their own social status with or without a husband.

However, that does not mean that women are always treated fairly. As we will see in Chapter 11, women are far more likely to experience significant downward mobility following divorce. In the workplace women are still paid less, and in the home they still assume most of the household chores. Women are also unlikely to be found in the highest SES levels; for example, very few women head corporations, hold high elected or appointed political office, or work at the upper administrative levels of colleges and universities.

Economics and Aging

For many people, growing old is not something that they can easily afford to do. Although the financial picture of older Americans improved considerably during the early 1970s, progress since then has been slow (Chen, 1985). In 1970 nearly 25% of older adults were officially designated as poor by the United States government; by 1975 this number had dropped to about 15%, where it hovers today. Estimating the number of poor elderly is difficult, however, because the income cut-offs change and because mere income does not reflect the numbers of people who experience downward mobility as a result of retirement. As will be noted in Chapter 12, retirees' income drops by nearly half. This decline is significant for everyone and, at least psychologically, strains even those who are relatively well off. Critics argue that people who are near the official poverty level should also be counted (Chen, 1985); if we include those with incomes up to 25% above the poverty line, the number of poor older adults would increase to around 25%. This compares with about 19% of the adult population under 65 who are poor or nearly poor.

The point is that many older adults in the United States are barely making ends meet. Roughly 90% of all older adults receive Social Security payments. Two thirds of older adults receive interest or dividend income, approximately one third receive some type of pension, and only about one quarter have earnings (Upp, 1983). As might be expected, elderly people in the lowest income brackets rely more heavily on Social Security than any other group, and for many in this category it is their only source of income. Although the Social Security system was in financial danger in the early 1980s, the U.S. Congress took steps to protect it into the next century. However, the problem of increasing the income for those who are on the minimum Social Security payments remains (Clark & Baumer, 1985).

Special Problems of Some Elderly. Three subgroups of older adults are in the worst financial situation: unmarried women, minority ethnic groups, and the very old (Chen, 1985).

According to the 1980 census, unmarried women (including the never married, the divorced, and the widowed) made up nearly half of all households headed by a person over age 65. Unmarried elderly women have lower average incomes than unmarried elderly men, with widows in worse shape than any other group, and they are half of the elderly poor (Chen, 1985). The increasing gap between the life expectancies of men and women will increase the number of unmarried elderly women over the foreseeable future, making the financial plight of older women a problem that will probably get worse in the short run.

A longer range forecast for unmarried older women is difficult to make, largely because of changes in the number of women who are employed outside the home. However, if women remain concentrated in lower paying jobs where pensions are not typically included in employee benefits, their financial problems will continue. In any event the next few decades will continue to bring a disproportionate number of poor elderly women (Chen, 1985).

A second segment of the elderly population facing continued economic problems is minority ethnic groups. Blacks and Hispanics have been shown to be disproportionately represented in the number of poor older adults; it is assumed that other minority ethnic groups are, as well, but statistics are scarce (Chen, 1985). For example, the poverty rate for elderly Blacks is three times higher than that for elderly Whites, and older Blacks' income is on average only 60% that of older Whites.

The plight of older minority-group members is due primarily to a lower participation in well-paying jobs, lower access to jobs with pension plans, fragmented employment histories, and fewer opportunities for advancement (J. J. Jackson, 1985). The increased emphasis on "high-tech" jobs holds little hope for minority ethnic groups who do not have access to educational opportunities. For these reasons the outlook for the coming decades for older minorities is poor (Markides & Levin, 1987); it is unlikely that the gap between minorities and Whites will close.

As noted in Chapter 1, the fastest growing segment of the population is the "old-old," especially people over age 80. Most of these individuals are women, who are already at a financial disadvantage. However, there are several important implications for the financial status of people over age 80 independent of sex.

Most obvious is the fact that increased life expectancy means a longer period of retirement, meaning, in turn, that more retirement income will be needed. One of the problems faced by pension plans and Social Security is that contributions are based on the assumption that people will live only a certain number of years in retirement; the amount of payments would roughly equal the amount of contributions made during the working years. As people live longer, however, a financial burden is placed on these programs when payments must exceed contributions. In part, this situation is what led to the Social Security crisis in the early 1980s.

A related point is that people on fixed incomes are harder hit by inflation. Thus, the longer one subsists on a fixed retirement income, the more difficult it becomes to make ends meet without more money. The problem is compounded by the rapidly increasing cost of health care. Because the likelihood of chronic disease increases with age, older adults are especially vulnerable financially. This is particularly true of families hit with a degenerative disease such as Alzheimer's disease.

Meeting the financial needs of the very old probably means addressing the cost of catastrophic illness and especially long-term care. Both are very expensive, and both will undoubtedly have to be financed by young and middle-aged taxpayers, making them rather controversial.

ETHNICITY AND ADULT DEVELOPMENT

Before the mid-1960s research on adult development and aging was largely limited to the study of White males. Racial and cultural diversity was ignored (Jackson, 1985). The growing field of **ethnogerontology** seeks to draw attention to the influence that ethnicity has on the aging process. One of the problems in examining ethnic variations in aging is a general lack of research (Jackson, 1985). This lack of data is apparent throughout this book; much of our knowledge about ethnic variations in aging is confined to demographics. Thus, we know about differences in marriage rates across ethnic groups but not very much about why those differences exist. In short, researchers tend to focus on ethnic groups, but not on the sense of ethnicity or ethnic identity as such.

Ethnic Groups

Before we address the issue of stratification and ethnicity, we need to define what we mean by an ethnic group. On the surface we probably have an intuitive feel for what ethnicity is when we use labels such as "Polish American" or "Korean American." However, providing a scientific definition of ethnicity is difficult. Several attempts have been made.

Schermerhorn (1970) defines an **ethnic group** as a collection of people within a larger society who have a common ancestry, memories of a shared historical past, and a cultural focus on one or more symbolic elements that they view as central to their identity as a people. These shared elements could involve kinship patterns, living patterns, religious affiliation, language, nationality, tribal identity, common physical features, or any of a host of other variables.

Although Schermerhorn's definition provides some precision, it also creates problems. For example, "Hispanic" would not qualify as an ethnic group because the Cubans, Puerto Ricans, Argentineans, Mexicans, and others do not share a common ancestry, nationality, or shared history. Moreover, ethnicity may not be easy to categorize. Children of a Hispanic father and a White mother would be difficult to classify in ethnic terms if the definition of ethnic group were based on biology.

Holzberg (1982) offers an alternative definition that defines ethnicity as social differentiation based on cultural criteria, such as a common language, customs, and voluntary associations, that foster ethnic identity and ethnic-specific social

institutions and values. By this definition "Hispanic" would qualify as an ethnic group because of shared values, language, customs, and so forth. An additional advantage of Holzberg's definition is that it distinguishes between ethnic group and minority group; for example, being Irish would reflect an ethnic identity, but not a minority group.

Ethnic Groups, Minority Groups, and Stratification

Just as age is used to stratify adults, ethnicity also provides a way. In American society stratification based on ethnicity often becomes combined with stratification based on minority-group status. Much of the research on stratification focuses on minority-group status rather than ethnicity per se. In the United States being White carries more status than being Black, Hispanic, Asian, or Native American. Discrimination based on minority-group membership is still a problem, despite major legislative efforts since the 1960s. Due to these social policies and to the factors that define minority groups themselves, there are many differences across minority ethnic groups in the United States on a host of demographic variables. Many of these differences were described in Chapter 1; differences in health and longevity were described in Chapter 4. For our purposes here we will focus on the fact that minority ethnic groups may be subject to additional disadvantages compared with Whites.

The most important way in which the stratifying of society based on minority-group ethnicity influences the process of adult development is by creating a situation termed **double jeopardy**. Talley and Kaplan (1956) originally used the term to refer to the problem of being simultaneously old and Black. Elderly Blacks were perceived to be doubly jeopardized because they carried into old age "a whole lifetime of economic and social in-dignities" caused by racial prejudice and discrim-ination (National Urban League, 1964, p. 2). Over the years the concept of double jeopardy has been expanded to include any individual, regard-less of race, who has two or more traits that are socially undesirable, thereby subjecting him or her to prejudice and discrimination (R. C. Crandall, 1980).

Double jeopardy for elderly members of mi-nority ethnic groups makes intuitive sense. For example, we have already seen that older adults normatively lose status. Coupled with the already lowered status of a minority ethnic group, becom-ing old would appear to put such individuals at a severe disadvantage. But as intuitively appealing as double jeopardy is, it turns out to be very diffi-cult to document.

The problem appears to be twofold. First, re-searchers disagree over how to measure double jeopardy. M. Jackson and Wood (1976) operation-alize it as existing whenever Blacks are more dis-advantaged than Whites in the same birth cohort. Jackson, Kolody, and Wood (1982) define it as occurring when Blacks over age 65 are more disadvantaged than Whites between 18 and 39 years old. Others (Cuellar & Weeks, 1980; Dowd & Bengtson, 1978) rely on subjective reports of members of minority ethnic groups concerning life satisfaction to define double jeopardy. Clearly, the lack of definitional consistency presents a problem: if researchers cannot agree on what dou-ble jeopardy is and how to measure it, then draw-ing conclusions from research is difficult.

Indeed, the second problem with the research literature on double jeopardy is inconsistent re-sults. For one thing, cross-sectional research de-signs cannot address the notion that double jeopardy represents "a whole lifetime of economic and social indignities," as argued by the National Urban League (J. J. Jackson, 1985). Only longi-tudinal designs can address such questions, as

Ethnic minority groups are the fastest growing segment of the older adult population.

pointed out in Chapter 1. Unfortunately, vir-tually all of the research on double jeopardy is cross-sectional. But even the cross-sectional stud-ies yield conflicting results. Some report signifi-cant differences between elderly minority ethnic groups and elderly Whites (M. Jackson et al., 1982; Register, 1981), while others find no differ-ences (J. J. Jackson & Walls, 1978; Ward & Kil-burn, 1983).

What are we to conclude? Perhaps the most reasonable position is to note that double jeopardy may not be a useful concept, because it focuses exclusively on social inequities without examin-ing age changes in them and tends to ignore un-derlying variables other than ethnicity that may be the real causal factors (J. J. Jackson, 1985). For example, it is true that the average elderly White woman is better off financially than the average elderly Black woman. As Jackson points out, however, marital stability and occupational and wage histories also differ between the two. Thus, whether differences in life statisfaction be-tween the groups, for example, is due to racial differences that led to double jeopardy may be the wrong question. Rather, we need to learn how the marital, occupational, wage-history, and other variables are related to disadvantages in old age that happen to correlate with ethnicity (Jackson, 1985; Schaie, Orchowsky, & Parham, 1982).

The role of ethnicity in adult development and aging is certainly important. What are needed, however, are longitudinal investigations of the unique contributions of ethnicity to the experience of adulthood, a stronger focus on variables other than race, and work on how changes in society affect changes in the aging process of minority ethnic groups (Cool, 1987; Jackson, 1985).

Ethnicity, Age Norms, and Generations: Two Examples

Two topics that have been the focus of considerable research in gerontology are age-appropriate behavior and intergenerational behavior. Although most of this work has focused on White samples, some investigators have studied specific ethnic groups. In this section we will consider two examples of the latter research. First, we will look at sex-typed age norms among older Hispanic Americans. Second, we will examine intergenerational relations among elderly Koreans living in the United States.

Sex-Typed Age Norms Among Older Hispanics. As we discovered earlier in this chapter, the aged in the United States tend to have few well-defined roles. However, a case can be made that certain activities are reserved for older people by each social or ethnic group (Ward, 1984). Bastida (1987) examined such a set in older Hispanic Americans.

A more detailed summary of the results of Bastida's study can be found in "How Do We Know?" In general, she found that Mexican, Puerto Ri-

can, and Cuban elderly people living in the United States were fairly similar to one another. Her most important discovery was that older Hispanics were quite realistic about their own aging: they knew that they were no longer able to do certain things. Sexual behaviors were not considered appropriate topics for conversation, and violators were sanctioned. Restrictions on behavior were generally more rigid on women than on men; interestingly, women were usually the enforcers of the norms.

Intergenerational Relations Among Korean Americans. Korean Americans increased faster between 1970 and 1980 than any other ethnic group, with the exception of Mexicans and Filipinos (Kiefer et al., 1985). Koh and Bell (1987) were concerned about the adjustment of these immigrants, especially about potential disruptions in family relationships for the elderly. Elderly Koreans residing in the New York City area were asked about their relationships with children and grandchildren, living arrangements, and need for services.

Koh and Bell report that nearly 70% of the participants wanted to live independently, a figure comparable to that for Whites (see Chapter 13). Moreover, older Koreans reported frequent contact with their children, at least by phone; this is also characteristic of other ethnic groups (see Chapter 11). Older Koreans faced many problems common to immigrants: language barriers, poor housing, loneliness, low income, and transportation difficulties. Two-thirds of the older Koreans could not read or speak English, which created serious problems in dealing with the majority culture. In contrast to life in Korea, where one's children represented the only source of assistance, older immigrants were more likely to go to social-service agencies for help.

In sum, Koh and Bell found that older Korean immigrants became similar to other ethnic groups

HOW · DO · WE · KNOW?

Sex-Typed Age Norms Among Older Hispanics

Whether there are age-related norms for behavior has been a topic of research in social gerontology for several decades (Wood, 1984). Expectations that people should act their age are fairly common, from childhood through adulthood. An important issue for gerontologists is whether these age norms actually constrain behavior, and, if so, how they are enforced. It would also be important to know whether these constraints can be documented in different ethnic groups.

To find out, Bastida (1987) conducted an investigation of age norms and their enforcement among older Hispanic Americans. She used three methods to examine the norms: extensive fieldwork, during which structured interviews were conducted; detailed content analyses of the responses; and a three-member panel to check the interpretation of the transcripts of the interviews. Bastida studied 160 older adults representing Mexican, Puerto Rican, and Cuban groups who lived in predominantly Hispanic communities, or barrios, and whose dominant language was Spanish. Information was

collected about age identification; aging; heterosexual relationships, including courtship, marriage, and sexual behavior; demographic characteristics; and observations from the field team, which spent at least 5 hours a day at the senior centers where the participants were interviewed.

Extensive content analyses revealed that around 70% of the men and nearly 85% of the women used realistic qualifiers concerning their age when responding to questions. For example, one 76-year-old woman explained: "What do these wrinkles tell you? Well, I'm old and must be realistic about it." Despite the fact that half of the sample was between 55 and 66, none of the participants labeled themselves middle-aged; the younger portion of the sample preferred the term *of advanced age*, whereas the oldest of the group preferred the expression *anciano*, or "very old." Participants openly admitted that age norms existed for grooming, courtship, marriage, and the ability to discuss sexuality. For example, there was a strong belief that one should dress according to his or her age, avoid flirting and courting, and never

discuss his or her sexual practices.

It turned out that women were much harsher than men when it came to enforcement of the norms. Over 80% of the women expressed disapproval of other women who violated the norms, whereas only a third of the men expressed the same sentiment. Punishment was usually meted out by women in the same age group; thus, there was a strong tendency for each age group to police its own members concerning conformity to age norms. Sex differences were also noted in how men and women actively listened and in how they described their lovers.

Bastida's research is one of the best attempts at understanding how age norms operate naturalistically in a particular ethnic group. One important point that she noted was the general lack of differences among the three groups she studied, indicating that the age norms identified generalize across different Hispanic groups. Considerably more work remains to be done, not only with Hispanic Americans but with other minority ethnic groups as well.

in many respects in their living and relationship patterns. Their data suggest that these individuals accepted an intergenerational pattern more like that in the United States than that in their native Korea.

The Importance of Ethnic Identity in Later Life

The study by Koh and Bell on Korean immigrants raises an important issue. That is, to what extent is it important or beneficial to maintain ethnic identity across adulthood?

Cool (1987) provides an analysis of this point. The pressure to maintain one's **ethnic identity**, or shared values and behaviors, is often pitted against the pressure to assimilate into the larger society. Many researchers have explored the notion that ethnic identity, in fact, serves as a source of support for the elderly. For example, elderly Jewish residents of communities and nursing homes show a strong ethnic identity, whether or not Jewish traditions are supported (Hendel-Sebestyen, 1979; Holzberg, 1983; Meyerhoff, 1978). Royce (1982) argues that ethnic identity is important to the elderly because it provides a source of solidarity for people who might otherwise be cut off from society.

Luborsky and Rubinstein (1987) argue that ethnic identity is a life-course phenomenon that becomes more important in later life than it is earlier in adulthood. They interviewed elderly Irish, Italian, and Jewish widowers and found that many of them had rediscovered their ethnic identities in old age. They identified four intertwined life-course concerns that were related to the meaning of ethnicity. First, the meaning of ethnic identity in later life is based on issues of life-span development and family history. These issues include the differentiation and separation of the self from the family and the simultaneous integration in, participation in, and attachment to the family. These issues are very similar to those involved in personal growth, as identified by Ryff (1984; see Chapter 8).

Second, ethnic identity derives meaning from the historical settings and circumstances in which key events are experienced. For example, the currently popular ethnic festivals engender a feeling of pride in one's heritage and a desire to identify with one's ethnic group. In contrast, times of national conflict, such as World War II, tend to lower the desire to identify with ethnic groups connected to the countries on the other side. Thus, many people of Japanese origin were sent to internment camps, and those of German heritage often tried to hide their background. The effect of timing and historical events on ethnic identity illustrates the point made in Chapter 1 about the importance of history-graded influences on development.

Third, Luborsky and Rubinstein found that current ethnic identity in these elderly men was situationally evoked depending on the needs and goals of the individuals. For example, many older men found themselves in the position of family historian after the death of their wives, who had fulfilled these roles earlier. Consequently, they became aware again of their family heritage and traditions, which fostered the reawakening of ethnicity.

Finally, past ethnic identity and experiences continue to be reworked as we consider our current ethnic identity. In other words, how we defined ourselves in the past is continually rethought, and updated throughout adulthood. During old age as we move toward integrity (see Chapter 8), we are especially prone to rethinking our earlier definitions of who we are. It turns out that our sense of self includes a healthy dose of ethnicity.

The importance of Luborsky and Rubinstein's research is that the aspects of ethnic identity that they uncovered may be common to many ethnic groups. Moreover, ethnic identity is inextricably intertwined with other personal characteristics in our sense of self, which is reworked across the life span. Thus, ethnic identity itself is truly a developmental concept and is not "fixed" within any person at any point. Indeed, ethnic identity may wax and wane, and it needs to be given more importance in psychosocial research.

CULTURE AND AGING AROUND THE WORLD

In this chapter and elsewhere in this book the word *culture* has been used relatively frequently as a focus of socialization, as a variable along which people differ, as a way to organize behavior, and in other ways. Whether a particular developmental theory holds up or whether a particular set of behaviors is observed "across cultures" is viewed as extremely important in evaluating its importance and generality. Even in our everyday speech we refer to people from different "cultures," meaning that we do not expect them to be the same as us (although we may want them to become like us).

Culture, then, is an often-used concept. It is not, however, very well defined, nor is it very old (Fry, 1988). The notion of **culture** dates only to the 19th century and the colonial expansion of Europe, when it was used as a way to convey obvious differences in the ways people did things in different parts of the world. Culture rapidly became the most important concept in anthropological research (Fry, 1988). Originally, it meant tradition or the complex set of customs that people are socialized into, but more recently culture

has been used to mean the ways in which people go about daily life (Fry, 1985; Ortner, 1984).

The study of aging in different cultures did not become a major area in anthropology until 1945 with the publication of Simmons' *Role of the Aged in Primitive Society*. Since the 1960s research in this area has grown considerably. Unfortunately, very little of this research has been conducted in a life-span developmental framework. Instead, the goal has been to describe the lives of older and younger members of societies. In this section we will consider how the elderly fare in different cultures and how age itself is viewed.

Age and Culture

We noted earlier that all societies consider age as one component of their organization (Halperin, 1987). How age-based organization is accomplished varies considerably from one culture to another. We will consider three types of societies as examples: egalitarian societies, ranked horticultural societies, and age-set systems.

Egalitarian Societies. **Egalitarian societies** are the oldest, smallest, and technologically simplest societies (Halperin, 1987). The members live by hunting and gathering in small, nomadic bands of extended families that come together or split apart according to seasonal variations in the availability of resources. Some examples of egalitarian societies in the world today are the Eskimo, the Kalahari !Kung, and the Tiwi of Australia.

Egalitarian societies rule themselves by consensus, and no individual has differential access to resources (Leacock, 1978). Class differences do not exist. Reciprocity and sharing the wealth form the basis for interaction; in times of need, everyone does without.

Age is an important characteristic of egalitarian societies. Among the !Kung, for example, older men and women assume the role of managers who control *the* most important resource: water (Biesele & Howell, 1981). Apparently, the !Kung reserve this most important task to those who have the most experience. Additionally, elderly !Kung are the keepers of essential technical information about the seasonal fluctuations in food supplies. This knowledge about plants and animals makes the elderly a critical element in the survival of the !Kung in the Kalahari Desert. Because of their knowledge and their participation in decision making, older !Kung are cared for by their children and grandchildren (R. B. Lee, 1968). Because some degree of sophistication and expertise are needed for hunting and gathering, most of the physical labor is given to younger and middle-aged people; children and the elderly live a relative life of leisure. Another interesting use of age grading concerns diet. The !Kung have strict age-graded norms concerning what foods may be eaten. For example, only children and the elderly may eat ostrich eggs; the !Kung believe that ostrich eggs, if eaten by people of reproductive age, will cause insanity (Biesele & Howell, 1981). A more scientific explanation is that the !Kung reserve a relatively scarce but excellent source of protein to those who may have difficulty chewing the hard-shelled alternative, the more plentiful mongongo nuts.

In other egalitarian societies expectations of people at different ages also vary with sex. For example, the Mundurucu of the Brazilian Amazon Basin have differing expectations of women at different points along the life span (Y. Murphy & Murphy, 1974). During their childbearing years women are to remain passive, retiring, and demure, are not to seek male company, and are to occupy separate physical and social domains. After menopause, however, women can sit anywhere, can speak freely and with authority, and are typically deferred to by men.

In general, egalitarian societies use age to organize roles that need to be performed. Older adults, to the extent that the society can provide for them, continue to fulfill important roles of teaching and socializing.

Ranked Horticultural Societies. The relationship between age and other aspects of society becomes more complicated in **ranked horticultural societies**. These societies are relatively permanent residents of a particular area and are much larger than egalitarian societies. The most notable differences between the two is a clear ranking system in which "big men" and chiefs acquire a larger proportion of goods and power than other members of the society (Halperin, 1987). Big men are those who achieve power by creating a loyal following, whereas chiefs attain power by virtue of kinship connections.

One example of a ranked horticultural society was that of the Coast Salish of the northwestern United States (Amoss, 1981). Among the Coastal Salish generational position defined the most important roles; political and economic power were in the hands of the old. In combination with high kinship rank, age was the basis for redistribution of wealth. The elderly among the Coastal Salish were valued for their knowledge and experience concerning such things as hunting, house building, and canoe making, as well as being the information source for rituals. Older members were also important in holding extended families together.

Holding older members of ranked horticultural societies in esteem for their experience and knowledge indicates that increased societal complexity does not necessarily bring with it devaluation of the elderly (Foner, 1984). This point argues against **modernization theory**, which holds that devaluing of old age comes as a by-product of technological change and the growing obsolescence of older adults' skills. In ranked horticultural societies age represents valued experience, not obsolescence. As pointed out in "Something

SOMETHING · TO · THINK · ABOUT

Modernization Theory and Respect for the Elderly

As we have noted, a major concern in studying aging in different cultures is to determine how older adults fare in different settings. One of the most influential theories that has guided this work is modernization theory. In brief, modernization theory provides a useful way of making comparisons between societies or within one society at different historical stages. It focuses on how a society is organized and differentiated, in an attempt to explain why the elderly are treated the way they are (Hendricks, 1982).

Modernization is a catch term closely associated with the Industrial Revolution of the 18th century, which began in Western Europe and continues to spread throughout the world today. The trend toward industrialization and subsequent urbanization, mass education, mass media, bureaucratization, wider dissemination of information, increased mobility, and rapid change brought about sweeping alterations in the traditional strata of society (Halperin, 1987; Silverman, 1987). As life got more complex, modernization had an enormous impact on the life course. Periods of the life span that were unimportant in nonin-

dustrialized societies, such as adolescence, became well recognized and formalized. Age grades became ways to label obsolete skills, as older people fell behind technological innovations.

Anthropologists and sociologists who examined the effects of these widespread changes on societies came to believe that modernization was largely responsible for the elderly's loss of prestige and power in industrialized societies (Cowgill & Holmes, 1972). Cowgill (1974) points to four major culprits: advances in health technology, which kept more people alive longer and led to the development of retirement; advances in economic technology, leading to new jobs that made the skills of the elderly obsolete; urbanization, which led to young adults' migration away from the rural homes of the elderly; and mass education, which gave the young an advantage over the old. Several researchers have presented data supporting modernization theory from a variety of countries such as Bangladesh, Chile, and Turkey (Bengtson et al., 1975; Gilleard & Gurkan, 1987).

Although modernization theory is very popular, it has come under severe attack from some

historians and anthropologists. Historians argue that there probably never was a time before the Industrial Revolution when older adults were uniformly treated with nothing but respect (Fischer, 1978; Quadagno, 1982; Stearns, 1977). Moreover, modernization theory tends to view all nonindustrialized societies alike in spite of their many differences. We have seen that these societies vary considerably in how they treat their elderly members, so to lump them all together is a serious oversimplification. Anthropologists point out that modernization of a society does not affect all cohorts similarly (Foner, 1984); thus, as initially younger cohorts age, the effects of modernization are extremely difficult to determine.

It is clear that modernization theory needs to account for variations among different societies and how they treat their aged. But one thing modernization theory has done is to point out that when societies undergo major and fundamental change, one of the hardest-hit groups is the old. Regardless of the adequacy of modernization theory in explaining how this happens, it still provides us with something to think about.

to Think About," however, in more technologically advanced countries modernization theory provides one, albeit controversial, explanation of devaluation in old age.

Age-Set Systems. One of the clearest examples of age grading occurs in some African cultures, in which age is a formalized principle of social organization that explicitly regulates the allocation of social roles (Foner & Kertzer, 1978, 1979; Kertzer & Madison, 1981). **Age-set systems** are groups of people who recognize common membership in a named grouping based on common age (Kertzer & Madison, 1981).

Although formalized age grading existed in many forms (Bernardi, 1985), it has been studied most in East African cultures (e.g., Kertzer & Madison, 1981). Among the Latuka, for example, both men and women past a certain age belong to an age set. The four age-set groupings in Latuka society are based solely on age; kinship and wealth are not considered. Within age sets there is no stratification for either sex. Labor is done by members of the two middle age sets; children and the elderly are exempt. In the Gada society each age set constitutes an egalitarian group collectively progressing through the social grades (Fry, 1988). Similar systems operate elsewhere in Africa.

There is some evidence that age-set systems existed in North and South America, but with some differences. For example, age sets were important only in young adulthood among the Akwe-Shavante of Brazil (Maybury-Lewis, 1984). On the Great Plains age sets and their accompanying rights were bought and sold to others as a means of passing through the age grades (Fry, 1988).

Formal age-set systems appear to share several commonalities (Fry, 1988). Because they are predominantly male, they tend to involve the distribution of power; for example, they determine who has the most political clout (Fortes, 1984). Phys-

iological age tends to be ignored; rather, age assumes a social-structural or organizational meaning (Bernardi, 1985). Status and rights tend to be uniquely assigned to each age set, such as novice, warrior, or elder. In contrast to inequality across age groups, there tends to be considerable equality among members of an age group (Fry, 1988).

Aging and Asian Cultures

Perhaps nowhere is the stereotype of revered older adults stronger in Americans' minds than in their view of how older people are treated in Asian cultures, especially in China and Japan. Americans hold a highly idealized image of honored elders who are held in great esteem, veritably worshipped for their wisdom (Tobin, 1987), an image that has been bolstered in the scientific literature (Palmore, 1975; Palmore & Maeda, 1985). The image is false in many respects; we will consider Japan as an example.

Tobin (1987) explored American ideas about aging in Japan by asking students in Chicago and Hawaii to complete questionnaires and by interviewing 40 Americans living in Tokyo. All respondents pictured the Japanese elderly to be highly respected, cared for, and happy with their lives. The actual state of affairs is quite different (Plath, 1980; Tobin, 1987). Japanese older people are faced with a gamut of pressing issues: declining health, housing shortages, and economic and familial problems. Younger Japanese wonder if their children will care for them when they grow old. The belief that Japanese culture fosters dependence has strongly influenced the interpretation of observed behavior (e.g., Campbell, 1984; Doi, 1973), which contrasts sharply with Americans' strong belief in independence. Tobin (1987) argues that Americans' belief in independence means that trying to get older adults in the United States to become dependent simply will not work;

Attitudes toward the elderly in Asian cultures may be changing as these countries become more urbanized and westernized.

what one is like in old age reflects the values in the culture that one learned while young.

A growing problem in Asia is that Western views on aging are beginning to whittle away at time-honored cultural traditions (Martin, 1988). Asian families are no longer so willing to care for their older members, due to increased migration, industrialization, and increased participation of women in the workplace. These changes in traditions are more apparent in urban areas than in rural areas. In response to these changes China and Japan have both passed legislation mandating that family members must care for frail elders (Goldstein & Goldstein, 1986; Kii, 1981).

Idealized images of honorable elders are damaging because they are merely one-dimensional pictures. The truth is that the problems faced in Western countries concerning health care and support for older adults are also pressing issues for countries around the world, including those in Asia.

Consequences of Inequality

Using age to divide societies into various strata is universal, as we have seen. An important consideration of such stratification is how age grading affects the members of each stratum. This issue is relevant only for societies that also have power differentiation through big men, chiefs, elected officials, and the like, since in these societies people in certain age strata control those in other age strata. In this section we will consider four consequences of the combination of age and unequal distribution of power (Foner, 1984): the presence of old men at the top, the presence of old women at the top, the losses of the old, and generational conflict.

Old Men at the Top. As we have noted earlier, in many societies older men are the leaders. They have an advantage over younger men in controlling material resources and other property, accumulating wives, and exercising authority both at home and in the wider community (Foner, 1984). They are also primary keepers of knowledge about rituals and other practices. This combination of factors typically leads to their being held in considerable esteem by other members of society.

Control of property and material resources is an important benefit of old age. Older men may be the only ones allowed to conduct property transfers, hold farming rights, and allocate re-

sources. Younger men depend on senior relatives for approval of marriages, which are often arranged among the elders.

Control of resources may include control of people as well. Such power allows those in charge to command the labor and support of others, and it is considered by some to be the most important source of older men's wealth and status (S. F. Moore, 1978). Having many children is a sign of power in many nonindustrial societies, as is the number of wives one has. Indeed, Moore (1978) argues that wives are the most treasured possessions of all. Having many children also enables the older men to show more hospitality, an important source of prestige, and to gain more wealth by marrying off many daughters.

Old Women at the Top. Later life is when women in many societies gain freedom, prestige, power, and respect (Foner, 1984). While they are young, women are at the mercy of both men and older women, and they are burdened with many restrictions in behavior and even diet.

Although the opportunities available to older women in nonindustrialized societies are not as great as they are for men, they are considerably better than they are for younger women. In many societies aging brings with it a freedom to engage in previously prohibited behavior and to speak one's mind, some access to positions of political power, respect as a repository of wisdom and expertise, and ultimate authority over the household (Foner, 1984). For example, there is considerable documentation that among West African societies an older woman called the Queen Mother wielded considerable power, from selecting the new chief or king to running the affairs of the society when the king was away (Foner, 1984; Fortes, 1950; Wallace, 1971).

Most of the power held by older women comes in the domestic arena (Foner, 1984; Fry, 1988). Older women have complete direction over younger adult women and children, with the senior wife in polygynous societies having the most authority. In many societies women gain prominence with age by becoming grandmothers. For example, LeVine (1978) notes that the most respected and powerful women in the Gusii culture were the oldest women with grandchildren, followed by other women with grandchildren, followed by women with married children. Married women with no children and unmarried adult women were at the bottom; they were at the mercy of everyone else. Similarly, in Chinese society older women who remained with the family could wield supreme authority over all other family members, even assuming control of the family's estate and affairs (Freedman, 1966).

With so much to gain, women in these societies eagerly anticipated growing old. Saddled with societal restrictions until after menopause, women greatly enjoyed their newfound freedom and respect. As Foner (1984) notes, the large discrepancy in power between men and women that is pointed out in sociological and psychological works about women diminishes significantly as women grow older.

Social Losses of the Old. The old are not always at the top in society. We know that well from observing our own culture, in which the elderly do not have a great deal of power. Putting older people at or near the bottom is not unique to Western culture, however.

In some societies physically and mentally competent older adults are stripped of their power and prestige in well-established ways. Ortner (1978) writes that among the Sherpa, property was dispersed before death, beginning with the first child's marriage. Sons were given a share of the land and a house; daughters were provided with cash, jewels, and utensils. Parents would do anything they could to delay children's marriages,

sometimes keeping them at home until they were in their 30s. However, eventually the youngest son married. According to custom, he inherited his parents' house. Parents became almost like servants, depending on the son for everything; they were left with virtually nothing. Property transfers before death also occurred in such diverse cultures as rural Ireland (Arensberg, 1968) and the Basque culture in Spain (Douglass, 1969).

Caring for physically or mentally incapacitated older adults was often difficult, especially in societies with few resources. In some cases frail older adults were cared for adequately, but in many they were not. Researchers have documented numerous societies that practiced abandonment or killing of incapacitated elderly (Glascock & Feinman, 1981; Maxwell, Silverman, & Maxwell, 1982; Simmons, 1945). In contrast, several reports have been made of societies like the !Kung who provide good care for their frail elderly (Goody, 1976; R. B. Lee, 1968; Simmons, 1945). Regardless of treatment, however, frail elderly people were usually stripped of any real or ceremonial authority they had.

Conflict Between Generations. One of the few universals in the study of aging in different cultures is the potential for **intergenerational conflict**. Young people the world over do not enjoy being subservient, believe that older people are out of touch, and want greater power for themselves (Foner, 1984). Yet these feelings are almost never expressed openly. Why do the strains between young and old so often remain hidden beneath the appearance of stable relationships?

For the most part bad feelings between generations remain suppressed for fairly logical reasons (Foner, 1984; Fry, 1985): open conflict could lead to homicide, which is outlawed; open conflict is disruptive to society; young people begin to grow old themselves and gain a share of the power; old and young simply accept inequality as a fact of life; intergenerational kinship ties defuse much of the hostility; and the age groups may simply avoid each other.

What we see in virtually every culture studied is a balance between the impatience in the young and the need for continuity in the old. The balance works by channeling the energy of youth into productive activities such as hunting and the wisdom and experience of age into decision-making activities. This balance is often precarious, but it drives home the point that the tensions between generations that we see in our own culture are not unique.

SUMMARY

The structural perspective holds that status and role are independent and can be combined to form four role types. Institutional roles have clear, formalized expectations; informal roles have clear expectations but no status; tenuous roles have status but no clear expectations; and nonroles have neither status nor expectations. Status and roles come through person-environment interactions.

The age stratification model is based on the fact that all societies organize themselves around different age grades, or age strata. Understanding cohort flow is a major goal. The societal significance attached to a cohort depends on its connection to others and its ability to wield power over others. Societal significance changes as cohorts age, increasing through middle age and declining thereafter. Socialization is the process by which people are taught age norms and behavioral expectations that are normative for that society. Anticipatory socialization before a transition

and resocialization afterwards are important for fitting in.

Gender differences are pervasive in adult development and aging. Although we have considerable evidence of this, we still do not understand the reasons for these differences.

Socioeconomic status (SES) is based mainly on income and occupation. There is a strong belief in mobility between social classes in the United States, but its reality is arguable. Both upward and downward mobility are stressful. Older adults are particularly at risk for financial problems due to their fixed incomes. Unmarried older women, minority ethnic groups, and the very old are the most likely groups to have financial crises.

An ethnic group is a collection of people who share similar values, language, and customs. Double jeopardy has been proposed as a condition describing people who are both elderly and from a minority ethnic group. However, it appears that other factors are better at explaining group differences and similarities. Ethnic identity often serves as a source of support for the elderly. It is a life-course phenomenon that is related to the events and experiences one has across adulthood. Ethnic identity is reworked throughout life.

The term *culture* is ill-defined; it usually refers to a group of people with similar customs who go about daily life in similar ways. Cultures differ in how they use age to organize. Many societies view the elderly as repositories of wisdom and experience and give them formal roles in teaching, rituals, and political power. Societies also differ in how women of various ages are given power and in how they deal with frail elderly people. How old men and old women at the top of the social hierarchy are given power provides insight into their formal roles. Intergenerational conflict is a universal experience; however, most societies keep conflict hidden through a variety of means.

GLOSSARY

age grades • Levels of age stratification that carry specific behavioral expectations; also known as age strata.

age norm • The expectations for behavior at a particular age.

age-set system • A group of people who recognize common membership in a named grouping based on common age.

age stratification model • A stratification system, based on age, that describes how society makes distinctions in behaviors, rights, and privileges.

allocation • The process of assigning and reassigning people of various ages to different roles.

amorphous position • A standing with clear status but no guidelines for specific behaviors.

anticipatory socialization • The process whereby people are prepared for role or status changes.

cohort flow • The movement of birth cohorts across time.

culture • The ways in which people go about everyday life.

double jeopardy • The risk of simultaneously being a member of two disfavored groups, such as the elderly and Blacks.

downward mobility • Movement from a higher SES to a lower SES.

egalitarian society • A group of people who live by hunting and gathering in small, nomadic bands of extended families that come together or split apart according to seasonal variations in the availability of resources.

ethnic group • A collection of people who have a common place of origin, language, customs, and voluntary associations, all of which foster ethnic identity and ethnic-specific social institutions and values.

ethnic identity • A sense of personal identification with one's ethnic group.

ethnogerontology • The study of the role that ethnicity has in aging.

informal role • In the structural perspective, a specific expected pattern of behavior unattached to status.

institutional role • In the structural perspective, a set of normative behaviors associated with a formal status.

interactionist perspective • The view that status and role are defined in terms of the interpretations that individuals put on their interactions with the environment.

intergenerational conflict • Discord between older and younger adults.

modernization theory • The belief that devaluing of old age comes as a by-product of technological change and the growing obsolescence of older adults' skills.

ranked horticultural society • A relatively permanent group of farming people who are hierarchically organized.

resocialization • A reorganization of one's expectations that occurs after a new role or status has been acquired.

role • In the structural perspective, the behaviors appropriate for any set of rights or duties.

socialization • The process by which individuals learn and internalize the norms and values of society, ensuring smooth transitions from one cohort to another.

societal significance • The degree of control one cohort has over another.

socioeconomic status (SES) • Position in society based on the amount of financial resources one has.

status • In the structural perspective, a formal position in society that can be clearly and unambiguously specified; it may denote particular rights, privileges, and duties for the person.

stratification system • A universal process of dealing with the distribution of valued things, such as prestige, esteem, wealth, privilege, and power.

structural perspective • The view that social structures define which statuses and roles are essential to societal functioning.

tenuous role • In the structural perspective, vaguely defined behaviors performed by those with a definite status.

titular position • An honorary standing entailing a type of tenuous role.

upward mobility • Movement from a lower SES to a higher SES.

ADDITIONAL READING

An excellent summary of stratification systems and age is

Riley, M. W. (1985). Age strata in social systems. In R. H. Binstock & E. Shanas (Eds.), *Handbook of aging and the social sciences* (2nd ed.) (pp. 369–411). New York: Van Nostrand Reinhold.

A survey of the major differences between men and women across adulthood can be found in

Rossi, A. S. (Ed.). (1985). *Gender and the life course.* New York: Aldine-Atherton.

Ethnic and cultural differences in aging are surveyed in

Gelfand, D. E., & Barresi, C. M. (Eds.). (1987). *Ethnic dimensions of aging.* New York: Springer.

Personal Relationships

James Wyeth, *Breakfast at Sea*, 1984. Private Collection. Courtesy of Adams Davidson Galleries, Washington, D.C.

OUR JOURNEY THROUGH LIFE IS NOT MADE alone. We are accompanied by our **social convoy**, those others who make up our lives (Antonucci, 1985). Indeed, the same point was made years ago by the songwriter who said that people who need people are the luckiest people in the world. The bonds we form with the members of our social convoy get us through the good and bad times. The good is so much better and the bad is so much easier to take if we have someone to share them with. It is from our social convoy that friends and spouses come, providing us with social support.

How we express our mutual interdependence with other people differs according to the situation, whether it be a family interaction, a love and sexual relationship, or a friendship. Relations that reflect love and attachment are especially important, since they are essential to survival and well-being throughout the life span. Although the nature of love in relationships is different at different ages, there is no doubt that men and women strive to attain it regardless of age (Reedy, Birren, & Schaie, 1981).

In this chapter we will explore some of the forms that interdependent relationships take. First, we will consider friendships and love relationships and how they change across adulthood. Since love relationships usually involve a couple, we will explore how it is that two persons find each other and marry and how marriages develop. We will also consider singlehood, divorce, remar-riage, and widowhood. Finally, we will take up some of the important roles associated with personal relationships, including parenting, family roles, and grandparenting.

FRIENDSHIPS

What is a friend? Someone who is there when you need to share? Someone not afraid to tell you the truth? Someone to have fun with? The question is surely difficult to answer. But we all have an intuitive understanding that friends are necessary, that they take work and time to develop, and that they play an important role in our daily lives.

Creating Friendships

A **friendship**, like any other intimate relationship, needs time to grow. It has been argued that friendships develop in three stages that reflect different levels of involvement. During the first phase there is only mutual awareness; people notice each other and make some judgment. This phase quickly passes to the second, termed surface contact, in which the two persons' behavior is governed by existing social norms, and little self-disclosure occurs. In these first two stages the people become what most of us call acquaintances. For a true friendship a third stage is necessary. As self-disclosure begins, the acquaintanceship

Friendships remain important throughout adulthood.

moves into the mutuality stage, marking the transition to friendship. At this point the individuals probably start feeling a sense of commitment to each other and begin to develop private norms to guide their relationship. It is during this last stage that characteristics typically associated with close friendships, such as honesty, sincerity, and emotional support, emerge (Newman, 1982).

Developmental Aspects of Friendships

On the average, people tend to have more friends and acquaintances during young adulthood than at any subsequent period (Antonucci, 1985). Several reasons account for this age-related decrease. First, age-segregated and highly concentrated college campuses, which foster the development of friendships, give way to age-integrated work settings and neighborhoods, which make friendships somewhat more difficult to establish. Second, our typical geographical mobility during adulthood makes long-term close friendships difficult to

maintain. Third, beyond the earliest years of adulthood, most people become too busy with their own families and careers to keep large friendship networks. Fourth, opposite-sex friendships typically diminish, probably because members of the opposite sex are perceived as threats to one's marriage (Huyck, 1982). Finally, the likelihood that members of one's friendship network will die increases with age.

Even though their numbers decline, friendships appear to become particularly important in later life. It may surprise you to learn that older adults' life satisfaction is largely unrelated to the quantity or quality of contact with the younger members of their own family but is substantially related to the quantity and quality of contacts with friends (Antonucci, 1985; Essex & Nam, 1987; Larson, 1978; G. R. Lee & Ellithorpe, 1982). Why are friends so important to the elderly? Some researchers believe that one reason may be older adults' concern that they not become burdens to their families (Roberto & Scott,

1986). As a result they help their friends foster independence. This reciprocity is a crucial aspect of friendship in later life, since it allows the paying back of indebtedness over time. Also important, though, is that friends are fun for people of all ages. The relationships we have with family members are not always positive, but we choose our friends for their pleasure value (Larson, Mannell, & Zuzanek, 1986).

Sex Differences in Friendships

Men and women tend to have different friendship patterns and derive different things out of friendships. These differences are most apparent during young adulthood (Fox, Gibbs, & Auerbach, 1985). Men tend to base friendships on shared activities or interests, whereas women tend to base them on more intimate and emotional sharing. Men are more likely to go bowling or talk sports with their friends, whereas women may ask friends over for coffee to discuss personal matters (Huyck, 1982). The differences become even more apparent when the aspects of the self that are disclosed to friends are examined. In one study (Hacker, 1981) 25% of the women surveyed said that they revealed only their weaknesses to friends, whereas 20% of the men revealed only their strengths.

Huyck (1982) speculates that male confiding is inconsistent with the need to compete and provides a reason for men's reluctance to do so. Interestingly, the female standard of friendship is the socially desirable model, one of the few times that women hold this position.

Sibling Friendships

The longest-term relationships we typically have in our lives are with our siblings, because siblings usually outlive parents. For people over age 60, 83% report that they feel close to at least one brother or sister (Dunn, 1984). This closeness dates to childhood and adolescence and is based on shared family experiences.

Despite the length and importance of sibling relationships, very little research has examined their developmental course. Gold (1988) has identified different types of sibling interactions that reflect different patterns of emotional and other kinds of support, closeness, and frequency of contact. Ties between sisters are typically the strongest, most frequent, and most intimate, (Cicirelli, 1980). Brother pairs tend to maintain less frequent contact (Connidis, 1988). Little is known about brother-sister relationships. Even though many older adults end up living with one of their siblings, we know virtually nothing about how or why this occurs. Clearly, we need much more research on how we interact with our brothers and sisters as we grow older.

LOVE RELATIONSHIPS

Love is one of those things that everybody can feel but nobody can define adequately or completely. (Test yourself: How would you explain what you mean when you look at someone and say, "I love you"?) Despite the difficulty in defining it, love underlies our most important relationships in life. In this section we will consider the components of love and how it develops across adulthood.

The Components of Love

There is little consensus about the nature of love. What most researchers do is identify important concepts of love and then use them to create different categories of love. Sternberg (1986) conducted a series of detailed studies on people's conceptions of love and how love is manifested in different ways. Based on this research, Sternberg developed a theory of love based on three components: (1) **passion**, an intense physiological desire for someone; (2) **intimacy**, the feeling that one can share all one's thoughts and actions with another; and (3) **commitment**, the willingness to stay with a person through good and bad times. Based on different combinations of these three components, Sternberg identifies seven forms of love:

1. *liking:* intimacy but no commitment or passion

2. *infatuation:* passion but no commitment or intimacy

3. *empty love:* commitment but no passion or intimacy

4. *romantic love:* intimacy and passion but no commitment

5. *fatuous love:* commitment and passion but no intimacy

6. *companionate love:* commitment and intimacy but no passion

7. *consummate love:* commitment, intimacy, and passion

Ideally, a true love relationship such as marriage has all three components, although the balance shifts as time passes.

Love Across Adulthood

The different combinations of love that Sternberg identifies can be used to understand how relationships develop. Early in a relationship passion is usually high, but intimacy and commitment tend to be low. This results in infatuation, an intense, physically based relationship in which the two persons have little understanding of each other and a high risk of misunderstanding and jealousy. Interestingly, this pattern seems to characterize all kinds of couples, married, unmarried, hetero-

sexual, and homosexual (Kurdek & Schmitt, 1986).

As the relationship continues, companionate love develops, a style characterized by greater intimacy and commitment but no passion. As Hatfield and Walster (1978) put it, "Passionate love is a fragile flower—it wilts in time. Companionate love is a sturdy evergreen; it thrives with contact." Sternberg (1986) compares infatuation to a drug addiction; in the beginning, even a small touch is enough to drive each partner into ecstasy. Gradually, though, one needs more and more stimulation to get the same feeling. Lovers eventually get used to the pleasures of passion with the same person, and passion fades. The wild passion of youth gives way to the deeper, committed love of adulthood.

Although the styles of love appear to differ with age, some important aspects of love relationships appear to maintain their same relative importance over time. Reedy, Birren, and Schaie (1981) examined six aspects of love relationships in 102 happily married couples: communication, sexual intimacy, respect, help and play behaviors, emotional security, and loyalty. As can be seen in Figure 11.1, the importance of some of love's aspects in satisfying relationships differs somewhat as a function of age. Overall, the findings support the idea that passion is relatively more important to younger couples, while tenderness and loyalty are relatively more important to older couples. Interestingly, sexual intimacy is equally important for young and middle-aged couples, and communication is more important to young couples than to any other group. Notice, however, that the relative rankings of the different components of love are the same for all age groups. Thus, although the particular weightings may vary, there are remarkable similarities across age in the nature of love relationships.

These results make intuitive sense. It is reasonable that young couples should focus more on

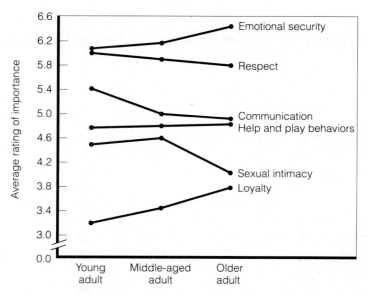

FIGURE 11.1 • Developmental differences in components of love. Note that there are differences across age in the ratings of the different components but that the rank orders of the components are the same.

(Source: "Age and Sex Differences in Satisfying Love Relationships Across the Adult Life Span" by M. N. Reedy, J. E. Birren, and K. W. Schaie, 1981, *Human Development, 24,* pp. 52–56. Copyright © 1981 by Karger. Reprinted with permission.)

communication, since they are still in the process of getting to know each other. Once this has occurred, and people begin to anticipate their partner's reactions, they move to a love based more on security, commitment, and loyalty. Of course, all of this assumes that one has a partner to love in the first place. How we find one of these is the topic of the next section.

Selecting a Partner

How do we find someone to love? The process of mate selection has been researched a great deal over the years. Murstein (1982) synthesized this large literature and concluded that mate selection occurred in three stages: the stimulus stage, the values stage, and the roles stage.

In the first stage one or more interesting stimuli, such as physical attractiveness, intellect, or social status, make the two individuals notice each other. Physical attractiveness is an especially strong stimulus for men. Women look for attractive men but are also drawn by status, preferring a leader rather than a follower and a person with good education or a good job. But preferences do not necessarily become choices. Both men and women compare their perceptions of themselves with their perceptions of someone they prefer and are likely to approach others only when these two perceptions are about equal.

The hallmark of the second stage is a comparison of values. Couples discuss their attitudes toward work, marriage, religion, society, culture, and a host of other topics. The more similar their values, the more likely it is that their attraction to each other will deepen; it is true that "birds of a feather flock together," at least in terms of stable relationships, not that "opposites attract."

Finally, as interactions become more frequent and intimate, each person develops roles within the relationship. Developing roles goes beyond the comparisons of values in the previous stage. It is a way to see how each partner copes with the day-to-day aspects of the relationship, and it provides a forum to see whether the person accepts or shirks responsibility, is honest or deceitful, is moody or even-keeled, and so forth. In short, the roles stage provides a way to understand what makes the other person tick.

Overall, men are quicker to think that they are compatible with their partner than women are. Perhaps this is because men and women have different ideas about love (Peplau & Gordon, 1985). Men tend to be more "romantic," believing in love at first sight, feeling that there is only one true love destined for them, and regarding love as magical and impossible to understand. Women, on the other hand, tend to be cautious "pragmatists" who believe that financial security is as important as passion in a relationship, that there are many people whom a person could learn to love, and that love does not conquer all differences.

LIFE-STYLES AND LOVE RELATIONSHIPS

Developing relationships is only part of the picture in understanding how adults live their lives with other people. Putting relationships in context is the goal of the following sections, as we explore the major life-styles of adults. Because most people eventually get married, we will con-

sider marriage first. Later, we will consider people who never get married, those who get divorced, people who are widowed, and those choosing homosexual relationships.

Marriage

Without question the vast majority of adults want their love relationships to result in marriage, although Americans are taking longer to get there. The median age at first marriage for adults in the United States has been rising for several decades. From 1960 to 1988 the median age for men rose about 3 years, from roughly 23 to 26, and the age for women rose nearly 4 years, from roughly 20 to 24 (U.S. Bureau of the Census, 1988). Although this increase in age at first marriage means that lifelong singlehood is also increasing, more than 90% of American adults are still likely to get married for the foreseeable future.

As anyone who has tried it or talked with married couples knows, marriage is hard work. Most of us also have an intuitive sense that certain factors, such as similarity of interests and values, age of the couple, and so forth, make a difference in the probability that a marriage will succeed. But we may not be aware of other important determinants. What is it, exactly, that keeps marriages going strong over time?

Factors Influencing the Success of Marriages. Although marriages, like other relationships, differ from one another, some general trends can be identified. One of the clearest is that marriages based on similarity of values and interests are the most likely to succeed (Diamond, 1986). Interestingly, the importance of **homogamy**, marriage based on similarity, extends across a wide variety of cultures and societies as diverse as Americans in Michigan and Africans in Chad (Diamond, 1986).

A second important factor in enduring marriages is the relative maturity of the two partners at the time they are married. In general, the younger the partners are, the lower the odds that the marriage will last, especially when the individuals are in their teens or early 20s (Kelly, 1982). In part, the age issue relates to Erikson's belief that intimacy cannot be achieved until after one's identity is established (see Chapter 8). Other reasons that marriages may or may not last include the degree of financial security present (low security is related to high risk of failure) and pregnancy at the time of the marriage (being a pregnant bride is related to high risk of failure, especially in very young couples) (Kelly, 1982).

The Developmental Course of Marital Satisfaction. Considerable research has been conducted on marital satisfaction across adulthood. As shown in Figure 11.2, overall marital satisfaction is highest at the beginning of the marriage, falls until the children begin leaving home, and rises again in later life (Berry & Williams, 1987).

In its early days marriage is at its most intense. During this honeymoon phase the couple spend considerable time together talking, going out, establishing their marital roles, arguing, making up, and making love. In good marriages, in which husband and wife share many activities and are open to new experiences together, this honeymoon phase results in bliss and high satisfaction (Olson & McCubbin, 1983). When the marriage is troubled, the intensity of the honeymoon phase creates considerable unhappiness (Swenson, Eskew, & Kohlhepp, 1981).

During the honeymoon phase the couple must learn to adjust to the different perceptions and expectations each person has for the other. Wives tend to be more concerned with keeping close ties with their friends. Women are also more likely to identify problems in the marriage and want to talk about them (Peplau & Gordon, 1985). The couple must also learn to handle confrontation. Wives tend to try to evoke sympathy, whereas husbands try to use logic or anger to win. A wife may bring up a problem and start to cry, resulting in the husband's storming out of the room, shouting at her to stop crying and start thinking. More successful ways of arguing need to be acquired.

As the bliss of the honeymoon phase becomes a memory, marital satisfaction tends to decline, especially for women. The decline in satisfaction holds for couples of diverse educational, religious, employment, age, and racial backgrounds (Glenn & McLanahan, 1981, 1982). The most common reason given for this drop is the birth of children. For most couples, having children means having substantially less time to devote to the marriage. As we will see in our discussion of parenthood, taking care of children is hard work, stealing energy that used to be spent on keeping the marriage alive and well (Glenn & Weaver, 1978). The fact that even childless couples experience a modest decline in marital satisfaction means that the drop is not totally due to having children. However, whether being childless is a voluntary decision or due to infertility may make a big difference in marital satisfaction, with the latter group experiencing considerable stress (Matthews & Matthews, 1986).

By mid-life, marital satisfaction hits rock bottom, and some differences between husbands and wives emerge (Turner, 1982). Husbands at all stages of the marriage tend to describe it in positive terms, whereas middle-aged wives tend to be more critical. For example, Lowenthal, Thurnher, & Chiriboga (1975) found that 80% of husbands, but only 40% of wives rated their marriages favorably in mid-life. Wives' chief complaint about their husbands was that they were too dependent and "clingy"; interestingly, this difference in feelings is sometimes noted in newlyweds,

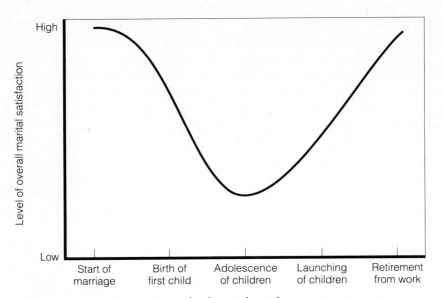

FIGURE 11.2 • Composite graph of marital satisfaction across adulthood. As noted in the text, however, some couples do not show a significant decline in satisfaction.

but it is husbands who describe their wives in such terms.

Marital satisfaction usually begins to rebound, at least temporarily, following the **launching** of adult children (Rhyne, 1981). The improvement is especially noteworthy in women, and it stems partly from the increased financial security after children leave, the relief from the day-to-day duties of parenting, and the additional time that wives have with their husbands.

For some middle-aged couples, however, marital satisfaction continues to be low. These couples tend to be ones who have grown apart but who continue to live together. In essence, they have become "emotionally divorced" (Fitzpatrick, 1984). For these couples, more time together is not a welcome change. Additionally, the physical appearance of one's partner is a contributor to marital satisfaction, particularly for men (Margo-

lin & White, 1987). Because age-related changes in women's appearance are viewed more negatively by society (see Chapter 3), some middle-aged men become increasingly disenchanted with their marriage.

Several studies report that marital satisfaction tends to be fairly high in older couples (e.g., S. A. Anderson, Russell, & Schumm, 1983; G. R. Lee, 1988; Maas & Kuypers, 1974). This level of satisfaction appears to be unrelated to the amount of past or present sexual interest or sexual activity (Bullock & Dunn, 1988) but is positively related to the degree of interaction with friends (Lee, 1988).

However, some researchers observe inconsistencies in satisfaction in long-term marriages (Ade-Ridder & Brubaker, 1983; Sporakowski & Axelson, 1984; Swenson & Trahaug, 1985). For example, Gilford (1984) reports that marital satisfaction among older couples increases shortly after retirement but decreases as health problems and age rise. Sporakowski and Axelson (1984) found that 80% of couples married at least 50 years recollected their marriages as being happy from their wedding day to the present. Surprisingly, however, only 28% of these couples named their spouse as being one of their closest friends.

The discrepant data concerning marital satisfaction in long-term marriages may be due to several factors. For one thing couples in this cohort were less likely to have divorced due to disagreement than those in more recent cohorts and may have simply developed detached, contented styles (Norton & Moorman, 1987). Older couples may also have different criteria for marital satisfaction than younger couples. Or they may simply not see the point in arguing anymore. Moreover, instrumental marriages, characteristic of most older couples, do not require that spouses be best friends to be satisfied. Indeed, Lee (1988) found lower marital satisfaction among older couples with working wives and retired husbands than among couples where both spouses were working or were retired. Unfortunately, our understanding of the dynamics of long-term marriages is extremely limited, so sorting out these possibilities must await further research.

Overall, marital satisfaction ebbs and flows over time. The pattern of a particular marriage over the years is determined by the nature of the dependence of each spouse on the other. When dependence is mutual and about equal, the marriage is strong and close. When the dependence of one partner is much higher than that of the other, however, the marriage is likely to be characterized by stress and conflict. Changes in individual lives over adulthood shift the balance of dependence from one partner to the other; for example, one partner may go back to school, become ill, or lose status. Learning how to deal with these changes is the secret to long and happy marriages.

What Are Long-Term Marriages Like? All of us have heard of or even know couples who have celebrated their golden wedding anniversary. Perhaps you have even participated in such a celebration for your grandparents. If you are like other inquiring minds, you may have wondered how they managed to stay together for so long.

The answer to this question lies in considering types of marriages. Over the years several attempts have been made at describing types of marriages. For example, Cuber and Harroff (1965) asked middle-aged couples to describe what their marriages had been like. This approach yields different categories, but such descriptions are static; that is, they simply describe what couples are like at one point. Although **point-in-time models** are helpful, they do not capture the dynamics of marriage over the long haul. To do this requires longitudinal research.

Weishaus and Field (1988) provide a longitudinal, dynamic model of marital types. Their model is based on a combination of point-in-time models and the hypothetical directions that marital satisfaction could take (e.g., decline, no change, or improvement); this combination yields six patterns. Weishaus and Field analyzed data from a longitudinal study of 17 couples married between 50 and 69 years that included measures of relationship quality over virtually the entire length of the couples' years together. The results of their research, described in more detail in "How Do We Know?" show that long-term marriages vary in their developmental trajectories. The only developmental patterns not found are continuous decline and continuous improvement. Moreover, couples show a real ability to "roll with the punches" and adapt with changing circumstances. For example, a serious illness to

HOW · DO · WE · KNOW?

Continuity and Change in Long-Term Marriages

It is usually heartening to learn that a couple are celebrating their 50th (or even higher) wedding anniversary. Couples who have stayed together that long must have a secret, we think. If not, they certainly must have learned how to cope with the changes that occur across adulthood.

It may be surprising to learn that researchers know very little about long-term marriages, especially from a developmental perspective. One of the only longitudinal studies of long-term marriages was conducted by Weishaus and Field (1988), who followed 17 couples in the Berkeley Studies. (Some of these people also served as participants in Maas and Kuypers's [1974] longitudinal study of personality, described in Chapter 8.) These couples had been married between 50 and 69 years and had been interviewed from time to time since their children were born in 1928 and 1929, most recently in 1982–1984.

Weishaus and Field set out to test a typology of marriages that combined aspects of cross-sectional studies with developmental changes. Their typology consists of six categories: (1) stable-positive marriages, which had maintained moderately high to high levels of satisfaction throughout their duration; (2) stable-neutral marriages, in which couples had never experienced high emotionality or intimacy; (3) stable-negative marriages, in which couples had experienced primarily negative emotions throughout; (4) curvilinear marriages, which had shown the typical drop in satisfaction in mid-life but which had risen in later life; (5) continuous-decline marriages, which had eroded gradually and continuously; and (6) continuous-increase marriages, in which happiness had begun very low and risen gradually throughout.

Weishaus and Field found couples that fit four of the six types; the two continuous types were not represented in the sample. Twelve of the marriages showed either the curvilinear or stable-positive patterns. All of the couples demonstrated shared and separate interests, and all showed commitment to the marriage and acceptance of each other. Couples with curvilinear or stable-positive marriages also demonstrated understanding, affection, and love and were uncritical of their mates and their marriages.

These findings point out the importance of a willingness to work at the marital relationship to keep it going. The continued sense of commitment to the relationship and to one's spouse is also key. The absence of the two continuous patterns probably indicates that couples involved in continuous-decline marriages get divorced before old age and that couples who do not love each other are unlikely to marry (which would be true in continuous-increase marriages).

one spouse is not detrimental to the relationship and may even make the bond stronger. Likewise, couples' expectations about marriage change over time, gradually becoming more congruent.

The Single Life

During the early years of adulthood most Americans are single. Current estimates are that 75% of men and 57% of women between the ages of 20 and 25 are unmarried. These percentages have been rising over the past few decades with the rise in median age of first marriage. Most single men and women enjoy this part of their lives, during which they have few responsibilities. For women, being single has the advantage of increasing the likelihood that they will go to college (Haggstrom, Kanouse, & Morrison, 1986).

Information about single people is very scarce. Beyond the contradictory popular images of them as swingers on cruise ships and getaway weekends or as lonely people existing in quiet desperation, few scientific data are available. Perhaps the lack of research is due to the fact that relatively few adults never marry, so singlehood is treated as a transient state of little inherent interest. Perhaps this situation will change as more people in recent cohorts remain single.

The Never-Married Across Adulthood.

Evidence drawn from several sources indicates that men and women typically decide whether to remain single between 25 and 30 (Phillis & Stein, 1983). One of the few consistent trends that emerges is a tendency for people with very little formal education (less than 5 years) and women with graduate training to remain single. Some speculate that some highly intelligent women choose career and personal freedom over marriage and that others stay single because they intimidate men with their superior earning power and career

success (Doudna & McBride, 1981; Unger, 1979).

How the decision to remain single occurs has been the subject of much speculation. Various explanations have been offered for delayed marriage, including changes in sexual standards, the increased financial independence of women, various liberation movements, changing economic conditions, and changing conceptions of marriage (Safilios-Rothschild, 1977; Stein, 1978). However, some adults may simply postpone the decision about whether to marry and slide into singlehood.

Because they spend a lifetime without a spouse, single adults develop long-standing alternative social patterns based on friendships. Women, especially, are highly involved with relatives, caring for an aged parent, living with a sibling, or actively helping nieces and nephews. Loneliness is typically not present; one study found that never-married women were comparable to married ones (Essex & Nam, 1987), and other evidence argues that they are not socially isolated (Rubinstein, 1987).

The Single Role.

Scientifically, we know very little about what it is really like to be a single adult. There is some evidence to suggest that many never-married adults have more-androgynous gender identities, have high achievement needs, are more autonomous, and want to maintain close relationships with others (Phillis & Stein, 1983). Many singles are acutely aware of their ambivalent feelings concerning their desires to have a successful career and their equally strong desires for intimacy. For many, this ambivalence is the reason they choose not to risk marriage.

Perhaps the two most difficult issues for single people are how to handle dating and others' expectations that they should marry. Both men and women experience role constrictions while dating: how sex should be handled, how to date without getting too serious too fast, and how to initiate a close friendship without coming on too strong. In addition, other people often assume that everyone gets married and sometimes force a single person to defend his or her status. This pressure to marry is especially strong for women as they near 30; frequent questions like "Any good prospects yet?" may leave women feeling conspicuous or left out as many of their friends marry.

Although attitudes are changing, it is still the case that people (especially women) who choose not to marry are often ostracized. Americans are extremely couple-oriented, and as their friends marry, single people find their friendship networks shrinking accordingly. Moreover, such social behaviors as "feeling sorry" for never-married people compound our basic lack of understanding of them. Still, many never-married people report that they are quite happy. For many, the satisfaction derived from careers and friendships is more than enough (Alwin, Converse, & Martin, 1985).

Cohabitation

Not being married does not mean having to live alone. Many unmarried adults live with other people who are not family members. Such living arrangements include sharing apartments and houses with other same-sex occupants. In the present context, however, we will define **cohabitation** as referring to two members of the opposite sex who live together but who are not married.

Over the last 25 years cohabitation has increased almost 60-fold. Proponents argue that it is a preparation for marriage; opponents may view it as living in sin. In this section we will consider who cohabits and why.

Who Cohabits? Although most attention is focused on college-age cohabitants, living to-

gether is certainly not confined to this age group. Research shows that cohabitants come from all socioeconomic backgrounds and represent all age groups. For instance, older couples sometimes choose cohabitation rather than marriage for financial reasons, and men who have less than a high school education or who are not attending college are more likely to cohabit (P. C. Glick & Norton, 1979). Other research shows that by the mid-1980s almost one third of all women between 20 and 29 had lived with an unrelated man (Tanfer, 1987).

Attitudes Toward Cohabitation. In general, college students see cohabitation more as a relevant step toward marriage than as a permanent alternative to it. This is especially true of women, who are much more eager to marry their partners than are men (Blumstein & Schwartz, 1983). Cohabitation seems acceptable to students in a strong, affectionate, monogamous relationship that, they believe, will eventually lead to marriage. Partners emphasize the educational and socializing value of cohabitation and describe it as a valuable learning experience that aids in personal growth and helps the couple evaluate their degree of commitment to each other (Macklin, 1978).

Sex differences in attitudes toward cohabitation have been noted. Men appear somewhat more open to cohabiting and do not feel the need for as strong an emotional commitment before living together. Women generally expect a deeper commitment and may feel exploited if it is absent (Macklin, 1978). Men are more likely to take it for granted that their partner will want to marry them, but, as noted earlier, women are more eager to get married in order to achieve commitment (Blumstein & Schwartz, 1983).

Cohabitation Versus Marriage. For many, choosing whether to cohabit or to marry is a difficult and emotionally charged decision. Indeed, most cohabiting couples either marry or end the relationship in a relatively short period (Blumstein & Schwartz, 1983). Cohabitants who do marry are very different from those who continue living together. Blumstein and Schwartz (1983) found that cohabitants who married held much more traditional views about the roles of men and women in society, were not avant-garde about their relationships, were more likely to pool their money and resources from the start, and saw each other in more flattering ways.

Considerable research has been aimed at uncovering differences between cohabiting and married couples. At first glance one might expect cohabiting couples to be more egalitarian than their married counterparts on the ground that they must be more liberal and open-minded. However, this does not seem to be the case. Decision making, division of labor, communication, and satisfaction with the relationship do not appear to distinguish cohabiting and married couples (Yllo, 1978). Cohabiting couples are not more "liberated" in making financial decisions than married couples; when women have more power over the finances, cohabiting couples tend to fight as well (Blumstein & Schwartz, 1983). Finally, cohabitants do not engage in sex outside of their relationship any more often than do married couples (Phillis & Stein, 1983). Differences in the rate of nonmonogamous relationships are more related to cohort than to type of relationship, with younger couples more likely to engage in sex outside of their primary relationship (Blumstein & Schwartz, 1983).

In summary, research consistently shows many similarities between people who cohabit and people who marry. Many cohabiting couples tend to reflect the predominant social values and gender roles to the same degree as the couples who get married. Perhaps this is not surprising. After all,

by their own admission many cohabiting couples view cohabitation as a prelude to, not a replacement for, marriage (Blumstein & Schwartz, 1983; DeMaris & Leslie, 1984).

Homosexual Couples

Less is known about the developmental course of homosexual relationships than about any other type. Perhaps this is because homosexual relationships are not widely viewed as an acceptable alternative to traditional marriage. Besides the usual problems of instability and guilt that sometimes accompany other forms of cohabitation, homosexual couples experience several additional problems resulting from the disapproval of much of society for gay relationships. For example, the loss of one's mate cannot be mourned as easily, since in many situations revealing one's homosexuality may put one's job in jeopardy (Kimmel, 1978).

One of the major differences between cohabiting and married couples, on the one hand, and gay or lesbian couples, on the other, is the frequency of sexual contact. On this dimension there is a difference between gay men and lesbian couples. On average, gay men have sex with each other early in the relationship more than any other type of couple (Blumstein & Schwartz, 1983). However, after the relationship has lasted a few years, they have sex far less than the average married couple. Lesbian couples are more likely to have intense, intimate, monogamous relationships than are gay men, and they tend to have sex far less frequently than any other group (Blumstein & Schwartz, 1983). Lesbian couples are also more likely to stay together than are gay men.

Once the couple are together, several choices must be made, as is the case in any intimate relationship. For example, decisions need to be made about the style of the relationship, whether there will be clearly defined roles of nurturer and provider, and whether the relationship will be sexually open (Blumstein & Schwartz, 1983).

Homosexual relationships are similar to traditional marriages in many ways; financial problems and decisions, household chores, and power differentials are issues for all couples. Yet homosexual couples lack adequate role models. Whether this is a serious problem, however, is open to debate. Peplau (1981) contends that it is actually an asset, since the model of a traditional marriage is less likely to be a strong influence. She also points out that both homosexual and heterosexual couples really want the same thing: a close, intimate relationship that allows for personal growth and sharing with another.

The Formerly Married

Through separation, divorce, desertion, and death, many adults make the transition from being married to being single each year. These transitions are always stressful and difficult. The transition from being married to being single brings with it important changes in both status and role expectations. For example, holidays may be difficult for individuals now unable to be with their children or deceased spouse. In this section we will consider the two largest groups of formerly married people, divorced and widowed adults.

Divorced Adults. Most adults enter marriage with the idea that the relationship will be permanent. Unfortunately, the dream of "till death us do part" is becoming less attainable for more and more couples. Their early intimacy fails to grow. Rather than growing together, they grow apart.

Many factors may disrupt a relationship to the extent that a couple seeks divorce. We will consider attitudes toward divorce, changing expectations of marriage, sex differences, and demographic factors. We will also look at some of the problems faced by divorced adults and the odds that they will enter into new relationships or marriages. But first it would be helpful to consider the facts: what are the odds of getting divorced?

Since reaching a post–World War II low during the 1950s, divorce rates for first marriages have been rising consistently at about 10% per year. (From 1960 to 1988 the actual increase was nearly 250%.) During the late 1980s the increase in the divorce rate seemed to be slowing, although it is still too early to tell whether that trend will continue. Presently, at least one in every three households is affected by divorce. Based on current trends it is now estimated that couples who have recently married have no better than a 50-50 chance of remaining married for life (Fisher, 1987).

Statistics worldwide and from different periods indicate that marriages fail relatively quickly. Internationally, the peak time for divorce is 3 or 4 years after the wedding, or when the couple are in their late 20s. The United States reflects that trend, with half of all divorces occurring within the first 7 years of marriage (Fisher, 1987).

Another way to approach the question of who is likely to get divorced is to examine personal demographic factors. One consistent factor related to divorce is race; Blacks are more likely than Whites to divorce or separate (Glenn & Supancic, 1984). Age is also important. The divorce rate for those who marry before age 20 is substantially higher than that for those who marry after age 20 (Glenn & Supancic, 1984). This difference is due in large part to the negative effects of premarital pregnancy on teenage couples. Higher frequency of attendance at religious services is related to lower divorce rates. Interestingly, in terms of religious preference, conservative Protestant denominations (for example, Nazarene, Pentecostal, Baptist) show relatively high divorce rates; rates for Protestants in general are higher than for either Catholics or Jews (Glenn & Supancic, 1984).

The factors that are good predictors of divorce are many of the same ones that argue against getting married in the first place (Udry, 1971). Differences on such dimensions as educational level, race, religion, or socioeconomic status produce marital discord more easily than do similarities.

One prominent reason given for the increase in divorce is that it is not perceived as negatively as it once was. Previous generations considered divorce the solution of last resort and held divorced adults in low regard, sometimes not allowing them to remarry. Even today, divorce is seen as a sign of failure, a pronouncement that the couple wish to end a relationship that they originally intended to last for a lifetime (Crosby, 1980). Still, divorced adults are not subjected to as many overt discriminations as they once were. So in some ways divorce has become a more acceptable, if not respectable, status.

Closely related to this change in attitude toward divorce is a shift in expectations for marriage. More people now expect marriage to be a positive experience and to be personally fulfilling. When a marriage fails to produce bliss, divorce is often considered as the way to a new and better partner. In the past husbands and wives did not expect to understand each other, because the sexes were opposites and a natural mystery. Today, middle-class marriage partners have a more flexible view and expect each other to be a friend, lover, wage earner, and caregiver (Blumstein & Schwartz, 1983).

These changes are evident in the reasons that people give for divorcing. In 1948 recently divorced women cited cruelty, excessive drinking, and nonsupport as the most common reasons (Goode, 1956). By 1985 the reasons had shifted to communication problems, basic unhappiness,

and incompatibility (Cleek & Pearson, 1985). Although women usually cite more reasons than men, as can be seen in Table 11.1 there is considerable agreement between the sexes. The differences are interesting: whereas 22% of women cite physical abuse as a significant cause of their divorce, only 3% of men do; and whereas 15% of men cite women's liberation as a cause, only 3% of women do.

These changes in reasons reflect a major shift toward no-fault divorce laws in the United States. In 1948 blame, such as infidelity or nonsupport, had to be established and was legally required for divorce. Today, blame is not a prerequisite, and reasons such as incompatibility are acceptable.

Although the changes in attitudes toward divorce have eased the social trauma associated with it, divorce still takes a high toll on the psyche of the couple. A nationwide survey revealed that divorce could impair individuals' well-being for at least 5 years after the event, producing a greater variety of long-lasting negative effects than even the death of a spouse (Nock, 1981). A longitudinal study of divorced people showed that they were more depressed than they had been when they were married (Menaghan & Lieberman, 1986).

Even though the psychological cost of divorce is high, divorced people do not wish they were still married. An intensive longitudinal study found that 5 years after the divorce only 20% of former partners thought that the divorce had been a mistake. Most approved of it, even if they had been initially opposed to it. However, most of the people said that they had underestimated the pain that the divorce would cause (Wallerstein & Kelly, 1980).

The nature of the effects of divorce changes over time. In the initial phase shortly after the breakup the partners often become even angrier and more bitter toward each other than they were

TABLE 11.1 · Main reasons men and women give for divorcing

Reasons Women Give		Reasons Men Give	
1. Communication problems	70%	1. Communication problems	59%
2. Basic unhappiness	60%	2. Basic unhappiness	47%
3. Incompatibility	56%	3. Incompatibility	45%
4. Emotional abuse	56%	4. Sexual problems	30%
5. Financial problems	33%	5. Financial problems	29%
6. Sexual problems	32%	6. Emotional abuse	25%
7. Alcohol abuse by spouse	30%	7. Women's liberation	15%
8. Infidelity by spouse	25%	8. In-laws	12%
9. Physical abuse	22%	9. Infidelity by spouse	11%
10. In-laws	11%	10. Alcohol abuse by self	9%

(Source: Summarized from "Perceived Causes of Divorce: An Analysis of Interrelationships" by M. D. Cleek and T. A. Pearson, 1985, *Journal of Marriage and the Family, 47,* pp. 179–191.)

before the separation. These feelings are often fostered by lawyers, who encourage partners to fight over property and custody of the children. Additionally, many partners underestimate their attachment to each other and may be overly sensitive to criticism from them. The increased hostility is often accompanied by periods of depression and disequilibrium, as patterns of eating, sleeping, drug and alcohol use, work, and residence change (Kelly, 1982).

Men have a more difficult time in the short run (Chiriboga, 1982). Most men report being shocked by the break, since it is usually the wife who files for divorce (Kelly, 1982). Husbands are more likely to be blamed for the problems, to accept the blame, to move out, and thereby to find their social life disrupted (Kitson & Sussman, 1982). Thus, although women are typically more distressed before the separation, men have more psychological and physical stress immediately after it (Bloom & Caldwell, 1981).

In the long run, however, women are much more seriously affected by divorce. The reasons are both social and economic. Women have fewer marriage prospects, find it more difficult to establish new relationships if they have custody of the children, and are at a major disadvantage financially. The financial problems of divorced women received considerable attention in the late 1980s as states passed laws to enforce child-support payments. Additionally, an ex-wife is not legally entitled to any of her former husband's Social Security benefits unless the divorce occurs after he has stopped working, nor does she share in pension or health benefits (Cain, 1982). These problems are especially important for middle-aged divorcées, who may have spent years as a homemaker and have few skills to obtain a job.

Divorce in middle age or late life has some special characteristics. In general, the older the individuals are, the greater the trauma (Chiriboga, 1982), largely because of the long period of investment in each other's emotional and practical lives. Longtime friends often turn away or take sides, causing additional disruption to the social network. Middle-aged and elderly women are at a significant disadvantage for remarriage, an especially traumatic situation for women who obtained much of their identity from their roles as wife and mother. An additional problem for elderly divorced people is that even if the divorce occurred many years earlier, children and other relatives may still blame them for breaking apart the family (Hennon, 1983).

The difficulty in adjusting to divorce often depends on whether there are children. Childless couples tend to adjust more readily, probably because they can make a clean break and a fresh start.

For divorced people with children, the trouble typically begins during the custody battle. Despite much public discussion of joint custody, it is far more typical that one parent gains custody and assumes the role of two parents, while the other is reduced to an occasional visitor. Over 90% of the time the mother receives custody. The price she pays is very high. At the same time that her responsibilities as a parent are increasing, her financial resources are decreasing. On average, divorced mothers experience a 73% decline in their standard of living within the first year following divorce. In contrast, their ex-husbands typically enjoy a 42% rise (Weitzman, 1985). Child care is expensive, and most divorced fathers contribute less than before the separation. In fact, only about one third of all child-support payments are actually made.

Divorced fathers pay a psychological price (Furstenberg & Nord, 1985). Although many divorced fathers would like to remain active in their children's lives, few actually are. Two or more years after the divorce, only one child in five ever stays overnight with the father, and half of all children of divorce have not even seen their father in the previous year. The fact that about one quarter of divorced couples end up as bitter enemies (Ahrons & Wallisch, 1986) only makes matters worse for all concerned.

The problems between divorced people with children can be overcome (Ahrons & Wallisch, 1986; Wallerstein & Kelly, 1980). Some former couples are able to get over their anger and cooperate with each other. Adjustment is also helped if both or neither remarries. Interestingly, it is easier for a new husband to accept his wife's friendly relationship with her former husband than it is for a new wife to accept her husband's friendly relationship with his ex-wife.

Remarriage. Although divorce is a traumatic event, it does not seem to deter people from eventually beginning new relationships that typically lead into another marriage. Nearly 80% of divorced people remarry within the first 3 years (Glick & Lin, 1986). Remarriage is much more likely if the divorced people are young, mainly because there are more partners available. Partner availability favors men at all ages, because men tend to marry women younger than themselves. For this reason the probability that a divorced woman will remarry declines with increasing age. Older divorced women with higher educational levels are the least likely to remarry (Glick & Lin, 1986), probably because of a shortage of eligible unmarried older men and a lower need for the financial security provided by a man.

Very little research has been conducted on second (or third or more) marriages. Remarried people report that they experience their second marriage differently. They claim to enjoy much better communication, to resolve disagreements with greater goodwill, to arrive at decisions more equitably, and to divide chores more fairly (Furstenberg, 1982). The truth, though, is another matter. Most couples believe that they will be more likely to succeed the second time around (Furstenberg, 1982). However, second marriages actually have a slightly higher risk of dissolution than first marriages if one spouse has custody of children from a previous marriage. Perhaps this optimism is the only way that people can overcome the feelings of vulnerability that usually accompany the breakup of the first marriage.

Adapting to new relationships in remarriage can be difficult. Hobart (1988) reports differences between remarried men and women in this regard. For remarried men, the preeminent relationship is with his new wife, and other relationships, especially those with his children from his first marriage, take a back seat. For remarried women, the relationship with their new husband remains more marginal than their relationship with their children from the first marriage. Thus, the higher failure rate for second marriages involving stepchildren may stem from differences in the centrality of particular relationships between husbands and wives.

Remarriage late in life tends to be happier than remarriage in young adulthood (Campbell, 1981), especially if the couple are widowed rather than divorced. The biggest problem faced by older remarried individuals is resistance from adult children, who may think that the new spouse is an intruder and may be concerned about an inheritance.

Because roughly 60% of all divorces involve children and because most divorced people remarry, most second-marriage families face the problems of integrating stepchildren. Unfortunately, we have almost no information about how stepparents interact with their new families. For example, we lack such basic information as the extent to which the factors that influence parent-child relationships in first marriages are modified in subsequent marriages.

What little information we have suggests that stepparents are more readily accepted by very young or adult children and by families that were split by divorce rather than by death. Male children tend to accept a stepparent more readily, especially when the new parent is a man. How-ever, children often feel that an opposite-sex stepparent "plays favorites" (Hetherington, Cox, & Cox, 1982). Adolescent stepchildren are especially difficult to deal with, and many second marriages fail because of this problem (White & Booth, 1985). To the extent that children still admire their absent biological parent, the stepparent may have feelings of inadequacy. Finally, stepparents and stepchildren alike often have unrealistic expectations for the relationship. Both parties need time to adjust to the new marriage (Hetherington et al., 1982).

There is essentially no socializing mechanism for becoming a stepparent. No consensus exists for how stepparents are supposed to behave, how stepparenting is to be similar or different from biological parenting, or how one's duties, obligations, and rights should be meshed with those of the absent biological parent. In many cases stepparents adopt their partner's children in order to surmount some of these problems. However, many of the emotionally charged issues remain. It is clear that much more needs to be learned about the experience of stepparenting, and the status, rights, and obligations of stepparents need to be clarified.

Widowhood. Traditional marriage vows proclaim that the union will last "till death us do part." Experiencing the death of a spouse is certainly a traumatic event, and it is one that is experienced by couples of all ages. Widowhood is more common for women; over half of all women over age 65 are widows, but only 15% of the same-aged men are widowers. The reasons for this discrepancy are related to biological and social forces: women have longer life expectancies and typically marry men older than themselves. Consequently, the average American married woman can expect to live 10 to 12 years as a widow.

The impact of widowhood goes far beyond the

ending of a partnership. Widowhood brings a special type of social stigma. Since they have been touched by death, widowed people are often left alone by family and friends who do not know how to deal with a bereaved person. As a result, widows and widowers often lose not only a spouse but also those friends and family who feel uncomfortable including a single person rather than a couple in social functions. Additionally, widowed individuals may feel awkward as the third party or may even view themselves as a threat to married friends. Since going to a movie or a restaurant by oneself may be unpleasant or unsatisfying to widows or widowers, they may just stay home. Unfortunately, others may assume that they simply wish or need to be alone.

Unlike some other cultures, U.S. society does not have well-defined social roles for widowed people. We even tend to show disapproval toward those who continue to grieve for too long. Since widowhood is most often associated with older women, the few social supports are largely organized for them.

Widowers and younger widows have substantially fewer resources, especially since their spouses are likely to have died unexpectedly and financial pressures are likely to be greater (Lowenthal et al., 1975).

Considerable research supports the notion that widowhood has different meanings for the two sexes. But the evidence is much less clear on the question of whether widowhood is harder for men or women. Let us consider what we know about these effects and meanings in order to appreciate the controversy.

In general, a woman's reaction to widowhood also depends on the kind of relationship she had with her husband. To the extent that women derived their identities from their husbands and did things as a couple, serious disruptions will result (Lopata, 1975). But women whose lives are cen-

tered in individual interactions will experience far less loss of identity and typically make only small changes in their life-style.

In a study of over 300 widows in Chicago, Lopata (1973, 1975) found six ways in which women dealt with the death of their spouse: (1) liberated women had worked through their loss and moved on to lead complex, well-rounded lives; (2) "merry widows" had life-styles filled with fun, dating, and entertainment; (3) working women were either still career-oriented or had simply taken any available job; (4) "widow's widows" lived alone, valued their independence, and preferred the company of other widows; (5) traditional widows lived with their children and took an active role in their children's and grandchildren's lives; and (6) grieving women were willingly isolated and could not work through their husbands' deaths or were isolated because they lacked interpersonal or job skills, but they wished to become more involved.

Gentry and Schulman (1988) studied remarriage as a coping response in older widows. They interviewed 39 widows who had remarried, 192 who had considered remarriage, and 420 who had not considered it. They found that women who had remarried reported significantly fewer concerns than either of the other groups. Interestingly, the remarried widows were also the ones who recalled the most concerns immediately after the death of their spouse. Apparently, remarriage helped these widows deal with the loss of their husband by alleviating loneliness and emotional distress.

Many people feel that the loss of one's wife presents a more serious problem than the loss of a husband. Perhaps this is because a wife is often a man's only close friend and confidant or because men are usually unprepared to live out their lives alone (Glick, Weiss, & Parkes, 1974). Men are often ill-equipped to handle such routine and necessary tasks as cooking, shopping, and keeping house, and they become emotionally isolated from family members. As more men become facile at housekeeping tasks, it remains to be seen whether these patterns will characterize future generations of widowers. It may be the social isolation of widowers that becomes the most important factor in poor adjustment (Turner, 1982).

Men are generally older when they are widowed than are women. Thus, to some extent the greater overall difficulties reported by widowers may be due to this age difference. Indeed, it turns out that if age is held constant, widows report higher anxiety than widowers (Atchley, 1975). Regardless of age, men have a clear advantage over women in the opportunity to form new heterosexual relationships; interestingly, though, older widowers are actually less likely to form new, close friendships than are widows. Perhaps this is simply a continuation of men's lifelong tendency to have few close friendships.

PARENTHOOD

Most Americans believe that it is normal, natural, and necessary to have children. We also tend to think that having children will be a joyful and fulfilling experience and that good parents are guided by their natural love for their children. These notions are applied especially to the mother, and belief in a maternal instinct is widespread (Skolnick, 1973). Unfortunately, it is unlikely that anyone possesses the innate ability to be a good parent. Perhaps this is the reason that adults often feel considerable anxiety over having children. They are pressured by family and friends. "When are you going to start a family?" is a question commonly asked of young couples. But once the child is here, adults often feel inadequate. In the words of one new parent, "It's scary being totally responsible for another person." In this section we will explore some of the aspects of parenthood, including the decision process itself and the joys and pains of having children.

Deciding Whether to Have Children

At some point during an intimate relationship, couples discuss whether to have children. This decision is more complicated than most people think, because a couple must weigh the many benefits with the many drawbacks. On the plus side children provide a source of personal satisfaction and love, fulfill the need for generativity, provide a potential source of companionship, and serve as a source of vicarious experience (Frieze, Parsons, Johnson, Ruble, & Zellman, 1978). Children also present problems. In addition to the financial burden, children also change established interaction patterns. For instance, they disrupt a couple's sexual relationship and decrease the amount of time for shared activities by up to half. Moreover, having children is stressful. Rossi (1968) summarizes some of the most important sources of stress accompanying parenthood: cultural pressure to have children, possible involuntary or unplanned parenthood, irrevocability of having a child, lack of formal education for parenting, and lack of consensus about how to be a good parent.

Although most couples still opt to have children even when they recognize the stresses and strains, an increasing number of couples are remaining childless. These couples have several advantages over those who choose to have children. Child-free couples report having happier marriages, more freedom, and higher standards of living. But they must also face social criticism from the larger child-oriented society and may run the risk of feeling more lonely in old age (Van Hoose & Worth, 1982).

For many couples, having children of their own is not an option: one or both partners may be infertile. About one in six couples experiences fertility problems, and experts believe the problem is increasing. Both psychological factors, such as anxiety or stress, and physical factors, such as disease, may cause infertility. In women physical problems that can cause infertility include the failure to ovulate, fallopian tube blockage, endometriosis, abnormalities in the vaginal mucus, and untreated gonorrhea or chlamydia. In men they include faulty or insufficient sperm, varicoceles, and blockages of the sperm ducts.

The Parental Role

The experience of being a parent is different for mothers than for fathers. Despite some recent changes, women are still responsible for meeting most of a child's day-to-day needs. Fathers are still expected to earn money and discipline the children. Being a mother and father, however, involves much more than these stereotypes.

In Western societies the status of being a full-time mother has varied over the last few decades. Traditionally, mothers have been thought to be crucial for the normal development of the child (Field & Widmayer, 1982). Concerns about attachment, social and emotional growth, and intellectual development have largely reinforced this belief. As a result women often report feeling trapped and depressed when their first child is born. They are made to feel guilty about leaving their child to return to work, and many feel torn between working outside the home and mothering. These feelings confront a majority of women in the United States; the government estimates that nearly two thirds of all mothers with children under age 6 will be employed by the early 1990s.

Only in the last 2 decades or so has research focused on fatherhood (Pleck, 1983). Much of the existing research on fathers is devoted to examining the impact of their absence rather than to the positive benefits that they bring to relationships with their children (Biller, 1982). Compared with mothers, fathers do not interact with their babies as much, and these interactions tend to involve play rather than caretaking (Powers & Parke, 1982). Timing of fatherhood in the marriage appears to make a major difference in the amount of time that fathers spend with their children. In general, men who become fathers in their 30s spend up to three times as much time in caring for preschool children as younger fathers (Daniels & Weingarten, 1982), feel less career pressure to divide their time, and have greater flexibility in their roles (Feldman, Nash, & Aschenbrenner, 1983).

Single Parents. One of the fastest growing groups of adults is single parents, most of whom are women. The increasing divorce rate, the large number of women who keep children born out of wedlock, and the desire of many single adults to have or adopt children are all contributing factors to this phenomenon. Being a single parent raises important questions: What happens when only one adult is responsible for child care? How do single parents meet their own needs for emotional support and intimacy? Certainly, how one feels about being single also has important effects.

Some of the personal and social situations of single parents have been studied with these issues in mind. Many divorced single parents report feelings of frustration, failure, guilt, and ambivalence about the parent-child relationship (Van Hoose & Worth, 1982). Frustration usually results from a lack of companionship and from loneliness, often in response to the fact that most social activities are typically reserved for couples. Feelings of guilt may lead to attempts to make up for the child's lack of a father or mother, or they may result when the parent indulges himself or herself. Since children are sometimes seen as hindrances to developing new relationships, parents may experience ambivalence toward them. These feelings may also arise if children serve as a reminder of a former failure.

Single parents, regardless of sex, face considerable obstacles. Financially, they are usually much less well-off than their married counterparts. Integrating the roles of work and parenthood are difficult enough for two persons; for the single parent the hardships are compounded. Financially, single mothers are hardest hit. Emotionally, single fathers may have the worst of it; according to some research their sleep, eating, play, work, and peer relations are badly affected, and they are more depressed than any other group of men (Pearlin & Johnson, 1977). Moreover, since most men are not socialized for child rearing, the lack of basic skills necessary to care for children may compound these problems.

One concern of particular importance to single parents is dating (Phillis & Stein, 1983). Indeed, the three most popular questions asked by single parents are "How do I become available again?" "How will my children react?" and "How do I cope with my own sexuality?" Clearly, initiating a new relationship is difficult for many single parents, especially those with older children. They may be hesitant to express this side of themselves in front of their children or may strongly dislike their children's questioning about or resentment of their dates. Moreover, access to social activities is more difficult for single parents; in response, organizations such as Parents Without Partners have been established to provide social outlets.

Overall, single parents seeking new relationships typically do so discreetly. Both mothers and fathers express concern about having dates stay overnight, although women feel more strongly about this (Greenberg, 1979). It would seem that single parents share the same needs as other adults; it is fulfilling them that is the problem. Of course, many single parents learn how to deal with the problem and find fulfilling relationships.

When the Children Leave

One of the biggest events in a family occurs when one's children leave home to establish their own careers and families. For most parents, children's departures are gradual; contact is still fairly frequent, and most ties are not cut. Eventually, the youngest child departs, creating a new situation for the middle-aged parents: the "empty nest," or **postparental family**.

The departure of the youngest child can be a traumatic time. This is especially true for mothers who had defined their identity mainly in terms of their children. The psychological effects of the empty nest can be important, as one mother complained: "My daughter was 21 when she married. It's not that I wanted her to stay with me, but I missed her terribly. I just felt so alone."

For many years this kind of reaction was thought to be universal in women. Children were thought to be a central source of satisfaction for mothers. This belief has not been supported by contemporary research (Turner, 1982). For most parents, the departure of the youngest child is not a particularly distressing event. Many people even perceive it as a change for the better (Nock, 1982). Adolescents can be difficult to live with, so to be rid of conflict and challenges to parental authority can be a relief. As one parent said: "It's fantastic. I have more free time, less laundry, lower expenses, and my husband and I can do what we want when we want."

This mother described another important aspect of the postparental period. For the first time in many years, a couple are living by themselves. They must learn about each other again and adjust to a different life-style without children. Most

Married couples are usually happier and more satisfied with their relationship after their children have left home.

couples feel contentment over the successful completion of child rearing. They may now have the time to continue developing the intimacy in their relationship that brought them together years earlier. Research on marital satisfaction and personal happiness supports these notions (Turner, 1982). Marital satisfaction typically rises from the low point when one's children are teenagers to a high during the postparental period that is second only to the period of newlywedded bliss. It seems that it is the opportunity to recreate the interpersonal relationship that originally led the couple to marry that accounts for this upswing. Thus, for most couples, an empty nest is a happy nest.

But what if the nest does not become empty? When children refuse to leave home or repeatedly return after nominally moving out, parental dis-tress is likely (Troll, 1975). This is especially true if the child is perceived to be delaying the transition to adulthood longer than the parents believe is reasonable. The outcome in this case is strained parent-child relationships. Empty nests are not only happy nests, they are the nests that parents expect to have.

FAMILY DYNAMICS AND MIDDLE AGE

Family ties across generations provide the basis for socialization and for continuity in the family's identity. These ties are particularly salient for members of the middle-aged generation, precisely because they are the link between their aging parents and their young-adult children. The pressure on this generation is considerable; in fact, middle-agers are often referred to as the **sandwich generation** to reflect their position between the old and the young.

In this section we will examine some of the dynamics between the middle-aged and their aging parents and between them and their young-adult children. Along the way we will clear up some popular misconceptions about neglect of elderly parents and war between the generations.

Middle-Agers and Their Children

The relationship between parents and children improves considerably as the children become young adults. In fact, parents are likely to view their young-adult children as friends (Troll & Bengtson, 1982). Middle-aged parents are still quite willing to help their adult children if needed, and they often provide financial assistance for college tuition, down payments on houses, and other major purchases. Young adults and their parents typically believe that they have strong, positive relationships, although the middle-aged parents tend to rate the relationship somewhat more positively than do their children. Still, most adult children and their middle-aged parents do not perceive a generation gap in their families (Troll & Bengtson, 1982).

Of course, this does not mean that conflicts are absent. About one third of middle-class fathers complain about their sons' lack of achievement and about their daughters' poor choice of husbands (Nydegger, 1986). And adult children do not necessarily approve of every aspect of their parents.

Despite these possible conflicts being a parent of a young adult beginning college or a career is usually a source of pride. Moreover, the younger

generation puts the middle generation, usually the mothers, in the role of **kinkeepers**, the people who gather the family together for celebrations and keep everyone in touch (Green & Boxer, 1986). Young-adult children may be a source of encouragement; many middle-aged mothers go to college because their young-adult children have urged them to, and many middle-aged fathers change life-styles for the same reason. Young adults benefit from the experience and perspective of their parents, making it a truly mutual sharing.

However, middle-aged parents may get squeezed by the younger generation as well. The number of young adults living with their parents increased sharply during the 1980s, reaching 30% by mid-decade (Glick & Lin, 1986). Roughly one third of them were unemployed and could not support themselves. Of divorced adults in their 20s, 40% live with their parents, finding more emotional and financial support there than on their own (Glick & Lin, 1986). Thankfully from the middle generation's perspective, this situation is temporary; by the 30s only 17% of divorced adults live with their parents. As we noted earlier, middle-aged parents take a dim view of adult children moving back home for long periods of time.

One of the most important ways in which middle-aged parents interact with their adult children comes when grandchildren arrive. Some of the best information on the relationship between parents and grandparents comes from studies of multigenerational families. For example, Cohler and Grunebaum (1981) studied the relationships among members of four multigeneration, working-class, Italian-American families. Most of their attention was directed toward the women, since they tended to be the key connectors between families (Troll, Miller, & Atchley, 1979).

Cohler and Grunebaum found that mothers and grandmothers maintained a close relationship due to socialization, role modeling, and the need for a source of information about parenting. The grandmothers in this study were not altogether pleased with the situation, however, and seemed annoyed that their daughters were demanding so much intimacy.

Similar close kinship bonds have been observed in several studies of Black families (Hayes & Mindel, 1973; Stack, 1972; Stanford & Lockery, 1984). These kinship networks provide a wide variety of support, from financial aid for single parents to role models of parenting to a source of additional child care.

The middle generation often serves as a mediator between grandparents and grandchildren (Wood & Robertson, 1978). In fact, nearly two thirds of young adults between 18 and 26 said in one study that their parents had influenced their involvement with their grandparents (Robertson, 1976). How parents control the grandparent-grandchild relationship has been interpreted as making the middle generation the "lineage bridge across the generations" (Hill, Foote, Aldonus, Carlson, & MacDonald, 1970, p. 62). We will consider additional aspects of grandparenting in a later section.

Middle-Agers and Their Aging Parents

In considering the relationship that middle-aged people have with their parents, two issues are most important. First, are they likely to ignore their elderly parents? Secondly, what do they do when confronted with a frail, elderly parent?

Frequency and Quality of Contact. One of the most widespread myths is that elderly parents are grossly neglected by their middle-aged children. At best, this myth has the middle-aged generation simply ignoring their parents; at worst, they put their parents into nursing homes and abandon them. The myth has been perpetuated by the beliefs that somewhere in the past, genera-

tions were much more devoted to each other than they are today and that today's children simply do not care for their parents the way they used to (G. R. Lee, 1985).

These myths are patently wrong. Although the proportion of older adults living with younger generations has declined over this century, the reason is financial independence of the elderly, *not* neglect (Lee, 1985). In 1900 programs such as Social Security or pension plans did not exist; older adults were forced to live with other family members just to make ends meet, not necessarily because they wanted to. What has increased is the number of older adults who live near one of their children; at least half of all older adults live within half an hour's drive of one of their children.

Frequency of contact between older parents and a middle-aged child remains high. Nearly 80% of elderly parents have seen their middle-aged child within the previous 2 weeks (L. Harris & Associates, 1981). This high visitation rate does not differ between rural and urban dwellers (Krout, 1988b) and continues even when older parents become ill. Adult children also seem to appreciate their parents more; middle age is a time for reevaluating one's relationships with parents (Farrell & Rosenberg, 1981; Helson & Moane, 1987).

Taking Care of Elderly Parents. Some middle-aged children, usually daughters, will have to care for at least one parent, most often a widowed mother in poor health. The decision to have a parent move in follows a relatively long period of time during which both generations live independently. This history of independence may create adjustment difficulties, since both parties must accommodate their life-styles. Because most family caregiving of the elderly is done by spouses, situations in which adult children enter the picture usually involve a very old mother who, after caring for her now-deceased husband, is herself in poor health. For this reason taking care of elderly parents is most likely to confront adult children as they themselves are approaching old age.

The minority of adult children who face caretaking are confronted with a dilemma. On the one hand, most feel a sense of responsibility to care for their parent and will do so if possible. But caring for aging parents is not without its price. Living together after years of separation is usually disliked by both parties; each would rather live alone. Conflicts typically arise due to differences in routines and life-styles. Stress seems to result in such relationships in two main ways (B. Robinson & Thurnher, 1979): (1) Adult children often have trouble coping with declines in their parents' functioning, especially mental deterioration. Misunderstandings of these changes may result in adult children's feeling ambivalent and antagonistic toward their parents. (2) Stress also results when the caretaking relationship is perceived as confining. If caring for aging parents seriously infringes on the adult child's life-style or routine, the situation is likely to be perceived negatively.

How well do families cope? Considerable research clearly documents that middle-aged adults spend great amounts of time, energy, and money helping their elderly parents (Cicirelli, 1981; Shanas, 1980; Stoller, 1983; Stoller & Earl, 1983). One study reports that 87% of a sample of 700 elderly people received at least half of the help they needed from their children and other relatives (J. N. Morris & Sherwood, 1984). In fact, care provided by the family helps to prevent or at least delay institutionalization (E. M. Brody, 1981; Cantor, 1980).

Caring for a frail parent is not without cost. Besides the obvious monetary expense, caring for a parent exacts a high psychological cost. Even the most devoted child has feelings of depression, resentment, anger, and guilt at times (Halpern, 1987). Many middle-aged adults have just come through the financial expenses associated with

child rearing and may need to plan for their own retirement. The additional burden of a frail parent puts considerable pressure on resources that were earmarked for other uses. These difficulties are especially acute for the children of victims of Alzheimer's disease and other chronic conditions (see Chapter 9).

Older adults may not be pleased with the prospect of living with their children. Independence and autonomy are important aspects of our lives, and their loss is not taken lightly. In fact, one study found that older adults were more likely than younger adults to express the desire to pay a professional for assistance than to ask a family member for help (Brody, Fulcomer, & Lang, 1983). Elderly parents may find it distasteful or demeaning to live with their children, and those who do may feel that they have no other choice (Lee, 1985). Moreover, most elderly parents, even when they are ill, have a strong desire to make decisions about their needs.

Whether older parents are satisfied with the help that their children provide appears to be a complex issue (Thomas, 1988). Older adults in fairly good health, those who prefer to live near relatives, and those who endorse the idea that families should help are most satisfied with the help that their middle-aged children provide. On the other hand, frail elderly parents, those who have little desire to live near their families, and those who prefer help from nonfamily sources are least satisfied.

Caring for an aging parent is clearly something that many people do, but it is often highly disruptive. Middle-aged adults often have few choices in how to provide care; many must quit their jobs because adequate alternatives are not available. One of the fastest growing issues pertaining to middle-aged adults is the availability of adult day care or other alternative programs. As explored in "Something to Think About," more and more adult children are being forced to search

---

SOMETHING · TO · THINK · ABOUT

Hiring Surrogates to Care for Frail Elderly Parents

"It gets scary sometimes. You know, Mom would wander off or would forget where she was. We had to do something." The situation in the Smith household is a typical problem for a growing number of middle-aged people who are caring for their frail elderly parents. As noted in the text, the situation is bad enough when everyone is in the same household. But it presents even bigger problems when parents and children live in different cities.

The answer that many middle-aged adults have discovered is to hire "surrogate children" to care for their parents while they are at work. Surrogate care is one of the fastest growing segments of

the health care industry, with over 600 companies in the United States by 1988, compared with fewer than 100 only 5 years earlier (Ricklefs, 1988). The increase reflects the rapid growth in the elderly population and the fact that most middle-aged caregivers must continue working to support themselves, their parents, and their own children. About half of the clients receiving surrogate care are elderly people whose children live far away, also indicative of the trend toward maintaining one's independence as long as possible.

Surrogate care costs as much as $30,000 a year for arranging and supervising 24-hour home care and other related services,

about the cost of a quality nursing home. But for many middle-aged adults the price is well worth it. Elderly people who may have been institutionalized are able to remain at home, and their children are able to provide for them.

Surrogate in-home services are not a panacea, however. They are largely unavailable outside of larger cities. Many health insurance plans do not pay for much of the service, which leaves out middle- and lower-income individuals. As the need for these services continues to grow into the next century, however, availability as well as subsidy programs will undoubtedly be hotly debated.

---

for other means of care, primarily because the cost of caring for an aging parent is extraordinarily high.

GRANDPARENTING

Becoming a grandparent is an exciting time for most people and represents the acquisition of new roles (Robertson, 1977). Many grandmothers see their role as easier than mothering, affording

pleasure and gratification without requiring them to assume major responsibility for the care and socialization of the child (Robertson, 1977). These days, becoming a grandparent usually happens while one is middle-aged rather than elderly, and it is frequently occurring as early as age 40 (Kivnick, 1982). Moreover, many younger grandparents have living parents themselves, making for truly multigenerational families.

Overall, surprisingly little research has been conducted on grandparents and their relationships with their grandchildren. We know that grandparents differ considerably in how they interact with grandchildren and in the meanings they derive from these interactions. We also know a little about how each group perceives the other and about the benefits of these relationships.

Styles of Grandparenting

Because grandparents, like all other groups, are diverse, how they interact with their grandchildren, termed their **grandparenting style**, differs (Neugarten & Weinstein, 1964). The most common style, characterizing about one third of grandparents, is called formal. These grandparents see their role in fairly traditional terms, occasionally indulging the grandchild, occasionally baby-sitting, expressing a strong interest in the grandchild, but maintaining a "hands-off" attitude toward child rearing, leaving that aspect to the parents. A second common style is used by the fun seeker, whose relationship is characterized by informal playfulness. The distant grandparent appears mainly on holidays, birthdays, or other formal occasions with ritual gifts for the grandchild but otherwise has little contact with him or her. A few grandmothers are surrogate parents, filling in for working mothers. Finally, a few grandfathers play the role of dispenser of family wisdom, assuming an authoritarian position and offering information and advice.

Little research has examined how grandparents develop different styles. It appears that grandparents under age 65 are more likely to be fun seeking, whereas those over 65 tend to be more formal. Whether this difference is due to the age of the grandparent, the age of the grandchild, or generational differences between younger and older grandparents is unclear. Some evidence points to a combination of factors. Grandparents tend to be more playful with younger grandchildren, but as both groups age, a more formal rela-

Although the meanings and styles of grandparenting vary across individuals, most grandparents are like this grandfather and enjoy the time they spend with their grandchildren.

tionship emerges (Kahana & Kahana, 1970; Kalish, 1975).

Robertson (1977) offers an alternative description of grandparenting styles based on her study of 125 grandmothers. She identifies a social and a personal dimension of grandparenting. The social dimension emphasizes societal needs and expectations, whereas the personal dimension focuses on personal factors and individual needs. Four combinations of these dimensions are possible. The *appointed* type is high on both dimensions of grandmothering. These grandmothers are very involved with their grandchildren and are equally concerned with indulging them and with doing what is morally right for them. The *remote* type is detached and has low social and personal expectations about the grandmothering role. *Symbolic* grandmothers emphasize the normative and moral aspects of the grandmothering role, and they have few personal expectations. *Individualized* grandmothers emphasize the personal aspects of grandmothering and ignore the social or moral side of the relationship.

Additional support for Robertson's notion of social and personal dimensions comes from investigations of how grandparents influence their grandchildren's attitudes and life-style. Many grandparents recommend religious, social, and vocational values through storytelling, giving friendly advice, or working together on special projects (Cherlin & Furstenberg, 1986). In return, grandchildren keep grandparents updated on current cultural trends.

The Meaning of Grandparenthood

Research has shown that people derive several positive meanings from grandparenthood. Kivnick (1982) administered a lengthy questionnaire to 286 grandparents. Based on the statistical procedure of factor analysis, Kivnick identified five meanings of grandparenting: centrality, or the degree to which grandparenting is a primary role in one's life; value as an elder, or being perceived as a wise, helpful person; immortality through clan, in that the grandparent leaves behind not one but two generations; reinvolvement with one's personal past, by recalling relationships with one's own grandparents; and indulgence, or getting satisfaction from having fun with and spoiling one's grandchildren.

When we compare the meanings derived by grandparents with the styles of grandparenting, there appear to be several similarities. For example, the notion that grandparents have a tendency to spoil or indulge their grandchildren appears as both a style and a meaning. Because of these apparent similarities, S. S. Miller and Cavanaugh (1987) decided to investigate whether there were any systematic relationships. They reported two major findings. First, most grandparents find several sources of meaning in being a grandparent. Second, there are few consistent relationships between the style of grandparenting and the various sources of meaning. J. L. Thomas, Bence, and Meyer (1988) also found that the symbolic meaning of grandparenthood was of little importance to the satisfaction derived from being a grandparent. Thomas (1986a, 1986b) reports that satisfaction with grandparenthood is higher in grandmothers and that the opportunity to nurture and support grandchildren is an important source of satisfaction.

What these results imply is that we may not be able to describe specific standardized styles or meanings of grandparenthood. This is not that surprising, because grandparents are so diverse. Moreover, to expect that there should be consistencies between how a 50-year-old grandfather interacts with a 2-year-old grandson and how an 80-year-old grandmother interacts with her 18-year-old grandson may be ridiculous. Grandparent-grandchild relationships may well be too idiosyncratic to be described in general terms (Bengtson & Robertson, 1985).

Grandparents and Grandchildren

The relationships between grandparents and grandchildren vary with the age of the child. Younger children (up to age 10 or so) tend to be closer to their grandparents than older children. Grandparents also tend to enjoy younger grandchildren more because they are so responsive (Kahana & Kahana, 1970). Still, many adolescents and young adults view their grandparents as a special resource and value their relationships with them (Robertson, 1976). Most young adults think that adult grandchildren have a responsibility to help their grandparents when necessary and without pay (Robertson, 1986).

Relationships between grandparents and grandchildren may also vary with the sex of the child. Some authors have suggested that grandmothers and granddaughters have better relationships than do grandfathers and grandsons (Atchley, 1977; Hagestad, 1978). According to these writers, this may be due to the fact that the relationships are along the maternal kinkeeping line, supporting the speculation made in the previous section about middle-aged women and their role as kinkeepers.

When the grandparent-grandchild relationship is viewed from the child's perspective, another set of interesting findings emerges. When asked to provide written descriptions of their grandparents, children use a greater variety of descriptors for the grandparent with whom they have the more reciprocal relationship (Schultz, 1980). Children also attribute more perspective-taking ability and more feelings of attachment to their favorite grandparent.

A growing concern among grandparents is maintaining contact with grandchildren after a divorce of the parents (Johnson, 1988; Johnson & Barer, 1987). In some cases contact is broken by the former in-laws. In other cases paternal grandmothers actually expand their family network by maintaining contact with their grandchildren from their sons' first marriage as well as subsequent ones (Johnson & Barer, 1987). Overall, however, maternal grandmothers whose daughters have custody have more contact with grandchildren following their daughters' divorces, and paternal grandmothers have less contact following their sons' divorces if their son does not have custody of the grandchildren (Cherlin & Furstenberg, 1986; Johnson, 1983).

Ethnic Differences. Grandparenting styles and interaction patterns differ somewhat among ethnic groups. In the United States, for example, Black Americans, Asian Americans, Italian Americans, and Hispanic Americans are more likely to be involved in the lives of their grandchildren than members of other groups are. Differences within these ethnic groups are also apparent. Italian-American grandmothers tend to be much more satisfied and involved with grandparenting than Italian-American grandfathers, who tend to be more distant. Among Hispanic groups, Cuban Americans are least likely and Mexican Americans most likely to be involved with the daily lives of their descendants (Bengtson, 1985). Black grandmothers under age 40 feel pressured to provide care for a grandchild that they were not eager for, whereas those over age 60 tend to feel that they are fulfilling an important role.

Kornhaber (1985) notes that styles of grandparenting vary with ethnic background. This fact is highlighted by the case of an 18-month-old girl who had grandparents from two very different ethnic backgrounds, one pair Latin and one pair Nordic. Her Latin grandparents tickled, frolicked with, and doted over her. Her Nordic grandparents let her be but loved her no less. Her Latin mother thought the Nordic grandparents were "cold and hard," and her Nordic father thought his in-laws were "driving her crazy." The child, though, was perfectly content with both sets of grandparents.

The Changing Role of Grandparents. Grandparenting is not what it used to be. **Detachment** rather than involvement seems increasingly to characterize grandparent-grandchild relations (Bengtson & Robertson, 1985; Kornhaber & Woodward, 1981; Rodeheaver & Thomas, 1986). The reasons for a more detached style are many and complex. Increased geographical mobility

means that many grandparents live far away from their grandchildren, making visits less frequent and the relationship less intimate. Grandparents today are more likely to live independent lives apart from their children and grandchildren. Grandmothers are more likely to be employed themselves, thereby having less time to devote to caring for their grandchildren. Because of the rising divorce rate, some grandparents rarely see grandchildren who are living with a former son- or daughter-in-law. Finally, grandparents are not seen as the dispensers of child-rearing advice that they once were, so they tend to take a background role in order to maintain family harmony.

Most grandparents are comfortable with their reduced role and are quite happy to leave child rearing to the parents. In fact, those who feel responsible for advising their grandchildren tend to be less satisfied with the grandparenting role than those who feel that their role is mainly to enjoy their grandchildren (Thomas, 1986a).

Great-Grandparenthood

With increasing numbers of people, especially women, living to a very old age, the number of great-grandparents is rising rapidly. However, cohort trends in age at first marriage and age at parenthood also play a role. When these factors are combined, we find that most great-grandparents are women who married relatively young and had children and grandchildren who also married and had children relatively early.

Although little research has been conducted on this group, it is becoming clear that their sources of satisfaction and meaning differ somewhat from those of grandparents (Doka & Mertz, 1988; Wentkowski, 1985). Three aspects of great-grandparenthood appear to be most important (Doka & Mertz, 1988).

First, being a great-grandparent provides a sense of personal and family renewal. Their grandchildren have produced new life, renewing their own excitement for life and reaffirming the continuance of their lineage. Seeing their families stretch across four generations may also provide psychological support through feelings of symbolic immortality that help them face death. That is, they know that their families will live many years beyond their own lifetime.

Second, great-grandchildren provide diversion in great-grandparents' lives. There are now new things to do, places to go, and new people to share them with.

Third, becoming a great-grandparent is a milestone, a mark of longevity. The sense that one has lived long enough to see the fourth generation is perceived very positively.

For many reasons, such as geographical distance and health, most great-grandparents maintain a distant relationship with their great-grandchildren. Still, the vast majority (over 90%) are proud of their new status (Wentkowski, 1985). As we enter the 21st century and the number of elderly people increases, four-generation families may become the norm.

SUMMARY

We are accompanied through life by our social convoy, which consists of all the people with whom we have personal relationships. Friendships are important across the entire adult life span. They evolve through a three-step process: awareness, surface contact, and mutuality. Men tend to have fewer close friends than women. Friends play a major role in the life satisfaction of older adults.

Love consists of the combination of passion, intimacy, and commitment. It evolves across adulthood from infatuation to companionate love. However, the important components of

good love relationships remain unchanged in importance over time. Partners are selected after a three-step process, moving from the stimulus stage to the values stage to the roles stage.

Age at first marriage has been steadily increasing for several decades. Marriages based on homogamy are more likely to survive than marriages based on differences. Marital satisfaction is high during the honeymoon phase, declines during the child-rearing years, and increases after children leave home. Several types of marriages have been identified, each representing a distinct developmental pattern in terms of satisfaction and happiness.

Most American adults remain single for several years before marriage, but only a few never marry. Never-married people appear to have high life satisfaction by old age, despite often being subject to expectations that they should marry. Although cohabitation has increased dramatically, it is not viewed as a replacement for marriage. Most cohabitants view it as a prelude to eventual marriage, but women are more eager for this than are men. Homosexual relationships appear to have many characteristics in common with heterosexual relationships in terms of satisfaction. However, lesbian couples tend to be more committed to monogamy than are gay male couples.

Divorce rates have been rising steadily for several decades. Most divorces occur early in the marriage. The psychological effects of divorce are considerable and long lasting for both men and women. However, women suffer most in the long run, due to a severe decline in income and restriction of their social network. The vast majority of divorced people remarry within 3 years. Remarriages involving stepchildren are more likely to fail than first marriages. Widowhood is not necessarily difficult. Several different styles of widowhood have been identified. Men are typically older when widowed and are more likely to remarry.

Parenthood is a major decision that involves both benefits and costs. Single parents face serious financial and social problems that are more serious than many anticipate. When children leave the home, parents are typically not distraught but, rather, welcome the opportunity to rediscover their mate.

Middle-aged parents typically have positive relationships with their adult children. Some are faced with caring for their aging parent. Evidence indicates that all generations remain in relatively close contact with one another.

Grandparenting is enjoyed by most people in that role. Several different styles of grandparenting have been noted, as well as various meanings derived from the experience. Modern grandparents are more likely to develop distant relationships with their grandchildren.

GLOSSARY

cohabitation • Living together by two members of the opposite sex.

commitment • The willingness to stay with a person through good and bad times.

detachment • The lack of an active, day-to-day interest or involvement in a relationship.

friendship • A close relationship with another person that involves mutuality.

grandparenting style • The way in which grandparents interact with their grandchildren.

homogamy • A marriage based on similarity of interests, values, and expectations.

intimacy • The feeling that one can share all one's thoughts and actions with another.

kinkeepers • Members of the family, usually women,

who gather members together for celebrations and keep them in touch with one another.

launching • The process by which grown children leave the home.

passion • An intense physiological desire for someone.

point-in-time model • A conceptual system based on cross-sectional research of a specific topic, such as marital satisfaction.

postparental family • The stage in the family cycle after all of the children have moved out.

sandwich generation • Middle-agers, so called because of their position between their adult children and their elderly parents.

social convoy • The group with whom we have personal relationships throughout life.

ADDITIONAL READING

One of the most complete and readable studies of all types of couple relationships (marriage, cohabitation, and homosexual relationships) is

Blumstein, P., & Schwartz, P. (1983). *American couples*. New York: Morrow.

A summary of family and marital relations in old age can be found in

Sussman, M. B. (1985). The family life of old people. In R. H. Binstock & E. Shanas (Eds.), *Handbook of aging and the social sciences* (2nd ed.) (pp. 415–449). New York: Van Nostrand Reinhold.

Work, Leisure, and Retirement

Jacob Lawrence, *Builders*, 1980. Courtesy SAFECO
Insurance Companies, Seattle, Washington.

One of the most interesting under-graduates I ever met was Earl. Earl was not a typical student. He was obviously older than the average undergraduate, but that's not why he stood out. What made Earl different was that he was preparing to embark on his third occupation. For 24 years he was in the Air Force, first as a pilot and later as a staff officer. His military experiences were often exciting but scary, especially when bullets ripped through his cockpit as he was flying missions over Vietnam. On returning to the United States, he taught a number of congress-men and senators how to fly. He transferred to the staff of NATO, but dealing with politicians became so frustrating that he retired. At age 44 he began his second occupation, as an insurance salesman. Although he was promoted and did well, he became disenchanted and resigned after 5 years. At age 50 he went back to college to prepare for a third occupation, in physical therapy.

Earl has worked for all of his adult life. None of us should find that terribly exciting or unusual by itself. It is hard to imagine what adulthood would be like if we did not work. In fact, Sigmund Freud once wrote that love and work were the two defining aspects of adulthood. Work is such an important part of our lives that many people view themselves in terms of their occupation and judge others by theirs. In this chapter we will seek answers to several questions: Why do people work? How do people choose occupations? How do oc-cupations develop? What factors produce individual differences in occupational patterns? How do people spend time when they are not working? What happens to them after they retire? Along the way, we will see to what extent Earl and other people like him are typical of workers in general.

As will become clear, addressing issues about work is considerably easier when we consider middle-class White men than when we consider women or minorities. To date, most of the research on occupational development has focused on male patterns. Although more research on women and minorities is being conducted, we must be careful in applying existing research and theory to these other groups until data have been compiled.

THE MEANING OF WORK

In the 1960s the phrase "different strokes for different folks" was used to get across the point that people's motives and needs differ. Thus, work has different meanings for different people. Studs Terkel, the author of the fascinating book *Working* (1974), writes that work is "a search for daily meaning as well as daily bread, for recognition as well as cash, for astonishment rather than torpor; in short, for a sort of life rather than a Monday through Friday sort of dying. Perhaps immortality, too, is part of the quest" (p. xiii).

For some people, then, work is a source of prestige, social recognition, and a sense of worth. For others, the excitement of the activity or its creative growth potential makes work meaningful. But for most people, the main purpose of work is to earn a living. This is not to imply, of course, that money is the only reward in a job; things like friendships, the chance to exercise power, and feeling useful are also important. It is both the money that can be exchanged for life's necessities (and maybe a few luxuries, too) and the possibility for personal growth that provide the incentive for most of us to work.

Regardless of what they do for a living, people view their job as a key element in their sense of identity. This feeling can be observed most readily when people introduce themselves socially: "Hi, I'm Kevin. I'm an accountant. What do you do?" One's job affects one's life in a whole host of ways, from living place to friends to clothes to how one talks. In short, the impact of work cuts across all aspects of life. Work, then, is a major social role of adult life. This role, termed one's occupation, provides an important anchor that complements our other anchor, love relationships.

Occupations and Careers

In understanding work roles, terminology is important. The term **occupation** is applied to all forms of work, but the term **career** is sometimes reserved for prestigious occupations. In this view a career is an elite institution in Western society (Stevens-Long, 1988). Ritzer (1977) argues that people who have careers stay in one occupational field and progress through a series of stages to achieve upward mobility, greater responsibility, mastery, and financial compensation. From this perspective, university professors and lawyers in a large firm have careers; assembly line workers and secretaries do not.

Other authors disagree, viewing career as any organized path an individual takes across time and space—that is, any consistent, organized involvement in any role (Van Maanen & Schein, 1977). In this perspective physicians, carpenters, and housewives have several careers simultaneously: as workers, spouses, citizens, and so forth.

In this chapter I will use the term *occupation* rather than *career* to refer to work roles. As we will see, occupations are highly developmental. Even young children are in the midst of the social preparation for work, as evidenced by pretend play and prodding questions from adults such as "What do you want to be when you grow up?" School curricula, especially in high school and college, are geared toward preparing people for particular occupations. We develop our interests in various occupations over time, and the changes that occur in occupations represent some of the most important events in the life cycle. Before we explore occupations as developmental phenomena, however, we need to consider how different occupations are associated with different levels of social status.

Social Status and Occupations

Workers in the United States are not all viewed as equally valuable. How people are treated is, in part, a function of the kind of work they do, which is given a particular status in society. Occupational status is correlated with intellectual ability and achievement, although not perfectly.

Five general levels of workers can be identified: marginal workers, blue-collar workers, pink-collar workers, white-collar workers, and executives and professionals. Where one falls in this hierarchy influences life-style, well-being, and social recognition. We will consider the characteristics of each level briefly.

Marginal workers work occasionally, but never long enough with one employer to establish a continuous occupational history. In this sense they are similar to Super's (1980) unstable, or multiple trial, occupational patterns. (Super's theory is discussed later in this chapter.) Marginal workers' unstable working patterns are due to several factors, such as a lack of necessary language or other abilities, discrimination, a criminal record, or physical or mental disorders. The lack of steady employment has serious negative effects on most other aspects of their lives, such as increased marital distress.

Blue-collar occupations are those that do not require formal education past high school and may be based more on physical than intellectual skills. Blue-collar occupations vary tremendously, however, from unskilled labor to the highly complex trades of electricians and pipe fitters, for example. In general, there is little mobility in blue-collar occupations; moves typically reflect changes for better pay or job security or result from unemployment. One problem faced by blue-collar workers is being looked down on by supervisors and upper-middle-class professionals, and many express inferiority feelings (Terkel, 1974).

Pink-collar occupations are held primarily by women. These positions include office and clerical worker, bank teller, receptionist, and the like. Typically, these occupations do not pay high wages. Although men may hold some of these positions, such as bank teller, they do so only for short periods before they are promoted.

White-collar occupations are in offices rather than in factories or outdoors. Although the skills required are thought to be more intellectual than those needed for blue-collar occupations, white-collar workers are not always paid better. What they do get, however, is higher status. Many white-collar jobs require formal education beyond high school, although there is very little evidence that this education is always directly related to job performance. Unhappiness among white-collar workers comes mostly from their feeling that the extra time and expense for more education is not

sufficiently rewarded, and from middle-level managers' feelings that they have little real effect on corporate decision making.

Executives and professionals have the highest status as well as the highest education. They are in the optimal position to control their own occupational development and to obtain the rewards that most other workers cannot. Comparisons among executives and professionals are usually not in terms of salaries but in how far and how quickly they progress.

CHOOSING AN OCCUPATION

Because our work life is a major source of our identity, provides us with an official position, and influences our life-style and social interactions, choosing an occupation is a serious matter. In this section we will explore how occupations are chosen and some of the influences on those choices.

Theories of Occupational Choice

Although we tend to think of occupational choice as something done during adolescence or young adulthood, recent theories and research have increasingly adopted a life-course perspective (e.g., Adler & Aranya, 1984). The main theoretical frameworks for occupational choice have focused on aspects of one's personality (see Chapter 8). Holland (1973, 1985) takes a **trait-factor approach**, whereas others (e.g., Betz & Hackett, 1986; Lent & Hackett, 1987) apply Bandura's notion of **self-efficacy** or compare occupational choice to personal development (Gottfredson, 1981). We will consider each of these theories, as well as the influences exerted by families.

Holland's Theory. One approach to understanding how people choose occupations is based

TABLE 12.1 • Summary of Holland's personality types and their relationship to occupational choices

Investigative

The model type is task-oriented, intraceptive, asocial; prefers to think through rather than act out problems; needs to understand; enjoys ambiguous work tasks; has unconventional values and attitudes. Vocational preferences include aeronautical design engineer, anthropologist, astronomer, biologist, botanist, chemist, editor of a scientific journal, geologist, independent research scientist, meteorologist, physicist, scientific research worker, writer of scientific or technical articles, zoologist.

Social

The model type is sociable, responsible, feminine, humanistic, religious; needs attention; has verbal and interpersonal skills; avoids intellectual problem solving, physical activity, and highly ordered activities; prefers to solve problems through feelings and interpersonal manipulations of others. Vocational preferences include assistant city school superintendent, clinical psychologist, director of welfare agency, foreign missionary, high school teacher,

juvenile delinquency expert, marriage counselor, personal counselor, physical education teacher, playground director, psychiatric case worker, social science teacher, speech therapist, vocational counselor.

Realistic

The model type is masculine; physically strong, unsociable, aggressive; has good motor coordination and skill; lacks verbal and interpersonal skills; prefers concrete to abstract problems; conceives of himself as being aggressive and masculine and as having conventional political and economic values. Persons who choose or prefer the following occupations resemble this type: airplane mechanic, construction inspector, electrician, filling station attendant, fish and wildlife specialist, locomotive engineer, master plumber, photoengraver, power shovel operator, power station operator, radio operator, surveyor, tree surgeon, tool designer.

Artistic

The model type is asocial; avoids problems that are highly structured or require gross physical skills; re-

(Source: John Holland, *Making Vocational Choices: A Theory of Vocational Personalities and Work Environments*, © 1985, pp. 19–22. Adapted by permission of Prentice-Hall, Inc., Englewood Cliffs, N.J.)

on the idea that they seek to optimize the fit between their individual traits, such as personality, intelligence, skills, and abilities, and their occupational interests. Holland (1973, 1985) developed a theory based on this idea. He categorizes occupations by the interpersonal settings in which people must function as well as their associated life-style. He identifies six personality types that combine these factors; they are summarized in Table 12.1.

Support for Holland's personality types comes from other research examining the relationship between personality and occupational choice. Re-

search comparing his types with Costa and McCrae's five dimensions of personality (see Chapter 8) suggests considerable overlap (Costa, McCrae, & Holland, 1984). For instance, his social and enterprising types fell into Costa and McCrae's extroversion dimension.

The congruence between traits and occupational selection in Holland's theory exists at the level of interest, not at the level of performance requirements per se. He predicts that people will choose the occupation that has the greatest similarity to their personality type. By doing this, they optimize their ability to express themselves, apply sembles the investigative type in being intraceptive and asocial; but differs from that type in that he has a need for individualistic expression, has less ego strength, is more feminine, and suffers more frequently from emotional disturbances; prefers dealing with environmental problems through self-expression in artistic media. Vocational preferences include art dealer, author, cartoonist, commercial artist, composer, concert singer, dramatic coach, free-lance writer, musical arranger, musician, playwright, poet, stage director, symphony conductor.

Conventional

The model type prefers structured verbal and numerical activities and subordinate roles; is conforming (extraceptive); avoids ambiguous situations and problems involving interpersonal relationships and physical skills; is effective at well-structured tasks; identifies with power; values material possessions and status. Vocational preferences include bank examiner, bank teller, bookkeeper, budget reviewer, cost estimator, court stenographer, financial analyst, computer equipment operator, inventory controller, payroll clerk, quality control expert, statistician, tax expert, traffic manager.

Enterprising

The model type has verbal skills for selling, dominating, leading; conceives of himself as a strong, masculine leader; avoids well-defined language or work situations requiring long periods of intellectual effort; is extraceptive; differs from the conventional type in that he prefers ambiguous social tasks and has a greater concern with power, status, and leadership; is orally aggressive. Vocational preferences include business executive, buyer, hotel manager, industrial relations consultant, manufacturer's representative, master of ceremonies, political campaign manager, real-estate salesperson, restaurant worker, speculator, sports promoter, stock and bond salesperson, television producer, traveling salesperson.

their skills, and take on new roles. Occupational satisfaction, for Holland, is maximized by having a good match between personality and occupation. Indeed, Spokane (1985) documented the relationship between such a congruence and occupational persistence, occupational choice, occupational stability, and work satisfaction.

Holland's theory does not mean that personality completely determines what occupation one chooses. The connection is that certain occupations are typically chosen by people who act or feel a certain way. Most of us would rather do something that we like to do than something we are forced to do. Thus, unless we have little choice due to financial or other constraints, we typically choose occupations on that basis. When mismatches occur, people usually adapt by changing jobs, changing interests, or adapting the job to provide a better match.

Although the relationships between personality and occupational choice are important, we must recognize that there are limits. Men and women are differentially represented in Holland's types (Costa et al., 1984). Regardless of age, women are more likely than men to be in the social, artistic, and conventional types. Additionally,

Holland's theory ignores the context in which the decision is made. For example, he overlooks the fact that many people may not have much choice in the kind of job they can get because of external factors such as family, financial pressures, or ethnicity. There are also documented changes in congruence between personality type and occupation across adulthood (Adler & Aranya, 1984). In short, we must recognize that what occupation we choose is related not only to what we are like but also to the dynamic interplay between us and the social situation we are in.

Self-Efficacy and Occupational Choice. Occupational choice is also strongly influenced by what we think of ourselves. All of us evaluate our abilities in terms of our strengths and weaknesses. Since we are likely to shy away from doing things that we think we have little ability to do, we tend to choose occupations that match what we think we may be able to do. Bandura (1982) terms this self-evaluation process self-efficacy.

Self-efficacy theory has had a considerable impact on conceptualizations of occupational choice (Lent & Hackett, 1987). In particular, it is becoming clear that it is what we *think* we are good at that determines occupational choice, not what we are *actually* good at. In fact, the two are often completely unrelated (Panek & Sterns, 1985). It turns out that the more efficacious that people judge themselves to be, the wider the range of occupational options they consider appropriate and the better they prepare themselves educationally for different occupational pursuits. People who have less confidence in themselves tend to limit their options, even when they have the true ability to engage in a wide range of occupations (Betz & Hackett, 1986; Lent & Hackett, 1987).

Self-efficacy theory also helps us understand differences between men and women and between Whites and minorities in occupational choices (Bandura, 1988). Cultural practices that convey lower expectations for women, stereotypical gender roles, sex-typed behaviors, and structural barriers to advancement eventually lower one's self-efficacy. Consequently, women and minorities may limit their interests and range of occupational options by the belief that they lack the ability for occupations traditionally occupied by White men, even though they do not differ from White men in actual ability.

Occupational Choice as Personal Development. Gottfredson (1981) points out that aspiring to various occupations parallels the development of the self. In particular, she argues that the development of self-concept during childhood and adolescence is a driving force behind occupational choices in adulthood. During childhood we develop an orientation to the size and power of people and things, to sex roles, to what society values, and to the unique self. This developmental sequence is strongly conditioned by cognitive development (see Chapter 6) and one's social environment. Gottfredson notes that all social groups share the same image of occupations but differ in their perceived opportunities for implementing their choices. In adulthood we learn how to compromise our choices and our priorities in our actual occupational selections.

Although Gottfredson's theory has not been widely adopted, it represents much promise. It is one of the only theories of occupational choice that takes cognitive development and social background into account, and it provides a rationale for the kinds of compromises that adults make.

Family Influences. Families may influence occupational choices directly by guiding children in specific directions, such as by sending them to a particular school, by getting them to participate in athletic activities, by providing musical or other instruction, or by exerting pressure on them to continue the family tradition. As the major socializing force, families are the context in which personality types and self-efficacy are shaped.

College freshmen typically express their tentative occupational choices in ways that reflect familial expectations and values by choosing majors that fit their parents' expectations (Venerable, 1974). Contrary to popular belief, however, as their education progresses, students become *less* certain about their initial occupational choices as they are exposed to more and different information about occupational options (Blocher & Raposa, 1981).

Families may also influence occupational selection by shaping children's values and interests. For example, parental attitudes toward certain occupations, whether highly positive or negative, often provide a way to learn how parents are likely to react when children eventually make their first tentative choices. Indeed, in a series of studies Mortimer found that the jobs chosen by sons tended to be similar to their fathers' in terms of work-related values (Mortimer, 1974, 1976; Mortimer & Kumka, 1982).

Furthermore, where a family lives indirectly influences occupational choice. Young people who grow up in large urban centers like New York or Los Angeles, for example, are far less likely to consider farming as an occupation than someone growing up in rural Iowa. Additionally, the overall socioeconomic status of the family is related to the occupational expectations and values that sons have. Sons of professional fathers may learn to aspire to professional occupations for themselves, and they will probably have the opportunity to acquire the education to achieve them. Whether this intergenerational transmission of occupational orientation is strong seems to depend on the closeness of the father-son relationship and on during what time in the child's life the father enjoyed high occupational status.

Whether the transmission of values is a major factor in women's occupational choices is less ap-

parent. There is some evidence of a relationship between high SES and the choice of a nontraditional occupation, such as science (Burlin, 1976). For women, it appears that the best predictors of occupational orientations, expectations, and achievements are whether their mother worked during childhood or adolescence and the nature of the father-daughter relationship. Women whose mother was employed are much more likely to have an occupation themselves (Auster & Auster, 1981), perhaps because working mothers serve as role models for their daughters. In addition, having a father who supports the daughter's choice for an occupation by encouraging her to achieve and by providing her the opportunity to do so is also important. Fathers who provide support show their daughters that having an occupation does not mean forgoing male approval (Weitz, 1977).

Grotevant and Cooper (1988) have considered all of these issues and incorporated them into a dynamic interactional model of occupational exploration by adolescents and young adults. They emphasize the importance of considering several variables in terms of how they are fostered by the family: parent-child relationships, individual competence, personality dimensions (self-esteem, ego control, ego resiliency), and potential intellectual ability. All of these variables are major influences on occupational choice. Additionally, they recognize that ethnicity and socioeconomic status have important effects on family dynamics and, by extension, occupational choice.

Sex Differences in Occupational Choice

Men and women differ on many dimensions in their occupational preparation. Different experiences begin early in life, during the period of occupational socialization, and continue even after retirement.

Men are groomed for future employment. Boys learn at an early age that men are known by the work they do, and they receive strong encouragement for thinking about what occupation they would like to have. Occupational achievement is stressed as a core element of masculinity. Important social skills are taught through team games, in which they learn how to play by the rules, to accept setbacks without taking defeat personally, to follow the guidance of the leader, and to move up the leadership hierarchy by demonstrating qualities that are valued by others.

Women have traditionally not been so well trained. The skills that they have been taught are quite different—how to be accommodative and supportive—and they have received little in the way of occupation-related skills (Shainess, 1984). However, the women's movement has stressed the importance of providing girls the necessary skills for occupations outside the home. Given that more than half of women are now employed and that this trend will probably continue, it is especially important that women be exposed to the same occupational socialization opportunities as men.

Attention to women's occupational choices is relatively recent (Betz & Fitzgerald, 1987), due mainly to the assumptions that women's primary roles were housewife and mother and that occupations were important only to single women. Perhaps as a result of the influence of these stereotypes, occupational choices and developmental patterns differ between men and women. For example, one study found that male college seniors with a "C+" average believed they were capable of earning a Ph.D. but that women with a "B+" average thought they were incapable of doing so (Baird, 1973). Even a year after graduation women with an "A" average were no more likely to be attending graduate or professional schools than were men with a "B" average

(Barnett & Baruch, 1978). These findings fit with the self-efficacy theory of occupational selection discussed earlier, and they indicate the strength of the effects that early differences in socialization can have on subsequent occupational achievement.

One controversial topic in occupational selection concerns women's decisions to "specifically and intentionally avoid high-prestige occupations" (Barnett & Baruch, 1978, p. 133). Although this conclusion fits data cited earlier on women's likelihood to seek postgraduate training and the notion that women have a fear of success, we must be careful not to read too much into these findings. That is, women may be reluctant to enter high-status occupations because of genuine roadblocks, such as hiring and pay discrimination, rather than because they are afraid to try.

Although it is still too early to tell, as women continue to move into the work force, the ways in which they choose occupations are likely to become more similar to the processes that men use. Whereas research on occupational choice before the 1970s tended to focus on men, more recent research routinely includes women. Over the next decade it is likely that we will see even fewer differences between men and women in the ways in which they decide to pursue occupations.

OCCUPATIONAL DEVELOPMENT

Deciding that one would like to become a computer programmer is only an initial step toward an occupation in computer science. Some of the additional steps are pretty obvious; for example, getting the proper training is essential, as is finding that first job. But for most of us, getting a first job is not enough. We would like not only to keep the job but also to advance in it. How quickly occupational advancement occurs (or does not) may lead to such labels as "fast-tracker" or "dead-ender" (Kanter, 1976). People who want to advance learn quickly how long to stay at one level and how to seize opportunities as they occur; others quickly learn the frustration of remaining in the same job with no chance for promotion.

How we advance through our occupation seems to be related to several factors beyond those important in choosing an occupation. Among these are expectations, support from co-workers, priorities, and job satisfaction. All of these help us face what psychologists call early professional socialization, in other words, what we are expected to do in our occupation. Before we consider these aspects, however, we will look at a general scheme of occupational development.

A General Framework of Occupational Development

No one is more responsible for conceptualizing occupations as developmental than Super. Over 4 decades Super (1957, 1980) developed a theory of occupational development based on self-concept. He proposes that occupations progress through five distinct stages that result from changes in individuals' self-concept and adaptation to an occupational role: implementation, establishment, maintenance, deceleration, and retirement. People are located along a continuum of **vocational maturity** through their working years; the more congruent their occupational behaviors are with what is expected of them at different ages, the more vocationally mature they are.

The implementation stage occurs during late adolescence. During this time people take a series of temporary positions in which they learn firsthand about work roles. This socialization process includes learning about responsibility and productivity, co-worker friendships, and life-styles of working adults. This series of positions helps individuals identify what types of occupations are attractive and fit their needs, self-concept, and expectations. Havighurst (1982) terms this period the trial work period and points out that it is typically very unstable.

The establishment stage begins with the selection of a specific occupation, which occurs during young adulthood, and continues through a period of years marked by stability, achievement, and advancement. During this time the typical worker may change jobs or positions within a company, but only rarely does he or she change occupations. For example, a person is likely to move from an entry-level to a supervisory position in the same company but is unlikely to go from working as an accountant to working as a plumber. During the establishment stage the worker's self-concept becomes more congruent with his or her occupation.

The third stage, termed the maintenance stage, is a period of transition that usually occurs during middle age (typically between ages 45 and 55). Workers begin to reduce the amount of time they spend in their work roles, mainly because they believe that they have either already accomplished their occupational goals or will never attain them. The drive to achieve diminishes, and simply maintaining one's occupation becomes dominant. This stage is reminiscent of Levinson and his colleagues' (1978) description of mid-life development, described in Chapter 8.

As workers near 60, they begin the deceleration stage. Preparation for retirement begins in earnest for most people, interest in leisure activities increases, and the process of separating oneself from one's occupation begins. Whether this separation process is easy or difficult depends on how much of one's identity comes from one's occupation. To the extent that one identifies very strongly with one's occupation, the separation process is more difficult.

Finally, most workers enter the retirement stage, in which they stop working full time. Because the final sections of this chapter deal with the specific issues involved with retirement, we will not consider them here.

Super's framework is important because it emphasizes that occupations are not static once they are chosen. Rather, they evolve in response to changes in the person's self-concept. Consequently, occupations are a developmental process that reflects and explains important life changes.

Women and Occupational Development

As noted earlier, interest in women's occupational choices is relatively recent. For many years research on women's occupational development was based on the assumption that most women saw their primary roles as housewife and mother (Betz & Fitzgerald, 1987). Consequently, descriptions of women's occupational development were predicated on this assumption, and continuous employment outside the home was viewed as nontraditional. More recently, researchers have changed their descriptions to reflect the fact that most women work outside the home.

Betz (1984) examined the occupational histories of 500 college women 10 years after graduation. Two thirds of these women were highly committed to their occupations, which for 70% were traditionally female ones. Most had worked continuously since graduation. Only 1% had been full-time homemakers during the entire 10-year period; 79% reported that they had successfully combined occupations with homemaking. Concerning occupational development, women in traditional female occupations were less likely to change occupations. If they did change, the move was more likely to be downward than were the changes made by women in nontraditional occupations.

Making It to the Top: Sex Discrimination. Women in high-status jobs are unusual. It was not until 1981 that a woman was appointed to the U.S. Supreme Court, few women serve in the highest ranks of major corporations, and women are largely outnumbered in the faculties of most universities and colleges.

One intuitively appealing reason for the paucity of women in top-level jobs is work overload. Overload results when women with occupations outside the home are also expected to perform most of the day-to-day housekeeping chores and child care. Instead of one occupation, these women are expected to have two. Contrary to intuition, however, work overload is usually not a factor. Far more important is **sex discrimination**, denying a job to someone solely on the basis of gender.

Baron and Bielby (1985) pull no punches in discussing sex discrimination. "Our analyses portray [sex] discrimination as pervasive, almost omnipresent, sustained by diverse organizational structures and processes. Moreover, this segregation drastically restricts women's career opportunities, by blocking access to internal labor markets and their benefits" (Baron & Bielby, 1985, p. 245). Women are being kept out of high-status jobs by the men at the top.

Women sometimes refer to a "glass ceiling," the level to which they may rise in a company but beyond which they may not go. This problem is most obvious in companies that classify jobs at various levels (as does the civil service). DiPrete and Soule (1988) found that the greatest disadvantage facing women occurred near the boundary between lower-tier and upper-tier job grades. Women tend to move to the top of the lower tier and remain there, whereas men are typically promoted to the upper tier, even when other factors, such as personal attributes and qualifications, are controlled.

Beyond discrimination in hiring and promotion, women are also the victims of pay discrimination. In many occupations men are paid substantially more than women in the same positions. Why? Traditionally, the attitude was that men had families to support, whereas women were working just to have something to do. Obviously, this is untrue. Many working women are the primary, if not the sole, source of support for their family and should not be paid less. This issue of **pay equity** for men and women in the same position has been expanded to include the issue of **comparable worth**. The principle behind comparable worth is that women in traditionally female occupations (secretaries, nurses, teachers, and so forth) should not be paid less than men in traditionally male occupations (construction workers, factory workers, and so on), providing that the skills required in the job, the job level, and the perceived importance of the work are comparable. Comparable worth continues to be a controversial legal area, and it will undoubtedly be debated for several years to come.

Sex and pay discrimination against women are even more unjustified given the amount of effort that women devote to work. Some authors (e.g., Becker, 1985) assert that family responsibilities keep women from devoting as much time to work as men. But Bielby and Bielby (1988) found no support for this assumption. In fact, they report that, on average, most women (65% to 70%) actually devote more time to work than do men with similar household responsibilities and occupations.

Although statutes have been passed to prohibit discrimination in the workplace, real change is unlikely without fundamental changes in social attitudes. Until we inculcate the belief that men and women should be provided equal opportunities for all occupations and that everyone should be paid on the basis of the kind of work done rather than gender, these problems will remain.

Age Discrimination and Occupational Development

Another structural barrier to occupational development is **age discrimination**, which involves denying a job or promotion to someone solely on the basis of age. The federal Age Discrimination in Employment Act is intended to promote the employment of workers between the ages of 40 and 70 based on their ability rather than their age. Under this law employers are banned from refusing to hire or to discharge workers solely on the basis of age or from segregating or classifying workers or otherwise affecting their status on that basis.

Age discrimination occurs in several ways (Snyder & Barrett, 1988). For example, employers can make certain types of physical or mental performance a job requirement and argue that older workers are incapable of it, or they can make cuts in the number of employees in an attempt to get rid of older workers by using mandatory retirement. Over 600 federal court cases have been filed since 1970 concerning age discrimination. Snyder and Barrett (1988) reviewed these cases and found that the employer had been favored about 65% of the time. Job-performance information was crucial in all cases; however, this information was usually presented in terms of general differences between young and old. Surprisingly, many courts did not question inaccurate information or stereotypical views of aging presented by employers, despite the lack of scientific data documenting age differences in actual job performance.

On the basis of their review Snyder and Barrett argue that findings from gerontological research need to be given to federal courts to help clarify their decision making. Indeed, much of the research in this chapter supports the conclusion that older workers are capable of performing at high levels of competence.

Social Status and Occupational Development

How does social status affect occupational development? In a comprehensive analysis of many studies, Jencks and his associates (1979) reached several important conclusions about men's occupational success defined in terms of who earns the most money. They found that occupational success was related to four factors: (1) Family and racial-ethnic background was the most important determinant. Sons of professional fathers earned the most, and Whites outearned Blacks. (2) Number of years of formal education was the second most important factor. (3) Intelligence was the third most important predictor of success. (4) Personality traits were also significant predictors.

The Jencks et al. study showed that there was no single determinant of occupational success. Many factors, from family to even luck, come together to influence how well we do in our occupation. It must also be remembered that not everyone defines occupational success in financial terms, so that the factors important in terms of pay may not be as important when success is defined in other ways (e.g., personal freedom, autonomy).

Occupational Expectations

Individuals form opinions about what it will be like to work in a particular occupation based on what they learn in school and from their parents. People tend to set goals regarding what they want to become and when they hope to get there. This tendency is so common, in fact, that in their theory of adult male development Levinson and his colleagues (1978) maintain that forming a **dream**, as they put it, is one of the young adult's chief tasks.

A major task throughout one's occupation is to refine and update occupational expectations. Refining the dream typically involves trying to live up to one's goal, monitoring one's progress toward the goal, and changing or even abandoning the goal as necessary. For some, modifying goals comes as a result of failure (such as changing from a business major because one is failing economics courses), racial or sexual discrimination, lack of opportunity, obsolescence of skills, economic reasons, or changing interests. In some cases one's initial choice may have simply been unrealistic; for example, nearly half of all young adults would like to become professionals (such as lawyers or physicians), but only one person in seven actually makes it (Cosby, 1974).

Whenever a person finds that he or she needs to modify occupational goals, the situation produces stress. And even though some modification is essential from time to time, it usually comes as a surprise that we could be wrong about what seemed to be a logical choice at the time. As Gina put it, "I really thought I wanted to be a flight attendant; the travel sounded really interesting. But it just wasn't what I expected."

Perhaps the rudest jolt for most of us comes during the transition from school to the "real world," where things just never seem to happen the way the textbooks say that they are supposed to. This **reality shock** (Van Maanen & Schein, 1977) befalls everyone, from the young mother who discovers that newborns demand an incredible amount of time to the accountant who learns that the financial forecast that took days to prepare may simply end up in a file cabinet. The visionary aspects of the dream may not disappear altogether, but a good hearty dose of reality goes a long way toward bringing a person down to earth and comes to play an increasingly important role in one's occupation and self-concept. For example, the woman who thought that she would receive the same rewards as her male counterparts for comparable work is likely to become increasingly angry and disillusioned when her successes result in smaller raises and fewer promotions.

Support for Levinson's idea that men build an occupational dream and the idea that the dream must contend with reality shock comes from a longitudinal study begun in 1956 by the American Telephone and Telegraph Company (AT&T). The goal of the research was to study the variables related to personality and ability that could predict occupational success and satisfaction (Bray, Campbell, & Grant, 1974). In the initial sample were 422 White males from a pool of lower-level managers from which future upper-level managers would be chosen. Some subjects were college graduates hired at the manager level, and the remainder were men without a college degree who had been promoted through the ranks.

The findings revealed considerable support for both Levinson's dream and a period of reality shock (A. Howard & Bray, 1980). Young managers began their occupations full of expectations but rapidly became more realistic. By the time the college-educated men were 29 years old, on average, and the noncollege men were 34, the strong desire to advance further through additional promotions had decreased markedly. Reasons for this decline included family disruption due to the need to move following a promotion and the lack of desire to devote more time to work, which would be required on entering upper-level management. Interestingly, these men were not dissatisfied with their jobs. In fact, they found a great deal of challenge, and their intrinsic motivation levels did not drop despite their reluctance to advance.

Although the AT&T study provided important insights, its limitations must be recognized. The inclusion of only White males means that the

developmental trends for other groups is largely unknown. Second, only white-collar workers with the potential of moving up the corporate ladder were studied. People in service, unskilled, and blue-collar jobs probably differ in important ways, since their potential for upward mobility is limited.

The Role of Mentors

Imagine how hard it would be to learn a new occupation with no support from other people around you. Fortunately, this is usually not necessary; most people are "shown the ropes" by another co-worker, typically an older, more experienced person. This person who provides the guidance has been called a **mentor** (Levinson et al., 1978).

A mentor is part teacher, part sponsor, part model, and part counselor. The mentor helps a young worker avoid trouble ("Beware of what you say around Bentley") and provides invaluable information about the many unwritten rules that govern day-to-day activities in the workplace (not working too fast on the assembly line, wearing the right clothes, and so on). As part of the relationship, a mentor makes sure that his or her protégé is noticed and receives credit for good work from supervisors. As a result, occupational success often depends on the quality of the mentor-protégé relationship. Consequently, mentors fulfill two main functions: improving the protégé's chances for advancement and promoting his or her psychological and social well-being (Kram, 1980, 1985; Kram & Isabella, 1985; Noe, 1987).

Playing the role of a mentor is also a developmental phase in one's occupation. Helping a younger employee learn the job fulfills aspects of Erikson's (1982) phase of generativity. In particular, the mentor is making sure that there is some continuity in the field by passing on the accumulated knowledge and experience he or she has

The guidance provided by an older worker through the mentor-protege relationship can be a key factor in successful career development.

gained by being in it for a while. This function of the mentor is part of middle-agers' attempts at ensuring the continuity of society and accomplishing or producing something worthwhile (Erikson, 1982).

The mentor-protégé relationship develops over time. Based on her in-depth study, Kram (1985) proposes a four-stage sequence. The first stage, initiation, constitutes the 6- to 12-month period during which the protégé selects a mentor and they begin to develop their relationship. The second stage, cultivation, lasts from 2 to 5 years and is the most active phase of the mentoring relationship. This is the period when the mentor provides considerable occupational assistance and serves as a confidant. The third stage, separation, is the most difficult. It begins when the protégé receives a promotion, often to the level of the mentor. The protégé must emerge from the protection of the mentor in order to demonstrate his or her own competence. Both parties experience

feelings of loneliness and separation. The final period is redefinition. In this period the protégé and mentor reestablish their relationship but with a new set of rules based more on friendship between peers.

Research on the selection of mentors by young adults reveals that potential mentors' interpersonal skills are the single most important factor (Olian, Carroll, Giannantonio, & Feren, 1988). Additonally, protégés are attracted to mentors who are connected in the organization and who are older than themselves.

Some authors think that women have a greater need for a mentor than men (Busch, 1985). However, women seem to have a more difficult time finding an adequate mentor. One reason is that female role models who could serve a mentoring function are scarce, especially in upper-level management. Only 7% of the women in the work force are in administrative, executive, or managerial jobs, compared with 12% of men

(U.S. Department of Labor, 1988). This is an unfortunate situation, especially in view of the fact that women who have female mentors are significantly more productive than women with male mentors (Goldstein, 1979). Although many young women report that they would feel comfortable with a male mentor (Olian et al., 1988), there are additional problems beyond productivity. Several researchers note that cross-sex mentor-protégé relationships produce conflict and tension resulting from possible sexual overtones, even when there has been no overtly sexual behavior on anyone's part (Kram, 1985).

Occupational Priorities

To a large extent the occupational aspirations one has are a function of one's **occupational priorities**. Such things as fame, money, and helping others may motivate people to run for public office, work at a second job, or enter social work. If we know a worker's priorities, what he or she values most, then we are in a good position to understand what things about an occupation are probably satisfying or unsatisfying.

Much has been written about an apparent shift in priorities among young people today compared with a generation ago. For example, it is asserted that young people are no longer willing to be just another person in a corporate machine and that they value personal growth above monetary gain. As with most generalizations part of this notion is true and part is not. It does seem to be the case that today's college students are more concerned with occupations that have positive social effects. They also seem to desire occupations that are challenging and that offer the chance for personal growth. However, they still believe that hard work leads to fame and fortune and that material gains are an appropriate goal (L. Y. Jones, 1980; Yankelovich, 1981).

Differences in occupational priorities were made clear in a second longitudinal study conducted by AT&T, begun in 1977, which was designed to parallel the original study started in 1956 (Howard & Bray, 1982). In the 1970s managers at AT&T were more diverse; almost half were women, and one third were minorities. No differences between the younger and older groups were found in intellectual ability (although the younger group was better educated), need for achievement, or personal work standards.

Key differences emerged in motivation for upward mobility, leadership, and desire for emotional support. The younger managers' expectations of rewards from work were much lower; they did not see most of their major rewards or life satisfactions coming from work. This view contrasted sharply with the older managers' high work motivation and early desire for promotion. The younger managers also had a lower desire to be responsible for subordinates and to direct others. Finally, they had a much stronger desire to provide emotional support to co-workers.

The findings at AT&T, depicted in Figure 12.1, are not unique. Other research has also documented the move away from materialism, power seeking, upward mobility, and competition toward an emphasis on individual freedom, personal growth, and cooperation (Jones, 1980; Yankelovich, 1981). Howard and Bray (1980) note that changes in workers' priorities may have significant implications for the effectiveness of our work socialization systems.

Expectation of a financially and personally rewarding occupation is praiseworthy. It may also be asking for trouble after reality shock hits, since very few jobs offer perfect combinations of material and personal reward. As a result many people become disenchanted with their jobs. Terkel (1974) documented many of these reactions: "I'm a machine" (a spot-welder). "A monkey could do what I do" (a receptionist). "I'm an object" (a model). Disillusionment occurs in all types of

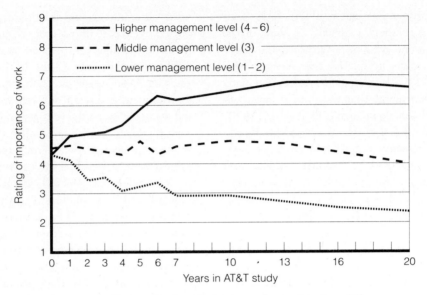

FIGURE 12.1 • Changes in the relative importance of work at different levels of management in the AT&T study.

(Source: *Career Motivation in Mid-Life Managers* by A. Howard and D. W. Bray, 1980, paper presented at the annual meeting of the American Psychological Association, Montreal. Reprinted with permission of the author.)

occupations, from the assembly-line worker who feels like a robot to the high-level corporate executive who feels like a small piece of a giant machine. Such shattered expectations must have an effect on another important factor in occupational development, job satisfaction.

Job Satisfaction

What does it mean to be satisfied with one's job or occupation? In a general sense **job satisfaction** is the positive feeling that results from an appraisal of one's work (Locke, 1976). In research, specific aspects such as satisfaction with working conditions, pay, and co-workers are considered. In practice, American workers actually have

a multidimensional conceptualization of job satisfaction.

Due to the complex nature of job satisfaction, most jobs end up being satisfying in some ways (e.g., achievement and power) and not in others (e.g., pay and working conditions). Factors that make jobs satisfying at one time may become less important the longer one is in an occupation or as new concerns are raised in society. For example, concern over health and safety problems played a much more important role in job satisfaction in the late 1970s than it did a decade earlier (Quinn & Staines, 1979). Additionally, occupational values change over time; military personnel and politicians have lost some of the prestige that they once had, while environmentally oriented jobs have increased in social worth. Given that the structural elements of a job (e.g., working conditions) affect satisfaction, an important question is whether the age of the worker is also related to his or her job satisfaction.

Almost all of the studies that have investigated the relationship between overall job satisfaction and age have found a low to moderate increase in satisfaction with increasing age (e.g., James & Jones, 1980; Schwab & Heneman, 1977). However, there are several important qualifications that need to be made in relation to this finding.

First, the relationship between worker age and job satisfaction is complex. Satisfaction does not increase in all areas with age. It appears that older workers are more satisfied with the intrinsic personal aspects of their jobs than they are with the extrinsic aspects, such as pay (Morrow & McElroy, 1987).

Second, increases in job satisfaction may not be due to age alone but, rather, to the degree to which there is a good fit between the worker and the job (Holland, 1985). From this perspective it is not surprising that increasing age should be related to increased job satisfaction: older workers have simply had more time to find a job that they like or may have simply resigned themselves to the fact that things are unlikely to improve, resulting in a better congruence between worker desires and job attributes (Barrett, 1978). A. T. White and Spector (1987) showed that the relationship between age and job satisfaction was due mainly to congruence and having an appropriate sense of control over one's job. Older workers also may have revised their expectations over the years so to better reflect the actual state of affairs. Because expectations become more realistic and are therefore more likely to be fulfilled, job satisfaction increases over time (Hulin & Smith, 1965).

Third, work becomes less of a focus in men's lives as they age and achieve occupational success (Bray & Howard, 1980). This process of disengagement from work can begin as early as the 30s for men who are not advancing rapidly in their occupations, but it comes somewhat later in men who achieve some degree of success. Consequently, for many men it takes less to keep them satisfied due to lower work motivation.

A fourth reason why job satisfaction increases with age may be that men discover different sources of satisfaction. As men stay in an occupation longer, they begin to find satisfaction in different ways. For example, they derive pleasure from accomplishing tasks and from becoming independent in their work (Bray & Howard, 1980). Interestingly, lower-level managers become more nurturant as time goes on, but the men at the top of the hierarchy become progressively more remote and detached and less sympathetic and helpful (A. Howard, 1984).

Finally, there is a growing awareness that job satisfaction may be cyclical. That is, it may show periodic fluctuations that are not related to age per se but, rather, to changes that people intentionally make in their occupations (Shirom & Mazeh, 1988). The idea is that job satisfaction increases over time because people change jobs or responsibilities on a regular basis, thereby keeping their occupation interesting and challenging. This provocative idea of periodicity in job satisfaction is explored further in "How Do We Know?"

CHANGING OCCUPATIONS

In the past it was quite common for people to choose an occupation during young adulthood and stay in it throughout their working years. Today, such one-time selections are far less common.

HOW · DO · WE · KNOW?

Periodicity and Job Satisfaction

As noted in the text, there is considerable evidence that job satisfaction tends to increase with age. Why this is true has been the subject of considerable debate. One hypothesis is that changes in job satisfaction are actually related to job seniority, or job tenure. The idea is that satisfaction tends to be high in the beginning of a job, to stabilize or drop during the middle phase, and to rise again later. Each time a person changes jobs, the cycle repeats.

Shirom and Mazeh (1988) decided to study the cyclical nature of job satisfaction systematically. They collected questionnaire data from a representative sample of 900 Israeli junior high school teachers with up to 23 years of seniority. The questionnaire contained items concerning teachers' satisfaction with salary, working hours, social status, contacts with pupils, autonomy, opportunities for professional growth, and opportunities for carrying out educational goals. The focus of analysis was on year-to-year changes in satisfaction.

Using a statistical technique called spectral analysis, Shirom and Mazeh were able to show that teachers' job satisfaction followed systematic 5-year cycles that were strongly related to seniority but unrelated to age. They noted that a major work-related change, a sabbatical leave, or a change in school characterized teachers' work approximately every 5 years. They concluded that each of these changes reinstated the cycle of high-lowered-high job satisfaction, which, when tracked over long periods, appear to be linear increases in overall job satisfaction.

An important implication of Shirom and Mazeh's data is that change may be necessary for long-term job satisfaction. Although the teaching profession has change built into it, such as sabbatical leaves, many occupations do not (Latack, 1984). This option of changes in job structure and other areas should be explored for more occupations.

It is now estimated that the average American will change jobs between 5 and 10 times (Toffler, 1970). Some authors view occupational changes as positive; Havighurst (1982), for example, strongly advocates such flexibility. According to his view, building change into the occupational life cycle may be one way to avoid disillusionment with one's initial choice. Changing occupations may be one way to guarantee challenging and satisfying work, and it may be the best option for those in a position to exercise it (Shirom & Mazeh, 1988).

Factors Influencing Occupational Change

Several factors have been identified as important in determining who will remain in an occupation and who will change. Some of these factors, such as personality, lead to self-initiated occupation changes. Others, such as obsolescence and economic factors, cause forced occupational changes.

Personality. One variable that is important in self-initiated occupational change is personality. Recall that Holland (1985) postulates that people with certain personality characteristics are suited to particular jobs. If a worker makes an initial selection and later comes to dislike an occupation, it may be because his or her personality does not match the job.

Several researchers have documented that personality factors and situational pressure combine to determine whether a person will remain in an occupation (e.g., Clopton, 1973; Wiener & Vaitenas, 1977). For example, Wiener and Vaitenas found that lack of interest, incongruity with one's occupation, lack of consistent and diversified interests, fear of failure, or a history of emotional problems predicted occupational change. Age was not a predictor.

Obsolescence and Economic Factors. Although some individuals have the luxury of opting for new occupations, occupational change is not self-initiated in many cases. For example, many people are forced to look for new occupations as a result of such developments as technological change or economic factors (both personal and societal).

Technological change is occurring at an ever-increasing rate, so that the skills that one learns today may be obsolete in only a few years. When this occurs, individuals may find that they are forced into making occupational changes. As an example, many Americans with skills important in heavy manufacturing, such as making steel, were displaced in the late 1970s and 1980s as domestic plants closed. Thus, workers are being forced to retrain themselves as never before either just to keep up with change or to learn about new employment opportunities. The latter reason is especially important; in 25 years at least one quarter of the readers of this book will hold jobs that currently do not exist.

Layoffs are one primary impetus to change oc-

cupations. In addition, some workers decide to seek a new occupation because of personal economic factors, such as insufficient pay. For example, recently divorced women may find themselves in this position, especially if child support payments are not received.

Loss of One's Job

Changing economic conditions in the United States over the past few decades, such as increased competition from foreign companies and changing demographics, have forced many people out of their jobs. The loss of jobs has hit heavy manufacturing and support businesses such as the steel, oil, and automotive industries and farming the hardest in recent years, but no one is immune. Indeed, the corporate takeover frenzy of the late 1980s put many middle- and upper-level corporate executives out of work as well.

Losing one's job has the potential for enormous personal impact (DeFrank & Ivancevich, 1986). Declines in physical health and self-esteem, depression, anxiety, and suicide are common (Lajer, 1982). Although the loss of one's job means the loss of income and status, these effects vary with age. Middle-aged men are more vulnerable than older or younger men (DeFrank & Ivancevich, 1986). Moreover, the extent of the effects of losing one's job are related to the degree of financial stress one is under and the timing of the loss (Estes & Wilensky, 1978). Childless couples and couples with young children suffer the most; couples whose children have left home or are independent fare better. Lajer (1982) reports that admission to a psychiatric unit is more likely for people who are over age 45 or have been unemployed for a long period.

The effects of losing one's job emphasize the central role that occupations play in forming a sense of identity in adulthood. How one perceives the loss of a job plays a major role in determining what the long-term effects will be.

DUAL-WORKER COUPLES

In dual-worker couples both partners work outside the home. This type of relationship is becoming the norm in American society, especially in families that cannot meet expenses with only one source of income. As we will see, there are both benefits and costs.

The experiences of most dual-worker couples are similar to those of Jan, a cashier at a local supermarket, and Tom, a worker at the nearby auto assembly plant. Jan and Tom are in their early 30s and have a 3-year-old daughter, Terri. Although they like the fact that their combined income lets them own a modest house, they also feel that there are many strains.

"You know, at times I feel overwhelmed," Jan related. "It's not that Tom doesn't help around the house. But it's not as much as he could. Most days after work I have to pick up Terri from Mom's and then come home and prepare dinner. After a hard day, that's about the *last* thing I want to do. I guess I'm not very good at being a superwoman, or whatever they call it. I also still feel a little guilty leaving Terri with Mom; there are times when I think I ought to be home with her rather than out working."

"But look at what we've got now," Tom responded. "You used to complain about things a lot more. You shouldn't feel guilty when you think about all the things we wouldn't have if you didn't work."

Jan and Tom's experiences point out the major gains and stresses reported by dual-worker couples. On the benefit side, their standard of living is higher, which allows them to have more mate-

rial goods and provide for their children better. However, as Jan indicated, there are several stresses as well. For most dual-worker couples, the biggest problem is the division of housework duties.

Division of Labor: Who Cleans and Cooks?

When both members of a couple are employed, who cleans the house and cooks the meals? Despite much media attention and claims of increased sharing in the duties, women still assume the lion's share of housework regardless of employment status. Wives spend about twice as many hours per week as their husbands in family work and bear the greatest responsibility for household and child-care tasks (Benin & Agostinelli, 1988). Indeed, it is this unequal division of labor that presents most dual-worker couples with a reason to argue and be unhappy.

Husbands and wives view the division of labor in very different terms. Benin and Agostinelli (1988) found that husbands were most satisfied with an equitable division of labor based on the number of hours spent, especially if the amount of time needed to perform household tasks was relatively small. Wives, on the other hand, are most satisfied if the division favors them; their satisfaction is unaffected by the total number of hours spent but, rather, by the husband's willingness to perform women's traditional chores. Broman (1988) reports similar results with Black dual-worker couples. In this study women were twice as likely as men to feel overworked by housework and to be dissatisfied with their family life.

Role conflict is another problem expressed by many dual-worker couples. Figuring out how to balance time at work and time with family confronts everyone. Many women were raised with motherhood as a major goal and feel torn between raising their children and continuing their

SOMETHING · TO · THINK · ABOUT

Division of Labor and Role Conflict in Dual-Worker Couples

One of the biggest issues facing American society in the 1990s is how dual-worker couples can balance their occupational and family roles. With the majority of couples now consisting of two wage earners, issues such as who does the household chores and how child care is arranged will become increasingly important.

The problems of the division of labor and role conflict began to move out of the domain of social science research and into American living rooms in the late 1980s. Television programs such as *thirtysomething* tackled most of these issues in ways never dreamed of by *Ozzie and Harriet*. Trying to decide who should take a promotion or who would clean the bathroom or who should stay home with sick children challenges the gender-role stereotypes that most Americans were taught.

As noted in the text, truly equitable divisions of labor are clearly the exception. Most American households with dual-worker couples still operate under a sex-segregated system: there are wives' chores and husbands' chores. There is no question that all of these tasks are important and must be performed to ensure domestic sanitation. There is also no question that these tasks take time. The important point for women is that it is not *how much* time is spent in performing household chores that matters but *which tasks* are performed. The research cited in the text indicates that what bothers wives the most is not that their husbands are lazy but that their husbands will not perform some "women's work." Men may mow the lawn, wash the car, and even cook, but they rarely run the vacuum, scrub the toilet, or change the baby's diaper.

It appears that husbands would be viewed much more positively by their wives if they performed more of the traditionally female tasks. Marital satisfaction would be likely to improve as a result. Moreover, the role modeling provided to children in these households would be a major step in breaking the transmission of age-old stereotypes. It's something to think about.

occupation (Shainess, 1984). Guilt feelings may be exacerbated by others who feel that a woman who places her children in day care is not a good mother. Her partner may also have his own views that do not agree with hers, further compounding the problem. Furthermore, spending time together is often difficult, especially if both work long hours (Kingston & Nock, 1987). The amount of time together is not necessarily the most important issue; rather, as long as the time is spent in shared activities such as eating, playing, and conversing, couples tend to be happy. Issues concerning division of labor and role conflict are important not only for research but, as discussed in "Something to Think About," in everyday life as well.

Despite these problems most dual-worker couples feel that the benefits, especially the extra income, are worth the costs. Many dual-worker couples, however, have no choice but to try to deal with the situation as best they can: both partners must work simply to pay the bills.

Impact on Occupational Development. Besides the impact on individuals' personal lives, dual-worker couples sometimes report negative effects on occupational development. The most obvious influence occurs when one partner decides to interrupt his or her occupation while the children are young and later reenters the labor force. Skills may have to be learned or relearned, and such returnees may find themselves competing with younger workers for the same positions.

The most important impact on couples who do not interrupt their occupations is on work decisions. The most common example of this problem involves the difficulty in deciding whose occupation is to advance. One partner may be offered a transfer and promotion that would involve moving to another city, which means that the other person's occupation would be seriously challenged. When this situation arises for most couples, it is the man's occupation that is usually given higher priority. One survey showed that 77% of women and 68% of men said that a woman should quit her job if her partner were offered a good position in another city. In contrast, only 10% of the women and 18% of the men said that the man should refuse the offer so that his partner could continue with her job (Roper Organization, 1980).

Some couples find alternative solutions to this dilemma. Rather than trying to decide whether the other partner should quit and move, an increasing number of people are living apart. Such living arrangements are common in some occupations, such as acting, politics, sports, and the military and are becoming more popular among professional couples (Moramarco, 1979). It must be recognized, however, that the stress of long-distance relationships can be severe. Some couples eventually decide that the costs of separation are higher than the benefits of maintaining one's occupation, and they reunite. Others decide to make the separation permanent, and break up.

LEISURE

Leisure is an important concept but a hard one to define. Many authors take the easy way out, and define it as the opposite of work. Leisure can also be viewed as a state of mind, like relaxation. One thing that is agreed on is that leisure is time left over when one is not working (Neulinger, 1974). From this perspective it involves what one chooses to do for pleasure. More formally, we can define **leisure** as "personally expressive discretionary activity, varying in intensity of involvement from relaxation and diversion . . . through personal development and creativity . . . up to sensual transcendence" (C. Gordon, Gaitz, & Scott, 1976). In this section we will examine the types of leisure and consider how leisure activities change over adulthood.

Types of Leisure

Virtually any activity that one engages in could be considered a leisure activity. To help organize the myriad of options, researchers have generally classified leisure activities into four categories: cultural, such as attending sporting events, concerts, church services, or meetings; physical, such as golf, hiking, aerobics, or gardening; social, such as visiting with friends or going to parties; and solitary, including reading, listening to music, or watching television (Bossé & Ekerdt, 1981; Glamser & Hayslip, 1985). Leisure activities can also be considered in terms of degree of personal involvement; examples of leisure activities

TABLE 12.2 · Forms of leisure activity and how they vary in intensity of cognitive, emotional, or physical involvement

Very high intensity	Sexual activity Highly competitive games or sports Dancing
Moderately high intensity	Creative activities (art, literature, music) Nurturance or teaching (children's arts and crafts) Serious discussion and analysis
Medium intensity	Attending cultural events Participating in clubs Sightseeing or travel
Moderately low intensity	Socializing Reading for pleasure Light conversation
Low intensity	Solitude Quiet resting Taking a nap

organized along this dimension are listed in Table 12.2.

An alternative description of leisure involves the distinction between preoccupations and interests (Rapoport & Rapoport, 1975). **Preoccupations** are more or less conscious "mental absorptions," the fundamental needs that channel behavior into some outlets and not others. A preoccupation is much like daydreaming. Sometimes, preoccupations become more focused and are converted to interests. **Interests** are ideas and feelings about things one would like to do, is curious about, or is attracted to. Expression of interests occurs through various activities, such as jogging, watching television, painting, and so on.

Rapoport and Rapoport's distinction draws attention to a key truth about leisure: any specific activity has different meaning and value depending on the individual involved. For example, cooking a gourmet meal is an interest, or leisure activity, for many people; for professional chefs,

however, it is work and thus is not leisure at all. Moreover, the same preoccupation (e.g., a sense of excitement) may be demonstrated in different activities, from watching a rare bird to climbing sheer rock cliffs.

Several factors have been identified as having considerable influence on what leisure activities people participate in (Burrus-Bammel & Bammel, 1985). The major ones are income, interest, health, abilities, transportation, education, and social characteristics. It is probable that how these factors influence leisure activities changes across adulthood (Burrus-Bammel & Bammel, 1985).

Developmental Changes in Leisure

A national survey found age and cohort differences in leisure activities (Harris and Associates, 1975). As age increased, fewer of the activities that adults considered leisure involved strenuous physical exertion, while more sedentary activities such as reading and watching television became more common.

Age differences have also been reported concerning the variety of leisure activities (Bray & Howard, 1978; Elder, 1974; Lowenthal, Thurnher, & Chiriboga, 1975). These studies indicate that young adults participate in a greater range of activities than middle-agers. Gordon et al. (1977) report that young adults prefer intense leisure activities, that middle-agers focus more on home- and family-oriented activities that are less intense, and that the elderly narrow the range of activities further and lower their intensity. It is important to realize, however, that older adults' choices of leisure activities may be restricted by what they are physically capable of doing and whether transportation is available (Hess & Markson, 1980). Unfortunately, little developmental research has been conducted to identify how these changes across adulthood take place.

RETIREMENT

Until 1935, when Social Security was inaugurated, retirement was rarely even considered by most Americans. Only since World War II have there been a substantial number of retired people in the United States. Today, the number is increasing rapidly, and the notion that individuals work a specified time and then retire is taken for granted.

The enactment of Social Security and the advent of various pension and savings plans have been accompanied by profound changes in attitudes toward retirement. Most people now view it as a right, a rather interesting view considering that working has long been considered virtually a moral obligation. It is this curious juxtaposition that makes retirement a very interesting topic.

As the number of retirees increases, several issues will be thrust to the forefront. Among them are early retirement, retirement planning, educational and work options for retirees, and health care for these individuals. We will explore many of these issues, as well as attitudes toward retirement and adjustment to it. But the first step in reaching these insights is to achieve a reasonably clear definition of it.

Defining Retirement

Like leisure, retirement is difficult to define. One way to look at retirement is to equate it with complete withdrawal from the work force. But this definition is inadequate; many "retired" people continue to work part time. Another possibility would be to define retirement as a self-described state. However, this definition will not work either, because some Blacks define themselves as "disabled" rather than "retired" in order to qualify for social service programs. The most useful way to view **retirement** is as a complex process by which people withdraw from full-time participation in an occupation. The decision to retire should not be made lightly, but it often is; many people spend more time planning for a 2-week vacation than they do for retirement. From this decision-making perspective retirement can be viewed in three ways: as a process, as a paradox, and as a change.

Retirement as a Process. The process of retirement begins as soon as one thinks about what life after employment might be like. More thinking usually leads to some sort of planning, even if it is only to check with one's employer about available financial benefits. The planning process

People who own their own businesses, like this couple, are among the groups least likely to look forward to retirement.

will be the topic of more detailed discussion in a later section.

Retirement as a Paradox. Retirement involves the loss of two very important things that we derive from work: income and status. Losing these key aspects of one's life should be reflected in poor adjustment, or so we might think. The paradox of retirement is that despite these losses the majority of retirees say that they are satisfied; they like and enjoy being retired.

Retirement as a Change. Retirement is both an end and a beginning. Although it involves change in almost every aspect of life, retirees have an advantage that is often overlooked. By the time they retire, they have already experienced several disruptive life transitions such as marriage, children leaving home, or moving; what they have learned from previous events provides the basis for adjusting to retirement. Clearly, retire-

ment is complex. In the next few sections we will review some of the information available on retirement, including how to prepare for it and how to make the best of it.

Deciding to Retire

The decision to retire is an intensely personal one that involves carefully weighing several factors. The major ones that we will consider are health, financial status, sex, race, and attitudes toward retirement.

Health. One of the most important influences on retirement decisions is health, regardless of whether one is approaching mandatory retirement. Clark and Spengler (1980) report that poor health is one of the two main reasons that people retire early; financial security is the other (Ward, 1984a, 1984b).

Financial Status. The importance of financial security is not surprising, since most people have plans that involve money, such as traveling, and because they would like to maintain their life-style. Many corporations offer preretirement planning programs that provide advice. We will consider some of their benefits later.

Sex. Although most research on retirement decisions has focused on men, some work has examined women. George, Fillenbaum, and Palmore (1984) found that a woman's decision to retire was predicted by age and the status of her husband, not by characteristics of her occupation. In contrast, Campione (1987) found that a woman's decision to retire was related not only to her husband's wages but also to her own financial status independent of her husband. These discrepant findings may be due to changing demographics. That is, only in the past few years have women remained in the work force long enough to make the decision to retire based on their own wage history.

Race. Another group that has been systematically overlooked in retirement research is Black Americans. Blacks may not label themselves as retired, for many reasons, from socialization to the need to adopt the disability role in order to maximize their benefits (Gibson, 1987). Because many Blacks do not have the financial or other resources to retire and must continue to work into old age, researchers have often excluded them.

A few investigators have examined the characteristics of retired Blacks (Gibson, 1986, 1987; Irelan & Bell, 1972; Jackson & Gibson, 1985; Murray, 1979). These studies show that Blacks often do not "decide" to retire, since many may not be working. Instead, they appear to label themselves as either retired or unretired based on subjective disability, work history, and source of income. An important finding is that gender differences are absent among Blacks; men and women base their self-labels on the same variables. Thus, findings based on White samples must not be generalized to Blacks, and separate theoretical models for Blacks may be needed (Gibson, 1987).

Attitudes Toward Retirement. People who have jobs that they feel are rewarding typically view retirement as less desirable than do people in unrewarding jobs. This conclusion is supported by several studies showing that blue-collar workers look forward to retirement (as long as they have enough money) but that professionals may not. Being autonomous and having responsibility in a job is associated with more negative attitudes toward retirement (Barfield & Morgan, 1978; Streib & Schneider, 1971).

Attitudes toward retirement for those in middle-level jobs, including clerical and service personnel, are best predicted by income. Workers with high incomes and those who have good pension plans are most favorable about retirement. This relationship is so strong and holds for such a wide range of middle-level jobs that some writers believe that it is the relationship between workers and money, not that between people and work, that should be researched (Shanas, 1972).

Educational level is another important predictor of attitudes, but the connection is complex. For men, it appears that more education is accompanied by more negative feelings, but this could be due to the likelihood that such men are in more autonomous jobs (Sheppard, 1976). The evidence is contradictory for women. Sheppard (1976) reports that the most highly educated women are positive about retiring and do so earlier. On the contrary, Streib and Schneider (1971) found that women with higher incomes, better education, and higher-status jobs tended to continue working longer. Clearly, more research is needed in order to sort out the relationship between education and retirement attitudes, especially for women.

Age and cohort differences also influence attitudes. At one time it was believed that younger workers were more favorably disposed to retirement than older workers (Atchley, 1976). Contradictory evidence has been reported, however; Barfield and Morgan (1978) found that older cohorts were more favorably disposed to retire. These differences may reflect two changes in viewing retirement. First, workers may be becoming more receptive to the idea that employment does not last forever. It should be remembered that retirees who participated in earlier studies had largely begun working before retirement was commonplace. Second, many researchers have changed their assumption that retirement is "a major disruption of an adult's role and would tend to have deleterious consequences for the individual" (Streib & Schneider, 1971, p. 5). Rather, many investigators are viewing retirement simply as another normative life transition to which most people adjust positively.

Adjustment to Retirement

Everyone agrees on one point about retirement: it is a life transition that produces stress. How people handle this stress is the process by which they adjust to the changes that retirement brings. Successful retirement requires responding to the challenges it presents and having a supportive network of relatives and friends. Before considering the research on whether people usually find retirement to their liking, we will look at two flexible theoretical frameworks that will help put the literature into perspective.

Work Styles. One way to conceptualize adjustment to retirement is by examining different combinations of work styles and life-styles. Lowenthal (1972) suggests that past behavior and attitudes during their employment years influence people's adjustment to retirement. Thus, individuals who have always been strongly work-oriented, viewing work as an end in itself, will be most likely to consider retirement as traumatic. Lowenthal argues that unless the highly work-oriented person finds a substitute for work, he or she is apt to find retirement an unpleasant experience.

People who are less strongly oriented toward work as a means to social acceptance may view retirement as a crisis, but they will eventually adjust. Lowenthal suggests that these instrumental, other-directed people may need to find a substitute for work, but usually this need is only temporary.

Three other groups complete Lowenthal's classification: the receptive-nurturant type, the autonomous type, and the self-protective type. Receptive-nurturant people are typically women who have lifelong commitments to emotional goals and intimacy. For them, the quality of the relationship with their partners is the key to adjustment in retirement. Provided the relationship is perceived as solid, retirement should present little difficulty.

Many autonomous individuals are in occupations that allow them to decide when to retire. These people present a complex pattern of creativity, varied goals, and self-generativity. If retirement is voluntary, little disruption should be expected; however, mandatory retirement may lead to depression until reorientation is achieved.

Finally, the self-protective person often sees nothing special about retirement; it is simply another chapter in a life full of struggles. Dependency on or responsibility for others is not allowed. These individuals have always been

When these workers retired in 1949, a gold watch may have been all they had to look forward to. Today, options for most people are far greater.

detached or disengaged. As long as retirement does not require radical change, it does not produce a crisis.

Lowenthal's approach clearly allows for a wide variety of possibilities. One common theme across the different types is that a redistribution of energy may be needed for successful adjustment to retirement; this change is reminiscent of the reevaluations that occurred earlier in development. Indeed, enduring aspects of personality and life-style are useful in predicting adjustment to retirement (Maas & Kuypers, 1974; Neugarten, 1977).

Values. A second theoretical framework, suggested by Atchley (1976), is compatible with Lowenthal's. Atchley proposes that how the individual views the role of the job in his or her life determines the extent to which retirement is a crisis. If the job fulfills goals not achieved by other activities and if it is considered important throughout adulthood, retirement will demand a major reorganization of one's values. However, if one's goals have been attained or if one's job was never considered of primary importance, little reorganization will be necessary. Atchley agrees with Lowenthal in concluding that strongly job-oriented people seek substitutes for work or even second occupations after retiring; these individuals are not able to reorganize their lives enough otherwise.

Satisfaction. Once people retire, do they like it? The evidence suggests that they do. Numerous national cross-sectional surveys conducted from the 1950s to the late 1970s documented that as long as income and health were maintained adequately, satisfaction with retirement was high (e.g., Barfield & Morgan, 1978; Streib & Schneider, 1971).

By 1980, however, retirees' responses had begun to change; a significantly higher proportion of them, although generally satisfied with retirement, felt that they would prefer to work (Harris & Associates, 1981). These findings probably reflect the increased concern over financial security expressed by many retirees. Indeed, two aspects of Harris's data support this conclusion. First, the increase during the 1970s in the proportion of retirees preferring to work paralleled the increase in the inflation rate in the United States. Second, retirees not collecting pensions were more likely to want to work than retirees on pensions. Still, overall satisfaction does not seem to drop, even in the most recent retirees (Ekerdt, Levkoff, & Bossé, 1981).

In sum, there is little evidence to support the stereotypical view of retirement as a major life crisis leading to poor adjustment. On the contrary, research since the 1950s has shown consistently that most people are satisfied with retirement living. Although an increasing number of people express a desire to work, this response comes largely from increased financial pressures and not from a fundamental dislike for retirement. Positive adjustment outcomes do not imply, however, that reorganization and change are unnecessary. Such changes are vital to maintaining one's psychological well-being. Reorientation occurs in most aspects of one's life; we will examine three contexts in the next section: family, friends, and community.

Family, Friendship, and Community

Retirement rarely affects only a single individual. No matter how personal the joys and sorrows of retirement may be, retirees' reactions are influenced by the social environment of their family, friends, and community. These social ties help us deal with the stresses of retirement, as they do in other life transitions. A long history of research verifies that social relationships help cushion the effect of life stress throughout adulthood. This support takes many forms: letting people know that they are loved; offering help if needed; providing advice; taking care of others' needs; just being there to listen. We should expect retirees who have close and strong social ties to have an edge over those who do not in dealing with change.

Family. Much attention has been focused on the role of intimate and family relationships in adjusting to retirement. Marriage has provided the framework for almost all of this work. Ideally, marital partners provide mutual support during the transition to retirement. Whether marriage actually serves this function is unclear. The few studies specifically dealing with the connection between marital status and satisfaction with retirement provide conflicting results. Some evidence suggests that the never-married are as satisfied as married retirees, whereas divorced, separated, or widowed retirees are much less happy (Barfield & Morgan, 1978; Larson, 1978). It could be that never-married people prefer singlehood and become accustomed to it long before retirement. Additionally, the difficulties encountered by those whose marriages were disrupted indirectly emphasize the stabilizing effects of marriage. But it seems that whatever relationship exists holds mainly for men; marital status alone has little effect on older women's satisfaction (Fox, 1979). Furthermore, we know almost nothing about the link between the quality of retirees' marriages and satisfaction with retirement.

Possible benefits aside, there is little doubt that retirement has profound effects on intimate relationships. It often disrupts long-established patterns of family interaction, forcing both partners (and others living in the house) to adjust. Simply being together more puts strain on the relationship. Daily routines need rearrangement, which may be stressful.

One common change that confronts most retired couples is the division of household chores. Although retired men tend to do more work around the home than they did before retirement, this situation does not always lead to desirable outcomes (Ingraham, 1974). For example, an employed husband may compliment his wife on her domestic skills; after retirement, however, he may suddenly want to teach her to do it "right." Part of the problem may be that such men are not used to taking orders about how chores are supposed to be done. One former executive told interviewers that before he retired, when he said "jump," highly paid employees wanted to know how high. "Now, I go home, I walk in the door and my wife says, 'Milton, take out the garbage.' I never saw so much garbage" (Quigley, 1979, p. 9). Finally, part of the problem may be in the perception of one's turf; after retirement men feel that they are thrust into doing things that they, and their partners, may have traditionally thought of as "women's work" (Troll, 1971).

Retirees maintain, and may increase, contact with their children, grandchildren, and other relatives. These contacts are viewed as an important component in retirees' lives. Still, independence

between generations is associated with high satisfaction among retirees (Riley & Foner, 1978). This need for independence is underscored by the fact that visits with children sometimes have a depressing rather than a positive effect on older (65 +) male retirees. Apparently, changing power relationships within the family are responsible; visiting children may serve to emphasize the father's loss of control over them.

Frequency of contact with other relatives does not appear to be related to life satisfaction among middle- and upper-middle-class retirees. That is, visiting relatives does not have negative effects, but it does not add to a retiree's overall satisfaction either (Lemon, Bengtson, & Peterson, 1972).

Friends. Intimate and family relationships are clearly important sources of support for retirees. However, they are not the only ones; friendship networks also provide support that often complements family networks. Friends sometimes provide types of support that, because of the strong emotional ties, families may be less able to provide: a compassionate, but objective listener; a companion for social and leisure activities; or a source of advice, transportation, and other assistance. The extent to which friends contribute to retirees' overall satisfaction is unclear, but seeing friends and having a confidant appears to be important (Lemon et al., 1972; Lowenthal & Haven, 1968).

Older men have fewer close personal friends for support than older women (Booth, 1972). This difference may help explain the sex difference between marital status and satisfaction discussed earlier. Men, because of their fewer close relationships, may be forced to rely more on their wives for support.

Community. Since social ties are generally related to retirees' satisfaction, an important consideration is whether the social environment

The Foster Grandparent Program, among others, provides a way for older adults to maintain meaningful personal roles.

facilitates continuing old ties and forming new ones. The past few decades have witnessed the rapid growth of organizations devoted to providing these opportunities to retirees. National associations such as the American Association of Retired Persons provide the chance to learn about what other retirees are doing and about services such as insurance and discounts.

Numerous smaller groups exist at the community level; these include senior centers and clubs. Many trade unions also have programs for their retired members. Additionally, there are many opportunities for retirees to help others. One federal agency, ACTION, administers four programs that have hundreds of local chapters: Foster Grandparents, Senior Companions, the Retired Senior Volunteer Program, and the Service Corps of Retired Executives.

Retirement Planning

To this point we have considered the characteristics and activities of retirees that affect how they feel about retirement. Now we are in a better position to ask what one should do to prepare for retirement. Perhaps by planning, retirees can anticipate and avoid some of the difficulties. For example, one common problem in adjusting to the retirement role is the abruptness of the transition from employment to unemployment. What processes might minimize the difficulties of this change?

One key element to successful retirement is preparation (Kamouri & Cavanaugh, 1986). Getting ready can take several forms: conscious or unconscious planning, informal or formal steps, and so on. One formal way to prepare for retirement is to participate in a **preretirement educa-tion program**. Such programs cover a wide variety of topics, from financial planning to adjustment; a typical content list is contained in Table 12.3. Campione (1988) found that men who do some preparing on their own, who are married and have families to plan for, who are healthy, and who have high occupational status are more likely to participate in formal preretirement programs. This profile reflects a strong bias in program participants; lower-income, minority individuals are not represented.

Every comprehensive planning program for retirement focuses on two key aspects: finances and attitudes. We will consider some of the ramifications of each.

Finances. Retirement, on average, involves a 50% reduction in income (Foner & Schwab, 1981). Obviously, if one is not prepared for this degree of income loss, financial pressures will be severe. Financial planning is necessary on several levels. First, most people are part of mandatory retirement plans such as Social Security. Although planning ends here for most people, it is not enough. If possible, individuals should also save funds in anticipation of income loss, such as in individual retirement accounts. It must be recognized, though, that the majority of American workers cannot set aside sufficient funds to carry them through their retirement years in the lifestyle they enjoyed before retirement.

Attitudes. Aside from finances, one's attitudes about retirement probably have the most important effect on satisfaction (Foner & Schwab, 1981). Even if it only involves thinking about when to retire and looking forward to it, developing a positive attitude is key to more rapid adjustment to and enjoyment of retirement (Barfield & Morgan, 1970; Kimmel, Price, & Walker,

1978). It appears that more formal preparation, such as participation in preretirement programs, is associated with more positive attitudes (Friedman & Orbach, 1974), but this relationship may be due to the fact that people who already hold favorable attitudes are the most likely to plan.

The relationship between attitudes and participation in preretirement programs has been addressed by Kamouri and Cavanaugh (1986). They compared four groups of workers: retired workers who had participated in a preretirement program, retired workers who had not participated, employees in a preretirement program, and employees on the waiting list for a program. Kamouri and Cavanaugh found that workers who had had the benefit of a program had a more realistic view of retirement than those who had not participated. The main benefit of participating in a preretirement program seemed to be realistic expectations that could be translated into a more positive attitude in the first few years of retirement. After about 3 years of retirement people who had not participated in the program were comparable in their attitudes to those who had, but they did note that their initial experiences had not been what they had expected.

SUMMARY

People view work as a key element in their sense of identity. Although most people work to earn a living, work also provides many other sources of satisfaction. An occupation develops over the entire life span and consists of an interaction between personal and social systems that change over time. The social status of different occupations varies across five levels: marginal workers, blue-collar workers, pink-collar workers, white-collar workers, and executives and professionals.

TABLE 12.3 · Topics in a typical preretirement education program

I. Deciding to retire: when is the right time?

II. Psychological aspects of aging
   A. Work roles and retirement
   B. Personal identity issues
   C. Retirement as a process, paradox, and change
   D. Effects on relationships with family and friends

III. Finances
   A. Social Security
   B. Pension
   C. Insurance
   D. Employment

IV. Legal aspects
   A. Wills
   B. Personal rights as senior citizens

V. Health
   A. Normal aging
   B. Medicare and Medicaid
   C. Issues in health insurance

VI. Where to live: the pros and cons of moving

VII. Leisure time activities
   A. Travel
   B. Hobbies
   C. Clubs and organizations
   D. Educational opportunities
   E. Volunteering

The choice of an occupation is influenced by several factors. Family influences are the most important, since they shape the early setting of goals, values, and expectations. Transmission of values is especially important for men. Personality factors are also important. Holland proposes six groupings of personality characteristics and specific occupations. Personal interests that are compatible with those of people in particular occupations are another factor. Self-efficacy has also been shown to be an important factor in occupational choice, as has the development of self-concept.

Occupational development proceeds through stages. Super has listed five: implementation, establishment, maintenance, deceleration, and retirement. Occupational development in women is limited by sex discrimination. People build expectations about their occupation that provide a plan for occupational development. This plan is often modified as a result of the "reality shock" that young adults face as they move into the job market. Support from co-workers, especially mentors, is very helpful in promoting occupational advancement and satisfaction. Periodic evaluation and modification of occupational priorities occurs throughout adulthood as individuals' needs and personal goals change. There is also evidence that occupational priorities change over generations, especially in mobility, leadership, and desire for emotional support. Job satisfaction tends to increase slightly with increasing age. However, this increase may be due to self-selection, increased experience, deemphasis of occupation, or changing sources of satisfaction.

Factors that influence the likelihood of changing occupations include personality, skill obsolescence, and economic conditions. Losing one's job may have a profound effect, but this depends on several factors such as length of unemployment and timing.

Dual-worker couples are becoming the norm. Although the benefits include a higher standard of living, there are costs such as less time to spend with the family and conflict over dividing up household chores. Most husbands still do fewer chores and avoid chores that are traditionally female.

Leisure activities are becoming an increasingly important aspect of workers' lives. Age differences in leisure activities are evident; older workers engage in fewer types than younger workers and in ones that are less physically demanding.

Retirement can be viewed as a process, a paradox, and a change. Attitudes toward retirement vary as a function of job type and whether the job is viewed as rewarding. The relationship of attitude toward retirement and age is complex, and it may reflect a generational shift toward a more positive outlook. Adjustment to retirement appears to be related to work styles, such as how strongly work-oriented a person is. Depending on the individual's work style, retirement can be a very good or a rather traumatic experience. Overall, most people are satisfied with retirement over the long run. There is no doubt that retirement has far-reaching effects; family and friendship relations must undergo a period of transition. Participation in preretirement programs is beneficial, especially in providing workers with a more realistic picture of what retirement is like.

GLOSSARY

age discrimination • Denying a person a job or promotion solely on the basis of age.

blue-collar occupation • A line of work that does not require formal education past high school and may be based more on physical than intellectual skills.

career • An organized progression through the various levels within the same occupational field; sometimes reserved for prestigious occupations.

comparable worth • The principle that people in traditionally sex-stereotyped jobs should be paid equally, based on the kinds of skills required.

dream • The aspirations and expectations one has for one's occupation.

executives and professionals • Those who hold jobs with the highest level of status.

interests • Ideas and feelings about things that one likes to do, is curious about, or is attracted to.

job satisfaction • Positive feelings about one's occupation.

leisure • Personal discretionary activities, which vary in intensity from very physically active to passive and sedentary.

marginal workers • People who work occasionally but never long enough with one employer to establish a continuous occupational history.

mentor • A co-worker, usually older, who provides guidance and psychological support.

occupation • What one does for a living; compare *career*.

occupational priorities • What one values most in an occupation.

pay equity • Paying men and women equally when they hold the same position.

pink-collar occupation • A line of work that is traditionally held by women.

preoccupations • Mental absorptions that occupy our time.

preretirement education program • A formal plan that offers information and socialization about health, financial, psychological, and other aspects of retirement.

reality shock • The realization that the "real world" is different than one had imagined it.

retirement • The process by which people withdraw from full-time participation in an occupation.

role conflict • The problem of balancing the time demands of work and family.

self-efficacy • The subjective evaluation of one's ability to perform in a specific situation or occupation.

sex discrimination • Denying a job to someone solely on the basis of gender.

trait-factor approach • A theory of occupational choice based on personality traits.

vocational maturity • A dimension in Super's theory of occupational development referring to the degree of congruence between one's self-concept and one's occupation.

white-collar occupation • Office work, which carries relatively high status and requires formal education beyond high school.

ADDITIONAL READING

An extensive review of research on older workers can be found in

Doering, M., Rhodes, S. R., & Schuster, M. (1983). *The aging worker: Research and recommendations*. Beverly Hills, CA: Sage Publications.

Excellent descriptions and case examples concerning couples and how they view work can be found in

Blumstein, P., & Schwartz, P. (1983). *American couples*. New York: Morrow.

An overview of retirement can be found in

Palmore, E. (Ed.). (1986). *Retirement: Causes and consequences*. New York: Springer.

Two journals that are especially good sources of information about occupational development and occupational choice are *Journal of Vocational Behavior* and *Journal of Counseling Psychology*.

Communities, Institutions, and Relocation

Grandma Moses, *Moving Day on the Farm*, 1951. Copyright © 1987, Grandma Moses Properties Co., New York. Anna Mary Robertson ("Grandma") Moses (1860–1961) became famous in old age for her paintings of American farmlife.

PEOPLE DO NOT BEHAVE IN A VACUUM; they behave in environments. As perfectly obvious as this statement seems, it has only been in the last few decades that the living environments in which people operate have been studied systematically. And it is only more recently that researchers in adult development have given them much thought. The principle concern in the field of **environmental psychology** has been the interaction of people with the communities or institution's in which they live. The basic assumption is that "a person's behavioral and psychological state can be better understood with knowledge of the context in which the person behaves" (Lawton, 1980, p.2).

In this chapter we will see how differences in the interaction between personal characteristics and the living environment can have profound effects on our behavior and our feelings about ourselves. Several theoretical frameworks will be described that can help us understand how to interpret person-environment interactions in a developmental context. We will consider the communities and neighborhoods that influence us and that partially determine whether we will be happy. Similarly, there are several aspects of housing that play important roles in our lives. Because some people do not live in the community, we will take a close look at institutional environments, especially nursing homes. Finally, we will look at people on the move and examine the effects of community-based and institutional relocation. Even though we must sometimes consider the person separately from the environment, keep in mind throughout the chapter that in the end it is the interaction of the two that we want to understand.

THEORIES OF PERSON-ENVIRONMENT INTERACTIONS

In order to appreciate the roles that different environments play in our lives, we need a framework for interpreting how people interact with them. Theories of person-environment interactions help us understand how individuals view their environments and how these views may change as people age. Because the field of environmental psychology has only recently been approached from a developmental perspective, few theories are well thought out (Scheidt & Windley, 1985). We will consider four that have received the most attention: competence and environmental press, congruence, stress and coping, and the loss-continuum concept.

All of these theories can be traced to a common beginning. Many years ago Kurt Lewin (1936) conceptualized **person-environment interactions** in the equation B = f(P,E). This relationship means that behavior (B) is a function of both the person (P) and the environment (E). What recent theorists did was to start with Lewin's equation and to describe the components in the equation in more detail. Specifically, their speculations concern what it is about people and about environments that combine to form behavior.

Competence and Environmental Press

One way to express the person-environment interaction is by focusing on competence and environmental press (Lawton, 1982; Lawton & Nahemow, 1973). **Competence** is defined as the theoretical upper limit of an individual's capacity to function. Lawton and Nahemow (1973) believe that competence involves five domains: biological health, sensory-perceptual functioning, motor skills, cognitive skills, and ego strength. These domains are thought to underlie all other abilities, and they are lifelong. Unfortunately, the components of competence are not easy to measure. The problem is that there are very few measures of the components that do not involve the environment in any way. As noted in Chapter 4, for example, biological health is strongly related to the type of environment in which we live. Thus, in most research one must settle for a rough approximation of a person's true competence.

Environments can be classified on the basis of the varying demands that they place on the individual. To reflect this idea, Lawton borrowed the term **environmental press** from Henry Murray (1938). The demands that environments put on people (environmental press) can be any combination of three types: physical, interpersonal, or social. Physical demands include such things as having to walk three flights of stairs to one's apartment. Interpersonal demands include the various pressures we feel to get along with other people. Social demands include such things as the local laws or social customs that affect our lives.

The model constructed by Lawton and Nahemow (1973) is a combination of these ideas. They assert that behavior is a result of a person of a particular competence level acting in an environment of a specific press level. Furthermore, behavior is placed on a continuum from positive to negative and is thought to be manifested at two levels, as observable behavior and as affect, or feelings. Each of these elements is represented schematically in Figure 13.1.

Low to high competence is represented in the figure on the vertical axis, and the horizontal axis represents weak to strong press level. Points in the graph show various combinations of person-environment interactions. Most important, the shaded areas demonstrate that adaptive behavior and positive affect result from many different combinations of competence and press levels, not just one. As one moves farther away from these areas—due to a change in press level, for example—behavior becomes increasingly maladaptive, and affect becomes more negative. Notice that maladaptive behavior and negative affect also result from many combinations of competence and press levels. Finally, the darkly shaded area labeled **adaptation level** represents points where press is average for particular levels of competence. The adaptation level is where behavior and affect are normal, so we are usually unaware of them. Awareness increases as we move away from adaptation level.

As an example of Lawton and Nahemow's model, consider Rick. Rick works in a store in an area of Omaha, Nebraska, where the crime rate is moderately high, representing a moderate level of environmental press. Because he is very good at self-defense, he has high competence; thus, he manages to cope. Because the Omaha police chief wants to lower the crime rate in that area, he increases patrols, thereby lowering the press level. If Rick maintains his high competence, maladaptive behavior may result because he has more competence than is optimal for the new environment.

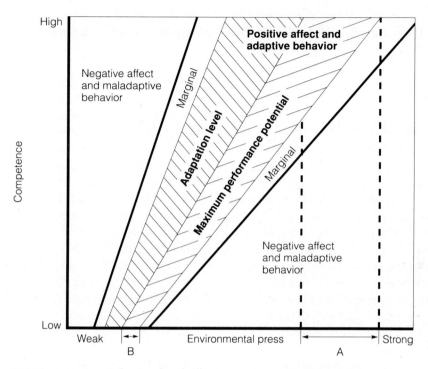

FIGURE 13.1 • Behavioral and affective outcomes of person-environment interactions based on the competence–environmental press model. This figure indicates that an individual of high competence will show maximum performance over a larger range of environmental situations than will a less competent person. The range of optimal environments occurs at a higher level of environmental press (A) for the most competent person than it does for the least competent person (B).

(Source: "Ecology and the Aging Process" (p. 661) by M. P. Lawton and L. Nahemow, 1973, in C. Eisdorfer and M. P. Lawton, Eds., *The Psychology of Adult Development and Aging*, Washington, DC: American Psychological Association. Copyright © 1973 by the American Psychological Association. Reprinted with permission of the publisher and author.)

But if instead of the police a street gang moved in, he would have to increase his competence and be more prepared in order to maintain his adaptation level. Other changes in the environment, such as arson threats, or in his competence, such as a broken arm, would create other combinations.

Before leaving Lawton and Nahemow's model, we need to note an important implication that it has for aging. Notice that the less competent the individual is, the greater the impact of environmental factors. To the extent that individuals experience declines in health, sensory processes, motor skills, cognitive skills, or ego strength, they will be able to cope with fewer environmental demands. Thus, in order for older adults to maintain good adaptational levels, either changes to lower environmental press or interventions to raise competence would need to be undertaken.

The Congruence Model

The **congruence model,** proposed by Kahana (1982), also includes the ideas of competence and environmental press, but in ways different from Lawton and Nahemow's model. In Kahana's view people vary in their needs, and environments differ in their ability to satisfy them. According to the congruence model, people with particular needs search for the environments that will meet them best. To the extent that a match exists, the individual feels content and satisfied; when a mismatch occurs, stress and discomfort result.

Congruence between the person and the environment is especially important when either individual or environmental options are limited. Limitations can occur for three reasons: environmental characteristics are restricted, such as when public transportation is unavailable for going shopping; an individual's freedom is limited, such as when he or she must always eat at the same time every day; and one believes that one has limited freedom, such as when one *thinks* that there is no way to get around despite a reliable bus system. Restricted environments are exemplified most clearly by institutions such as nursing homes and hospitals. Limits on individual freedom can result from age-related declines in competence. Self-perceptions of limited freedom reflect the belief that one's life is controlled by external forces, in the ways described in Chapter 9.

When applied specifically to the older adult, Kahana's congruence model shows that several points should be considered for optimizing the person-environment fit (Kahana & Kahana,

1983). Not only must the kind of situation be considered, such as whether the person is in a single-family, congregate, or institutional living arrangement, but personal factors must be considered as well. Personal factors are very important because people vary considerably in their needs. Some of us value autonomy and independence highly, for example, whereas others place less importance on them. We must be careful when designing programs and interventions for adults to take these individual differences into account. Otherwise, we may unintentionally increase the discrepancy between the person and the environment, resulting in increases in stress for the people we intended to help.

Kahana's model is especially useful when considering issues in institutional settings such as nursing homes and hospitals. Indeed, most of the research that has examined issues such as autonomy has been done in long-term care facilities (Collopy, 1988; Hofland, 1988). This makes sense when one realizes that it is in these settings that difficult decisions involving trade-offs between personal freedom and institutional requirements are made most often (Collopy, 1988). We will return to Kahana's congruence model later in the chapter when we focus on nursing homes.

Stress and Coping Theory

Schooler (1982) has applied Lazarus's cognitive theory of **stress and coping,** described in Chapter 4, to the understanding of the older person's interaction with the environment. The basic premise of Lazarus's theory is that people evaluate situations in order to assess their potential threat value. Situations may be evaluated as harmful, beneficial, or irrelevant. When situations are viewed as harmful or threatening, people also establish the range of coping responses that they have at their disposal for removing the harmful situation. This process results in making a coping response. Outcomes of coping may be positive or negative depending on many contextual factors.

Schooler (1982) argues that this perspective is especially helpful in understanding older adults because of their increased vulnerability to social and physical hazards. To test his ideas, Schooler evaluated retest data on a sample of 521 people drawn from a national sample of 4,000 institutionalized older adults. In particular, he examined the impact of three potential stressors (environmental change, residential mobility, and major life events) on health or morale. He also examined the buffering, or protective, effects of social support systems and ecological factors on the relationships among the stressors and outcomes. Consistent with the theory, Schooler showed that the presence of social support systems affected the likelihood that particular situations would be defined as threatening. For example, living alone is more likely to be viewed as stressful when one has little social support than when one has many friends who live nearby.

Schooler's work provides an important theoretical addition, because it deals with the relation between everyday environmental stressors and the adaptive responding of community-dwelling individuals. However, he admits that more research needs to be done, especially in the area of understanding how the threat-appraisal process varies with age across different environmental contexts.

The Loss-Continuum Concept

Pastalan (1982) views aging as a progressive series of losses that reduce one's social participation. This **loss continuum** includes children leaving, loss of social roles, loss of income, death of spouse or close friends and relatives, loss of sensory acuity, and loss of mobility due to poorer health. Because these losses reduce people's ability to partake fully in community resources, their own home and immediate neighborhood take on far greater importance. This increase in importance means that older adults are especially sensitive to even small environmental changes (Regnier, 1983; Rowles & Ohta, 1983).

One good example of the importance of the immediate neighborhood in the loss-continuum concept is the fact that a one-block radius around homes in cities is critical. Beyond this radius the rate at which elderly people make trips for shopping or other purposes drops sharply (Silverman, 1987). Consequently, well-planned environmental changes, even those on a small scale, can have significant payoffs for older adults. Pastalan (1982) himself views his approach as less a theory than a guide to practical change to facilitate the maintenance of competence and independence of older adults.

Common Theoretical Themes

It should be apparent that the four theories we have considered have much in common. Most important, all of them agree that the focus must be on the *interaction* between the person and the environment, not on one or the other. Another important theme in common is that no one environment will meet everyone's needs. Rather, a range of potential environments may be optimal.

As noted earlier, however, the study of person-environment interactions is very new and is not well systematized. There is little agreement on the set of environmental factors that must be accounted for or on which set of personal needs must be met for optimal satisfaction. It is also not clear whether there are developmental changes in person-environment interactions (Rowles & Ohta, 1983). Such transitions would be expected from a life-span perspective, but this approach has generally not been used in person-environment research (Silverman, 1987). One thing is clear, though: elderly people require a broad range of living environments to satisfy the variety of their personal needs.

COMMUNITIES, NEIGHBORHOODS, AND HOUSING

The most general levels at which we can examine person-environment interactions are communities and neighborhoods. Communities are usually defined as geographical or political units like cities and towns. Neighborhoods are the parts of the larger community that groups of people identify with and often label; Flatbush in Brooklyn, Buckhead in Atlanta, and Watts in Los Angeles are some examples. In this section we will examine several aspects of communities and neighborhoods that have an impact on us and some personal factors that are important in considering the composition of the environment. We will also take a brief look at some important aspects of housing for the elderly.

Community Size

Among the most important dimensions of a community that affect the life satisfaction of the residents is community size, conveniently represented along the **rural-urban continuum**. Hundreds of studies have examined the effects of size on all kinds of personal characteristics, from overall life satisfaction to knowledge about the availability of services (e.g., Krout, 1988a, 1988b; Silverman, 1987). Some marked differences have emerged that are important for understanding person-environment interactions, especially among the elderly. In interpreting differences between rural and urban communities, keep in mind that size alone does not tell us *why* the differences emerge. Other factors such as economic or ethnic differences that were not or could not be measured may also be responsible.

Overall Satisfaction. In terms of overall life satisfaction the effects of community size are complex. No clear trends emerge for young adults, but both direct and indirect effects have been documented for older adults. Liang and Warfel (1983) used the results of surveys done nationally and in three states to study urban-rural differences in life satisfaction. They found that the size of a community had a negative impact on the degree of actual and perceived integration into the community; people in large cities were less integrated than people in smaller communities. However, feeling that one is a part of the community does not affect the life satisfaction of people living in large cities as much as it does that of people in small communities. In large cities health factors are more important. The importance of health as a predictor of satisfaction is highlighted by Lawton's (1980) finding that when health factors are controlled, no differences in satisfaction as a function of community size are observed.

Liang and Warfel's findings support results from several other studies and generations of folk wisdom concerning the informal social network (Lawton, 1985). Rural communities often lack sufficient health care facilities, shopping centers, and so on. However, friends, neighbors, and family, collectively termed the **informal social network**, often make up for these shortcomings by providing some of the missing services, such as by visiting sick friends (Davis, 1980; Rowles, 1983). The more one feels like part of the community, the larger one's informal network is and the higher one's life satisfaction (Rowles, 1983).

Still, many elderly people prefer to live in large cities because of greater opportunities for

A sense of community and friendliness tend to be higher among rural residents compared with their urban-dwelling counterparts.

social interaction. In contrast to small towns, large cities have better public transportation, which greatly facilitates older adults' ability to maintain contact with their families, friends, and ethnic group (Rudzitis, 1984).

Complexity. A second way to examine urban-rural differences is to look at the complexity of the community (Taietz, 1975). **Complexity** refers to the degree of differentiation among the services available to a community. Taietz (1975; Taietz & Milton, 1979) and Krout (1988a) examined complexity in rural and urban communities in New York state in terms of older adults' knowledge of locally available social services, housing, retail trade, community planning, and medical specialties.

Taietz found that higher complexity was associated with accurate information about facilities only in urban areas. As complexity increased in smaller communities, accuracy of knowledge about available facilities decreased. Krout ex-

tended these findings by demonstrating that residents of smaller communities were less aware of services on average but that this relationship might vary with a particular personal need for a specific service. Krout's results are explored in more detail in "How Do We Know?"

Because accurate information is essential for appropriate use of community services, an accompanying decline in resource utilization would be expected in complex small communities. The end result is that individuals' life satisfaction may decline because they perceive needs that are not being adequately met. That is, even if services are available, as long as people think that they are not, their overall satisfaction may be adversely affected.

Ideal Communities. Finally, some studies have examined people's notions of what the ideal community ought to have. In a comprehensive investigation Blake and Lawton (1980) found that younger and older adults living in both

HOW · DO · WE · KNOW?

Awareness of Services and Community Size

Lack of awareness of public services among the elderly has been cited as a major reason why many services are underutilized. However, few studies have examined the awareness levels of rural and urban elderly residents at the community level. One exception to this lack of research is a study conducted by Krout (1988a).

Krout surveyed a random sample of 600 elderly residents of a metropolitan county and a nonmetropolitan county in western New York. He was interested in how aware people were of various services as a function of three types of factors: predisposing, enabling, and need. Predisposing factors affect the likelihood that people become aware of services; they include such things as age, sex, race, marital status, education, home ownership, and contact with children. Enabling factors facilitate or inhibit the use of services; household income and car ownership are two com-

mon ones. The need factor reflects various conditions, such as health problems, that affect the degree to which people seek out services.

Krout collected data in personal interviews. He asked respondents what they knew about eight types of services in their community: elderly visitors, home health, home help, home meals, hot luncheon sites, information-referral services, legal aid, and transportation. The greatest awareness was shown for transportation, home meals, and hot luncheon sites, all of which were familiar to at least 75% of the respondents. However, people living in the metropolitan county were more aware of services, in general, than were the nonmetropolitan residents.

When Krout subjected his data to further statistical analyses, he found that community size was the best predictor of awareness. However, additional

characteristics related to the personal factors were also important. For predisposing factors, "young-old," nonwhite, better educated, married homeowners were more aware of services. For enabling factors, income was related to awareness. Finally, people with health problems or those who needed help with activities of daily living were more aware of services.

Krout's research shows that awareness of services available in one's community is more than a function of community size. It also appears that those who have specific reasons to know about services are also the ones who are aware of them. Krout's results must be interpreted with some caution, however, since he studied only elderly residents of two counties in New York. Whether the factors he found would generalize to other parts of the United States or to other Western countries remains to be seen.

rural and urban communities agreed that high-quality medical care, good schools, adequate numbers of good jobs, and a variety of stores should be available. However, several age and community differences emerged when comparisons were made of the absolute level of impor-

tance of these factors. Younger adults were most concerned about jobs and schools, and urbanites were more concerned about social facilities. Overall, older adults were more satisfied with the facilities available in their community than were younger adults.

Neighborhoods

Neighborhoods provide a setting for social inter-action as well as a convenient location for obtaining goods and services. Most research on neighborhoods from a developmental perspective concerns people's perceptions of their neighborhood as a good place to live and the utilization of local services. One general finding from this work is that as people age, they become more dependent on their local environment (Regnier, 1983). With this in mind, we will focus on the factors of the neighborhood that are particularly important to the elderly.

People's perceptions of their neighborhoods not only affect how they behave there but also have an impact on their overall psychological well-being. The important point here is that it is often the perception of the environment that matters, not necessarily the way things really are. It turns out that the relationship between objective neighborhood characteristics, such as the actual number of stores, and well-being is modest at best (Lawton & Nahemow, 1979).

Crime. Crime is one important dimension related to individuals' perceptions of their neighborhoods. More than anything else, it is the fear of crime, rather than actually being a victim of crime, that affects overall well-being (Lawton & Yaffe, 1980). Moreover, a survey of middle-aged and elderly residents of Los Angeles showed that concern about being a victim of crime was more related to neighborhood crime rate than it was to age. However, this positive relationship between concern and crime rate was not constant for Blacks, Mexican Americans, and Anglos. That is, Blacks and Mexican Americans are less easily influenced by neighborhood crime rates than are Anglos (Janson & Ryder, 1983). In general, the data suggest that there is little evidence to support the view that most older adults live like prisoners in their homes out of fear (Lawton, 1985). It appears that the perception of safety is the important consideration in satisfaction with one's neighborhood (Jirovec, Jirovec, & Bossé, 1985).

Structural Features. The age structure of neighborhoods as a factor in well-being has been examined in several studies. Lawton and Nahemow (1979) conducted an extensive examination of 31 characteristics of neighborhoods as factors in the well-being of 2,400 elderly tenants of planned-housing projects. They found that living in a neighborhood with a high proportion of older adults was related to greater participation in activities, higher satisfaction with housing, and more interpersonal interactions with other tenants. Although these findings support the idea that there are benefits of living in a neighborhood with many similarly aged people, Lawton and Nahemow point out that the size of the benefits is small. Indeed, some older adults are more satisfied living where they have few age peers. It appears that the benefits of living near age peers depend on the particular person; individual differences are large.

A study conducted by the Veterans Administration of 100 elderly men in Boston showed that perceived safety was by far the most important consideration in choosing a neighborhood (Jirovec et al., 1985). Interestingly, the other major characteristics listed, such as beauty, space, and antiquity, were aesthetic ones reflecting subjective, personal perception of the environment. Absent from this list were more traditional factors such as accessibility of resources or concentration of age peers.

When Lawton and Nahemow (1979) examined racial factors and neighborhood structure, they found parallel results. Specifically, friendship and activity patterns were highest for Black elderly people when they lived in neighborhoods that had higher concentrations of Blacks. Overall, though, the results indicated that Whites and Blacks were affected similarly by structural factors in the neighborhood.

Finally, people sometimes become attached to their neighborhoods. This may be especially true for older adults who have lived in the same place for decades and have become dependent on local services. This attachment may feed into one's general well-being by providing opportunities to reminisce about the past. Rowles (1980) suggests that reminiscing about the neighborhood may complement and accompany age-related increases in spatial constriction and dependence on the local area. As our society continues to be increasingly mobile, however, fewer of us will live in the same neighborhood all of our lives. Thus, it will be interesting to see whether our feelings of attachment to where we live change over the next few decades.

Housing

Over 20% of the households in the United States are headed by an adult over age 65, and the number of such households is growing more rapidly than the proportion of elderly in the general population (Silverman, 1987). Of these households headed by older adults, nearly 70% are owner-occupied. Unfortunately, these homes are often older, in poorer condition, and in less desirable neighborhoods than housing for younger and middle-aged adults. However, elderly homeowners have some clear advantages over renters; 86% of the homeowners have paid off their mortgage, whereas the renters spend an average of 30% of their income on housing. Elderly renters also tend to live in poorer quality apartments than their younger counterparts.

Golant (1984) points out an important consideration about housing that is often overlooked. Most elderly homeowners and renters live in homes designed for younger cohorts that are in-

appropriate for the changing needs of older adults. For example, most housing is too large, built on multiple levels, and designed with few fixtures to compensate for changing perceptual and motor skills.

Despite the range of housing options little developmental research has been conducted to examine the effects of these different arrangements on adults of various ages. Instead, gerontologists have primarily focused on age-segregated versus age-integrated housing. This research has been conducted in four main settings: apartment complexes for the elderly, retirement communities, congregate housing, and single-room-occupancy (SRO) hotels.

Age-Segregated Versus Age-Integrated Housing. Most older adults live in **age-integrated** communities, where there are people of all ages. Increasingly, however, the elderly are opting for communities that are **age-segregated**, that is, exclusively for older adults. In the United States federally assisted age-segregated housing projects began in 1956. Although roughly 6% of older adults live in age-segregated housing, this number is still well below that in some European countries such as the Netherlands, Sweden, France, and West Germany (Silverman, 1987). Since the 1960s the impact of age-segregated housing on older adults has been the topic of considerable research.

Early studies by Rosow (1967) on middle- and working-class elderly people in Cleveland and by Messer (1968) on public housing residents in Chicago showed that high concentrations of older adults resulted in higher levels of social contacts and morale, especially for women. Later research supported these findings, but added some important cautions. For example, Lawton confirmed that age-segregated housing resulted in increased social participation, interaction with other tenants, and satisfaction with housing (Lawton,

1980; Lawton, Moss, & Moles, 1984). However, Lawton (1980) and Carp (1976) both point out that these findings may be a function of the kind of housing and the particular neighborhood studied. For example, the people whom Rosow studied lived in an old, established neighborhood with long-term friendship patterns already in place. Whether the benefits of age-segregated housing extend to newer neighborhoods is a topic we will explore in the next few sections.

Several researchers have conducted excellent studies of people living in *apartment complexes for the elderly*. Two research methods have been used, interviews and participant observation.

The classic interview study of apartment residents was done by Carp (1966, 1976) at Victoria Plaza in San Antonio. Carp not only collected baseline data but also conducted follow-up interviews for 8 years following initial occupancy. In general, Carp found that the move to Victoria Plaza was associated with improved social and psychological well-being, lower mortality, a lower rate of institutionalization, improved health, and increased social participation as compared with remaining in one's original home. Although the people who moved to Victoria Plaza chose to do so and may not represent older people in general, they received many benefits.

Although the findings from other interview studies have not always been as impressive, they do tend to agree with Carp's overall conclusions that age-segregated apartments produce many benefits. For example, Lawton and Cohen (1974) and Messer (1967) both found improved well-being following a move to an age-segregated housing complex.

In contrast to interview studies, the investigator in **participant observation research** actually lives in the housing project. One of the best examples of such research was done by Hochschild (1973), who studied 46 low-income elderly residents, mostly widows, in San Francisco. An im-

portant characteristic of this project was the development of a **subculture**, or a strong positive feeling distinctive to the occupants. That is, although they did not have a great awareness of what was happening in the community around them, they were well informed on the events that were relevant to their lives. They celebrated birthdays together; looked in on one another; shared information, shopping, and costs; and communicated with one another extensively. Hochschild viewed these new shared roles as replacements for roles lost in their former communities that protected the residents against loneliness.

In a much larger study Jacobs (1975) examined a high-rise apartment building for working-class elderly people on a college campus in Syracuse, New York. Unlike the complex studied by Hochschild, the one in Syracuse was large, with over 400 residents, and ethnically diverse, with obvious tensions between the majority Whites and the small number of Blacks. Additionally, the fact that some of the residents were frail was resented by many others, who feared that the project would turn into a nursing home. Jacobs found that many residents were apathetic, passive, and isolated. Consequently, Jacobs concluded that a cohesive subculture would not result from simply putting people of the same age together. Rather, the emergence of a subculture depends on such factors as number, ethnicity, and health status.

In short, what we have learned from research on apartment complexes is that it takes much more than a collection of same-aged people to make a coherent, satisfying community. From a life-course perspective, past experiences, attitudes, and needs must be considered and taken into account. When these factors are considered and a subculture emerges, the positive impact of living in such settings is substantial (Longino, 1981).

Another rapidly growing form of age-segregated housing is **retirement communities**. In retirement communities not only is housing restricted to people of a given age, but the whole community is designed to cater to the needs of the elderly. For example, housing units are often one-story, electric golf carts are a preferred mode of transportation, and activities are planned with the older adult in mind. From their beginning in the Sun Belt states, retirement communities are now appearing across the United States.

Despite the considerable publicity that retirement communities have received, surprisingly little research has been done on their effects on residents. What little there is points to two opposite conclusions. Survey studies show that retirement communities tend to have overwhelmingly White, relatively affluent, better educated, healthier, married older adults (e.g., Heintz, 1976). Life satisfaction among residents is high, few wish to move out, and social participation is high.

In sharp contrast, participant observation research paints a very different picture. Jacobs (1974, 1975) studied the geographically isolated community of Fun City southeast of Los Angeles. The typical resident there was lonely, unhappy, and in despair. Social participation was low; only around 500 of the nearly 6,000 residents were active in a club or organization. In terms of Lawton and Nahemow's environmental press model, an imbalance existed between high personal competence and low environmental demands, resulting in poor adaptation. Jacobs also reported strong racist attitudes toward Blacks, Hispanics, and Native Americans, which was thought to be responsible for the lack of minority residents.

It is unclear why the findings in the survey and participant observation studies were so discrepant. It may be that residents want to highlight only the good aspects on a survey and that the negative aspects must be uncovered by personal observations. Geographical location could also be a factor, as well as how good the match is between

competence and environmental demands. Further research is clearly needed in order to resolve these issues.

Congregate housing represents an intermediate step between living independently and living in an institutional setting. Congregate housing includes what is sometimes called intermediate, communal, or community housing. The importance of congregate housing is that it provides a viable alternative to institutionalization for people who need supportive services in order to maintain their independence.

Great Britain has led the way in developing congregate housing. The complex usually has self-contained apartments that are linked to a central office for emergencies. A medical clinic with a full-time nursing staff is on the premises. Planned social activities are organized by a trained staff. Heumann and Boldy (1982) surveyed several British facilities and concluded that residents remained functionally independent longer and were more likely to avoid institutionalization than elderly residents of conventional housing.

Congregate housing in the United States has adopted the British model. Carlin and Mansberg (1984) showed that residents of a congregate facility in the northeastern United States were remarkably active in organizing and participating in activities. Their strong sense of cohesiveness was demonstrated by their sense of pride and mutual concern for the home and the residents. The sense of cohesiveness, or "we-feeling," was also noted by Ross (1977) in her study of a congregate home for the working-class elderly in Paris.

The need for increased congregate facilities is one of the most pressing housing needs in the United States (U.S. Office of Technology Assessment, 1984). Estimates are that 3 million elderly people in the United States need some sort of assisted housing, with the number expected to increase dramatically over the next few decades. Because little is known about the optimal design of congregate facilities and the type of resident who will benefit most, however, social policy awaits more research on these issues. Such research would benefit from the theoretical perspectives outlined at the outset, with special attention on the relationship between competence and demands and the congruence between needs and services.

Rather than living in congregate facilities, some elderly want to maintain their independence. The **single-room-occupancy (SRO) hotel** offers an alternative for people who desire a high degree of autonomy. SRO hotels are usually located in dangerous and dilapidated areas of inner cities (Lawton, 1980).

Erickson and Ekert (1977) classify SROs into three types: skid row hotels, the most deteriorated type, with mainly male, low-income occupants; working-class hotels, relatively clean, with housekeeping services and mostly male occupants; and middle-class hotels, more comfortable and expensive, with equal numbers of male and female occupants and some activities. Several participant observation studies have shown that residents of skid-row and working-class hotels are fiercely independent, have large social networks, have marginal relationships with family, show high mutual support, and are usually poor (Ekert, 1980; Sokolovsky & Cohen, 1983; J. Stephens, 1976; Teski, 1981). Survey research has documented similar findings; men living in SROs and on the street are in generally poorer health than their community-dwelling counterparts, and these health problems are related to stress, unfulfilled needs, relative youth, and contacts with agencies (C. I. Cohen, Teresi, & Holmes, 1988). Unfortunately, almost none of these data have been analyzed from a life-course perspective.

Most researchers agree that SROs play an important role in serving poor, independently minded elderly people. However, the number of SROs is rapidly diminishing, often because of urban renewal. For example, 89% of the SROs in New York City disappeared between 1970 and 1983 and were replaced with luxury housing (Sanjek, 1984). This substantial loss of SROs may be partially responsible for the increase in the homeless elderly, a connection that needs to be explored.

Conclusions. Although most of the research on communities, neighborhoods, and housing reviewed here focuses on how old people make out in various communities, it is important to realize that living arrangements in old age come from many decisions over the life span. Decisions about family size, kinship pattern, health care, occupational choices, and personal priorities all contribute to housing decisions in later life. Disruptions in these areas earlier in adulthood may have long-term carryover effects in old age.

The most important point to remember about communities, neighborhoods, and housing is that optimizing of the person-environment fit is the goal. Wiseman (1981) argues that the first step should be changing the person's level of competence or personal resources through such interventions as better health care and economic security. The second step would be to change the environment through relocation. The final strategy is to facilitate environmental interactions for the elderly, such as by instituting better transportation. What we need to know most of all is whether the success of these suggestions is related to normative developmental changes.

INSTITUTIONS

Although the majority of older adults live in the community, some do reside in institutions. At any moment approximately 5% of the population over 65 is living in an institution. This may seem to be a small number of people, especially in view of the dominant stereotype of disability and sickness in old age. Before we feel too relieved, however, we must also recognize that the probability that someone who lives past age 85 will spend at least *some* time in an institution is much higher than 1 in 20—it is more like 1 in 4 (Johnson, 1987). Thus, the number of people who are potentially affected by institutions is rather large.

Institutions are very different environments from those we have considered so far. As we will see, the inhabitants of institutions differ on many dimensions from their community-dwelling counterparts. Likewise, the environment itself is markedly different from neighborhood and community contexts. But because many aspects on the institutional environment are controlled, it offers a unique setting to examine person-environment interactions in more detail than is possible in other settings.

In this section we will examine types of institutions, the typical resident, and the psychosocial environment in institutions. Since virtually all of the adult developmental research in this field focuses on the elderly, we will concentrate on the older individual's experience of institutionalization.

Types of Institutions

The main types of institutions for elderly residents are nursing homes, personal-care and boarding homes, and psychiatric hospitals. **Nursing homes** house the largest number of elderly residents of institutions. They are governed by state and federal regulations that establish minimum standards for care. Two levels of care in nursing homes are defined in the federal regulations (Johnson & Grant, 1985). **Skilled nursing care** consists of 24-hour care requiring skilled medical and other health services, usually from nurses. **Intermediate**

care is also 24-hour care necessitating nursing supervision, but at a less intense level. In actual practice the major differences between the two are the types and numbers of health care workers on the staff. Perhaps for this reason, the distinction between skilled and intermediate care is undergoing governmental review.

Personal-care homes and **boarding homes** may also be regulated by states; however, no federal guidelines for these types of institutions exist. These institutions are primarily very small, and they house people who need assistance with daily needs because of disabilities or chronic disorders such as arthritis but who otherwise are in fairly good health. The quality of care in these institutions varies widely.

In the past, **psychiatric hospitals** housed many more older adults than they do now. Since the mid-1960s elderly psychiatric patients have been increasingly dismissed and relocated in the community or in other institutions. Unfortunately, little research has been conducted to measure the adjustment of these individuals after relocation. Today, older adults who suffer severe emotional or cognitive deficits are often placed in nursing homes rather than psychiatric hospitals. Elderly patients who are admitted to psychiatric hospitals due to serious psychological disorders such as paranoia or severe depression stay there for a much shorter period than even 20 years ago.

Because they contain the majority of older adults who live in institutions, nursing homes have been the setting for almost all of the research on the effects of institutionalization. For this reason nursing homes will be the focus of the remainder of this section. Caution should be exercised in generalizing the results from nursing home research to other types of institutions. Differences in structure, staffs, and residents' characteristics make comparisons of different types of institutions difficult. As a result we need more research

on the experience of older residents of other types of institutions and on how these experiences compare with those of nursing home residents. Additionally, as noted in "Something to Think About," funding for nursing homes will be an increasingly important issue in the coming decades.

Who Is Likely to Live in Nursing Homes?

Who is the typical resident of a nursing home? She is very old, White, financially disadvantaged, probably widowed or divorced, and possibly without living children. These characteristics are not similar to the population at large, as discussed in Chapter 1. For example, men are underrepresented in nursing homes, as are minorities. However, at least some of the ethnic differences may be a matter of personal choice rather than institutional policy. For example, some older Mexican Americans remain in the community to be cared for by family and friends regardless of their degree of impairment (Eribes & Bradley-Rawls, 1978).

What problems do typical nursing home residents have? For the most part, the average nursing home resident is clearly impaired, both mentally and physically. Indeed, the main reason for institutionalization for almost 80% of nursing home residents is health. Still, placement in a nursing home is usually done only as a last resort; over half of the residents come from other institutions such as general hospitals (Lawton, 1980).

Clearly, frail elderly people and their relatives alike do not see nursing homes as an option until other avenues have been explored. This may account for the numbers of truly impaired individuals who live in nursing homes; the kinds and amount of problems make life outside the nursing home very difficult on them and their families. In fact, if all other things are equal, the best predictor of who will be placed in a nursing home is the

absence of a viable social support system (George, 1980).

The fact that older adults and their families do not see nursing homes as the placement of choice means that the decision was probably made reluctantly. In some cases individuals other than family members enter the decision process. One common situation involves older adults living in age-segregated housing projects, most of which have some type of policy concerning the level of functioning that residents must have to remain. In actual practice most housing projects have explicit policies in areas concerning safety and liability; for example, some have regulations that tenants who need constant monitoring or who are nonambulatory must move out. However, most of these regulations are deliberately vague concerning basic skills needed for daily living, such as the ability to maintain one's own apartment, and about areas of personal behavior involving mental confusion, emotional instability, and drinking problems (Bernstein, 1982).

Bernstein surveyed the managers of 136 housing projects concerning their criteria for asking tenants to leave. She found substantial agreement across policies, which are summarized in Table 13.1. As can be seen, the most frequent reason for asking tenants to leave involved psychological functioning (mental ability, emotional stability, and so on). Tenants most often left voluntarily because they needed constant supervision. Notice that these reasons (and most of the other criteria listed) are similar to the characteristics of the typical nursing home resident.

Characteristics of Nursing Homes

We can examine nursing homes on two dimensions: physical and psychosocial. Physical characteristics include factors such as size, staff-to-resident ratio, numbers and types of activities,

S O M E T H I N G · T O · T H I N K · A B O U T

Financing Long-Term Care

The current system of financing long-term care in the United States is in very serious trouble. Nursing home costs in 1988 averaged over $22,000 per year and were far and away the leading catastrophic health care expense (Wiener, 1988). Contrary to popular belief, Medicare pays only 2% of nursing home expenses, and the typical private insurance plan pays only an additional 1%. Most often, the typical nursing home patient must deplete his or her life savings to pay for care. Once patients become totally impoverished, they become dependent on Medicaid. This public subsidy for nursing home care cost roughly $20 billion in 1988 and is increasing rapidly. For example, governmental support of long-term care, which represented 0.45% of the gross national product in 1988, is expected to grow to 1.42% by 2050 (Wiener, 1988). How will we be able to finance the long-term health care system?

One option is through the private sector. This approach includes long-term-care insurance, individual retirement accounts for long-term care, health-maintenance organizations, and alternative housing arrangements such as congregate housing. Many of these options place the burden on individuals to come up with ways of financing their own care. The Brookings Institution estimates that by 2018 private long-term-care insurance will be affordable by as many as 45% of older adults. However, these projections also indicate that at best, private insurance will lower Medicaid expenditures by only 2% to 5%. Such modest reductions in public support would also accompany individual retirement accounts, alternative housing, health-maintenance organizations, and other options. Consequently, large subsidies from government will still be needed for long-term care regardless what the private sector does.

Given that governmental subsidies for long-term care will be required for the foreseeable future, the question becomes how to finance them. Under the current Medicaid system older adults are not protected from becoming impoverished. Moreover, the way that the system is designed, the substantial majority of people needing care will ultimately qualify for the program once their savings are depleted. With the aging of the baby boom generation, Medicaid costs will skyrocket. If we want to continue the program in its current form, it is likely that additional revenues will be needed, perhaps in the form of taxes.

The questions facing us are whether we want to continue forcing older adults to become totally impoverished when they need long-term care, whether we want the government to continue subsidy programs, and whether we would be willing to pay higher taxes for this subsidy. How we answer these questions will have a profound impact on the status of long-term care over the next few decades. It's something to think about.

TABLE 13.1 • Most frequently mentioned reasons for asking tenants to leave housing projects or for their leaving voluntarily

	Projects Asked Tenants to Leave (%)	Projects' Tenants Left Voluntarily (%)
Tenant showed mental decline (senility, not mentally alert) or had problems such as emotional imbalance, aggressive behavior, paranoia, depression, etc.	61	27
Tenant was a potential health or safety hazard to self or others (accidents, fire, flooding, etc.).	32	10
Tenant needed daily supervision of activities, medication, and personal well-being.	30	67
Tenant had an alcohol abuse problem.	29	6
Tenant was bedridden and/or needed skilled nursing care facility (24-hour).	25	55
Tenant was a major disturbance or had a difficult personality.	22	0
Tenant had severe illness (stroke, heart, cancer, etc.).	18	39
Tenant had a general decline in health (frailty, deterioration, going downhill).	16	30
Tenant left to be with family members.	0	60
Tenant needed to have meals cooked or provided (if meals were on-site, they were not frequent enough or tenant was unable to get to them).	0	20

(Source: "Who Leaves—Who Stays: Residency Policy in Housing for the Elderly, by J. Bernstein, 1982, *Gerontologist, 22*, pp. 305–313. Copyright © 1982 by the Gerontological Society of America. Reprinted with permission.)

and certification requirements. Unfortunately, very little research has been done comparing institutions on these dimensions. As a result we do not have a good idea of how much variance there is on these dimensions across nursing homes and when differences become important.

More is known about the effects of these dimensions on residents' psychosocial well-being. The combination of the physical, personal, staff-related, and service-related aspects of the nursing home makes up a *milieu*, a higher-order abstraction of the environmental context (Lawton, 1980).

Over the last decade several researchers have been conceptualizing the effects of the institutional milieu on residents. We are already familiar with Kahana's ideas; an expansion of the previous discussion will be presented here. A second investigator, Moos, has taken a somewhat different approach that emphasizes measurement; we will also

Maintaining a social network is important, especially when living
in a nursing home.

consider his views in detail. Finally, we will consider some work by Langer from a social-psychological perspective.

The Congruence Approach. In describing her congruence theory, Kahana (1982) also discusses several dimensions along which person-environment congruence can be classified (see Table 13.2). She is especially interested in describing institutions, so most of her research is aimed at documenting her dimensions in these settings.

Kahana's approach emphasizes that personal well-being is not just the product of the characteristics of the institution and of the individual but also of the congruence between the individual's needs and the ability of the institution to meet them. People whose needs are congruent with the control provided by the institution should have the highest well-being. However, any number of factors could potentially be important in determining congruence, as is demonstrated by the large number of subdimensions in the congruence model.

Harel (1981) investigated which of these many factors in determining congruence was the most important in predicting well-being. Based on 125 interviews in 14 nursing homes, Harel found that continuing ties with preferred members of the resident's social network was the most important variable. Meeting social needs, then, should constitute a major goal for institutions. Harel suggested that a resident services department be established in nursing homes as well as policies allowing greater opportunities for choice in socializing.

Attempting to establish congruence in the social domain may have direct benefits. Greene and Monahan (1982) demonstrated that the frequency of family visitation affected residents' level of impairment. Specifically, those residents who were visited often by their families had significantly higher levels of psychosocial functioning.

This suggests that meeting social needs through visitation has a positive and direct effect on residents' well-being.

Moos's Approach. A second way to examine the person-environment interaction in institutions has been offered by Moos and his colleagues (Moos & Lemke, 1984, 1985). Moos believes that institutions can be evaluated in physical, organizational, supportive, and social-climate terms. Each of these areas is thought to have an effect on the well-being of the residents.

Several scales have been developed to assess institutions on these dimensions. The **Multiphasic Environmental Assessment Procedure (MEAP)**, one of the most comprehensive, assesses four aspects of the facility: physical and architectural features; administrative and staff policies and programs; resident and staff characteristics; and social climate. Each area is measured by separate multidimensional scales. Together, information from the MEAP provides a complete picture that allows a judgment to be made about how well the facility meets residents' needs.

Moos's approach has the advantage that separate dimensions of the person-environment interaction can be measured and examined independently. For one thing, it establishes areas of strength and weakness so that appropriate programs can be devised. But perhaps more importantly it may provide a basis for future efforts at developing rating systems for evaluating the overall quality of an institution. At present, questions like what really distinguishes good and bad nursing homes, for example, are unanswerable. Only further refinement of measures like those developed by Moos will give us a clue.

Social-Psychological Perspectives. Langer approaches the issue of person-environment interactions quite differently from either Kahana or Moos. She believes that the important factor in residents' well-being is the degree to which they perceive that they are in control of their lives (Langer, 1985).

To demonstrate her point, she conducted an ingenious experiment. One group of nursing home residents were told that staff members were there to care for them and to make decisions for them about their daily lives. In contrast, a second group of residents were encouraged to make their own decisions concerning meals, recreational activities, and so forth. This second group showed marked improvements in well-being and activity level compared with the first group (Langer & Rodin, 1976). These improvements were still seen 18 months later; in fact, the second group also seemed to have lower mortality rates (Rodin & Langer, 1977).

Based on her findings, Langer became convinced that making residents feel competent and in control were key factors in promoting positive person-environment interactions in nursing homes. Langer (1985) points to several aspects of the nursing home environment that fail in this regard. First, the decision to institutionalize is often made by persons other than the individual involved. Staff members may communicate their belief that the resident is simply incapable of making any decision or may treat him or her like a child, rather than like an adult who is moving to a new home.

Second, the label "nursing home resident" may have strong negative connotations. This is especially true if as a younger adult the person had negative preconceived ideas about why people go to nursing homes. A long history of social-psychological research shows that the individual may begin to internalize these stereotypical beliefs, even if they are unwarranted (e.g., Kelley, 1967). Other labels such as "patient" may have similar effects.

TABLE 13.2 · Environmental and individual dimensions of Kahana's congruence model with descriptions of important aspects of each.

Segregate Dimension	
Environment	*Individual*
a. Homogeneity of composition of environment. Segregation based on similarity of resident characteristics (sex, age, physical functioning and mental status).	a. Preference for homogeneity, i.e., for associating with like individuals. Being with people similar to oneself.
b. Change vs. sameness. Presence of daily and other routines, frequency of changes in staff and other environmental characteristics.	b. Preference for change vs. sameness in daily routines, activities.
c. Continuity or similarity with previous environment of resident.	c. Need for continuity with the past.

Congregate Dimension	
Environment	*Individual*
a. Extent to which privacy is available in setting.	a. Need for privacy.
b. Collective vs. individual treatment. The extent to which residents are treated alike. Availability of choices in food, clothing, etc. Opportunity to express unique individual characteristics.	b. Need for individual expression and idiosyncracy. Choosing individualized treatment whether that is socially defined as "good" treatment or not.
c. The extent to which residents do things alone or with others.	c. Preference for doing things alone vs. with others.

Institutional Control	
Environment	*Individual*
a. Control over behavior and resources. The extent to which staff exercises control over resources.	a. Preference for (individual) autonomy vs. being controlled.
b. Amount of deviance tolerated. Sanctions for deviance.	b. Need to conform.
c. Degree to which dependency is encouraged and dependency needs are met.	c. Dependence on others. Seeks support or nurturance vs. feeling self-sufficient.

(Source: "A Congruence Model of Person-Environment Interaction" by E. Kahana, 1982, in M. P. Lawton et al., Eds., *Aging and the Environment: Theoretical Approaches.* New York: Springer. Reprinted by permission of Dr. Eva Kahana.)

Structure

Environment	Individual
a. Ambiguity vs. specification of expectations. Role ambiguity or role clarity (e.g., rules learned from other residents).	a. Tolerance of ambiguity vs. need for structure.
b. Order vs. disorder.	b. Need for order and organization.

Stimulation–Engagement

Environment	Individual
a. Environmental input (stimulus properties of physical and social environment).	a. Tolerances and preference for environmental stimulation.
b. The extent to which resident is actually stimulated and encouraged to be active.	b. Preference for activities vs. disengagement.

Affect

Environment	Individual
a. Tolerance for or encouragement of affective expression. Provision of ritualized show of emotion (e.g., funerals).	a. Need for emotional expression. Display of feelings, whether positive or negative.
b. Amount of affective stimulation. Excitement vs. peacefulness in environment.	b. Intensity of affect, for example, need for vs. avoidance of conflict and excitement (shallow affect).

Impulse Control

Environment	Individual
a. Acceptance of impulsive life vs. sanctions against it. The extent to which the environment gratifies needs immediately vs. postponed need gratification. Gratification-deprivation ratio.	a. Ability to delay need gratification. Preference for immediate vs. delayed reward. Degree of impulse need.
b. Tolerance of motor expression—restlessness, walking around in activities or at night.	b. Motor control; psychomotor inhibition.
c. Premium placed by environment on levelheadedness and deliberation.	c. Impulsive closure vs. deliberate closure.

Third, the demonstration of "tender loving care" may serve mainly to reinforce the belief in one's incompetence. That is, in helping people perform basic tasks such as getting dressed, we run the risk of increasing their level of incompetence and dependence on others. Again, providing assistance where none is needed may be a way in which the staff communicates its belief that the individual cannot fend for himself or herself at all.

The physical aspects of the environment may also reinforce the belief of no control. To the extent that the environment is unfamiliar or is difficult to negotiate, persons living in it may feel incompetent. Mastering the environment increases feelings of control, but if this process is either not allowed or is made too easy, the outcome may be negative.

Finally, Langer (1985) argues that routine is also detrimental to well-being. If the environment is too predictable, there is little for people to think about; in Langer's terms we become mindless. In this state we are typically not aware of what we do; we behave as if we were on automatic pilot. If nursing home environments promote mindlessness, then individuals behave automatically and have difficulty remembering what happened even a short time before. When this occurs, the staff may view the person as incompetent. But since we all engage in mindless activity (e.g., performing a series of complex but automatic functions while driving) about which we have no recollection (one often cannot recall anything about driving the last several miles), immediately considering it as indicative of incompetence in the elderly but not in ourselves is difficult to justify.

Although some researchers have failed to replicate Langer's research when residents are reexamined over longer periods (e.g., Schulz & Hanusa, 1978), the points raised concerning how

nursing home residents should be treated are still very important. Whether the benefits of increased control last over the long run is still an open issue. Whether we should treat nursing home residents with respect is not.

RELOCATION

The United States is a highly mobile society. The time when people lived their entire lives in the same neighborhood has largely passed. Relocation is experienced by adults of all ages, many of whom are already veterans by the time they reach 21. Regardless of one's age or previous experience, relocation is a challenge. Whether it is moving to a different floor in the dorm or across the country, moving disrupts our physical and social environments and tests our coping skills. Living in a house full of boxes and moving cartons is a hassle; leaving friends and family for a strange city hundreds of miles away is emotionally traumatic. But as any veteran of many relocations will attest, lots of things determine whether a move will be psychologically tolerable or a nightmare. Exactly what impact does moving have on psychological well-being? Does the type of relocation make a difference? What factors make adjustment after moving easier or more difficult?

In order to answer these questions, we will examine two types of relocation: community-based and institutional. Community-based moves involve moving from one residence to another, regardless whether the two are in the same neighborhood or a great distance apart. The key ingredient is that the person maintains an independent residence. In contrast, institutional relocations involve moving either from a community-based residence to an institution or from one institution

to another. The major factor here is that the individual is not able to live independently in the community.

Community-Based Relocation

Community-based relocations are fairly common. Although younger adults are the most likely to move, middle-aged and older adults do relocate. Indeed, in 1987 nearly one third of adults over age 45 had moved within the previous 5 years. Clearly, community-based relocation is fairly common.

Why People Move. Although many older adults head to the Sun Belt, many do not. In fact, recent trends indicate that the flight to warmer climates is slowing, and many elderly people choose to relocate to retirement communities in the North (Meyer, 1987). Regardless of where they go, why do they move in the first place?

In one of the few developmental studies on mobility, Speare and Meyer (1988) identified four reasons for moving mentioned by movers 55 and older that corresponded to changes in later life: amenity, kinship, retirement, and widowhood. **Amenity mobility** is based on a primary or secondary reason of climate change. **Kinship mobility** occurs because the person wants to be closer to relatives. **Retirement mobility** takes place in response to retirement, with climate and distance from relatives not a factor. **Widowhood mobility** occurs when a person desires to be closer to important members of the social support system other than the immediate family.

The characteristics of elderly movers differ somewhat based on the reason for moving. As summarized in Table 13.3, amenity and retirement movers are similar in that both groups are richer and better educated, own their own home, and are married. Kinship movers tend to be older than other types but in other respects are similar to other groups. Widowhood movers have significantly lower income, are older, but are also well educated and own homes. Additionally, amenity and retirement movers head to the South and West more often than other types, who relocate to all regions.

Factors Affecting Adjustment. Simply because relocation happens frequently does not diminish its psychological impact. One way to think about this aspect of relocation is to consider moving in terms of the psychological stress it introduces and the effects that stress has on a person's adjustment. When relocation is viewed this way, an important question comes to mind. Given that any relocation is potentially stressful, what variables influence an individual's perception of stress in community-based relocations?

Four variables appear to be important. Obviously, the degree to which familiar behavior patterns are disrupted is a consideration. Second, the sense of personal loss at leaving one's former residence also affects subsequent adjustment. To the extent that one was very attached to one's old home, adjustment to one's new home may be harder. A third variable is the distance involved in the move; the farther one moves, the greater the disruption of routines is likely to be. Finally, the reason for the move is very important. It is generally true that people who make voluntary moves perceive the relocation more positively than people who make involuntary moves.

Although the four variables of disruption, loss, distance, and reason are good predictors of stress in community-based moves, there are substantial individual differences in people's adjustment even for identical levels of loss, for example. How well one adjusts to relocation, then, is a function not only of disruption and so forth but also of several personal factors involving social

TABLE 13.3 • Characteristics of different types of movers and nonmovers aged 55 and older

Independent Variables	Movers, by Reason					Nonmovers
	Amenity	*Kinship*	*Retirement*	*Widowed*	*Other*	
Age groups						
55 to 64	53.6	41.4	59.2	35.4	57.8	41.3
65 to 74	25.5	33.8	29.4	32.1	26.9	34.9
75 and over	21.0	24.8	11.5	32.5	15.3	23.8
Total	100.0	100.0	100.0	100.0	100.0	100.0
Household types						
Single person	32.9	48.4	18.5	89.5	45.8	33.0
2 + persons	8.7	9.9	0.0	10.5	13.1	11.0
Married couple	58.4	41.7	81.5	0.0	41.1	56.0
Total	100.0	100.0	100.0	100.0	100.0	100.0
Previous tenure						
Homeowner	70.8	48.7	78.6	62.8	29.7	78.2
Renter	29.2	51.3	21.4	37.2	70.3	21.8
Total	100.0	100.0	100.0	100.0	100.0	100.0
Education (in years)						
0 to 7	8.7	13.2	6.9	17.4	20.2	14.5
8 to 11	27.1	39.6	25.2	25.2	28.3	30.9
12 to 15	50.3	34.8	55.7	33.7	39.5	41.8
16 +	13.9	12.3	12.2	23.7	12.0	12.9
Total	100.0	100.0	100.0	100.0	100.0	100.1
Income/poverty						
Below poverty	13.1	20.9	8.7	39.8	28.9	16.3
Below 2 × poverty	21.8	32.5	27.6	28.7	27.0	28.1
Above 2 × poverty	65.1	46.6	63.6	31.5	44.1	55.6
Total	100.0	100.0	100.0	100.0	100.0	100.0

(Source: "Types of Elderly Residential Mobility and Their Determinants" by A. Speare, Jr., and J. W. Meyer, 1988, *Journal of Gerontology, 43,* pp. 574–581. Copyright © 1988 by the Gerontological Society of America. Reprinted with permission.)

status, social support, environmental variables, and perception of the move. These personal factors affect the perception of stress and facilitate or hinder the adjustment process. Since they are important factors in understanding how individuals cope with relocation, they will be considered more thoroughly in the following sections.

Social status factors such as occupation, education, and socioeconomic status provide an indication of where a person fits in the community and an index of life experience. Of the many social status variables that could influence adjustment to community-based relocation, only two have been studied systematically. Higher levels of education lead to better adjustment (Storandt, Wittels, & Botwinick, 1975), as does higher socioeconomic status, reflected in occupation and income (Rosow, 1967; Storandt et al., 1975). Because more highly educated people tend to have higher socioeconomic status, the two factors may operate together.

One thing is clear from this work. Our understanding of the influence of social status on adjustment to relocation is quite limited. Important factors such as marital status, race, and sex have not been examined very thoroughly as potential influences. Until such multivariate research is done, we will not know whether the influence of education and socioeconomic status holds independent of these other factors.

Social support systems provide both emotional and other types of assistance during relocation. We have already seen that maintaining friendships is an important factor in nursing home residents' well-being; the same is true for people who move. Research shows that good relationships with family and friends facilitate adjustment to relocation (George, 1980; Lawton, 1980).

Some research has examined changes in social support systems following relocation. Interestingly, it appears that people do not substitute relationships with one group for missing relationships with another. For instance, older adults whose children or other close relatives move away do not substitute friendships with age peers for the missing familial ties (Hochschild, 1973). The best possible situation is one in which old friendship and family bonds can be maintained and new ones developed.

Environmental variables such as the physical characteristics of the new residence and the nature of the new community affect adjustment. In particular, the issues of space, privacy, and convenience are important physical factors. Improvements on these dimensions will lead to better adjustment (Lawton, 1980). Additionally, people who move to communities having high proportions of same-age peers tend to adjust better (Rosow, 1967; Teaff, Lawton, Nahemow, & Carlson, 1978). This effect is probably due to the greater ease of forming new friendships when one is surrounded by people of similar age and background, thereby helping to build a new social support system.

People's *perception of the move,* such as what they believe to be their degree of control, has a direct bearing on how well they adjust, independent of the true situation. In general, if people think that they are being forced to move, adjustment problems are more likely to result (George, 1980).

If perception is viewed as a function of advance knowledge of the move, a contrasting picture emerges. Schooler (1982) found that when moves were expected, the outcomes were worse than when they were unexpected. He speculated that advance knowledge of an impending relocation might induce anxiety, which might be exacerbated by the trauma of the move itself. Interestingly, when expected relocations resulted in a better environment or when a confidant was available, the negative impact was reduced.

However, Schooler did not take into account why people were moving or their attitudes about it, so the overall meaning of his results is somewhat unclear. Still, we should not dismiss his results; they point out that even when individuals know that they are going to move, some people may suffer from the anxiety induced by this knowledge.

Long-Term Effects. Most studies of adjustment to community-based relocation have followed the participants for only a short time after they move. Because short-term effects may differ from long-term effects, longitudinal investigations are required to address this possibility. All of the psychological consequences of moving that we have considered thus far are based on short-term assessments. In this section we will consider what we know about the long-term effects of moving in the community.

Two projects have examined adjustment of movers approximately a year after their voluntary relocation. Both involved older adults moving from independent community residences to housing projects designed specifically for the elderly, and both involved comparisons between movers and people who were on the waiting list for admission to the housing complex, termed "nonmovers" in this study.

In the first project participants were all eligible for low-income housing and had limited financial assets. They were tested on four areas relating to psychological adjustment: cognitive and psychomotor performance, health, activity level, and morale and well-being. Testing was done twice, 5 months before the move and 9 months after. The results showed no differences between movers and nonmovers on any of the measures, so the investigators concluded that moving had no long-term adverse effects (Storandt & Wittels, 1975; Storandt et al., 1975; Wittels & Botwinick, 1974).

The second project involved individuals who wanted to move to Victoria Plaza in San Antonio. For those people who were successful getting into the project, the new residences offered considerably improved surroundings than had been available in the previous residence. Movers and nonmovers were tested three times: 6 months before the move and 1 and 8 years after the move. Health, mortality rates, and well-being were measured. Results showed that on each test the movers were significantly better off than the nonmovers on every measure. Thus, when relocation involves significant improvements in one's physical surroundings, the benefits of moving or the costs of not moving are potentially very long-lasting (Carp, 1966, 1975a, 1975b, 1977).

Institutional Relocation

We saw in the earlier discussion of institutions that although only about 5% of the people over age 65 reside in them at any one time, many more people spend at least part of their lives there. This means that many people face the transition from living in the community to living in an institution each year. As in community-based relocation, there is disruption in routines and in social relationships and a sense of loss from leaving the previous home.

From the previous discussion, and perhaps from personal experience, we might expect institutional relocation to be more difficult to deal with psychologically. After all, older and younger people view institutionalization with dread and see it as an admission that they are no longer competent enough to care for themselves. Admission to an institution also involves giving up a great deal of personal freedom and privacy. But do these factors necessarily imply that all institutional relocations result in negative outcomes?

Personal Factors Affecting Adjustment. To answer this question, we must consider many of

the same personal factors affecting adjustment that are important in community-based moves: social status, social support, and involuntary versus voluntary relocation. Moreover, there are several other variables that must be considered in institutional relocation: physical and cognitive resources, personality factors, and preparation experiences.

Relocation to an institution is not random. As noted earlier, very old White women who are widowed or unmarried and who have minimal financial resources are the most likely to be institutionalized when they face serious health problems. Although these variables of *social status* accurately predict who the typical relocator will be, they do not appear to predict level of adjustment in the institution.

Physical health and cognitive abilities facilitate institutional relocation (Tobin & Lieberman, 1976). Specifically, people in poor health and those who have experienced severe cognitive declines are more likely to have adjustment problems. Although inadequate physical and cognitive resources predict maladjustment, adequate resources do not guarantee successful relocation.

The importance of *social support* as a factor in adjustment to institutional relocation cannot be overemphasized. As indicated earlier, lack of a viable social support system is the best predictor of institutionalization (George, 1980). The maintenance of old support systems and the development of new ones after relocation to a nursing home eases adjustment (Greene & Monahan, 1982; Harel, 1981). Furthermore, close primary relationships are associated with better adjustment following relocation from one institution to another (Wells & Macdonald, 1981). These relationships provide residents with a source of continuity that enable them to deal better with an emotionally stressful event.

There appears to be a cluster of *personality traits* that is related to survival among nursing home residents. These traits include aggression, hostility, assertiveness, and narcissism (Tobin & Lieberman, 1976). Since people with these traits are not usually the easiest to get along with, it may seem surprising that such unpleasant characteristics are related to at least one aspect of adjustment. However, these traits may represent the only means by which a person can assert his or her individuality and dislike for the lack of personal freedom in the institution. In this sense these characteristics may represent a more adaptive response than passive acceptance, even though the latter behavior will win more friends among the staff.

Preparation for institutional relocation involves not only formal programs but also informal ones through friendship networks. A number of studies have shown that adjustment following relocation from one institution to another is better if residents are given a formal preparation program (e.g., Pastalan, 1976; Pino, Rosica, & Carter, 1978). Borup (1981) concluded that the major objective of these programs should be to help reduce the stress and anxiety associated with the relocation.

Recall that a good predictor of adjustment in community-based relocation was whether the move was *voluntary or involuntary*. Knowing this, we might predict that involuntary moves to institutions would also be more stressful. Unfortunately, almost no research has examined this issue. The problem is that most institutional relocations are involuntary, so researchers have not considered this factor.

Type of Relocation and Adjustment. We have seen that many personal factors influence adjustment following institutional relocation. In order to understand the adjustment process itself, however, we must consider two types of institutional relocation: relocation from the community

to an institution and relocation from one institution to another. We have alluded to these different types in our discussion of personal factors; we will now examine them in more detail. Since almost all of the relevant studies have concentrated on nursing homes as the setting, our survey will focus on this institution.

Three issues that are important in the adjustment process following *relocations from the community to a nursing home* have been investigated fairly intensely: person-environment fit, short-term versus long-term adjustment patterns, and factors immediately before institutionalization.

The appropriateness of the nursing home and of the services it provides is related to level of residents' morale 1 year after their relocation (J. N. Morris, 1975). People who are placed in inappropriate nursing homes have significantly lower morale than those who are appropriately placed. These findings once again show the importance of Kahana's (1982) notion of congruence, or person-environment fit.

In examining adjustment after a move from the community to a nursing home, a researcher must be careful to follow the residents long enough. This point was nicely demonstrated by Spasoff and his colleagues (1978). They found that life satisfaction was consistently high at 1 month and 1 year after relocation. However, 25% of the original sample had died, and 15% had been moved to other nursing homes during the first year. Clearly, the sample that was tested after 1 year was different from the one tested initially. Spasoff et al. (1978) demonstrated that investigators need to be sensitive to these changes in sample characteristics in order to avoid incorrect conclusions about long-term adjustment.

Tobin and Lieberman conducted a major longitudinal investigation of adjustment to moves from the community to nursing homes (Tobin & Lieberman, 1976). They were able to isolate the effects of relocation itself by examining three

groups of people: a group that was waiting for admission to a nursing home, a group that had been in a nursing home for 1 to 3 years, and a sample that stayed in the community throughout the study. Five factors in adjustment (physical health, cognitive functioning, emotional states, emotional responsiveness, and self-perception) were measured at three times: before the institutionalization of the relocation group, 2 months after relocation, and 1 year after.

Most important, Tobin and Lieberman found that even before institutionalization the relocation group resembled the institutional group more than the community group. Moreover, the main influences on adjustment and identity after placement are those that lead to institutionalization in the first place. Following relocation, the first few months seem to be the most difficult, although some people experience relocation stress up to a year later. Thus, Tobin and Lieberman's results show that it is the elderly with the fewest personal resources to handle stress who are most likely to be involved in the stress of relocation from the community to a nursing home.

Few studies have examined the psychological adjustment process following *relocation from one institution to another*. Rather, investigators have looked at mortality rates as the measure of successful relocation. A highly controversial series of studies by Borup and his associates in the late 1970s and early 1980s spurred a heated debate over the connection between interinstitutional relocation and mortality (Borup, 1981, 1982, 1983; Borup & Gallego, 1981; Borup, Gallego, & Heffernan, 1979, 1980).

Borup concluded from his own and others' research that relocation alone had no effect on residents' mortality. He argues that in some cases a moderate environmental change can even have a positive effect, for reasons similar to Langer's concerning mindlessness. Finally, Borup attributes most of the apparent negative consequences of

relocation to the length of time spent in the nursing home. That is, he feels that the same observations of decline would be made if residents remained in the same nursing home for the same period.

Borup's conclusions have been attacked by several authors (Bourestom & Pastalan, 1981; Horowitz & Schulz, 1983). Criticisms of Borup's research design and interpretations of his own and others' findings have been the main focus of these debates. These authors are also concerned that nursing homes will misapply Borup's results and abandon all attempts to make relocation less stressful. These critics force the reader to evaluate the evidence carefully and stimulate discussion on a very important topic.

The weight of the evidence points to the conclusion that interinstitutional relocation per se has little if any direct effect on mortality. Future researchers will be focusing on the question of psychological adjustment following such moves. It remains to be seen whether the findings from this research will prove as controversial as those from mortality research.

Relocation within the same institution occurs relatively frequently, such as when a new wing is built or a resident requests the move. As with interinstitutional relocation, past research has resulted in confusing data. In an attempt to clarify the issues, Pruchno and Resch (1988) examined 1-year mortality rates in one group following room changes for reasons other than health and in a nonmover group matched for competence. Through advanced statistical analyses, Pruchno and Resch showed that the connection between mortality after relocation and initial competence was complex. Mortality rates for movers who had high or low initial competence were lower than for the nonmover group. However, movers with moderate initial competence showed higher mortality levels. Pruchno and Resch argue that moving represented a positive and stimulating ex-

perience for residents with high or low competence, whereas those with moderate competence viewed the move as disruptive and confusing. The important point from this research is that mortality effects following a move may be related to the environmental cues that are most salient to the residents. That is, residents who notice the negative features of the move may be more at risk than those who focus on the positive aspects.

SUMMARY

Environmental psychology is based on the assumption that people can be understood better when they are considered within the context in which they behave. Four models of person-environment interactions were discussed: the competence and environmental press model, the congruence model, stress and coping theory, and the loss-continuum model. According to the competence and environmental press model, behavior is the result of a person with a particular level of ability, or competence, acting in an environment that puts certain demands, or press, on him or her. Adaptive and maladaptive behavior both result from many possible combinations of competence and press. According to the congruence model, people with particular needs search for environments that will meet them best. Congruence is most important when the individual's options are limited. The stress and coping theory is based on Lazarus and Folkman's notion that people evaluate the perceived threat in their environment. This theory is especially useful in understanding people at risk. The loss-continuum concept analyzes person-environment interactions in terms of personal losses, with emphasis on the growing importance of the immediate neighborhood with increasing age.

Several aspects of communities, neighborhoods, and housing affect the well-being of their residents. The size of a community influences the degree to which one feels part of it; this feeling is increased as towns get smaller. Complexity in small towns is associated with less knowledge about what local services are available; in large cities, however, complexity is associated with more knowledge of services. Neighborhood factors such as concern about crime, the age and racial structure of the neighborhood, and the degree of attachment to a neighborhood all affect satisfaction with where one lives. The issue of age-segregated versus age-integrated housing has been the focus of considerable research. A key issue in apartment complexes is that the emergence of a subculture is necessary for positive effects to accrue. Research on retirement communities has resulted in opposite conclusions: that they are either very good or very bad for social participation, depending on geographical location, research method used, and quality of the environment. Congregate housing represents a viable alternative to institutionalization for many elderly people. Single-room-occupancy hotels are steadily decreasing in number, limiting the poor who want to maintain their autonomy.

Nursing homes house the majority of older adults who reside in institutions. The typical nursing home resident is a very elderly woman who is unmarried, financially disadvantaged, and without a viable social support network. The well-being of nursing home residents is increased when there is congruence between their needs and the ability of the institution to meet them. Attempts to assess nursing home quality emphasize the importance of congruence. Suggestions for improving the overall environment (e.g., staff attitudes, routinization, labeling) have come from concerns about the psychosocial well-being of residents.

Little research has been conducted on the factors influencing well-being after community-based relocation. Personal resources, especially the social support system, appear to be most important. Adjustment to institutional relocation depends on level of cognitive and physical impairment, social support, personality, whether the move is voluntary, and degree of preparation.

GLOSSARY

adaptation level • Points where environmental press are average for particular levels of competence.

age-integrated • Having people of all ages.

age-segregated • Having age restrictions.

amenity mobility • Relocation based on personal preferences for climate.

competence • The theoretical upper limit of an individual's capacity to function.

complexity • The degree to which formal services to individuals are differentiated into various agencies in a community.

congregate housing • An intermediate living arrangement between independent housing and an institution; some supportive services are available.

congruence model • An approach to person-environment interactions that emphasizes the fit between individuals' needs and the degree to which they are met by the environment.

environmental press • The demands put on the individual by the environment.

environmental psychology • The study of the interaction of people with their living environment.

informal social network • Friends, family, and neighbors who provide care and support.

intermediate care • Full-time attention by a trained health care staff that is less intensive than skilled nursing care.

kinship mobility • Relocation based on a desire to live closer to relatives.

loss-continuum • Concept A model of person-environment interaction that postulates reduction in life space resulting from progressive series of losses, such as death of friends.

Multiphasic Environmental Assessment Procedure (MEAP) • A comprehensive scale to measure how well an institution is meeting the needs of residents.

nursing home • The most common type of institution for the elderly, providing various levels of care.

participant observation research • A study in which the investigator lives with residents.

personal-care and boarding homes • Small residences for the elderly that cater to individuals who have chronic diseases but are otherwise in reasonably good health.

person-environment interactions • A set of theories based on the idea that behavior is a function of the person and the environment.

psychiatric hospital • An institution that provides care for mentally ill individuals; at one time such places housed many older adults.

retirement community • An age-segregated town catering to the needs of the elderly.

retirement mobility • Relocation based on a response to retirement, with climate and distance from relatives not considered.

rural-urban continuum • The dimension along which communities vary in terms of size.

single-room-occupancy (SRO) hotel • A residential hotel catering to elderly residents; there are three types: skid row, working-class, and middle-class.

skilled nursing care • Full-time attention by skilled medical or other health professionals; usually provided in a nursing home.

stress and coping theory • A model of person-environment interaction based on Lazarus's theory of stress (described in Chapter 4).

subculture • A strong positive feeling distinctive to residents of a particular location.

widowhood mobility • Relocation based on a desire after the death of one's spouse to be closer to members of one's social support system other than family.

ADDITIONAL READING

A good overview of person-environment interactions can be found in

Lawton, M. P., Windley, P. G., & Byerts, T. O. (1982). *Aging and the environment: Theoretical approaches.* New York: Springer.

Two chapters in a book edited by Philip Silverman summarize research on living arrangements:

Johnson, C. L. (1987). The institutional segregation of the aged. And Silverman, P. (1987). Community settings. In P. Silverman (Ed.), *The elderly as modern pioneers.* Bloomington: Indiana University Press.

Death and Dying

Andrew Wyeth, *Beckie King*, 1946. Dallas Museum of Art, Gift of Everett L. DeGolyer

The human mind is as little capable to contemplate death for any length of time as the eye is able to look at the sun.

La Rochefoucauld

PEOPLE HAVE A PARADOXICAL RELATIONship with death. On the one hand, we have almost a fascination with it. The popularity of news stories about murders or wars and the crowds of onlookers at accidents testify to that. But when it comes to pondering our own death or that of people close to us, we have considerable problems, as La Rochefoucauld wrote over 300 years ago. When death is personal, we become uneasy. It is hard indeed to look at the sun.

In this chapter we will consider death from many perspectives. We will examine some of the issues surrounding how death is defined. The reasons why most of us avoid thinking about death will be considered. What it is like to die and how dying people are cared for will be explored. Since death affects not only the dying but the survivors as well, the ways in which people grieve are also described. Finally, the issue of an afterlife and the near-death experience will be considered.

DEFINITIONS AND ETHICAL ISSUES

Death can be viewed as a transition between being alive and being dead. Dying, like aging, is a process. Being dead, like being young or old, is a status. Each of these terms seems clear enough, but in fact each is very hard to define. For example, exactly what is death? When does death occur? These are two of the questions we will address in this section.

Sociocultural Definitions of Death

What comes to mind when you hear the word *death*? Black crepe paper or a cemetery? A driver killed in a traffic accident? Old people in nursing homes? A gathering of family and friends? A transition to an eternal reward? A car battery that doesn't work anymore? An unknowable mystery? Each of these possibilities represents one of the ways in which death can be considered (Kastenbaum, 1975). But each of these possibilities reflects Western culture (Kalish, 1987). People in other traditions view death differently. Because beliefs about death are not universal, it is important at the outset to realize that just because people around the world appear to use the same words or concepts that we do, they may not mean the same things.

For example, Westerners tend to divide people into groups based on chronological age, even though we recognize the limitations of this concept (see Chapter 1). Although we would like to divide people along more functional grounds, practicality dictates that chronological age will have to do. However, other cultures divide people differently. Among the Melanesians the term *mate* includes the very sick, the very old, and the dead; the term *toa* refers to all other living people. This distinction is the most important one, not the one between the living and the dead as in our culture (Counts & Counts, 1985). Other South Pacific cultures believe that the life force may leave the body during sleep or illness, suggesting that sleep, illness, and death are considered together. In this way people "die" several times before experiencing "final" death (Counts & Counts, 1985). For example, among the Kaliai, "the people . . . are prepared to diagnose as potentially fatal any fever or internal pain or illness that does not respond readily to treatment" (p. 150). Mourning rituals and definitions of states of bereavement also vary across cultures (Simmons, 1945). Thus, in considering death, dying, and bereavement, we must keep in mind that the experiences of our culture may not generalize to others.

Kastenbaum's Approach. Kastenbaum (1975) feels that death can be viewed in at least six ways: as a variable, a statistic, an event, a state, an analogy, and a mystery. These different ways of viewing death are a reflection of the diverse ways in which society deals with death. Kalish agrees with Kastenbaum's ideas: "Death means different things to the same person at different times; and it means different things to the same person at the same time" (Kalish, 1976, p. 483). Let us consider what these "different things" are.

In every culture there are *particular images or objects* that serve as reminders of death. For instance, a flag at half staff, sympathy cards, and tombstones all bring death to mind. People may try to avoid thinking about or viewing these reminders. Others may see these images and feel uneasy or may simply think about their own inevitable death.

Each year, numerous reports summarize death-related information: how many people died from certain diseases, traffic accidents, or murders, for example. These *mortality statistics* are vital to many organizations such as insurance companies, which use them to set premium rates for health and life insurance, and community planners, who use them to project needs for various services. But they also tend to sanitize and depersonalize death by removing the personal context and presenting death as a set of numbers.

Whenever someone dies, it is an *event*. The legal community marks it with official certificates and procedures. Family and friends gather to mourn and comfort one another. Funerals or memorial services are held. Memorial funds may be established. All of these actions serve to mark a person's death and illustrate how death brings people together. The gathering is sometimes seen on a societal level; the national mourning following the Challenger tragedy is an example.

What is it like to be dead? All answers to this question are examples of our belief in death as a *state of being*. Individual differences are the rule here, and particular beliefs are mainly a product of personal experiences and religious beliefs. Death may be thought of as a state of perpetual being, a state of nothingness, a time of waiting or of renewal, an experience that is much like this life, or an existence that involves a transformation of being. While we are alive, each of these views is equally valid; perhaps we will learn more when we make the transition ourselves.

In our language we have many sayings that use the notion of death as an *analogy* to convey the uselessness of people or objects: "that's a dead battery" or "you're a deadhead." In addition, some animals, such as opossums, use playing dead as a defense against predators. Finally, a person who is considered totally unimportant by family or acquaintances may be disowned and treated as if he or she were dead.

Even though we know that death is inevitable, it is rarely a major topic for discussion or consideration. More important, because we have so little scientifically valid information about death, it remains an unanswered question, the ultimate *mystery* in our lives. Try as we might, death is one life event (like the moment that life begins) that is understood only when it is experienced. Which, of course, is a major reason that we are typically afraid to die.

Kalish's Approach. Kalish (1987) also views death as having many meanings. However, he describes them a bit differently than Kastenbaum does, thereby emphasizing different aspects. Four of Kalish's topics are important here: death as a boundary, death as the thief of meaning, death as the basis for fear and anxiety, and death as reward or punishment.

Regardless of how one views the state of death, it is seen as an end, or *boundary*, of one's earthly existence. When the end of a period of time is approaching, we tend to pay greater attention to it and to use the time remaining more effectively. For example, as students near the end of their undergraduate careers, they typically change the way in which they spend the remaining time, based on their priorities. Consider how your use of time would change if you could assume 400 more years of life rather than 50 or 60. Would you continue doing what you are right now? Or would you do something different?

By the same token, as people's death becomes more imminent, how they use their remaining time becomes more important. For example, Kalish and Reynolds (1981) found that 29% of people over 60 thought about their death every day, compared with 15% under 40 and 11% between 40 and 60.

Interestingly, it also appears that people allot themselves a certain number of years to which they feel entitled. Although the exact number of years varies across the life span, most people feel that this amount of time is only fair; this view is termed the **just world view** by social psychologists (Kalish, 1987). If death becomes imminent many years before this "entitled" length of life, the person is liable to feel cheated. If the number of expected years of life is exceeded, then death is seen to be playing by the rules; it is now all right to die.

Intellectually, we all know that we may die at any time, but in modern society the probability of death before old age is relatively low. This was not always true. In earlier centuries death occurred almost randomly across the life cycle, with many deaths among infants, young children, and women in childbirth. Ariès (1974) believes that people in earlier times lived each day to the fullest because they knew firsthand that death really did occur to people of all ages.

Today, we are so convinced that we will live a long life that we let many days simply slip by. We delay fulfillment of dreams or ambitions until the later years, when illness or limited finances may restrict our ability to do what we had planned. In this sense death has *robbed us of the meaning of life.* We no longer take each day and use it for everything it is worth. As a result the conflicts of the later years (Erikson, 1980; see Chapter 8) involve questions of what life means, such as why we should bother learning new things since death is so close (Kalish, 1987).

Thinking about death may bring about feelings of *fear and anxiety.* Because so much research has examined this topic, we will consider it in detail later.

Many people believe that the length of life is a *reward or punishment* for how righteously or sinfully one lives. For example, the Hopi Indians believe that kindness, good thoughts, and peace of mind lead to a long life (Simmons, 1945). Similarly,

Among the Hopi, the length of life is believed to be tied to good deeds.

a study of four ethnic communities in Los Angeles (Black, Hispanic, Japanese-American, and Anglo) found that over half of the respondents over 65 and about 30% of younger respondents agreed with the statement "Most people who live to be 90 years old or older must have been morally good people" (Kalish & Reynolds, 1981). Finally, the Managalase, an Oceanic society, believe that simply remaining alive into old age is a sign of strength of "soul," and their elderly are treated with more respect than in most societies (McKellin, 1985).

Legal and Medical Definitions

Sociocultural approaches to defining death help us understand the different ways in which people view it. But these views do not address a very fundamental question: how do we determine that someone has died? To answer this question, we must turn our attention to the medical and legal definitions of death.

Determining when death occurs has always been a judgment. Just as there is considerable debate over when life begins, so there is over when life ends. The solution typically has been for experts to propose a set of criteria, which are then adopted by society (Jeffko, 1979). For hundreds of years people accepted and applied the criteria known today as those defining **clinical death**, a lack of heartbeat and respiration. Today, however, the most widely accepted criteria are those termed **brain death**:

1. no spontaneous movement in response to any stimuli

2. no spontaneous respirations for at least 1 hour

3. total lack of responsiveness to even the most painful stimuli

4. no eye movements, blinking, or pupil responses

5. no postural activity, swallowing, yawning, or vocalizing

6. no motor reflexes

7. a flat electroencephalogram (EEG) for at least 10 minutes

8. no change in any of these criteria when they are tested again 24 hours later

In order for a person to be declared brain dead, all of these eight criteria must be met. Moreover, other conditions that might mimic death, such as deep coma, hypothermia, or drug overdose, must be ruled out.

It should be noted that the lack of brain activity in this definition is interpreted by most hospitals to require the complete absence of both brainstem and cortical activity. This point is important, as the famous case of Karen Ann Quinlan demonstrated. Quinlan's cortical functioning had stopped as the result of a deadly mixture of alcohol and barbiturates; however, because her brainstem was still functioning, she continued to survive on her own.

Based on this and similar cases, some professionals are beginning to argue that the criteria for death should include only cortical functioning. This approach, termed **cortical death**, would allow physicians to declare an individual who had no cortical functioning dead even when brainstem functioning continued. Under a definition of cortical death, Quinlan would have been declared legally dead years before she actually died. Proponents of a cortical death definition point out that those functions that we typically use to define humanness, such as thinking and personality, are located in the cortex. When these functions are destroyed, it is argued, the "person" no longer exists. Although the idea of cortical death as a definition has many adherents, it is not used as a legal definition anywhere in the United States.

Ethical Issues

An ambulance screeches to a halt. Emergency personnel quickly wheel a woman into the emergency room. She has no pulse and no respiration. Working rapidly, the trauma team reestablishes a heartbeat through electric shock. A respirator is connected. An EEG and other tests reveal extensive and irreversible brain damage, but her brainstem is not completely destroyed. What should be done?

This is an example of the kinds of problems faced in the field of **bioethics**, the study of the interface between human values and technological advances in health and life sciences. Specific issues range from whether to conduct research involving genetic engineering to whether someone should be kept alive by forced feeding or by a machine. In the arena of death and dying the most important bioethical issue is euthanasia.

Derived from the Greek word meaning "good death," **euthanasia** refers to the act or practice of ending a life for reasons of mercy. The moral dilemma posed by euthanasia becomes apparent when we try to decide the circumstances under which a person's life should be ended. In our society this dilemma occurs most often when individuals are being kept alive by machines or when someone is suffering from a terminal illness.

Euthanasia can be carried out in two very different ways. **Active euthanasia** involves the deliberate ending of someone's life. This can be done by the patient or someone else administering a drug overdose or using other means; by making it known that no extraordinary means are to be used to keep the person alive, through a "living will" or other means; or through ending a person's life without his or her permission, by so-called mercy killing. The purpose of a living will is to make one's wishes about the use of life support known in the event one is unconscious or otherwise incapable of expressing them. Although there is considerable support for the living will concept, there are several problems with it as well. Foremost among these is that many people fail to inform their relatives about their living will and do not make their wishes known. Obviously, this puts relatives at a serious disadvantage if decisions concerning the use of life-support systems need to be made.

The second form of euthanasia, **passive euthanasia**, involves allowing a person to die by withholding an available treatment. For example, chemotherapy might be withheld from a cancer patient, a surgical procedure might not be performed, or food could be withdrawn.

Most people find it difficult to decide how they feel about euthanasia. They opt for making case-by-case decisions that would vary with the circumstances. Physicians report that they would usually agree with passive euthanasia but only if authorized by the family. Active euthanasia is not generally supported, usually out of fear that it might be used against people who were not terminally ill or who were defenseless against such movements, such as the cognitively impaired (Kieffer, 1979). The belief that one person should not kill another is deeply rooted in our society; for

that reason euthanasia is likely to be a much-debated topic for many years to come. "Something to Think About" explores some of the topics likely to be controversial.

THINKING ABOUT DEATH: PERSONAL COMPONENTS

Most modern authors tend to agree that death is a paradox (Schulz, 1978). That is, we are afraid of or anxious about death, but it is this same fear or anxiety that directly or indirectly causes much of our behavior. We will examine this paradox in the following sections. Specifically, we will focus on two questions: What is it about death that we fear or that makes us anxious? How do we show our fear or anxiety?

Fear and Anxiety Over Death

Being afraid to die is considered normal by most people. As one research participant put it, "You are *nuts* if you aren't afraid of death" (Kalish & Reynolds, 1976). The feeling expressed by this person, **fear**, refers to becoming aroused in response to a specific event or object. **Anxiety**, another way in which we feel aroused, is negative feelings that cannot be tied to a specific source. In reference to death we experience both fear and anxiety.

Fear of Death. Fear of death takes many forms (Kalish, 1985; Schulz, 1978). We fear physical suffering; we are afraid that death will be long and painful, and we do not want to experience that. We may also fear death because it will interrupt our goals. We want to accomplish many things with our lives, and sometimes we are afraid that we will die first. Our death is also feared

SOMETHING · TO · THINK · ABOUT

Bioethics, Euthanasia, and Controversy

As noted in the text, there is no universally accepted definition of death that is free from problems. In fact, each time the legal or medical definition of death is changed, a host of ethical issues must be confronted. Although most people in the United States now accept the brain-death definition, when this criterion was being implemented it caused several problems. Perhaps the most troublesome was the introduction of life-support technology, both to prolong life and to keep organs available for transplant surgery. Under the prevailing definition of death at the time, clinical death, the act of turning off a life-support system was considered murder, since death was defined solely as the lack of pulse and respiration. Since these bodily functions were present, even though artificially so, stopping them fell under the rubric of homicide in the criminal codes. Due to court decisions in cases like Karen Ann Quinlan's, the issue was resolved, and a different criterion of death was implemented.

Moving from a brain-death criterion to a cortical-death criterion would create new problems for bioethicists. Because this criterion requires only that activity cease in the cerebral cortex, the brainstem may still be intact and functional. In this case the patient might even have spontaneous pulse and respiration but would be considered dead. At this point some type of intervention would be needed to stop the brainstem functions. Would this be euthanasia? Under a cortical-death criterion, no; the patient is already dead. But under a brain-death criterion such intervention would be active euthanasia and might even be viewed as murder. And under a clinical death criterion the patient would be considered to still be alive! Thus, the issues confronting physicians would be similar to those encountered during the shift from a clinical-death criterion to a brain-death criterion.

Whether American society will ever adopt a cortical-death criterion remains to be seen. What is clear is that bioethicists must make the dilemmas clear, and we must make ourselves aware of the issues. What is at stake is literally a matter of life and death. It's something to think about.

---

because of the impact it has on others. For instance, parents worry about who would care for the children if they should die. Finally, we may fear the state we enter after we die.

Strange as it may seem, fear of death may have a beneficial side. For one thing being afraid to die means that we often go to great lengths to make sure we stay alive. And since staying alive helps to ensure the continuation and socialization of the species, fear of death may serve to help the next generation.

Death Anxiety. It is the ethereal nature of death anxiety that makes us feel so uncomfortable. We cannot put our finger on something about death and identify what is causing us to feel uneasy. Because of this, we must look for behavioral evidence to document death anxiety. Techniques have varied considerably: projective personality tests, such as the Rorschach Inkblots; paper-and-pencil tests, such as Templer's Death Anxiety Scale; and measures of physiological arousal, such as galvanic skin response. Research findings suggest that death anxiety is a complex, multidimensional construct.

On the basis of several diverse studies using many different measures, it appears that death anxiety consists of several components. Each of these components is most easily described with terms that resemble examples of fear but cannot be tied to anything specific. Schulz (1978) concluded that the components of death anxiety included pain, body malfunction, humiliation, rejection, nonbeing, punishment, interruption of goals, and negative impact on survivors. To complicate matters further, it is possible to assess any of these components at any of three levels: public, private, and nonconscious. That is, what we admit feeling about death in public may differ considerably from what we feel when we are alone with our own thoughts. In short, the measurement of death anxiety is complex, and researchers need to specify which aspect(s) they are assessing.

Considerable research has been conducted to learn what demographic and personality variables are related to death anxiety. Although the results are often ambiguous, some patterns have emerged.

Sex differences in death anxiety have been found inconsistently. Some researchers find that women score higher than men on questionnaire measures of death anxiety (e.g., Iammarino, 1975; Templer, Ruff, & Franks, 1971), but others do not (Dickstein, 1972; Nehrke, Bellucci, & Gabriel, 1977). When differences are observed, women tend to view death in more emotional terms, whereas men tend to view it in more cognitive terms (Degner, 1974; Krieger, Epsting, & Leitner, 1974; Wittkowski, 1981). Keith (1979) offers perhaps the best way of understanding the controversy. Keith's questionnaire combines items that measure death anxiety, perceptions of life after death, and general acceptance. Women apparently find the prospect of their own death more anxiety-producing than men do, but they simultaneously have a greater acceptance of their own death. Acceptance and anxiety had always been thought to be antithetical, but they may not be (Kalish, 1985).

Several studies have demonstrated a complex relationship between death anxiety and religiosity, defined as being a churchgoing, denomination-affiliated person or as adhering to a traditional belief system (Feifel & Nagy, 1981; Templer, 1972). Although studies have documented the link between belief in an afterlife and degree of religiosity, the relationship between belief in an afterlife and death anxiety independent of religiosity needs further exploration (Kalish, 1985).

Few investigators have examined death anxiety in relation to ethnicity. J. E. Myers, Wass, and Murphey (1980) found that elderly Black respondents in the American South expressed higher death anxiety than their White counterparts. Bengtson, Cuellar, and Raga (1977) observed declines in death anxiety with age among three ethnic communities (Blacks, Mexican Americans, and Whites) but did not find differences across the ethnic groups. Bengtson et al. (1977) also found that elderly Blacks were much more likely to expect a long life than either Mexican Americans or Whites, confirming results obtained earlier by Reynolds and Kalish (1974).

Although the elderly think more about death than any other age group, they are less fearful and more accepting of it (e.g., Bengtson et al., 1977; Kalish & Reynolds, 1981; Keller, Sherry, & Piotrowski, 1984). Several reasons have been offered for this consistent finding (Kalish, 1987): older adults have more chronic diseases, and they realistically know that these health problems are unlikely to improve over time; the probabilities are high that many members of their family and friendship network have died already; the most important tasks of life have been completed; and they have thought a great deal about their death.

Kalish (1987) also suggests that a major reason for reduced death anxiety in later life is that the value and satisfaction of living are not as great.

Finally, death anxiety may also be related to the occupation one has, the experiences one has had with the death of others, and how one views aging. Vickio and Cavanaugh (1985) found that among nursing home employees those who had positive outlooks on older adults and on their own aging tended to have lower death anxiety. They also found that level of death anxiety was related to job; cooks and housekeepers tended to have higher anxiety than nurses and social service workers. The level of death anxiety was unrelated to the number of deaths among friends or relatives of the employee, but it was inversely related to the number of deaths among residents known by the employee.

Clearly, death anxiety is complex. We are uncertain on many of its aspects, partly because it comprises many components that we do not fully understand. Yet we can see death anxiety and fear in action all the time in the many behaviors that we show.

How Do We Show Death Anxiety and Fear?

When we are afraid or anxious, our behavior changes in some way. One of the most common ways in which this occurs in relation to death is through **avoidance** (Kastenbaum, 1975). Avoiding situations that remind us of death occurs at both the unconscious and conscious levels. People who refuse to go to funerals because they find them depressing or who will not visit dying friends or relatives may be consciously avoiding death. Unconscious avoidance may take the form of being too busy to help out a dying person. Society provides several safeguards to help us avoid the reality of death, from isolating dying people in institutions to providing euphemisms for referring to death, such as saying that a person has "passed away."

A second way of showing fear or anxiety is the opposite of the first; rather than avoiding death, we challenge it (Kalish, 1984). In this case people deliberately and repeatedly put themselves in dangerous, life-threatening situations such as skydiving, auto racing, war, and so forth. These people have not been studied sufficiently to know whether they feel a need to assert their superiority over death. But interestingly enough, a study of pedestrian behavior at a busy intersection in Detroit revealed that people who took chances in crossing the street (for example, not looking before crossing, walking against the light, and jaywalking) were more likely to have thought about suicide and expected to live a significantly shorter time than more cautious pedestrians (Kastenbaum & Briscoe, 1975).

Other ways of exhibiting a fear of death are numerous. Some of the more common include changing life-styles, dreams and fantasies, using humor, displacing fear or anxiety onto something else such as work, and becoming a professional who deals with death (Kalish, 1984). Such behaviors are indicative of large individual variations in how we handle our feelings about death. Still, each of us must come to grips with death and learn how to deal with it.

Learning to Deal With Death Anxiety and Fear

Although some degree of death anxiety and fear may be appropriate, we must guard against their becoming powerful enough to interfere with our normal daily routines. Several ways exist to help us in this endeavor. Perhaps the one most often used is to live life to the fullest. Kalish (1984, 1987) argues that people who do this enjoy what they have; although they may still fear death and feel cheated, they have few regrets. In a sense they "realize that [they] might die any moment, and yet live as though [they] were never going to die" (Lepp, 1968, p. 77).

Koestenbaum (1976) proposes several exercises and questions to increase one's death awareness. Some of these are to write your own obituary and plan your own death and funeral services. You can also ask yourself: "What circumstances would help make my death acceptable?" "Is death the sort of thing that could happen to me?"

These questions serve as a basis for an increasingly popular way to reduce fear and anxiety, death education. Most death education programs combine factual information about death with issues aimed at reducing anxiety and fear in order to increase sensitivity to others' feelings. These programs vary widely in orientation, since they can include such topics as philosophy, ethics, psychology, drama, religion, medicine, art, and many others. Additionally, they can focus on death, the process of dying, grief and bereavement, or any combination of them. In general, death education programs appear to help mainly by increasing our awareness of the complex emotions that are felt and expressed by dying individuals and their families.

THINKING ABOUT DEATH: THEORIES OF DYING

What is it like to die? How do terminally ill people feel about dying? Are people more concerned about dying as they grow older? To answer these questions, a few scholars have developed theories of dying that are based on interviews and other methods. The point of these theories is to show that dying is a complex process and that our thoughts, concerns, and feelings change as we move closer to death. We will examine two ways of conceptualizing the dying process: a **stage approach** and a **phase approach**. We will also consider how the thoughts and feelings of dying people vary as a function of age.

The Stage Theory of Dying

Elisabeth Kübler-Ross became interested in the experience of dying as an instructor on psychiatry at the University of Chicago in the early 1960s. Over 200 interviews with terminally ill people convinced her that most people followed a sequence of emotional reactions. Using her experiences, she developed a sequence of five stages that described the process of an appropriate death: denial, anger, bargaining, depression, and acceptance (Kübler-Ross, 1969).

When people are told that they have a terminal illness, their first reaction is likely to be shock and disbelief. Denial is a normal part of getting ready to die. Some want to shop around for a more favorable diagnosis, and most feel that a mistake has been made. Others try to find assurance in religion. Eventually, though, most people accept the diagnosis and begin to feel angry.

In the anger stage, people express hostility, resentment, and envy toward health care workers, family, and friends. Individuals ask, "Why me?" and express a great deal of frustration. The fact that they are going to die when so many others will live seems so unfair. As these feelings begin to be dealt with and to diminish, the person may begin to bargain.

In the bargaining stage people look for a way out. Maybe a deal can be struck with someone, perhaps God, that would allow survival. For example, a woman might promise to be a better mother if only she could live. Eventually, the individual becomes aware that these deals will not work.

When one can no longer deny the illness, perhaps due to surgery or pain, feelings of depression are very common. People report feeling deep loss, sorrow, guilt, and shame over their illness and its consequences. Kübler-Ross believes that allowing people to discuss their feelings with others helps move them to an acceptance of death.

In the acceptance stage the person accepts the inevitability of death and often seems detached from the world and at complete peace. "It is as if the pain is gone, the struggle is over, and there comes a time for the 'final rest before the journey' as one patient phrased it" (Kübler-Ross, 1969, p. 100).

Although she believes that these five stages represent the typical course of emotional development in the dying, Kübler-Ross (1974) cautions that not everyone goes through all of them or progresses through them at the same rate or in the same order. In fact, we could actually harm dying individuals by considering these stages as fixed and universal. Individual differences are great, as Kübler-Ross points out. Emotional responses may vary in intensity throughout the dying process. Thus, the goal in applying Kübler-Ross's theory to real-world settings would be to help people achieve an appropriate death. An appropriate death is one that meets the needs of the dying person, allowing him or her to work out each problem as it comes.

The Phase Theory of Dying

Instead of offering a series of stages, some writers view dying as a process with three phases: an acute phase, a chronic living-dying phase, and a terminal phase (Pattison, 1977a; Weisman, 1972). These phases are represented in Figure 14.1.

The acute phase begins when the individual becomes aware that his or her condition is terminal. This phase is marked by a high level of anxiety, denial, anger, and even bargaining. In time, the person adjusts to the idea of being terminally ill, and anxiety gradually declines. During this chronic living-dying phase, a person generally has many contradictory feelings that must be integrated. These include fear of loneliness, fear of the unknown, and anticipatory grief over the loss of friends, of body, of self-control, and of identity (Pattison, 1977b). These feelings of fear and grief exist simultaneously or alternate with feelings of hope, determination, and acceptance (Shneidman, 1973). Finally, the terminal phase begins when the individual begins withdrawing from the world. This last phase is the shortest, and it ends with death.

The notion of a **dying trajectory** was introduced to describe these three phases more clearly. A dying trajectory describes the length and the form of one's dying process. Four dying trajectories have been suggested, differing mainly in whether death is certain or uncertain (Glaser & Strauss, 1965, 1968; Strauss & Glaser, 1970):

1. Certain death is expected at a known time, such as when a woman is told that she has 6 months to live.

2. Certain death is expected but at an unknown time, such as when the woman may be told that she has between 6 months and 5 years.

3. It is uncertain whether the woman will die, but the answer will be clear in a known period of time; for example, exploratory surgery will resolve the issue.

4. It is uncertain whether the woman will die, and there is no known time when the question will be answered; for example, she has a heart problem that may or may not be fatal and could cause problems at some point in the future.

The last two trajectories are thought to produce the most anxiety due to their higher degrees of ambiguity and uncertainty. The acute phase is lengthened, and the overall trajectory is more

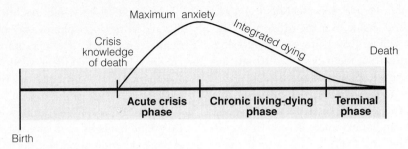

FIGURE 14.1 · The phase theory of dying

difficult. It seems that knowing whether one is going to die plays an important role in the ability to deal with the problem and the degree of overall adjustment.

Although stages and phases of dying have not been researched very thoroughly, it seems that how people deal with their own death is a complicated process. Denial and acceptance can take many forms and may even occur simultaneously. People take a last vacation and update their will at the same time. It is becoming increasingly clear that it is not the task of health care workers or mental health workers to force someone to die in a particular way. There is no such thing as one right way to die. The best we can do is to make sure that we stay in touch with the dying person's (and our own) feelings and are available for support. In this way we may avoid contributing to what could be considered a "wrong" way to die: being abandoned and left to die alone.

An Adult Developmental Perspective on Dying

Dying is not something that happens only to one age group. Most of us tend not to think about it, because we associate dying with old age. But babies die of sudden infant death syndrome, children die in accidents, and adolescents and young

adults die from cancer. Death knows no age limits. Yet one person's death often seems more acceptable than another's (Kastenbaum, 1985). The death of a 95-year-old woman is considered natural; she had lived a long, full life. But the death of an infant is considered to be a tragedy. Whether or not such feelings are justified, they point to the fact that death is experienced differently depending on age: treatment differs, and responses to others' losses differ. In this section we will briefly examine the personal side of how the age of a dying person changes the meaning of death.

The old die mainly from chronic diseases, such as heart disease and cancer; the young die mainly from accidents (Kalish, 1987). The diseases of older adults typically incapacitate before they kill, resulting in a dying trajectory of slow decline and eventual death. Because older adults and younger adults die in different ways, their dying processes differ (Kalish, 1985):

1. Financial costs for the elderly are higher due to the need for long-term care.

2. The elderly's need for health and human care is greater.

3. The elderly have more potential for leading a normal life during the early part of the dying process.

4. The elderly have a longer period to contemplate and plan for their death.

5. The elderly have more opportunity to see old friends or visit important places.

6. The elderly are more likely to die in institutions and are more likely to be confused or comatose immediately before their death.

7. More elderly women die without a spouse or sibling to participate in care, making them more dependent on adult children.

In short, the elderly take longer to die and are more likely to die in isolation than any other age group.

Many of the concerns of dying individuals seem to be specific to how old they are (Kalish, 1987). The most obvious difference comes in the extent to which people feel cheated. Younger adults are more likely to feel deprived of the opportunity to experience a full life than are middle-agers or older adults. Younger adults feel that they are losing what they might attain; older adults feel that they are losing what they have. Beyond these general differences, however, not much is known about how adults of various ages differ in how they face death. Most of the literature focuses on older adults. Clearly, we badly need more information about what it is like to be young or middle-aged and to be dying.

One important factor that affects dying older adults is that their deaths are viewed by the community as less tragic than the deaths of younger people (Kalish & Reynolds, 1976; Kastenbaum, 1985). Consequently, older adults receive less intense life-saving treatment and are perceived as less valuable and not worth a large investment of time, money, or energy: "The terminally aged may be as helpless as a child, but they seldom arouse tenderness" (Weisman, 1972, p. 144). Many dying older adults reside in long-term care facilities where contacts with family and friends are fewer. Kalish (1987) writes that the elderly, especially the ill and those with diminished functional competence, offer less to their communities. Consequently, when their death occurs the emotional pain is not as great because the resulting losses are viewed as less significant and meaningful.

WHERE WILL WE DIE?

Where do most of us want to die? Surveys indicate that most older people would rather die at home but that this wish is not as important to middle-aged people (Kalish & Reynolds, 1976). Family members who had cared for relatives who died at home usually feel glad that it happened that way, even though about one third wonder whether home care was the right decision (Cartwright, Hockey, & Anderson, 1973).

Despite the expressed wishes of most people, the vast majority of us will not die at home among family and friends. Rather, approximately 75% of deaths occur in institutions such as hospitals and nursing homes (Lerner, 1970; Marshall, 1980). This increasing institutionalization of death has two major consequences (Schulz, 1978). First, health care professionals are playing a more important role in dying people's lives. This means that the medical staff is being forced to provide emotional support in situations largely antithetical to their main mission of healing and curing. This dilemma presents health care workers with problems that we will consider later.

A second important result of the **institutionalization of death** is that dying is being removed from our everyday experience. Not long ago, each of us would have known what it was like to interact with a dying person and to be present when someone died. Institutions isolate us from death, and some argue that they are largely to blame for our increasing avoidance. Unfortunately, we will probably never be able to know whether this opinion is accurate, because it is impossible to evaluate. For ethical reasons, we cannot randomly have some people die at home and others die at hospitals in order to compare the effects of each.

Dying in a Hospital Versus Dying at Home

As indicated earlier, the trend during the 20th century has been away from dying at home. What implications does this trend have? Certainly, some people still die at home either because their deaths occur unexpectedly or because they have chosen to remain at home. Yet even in these cases most people are still rushed to a hospital where the official declaration is made (Marshall, 1980). In a technical sense, then, virtually everyone dies at a hospital or other health care facility.

Perhaps the best explanation for this change relates to advances in health care itself. As health care became more effective, efficient, and technologically advanced, people needed to take advantage of hospital facilities in order to make certain that everything possible had been done. Even when a person's illness is terminal, there is a good chance that a lengthy hospital stay will result. Hospitals offer another major advantage compared to home: continuous care. Caring for a dying person is often time-consuming and draining and may require special medical expertise. Hospitals are typically better equipped to handle these demands.

All is not on the hospital's side, however. Autonomy and personal relationships usually suffer when people are in a hospital (Kalish, 1984). People remaining at home have less difficulty on these dimensions; rigid visitation hours are the exception at home.

What, then, determines where we will die?

Kalish (1984) offers six factors: physical condition, availability of care, finances, competence of institutions, age, and personal preference. Clearly, the particular health problem that a person has may dictate the context for dying. If it demands intensive or sophisticated medical treatment or if the degree of incapacitation is great, a medical facility is likely to be chosen.

Kalish notes that the availability of caretakers outside the health care institution plays a very important role. If an individual has several people who can care for him or her at home, an institution is a less likely choice. Overall, then, the best predictor of nursing home admission is the degree of social support available (George & Gwyther, 1986). However, caretakers must be more than just available; they must be willing to make the necessary sacrifices as well.

Finally, personal preference plays a role. Some people simply prefer to be at home in familiar surroundings with their family and friends when they die. Others, who fear that they will burden their loved ones or that emergency medical assistance may be unavailable, choose a hospital or nursing home. Kalish (1985) writes that dying at home is most appropriate when the person is reasonably alert and capable of interaction with others, when his or her health condition is beyond treatment, when dying at home would provide something meaningful to the person, and when death is imminent.

The Hospice Alternative

As we have seen, most people would like to die at home among family and friends. An important barrier to this choice is the availability of support systems when the individual has a terminal disease. In this case most people believe that they have no choice but to go to a hospital or nursing home. However, another alternative exists, a **hospice** (Koff, 1981). The emphasis in a hospice

Hospices emphasize the importance of maintaining dignity and involving family members throughout the dying process.

is on the quality of life. This approach grows out of an important distinction between the prolongation of life and the prolongation of death. In a hospice the concern is to make the person as peaceful and comfortable as possible, not to delay an inevitable death. Although medical care is available at a hospice, it is aimed primarily at controlling pain and restoring normal functioning. This orientation places hospices between hospitals and homes in terms of contexts for dying.

Modern hospices are modeled after St. Christopher's Hospice in England, founded in 1967 by Dr. Cicely Saunders. The services offered by a hospice are requested only after the person or physician believes that no treatment or cure is possible, making the hospice program markedly different from hospital or home care. The differences are evident in the principles that underlie hospice care: clients and their families are viewed as a unit; clients should be kept free of pain; emotional and social impoverishment must be minimal; clients must be encouraged to maintain competencies; conflict resolution and fulfillment of realistic desires must be assisted; clients must be free to begin or end relationships; and staff members must seek to alleviate pain and fear (Saunders, 1977).

Two types of hospices exist: inpatient and outpatient. Inpatient hospices provide all care for clients; outpatient hospices provide services to clients who remain in their own homes. This latter variation is becoming increasingly popular, largely because more clients can be served at a lower cost.

Hospices do not follow a hospital model of care. The role of the staff in a hospice is not so much to do *for* the client as it is just to be *with* the client. A client's dignity is always maintained; often more attention is paid to appearance and personal grooming than to medical tests. Hospice staff members also provide a great deal of support to the client's family. At inpatient hospices visiting hours are unrestricted, and families are strongly encouraged to take part in the client's care (VandenBos, DeLeon, & Pallack, 1982).

Researchers have documented important differences between inpatient hospices and hospitals (Hinton, 1967; Parkes, 1975; VandenBos et al., 1982). Hospice clients were more mobile, less anxious, and less depressed; spouses visited hospice clients more often and participated more in their care; and hospice staff members were perceived as more accessible. In addition, E. K. Walsh and Cavanaugh (1984) showed that most hospice clients who had been in hospitals before coming to a hospice strongly preferred the care at the hospice.

Although the hospice is a valuable alternative for many people, it may not be appropriate for everyone. Some disorders require treatments or equipment not available at inpatient hospices, and some people may find that a hospice does not meet their needs or fit with their personal beliefs. Walsh and Cavanaugh found that the perceived needs of hospice clients, their families, and the staff did not always coincide. In particular, the staff and family members emphasized pain management, whereas many of the clients wanted more attention paid to personal issues. The important point from this study is that the staff and family members may need to ask clients what they need more often, rather than making assumptions about what they need.

Although a hospice offers an important alternative to a hospital or other institution as a place to die, it is not always available. For example, older adults who are slowly dying but whose time of death is uncertain may not be eligible. Meeting the needs of these individuals will be a challenge for future health care providers.

CARING AND HELPING RELATIONSHIPS

The growing awareness that death is a developmental process and the fact that death no longer occurs as frequently at home have led to a substantial increase in the number of people who work with the dying. The contexts may vary (hospitals, hospices, nursing homes), but the skills that are required and the kinds of relationships that develop are similar. With this in mind, we will focus on the helping done by health care and mental health workers. As a prelude to this discussion, let us consider what it is like to work with the dying and the basic needs that must be met.

Working With Dying People

Most people think that it must be hard to work with individuals who are dying. They serve as reminders that we, too, will die someday. As indicated earlier, this is a scary proposition. The realization that we will die makes us question the value of things, since dying people are proof that we cannot control all aspects of our lives. Few of us really control when or how we die. Many dying people experience pain, are unpleasant to look at or be near, and have a limited future. Most of us do not like to be reminded of these things. Finally, dying involves loss, and most of us do not seek out relationships with people when we know they are going to end painfully.

Despite these issues many people work with the dying and have extremely positive experiences. Most of these individuals chose their occupation because of their interests. Yet they still experience stress and psychologically withdraw from their work. Although common, this withdrawal is not an inevitable part of working with people who are dying. As presented in the following sections, information about dying people and their needs may alleviate the need to pull away.

Needs of Dying People

There is consensus that dying people have three especially important needs: the need to control pain, the need to retain dignity and feelings of self-worth, and the need for love and affection (Schulz, 1978). The mission of the people who work with the dying is meeting these needs.

When a terminal disease is painful, an important need is pain management. Several approaches are available, such as surgery, drugs, hypnosis, and biofeedback. Especially in the case of chemotherapy for cancer, the management of pain can sometimes become the major focus of intervention. In such cases it is especially important to consider additional issues such as compliance with the treatment.

The need for dignity and self-worth is extremely important. Recall that this was one of the needs stated most often by hospice clients in the Walsh and Cavanaugh (1984) study. Dignity can be enhanced especially by including the dying person in all decisions that affect him or her, including control over the end of life. Loss of a sense of control can create serious psychological stress, which can have physical implications as well.

Showing love and affection to the dying can help reduce the fear of abandonment that many of us have. Love and affection can be communicated by touching or other physical contact, but it can also be shown by simply being present and listening, supporting, and reassuring the person that he or she is not alone.

How are these needs met? In addition to the family, health care and mental health workers share the responsibility. Let us consider how well they treat dying people.

Helping the Dying: Health Care Workers

How do health care workers deal with dying people? Do they confront the issues? What do they tell dying people about their condition? How do their clients feel about it? These are some of the questions that will concern us in this section. Although there is little research on these important topics, we can get some feel for the ways in which health care professionals handle death and dying.

Attitudes and Behaviors. Because the medical profession is oriented toward helping people and saving lives, death could be seen as a failure.

Several researchers have shown that this was the perspective taken by many physicians and nurses in the past (Glaser & Strauss, 1965; Kastenbaum & Aisenberg, 1976; Pearlman, Stotsky, & Dominick, 1969). Most of this research documented that medical personnel in hospitals tended to avoid patients once it was known that they were dying. Indeed, one study found that nurses were slower to respond to the call lights of terminally ill patients than to those of other patients (Le Shan, in Kastenbaum & Aisenberg, 1976). Furthermore, when dying patients confront doctors or nurses with statements about death, such as "I think I'm going to die soon," the most common responses are fatalism ("We all die sometime"), denial ("You don't really mean that"), and changing the subject. These responses represent ways of not dealing with death.

How comfortable health care workers are in discussing death with dying people seems to be related to the amount of experience they have had with death, although the nature of the relationship is unclear. For example, some studies find that nurses' uneasiness increases with experience (Pearlman et al., 1969), while others find that experience makes it easier (Vickio & Cavanaugh, 1985). These discrepancies may stem from using interviews as opposed to questionnaires or from the general trend toward being open, honest, and supportive with people who want to talk about death. Indeed, there have been many calls in the medical literature for better communication with dying people (Kalish, 1985).

Changes in attitudes and behavior toward the dying may well reflect the spirit of the times (Kalish, 1987). During the 1980s there was a movement away from viewing science and technology as producing the ultimate in health care. Instead, the emphasis was increasingly on the relationship between health care workers and the dying person. At the same time the basic rights of the dying were being demanded, including the right to die with dignity. These changes at the societal level are probably the most important reasons for the shift in attitudes and behaviors over the past few decades.

Informing the Client. Should a patient be told that he or she is going to die? In the past this was only rarely done; most patients remained uninformed. The reasoning seemed to be that admitting the truth might accelerate the patient's decline, although it is also likely that it was done to protect the health care workers from facing death. This policy was typically followed regardless of the patient's wishes. For example, one comprehensive survey revealed that even though 75% to 90% of terminally ill patients indicated that they wanted to be told if they were dying, 70% to 90% of the physicians withheld that information (Feifel, 1965).

The majority practice today among medical personnel is to tell the patient the truth. Still, deciding whether to confront a person with the news that he or she is dying is a complex decision. For instance, sometimes it is just not known for certain whether a person will live or die. Full disclosure often depends on the physical and mental health of the patient. However, most investigators believe that the physician or nurse can help the client achieve a good death by being honest, by letting clients take the initiative in requesting information, and by being available for support (Hinton, 1976).

Most terminally ill people understand that there is something seriously wrong with them even before they are officially informed. With this growing awareness comes the additional recognition that others know as well. If others are unwilling to talk about it, patients may engage in a **mutual pretense** with family, friends, and professionals. In mutual pretense everyone knows that death is coming soon, but everyone acts as if nothing serious is the matter. Mutual pretense is difficult to carry out over a long period, however, because it is likely that someone will break the rules and talk about the disease. Providing a supportive context in which the impending death can be discussed avoids the problem altogether.

When death occurs in a health care setting, it is often hidden from public view. In some cases extreme measures are taken, such as disguising bodies or hiding them in order to protect other patients. Such actions are interpreted by some as additional examples of health care workers' denial of death. Although the therapeutic value of protecting other patients has never been demonstrated, these practices continue in some places.

Helping the Dying: Mental Health Workers

Not all of the concerns of dying people involve their medical problems. Caring for the dying also entails meeting the psychological needs described by Kübler-Ross and others. We can separate the work done by mental health workers into two types: psychotherapy and paraprofessional counseling.

Psychotherapy. Dying people seek psychotherapy for many reasons. Dying can be a very stressful time. Sometimes, confronting our fears and anxieties is too difficult to handle on our own, and some professional help is needed. Concerns about work, conflicts with family, and financial matters may interfere with the ability to resolve the difficult psychological issues.

Conducting psychotherapy with the dying is often difficult. Use of the traditional hour-long session may be stressful if the client cannot sit that long or inconvenient if medical treatment needs to be continuous. Moreover, many psychotherapists have the same problems in dealing with death as medical personnel. When the therapist is forced to confront his or her own death anxiety and fear, it may hinder the psychotherapeutic process. And since many therapists use a medical model of pathology, dying people may not fit with their particular viewpoint. Most psychotherapists tend to focus on current problems and functioning rather than probing the distant past. Perhaps the best idea is to use the therapy to foster personal growth (Le Shan, 1969).

Paraprofessional Counseling. Working through anxieties and fears when one is dying does not always require a psychotherapist. In fact, most of the time it is accomplished by talking to relatives, friends, clergy, social workers, and medical personnel. The issues that are discussed are the same, for the most part, as those discussed with psychotherapists, and the feelings that are expressed are just as intense. Many people believe that having friends and family who are willing to listen and provide support is a key factor in resolving problems, although there is little research dealing with dying people.

SURVIVORS: THE GRIEVING PROCESS

Each of us suffers many losses over a lifetime. Whenever we lose someone close to us through death or other separation, we experience both grief and mourning. **Grief** refers to the sorrow, hurt, anger, guilt, confusion, and other feelings that arise after suffering a loss. **Mourning** concerns the ways in which we express our grief. These expressions are highly influenced by culture; for some mourning may involve wearing black, attending funerals, and observing an official period of grief, while for others it means drinking, wearing white, and marrying the deceased spouse's sibling. Thus, grief corresponds to the emotional reactions following loss, while mourning refers to the culturally approved behavioral manifestations of our feelings.

In this section we will examine how people deal with loss. Since the grieving process is affected by the circumstances surrounding the death, we must first differentiate between expected and unexpected loss. Next, because grief can be expressed in many ways, the differences between normal and abnormal reactions will be explored. Finally, how well we cope with the death of a loved one is related to the kind of relationship that existed. Thus, we will compare grieving following different kinds of loss.

Expected Versus Unexpected Death

For many years it has been believed that the intensity and course of grief depend on whether the death was expected or occurred suddenly and unexpectedly (Shand, 1920). Fulton (1970) labeled the two situations as high-grief death and low-grief death. A high-grief death is one that is unexpected, for example, an accidental death. Low-grief deaths are expected; an example would be the death of a spouse following a long illness. According to Fulton, the main difference is not that people in one situation necessarily grieve more (or less) than those in another situation. Rather, when death is anticipated, people go through a period of anticipatory grief before the death that serves to buffer the impact of the loss when it comes.

Research on grief following expected versus unexpected deaths supports the basic point raised by Fulton. The opportunity for anticipatory grieving has been shown to result in a lower likelihood of psychological problems 1 year after the death of a spouse (Ball, 1976–1977; Parkes, 1975), greater acceptance by parents following the death of a child (Binger et al., 1969), and more rapid recovery of effective functioning and subsequent happiness (Glick, Weiss, & Parkes, 1974).

The grief expressed by the Japanese following the death of Hirohito exemplifies the point that grief is experienced even though death may be anticipated.

However, anticipating the death of someone close does produce considerable stress in itself (Norris & Murrell, 1987).

The reasons why anticipated deaths result in quicker recovery are not yet fully understood. We know that stressful events, in general, are less problematic if they are expected, so that the same principles probably hold for death. Perhaps it is the opportunity to rehearse what it would be like without the dying person and the chance to make appropriate arrangements that helps. In practicing, we may realize that we need support, may feel lonely and scared, and may take steps to get ourselves ready. Moreover, if we recognize that we are likely to have certain feelings, they may be easier to understand and deal with when they come.

Another difference between expected and unexpected deaths is that an anticipated death is often less mysterious. Most of the time we know why the person died. A sudden death from an accident is not as easy to comprehend, as there does not seem to be a good explanation for it. There is no disease to blame, and survivors may fear that it could just as easily happen to them. Knowing the real reason why someone dies makes adjustment easier.

Stages of Grief

How do people grieve? What do they experience? The process of grieving is a complicated and personal one. Just as there is no right way to die, there is no right way to grieve. Recognizing that there are plenty of individual differences, we will consider these patterns in this section.

Writers on the process of grieving have found it convenient to describe it as consisting of several phases. Like the stages and phases of dying, the phases of grieving are not clearly demarcated, nor does one pass from one to another cleanly. The goal of this approach is simply to describe the major steps of recovery following a death. The phases reflect the fact that when someone close to us dies, we must reorganize our lives, establish new patterns of behavior, and redefine relationships with family and friends. Although there is an implied sequence to the phases, we must keep in mind that some people reexperience them over time and that progress through them is not always even or predictable.

The grieving process can be divided into three main phases: initial phase, intermediate phase, and recovery phase (Averill, 1968; Parkes, 1972; Pincus, 1976). Each phase has certain characteristics, and particular issues are more important at some points than others.

When the death occurs, and usually for a few weeks afterward, the survivor's reaction is shock, disbelief, and numbness. People often report feeling empty, cold, and confused, which serves to protect them from the pain of bereavement. The shock and disbelief typically continue for several days following the death and then give way to several weeks of sorrow and sadness, which are expressed mainly through crying.

Over time, one is expected to begin recovering from these feelings. As a result of this pressure survivors may suppress emotions. Unfortunately, suppression of feelings is often interpreted as a sign of recovery, which it certainly is not. Along with learning how to deal with sorrow, survivors must handle feelings of not being able to make it. Fortunately, most people eventually realize that their anxieties are not well-founded and are actually hindering recovery, and they eventually come to some resolution.

Several weeks after the death, people begin to realize what life without the deceased person means. Researchers point to three behavior patterns that characterize this second, or intermedi-

ate, phase. First, the bereaved person thinks about the death a great deal; feelings of guilt or responsibility are common. Second, survivors try to understand why the person died. They search for some reason for the death, to try to put it in a meaningful context. Finally, people search for the deceased. They feel the person's presence and dream or even converse with him or her. Such behavior demonstrates a longing to be with the deceased, and it is often a reaction to feelings of loneliness and despair. Eventually, these feelings and behaviors diminish, and the bereaved person moves to the final phase.

Entry into the recovery phase of grief often results from a conscious decision that continued dwelling on the past is pointless and that one's life needs to move froward. Once this is recognized, recovery can begin. Behaviorally, the process takes many forms, with increased socializing one common example. It is not unusual to see marked improvement in the survivor's self-confidence. Emerging from a bereavement experience is an achievement. People are often more capable and stronger as a result of coping with such a tragic event. New skills may be developed, whether they be cooking, balancing a checkbook, or home repair.

In considering these phases of grief, we must avoid making several mistakes. First, grieving ultimately is an individual experience. The optimal process for one person may not be the best for someone else. Second, we must not underestimate the amount of time it takes to progress from the initial shock to recovery. To a casual observer, this may seem to occur over a few weeks. Actually, it takes much longer to resolve the complex emotional issues that we face during bereavement. Researchers and therapists alike agree that it takes at least a year for a person to be reasonably recovered, and 2 years is not uncommon. Interestingly, a 2-year period was proposed by Weiss (1975) as the time needed for most people to recover from divorce. Finally, it should also be noted that *recovery* may be a misleading term. It is probably more accurate to say that we learn to live with our loss, rather than that we recover. The impact of the loss of a loved one lasts a very long time, perhaps for the rest of one's life.

Normal Grief Reactions

The feelings experienced during grieving are intense, which not only makes it difficult to cope but also may cause one to wonder whether he or she is normal. A summary of college students' perceptions of normal responses is presented in Table 14.1. Many authors refer to the psychological side of coming to terms with bereavement as **grief work**. Vickio, Cavanaugh, and Attig (in press) found that college students were well aware of the need for grief work, correctly recognized the need for at least a year to do it, and were very sensitive to the range of emotions and behaviors demonstrated by the bereaved. In the following sections we will consider some of the most common reactions to bereavement.

Grief provides a way to channel emotions, as in the Names Project, a memorial to people who died from AIDS.

Sorrow and Sadness. All the evidence we have suggests that intense feelings are the most common ones experienced during the grieving process (Kalish, 1985). Some studies have even found that these feelings of sadness can be so intense that they make the individual appear clinically depressed. For example, in the month following the death of their spouse, many widows display symptoms similar to those of depressed psychiatric clients. Many of these women lack a strong support system of family and friends (Kalish, 1981).

Denial and Disbelief. When death happens unexpectedly, a very common response is denial. Usually this response involves an intellectual recognition that the person has died but an inability or unwillingness to believe it. Sometimes denial is seen when a family starts to make plans that would normally have included the deceased person and then realizes the problem. At other times denial is shown when parents refuse to change the room of their deceased child or a widower continues to say "we." We must recognize that denial is sometimes adaptive and protective. Without denial during the first few days after the death, the pain might be overwhelming. Taken to extremes, however, denial can become very maladaptive.

Guilt. Guilt is probably the most complex reaction to death. Sometimes guilt arises because we have mixed feelings toward the person who died. We may be angry that he or she died yet relieved that we are not burdened with caretaking

TABLE 14.1 • Perceptions of typical grief reactions following the death of a loved one

Type of Reaction	Occurs During Initial Period of Grieving (Percent Citing the Reaction)	Occurs During Intermediate or Long-Term Grieving (Percent Citing the Reaction)	Sign That Grieving Is Abnormal If Occurring Long After Loss (Percent Citing the Reaction)
Disbelief	32.5%	0.8%	2.7%
Denial	24.4	8.1	5.5
Shock	48.0	1.6	8.2
Sadness	80.5	80.5	0
Anger	52.8	39.0	10.0
Hatred	8.1	5.7	9.1
Guilt	12.2	10.6	0
Fear	8.9	1.6	0.9
Anxiety	4.9	4.9	0.9
Confusion	9.8	6.5	0
Helplessness	4.9	0.8	0
Emptiness	10.6	6.5	0
Loneliness	13.0	16.3	0
Acceptance	2.4	2.4	1.8
Relief	3.3	0.8	5.5
Happiness that person died	4.1	0.8	66.4
Lack of enthusiasm	0	3.3	0
Absence of emotions	1.6	1.6	4.5

(Source: *Perceptions of Grief Among University Students* by C. J. Vickio, J. C. Cavanaugh, and T. Attig, in press, *Death Studies.*)

duties any longer. Perhaps the most common source of guilt is what Kalish (1981) calls the "If only I had . . ." syndrome: "If only I had gotten home in time"; "If only I had made him go to the doctor's earlier"; "If only I had expressed my feelings toward Mom while she was still alive." Guilt most often results from feeling that there was something one could have done to prevent the death, that one should have treated the person better while he or she was still alive, or that one is actually relieved that the person died. Such feelings are commonplace in normal grief, but they must be monitored so that they do not become overwhelming.

Anniversary Reactions. Resolving grief takes time, as we have seen. During that time, and for many years to come, certain dates that have personal significance may reintroduce feelings of grief. For example, holidays such as

Thanksgiving that were spent with the deceased person may be difficult times. The actual anniversary of the death can be especially troublesome. The term *anniversary reaction* itself refers to changes in behavior related to feelings of sadness on this date. Personal experience and research show that recurring feelings of sadness or other examples of the anniversary reaction are very common in normal grief (Bornstein & Clayton, 1972).

Longitudinal Research Findings. Most research on how people react to the death of a loved one is cross-sectional. Norris and Murrell (1987) conducted a longitudinal study of grief work in which three interviews were conducted before the death, and one after. The results of their research are described in more detail in "How Do We Know?" Briefly, Norris and Murrell reported that bereavement did not affect health; family stress increased as the death approached but diminished afterwards; before the death, family stress was associated with worsening health; after the death, health worsened only if there had been no family stress before the death; and after the death, psychological stress always increased. The results of this study have important implications for interventions. That is, interventions aimed at reducing stress or promoting health may be more effective if done before the death. Additionally, because health problems increased only among those who felt no stress before the death, it may be that the stress felt before the death is a product of anticipating it. Lundin (1984) also found this to be the case, in that health problems increased only for those experiencing sudden death.

Abnormal Grief Reactions

Not everyone is able to move through the phases of grief and begin rebuilding his or her life. Sometimes the feelings of hurt, loneliness, or guilt are so overwhelming that they become the focus of the survivor's life. Thus, what distinguishes normal from abnormal grief is not the kind of reaction but, rather, its intensity and duration (Schulz, 1985). For example, statements such as "I really feel that if I had gotten home from the store even 5 minutes earlier my husband would be alive" would be considered normal if made a month or so after the death. When made 3 years afterward, however, they would be considered abnormal. Likewise, intense feelings are normal early in the process, but if they never diminish they are classified as abnormal.

Elderly people who had difficulty coping with a death 2 years later were found to be different from good copers (Lund et al., 1985–1986). Poor copers expressed lower self-esteem before bereavement, were more confused, had a greater desire to die, cried more, and were less able to keep busy shortly after the death.

Overall, the most common manifestation of abnormal grief is excessive guilt and self-blame. In some people guilt results in a disruption of everyday routines and a diminished ability to function. People begin to make judgment errors, may reach a state of agitated depression, may experience problems sleeping or eating, and may have intense recurring thoughts about the deceased person. Many of these individuals either seek professional help voluntarily or are referred by concerned family members or friends. Unfortunately, the long-term prognosis for people suffering abnormal grief responses is not good (Schulz, 1985).

Types of Loss and Grieving

Consider the following deaths from cancer: an adolescent, a middle-aged mother, and an elderly man. Our reaction to each of them is different, even though all of them died from the same disease. The way we feel when someone dies is

Dealing with the death of one's spouse is often a very difficult process.

partially determined by how old that person was. Our society tends to view some deaths as more tragic or as easier to accept than others. Even though we really know that this approach has no research support, people nevertheless act as if it did. For example, people typically consider the death of a child as extremely traumatic, unless it occurred at birth. Or if one's parent dies when one is young, the loss is considered greater than if one is middle-aged and the parent is old. The point is that our society in a sense makes judgments about how much grief one should have following different types of loss. We have noted that death is always a traumatic event for survivors. But unfortunately the survivors are not always allowed to express their grief over a period of time or even to talk about their feelings. These judgments that society makes serve to impose arbitrary time limits on the grieving process, despite the fact that virtually all the evidence we have indicates that we should not do that. Let us consider three types of loss and see how these judgments occur.

Death of One's Parent. Most parents die after their children have grown. But whenever it occurs, parental death hurts. We lose not only a key relationship but also an important psychological buffer between us and death. We, the children, are now next in line. Indeed, when one's parent dies, it often leads the surviving children to redefine the meaning of parenthood and the importance of time together (Malinak, Hoyt, & Patterson, 1979).

For most people, the death of a parent deprives them of many important things: a source of guidance and advice, a source of love, and a model for their own parenting style. It may also deny them

HOW · DO · WE · KNOW?

Family Stress and Adaptation Before and After Bereavement

What happens to a family that experiences the death of a loved one? Norris and Murrell (1987) sought to answer this question by tracking families before and after bereavement. As part of a very large normative longitudinal study, they conducted detailed interviews approximately every 6 months. The data concerning grief reactions constitute a subset of this larger study, in which 63 older adults in families experiencing the death of an immediate family member were compared with 387 older adults in families who had not been bereaved.

The measures obtained extensive information on physical health, including functional abilities and specific ailments; psychological distress; and family stress. The psychological-distress measure tapped symptoms of depression. The family-stress measure assessed such things as new serious illness of a family member, having a family member move in, additional family responsibilities, new family conflict, or new marital conflict.

The results were enlightening. Among bereaved families, overall family stress increased before the death and then

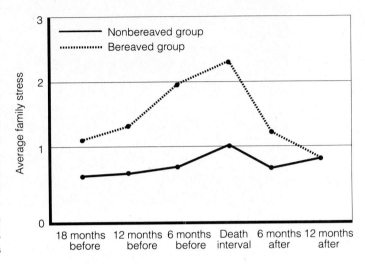

a

FIGURE 14.2 • Family stress experienced by bereaved and nonbereaved groups. Part *a* shows stress over a 30-month period. Part *b* shows the relationship between health and stress before and after bereavement.

(Source: "Older Adult Family Stress and Adaptation Before and After Bereavement" by F. N. Norris and S. A. Murrell, 1987, *Journal of Gerontology, 42*, pp. 609 and 610. Copyright © 1987 by the Gerontological Society of America. Reprinted by permission of the publisher and author.)

decreased. The level of stress experienced by these families was highest in the period right around the death. Moreover, bereavement was the only significant predictor of family stress, meaning that it was the anticipation and experience of bereavement that caused stress. Even more interesting were the findings concerning the relationship between health and stress. Bereaved individuals who reported stress before the death were in poorer health be-

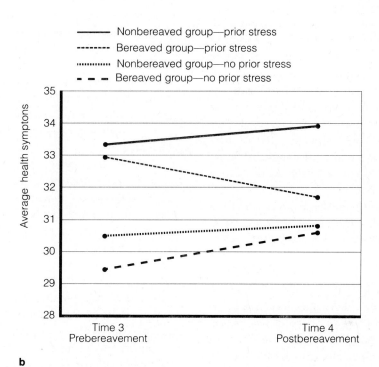

b

fore the death than were bereaved persons who were not experiencing stress. However, bereaved individuals reporting prior stress showed a significant *drop* in physical symptoms 6 months after the death; bereaved persons reporting no prior stress reported no change. The net result was that both groups ended up with about the same level of physical symptoms 6 months after bereavement. Both sets of results are depicted in Figure 14.2.

The Norris and Murrell study has two major implications. First, bereavement does not appear to cause poor health; the bereaved groups were not much different from the group of nonbereaved people in nonstressful families. Second, bereavement *does* appear to result in a marked increase in psychological distress. In sum, marked changes in psychological distress following bereavement are normal, but marked changes in physical health are not.

the opportunity to improve aspects of their relationship with a parent. The loss of a parent is perceived as a very significant one; society allows us to grieve for a reasonable length of time.

Death of One's Child. The death of a child is generally perceived as a great tragedy, since children are not supposed to die before their parents. It is as if the natural order of things has been violated. The loss is especially traumatic if it occurs suddenly, such as in sudden infant death syndrome or an automobile accident. But parents of terminally ill children still suffer a great deal, even with the benefit of anticipatory grieving. Mourning is always intense, and some parents never recover or attempt to reconcile the death of their child.

One of the most overlooked losses is the loss of a child through stillbirth, miscarriage, abortion, or neonatal death (Borg & Lasker, 1981). Attachment to one's child begins prenatally. His or her death hurts deeply, so to contend that the loss of a child before or at birth is not as tragic as the loss of an older child makes little sense. Yet parents who experience this type of loss are expected to recover very quickly and are often the recipients of unfeeling comments if these societal expectations are not met.

Finally, grandparents' feelings can easily be overlooked. They, too, feel the loss when their grandchild dies. Moreover, they grieve not only for the grandchild but also for their own child's loss (Hamilton, 1978). Grandparents must also be included in whatever rituals or support groups the family chooses.

Death of One's Spouse. More has been written about the death of a spouse than about any other type of loss. It clearly represents a deep personal loss, especially when the couple had a very long and close relationship. In a very real way when one's spouse dies, a part of oneself dies, too.

The death of a spouse is different from other losses. There is pressure from society to mourn for a period of time. Typically, this pressure is manifested if the survivor begins to show interest in finding another mate before an acceptable period of mourning has passed. Although Americans no longer define the length of such periods, many feel that about a year is appropriate. That such pressure and negative commentary usually do not accompany other losses is another indication of the seriousness with which most people take the death of a spouse.

Another important point concerning the loss of one's spouse involves the age of the survivor. Young adult spouses tend to show more intense grief reactions immediately following the death than do older spouses. However, the situation 18 months later is reversed. At that time older spouses report more grief than do younger spouses (Sanders, 1980–1981). The differences seem to be related to four factors: the death of a young spouse is more unexpected, there are fewer same-aged role models for young widows or widowers, the dimensions of grief vary with age, and the opportunities for remarriage are greater for younger survivors. Older widows anticipate fewer years of life and prefer to cherish the memory of their deceased spouse rather than to attempt a new marriage (Raphael, 1983).

Some longitudinal studies have examined the grief process in reaction to the death of a spouse. Dimond, Lund, and Caserta (1987) found that social support played a significant role in the outcome of the grieving process during the first 2 years after the death of a spouse. In particular, it is the quality of the support system, rather than number of friends, that is particularly important.

IS THERE LIFE AFTER DEATH?

Most people believe that death does not mark the end of being. Although the exact nature of this belief in an afterlife varies widely across individuals and cultures, the themes are the same. We can examine these themes with two questions in mind. Is the belief in an afterlife just wishful thinking? Do we have any scientific indication that there may be reason to suspect another life or type of existence?

These were the questions that prompted Moody (1975) to interview people who had had close calls with death, that is, **near-death experiences**. In many cases these people had been clinically dead, and in other cases they had come very close to dying. On the basis of these interviews Moody was able to identify several common reports, although individual experiences differed somewhat. The common aspects of the experiences include (1) an awareness of a buzzing or drumming sound or possibly hearing oneself declared dead; (2) feeling oneself moving out of one's body and then quickly down a tunnel, funnel, or cave toward an intense light; (3) seeing or feeling the presence of dead relatives who are present to help one make the transition from this life; (4) sensing the light as a power or presence, sometimes interpreted or experienced as love, that makes one review one's own life rather than be judged; (5) "seeing" one's life pass in front of one's eyes as a kaleidoscopic view of one's own thoughts and deeds; (6) being aware or being told that the time for one's death has not yet come and that one must return to finish the normal life span.

Some of the people whom Moody interviewed resented having survived. For them, the near-death experience was extraordinarily pleasant, and they felt cheated. For most people, the close encounter with death gave them a new and more positive outlook on life. Many people changed their life-styles, and some acquired a deep spiritual commitment. Most no longer feared death, because they felt that the knowledge of what it would be like had removed the mystery and doubt.

Moody makes no claims that these experiences "prove" that there is life after death. Nevertheless, he does believe that these data are significant, if for no other reason than that the experiences reported by his participants were remarkably similar. Subsequent verification of these reports have been offered (Moody, 1977; Siegel, 1980). As a result many people see the themes and consistency of the reports as evidence that there is life after death. Because belief in an afterlife is so common, this is not very surprising.

The believers in the evidence are not without their critics, however. Siegel (1980) uses evidence from biology, psychology, and anthropology to dismiss claims that the reports reflect experiences of an afterlife. Siegel tries to show how each of the common themes in these reports can be explained by known processes (e.g., hallucinations similar to those induced by drugs). He argues that because we know so little about the workings of the brain, it is more likely that the experiences reflect neurological processes than actual experiences of an afterlife.

Whose interpretation is correct? Unfortunately, the question is presently unanswerable and is likely to stay that way. But even if the claims of an afterlife are exaggerated, the belief in its potential existence is probably adaptive in this life. Many people are more likely to use death as a stimulus for personal growth if they think that something might follow it. Additionally, without the concept of an afterlife, death could result for some people in a devastating fear of total nonbeing. A belief in an afterlife may be nothing more than a way of denying the reality and possibility the finality of death. But the adaptive value of this belief is truly great. If nothing else, it allows us to keep on living life to the fullest. And in the end, that is what it's all about.

SUMMARY

Defining death has been difficult because it means many different things. Medical definitions currently focus on biological functioning (brain activity), and sociocultural definitions reflect the many ways of conceptualizing death (as a variable, statistic, event, state, analogy, or mystery). Because death involves complex issues, ethical problems such as euthanasia present society with difficult challenges.

Fear of death and death anxiety are pervasive in our society. Unfortunately, research on these topics is inconclusive. Measurement difficulties abound, and the most important correlates of death anxiety remain unclear. Nevertheless, many people believe that we base our behavior on feelings of fear and anxiety. Some examples include denying death or challenging it by putting our lives in danger. We can learn to overcome our fear and anxiety by thinking and preparing for our death.

The process of dying can be viewed as a sequence of stages or phases. Kübler-Ross proposes five stages: denial, anger, bargaining, depression, and acceptance. She emphasizes that the rate of progression through the stages varies from person to person and that individuals should not be forced through them. An alternative view suggests three phases: an acute phase, a chronic living-dying phase, and a terminal phase. Again, rates of progression reflect individual differences. How one approaches dying varies as a function of age; for example, younger adults feel more cheated than older adults.

Although most people say that they would prefer to die at home, few actually do so. Factors that enter into the decision of where to die include type of care needed, finances, and personal choice. Besides hospitals and nursing homes, people may opt for dying at a hospice. In this latter setting the family takes a much more active role, and the goal is to reduce pain while maintaining dignity.

Both medical workers and mental health workers care for the dying. A problem faced by all is balancing their feelings while treating the client. Attitudes often interfere with this process. For example, physicians and nurses may respond to calls from dying persons more slowly. Informing a person that he or she is dying also presents difficulties. The current emphasis is on open, honest communication.

Grief is the emotional response to loss. Mourning is the behavioral manifestation of grief. Deaths that are expected result in less grief after the loss than do unexpected or sudden deaths. Grief seems to progress through phases: an initial phase of shock and denial, an intermediate phase of searching and questioning, and a final phase of recovery. Many feelings are normal in the sense that they are experienced by nearly everyone after a loss, including sorrow, denial, and guilt. Abnormal grief occurs when these feelings remain very intense for an extended period. The type of loss also affects the grieving process; that is, we grieve differently over losses depending on the nature of the relationship.

GLOSSARY

active euthanasia • Deliberate ending of another person's life as an act of mercy.

avoidance • Not confronting a situation that reminds us of death, either at a conscious or an unconscious level.

bioethics • Study of the interface between human values and technological advances in health and the life sciences.

brain death • The lack of spontaneous movement, respiration, responsiveness, reflexes, and brain wave activity.

clinical death • The absence of pulse and respiration.

cortical death • The lack of brain activity in the cortex.

death anxiety • General, nonspecific feelings of uneasiness concerning death.

dying trajectory • A description of the length and form of the dying process in the phase approach.

euthanasia • The act or practice of ending life for reasons of mercy.

fear of death • A feeling of dread directly related to some specific aspect of dying.

grief • Feelings of sorrow, hurt, anger, guilt, confusion, and so forth that follow a loss.

grief work • The job of coming to terms with one's grief.

hospice • An alternative care model for the dying that emphasizes the quality of life and relief from pain.

institutionalization of death • Removing dying from everyday experience and placing it in the context of hospitals and other institutions.

just world view • The belief that the world operates under a law of fairness.

mourning • The ways in which people express grief.

mutual pretense • Acting as if everything is normal despite the imminence of death.

near-death experience • A brush with dying that some people interpret as representative of life after death.

passive euthanasia • Allowing a person to die by withholding an available treatment.

phase approach • A conceptualization of the dying process as consisting of a continuous process.

stage approach • A conceptualization of the dying process as consisting of distinct periods.

ADDITIONAL READING

Several excellent books on death, dying, and bereavement are available. Summaries of the research can be found in

Kalish, R. A. (1987). Death and dying. In P. Silverman (Ed.), *The elderly as modern pioneers* (pp. 320–334). Bloomington: Indiana University Press.

Kastenbaum, R. (1985). Death and dying: A life-span approach. In J. E. Birren & K. W. Schaie (Eds.), *Handbook of the psychology of aging* (2nd ed.) (pp. 619–643). New York: Van Nostrand Reinhold.

Heading Toward
The 21st Century

Marc Chagall, *Forward!*, 1917. Art Gallery of Ontario, Toronto. Gift of Sam and Ayala Zacks. Copyright © 1989, ARS/ADAGP, New York.

By the time you reach old age, the 21st century will be well along. Technology will have made major advances that will make commonplace what is only science fiction today. Our daily lives may be vastly different than they are right now. Life will undoubtedly be more complicated. You will probably have experienced first-hand many of the things discussed in this book: marriage, children, career changes, relocation, personal development, physical and cognitive changes, and so on. You will know what adult development is like.

For now, though, we must be content with gazing into a crystal ball. We know many things about adult development and aging to guide us, but there are many unknowns, too. Throughout this book we have encountered predictions about this future and how older people may fare. Some of these predictions are positive; for example, it is likely that more people will live to advanced ages. Other forecasts are not so rosy; as more people live to a very old age, there will be more need for long-term care. These predictions represent our best guess about what life will be like in 40 years or so, based on what we know now and what is likely to happen if we continue the way we are going.

The purpose of this chapter is to pull together several crucial issues facing gerontologists as we approach the 21st century. This survey will not be exhaustive; rather, we will focus on two things: points that have been singled out for special concern and areas where major advances may have a dramatic impact on our own development.

Three issues have been identified as trouble spots for the future. The first is the need for better research, a problem that underlies all others. Second, we will examine the growing crisis in health care and health policy. Third, we will consider the need for creating productive roles for the elderly.

Other issues concern areas of ongoing research that have the potential to revolutionize our own developmental course. Chief among these is research on biological and physiological aspects of aging. Also important are discoveries that are being made in the cognitive domain that challenge age-old stereotypes of aging.

IDENTIFYING ISSUES OF CONCERN

Throughout this book we have seen that adult development and aging are complex processes that we are far from understanding. Because the number of older people is rising and because we need more and better information, three issues need to be addressed in the near future if we are to optimize our own development into the next century. These are better research, health care, and productive roles.

The Need for Better Research

In Chapter 1 we considered various methods for conducting research on adult development and aging. Recall that of the major methods (cross-sectional, longitudinal, time-lag, and sequential), longitudinal and sequential designs are the ones that tell us what we really want to know: whether a particular process or behavior *changes* over time. Cross-sectional research identifies only differences that are related to age; they may reflect true age change or merely cohort differences. But the vast majority of research we have considered in this book is cross-sectional. Longitudinal and sequential work is confined mainly to topics in cognitive and personality development. Where does this leave us?

The problem we are faced with is the possibility that much of what we know about adult development and aging may not reflect true age changes. Rather, it may largely reflect cohort differences that are, in turn, a reflection of the changes that have occurred in society over this century. Recall from Chapter 10 that the modernization of society has a strong influence that may differ across generations. This may mean that differences in intellectual skills or memory performance are due to changes in the skills needed by each succeeding generation to survive and adapt in daily life.

Cross-sectional research will never solve the problem, since age and cohort are always confounded. Longitudinal research addresses the issue of age change, but it is severely limited because the results may not generalize across cohorts. Sequential research appears to be our best, and only, way out. We must have reliable data on whether the differences we observe between age groups are something innate in humans or whether they are due more to historical experiential factors.

But improved research does not only mean using a different, more sophisticated design. It also means cutting across disciplines and incorporating findings from one field to interpret data from another. A good example is the need for a blend between biological-physiological research and behavioral research. The search for the genetic link in Alzheimer's disease, for instance, may also yield the key to why cognitive processes fail (see Chapter 9). Cognitive scientists and neurological scientists working together will make substantially more progress than either group working alone. Likewise, there may be a connection between changing levels of neurotransmitters and aspects of personality, mainly studied through psychopathology (see the discussion on depression in Chapter 9).

The point is that we need better research not only to understand more about adult development and aging but also to know how better to commit resources for the future. As we will see, the most serious problem facing the United States concerning the elderly is health care; the lack of data collected over time from multiple cohorts seriously impairs our ability to plan for the future. Getting better information also means changing our research priorities from a system that rewards quantity, which promotes more cross-sectional research, to one that rewards high quality, which would promote more longitudinal and sequential research. Perhaps changing our priorities should be the place to start; otherwise, the future will arrive and we will still not have a data base.

The Crisis in Health Care

No problem in the United States will be more pressing in the coming years than the need for health care for older adults (J. A. Brody, 1988; Wallack & Cohen, 1988). The number of elderly will increase dramatically over the next 30 to 40 years, most rapidly in the over-80 age group. By the year 2000 the over-80 group will constitute the largest single federal entitlement group, receiving nearly $83 billion a year in benefits (Torrey, 1985). Health care costs for adults over age 65 will soar as the expenses for chronic and debilitating diseases mount. Long-term care is already in crisis; beds are in short supply, and the cost of the average nursing home is beyond the means of many (see Chapter 13). Information is also scarce, and statistical tools for analyzing it are often inadequate (National Research Council, 1988).

The growing concern over health care for the elderly prompted the National Research Council (NRC) to study the situation and to make several recommendations concerning future health care policy (NRC, 1988). These recommendations address several areas of special concern, as well as general issues.

The NRC identifies the financing of medical care for the elderly as the most important health policy issue facing the United States in the 1990s. The cost of care, who will pay for it, and how it will be financed are issues that *must* be addressed. The changes in Medicare and Medicaid during the 1980s and the growing realization that private insurance will need to become more heavily involved have had a significant impact on how health care is financed. We noted in Chapters 9 and 13 that many public and private insurance programs do not adequately cover the cost of quality long-term care. The trend toward increased reliance on individuals to either have their own health coverage or pay for care themselves has profound implications for people facing chronic debilitating conditions such as Alzheimer's disease. The NRC points to a lack of adequate data on the cost burden of such care, and it places high priority on obtaining them.

How health care is delivered is a second issue facing American society. The diminishing number of physicians in rural areas and in some specialties, the closing of inner-city hospitals, and the lack of transportation to health care centers present significant problems to older adults, especially minority groups and the frail. The growth of for-profit care and business-oriented approaches to health care, not recognizing age differences in recovery time from illness, and

increased competition also create barriers to quality health care for the elderly.

The NRC identifies the need for and cost of long-term care as major factors in the overall financing picture. Moreover, many of the issues cited earlier apply to long-term-care facilities. Many nursing homes do not take Medicaid patients, for example, forcing many elderly poor to settle for lower-quality care or no care. We have no consistent program of data collection to determine how many people are likely to need long-term care in the future. Surveys also need to include facilities other than nursing homes, such as chronic disease hospitals, mental health facilities, rehabilitation centers, group homes, halfway houses, and residential facilities.

A smart investment strategy, according to the NRC, would be to spend health care dollars on health promotion and disease prevention. This approach would emphasize keeping oneself in good health in order to avoid the more expensive treatment programs. Generally speaking, paying for checkups and needed treatment early in the disease process is markedly less expensive than waiting until the disease has spread. Important intervention goals include promoting healthy activities and life-style among older adults. Whether the federal government should finance prevention and promotion is an important policy decision.

Monitoring health care systems to ensure that people get the best care for their money and that care quality meets high standards are also important. Simply solving the financing problem is only half the battle. The health care industry must be held accountable for its actions.

Carrying out the NRC's recommendations will be expensive. By its own estimate, data collection alone may cost $15 billion to $20 billion or more. Such a high price tag makes one wonder whether the benefits would justify the expense. The answer is a resounding yes. We have too little information now to address the coming crisis in health care adequately (Hollander & Becker, 1988). Policymakers need reliable data on which to base decisions about where to allocate federal dollars in order to do the most good for the most people. Not collecting adequate information and not making appropriate policy decisions would be far more expensive, both in terms of dollars and in the quality of life of older people. Our goals should be to enable the elderly to stay healthy and functionally independent as long as possible, to provide access to quality health care of whatever type is appropriate, and to provide care in the least restrictive and most cost-effective environment (Somers, 1987). The issue facing us is whether we are willing to assume the cost burden. If not, the alternatives are not pleasant to think about.

Productive Roles for Older Adults

One of the key issues facing older adults that was identified in Chapter 10 is the lack of formal social roles. Adults currently relinquish many of the major roles of adulthood by the time they reach old age. We have noted that older cohorts experience major declines in societal significance as a result of these role losses. One of the most important of these relinquished roles is work. As more people enter retirement over the coming decades, the issue of how to keep older adults connected with society will become more critical.

In an effort to draw up guidelines for addressing the need to develop productive roles for older adults, the Committee on an Aging Society (CAS) of the Institute of Medicine and the National Research Council explored unpaid productive roles as one alternative (CAS, 1986). Unpaid productive roles are ones in which individuals make a significant contribution to society but are not given wages. The difference between paid and unpaid productive roles is sometimes arbitrary, and the work is often similar.

Voluntarism has a long, distinguished tradition in the United States. From Boy Scout troop leaders to friendly visitors in hospitals and nursing homes, millions of people donate their time freely each year. The CAS argues that we should look to older adults as a major source of volunteers in social and health services. It proposes that a systematic effort at providing unpaid productive roles for older adults would accomplish two things. First, it would increase the availability of some social and health services that could be provided by nonprofessionals. For example, existing programs such as Foster Grandparents could be enhanced, and new programs such as home visitation for the frail elderly could be started in many communities. Second, unpaid productive roles would give older people a formal way to maintain self-esteem and identity after retirement without having to be employed. Unpaid productive roles would enable them to retain societal significance by using their accumulated years of experience and expertise.

An important issue not directly addressed by the CAS is that volunteers often end up in clerical or social tasks, with little opportunity to have a direct say in the operation of the program. This is not an optimal situation, of course, since volunteers often come into the program with years of experience. This is especially true for older adults, who may view volunteer positions as low-status roles that do not take advantage of their experience.

The CAS gives most attention to the prospect of older volunteers (providing, of course, that the status and menial nature of volunteer work are addressed). It points out that declining federal and state support of social service programs through the 1980s has led to a serious shortage of people to provide these much-needed services.

Having older adults share their experiences and wisdom is one way
of providing productive roles for them in society.

The growing number of older people could be a resource in easing the impact of personnel cuts that have been made as a result of fewer dollars. Estimates are that between 35% and 40% of older adults already perform some sort of volunteer work, and projections are that this figure will increase (Kieffer, 1986). Thus, the potential pool is relatively large.

If a concerted effort is to be made to provide older adults with formalized roles through unpaid productive activities, several impediments to participation need to be addressed (CAS, 1986). Older people are often not actively recruited by organizations or are not encouraged to remain. Individuals are often expected to cover expenses such as transportation, with little hope for tax deductions to help defray such costs. Unions are often reluctant to accept volunteers, viewing them as a way to displace paid employees. Some older adults themselves view voluntarism as a form of exploitation, feeling that volunteers are

considered second-class citizens in organizations. The lack of adequate transportation for elderly people who do not drive means that people who might otherwise volunteer will not do so because they cannot get there.

How can we eliminate these barriers? First of all, we need to explicitly recognize that older adults have a wealth of experience and expertise that should not be allowed to go to waste. Kieffer (1986) notes that this expertise of the elderly has been systematically and increasingly thrown away since the 1940s. We need to begin to draw on older adults as experts in much the same way as members of some nonindustrialized societies do. Second, we need to make positive appeals to older adults to become volunteers and share their knowledge. Third, there need to be incentives for volunteers, including increased recognition. Fourth, we need improved supervision, development, and management of volunteer programs. Providing services takes coordination of both government and business. Careful planning needs to be done, and programs have to be monitored to ensure that they provide optimal services. Finally, the impediments outlined earlier need to be removed. Most important, transportation to and from the volunteer site should be provided to those who want to participate.

Well-planned and well-managed volunteer programs could become extremely cost-effective, both in terms of the services they provide and the benefits to the volunteers. Social and health services that are currently unavailable could be provided at a fraction of the cost of identical programs using only a paid staff. Volunteers benefit by feeling more useful in society and regaining aspects of identity lost after retirement.

Volunteer programs are not a panacea, however. The CAS notes that volunteer programs should never be used as a way to cut corners or to eliminate needed professionals. Such programs should be viewed as a way to supplement existing services, not as a replacement for them. Used appropriately, however, voluntarism could be an effective way to reconnect older adults to society.

THE REALM OF DISCOVERY

Insights into the experience of adult development and aging are being achieved at an ever-quickening pace. Two areas that have had major impacts on the day-to-day experience of growing old are biological-physiological research and cognitive-developmental research.

Unlocking the Secrets of Aging

As we noted in Chapters 3 and 4, we have learned a great deal about the biology and physiology of aging. Our knowledge is increasing even more through research on diseases of aging, especially Alzheimer's disease. As noted in Chapter 9, Alzheimer's disease is thought by many to be qualitatively similar to normal aging. By combining research on both normal and abnormal aging, we may unlock the genetic basis of human aging in our own lifetime. Not even Ponce de León could have imagined that.

We already have the technology to greatly prolong life by curing diseases that only a few decades ago were major killers. High-tech surgical techniques make cataract operations routine. Open-heart surgery and cancer treatments that were only dreams in the 1960s are commonplace. Diagnostic techniques through computer-enhanced imaging allow physicians to detect problems even before they are manifested.

What might these changes mean to us? For one thing, they almost ensure that, barring accidents, virtually everyone will have the chance to live to a very old age. But more important is the prospect that in our lifetime we may have the ability to reverse the aging process itself. The implications of this possibility are mind-boggling. Bioethicists (see Chapter 14) would have to deal with the question of whose aging process could be reversed and under what circumstances it would be done. Would genetic engineering be routinely performed on victims of Alzheimer's disease or other genetic disorders? Could the average person have his or her aging process slowed? Who would decide? What impact would significant slowing of aging have on society? How would we deal with the population increase?

These and other questions bring home the sobering fact that understanding the biological and physiological process of aging may create more problems than it solves. As pointed out many times in the text, we need to approach the problem from a life-course perspective and ask ourselves whether the outcome is in our best interest.

Interestingly, unlocking the secrets of aging would tend to exacerbate the health care problems facing the United States. Larger numbers of people living to unprecedented old age might completely overburden the system. This problem emphasizes the point that progress in one area may create additional dilemmas elsewhere. It also points out the need for careful planning and policy-making in the years ahead.

Understanding How We Think

Perhaps no other area of research in adult development and aging has forced more rethinking of stereotypes than work on intellectual and memory skills. From the earliest descriptions of older people to the present, the belief has been that with old age comes a marked diminution of cognitive ability. As we learned in Chapters 6 and 7, however, researchers over the past 2 decades have discovered that this stereotype is only partially true.

In fact, aging does bring changes in cognitive abilities. Some people do decline, but others do not. Moreover, it is beginning to appear that even cognitive skills that we thought declined may actually be amenable to remediation. The discovery that one's predominant mode or style of thinking may change as one ages and that thought becomes reunited with the inner self are revolutionizing the way in which psychologists view older adults. The effects are dramatic. We have gone from questioning whether we even needed to document the decline because we were so certain of it, in the 1950s, to being very cautious in discussing the developmental trends in relatively specific abilities, because we accept the fact that not all abilities change.

We are also witnessing a movement toward wondering how adults think in their everyday lives. This naturalistic shift, while not encompassing most cognitive-developmental research, nevertheless brings attention to the fact that adults develop compensatory strategies for dealing with cognitive aging. Differences that are obtained in the laboratory may be moot in the real world because we have learned how to deal with our limitations. In short, we may be realistic in our everyday cognitive activity without even knowing it.

What does the continued discovery of cognitive change across adulthood mean for the future? Perhaps above all, the discoveries since the early 1970s mean that a focus on lifelong learning will be even more pronounced in the 21st century. Colleges and universities may begin to recruit older adults actively into their academic programs. The image of older people being incapable of learning may be laid to rest, replaced by an image of older people teaching the young and learning from them.

SOME FINAL THOUGHTS

In this book you have seen a snapshot of what adult development and aging are like today. You have learned about their complexities, myths, and realities. But more than anything else, you have learned what we really know about the pioneers who have blazed the trail ahead of us.

In a short time it will be your turn to lead the journey. The decisions you make will have enormous impact on those who will be old: your parents, grandparents, and the people who taught you. The decisions will not be easy ones. But you have an advantage that the pioneers did not. You have the collected knowledge of gerontologists to help. With a continued concerted effort you will be able to address the problems and meet the challenges that lie ahead. Then, when you yourself are old, you will be able to look back on your life and say, "I lived long—and I prospered."

Adams, P., Davies, G. T., & Sweetname, P. (1970). Osteoporosis and the effect of aging on bone mass in women. *Quarterly Journal of Medicine, 39*, 601–615.

Adams, R. D. (1980). Morphological aspects of aging in the human nervous system. In J. E. Birren & R. B. Sloane (Eds.), *Handbook of mental health and aging* (pp. 149–160). Englewood Cliffs, NJ: Prentice-Hall.

Ade-Ridder, L., & Brubaker, T. H. (1983). The quality of long-term marriages. In T. H. Brubaker (Ed.), *Family relationships in later life* (pp. 21–30). Beverly Hills, CA: Sage Publications.

Adler, S., & Aranya, N. (1984). A comparison of the work needs, attitudes, and preferences of professional accountants at different career stages. *Journal of Vocational Behavior, 25*, 574–580.

Ahrons, C., & Wallisch, L. (1987). The relationship between former spouses. In D. Perlman & S. Duck (Eds.), *Intimate relationships: Development, dynamics, and deterioration* (pp. 269–296). Beverly Hills, CA: Sage Publications.

Alwin, D. F., Converse, P. E., & Martin, S. S. (1985). Living arrangements and social integration. *Journal of Marriage and the Family, 47*, 319–334.

American Association of Retired Persons (AARP). (1988). *A portrait of older minorities*. Washington, DC: Author.

American Heart Association. (1983). *Eat well but eat wisely*. New York: Author.

American Psychiatric Association. (1987). *Diagnostic and statistical manual (DSM III-R)*. Washington, DC: Author.

Amoss, P. T. (1981). Coast Salish elders. In P. T. Amoss & S. Harrell (Eds.), *Other ways of growing old* (pp. 227–238). Stanford, CA: Stanford University Press.

Amoss, P. T., & Harrell, S. (1981). Introduction: An anthropological perspective on aging. In P. T. Amoss & S. Harrell (Eds.), *Other ways of growing old* (pp. 1–24). Stanford, CA: Stanford University Press.

Anastasi, A. (1958). Heredity, environment, and the question "how?" *Psychological Review, 65*, 197–208.

Anderson, J. R. (1982). Acquisition of cognitive skill. *Psychological Review, 89*, 369–406.

Anderson, P. W. (1972). More is different. *Science, 177*, 393–396.

Anderson, R. G., & Meyerhoff, W. L. (1982). Otologic manifestations of aging. *Otolaryngologic Clinics of North America, 15*, 353–370.

Anderson, S. A., Russell, C. S., & Schumm, W. R. (1983). Perceived marital quality and family life-cycle categories: A further analysis. *Journal of Marriage and the Family, 45*, 127–139.

Andrasik, F., Blanchard, E. B., & Edlund, S. R. (1985). Physiological responding during biofeedback. In S. R. Burchfield (Ed.), *Stress: Psychological and physiological interactions* (pp. 282–306). Washington, DC: Hemisphere.

Anlezark, G. M., Crow, T. J., & Greenway, A. P. (1973). Impaired learning and decreased cortical norepinephrine after bilateral locus coeruleus lesions. *Science, 181*, 682–684.

Anschutz, L., Camp, C. J., Markley, R. P., & Kramer, J. J. (1985). Maintenance and generalization of mnemonics for grocery shopping by older adults. *Experimental Aging Research, 11*, 157–160.

Anschutz, L., Camp, C. J., Markley, R. P., & Kramer, J. J. (1987). Remembering mnemonics: A three-year follow-up on the effects of mnemonic training in elderly adults. *Experimental Aging Research, 13,* 141–143.

Antonucci, T. C. (1985). Personal characteristics, social support, and social behavior. In R. H. Binstock & E. Shanas (Eds.), *Handbook of aging and the social sciences* (pp. 94–128). New York: Van Nostrand Reinhold.

Arensberg, C. (1968). *The Irish countryman: An anthropological study.* New York: Peter Smith.

Ariès, P. (1974). *Western attitudes toward death: From the Middle Ages to the present* (P. N. Ranum, Trans.). Baltimore: Johns Hopkins University Press.

Arlin, P. K. (1975). Cognitive development in adulthood: A fifth stage? *Developmental Psychology, 11,* 602–606.

Armor, D. J., Polich, J. M., & Stambul, H. B. (1976). *Alcoholism and treatment.* Santa Monica, CA: Rand.

Aronson, M. K. (Ed.). (1988). *Understanding Alzheimer's disease.* New York: Scribner's.

Atchley, R. C. (1975). The life course, age grading, and age-linked demands for decision making. In N. Datan & L. H. Ginsberg (Eds.), *Life-span developmental psychology: Normative life crises* (pp. 261–278). New York: Academic Press.

Atchley, R. C. (1976). *The sociology of retirement.* Cambridge, MA: Schenkman.

Atchley, R. C. (1977). *The social forces in later life.* Belmont, CA: Wadsworth.

Attig, M. S. (1983, November). *The processing of spatial information by adults.* Paper presented at the meeting of the Gerontological Society of America, San Francisco.

Auster, C. J., & Auster, D. (1981). Factors influencing women's choice of nontraditional careers: The role of family, peers, and counselors. *Vocational Guidance Quarterly, 29,* 253–263.

Averill, J. R. (1968). Grief: Its nature and significance. *Psychological Bulletin, 70,* 721–748.

Avioli, L. V. (1982). Aging, bone, and osteoporosis. In S. G. Korenman (Ed.), *Endocrine aspects of aging* (pp. 199–230). New York: Elsevier Biomedical.

Avolio, B. J., & Waldman, D. A. (1987). Personnel aptitude-test scores as a function of age, education, and job type. *Experimental Aging Research, 13,* 109–113.

Axelrod, S., & Cohen, L. D. (1961). Senescence and embedded-figure performance in vision and touch. *Perceptual and Motor Skills, 12,* 283–288.

Bäckman, L. (1985). Further evidence for the lack of adult age differences on free recall of subject performed tasks: The importance of motor action. *Human Learning, 4,* 79–87.

Bäckman, L., & Nilsson, L.-G. (1984). Aging effects in free recall: An exception to the rule. *Human Learning, 3,* 53–69.

Bäckman, L., & Nilsson, L.-G. (1985). Prerequisites for the lack of age differences in memory performance. *Experimental Aging Research, 11,* 67–73.

Baddeley, A. (1981). The cognitive psychology of everyday life. *British Journal of Psychology, 72,* 257–269.

Bahrick, H. P., Bahrick, P. P., & Wittlinger, R. P. (1975). Fifty years of memory for names and faces: A cross-sectional approach. *Journal of Experimental Psychology, 104*, 54–75.

Baird, L. (1973). *The graduates.* Princeton, NJ: Educational Testing Service.

Baker, H., Frank, O., Thind, S., Jaslow, J. P., & Louria, D. B. (1979). Vitamin profiles in elderly persons living at home or in nursing homes versus profiles in healthy young subjects. *Journal of the American Geriatrics Society, 27*, 444–450.

Baldessarini, R. J. (1978). Chemotherapy. In A. M. Nicholi (Ed.), *The Harvard guide to modern psychiatry* (pp. 387–432). New York: Belknap.

Ball, J. F. (1976–1977). Widow's grief: The impact of age and mode of death. *Omega: Journal of Death and Dying, 7*, 307–333.

Baltes, M. M., & Baltes, P. B. (Eds.) (1986). *The psychology of control and aging.* Hillsdale, NJ: Erlbaum.

Baltes, P. B. (1979). Life-span developmental psychology: Some converging observations on history and theory. In P. B. Baltes & O. G. Brim, Jr. (Eds.), *Life-span development and behavior: Vol. 2* (pp. 255–279). New York: Academic Press.

Baltes, P. B., Dittmann-Kohli, F., & Dixon, R. A. (1984). New perspectives on the development of intelligence in adulthood: Toward a dual-process conception and a model of selective optimization with compensation. In P. B. Baltes & O. G. Brim, Jr. (Eds.), *Life-span development and behavior: Vol. 6* (pp. 33–76). New York: Academic Press.

Baltes, P. B., Reese, H. W., & Lipsitt, L. P. (1980). Life-span developmental psychology. *Annual Review of Psychology, 31*, 65–100.

Baltes, P. B., Reese, H. W., & Nesselroade, J. R. (1977). *Life-span developmental psychology: Introduction to research methods.* Pacific Grove, CA: Brooks/Cole.

Baltes, P. B., & Schaie, K. W. (1974). Aging and IQ: The myth of the twilight years. *Psychology Today, 7*, 35–40.

Baltes, P. B., & Willis, S. L. (1982). Enhancement (plasticity) of intellectual functioning: Penn State's Adult Development and Enrichment Project (ADEPT). In F. I. M. Craik & S. Trehub (Eds.), *Aging and cognitive processes* (pp. 353–389). New York: Plenum.

Bandura, A. (1986). *Social foundations of thought and action: A social cognitive theory.* Englewood Cliffs, NJ: Prentice-Hall.

Bandura, A. (in press). Reflections on non-ability determinants of competence. In J. Kolligan, Jr., & R. J. Sternberg (Eds.), *Competence considered: Perceptions of competence and incompetence across the lifespan.* New Haven, CT: Yale University Press.

Barfield, R. E., & Morgan, J. N. (1978). Trends in satisfaction with retirement. *Gerontologist, 18*, 19–23.

Barnes, R. F., Raskind, M., Gumbrecht, G., & Halter, J. B. (1982). The effects of age on the plasma catecholamine response to mental stress in man. *Journal of Clinical Endocrinology and Metabolism, 54*, 64–69.

Baron, J. N., & Bielby, W. T. (1985). Organizational barriers to gender equality: Sex segregation of jobs and opportunities. In A. S. Rossi (Ed.), *Gender and the life course* (pp. 233–251). New York: Aldine.

Barrett, G. V. (1978). Task design, individual attributes, work satisfaction, and productivity. In A. Negandhi & B. Wilpert, (Eds.), *Current research in work organizations.* Kent, OH: Kent State University Press.

Barrett, G. V., Alexander, R. A., & Forbes, J. B. (1977). Analysis of performance measurement and training requirements for driving decision making in emergency situations. *JSAS Catalogue of Selected Documents in Psychology, 7*, 126 (Ms. No. 1623).

Barrett, T. R., & Wright, M. (1981). Age-related facilitation in recall following semantic processing. *Journal of Gerontology, 36*, 194–199.

Bartoshuk, L. M., Rifkin, B., Marks, L. E., & Bars, P. (1986). Taste and aging. *Journal of Gerontology, 41*, 51–57.

Bartus, R., Dean, R. L., & Fisher, S. K. (1986). Cholinergic treatment for age-related memory disturbances: Dead or barely coming of age. In

T. Crook, R. Bartus, S. Ferris, & S. Gershon (Eds.), *Treatment development strategies for Alzheimer's disease* (pp. 421–450). New Caanan, CT: Mark Powley Associates.

Baruch, G. K. (1984). The psychological well-being of women in the middle years. In G. K. Baruch & J. Brooks-Gunn (Eds.), *Women in midlife* (pp. 161–180). New York: Plenum.

Baruch, G. K., Barnett, R., & Rivers, C. (1983). *Life prints: New patterns of love and work for today's women.* New York: McGraw-Hill.

Basseches, M. (1984). *Dialectical thinking and adult development.* Norwood, NJ: Ablex.

Bastida, E. (1987). Sex-typed age norms among older Hispanics. *Gerontologist, 27,* 59–65.

Baylor, A. M., & Spirduso, W. W. (1988). Systemic aerobic exercise and components of reaction time in older women. *Journal of Gerontology, 43,* P121–P126.

Beck, A. T. (1967). *Depression: Clinical, experimental, and theoretical aspects.* New York: Harper & Row.

Beck, A. T. (1976). *Cognitive therapy and the emotional disorders.* New York: International Universities Press.

Beck, A. T., Rush, J., Shaw, B., & Emery, G. (1979). *Cognitive therapy of depression.* New York: Guilford.

Beck, A. T., Ward, C. H., Mendelson, M., Mock, J., & Erbaugh, J. (1961). An inventory for measuring depression. *Archives of General Psychiatry, 4,* 561–571.

Bellezza, F. S. (1981). Mnemonic devices: Classification characteristics, and criteria. *Review of Educational Research, 51,* 247–275.

Belloc, N. B., & Breslow, L. (1972). Relationship of physical health status and health practices. *Preventive Medicine, 1,* 409–421.

Bengtson, V. L. (1985). Diversity and symbolism in grandparental roles. In V. L. Bengtson & J. F. Robertson (Eds.), *Grandparenthood* (pp. 11–25). Beverly Hills, CA: Sage Publications.

Bengtson, V. L., Cuellar, J. B., & Raga, P. K. (1977). Stratum contrasts and similarities in attitudes toward death. *Journal of Gerontology, 32,* 76–88.

Bengtson, V. L., Dowd, J. J., Smith, D. H., & Inkles, A. (1975). Modernization, modernity and perceptions of aging: A cross-cultural study. *Journal of Gerontology, 30,* 688–695.

Bengtson, V. L., & Morgan, L. A. (1983). Ethnicity and aging: A comparison of three ethnic groups. In J. Sokolovsky (Ed.), *Growing old in different societies: Cross-cultural perspectives* (pp. 157–167). Belmont, CA: Wadsworth.

Bengtson, V. L., & Robertson, J. F. (Eds.). (1985). *Grandparenthood.* Beverly Hills, CA: Sage Publications.

Benin, M. H., & Agostinelli, J. (1988). Husbands' and wives' satisfaction with the division of labor. *Journal of Marriage and the Family, 50,* 349–361.

Benjamin, B. J. (1982). Phonological performance in gerontological speech. *Journal of Psycholinguistic Research, 11,* 159–167.

Berg, C., Hertzog, C., & Hunt, E. (1982). Age differences in the speed of mental rotation. *Developmental Psychology, 18,* 95–107.

Bergman, M. (1971). Hearing and aging: Implications of recent research findings. *Audiology, 10,* 164–171.

Bergman, M., Blumenfeld, V. G., Cascardo, D., Dask, B., Levitt, H., & Margulies, M. K. (1976). Age-related decrement in hearing for speech: Sampling and longitudinal studies. *Journal of Gerontology, 31,* 533–538.

Bergström, B. (1978). Morphology study of the vestibular nerve fibers in man at various ages. *Acta Otolaryngolica, 76,* 331–338.

Berkman, L. F., Breslow, L., & Wingard, D. L. (1983). Health practices and mortality risk. In L. F. Berkman & L. Breslow (Eds.), *Health and ways of living: The Alameda County study* (pp. 61–112). New York: Oxford University Press.

Berkow, R. (Ed.). (1987). *The Merck manual of diagnosis and therapy* (15th ed.). Rahway, NJ: Merck, Sharp, & Dohme Research Laboratories.

Bernardi, B. (1985). *Age class systems: Social institutions and politics based on age.* Cambridge: Cambridge University Press.

Bernstein, J. (1982). Who leaves — who stays: Residency policy in housing for the elderly. *Gerontologist, 22,* 305–313.

Berry, J. M. (1986). *Memory complaints and performance in older women: A self-efficacy and causal attribution model.* Unpublished doctoral dissertation, Washington University, St. Louis.

Berry, J. M., West, R. L., & Scogin, F. (1983, November). *Predicting everyday and laboratory memory skill.* Paper presented at the meeting of the Gerontological Society of America, San Francisco.

Berry, R. E., & Williams, F. L. (1987). Assessing the relationship between quality of life and marital and income satisfaction: A path analytic approach. *Journal of Marriage and the Family, 49,* 107–116.

Berscheid, E., Walster, E., & Bohrnstedt, G. (1973). Body image. The happy American body: A survey report. *Psychology Today, 7*(6), 119–131.

Betz, E. L. (1984). A study of career patterns of women college graduates. *Journal of Vocational Behavior, 24,* 249–263.

Betz, N., & Fitzgerald, L. F. (1987). *The career psychology of women.* New York: Academic Press.

Betz, N. E., & Hackett, G. (1986). Applications of self-efficacy theory to understanding career choice behavior. *Journal of Social and Clinical Psychology, 4,* 279–289.

Bielby, D. D., & Bielby, W. T. (1988). She works hard for the money: Household responsibilities and the allocation of work effort. *American Journal of Sociology, 93,* 1031–1059.

Bierman, E. L. (1985). Arteriosclerosis and aging. In C. E. Finch & E. L. Schneider (Eds.), *Handbook of the biology of aging* (2nd ed.) (pp. 842–858). New York: Van Nostrand Reinhold.

Biesele, M., & Howell, N. (1981). The old people give you life: Aging among !Kung hunter-gatherers. In P. T. Amoss & S. Harrell (Eds.), *Other ways of growing old* (pp. 77–98). Stanford, CA: Stanford University Press.

Biller, H. B. (1982). Fatherhood: Implications for child and adult development. In B. B. Wolman (Ed.), *Handbook of developmental psychology* (pp. 702–725). Englewood Cliffs, NJ: Prentice-Hall.

Binet, H. (1903). *L'étude expérimentale de l'intelligence.* Paris: Schleicher.

Binger, C. M., Ablin, A. R., Feuerstein, R. C., Kushner, J. H., Zoger, S., & Mikkelson, C. (1969). Childhood leukemia — Emotional impact on patient and family. *New England Journal of Medicine, 280,* 414.

Birren, J. E. (1969). Age and decision strategies. In A. T. Welford & J. E. Birren (Eds.), *Decision making and age: Interdisciplinary topics in gerontology: Vol. 6.* Basel: Karger.

Birren, J. E., & Cunningham, W. (1985). Research on the psychology of aging: Principles, concepts, and theory. In J. E. Birren & K. W. Schaie (Eds.), *Handbook of the psychology of aging* (2nd ed.) (pp. 3–34). New York: Van Nostrand Reinhold.

Birren, J. E., & Renner, V. J. (1977). Research on the psychology of aging. In J. E. Birren & K. W. Schaie (Eds.), *Handbook of the psychology of aging* (pp. 3–38). New York: Van Nostrand Reinhold.

Birren, J. E., & Renner, V. J. (1979). A brief history of mental health and aging. In *Issues in mental health and aging: Vol. 1. Research* (pp. 1–26). Washington, DC: National Institute of Mental Health.

Birren, J. E., & Renner, V. J. (1980). Concepts and issues of mental health and aging. In J. E. Birren & R. B. Sloane (Eds.), *Handbook of mental health and aging* (pp. 3–33). Englewood Cliffs, NJ: Prentice-Hall.

Black, P., Markowitz, R. S., & Cianci, S. (1975). Recovery of motor function after lesions in motor cortex of monkey. In R. Porter & D. W. Fitzsimmons (Eds.), *Outcome of severe damage to the central nervous system* (pp. 65–70). Amsterdam: Elsevier.

Blake, B. F., & Lawton, M. P. (1980). Perceived community functions and the rural elderly. *Educational Gerontology, 5,* 375–386.

Blanchard-Fields, F. (1986). Reasoning on social dilemmas varying in emotional saliency: An adult developmental study. *Psychology and Aging, 1,* 325–333.

Blanchard-Fields, F., & Irion, J. C. (1988). The relation between locus of control and coping in two contexts: Age as a moderator variable. *Psychology and Aging, 3,* 197–203.

Blass, J. P., & Barclay, L. L. (1985). New developments in the diagnosis of dementia. *Drug Development Research, 5,* 39–58.

Blazer, D., George, L. K., & Hughes, D. C. (1988). Schizophrenic symptoms in an elderly community population. In J. A. Brody & G. L. Maddox (Eds.), *Epidemiology and aging: An international perspective* (pp. 134–149). New York: Springer.

Blazer, D., Hughes, D. C., & George, L. K. (1987). The epidemiology of depression in an elderly community population. *Gerontologist, 27,* 281–287.

Blazer, D., & Williams, C. D. (1980). Epidemiology of dysphoria and depression in the elderly populations. *American Journal of Psychiatry, 137,* 439–444.

Blessed, G., Tomlinson, B. E., & Roth, M. (1968). The association between quantitative measures of dementia and of senile changes in the cerebral grey matter of elderly subjects. *British Journal of Psychiatry, 114,* 797–811.

Blocher, D. H., & Ropoza, R. S. (1981). Professional preparation. In A. W. Chickering & Associates (Eds.), *The modern American college* (pp. 212–231). San Francisco: Jossey-Bass.

Block, R., DeVoe, M., Stanley, B., Stanley, M., & Pomara, N. (1985). Memory performance in individuals with primary degenerative dementia: Its similarity to diazepam-induced impairments. *Experimental Aging Research, 11,* 151–155.

Bloom, B. L., & Caldwell, R. A. (1981). Sex differences in adjustment during the process of marital separation. *Journal of Marriage and the Family, 43,* 693–701.

Blum, E. M. (1966). Psychoanalytic views of alcoholism: A review. *Quarterly Journal of Studies of Alcohol, 27,* 259–299.

Blum, J. E., & Jarvik, L. F. (1974). Intellectual performance of octogenarians as a function of education and initial ability. *Human Development, 17,* 364–375.

Blume, S. B. (1985). Psychodrama and the treatment of alcoholism. In S. Zimberg, J. Wallace, & S. B. Blume (Eds.), *Practical approaches to alcoholism psychotherapy* (pp. 87–108). New York: Plenum.

Blumenthal, J. A., Emery, C. F., Cox, D. R., Walsh, M. A., Kuhn, C. M., Williams, R. B., & Williams, R. S. (1988). Exercise training in healthy Type A middle-aged men: Effects on behavioral and cardiovascular responses. *Psychosomatic Medicine, 50,* 418–433.

Blumenthal, J. A., & Madden, D. J. (1988). Effects of aerobic exercise training, age, and physical fitness on memory-search performance. *Psychology and Aging, 3,* 280–285.

Blumstein, P., & Schwartz, P. (1983). *American couples.* New York: Morrow.

Bobrow, D. G., & Collins, A. (1975). *Representation and understanding: Studies in cognitive science.* New York: Academic Press.

Bohannon, P. (1980). Time, rhythm, and pace. *Science 80, 1*(3), 18, 20.

Boller, F. (1980). Mental status of patients with Parkinson disease. *Journal of Clinical Neuropsychology, 2,* 157–172.

Boller, F., Mizutani, T., & Roessman, V. (1980). Parkinson's disease, dementia, and Alzheimer's disease: Clinicopathological correlations. *Annals of Neurology, 7,* 329–335.

Bondareff, W. (1983). Age and Alzheimer's disease. *Lancet, 1,* 1447.

Bondareff, W. (1985). The neural basis of aging. In J. E. Birren & K. W. Schaie (Eds.), *Handbook of the psychology of aging* (2nd ed.) (pp. 95–112). New York: Van Nostrand Reinhold.

Bondareff, W., Mountjoy, C. Q., & Roth, M. (1982). Loss of neurons or origin of the adrenergic projection to cerebral cortex (nucleus locus ceruleus) in senile dementia. *Neurology, 32,* 164–168.

Booth, A. (1972). Sex and social participation. *American Sociological Review, 37*, 183–192.

Bootzin, R. R. (1977). Effects of self-control procedures for insomnia. In R. B. Stuart (Ed.), *Behavioral self-management: Strategies, techniques, and outcomes* (pp. 176–195). New York: Brunner/Mazel.

Bootzin, R. R., & Engle-Friedman, M. (1981). The assessment of insomnia. *Behavioral Assessment, 3*, 107–126.

Bootzin, R. R., & Engle-Friedman, M. (1987). Sleep disturbances. In L. L. Carstensen & B. A. Edelstein (Eds.), *Handbook of clinical gerontology* (pp. 238–251). New York: Pergamon Press.

Bootzin, R. R., Engle-Friedman, M., & Hazelwood, L. (1983). Insomnia. In P. M. Lewinsohn & L. Teri (Eds.), *Clinical geropsychology: New directions in assessment and treatment* (pp. 81–115). New York: Pergamon Press.

Borg, S., & Lasker, J. (1981). *When pregnancy fails.* Boston: Beacon.

Borgatta, E. F., & Corsini, R. J. (1964). *Manual for the Quick Word Test.* New York: Harcourt, Brace, & World.

Borkan, G. A., & Norris, A. H. (1980). Assessment of biological age using a profile of physiological parameters. *Journal of Gerontology, 35*, 177–184.

Borkovec, T. D. (1982). Insomnia. *Journal of Consulting and Clinical Psychology, 50*, 880–895.

Bornstein, P. E., & Clayton, P. J. (1972). The anniversary reaction. *Diseases of the Nervous System, 33*, 470–472.

Bortz, W. M. (1982). Disuse and aging. *JAMA, 248*, 1203–1208.

Borup, J. H. (1981). Relocation: Attitudes, information network, and problems encountered. *Gerontologist, 21*, 501–511.

Borup, J. H. (1982). The effects of varying degrees of interinstitutional environmental change on long-term care of patients. *Gerontologist, 22*, 409–417.

Borup, J. H. (1983). Relocation and mortality research: Assessment, reply, and the need to refocus the issues. *Gerontologist, 23*, 235–242.

Borup, J. H., & Gallego, D. T. (1981). Mortality as affected by interinstitutional relocation: Update and assessment. *Gerontologist, 21*, 8–16.

Borup, J. H., Gallego, D. T., & Heffernan, P. G. (1979). Relocation and its effect on mortality. *Gerontologist, 19*, 135–140.

Borup, J. H., Gallego, D. T., & Heffernan, P. G. (1980). Relocation: Its effect on health, functioning, and mortality. *Gerontologist, 20*, 468–479.

Bossé, R., & Ekerdt, D. J. (1981). Change in self-perception of leisure activities with retirement. *Gerontologist, 21*, 650–653.

Botwinick, J. (1977). Intellectual abilities. In J. E. Birren & K. W. Schaie (Eds.), *Handbook of the psychology of aging* (pp. 580–605). New York: Van Nostrand Reinhold.

Botwinick, J. (1984). *Aging and behavior* (3rd ed.). New York: Springer.

Botwinick, J., & Brinley, J. F. (1962). An analysis of set in relation to reaction time. *Journal of Experimental Psychology, 63*, 568.

Botwinick, J., Robbin, J. S., & Brinley, J. F. (1959). Reorganization of perceptions with age. *Journal of Gerontology, 14*, 85–88.

Botwinick, J., & Storandt, M. (1974). *Memory, related functions and age.* Springfield, IL: Charles C Thomas.

Bourestom, N., & Pastalan, L. (1981). The effects of relocation on the elderly: A reply. *Gerontologist, 21*, 4–7.

Bowles, N. L., & Poon, L. W. (1982). An analysis of the effect of aging on memory. *Journal of Gerontology, 37*, 212–219.

Bray, D. W., Campbell, R. J., & Grant, D. L. (1974). *Formative years in business.* New York: Wiley.

Bray, D. W., & Howard, A. (1983). The AT&T longitudinal studies of managers. In K. W. Schaie (Ed.), *Longitudinal studies on adult psychological development* (pp. 266–312). New York: Guilford.

Breitner, J. C. S. (1988). Alzheimer's disease: Possible evidence for genetic causes. In M. K. Aronson (Ed.), *Understanding Alzheimer's disease* (pp. 34–49). New York: Scribner's.

Brent, S. B. (1984). *Psychological and social structure: Their organization, activity, and development.* Hillsdale, NJ: Erlbaum.

Breslow, R., Kocsis, J., & Belkin, B. (1981). Contribution of the depressive perspective to memory function in depression. *American Journal of Psychiatry, 138,* 227–230.

Brickel, C. M. (1984). The clinical use of pets with the aged. *Clinical Gerontologist, 2,* 72–74.

Brim, O. G., Jr. (1968). Adult socialization. In J. A. Clausen (Ed.), *Socialization and society.* Boston: Little, Brown.

Brim, O. G., Jr., & Kagan, J. (1980). Constancy and change: A view of the issues. In O. G. Brim, Jr., & J. Kagan (Eds.), *Constancy and change in human development* (pp. 1–25). Cambridge, MA: Harvard University Press.

Brizzee, K. R. (1975). Gross morphometric analyses and quantitative histology of the aging brain. In J. M. Ordy & K. R. Brizzee (Eds.), *Neurobiology of aging* (pp. 401–424). New York: Plenum.

Brody, E. M. (1981). Women in the middle and family help to older people. *Gerontologist, 21,* 471–480.

Brody, E. M. (1985). Parent care as a normative family stress. *Gerontologist, 25,* 19–29.

Brody, E. M., Johnsen, P. T., Fulcomer, M. C., & Lang, A. M. (1983). Women's changing roles and help to elderly parents: Attitudes of three generations of women. *Journal of Gerontology, 38,* 597–607.

Brody, E. M., Kleban, M. H., Johnsen, P. T., Hoffman, C., & Schoonover, C. B. (1987). Work status and parent care: A comparison of four groups of women. *Gerontologist, 27,* 201–208.

Brody, J. (1988, August 29). New test for Huntington's creates difficult choices. *Atlanta Journal,* p. 2B.

Brody, J. A. (1988). Changing health needs of the ageing population. In D. Evered & J. Whelan (Eds.), *Symposium on research and the ageing population* (pp. 208–215). Chichester, England: Wiley.

Brody, J. A., & Brock, D. B. (1985). Epidemiologic and statistical characteristics of the United States elderly population. In C. E. Finch & E. L. Schneider (Eds.), *Handbook of the biology of aging* (2nd ed.) (pp. 3–26). New York: Van Nostrand Reinhold.

Brody, J. E. (1982). *The New York Times guide to personal health.* New York: Times Books.

Broman, C. L. (1988). Household work and family life satisfaction of Blacks. *Journal of Marriage and the Family, 50,* 743–748.

Brown, J. K. (1982). Cross-cultural perspectives on middle-aged women. *Current Anthropology, 23,* 143–156.

Brownell, K. D., Bachorik, P. S., & Ayerle, R. S. (1982). Changes in plasma lipid and lipoprotein levels in men and women after a program of moderate exercise. *Circulation, 65,* 477–484.

Bruce, P. R., Coyne, A. C., & Botwinick, J. (1982). Adult age differences in metamemory. *Journal of Gerontology, 37,* 354–357.

Buell, S. J., & Coleman, P. D. (1979). Dendritic growth in the aged human brain and failure of growth in senile dementia. *Science, 206,* 854–856.

Buell, S. J., & Coleman, P. D. (1981). Quantitative evidence for selective dendritic growth in normal human aging but not in senile dementia. *Brain Research, 214,* 23–41.

Bullock, W. A., & Dunn, N. J. (1988, August). *Aging, sex, and marital satisfaction.* Paper presented at the meeting of the American Psychological Association, Atlanta.

Burdman, G. M. (1986). *Healthful aging.* Englewood Cliffs, NJ: Prentice-Hall.

Burdz, M. P., Eaton, W. D., & Bond, J. B. (1988). Effect of respite care on dementia and nondementia patients and their caregivers. *Psychology and Aging, 3,* 38–42.

Burgio, K. L., & Engel, B. T. (1987). Urinary incontinence: Behavioral assessment and treatment. In L. L. Carstensen & B. A. Edelstein (Eds.), *Handbook of clinical gerontology* (pp. 252–266). New York: Pergamon Press.

Burke, D. M., & Light, L. L. (1981). Memory and aging: The role of retrieval processes. *Psychological Bulletin*, 90, 513–546.

Burlin, F. (1976). The relationship of parental education and maternal work and occupational status to occupational aspiration in adolescent females. *Journal of Vocational Behavior*, 9, 99–104.

Burrus-Bammel, L. L., & Bammel, G. (1985). Leisure and recreation. In J. E. Birren & K. W. Schaie (Eds.), *Handbook of the psychology of aging* (2nd ed.) (pp. 848–889). New York: Van Nostrand Reinhold.

Busch, J. W. (1985). Mentoring in graduate schools of education: Mentors' perceptions. *American Educational Research Journal*, 22, 257–265.

Buskirk, E. R. (1985). Health maintenance and longevity: Exercise. In C. E. Finch & E. L. Schneider (Eds.), *Handbook of the biology of aging* (2nd ed.) (pp. 894–931). New York: Van Nostrand Reinhold.

Busse, E. W., & Maddox, G. L. (1985). *The Duke longitudinal studies of normal aging: 1955–1980*. New York: Springer.

Butler, R. N., & Lewis, M. I. (1982). *Aging and mental health* (3rd ed.). St. Louis: C. V. Mosby.

Cain, B. S. (1982, December 12). Plight of the grey divorcée. *New York Times Magazine*, pp. 89–90, 92, 95.

Cain, L. (1987). Alternative perspectives on phenomena in human aging: Age stratification and age status. *Journal of Applied Behavioral Science*, 23, 227–294.

Caird, F. I., & Judge, T. C. (1974). *Assessment of the elderly patient*. London: Pittman Medical.

Cameron, P. (1975). Mood as an indicant of happiness: Age, sex, social class, and situational differences. *Journal of Gerontology*, 30, 216–224.

Cameron, R., & Meichenbaum, D. (1982). The nature of effective coping and the treatment of stress related problems: A cognitive-behavioral perspective. In L. Goldberger & S. Breznitz (Eds.), *Handbook of stress: Theoretical and clinical aspects* (pp. 695–710). New York: Free Press.

Camp, C. J. (1989). World knowledge systems. In L. W. Poon, D. C. Rubin, & B. Wilson (Eds.), *Everyday cognition in adulthood and late life*. New York: Cambridge University Press.

Camp, C. J., Markley, R. P., & Kramer, J. J. (1983). Spontaneous use of mnemonics by elderly individuals. *Educational Gerontology*, 9, 57–71.

Campbell, A. (1981). *The sense of well-being in America: Recent patterns and trends*. New York: McGraw-Hill.

Campbell, R. (1984). Nursing home and long-term care in Japan. *Pacific Affairs*, 51, 78–89.

Campione, W. A. (1987). The married woman's retirement decision: A methodological comparison. *Journal of Gerontology*, 42, 381–386.

Campione, W. A. (1988). Predicting participation in retirement preparation programs. *Journal of Gerontology*, 43, S91–S95.

Canestrari, R. E., Jr. (1963). Paced and self-paced learning in young and elderly adults. *Journal of Gerontology*, 18, 165–168.

Cantor, M. H. (1980). The informal support system: Its relevance in the lives in the elderly. In E. Borgatta & N. McCluskey (Eds.), *Aging and society* (pp. 111–146). Beverly Hills, CA: Sage Publications.

Carlin, V. F., & Mansberg, R. (1984). *If I live to be 100 . . . Congregate housing for later life*. West Nyack, NY: Parker.

Carp, F. M. (1966). *A future for the aged*. Austin: University of Texas Press.

Carp, F. M. (1975). User evaluation of housing for the elderly. *Gerontologist*, 16, 102–111.

Carp, F. M. (1976). Housing and living environments of older people. In R. H. Binstock & E. Shanas (Eds.), *Handbook of aging and the social sciences* (pp. 244–271). New York: Van Nostrand Reinhold.

Carp, F. M. (1977). Impact of improved living environment on health and life expectancy. *Gerontologist*, 17, 242–249.

Carruthers, M. (1983). Instrumental stress tests. In H. Selye (Ed.), *Selye's guide to stress* (Vol. 2) (pp. 331–362). New York: Scientific and Academic Editions.

Cartwright, A., Hockey, L., & Anderson, J. L. (1973). *Life before death.* London: Routledge & Kegan Paul.

Case, R. B., Heller, S. S., Case, N. B., & Moss, A. J. (1985). Type A behavior and survival after acute myocardial infarction. *New England Journal of Medicine, 312,* 737–741.

Caserta, M. S., Lund, D. A., Wright, S. D., & Redburn, D. E. (1987). Caregivers to dementia patients: The utilization of community services. *Gerontologist, 27,* 209–214.

Cauna, N. (1965). The effects of aging on the receptor organs of the human dermis. In W. Montagna (Ed.), *Advances in biology of skin: Vol. 6. Aging* (pp. 63–96). New York: Pergamon Press.

Cavanaugh, J. C. (1983). Comprehension and retention of television programs by 20- and 60-year olds. *Journal of Gerontology, 38,* 190–196.

Cavanaugh, J. C. (1984). Effects of presentation format on adults' retention of television programs. *Experimental Aging Research, 10,* 51–53.

Cavanaugh, J. C. (1986–1987). Age differences in adults' self-reports of memory ability: It depends on how and what you ask. *International Journal of Aging and Human Development, 24,* 241–277.

Cavanaugh, J. C. (1989). The importance of awareness in memory aging. In L. W. Poon, D. C. Rubin, & B. Wilson (Eds.), *Everyday cognition in adulthood and late life.* New York: Cambridge University Press.

Cavanaugh, J. C., Grady, J. G., & Perlmutter, M. (1983). Forgetting and use of memory aids in 20 to 70 year olds' everyday life. *International Journal of Aging and Human Development, 17,* 113–122.

Cavanaugh, J. C., Kramer, D. A., Sinnott, J. D., Camp, C. J., & Markley, R. J. (1985). On missing links and such: Interfaces between cognitive research and everyday problem solving. *Human Development, 28,* 146–168.

Cavanaugh, J. C., & Morton, K. R. (1989). Contextualism, naturalistic inquiry, and the need for new science: A rethinking of everyday memory aging and childhood sexual abuse. In D. A. Kramer & M. Bopp (Eds.), *Transformation in clinical and developmental psychology* (pp. 89–114). New York: Springer-Verlag.

Cavanaugh, J. C., Morton, K. R., & Tilse, C. R. (1989). A self-evaluation framework for understanding everyday memory aging. In J. D. Sinnott (Ed.), *Everyday problem solving: Theory and application* (pp. 266–284). New York: Praeger.

Cavanaugh, J. C., & Murphy, N. Z. (1986). Personality and metamemory correlates of memory performance in younger and older adults. *Educational Gerontology, 12,* 387–396.

Cavanaugh, J. C., & Perlmutter, M. (1982). Metamemory: A critical examination. *Child Development, 53,* 11–28.

Cavanaugh, J. C., & Poon, L. W. (in press). Metamemorial predictors of memory performance in young and old adults. *Psychology and Aging.*

Cavanaugh, J. C., & Stafford, H. (1989). Being aware of issues and biases: Directions for research on post-formal thought. In M. L. Commons, J. D. Sinnott, F. A. Richards, & C. Armon (Eds.), *Adult development: Vol. 1. Comparisons and applications of adolescent and adult developmental models* (pp. 272–292). New York: Praeger.

Cerella, J., Poon, L. W., & Fozard, J. L. (1982). Age and iconic read-out. *Journal of Gerontology, 37,* 197–202.

Cerella, J., Poon, L. W., & Williams, D. M. (1980). Age and the complexity hypothesis. In L. W. Poon (Ed.), *Aging in the 1980s.* Washington, DC: American Psychological Association.

Chaffin, R., & Herrmann, D. J. (1983). Self reports of memory abilities by old and young adults. *Human Learning, 2,* 17–28.

Chalke, H. D., Dewhurst, J. R., & Ward, C. W. (1958). Loss of sense of smell in old people. *Public Health, 72,* 223–230.

Chance, J., Overcast, T., & Dollinger, S. J. (1978). Aging and cognitive regression: Contrary findings. *Journal of Psychology, 98,* 177–183.

Chandler, M. J. (1980). Life-span intervention as a symptom of conversion hysteria. In R. R. Turner & H. W. Reese (Eds.), *Life-span developmental psychology: Intervention* (pp. 79–91). New York: Academic Press.

Charness, N. (1981). Aging and skilled problem solving. *Journal of Experimental Psychology, 110,* 21–38.

Chen, Y.–P. (1985). Economic status of the aging. In R. H. Binstock & E. Shanas (Eds.), *Handbook of aging and the social sciences* (2nd ed.) (pp. 641–665). New York: Van Nostrand Reinhold.

Chenoweth, B., & Spencer, B. (1986). Dementia: The experience of family caregivers. *Gerontologist, 26,* 266–272.

Cherkin, A. (1984). Effects of nutritional status on memory function. In H. J. Armbrecht, J. M. Prendergast, & R. M. Coe (Eds.), *Nutritional intervention in the aging process* (pp. 229–249). New York: Springer-Verlag.

Cherlin, A. J. (1981). *Marriage, divorce, remarriage.* Cambridge, MA: Harvard University Press.

Cherlin, A. J., & Furstenberg, F. F., Jr. (1986). *The new American grandparent: A place in the family, a life apart.* New York: Basic Books.

Chiriboga, D. A. (1982). Adaptation to marital separation in later and earlier life. *Journal of Gerontology, 37,* 109–114.

Chiriboga, D. A. (1984). Social stressors as antecedents of change. *Journal of Gerontology, 39,* 468–477.

Chiriboga, D. A. (1985, November). *Stress and personal continuity.* Paper presented at the meeting of the Gerontological Society of America, New Orleans.

Cicirelli, V. G. (1980). Sibling relationships in adulthood: A life-span perspective. In L. W. Poon (Ed.), *Aging in the 1980s* (pp. 455–474). Washington, DC: American Psychological Association.

Cicirelli, V. G. (1981). *Helping elderly parents: The role of adult children.* Boston: Auburn House.

Cicirelli, V. G. (1986). Family relationships and care/management of the dementing elderly. In M. Gilhooly, S. Zarit, & J. E. Birren (Eds.), *The dementias: Policy and management* (pp. 89–103). Englewood Cliffs, NJ: Prentice-Hall.

Clark, R. L., & Baumer, D. L. (1985). Income maintenance policies. In R. H. Binstock & E. Shanas (Eds.), *Handbook of aging and the social sciences* (2nd ed.) (pp. 666–696). New York: Van Nostrand Reinhold.

Clark, R. L., Maddox, G. L., Schrimper, R. A., & Sumner, D. A. (1984). *Inflation and the economic well-being of the elderly.* Baltimore: Johns Hopkins University Press.

Clark, R. L., & Spengler, J. J. (1980). *The economics of individual and population aging.* New York: Cambridge University Press.

Clark, W. C., & Mehl, L. (1971). Thermal pain: A sensory decision theory analysis of the effect of age and sex on d', various response criteria, and 50 percent pain threshold. *Journal of Abnormal Psychology, 78,* 202–212.

Clausen, J. A. (1981). Men's occupational careers in the middle years. In D. H. Eichorn, N. Haan, J. Clausen, M. Honzik, & P. Mussen (Eds.), *Present and past in middle life* (pp. 321–351). New York: Academic Press.

Clausen, J. A. (1986). *The life course: A sociological perspective.* Englewood Cliffs, NJ: Prentice-Hall.

Clayton, V. P. (1975). Erikson's theory of human development as it applies to the aged: Wisdom as contradictory cognition. *Human Development, 18,* 119–128.

Clayton, V. P. (1982). Wisdom and intelligence: The nature and function of knowledge in the later years. *International Journal of Aging and Human Development, 15,* 315–323.

Clayton, V. P., & Birren, J. E. (1980). The development of wisdom across the life-span: A reexamination of an ancient topic. In P. B. Baltes & O. G. Brim, Jr. (Eds.), *Life-span development and behavior: Vol. 3* (pp. 104–135). New York: Academic Press.

Clayton, V. P., & Overton, W. F. (1973, November). *The role of formal operational thought in the aging process*. Paper presented at the meeting of the Gerontological Society of America, Miami.

Cleek, M. B., & Pearson, T. A. (1985). Perceived causes of divorce: An analysis of interrelationships. *Journal of Marriage and the Family, 47*, 179–191.

Clopton, W. (1973). Personality and career change. *Industrial Gerontology, 17*, 9–17.

Cohen, C. I., Teresi, J. A., & Holmes, D. (1988). The physical well-being of old homeless men. *Journal of Gerontology, 43*, S121–S128.

Cohen, G. (1979). Language comprehension in old age. *Cognitive Psychology, 11*, 412–429.

Cohen, G. (in press). Age differences in memory for tests: Production deficiency of processing limitations? In D. M. Burke & L. L. Light (Eds.), *Language, memory, and aging*. New York: Academic Press.

Cohen, G., & Faulkner, D. (1989). The effects of aging on perceived and generated memories. In L. W. Poon, D. C. Rubin, & B. Wilson (Eds.), *Everyday cognition in adulthood and late life*. New York: Cambridge University Press.

Cohen, R. M., Weingartner, H., Smallberg, S. A., Pickar, D., & Murphy, D. L. (1982). Effort and cognition in depression. *Archives of General Psychiatry, 39*, 593–597.

Cohen, S. (1980). Aftereffects of stress on human performance and social behavior: A review of research and theory. *Psychological Bulletin, 88*, 82–108.

Cohler, B. J., & Grunebaum, H. U. (1981). *Mothers, grandmothers, and daughters: Personality and child care in three-generation families*. New York: Wiley.

Coleman, R. M., Miles, L. E., Guilleminault, C. C., Zarcone, V. P., van den Hoed, J., & Dement, W. C. (1981). Sleep wake disorders in the elderly: A polysomnographic analysis. *Journal of the American Geriatrics Association, 29*, 289–296.

Colerick, E. J., & George, L. K. (1986). Predictors of institutionalization among caregivers of patients with Alzheimer's disease. *Journal of the American Geriatrics Association, 34*, 493–498.

Collopy, B. J. (1988). Autonomy in long term care: Some crucial distinctions. *Gerontologist, 28*(Suppl.), 10–17.

Comalli, P. E., Jr. (1970). Life-span changes in visual perception. In L. R. Goulet & P. B. Baltes (Eds.), *Life-span developmental psychology: Research and theory* (pp. 211–226). New York: Academic Press.

Comalli, P. E., Jr., Wapner, S., & Werner, H. (1962). Interference effects of Stroop Color-Word Test in children, adulthood, and aging. *Journal of Genetic Psychology, 100*, 47–53.

Committee on an Aging Society. (1986). *Productive roles in an older society*. Washington, DC: National Academy Press.

Commons, M. L., & Richards, F. A. (1984). A general model of stage theory. In M. L. Commons, F. A. Richards, & C. Armon (Eds.), *Beyond formal operations: Late adolescent and adult cognitive development* (pp. 120–140). New York: Praeger.

Commons, M. L., Richards, F. A., & Armon, C. (Eds.). (1984). *Beyond formal operations: Late adolescent and adult cognitive development*. New York: Praeger.

Commons, M. L., Richards, F. A., & Kuhn, D. (1982). Systematic and metasystematic reasoning: A case for levels of reasoning beyond Piaget's stage of formal operations. *Child Development, 53*, 1058–1069.

Commons, M. L., Sinnott, J. D., Richards, F. A., & Armon, C. (Eds.). (1989). *Adult development: Vol. 1. Comparisons and applications of adolescent and adult developmental models*. New York: Praeger.

Connidis, I. (1988, November). *Sibling ties and aging*. Paper presented at the Gerontological Society of America, San Francisco.

Connor, C. L., Walsh, R. P., Lintzelman, D. K., & Alvarez, M. G. (1978). Evaluation of job applicants: The effects of age versus success. *Journal of Gerontology, 33*, 246–252.

Cook-Greuter, S. (1989). Maps for living: Ego development theory from symbiosis to conscious universal embeddedness. In M. L. Commons, J. D. Sinnott, F. A. Richards, & C. Armon (Eds.), *Adult*

REFERENCES

development: Vol. 1. Comparisons and application of adolescent and adult developmental models. New York: Praeger.

Cool, L. E. (1987). The effects of social class and ethnicity on the aging process. In P. Silverman (Ed.), *The elderly as modern pioneers* (pp. 211–227). Bloomington: Indiana University Press.

Cooper, S. J. (1984). Drug treatments, neurochemical change and human memory impairment. In B. Wilson & N. Moffat (Eds.), *Clinical management of memory problems* (pp. 132–147). Rockville, MD: Aspen.

Corkin, S., Growdon, J. H., Sullivan, E. V., Nissen, M. J., & Huff, F. J. (1986). Assessing treatment effects: A neuropsychological battery. In L. W. Poon (Ed.), *Handbook for clinical memory assessment of older adults* (pp. 156–167). Washington, DC: American Psychological Association.

Corso, J. F. (1981). *Aging sensory systems and perception.* New York: Praeger.

Corso, J. F. (1984). Auditory processes and age: Significant problems for research. *Experimental Aging Research, 10,* 171–174.

Corso, J. F. (1987). Sensory-perceptual processes and aging. In K. W. Schaie (Ed.), *Annual review of gerontology and geriatrics: Vol. 7* (pp. 29–55). New York: Springer.

Cosby, A. (1974). Occupational expectations and the hypothesis of increasing realism of choice. *Journal of Vocational Behavior, 5,* 53–65.

Costa, P. T., Jr., & McCrae, R. R. (1977). Cross-sectional differences in masculinity-femininity in adult men. *Gerontologist, 17,* 50.

Costa, P. T., Jr., & McCrae, R. R. (1978). Objective personality assessment. In M. Storandt, I. C. Siegler, & M. F. Elias (Eds.), *The clinical psychology of aging* (pp. 119–143). New York: Plenum.

Costa, P. T., Jr., & McCrae, R. R. (1980a). Somatic complaints in males as a function of age and neuroticism: A longitudinal analysis. *Journal of Behavioral Medicine, 3,* 245–258.

Costa, P. T., Jr., & McCrae, R. R. (1980b). Still stable after all these years: Personality as a key to some issues in adulthood and old age. In P. B. Baltes & O. G. Brim, Jr. (Eds.), *Life-span development and behavior: Vol. 3* (pp. 65–102). New York: Academic Press.

Costa, P. T., Jr., & McCrae, R. R. (1988). Personality in adulthood: A six-year longitudinal study of self-reports and spouse ratings on the NEO Personality Inventory. *Journal of Personality and Social Psychology, 54,* 853–863.

Costa, P. T., Jr., McCrae, R. R., & Arenberg, D. (1980). Enduring dispositions in adult males. *Journal of Personality and Social Psychology, 38,* 793–800.

Costa, P. T., Jr., McCrae, R. R., & Holland, J. L. (1984). Personality and vocational interests in an adult sample. *Journal of Applied Psychology, 42,* 390–400.

Cotman, C. W., & Holets, V. R. (1985). Structural changes at synapses with age: Plasticity and regeneration. In C. E. Finch & E. L. Schneider (Eds.), *Handbook of the biology of aging* (pp. 617–644). New York: Van Nostrand Reinhold.

Counts, D. A., & Counts, D. R. (1985). I'm not dead yet! Aging and death: Processes and experiences in Kalia. In D. A. Counts & D. R. Counts (Eds.), *Aging and its transformations* (pp. 131–156). Langham, MD: University of America Press.

Coward, R., & Lee, G. (Eds.). (1985). *The elderly in rural society.* New York: Springer.

Cowgill, D. (1974). Aging and modernization: A revision of the theory. In J. Gubrium (Ed.), *Late life: Communities and environmental policy* (pp. 123–146). Springfield, IL: Charles C Thomas.

Cowgill, D., & Holmes, L. D. (1972). *Aging and modernization.* New York: Appleton-Century-Crofts.

Coyne, A. C. (1983, November). *Age, task variables, and memory knowledge.* Paper presented at the meeting of the Gerontological Society of America, San Francisco.

Craik, F. I. M. (1968). Two components in free recall. *Journal of Verbal Learning and Verbal Behavior, 7,* 996–1004.

Craik, F. I. M. (1977). Age differences in human memory. In J. E. Birren & K. W. Schaie (Eds.), *Handbook of the psychology of aging* (pp. 384–420). New York: Van Nostrand Reinhold.

Craik, F. I. M., & Lockhart, R. S. (1972). Levels of processing: A framework for memory research. *Journal of Verbal Learning and Verbal Behavior, 11,* 671–684.

Craik, F. I. M., & Rabinowitz, J. C. (1984). Age differences in the acquisition and use of verbal information. In J. Long & A. Baddeley (Eds.), *Attention and performance: Vol. 10.* Hillsdale, NJ: Erlbaum.

Crandall, J. E., & Lehman, R. E. (1977). Relationship of stressful life events to social interest, locus of control, and psychological adjustment. *Journal of Consulting and Clinical Psychology, 45,* 1208.

Crandall, R. C. (1980). *Gerontology: A behavioral science approach.* Reading, MA: Addison-Wesley.

Crook, T. (1987). Dementia. In L. L. Carstensen & B. A. Edelstein (Eds.), *Handbook of clinical gerontology* (pp. 96–111). New York: Pergamon Press.

Crook, T., & Cohen, G. (1983). *Physician's guide to the diagnosis and treatment of depression in the elderly.* New Canaan, CT: Mark Powley Associates.

Crosby, J. F. (1980). Critique of divorce statistics and their interpretation. *Family Relations, 29,* 51–58.

Crystal, H. A. (1988). The diagnosis of Alzheimer's disease and other dementing disorders. In M. K. Aronson (Ed.), *Understanding Alzheimer's disease* (pp. 15–33). New York: Scribner's.

Cuber, J. F., & Harroff, P. B. (1965). *Sex and the significant Americans.* Baltimore: Penguin.

Cuellar, J. B., & Weeks, J. R. (1980). *Minority elderly Americans: A prototype for area offices on aging* (executive summary). San Diego: Allied Home Health Association.

Cunningham, W. R. (1987). Intellectual abilities and age. In K. W. Schaie (Ed.), *Annual review of gerontology and geriatrics: Vol. 7* (pp. 117–134). New York: Springer.

Curcio, C. A., Buell, S. J., & Coleman, P. D. (1982). Morphology of the aging central nervous system: Not all downhill. In J. A. Mortimer, F. J. Pirozzola & G. I. Maletta (Eds.), *Advances in neurogerontology: Vol. 3. The aging motor system* (pp. 7–35). New York: Praeger.

Currey, J. D. (1984). Effects of differences in mineralization on the mechanical properties of bone. *Philosophical Transactions of the Royal Society of London (Biology), 304*(1121), 509–518.

Dakof, G. A., & Mendelsohn, G. A. (1986). Parkinson's disease: The psychological aspects of a chronic illness. *Psychological Bulletin, 99,* 375–387.

Daniels, P., & Weingarten, K. (1982). *Sooner or later: The timing of parenthood in adult lives.* New York: Norton.

Dannefer, D. (1988). What's in a name? An account of the neglect of variability in the study of aging. In J. E. Birren & V. L. Bengtson (Eds.), *Emergent theories of aging* (pp. 356–384). New York: Springer.

Danziger, W. L., & Salthouse, T. A. (1978). Age and the perception of incomplete figures. *Experimental Aging Research, 4,* 67–80.

Davidson, J. M., Chen, J. J., Crapo, L., Gray, G. D., Greenleaf, W. J., & Catania, J. A. (1983). Hormonal changes and sexual function in aging men. *Journal of Clinical Endocrinology and Metabolism, 57,* 71–77.

Davidson, R. J., Schwartz, G. E., Saron, C., Bennett, J., & Goleman, D. J. (1979). Frontal vs. parietal EEG asymmetry during positive and negative affect. *Psychophysiology, 16,* 202–203.

Davies, P. (1988). Alzheimer's disease and related disorders: An overview. In M. K. Aronson (Ed.), *Understanding Alzheimer's disease* (pp. 3–14). New York: Scribner's.

Davies, P., & Maloney, A. J. F. (1976). Selective loss of central cholinergic neurons in Alzheimer's disease. *Lancet, 2,* 1403.

DeFrank, R., & Ivancevich, J. M. (1986). Job loss: An individual level review and model. *Journal of Vocational Behavior, 19,* 1–20.

DeLongis, A., Coyne, J. C., Dakof, G., Folkman, S., & Lazarus, R. S. (1982). Relationship of daily hassles, uplifts, and major life events to health status. *Health Psychology, 1,* 119–136.

DeMaris, A., & Leslie, G. R. (1984). Cohabitation with the future spouse: Its influence upon marital satisfaction and communication. *Journal of Marriage and the Family, 46,* 77–84.

Denney, N. W. (1974). Classification abilities in the elderly. *Journal of Gerontology, 29,* 309–314.

Denney, N. W. (1982). Aging and cognitive changes. In B. B. Wolman (Ed.), *Handbook of developmental psychology* (pp. 807–827). Englewood Cliffs, NJ: Prentice-Hall.

Denney, N. W., & Cornelius, S. W. (1975). Class inclusion and multiple classification in middle and old age. *Developmental Psychology, 11,* 521–522.

deVries, H. A. (1980). *Physiology of exercise for physical education and athletics* (3rd ed.). Dubuque, IA: William C. Brown.

deVries, H. A. (1983). Physiology of exercise and aging. In D. W. Woodruff & J. E. Birren (Eds.), *Aging: Scientific perspectives and social issues* (pp. 285–304). Pacific Grove, CA: Brooks/Cole.

Dewey, J. (1908). Does reality possess practical character? In J. Dewey (Ed.), *Essays, philosophical and psychological, in honor of William James* (pp. 53–80). New York: Longmans, Green.

Diamond, J. (1986). I want a girl just like the girl . . . *Discover, 7*(11), 65–68.

Dickstein, L. S. (1972). Death concern: Measurement and correlates. *Psychological Reports, 30,* 563–571.

Dignam, J. M., & Takemoto-Chock, N. K. (1981). Factors in the natural language of personality: Re-analysis, comparison, and interpretation of six major studies. *Multivariate Behavioral Research, 16,* 149–170.

Dillingham, A. E. (1981). Age and workplace injuries. *Aging and Work, 4,* 1–10.

DiLollo, V., Arnett, J. L., & Kruk, R. V. (1982). Age-related changes in rate of visual information processing. *Journal of Experimental Psychology: Human Perception and Performance, 8,* 225–237.

Dimond, M., Lund, D. A., & Caserta, M. S. (1987). The role of social support in the first two years of bereavement in an elderly sample. *Gerontologist, 27,* 599–604.

Dimsdale, J. E., Gilbert, J., Hutter, A. M., Hackett, T. P., & Block, P. C. (1981). Predicting cardiac morbidity based on risk factors and coronary angiographic findings. *American Journal of Cardiology, 47,* 73–76.

DiPrete, T. A., & Soule, W. T. (1988). Gender and promotion in segmented job ladder systems. *American Sociological Review, 53,* 26–40.

Dittmann-Kohli, F., & Baltes, P. B. (in press). Toward a neofunctionalist conception of adult intellectual development: Wisdom as a prototypical case of intellectual growth. In C. Alexander & E. Langer (Eds.), *Beyond formal operations: Alternative endpoints to human development.* New York: Oxford University Press.

Dixon, R. A. (1989). Questionnaire research on metamemory and aging: Issues of structure and function. In L. W. Poon, D. C. Rubin, & B. A. Wilson (Eds.), *Everyday cognition in adulthood and late life.* New York: Cambridge University Press.

Dixon, R. A., & Hultsch, D. F. (1983a). Metamemory and memory for text relationships in adulthood: A cross-validation study. *Journal of Gerontology, 38,* 689–694.

Dixon, R. A., & Hultsch, D. F. (1983b). Structure and development of metamemory in adulthood. *Journal of Gerontology, 38,* 682–688.

Dixon, R. A., Kramer, D. A., & Baltes, P. B. (1985). Intelligence: A life-span developmental perspective. In B. B. Wolman (Ed.), *Handbook of developmental psychology* (pp. 301–350). New York: Wiley.

Dixon, R. A., & von Eye, A. (1984). Depth processing and text recall in adulthood. *Journal of Reading Behavior, 26,* 109–117.

Dohrenwend, B. P. (1979). Stressful life events and psychopathology: Some issues of theory and method. In J. E. Barrett, B. M. Rose, & G. L. Klerman (Eds.), *Stress and mental disorder.* New York: Raven.

Dohrenwend, B. S., Krasnoff, L., Askenasy, A. R., & Dohrenwend, B. P. (1978). Exemplification of a method for scaling life events: The PERI Life Event Scale. *Journal of Health and Social Behavior, 19*, 205–229.

Dohrenwend, B. S., Krasnoff, L., Askenasy, A. R., & Dohrenwend, B. P. (1982). The Psychiatric Epidemiology Research Interview Life Events Scale. In L. Goldberger & S. Breznitz (Eds.), *Handbook of stress: Theoretical and clinical aspects* (pp. 332–363). New York: Free Press.

Doi, T. (1973). *The anatomy of dependence*. Tokyo: Kodansha.

Doka, K. J., & Mertz, M. E. (1988). The meaning and significance of great-grandparenthood. *Gerontologist, 28*, 192–197.

Doty, R. L., Shaman, P., Appelbaum, S. L., Giberson, R., Sikorski, L., & Rosenberg, L. (1984). Smell identification ability: Changes with age. *Science, 226*, 1441–1443.

Doudna, C., & McBride, F. (1981). Where are the men for the women at the top? In P. Stein (Ed.), *Single life: Unmarried adults in social context*. New York: St. Martin's.

Douglass, W. A. (1969). *Death in Murelaga: Funerary ritual in a Spanish Basque village*. Seattle: University of Washington Press.

Dowd, J. J. (1980). *Stratification among the aged*. Pacific Grove, CA: Brooks/Cole.

Dowd, J. J., & Bengtson, V. L. (1978). Aging in minority populations: An examination of the double jeopardy hypothesis. *Journal of Gerontology, 33*, 427–436.

Doyle, K. O., Jr. (1974). Theory and practice of ability testing in ancient Greece. *Journal of the History of the Behavioral Sciences, 10*, 202–212.

Drachman, D. A. (1977). Memory and cognitive function in man: Does the cholinergic system have a specific role? *Neurology, 27*, 783–790.

Drachman, D. A., Noffsinger, D., Sahakian, B. J., Kurdziel, S., & Fleming, P. (1980). Aging, memory, and the cholinergic system: A study of dichotic listening. *Neurobiology of Aging, 1*, 39–43.

Duara, R., London, E. D., & Rapoport, S. I. (1985). Changes in structure and energy metabolism of the aging brain. In C. E. Finch & E. L. Schneider (Eds.), *Handbook of the biology of aging* (2nd ed.) (pp. 595–616). New York: Van Nostrand Reinhold.

Dublin, L. I., Lotka, A. J., & Spiegelman, M. (1946). *The money value of a man*. New York: Ronald.

DuBois, P. H. (1968). A test dominated society: China 1115 B.C.–1905 A.D. In J. L. Barnette (Ed.), *Readings in psychological tests and measurements* (pp. 249–255). Homewood, IL: Dorsey Press.

Dunn, J. (1984). Sibling studies and the developmental impact of critical incidents. In P. B. Baltes & O. G. Brim, Jr. (Eds.), *Life-span development and behavior: Vol. 6*. New York: Academic Press.

Dychtwald, K. (Ed.). (1986). *Wellness and health promotion for the elderly*. Rockville, MD: Aspen.

Dye, C. J., & Koziatek, D. A. (1981). Age and diabetes effects on threshold and hedonic perception of sucrose solutions. *Journal of Gerontology, 36*, 310–315.

Eckhardt, M. J., Harford, T. C., Kaelber, C. T., Parker, E. S., Rosenthal, L. S., Ryback, R. S., Salmoiraghi, G. C., Vanderveen, E., & Warren, K. R. (1981). Health hazards associated with alcohol consumption. *JAMA, 246*, 648–666.

Eeg-Olofsson, O. (1971). The development of the electroencephalogram in normal children and adolescents from the age of 1 through 21 years. *Acta Pediatrica Scandinavica Supplementum, 208*, 1–46.

Eisdorfer, C., & Wilkie, F. (1977). Stress, disease, aging, and behavior. In J. E. Birren & K. W. Schaie (Eds.), *Handbook of the psychology of aging* (pp. 251–275). New York: Van Nostrand Reinhold.

Eisner, D. A. (1972). Developmental relationships between field independence and fixity-mobility. *Perceptual and Motor Skills, 34*, 767–770.

Eisner, D. A. (1973). *The effect of chronic brain syndrome upon concrete and formal operations in elderly men.* Unpublished manuscript cited in Papalia & Bielby (1974).

Ekerdt, D. J., Levkoff, S., & Bossé, R. (1981, November). *Adapting to retirement: Is there a honeymoon?* Paper presented at the meeting of the Gerontological Society of America, Toronto.

Ekert, J. K. (1980). *The unseen elderly: A study of marginally subsistent hotel dwellers.* San Diego: Campanile.

Ekstrom, R. B., French, J. W., & Harman, H. H. (1979). Cognitive factors: Their identification and replication. *Multivariate Behavioral Research Monographs,* No. 79.2.

Elder, G. H., Jr. (1974). *Children of the great depression.* Chicago: University of Chicago Press.

Engen, T. (1982). *The perception of odors.* New York: Academic Press.

Enns, M. P., Van Itallie, T. B., & Grinker, J. A. (1979). Contributions of age, sex, and degree of fatness on performances and magnitude estimation for sucrose in humans. *Physiology and Behavior, 22,* 999–1003.

Epstein, L. J. (1976). Depression in the elderly. *Journal of Gerontology, 31,* 278–282.

Epstein, L. J. (1978). Anxiolytics, anti-depressants and neuroleptics in the treatment of geriatric patients. In M. A. Lipton, A. D. Mascio, & K. F. Killam (Eds.), *Psychopharmacology: A generation of progress* (pp. 1517–1523). New York: Raven.

Erber, J. T. (1981). Remote memory and age: A review. *Experimental Aging Research, 7,* 189–199.

Eribes, R. A., & Bradley-Rawls, M. (1978). Under-utilization of nursing home facilities by Mexican American elderly in the Southwest. *Gerontologist, 18,* 363–371.

Erickson, R., & Ekert, K. (1977). The elderly poor in downtown San Diego hotels. *Gerontologist, 17,* 440–446.

Erickson, R. C., Poon, L. W., & Walsh-Sweeney, L. (1980). Clinical memory testing of the elderly. In L. W. Poon, J. L. Fozard, L. S. Cermak, D. Arenberg,

& L. W. Thompson (Eds.), *New directions in memory aging* (pp. 379–402). Hillsdale, NJ: Erlbaum.

Erikson, E. H. (1968). *Identity: Youth and crisis.* New York: Norton.

Erikson, E. H. (1982). *The life cycle completed: Review.* New York: Norton.

Esler, M., Skews, H., Leonard, P., Jackman, G., Bobik, A., & Korner, P. (1981). Age-dependence of noradrenaline kinetics in normal subjects. *Clinical Science, 60,* 217–219.

Essex, M. J., & Nam, S. (1987). Marital status and loneliness among older women. *Journal of Marriage and the Family, 49,* 93–106.

Estes, C. L., Fox, S., & Mahoney, C. W. (1986). Health care and social policy: Health promotion and the elderly. In K. Dychtwald (Ed.), *Wellness and health promotion for the elderly* (pp. 55–70). Rockville, MD: Aspen.

Estes, R. J., & Wilensky, H. L. (1978). Life cycle squeeze and the morale curve. *Social Problems, 25,* 277–292.

Evans, G. W., Brennan, P. L., Skorpanich, M. A., & Held, D. (1984). Cognitive mapping and elderly adults: Verbal and location memory for urban landmarks. *Journal of Gerontology, 39,* 452–457.

Exton-Smith, A. N. (1985). Mineral metabolism. In C. E. Finch & E. L. Schneider (Eds.), *Handbook of the biology of aging* (2nd ed.) (pp. 511–539). New York: Van Nostrand Reinhold.

Farmer, P. M., Peck, A., & Terry, R. D. (1976). Correlations among neuritic plaques, neurofibrillary tangles, and the severity of senile dementia. *Journal of Neuropathology and Experimental Neurology, 35,* 367–376.

Farrell, M. P., & Rosenberg, S. D. (1981). *Men at midlife.* Boston: Auburn House.

Featherman, D. L. (1980). Schooling and occupational careers: Constancy and change in worldly success. In O. G. Brim, Jr., & J. Kagan (Eds.), *Constancy and change in human development.* Cambridge, MA: Harvard University Press.

REFERENCES

Featherman, D. L. (1981). The life-span perspective in social science research. In American Association for the Advancement of Science (Ed.), *Policy outlook: Science, technology, and the issues of the eighties Vol. 2: Sources.* Washington, DC: U.S. Government Printing Office.

Feifel, H. (1965). The function of attitudes toward death. In Group for the Advancement of Psychiatry (Eds.), *Death and dying: Attitudes of patient and doctor* (pp. 632–641). New York: Mental Health Materials Center.

Feifel, H., & Nagy, V. T. (1981). Another look at fear of death. *Journal of Consulting and Clinical Psychology, 49,* 278–286.

Feinberg, I., Fein, E., Floyd, T. C., & Aminoff, M. J. (1982). Delta (0.5–3Hz) EEG waveforms during sleep in young and elderly normal subjects. In E. Weitzman (Ed.), *Advances in sleep research* (Vol. 7). New York: Plenum.

Feinson, M. C. (1987). Mental health and aging: Are there gender differences? *Gerontologist, 27,* 703–711.

Feldman, S. S., Biringen, Z. C., & Nash, S. C. (1981). Fluctuations of sex-related self-attributions as a function of the family life cycle. *Developmental Psychology, 17,* 24–35.

Feldman, S. S., Nash, S. C., & Aschenbrenner, B. G. (1983). Antecedents of fathering. *Child Development, 54,* 1628–1636.

Felton, B. J., & Revenson, T. A. (1987). Age differences in coping with chronic illness. *Psychology and Aging, 2,* 164–170

Fernie, G. R., Gryfe, C. I., Holliday, P. J., & Llewellyn, A. (1982). The relationship of postural sway in standing to the incidence of falls in geriatric subjects. *Age and Ageing, 11,* 11–16.

Ferris, S. H., & Crook, T. (1983). Cognitive assessment in mild to moderately severe dementia. In T. Crook, S. Ferris, & R. Bartus (Eds.), *Assessment in geriatric psychopharmacology.* New Canaan, CT: Mark Powley Associates.

Ferris, S. H., Crook, T., Flicker, C., Reisberg, B., & Bartus, R. T. (1986). Assessing cognitive impairment and evaluating treatment effects: Psychometric and performance tests. In L. W. Poon (Ed.), *Handbook for clinical memory assessment of older adults* (pp. 139–148). Washington, DC: American Psychological Association.

Fields, T. M., & Widmayer, S. M. (1982). Motherhood. In B. B. Wolman (Ed.), *Handbook of developmental psychology* (pp. 681–701). Englewood Cliffs, NJ: Prentice-Hall.

Finch, C. E. (1982). Rodent models for aging processes in the human brain. In S. Corkin, K. L. Davis, J. H. Growden, E. Usdin, & R. J. Wurtman (Eds.), *Aging: Vol. 19. Alzheimer's disease: A report of progress* (pp. 249–258). New York: Raven.

Fischer, D. H. (1978). *Growing old in America.* New York: Oxford University Press.

Fisher, H. E. (1987). The four-year itch. *Natural History, 96*(10), 22–33.

Fiske, M., & Chiriboga, D. A. (1985). The interweave of societal and personal change in adulthood. In J. Munnichs, P. Mussen, E. Olbrich, & P. G. Coleman (Eds.), *Life-span and change in gerontological perspective* (pp. 177–209). New York: Academic Press.

Fitzpatrick, M. A. (1984). A topological approach to marital interaction — Recent theory and research. *Advances in Experimental Sociology, 18,* 1–47.

Fleming, B. (1982). The vitamin status and requirements of the elderly. In G. B. Moment (Ed.), *Nutritional approaches to aging research* (pp. 83–117). Boca Raton, FL: CRC.

Folkins, C. H., & Sime, W. E. (1980). Physical fitness training and mental health. *American Psychologist, 36,* 373–389.

Folkman, S., Lazarus, R. S., Pimley, S., & Novacek, J. (1987). Age differences in stress and coping processes. *Psychology and Aging, 2,* 171–184.

Folstein, M. F., Folstein, S. E., & McHugh, P. R. (1975). Mini-mental state: A practical method for grading the cognitive state of patients for the clinician. *Journal of Psychiatric Research, 12,* 189–198.

REFERENCES

Foner, A. (1986). *Aging and old age: New perspectives.* Englewood Cliffs, NJ: Prentice-Hall.

Foner, A., & Kertzer, D. I. (1978). Transitions over the life course: Lessons from age-set societies. *American Journal of Sociology, 83,* 1081–1104.

Foner, A., & Kertzer, D. I. (1979). Intrinsic and extrinsic sources of change in life course transitions. In M. W. Riley (Ed.), *Aging from birth to death: Interdisciplinary perspectives* (pp. 121–136). Boulder, CO: Westview.

Foner, A., & Schwab, K. (1981). *Aging and retirement.* Pacific Grove, CA: Brooks/Cole.

Foner, N. (1984). *Ages in conflict: A cross-cultural perspective on inequality between old and young.* New York: Columbia University Press.

Fortes, M. (1950). Kinship and marriage among the Ashanti. In A. R. Radcliffe-Brown & D. Forde (Eds.), *African systems of kinship and marriage* (pp. 252–284). London: Oxford University Press.

Fortes, M. (1984). Age, generation and social structure. In D. I. Kertzer & J. Keith (Eds.), *Age and anthropological theory* (pp. 99–122). Ithaca, NY: Cornell University Press.

Fox, A. (1979, January). Earnings replacement rates of retired couples: Findings from the Retirement History Study. *Social Security Bulletin, 42,* 17–39.

Fox, M., Gibbs, M., & Auerbach, D. (1985). Age and gender dimensions of friendship. *Psychology of Women Quarterly, 9,* 489–502.

Fozard, J. L. (1980). The time for remembering. In L. W. Poon (Ed.), *Aging in the 1980s* (pp. 273–287). Washington, DC: American Psychological Association.

Fozard, J. L., & Popkin, S. J. (1978). Optimizing adult development: Ends and means of an applied psychology of aging. *American Psychologist, 33,* 975–989.

Fozard, J. L., Thomas, J. C., & Waugh, N. C. (1976). Effects of age and frequency of stimulus repetitions on two-choice reaction time. *Journal of Gerontology, 31,* 556–563.

Freedman, M. (1966). *Chinese lineage and society: Fukien and Kwangtung.* London: Athlone.

Freeman, J. T. (1979). *Aging: Its history and literature.* New York: Human Sciences Press.

Friedman, E. A., & Orbach, H. L. (1974). Adjustment to retirement. In S. Arieti (Ed.), *American handbook of psychiatry: Vol. 1* (2nd ed.) (pp. 609–645). New York: Basic Books.

Friedman, L. A., & Kimball, A. W. (1986). Coronary heart disease mortality and alcohol consumption in Framingham. *American Journal of Epidemiology, 124,* 481–489.

Friedman, M., & Rosenman, R. H. (1974). *Type A behavior and your heart.* New York: Random House.

Fries, J. F., & Crapo, L. M. (1986). The elimination of premature disease. In K. Dychtwald (Ed.), *Wellness and health promotion for the elderly* (pp. 19–38). Rockville, MD: Aspen.

Frieze, I. H., Parsons, J. E., Johnson, P. B., Ruble, D. N., & Zellman, G. L. (1978). *Women and sex roles: A social psychological perspective.* New York: Norton.

Frolkis, V. V., & Bezrukov, V. V. (Eds.). (1979). *Aging of the central nervous system: Vol. 11. Interdisciplinary topics in human aging.* New York: Karger.

Fry, C. L. (1985). Culture, behavior, and aging in the comparative perspective. In J. E. Birren & K. W. Schaie (Eds.), *Handbook of the psychology of aging* (2nd ed.) (pp. 216–244). New York: Van Nostrand Reinhold.

Fry, C. L. (1988). Theories of age and culture. In J. E. Birren & V. L. Bengtson (Eds.), *Emergent theories of aging* (pp. 447–481). New York: Springer.

Fry, P. S. (1986). *Depression, stress, and adaptation in the elderly.* Rockville, MD: Aspen.

Fulton, R. (1970). Death, grief, and social recuperation. *Omega: Journal of Death and Dying, 1,* 23–28.

Furstenberg, F. F., Jr. (1982). Conjugal succession: Reentering marriage after divorce. In P. B. Baltes & O. G. Brim, Jr. (Eds.), *Life-span development and behavior: Vol. 5* (pp. 108–146). New York: Academic Press.

Furstenberg, F. F., Jr., & Nord, C. W. (1985). Parenting apart: Patterns of childbearing after marital disruption. *Journal of Marriage and the Family, 47,* 893–912.

Gajdusek, D. C. (1977). Unconventional viruses and the origin and disappearance of kuru. *Science, 197,* 943–960.

Gallagher, D., & Thompson, L. W. (1983). Depression. In P. M. Lewinsohn & L. Teri (Eds.), *Clinical geropsychology* (pp. 7–37). New York: Pergamon Press.

Garber, J., & Seligman, M. E. P. (Eds.). (1980). *Human helplessness: Theory and applications.* New York: Academic Press.

Garland, C., Barrett-Connor, E., Suarez, L., Criqui, M. H., & Wingard, D. L. (1985). Effects of passive smoking on ischemic heart disease mortality of nonsmokers: A prospective study. *American Journal of Epidemiology, 121,* 645–650.

Garn, S. M. (1975). Bone loss and aging. In R. Goldman & M. Rockstein (Eds.), *The physiology and pathology of aging* (pp. 39–57). New York: Academic Press.

Gatz, M., & Siegler, I. C. (1981, August). *Locus of control: A retrospective.* Paper presented at the meeting of the American Psychological Association, Los Angeles.

Gaylord, S. A., & Zung, W. W. K. (1987). Affective disorders among the aging. In L. L. Carstensen & B. A. Edelstein (Eds.), *Handbook of clinical gerontology* (pp. 76–95). New York: Pergamon Press.

Gentry, M., & Schulman, A. D. (1988). Remarriage as a coping response for widowhood. *Psychology and Aging, 3,* 191–196.

George, L. K. (1980). *Role transitions in later life.* Pacific Grove, CA: Brooks/Cole.

George, L. K., Fillenbaum, G., & Palmore, E. (1984). Sex differences in the antecedents and consequences of retirement. *Journal of Gerontology, 39,* 364–371.

George, L. K., & Gwyther, L. P. (1986). Caregiver well-being: A multidimensional examination of family caregivers of demented adults. *Gerontologist, 26,* 253–259.

Georgoudi, M., & Rosnow, R. L. (1985). Notes toward a contextualist understanding of social psychology. *Personality and Social Psychology Bulletin, 11,* 5–22.

Gerner, R. (1980). Depression in the elderly. In O. Kaplan (Ed.), *Psychopathology of aging* (pp. 97–148). New York: Academic Press.

Gerner, R. H., & Jarvik, L. F. (1984). Antidepressant drug treatment in the elderly. In E. Friedman, F. Mann, & S. Gerson (Eds.), *Depression and antidepressants: Implications for consideration and treatment.* New York: Raven.

Gerstenblith, G. (1980). Noninvasive assessment of cardiovascular function in the elderly. In M. L. Weisfeldt (Ed.), *Aging: Vol. 12. The aging heart: Its function and response to stress* (pp. 247–268). New York: Raven.

Gescheider, G. A. (1985). *Psychophysics: Method and theory* (2nd ed.). Hillsdale, NJ: Erlbaum.

Giambra, L. M., & Quilter, R. E. (1988). Sustained attention in adulthood: A unique, large-sample, longitudinal and multicohort analysis using the Mackworth Clock Test. *Psychology and Aging, 3,* 75–83.

Gibbs, J. C., Gajdusek, D. C., Asher, D. M., Alpers, M. P., Beck, E., Daniel, P. M., & Matthews, W. B. (1968). Creutzfeld-Jakob disease (spongiform encephalopathy): Transmission to the chimpanzee. *Science, 161,* 388–389.

Gibson, R. C. (1986). *Blacks in an aging society.* New York: Carnegie Corporation.

Gibson, R. C. (1987). Reconceptualizing retirement for Black Americans. *Gerontologist, 27,* 691–698.

Gilewski, M. J., & Zelinski, E. M. (1986). Questionnaire assessments of memory complaints. In L. W. Poon (Ed.), *Handbook for clinical memory assessment of older adults* (pp. 93–107). Washington, DC: American Psychological Association.

Gilford, R. (1984). Contrasts in marital satisfaction throughout old age: An exchange theory analysis. *Journal of Gerontology, 39,* 325–333.

Gilhooly, M. L. M. (1984). The impact of care-giving on caregivers: Factors associated with the psychological well-being of people supporting a demented relative in the community. *British Journal of Medical Psychology, 57,* 35–44.

Gilhooly, M. L. M. (1986). Senile dementia: Factors associated with caregivers' preference for institutional care. *British Journal of Medical Psychology, 59,* 165–171.

Gill, J. S., Zezulka, A. V., Shipley, M. J., Gill, S. K., & Beevers, D. G. (1986). Stroke and alcohol consumption. *New England Journal of Medicine, 315,* 1041–1046.

Gilleard, C. J., & Gurkan, A. A. (1987). Socio-economic development and the status of elderly men in Turkey: A test of modernization theory. *Journal of Gerontology, 42,* 353–357.

Glamser, F., & Hayslip, B., Jr. (1985). The impact of retirement on participation in leisure activities. *Therapeutic Recreation Journal, 19,* 28–38.

Glascock, A. P., & Feinman, S. (1981). Social asset of social burden: Treatment of the aged in non-industrial societies. In C. L. Fry (Ed.), *Dimensions: Aging, culture, and health* (pp. 13–32). New York: Praeger.

Glaser, B. G., & Strauss, A. L. (1965). *Awareness of dying.* Chicago: Aldine-Atherton.

Glaser, B. G., & Strauss, A. L. (1968). *Time for dying.* Chicago: Aldine-Atherton.

Glass, R. B. (1986). Infertility. In S. S. C. Yen & R. B. Jaffe (Eds.), *Reproductive endocrinology: Physiology, pathophysiology, and clinical management* (2nd ed.) (pp. 571–613). Philadelphia: Saunders.

Glenn, N. D., & McLanahan, S. (1981). The effects of offspring on the psychological well-being of older adults. *Journal of Marriage and the Family, 43,* 409–421.

Glenn, N. D., & McLanahan, S. (1982). Children and marital happiness: A further specification of the relationship. *Journal of Marriage and the Family, 44,* 63–72.

Glenn, N. D., & Supancic, M. (1984). The social and demographic correlates of divorce and separation in the United States: An update and reconsideration. *Journal of Marriage and the Family, 46,* 563–575.

Glenn, N. D., & Weaver, C. N. (1978). The marital happiness of remarried divorced persons. *Journal of Marriage and the Family, 40,* 269–282.

Glick, I. O., Weiss, R. S., & Parkes, C. M. (1974). *The first year of bereavement.* New York: Wiley.

Glick, P. C., & Lin, S.–L. (1986). Recent changes in divorce and remarriage. *Journal of Marriage and the Family, 48,* 737–748.

Glick, P. C., & Norton, A. J. (1979). Marrying, divorcing, and living together in the U.S. today. *Population Bulletin, 32,* 1–41.

Golant, S. M. (1984). The effects of residential and activity behaviors on old people's environmental experiences. In I. Altman, J. Wohlwill, & M. P. Lawton (Eds.), *Human behavior and the environment: Elderly people and the environment* (pp. 239–278). New York: Plenum.

Gold, D. T. (1988, November). *Late-life sibling relationships: Does race affect typological distribution?* Paper presented at the meeting of the Gerontological Society of America, San Francisco.

Goldstein, A., & Goldstein, S. (1986). The challenge of an aging population in the People's Republic of China. *Research on Aging, 8,* 179–199.

Goldstein, E. (1979). Effect of same-sex and cross-sex role models on the subsequent academic productivity of scholars. *American Psychologist, 34,* 407–410.

Gollin, E. S. (1985). Ontogeny, phylogeny, and causality. In E. S. Gollin (Ed.), *The comparative development of adaptive skills* (pp. 1–18). Hillsdale, NJ: Erlbaum.

Gonda, J. (1980). Relationship between formal education and cognitive functioning: A historical perspective. *Educational Gerontology, 5,* 283–291.

Goode, W. J. (1956). *After divorce.* Glencoe, IL: Free Press.

Goody, J. (1976). Aging in non-industrial societies. In R. H. Binstock & E. Shanas (Eds.), *Handbook of aging and the social sciences* (2nd ed.) (pp. 117–129). New York: Van Nostrand Reinhold.

Gordon, C., Gaitz, C. M., & Scott, J. (1976). Leisure and lives: Personal expressivity across the life span. In R. H. Binstock & E. Shanas (Eds.), *Handbook of aging and the social sciences* (2nd ed.) (pp. 310–341). New York: Van Nostrand Reinhold.

Gordon, T., & Doyle, J. T. (1987). Drinking and mortality : The Albany study. *American Journal of Epidemiology, 125*, 263–270.

Gordon, T., & Kannel, W. B. (1984). Drinking and mortality: The Framingham study. *American Journal of Epidemiology, 120*, 97–107.

Gottfredson, L. S. (1981). Circumscription and compromise: A developmental theory of occupational aspirations. *Journal of Counseling Psychology, 28*, 545–579.

Gottfries, C. G. (1985). Alzheimer's disease and senile dementia: Biochemical characteristics and aspects of treatment. *Psychopharmacology, 86*, 245–252.

Gottfries, C. G., Gottfries, I., & Roos, B. E. (1969). The investigation of homovanillic acid in the human brain and its correlation to senile dementia. *British Journal of Psychiatry, 115*, 563–574.

Gottfries, C. G., Roos, B. E., & Winblad, B. (1976). Monoamine and monoamine metabolites in the human brain post mortem in senile dementia. *Aktuelle Gerontologie, 6*, 429–435.

Gottlieb, G. (1970). Conceptions of prenatal behavior. In L. R. Aronson, E. Tobach, D. S. Lehrman, & J. S. Rosenblatt (Eds.), *Development and evolution of behavior: Essays in memory of T. C. Schneirla* (pp. 111–137). San Francisco: W. H. Freeman.

Gould, R. (1978). *Transformations: Growth and change in adult life.* New York: Simon & Schuster.

Gould, S. J. (1977). *Ontogeny and phylogeny.* Cambridge, MA: Belknap.

Granick, S., & Friedman, A. S. (1973). Effect of education on decline of psychometric test performance with age. *Journal of Gerontology, 22*, 191.

Green, A. L., & Boxer, A. M. (1986). Daughters and sons as young adults. In N. Datan, A. L. Green, & H. W. Reese (Eds.), *Life-span developmental psychology: Intergenerational relations* (pp. 125–150). Hillsdale, NJ: Erlbaum.

Green, L. W. (1980). To educate or not to educate — Is that the question? *American Journal of Public Health, 70*, 625–626.

Green, R. F. (1969). Age-intelligence relationships between ages sixteen and sixty-four: A rising trend. *Developmental Psychology, 1*, 618–627.

Greenberg, J. B. (1979). Single parenting and intimacy: A comparison of mothers and fathers. *Alternative Lifestyles, 2*, 308–330.

Greene, V. L., & Monahan, D. J. (1982). The impact of visitation on patient well-being in nursing homes. *Gerontologist, 22*, 418–423.

Greenough, W. T., & Green, E. J. (1981). Experience and the changing brain. In J. L. McGaugh & S. B. Kiesler (Eds.), *Aging: Biology and behavior* (pp. 159–200). New York: Academic Press.

Greenwood, J., Love, E. R., & Pratt, O. E. (1983). The effects of alcohol or of thiamine deficiency upon reproduction in the female rat and fetal development. *Alcohol and Alcoholism, 18*, 45–51.

Grey, R. (1756). *Memoria technica* (4th ed.). London: Hinton.

Grimby, G., & Saltin, B. (1983). The aging muscle. *Clinical Physiology, 3*, 209–218.

Grotevant, H. D., & Cooper, C. R. (1988). The role of family experience in career exploration: A life-span perspective. In P. B. Baltes, D. L. Featherman, & R. M. Lerner (Eds.), *Life-span development and behavior: Vol. 8* (pp. 231–258). Hillsdale, NJ: Erlbaum.

Guigoz, Y., & Munro, H. N. (1985). Nutrition and aging. In C. E. Finch & E. L. Schneider (Eds.), *Handbook of the biology of aging* (2nd ed.) (pp. 878–893). New York: Van Nostrand Reinhold.

REFERENCES

Guilford, J. P. (1959). *Personality*. New York: McGraw-Hill.

Guilford, J. P. (1980). Fluid and crystallized intelligence: Two fanciful concepts. *Psychological Bulletin, 88*, 406–412.

Gurland, B. J. (1974). A broad clinical assessment of psychopathology in the aged. In C. Eisdorfer & M. P. Lawton (Eds.), *The psychology of adult development and aging* (pp. 343–377). Washington, DC: American Psychological Association.

Gurland, B. J. (1976). The comparative frequency of depression in various adult age groups. *Journal of Gerontology, 31*, 283–292.

Guthrie, H. A. (1988). Nutrient requirements of the elderly. In R. Chernoff & D. A. Lipschitz (Eds.), *Health promotion and disease prevention in the elderly* (pp. 33–43). New York: Raven Press.

Gutmann, D. (1977). The cross-cultural perspective: Notes toward a comparative psychology of aging. In J. E. Birren & K. W. Schaie (Eds.), *Handbook of the psychology of aging* (pp. 302–326). New York: Van Nostrand Reinhold.

Gutmann, D. (1978). *Personal transformation in the post-parental period: A cross-cultural view*. Washington, DC: American Association for the Advancement of Science.

Haan, N. (1976). Personality organization of well-functioning younger people and older adults. *International Journal of Aging and Human Development, 7*, 117–127.

Haan, N. (1981). Common dimensions of personality: Early adolescence to middle life. In D. H. Eichorn, N. Haan, J. Clausen, M. Honzik, & P. Mussen (Eds.), *Present and past in middle life* (pp. 117–151). New York: Academic Press.

Haan, N. (1985). Common personality dimensions or common organization across the life span? In J. M. Munnichs, P. Mussen, E. Olbrich, & P. G. Coleman (Eds.), *Life-span and change in gerontological perspective* (pp. 17–44). New York: Academic Press.

Haan, N., Millsap, R., & Hartka, E. (1986). As time goes by: Change and stability in personality over fifty years. *Psychology and Aging, 1*, 220–232.

Hachinski, V. C., Lassen, N. A., & Marshall (1974). Multi-infarct dementia — A cause of mental deterioration in the elderly. *Lancet, 2*, 207–210.

Hacker, H. M. (1981). Blabbermouths and clams — Sex differences in self-disclosure in same-sex and cross-sex friendship dyads. *Psychology of Women Quarterly, 5*, 385–401.

Hagestad, G. (1978). *Patterns of communication and influence between grandparents and grandchildren*. Paper presented at the World Conference on Sociology, Helsinki, Finland.

Hagestad, G. O., & Neugarten, B. L. (1985). Age and the life course. In R. H. Binstock & E. Shanas (Eds.), *Handbook of aging and the social sciences* (2nd ed.) (pp. 35–61). New York: Van Nostrand Reinhold.

Haggstrom, G. W., Kanouse, D. E., & Morrison, P. A. (1986). Accounting for education shortfalls of mothers. *Journal of Marriage and the Family, 48*, 175–186.

Hahn, L. E. (1942). *A contextualist theory of perception*. Berkeley, CA: University of California Press.

Hakim, S., & Adams, R. D. (1965). The special clinical problem of symptomatic hydrocephalus with normal cerebrospinal fluid pressure: Observations on cerebrospinal fluid hydrodynamics. *Journal of the Neurological Sciences, 2*, 307–327.

Haley, J. (1971). Family therapy. *International Journal of Psychiatry, 9*, 233–242.

Haley, W. E., Levine, E. G., Brown, S. L., Berry, J. W., & Hughes, G. H. (1987). Psychological, social, and health consequences of caring for a relative with senile dementia. *Journal of the American Geriatrics Society, 35*, 405–411.

Halperin, R. H. (1987). Age in cross-cultural perspective: An evolutionary approach. In P. Silverman (Ed.), *The elderly as modern pioneers* (pp. 228–252). Bloomington: Indiana University Press.

Halpern, J. (1987). *Helping your aging parents*. New York: McGraw-Hill.

Hamberger, K., & Lohr, J. (1984). *Stress and stress management: Research and applications.* New York: Springer.

Hamilton, J. (1978). Grandparents as grievers. In J. O. Sahler (Ed.), *The child and death.* St. Louis: C. V. Mosby.

Hamilton, M. (1967). Development of a rating scale for primary depressive illness. *British Journal of Social and Clinical Psychology, 6,* 278–296.

Hanley, T. (1974). "Neuronal fall-out" in the aging brain: A critical review of the quantitative data. *Age and Ageing, 3,* 133–151.

Hanley-Dunn, P., & McIntosh, J. L. (1984). Meaningfulness and recall of names by young and old adults. *Journal of Gerontology, 39,* 583–585.

Harbin, T. J., & Blumenthal, J. A. (1985). Relationship among age, sex, the Type A behavior pattern, and cardiovascular reactivity. *Journal of Gerontology, 40,* 714–720.

Harel, Z. (1981). Quality of care, congruence, and well-being among institutionalized aged. *Gerontologist, 21,* 523–531.

Harker, J. O., Hartley, J. T., & Walsh, D. A. (1982). Understanding discourse: A life-span approach. In B. A. Hutson (Ed.), *Advances in reading/language research: Vol. 1* (pp. 155–202). Greenwich, CT: JAI.

Harkins, S. W., & Kwentus, J. (in press). Pain, discomfort, and suffering in the elderly. In J. J. Bonica (Ed.), *Clinical management of pain.* Philadelphia: Lea & Febinger.

Harkins, S. W., Price, D. D., & Martelli, M. (1986). Effects of age on pain perception: Thermonociception. *Journal of Gerontology, 41,* 58–63.

Harman, S. M., & Talbert, G. B. (1985). Reproductive aging. In C. E. Finch & E. L. Schneider (Eds.), *Handbook of the biology of aging* (2nd ed.) (pp. 457–510). New York: Van Nostrand Reinhold.

Harris, D. B. (Ed.). (1957). *The concept of development.* Minneapolis: University of Minnesota Press.

Harris, J. E. (1980). Memory aids people use: Two interview studies. *Memory and Cognition, 8,* 31–38.

Harris, J. E. (1984a). Methods of improving memory. In B. Wilson & N. Moffat (Eds.), *Clinical management of memory problems* (pp. 46–62). Rockville, MD: Aspen.

Harris, J. E., (1984b). Remembering to do things: A forgotten topic. In J. E. Harris & P. E. Morris (Eds.), *Everyday memory, actions, and absentmindedness* (pp. 71–92). London: Academic Press.

Harris, J. E., & Sunderland, A. (1981). A brief survey of the management of memory disorders in rehabilitation units in Britain. *International Rehabilitation Medicine, 3,* 206–209.

Harris, L., & Associates (1975). *The myth and reality of aging in America.* Washington, DC: National Council on the Aging.

Harris, L., & Associates (1981). *Aging in the 80s: America in transition.* Washington, DC: National Council on the Aging.

Harris, R. L., Ellicott, A. M., & Holmes, D. S. (1986). The timing of psychosocial transitions and changes in women's lives: An examination of women aged 45 to 60. *Journal of Personality and Social Psychology, 51,* 409–416.

Hartford, M. E. (1980). The use of group methods for work with the aged. In J. E. Birren & R. B. Sloane (Eds.), *Handbook of mental health and aging* (pp. 806–826). Englewood Cliffs, NJ: Prentice-Hall.

Hartley, J. T. (1989). Memory for prose: Perspectives on the reader. In L. W. Poon, D. C. Rubin, & A. Wilson (Eds.), *Everyday cognition in adult and late life.* New York: Cambridge University Press.

Hartley, J. T., Harker, J. O., & Walsh, D. A. (1980). Contemporary issues and new directions in adult development of learning and memory. In L. W. Poon (Ed.), *Aging in the 1980s: Psychological issues* (pp. 239–252). Washington, DC: American Psychological Association.

Haskell, W. L., Camargo, C., Jr., Williams, P. T., Vranizan, K. M., Krauss, R. M., Lindgren, F. T., & Wood, P. D. (1984). The effect of cessation and resumption of moderate alcohol intake on serum high-density lipoprotein subfractions. *New England Journal of Medicine, 310,* 805–810.

Hatfield, E., & Walster, E. (1978). *A new look at love.* Reading, MA: Addison-Wesley.

Haun, P. (1965). *Recreation: A medical viewpoint.* New York: Teachers College, Columbia University Press.

Hauri, P. (1982). *The sleep disorders.* Kalamazoo, MI: Upjohn.

Havighurst, R. J. (1982). The world of work. In B. B. Wolman (Ed.), *Handbook of developmental psychology* (pp. 771–787). Englewood Cliffs, NJ: Prentice-Hall.

Hays, W. C., & Mindel, C. (1973). Extended kinship relations in Black and White families. *Journal of Marriage and the Family, 35,* 51–56.

Hayslip, B., Jr. (1986, August). *Alternative mechanisms for improvements in fluid ability in the aged.* Paper presented at the meeting of the American Psychological Association, Washington, DC.

Hayslip, B., Jr. (1988). Personality-ability relationships in aged adults. *Journal of Gerontology, 43,* P79–P84.

Healey, E. S., Kales, A., Monroe, L. J., Bixler, E. O., Chamberlin, K., & Soldatos, C. R. (1981). Onset of insomnia: Role of life-stress events. *Psychosomatic Medicine, 43,* 439–451.

Heaney, R. P. (1982). Age-related bone loss. In M. E. Reff & E. L. Schneider (Eds.), *Biological markers of aging* (pp. 161–167) (NIH Publication No. 82–2221). Washington, DC: U. S. Government Printing Office.

Heaney, R. P., Gallagher, J. C., Johnston, C. C., Neer, R., Parfitt, A. M., & Whedon, G. D. (1982). Calcium nutrition and bone health in the elderly. *American Journal of Clinical Nutrition, 36,* 987–1013.

Heintz, K. M. (1976). *Retirement communities.* New Brunswick, NJ: Rutgers University Center for Urban Policy Research.

Helson, R., & Moane, G. (1987). Personality change in women from college to midlife. *Journal of Personality and Social Psychology, 52,* 1176–1186.

Hendel-Sebestyen, G. (1979). Role diversity: Toward the development of community in a total institutional setting. *Anthropological Quarterly, 52,* 19–28.

Henderson, G., Tomlinson, B., & Gibson, P. H. (1980). Cell counts in human cerebral cortex in normal adults throughout life using an image analyzing computer. *Journal of the Neurological Sciences, 46,* 113–136.

Hendricks, J. (1982). The elderly in society: Beyond modernization. *Social Science History, 6,* 321–345.

Hendricks, J., & Hendricks, C. (1986). *Aging in mass society: Myths and realities* (3rd ed.). Boston: Little, Brown.

Hennon, C. B. (1983). Divorce and the elderly: A neglected area of research. In T. H. Brubaker (Ed.), *Family relationships in later life* (pp. 149–172). Beverly Hills, CA: Sage Publications.

Henretta, J. C. (1988). Conflict and cooperation among age strata. In J. E. Birren & V. L. Bengtson (Eds.), *Emergent theories of aging* (pp. 385–404). New York: Springer.

Hensel, H. (1981). *Thermoreception and temperature regulation.* New York: Academic Press.

Herberman, R. B., & Callewaert, D. M. (Eds.). (1985). *Mechanisms of cytotoxicity by NK cells.* Orlando, FL: Academic Press.

Herbert, V. (1988). Megavitamins, food fads, and quack nutrition in health promotion: Myths and risks. In R. Chernoff & D. A. Lipschitz (Eds.), *Health promotion and disease prevention in the elderly* (pp. 45–66). New York: Raven Press.

Herman, J. F., & Coyne, A. C. (1980). Mental manipulations of spatial information in young and elderly adults. *Developmental Psychology, 16,* 537–538.

Herr, J., & Weakland, J. (1979). *Counseling elders and their families: Practical techniques for applied gerontology.* New York: Springer.

Hertzog, C., Dixon, R. A., Schulenberg, J., & Hultsch, D. F. (1987). On the differentiation of memory beliefs from memory knowledge: The factor structure of the Metamemory in Adulthood scale. *Experimental Aging Research, 13,* 101–107.

Hertzog, C., Hultsch, D. F., & Dixon, R. A. (in press). Evidence for the convergent validity of two self-report metamemory questionnaires. *Developmental Psychology.*

Hess, B., & Markson, E. W. (1980). *Aging and old age: An introduction to social gerontology*. New York: Macmillan.

Hesse, M. (1980). *Revolutions and reconstructions in the philosophy of science*. Bloomington: Indiana University Press.

Hetherington, E. M., Cox, M., & Cox, R. (1982). Effects of divorce on parents and children. In M. E. Lamb (Ed.), *Nontraditional families: Parenting and child development*. Hillsdale, NJ: Erlbaum.

Heumann, L., & Boldy, D. (1982). *Housing for the elderly: Policy and planning formulation in Western Europe and North America*. London: Croom Helm.

Hill, R., Foote, N., Aldonus, J., Carlson, R., & MacDonald, R. (1970). *Family development in three generations*. New York: Schenkman.

Himmelfarb, S. (1984). Age and sex differences in the mental health of older persons. *Journal of Consulting and Clinical Psychology, 52*, 844–856.

Hinton, J. M. (1967). *Dying*. Harmondsworth, England: Penguin.

Hinton, J. M. (1979). Comparison of places and policies for terminal care. *Lancet, 1*, 29–32.

Hirschenfield, R. M. A., & Cross, C. K. (1982). Epidemiology of affective disorders: Psychosocial risk factors. *Archives of General Psychiatry, 39*, 35–46.

Hobart, C. (1988). The family system in remarriage: An exploratory study. *Journal of Marriage and the Family, 50*, 649–661.

Hochschild, A. R. (1973). *The unexpected community*. Englewood Cliffs, NJ: Prentice-Hall.

Hoff, S. F., Scheff, S. W., Bernardo, L. S., & Cotman, C. W. (1982). Lesion-induced synaptogenesis in the dentate gyrus of aged rats. 1: Loss and reacquisition of normal synaptic density. *Journal of Comparative Neurology, 205*, 246–252.

Hoff, S. F., Scheff, S. W., & Cotman, C. W. (1982). Lesion-induced synaptogenesis in the dentate gyrus of the aged rat. 2: Demonstration of an impaired degeneration clearing response. *Journal of Comparative Neurology, 205*, 253–259.

Hofland, B. F. (1988). Autonomy in long term care: Background issues and a programmatic response. *Gerontologist, 28*(Suppl.), 3–9.

Holland, J. L. (1966). *The psychology of vocational choice*. Waltham, MA: Blaisdell.

Holland, J. L. (1973). *Making vocational choices: A theory of careers*. Englewood Cliffs, NJ: Prentice-Hall.

Holland, J. L. (1985). *Making vocational choices: A theory of vocational personalities and work environments*. Englewood Cliffs, NJ: Prentice-Hall.

Hollander, C. F., & Becker, H. A. (1988). Planning for health services for the elderly. In D. Evered & J. Whelan (Eds.), *Symposium on research and the ageing population* (pp. 221–228). Chichester, England: Wiley.

Holmes, T. H., & Masuda, M. (1974). Life change and illness susceptibility. In B. S. Dohrenwend & B. P. Dohrenwend (Eds.), *Stressful life events: Their nature and effects*. New York: Wiley.

Holmes, T. H., & Rahe, R. H. (1967). The Social Readjustment Rating Scale. *Journal of Psychosomatic Research, 11*, 213–218.

Holyroyd, K. A., Appel, M. A., & Andrasik, F. (1983). A cognitive-behavioral approach to psychophysiological disorders. In D. Meichenbaum & M. E. Jarenko (Eds.), *Stress reduction and prevention*. New York: Plenum.

Holzberg, C. S. (1982). Ethnicity and aging: Anthropological perspectives on more than just the minority elderly. *Gerontologist, 22*, 249–257.

Holzberg, C. S. (1983). Anthropology, life histories, and the aged: The Toronto Baycrest Center. *International Journal of Aging and Human Development, 18*, 255–275.

Horn, J. L. (1978). Human ability systems. In P. B. Baltes & O. G. Brim, Jr. (Eds.), *Life-span development and behavior: Vol. 1* (pp. 211–256). New York: Academic Press.

Horn, J. L. (1982). The aging of human abilities. In B. B. Wolman (Ed.), *Handbook of developmental psychology* (pp. 847–870). Englewood Cliffs, NJ: Prentice-Hall.

Horn, J. L., & Donaldson, G. (1980). Cognitive development in adulthood. In O. G. Brim, Jr., & J. Kagan (Eds.), *Constancy and change in human development* (pp. 445–529). Cambridge, MA: Harvard University Press.

Horn, J. L., Donaldson, G., & Engstrom (1981). Apprehension, memory, and fluid intelligence decline through the "vital years" of adulthood. *Research on Aging, 3,* 33–84.

Hornblum, J. N., & Overton, W. F. (1976). Area and volume conservation among the elderly: Assessment and training. *Developmental Psychology, 12,* 68–74.

Horowitz, M. J., & Schulz, R. (1983). The relocation controversy: Criticism and commentary on five recent studies. *Gerontologist, 23,* 229–234.

Howard, A. (1984, August). *Cool at the top: Personality characteristics of successful executives.* Paper presented at the meeting of the American Psychological Association, Toronto.

Howard, A., & Bray, D. W. (1980, August). *Career motivation in mid-life managers.* Paper presented at the meeting of the American Psychological Association, Montreal.

Howard, D. V. (1983). *Cognitive psychology: Memory, language, and thought.* New York: Macmillan.

Howard, G. S. (1985). The role of values in the science of psychology. *American Psychologist, 40,* 255–265.

Howe, M. L. (1988). Measuring memory development in adulthood: A model-based approach to disentangling storage-retrieval contributions. In M. L. Howe & C. J. Brainerd (Eds.), *Cognitive development in adulthood* (pp. 39–64). New York: Springer-Verlag.

Hoyer, W. J. (1984). Aging and the development of expert cognition. In T. M. Schlechter & M. P. Toglia (Eds.), *New directions in cognitive science* (pp. 69–87). Norwood, NJ: Ablex.

Huff, F. J., Growdon, J. H., Corkin, S., & Rosen, T. J. (1987). Age at onset and rate of progression of Alzheimer's disease. *Journal of the American Geriatrics Association, 35,* 27–30.

Hughston, G. A., & Protinsky, H. W. (1978). Conservation abilities of elderly men and women: A comparative investigation. *Journal of Psychology, 98,* 23–26.

Hulin, C. L., & Smith, P. C. (1965). A linear model of job satisfaction. *Journal of Applied Psychology, 49,* 209–216.

Hultsch, D. F. (1971). Adult age differences in free classification and free recall. *Developmental Psychology, 4,* 338–342.

Hultsch, D. F., & Dixon, R. A. (1983). The role of pre-experimental knowledge in text processing in adulthood. *Experimental Aging Research, 9,* 17–22.

Hultsch, D. F., & Dixon, R. A. (1984). Memory for text materials in adulthood. In P. B. Baltes & O. G. Brim, Jr. (Eds.), *Life-span development and behavior: Vol. 6* (pp. 77–108). New York: Academic Press.

Hultsch, D. F., & Plemons, J. K. (1979). Life events and life-span development. In P. B. Baltes & O. G. Brim, Jr. (Eds.), *Life-span development and behavior: Vol 2* (pp. 1–36). New York: Academic Press.

Hussian, R. A., & Brown, D. C. (1987). Use of two-dimensional grid patterns to limit hazardous ambulation in demented patients. *Journal of Gerontology, 42,* 558–560.

Hussian, R. A., & Davis, R. L. (1985). *Responsive care: Behavioral interventions with elderly persons.* Champaign, IL: Research Press.

Huyck, M. H. (1982). From gregariousness to intimacy: Marriage and friendship over the adult years. In T. M. Field, A. Huston, H. C. Quay, L. Troll., & G. E. Finley (Eds.), *Review of human development* (pp. 471–484). New York: Wiley.

Iammarino, N. K. (1975). Relationship between death anxiety and demographic variables. *Psychological Reports, 17,* 262.

Ingraham, M. (1974). *My purpose holds: Reactions and experiences in retirement of TIAA–CREF annuitants.* New York: Educational Research Division, Teachers Insurance and Annuity Association College Retirement Equities Fund.

Irelan, L. M., & Bell, D. B. (1972). Understanding subjectively defined retirement: A pilot analysis. *Gerontologist, 12,* 354–356.

Isaksson, B. (1973). Clinical nutrition: Requirements of energy and nutrients in diseases. *Bibliography of Nutrition and Dietetics, 19,* 1.

Ivancevich, J. M., & Matteson, M. T. (1988). Type A behavior and the healthy individual. *British Journal of Medical Psychology, 61,* 37–56.

Jackson, J. J. (1985). Race, national origin, ethnicity, and aging. In R. H. Binstock & E. Shanas (Eds.), *Handbook of aging and the social sciences* (2nd ed.) (pp. 264–303). New York: Van Nostrand Reinhold.

Jackson, J. J., & Walls, B. E. (1978). Myths and realities about aged Blacks. In M. R. Brown (Ed.), *Readings in gerontology* (2nd ed.) (pp. 95–113). St. Louis: C. V. Mosby.

Jackson, J. S., & Gibson, R. C. (1985). Work and retirement among the black elderly. In Z. Blau (Ed.), *Current perspectives on aging and the life cycle* (pp. 193–222). Greenwich, CT: JAI.

Jackson, M., Kolodny, B., & Wood, J. L. (1982). To be old and Black: The case for double jeopardy on income and health. In R. C. Manuel (Ed.), *Minority aging, sociological and social psychological issues* (pp. 161–170). Westport, CT: Greenwood.

Jackson, M., & Wook, J. L. (1976). *Aging in America: Implications for the Black aged.* Washington, DC: National Council on the Aging.

Jacobs, J. (1974). *Fun city: An ethnographic study of a retirement community.* New York: Holt, Rinehart, & Winston.

Jacobs, J. (1975). *Older persons and retirement communities.* Springfield, IL: Charles C Thomas.

Jacobson, E. (1938). *Progressive relaxation.* Chicago: University of Chicago Press.

James, L. R., & Jones, A. P. (1980). Perceived job characteristics and job satisfaction: An examination of reciprocal causation. *Personnel Psychology, 33,* 97–135.

James, W. (1890). *The principles of psychology.* New York: Holt.

Jamison, K. R., Gerner, R. H., & Goodwin, F. K. (1979). Patient and physician attitudes toward lithium: Relationships to compliance. *Archives of General Psychiatry, 36,* 866–869.

Janson, P., & Ryder, L. K. (1983). Crime and the elderly: The relationship between risk and fear. *Gerontologist, 23,* 207–212.

Jaques, E. (1965). Death and the mid-life crisis. *International Journal of Psychoanalysis, 46,* 502–514.

Jaremko, M. E. (1983). Stress inoculation training for social anxiety with emphasis on dating anxiety. In D. Meichenbaum & M. E. Jaremko (Eds.), *Stress reduction and prevention.* New York: Plenum.

Jeffko, W. G. (1979, July 6). Redefining death. *Commonweal,* pp. 394–397.

Jemmott, J. B., Borysenko, J. Z., Borysenko, M., Mcclelland, D. C., Chapman, R., Meyer, D., & Benson, H. (1983). Academic stress, power motivation, and decrease in secretion rate of salivary secretory immunoglobulin A. *Lancet, 1,* 1400–1402.

Jirovec, R. L., Jirovec, M. M., & Bossé, R. (1985). Environmental determinants of neighborhood satisfaction among urban elderly men. *Gerontologist, 24,* 261–265.

Johanson, D. C., & Edey, M. A. (1981). *Lucy: The beginnings of humankind.* New York: Simon & Schuster.

Johnson, C. L. (1983). A cultural analysis of the grandmother. *Research on Aging, 5,* 547–567.

Johnson, C. L. (1987). The institutional segregation of the elderly. In P. Silverman (Ed.), *The elderly as modern pioneers* (pp. 307–319). Bloomington: Indiana University Press.

Johnson, C. L. (1988). Active and latent functions of grandparenting during the divorce process. *Gerontologist, 28,* 185–191.

Johnson, C. L., & Barer, B. (1987). Marital instability and the changing kinship networks of grandparents. *Gerontologist, 27,* 330–335.

Johnson, C. L., & Grant, L. (1985). *The nursing home in American society.* Baltimore: Johns Hopkins University Press.

Jones, K. H., & Enist, D. L. (1985). Mechanism of age-related changes in cell mediated immunity. In M. Rothstein (Ed.), *Review of biological aging research: Vol. 2* (pp. 155–177). New York: Liss.

Jones, L. Y. (1980). *Great expectations: America and the baby boom generation.* New York: Coward, McCann, & Geoghegan.

Jones, M. K., & Jones, B. M. (1980). The relationship of age and drinking habits to the effects of alcohol on memory in women. *Journal of Studies on Alcohol, 41,* 179–186.

Kahana, B., & Kahana, E. (1970). Grandparenthood from the perspective of the developing grandchild. *Developmental Psychology, 3,* 98–105.

Kahana, E. (1982). A congruence model of person-environment interaction. In M. P. Lawton, P. G. Windley, & T. O. Byerts (Eds.), *Aging and the environment: Theoretical approaches* (pp. 97–121). New York: Springer.

Kahana, E., & Kahana, B. (1983). Environmental continuity, futurity, and adaptation of the aged. In G. D. Rowles & R. J. Ohta (Eds.), *Aging and milieu: Environmental perspectives on growing old* (pp. 205–230). New York: Academic Press.

Kahn, R. L., Goldfarb, A. I., Pollack, M., & Peck, A. (1960). Brief objective measures for the determination of mental status in the aged. *American Journal of Psychiatry, 117,* 326–328.

Kales, A., Allen, W. C., Scharf, M. B., & Kales, J. D. (1970). Hypnotic drugs and effectiveness: All-night EEG studies of insomniac subjects. *Archives of General Psychiatry, 23,* 226–232.

Kales, A., Scharf, M. B., & Kales, J. D. (1978). Rebound insomnia: A new clinical syndrome. *Science, 201,* 1039–1040.

Kalish, R. A. (1975). *Late adulthood.* Pacific Grove, CA: Brooks/Cole.

Kalish, R. A. (1976). Death in a social context. In R. H. Binstock & E. Shanas (Eds.), *Handbook of aging and the social sciences* (pp. 483–507). New York: Van Nostrand Reinhold.

Kalish, R. A. (1984). *Death, grief, and caring relationships* (2nd ed.). Pacific Grove, CA: Brooks/Cole.

Kalish, R. A. (1985). The social context of death and dying. In R. H. Binstock & E. Shanas (Eds.), *Handbook of aging and the social sciences* (2nd ed.) (pp. 149–170). New York: Van Nostrand Reinhold.

Kalish, R. A. (1987). Death and dying. In P. Silverman (Ed.), *The elderly as modern pioneers* (pp. 320–334). Bloomington: Indiana University Press.

Kalish, R. A., & Reynolds, D. (1976). *Death and ethnicity: A psychocultural study.* Los Angeles: University of Southern California Press.

Kalish, R. A., & Reynolds, D. K. (1981). *Death and ethnicity: A psychocultural study.* Farmingdale, NY: Baywood.

Kallmann, F. J. (1957). Twin data on the genetics of aging. In G. E. Wolstenhoime & C. M. O'Connor (Eds.), *Methodology of the study of ageing* (pp. 131–143). London: Churchill.

Kaminsky, M. (1978). Pictures from the past: The use of reminiscence in casework with the elderly. *Journal of Gerontological Social Work, 1,* 19–31.

Kamouri, A., & Cavanaugh, J. C. (1986). The impact of pre-retirement education programs on workers' pre-retirement socialization. *Journal of Occupational Behavior, 7,* 245–256.

Kannel, W. B. (1985). Hypertension and aging. In C. E. Finch & E. L. Schneider (Eds.), *Handbook of the biology of aging* (2nd ed.) (pp. 859–877). New York: Van Nostrand Reinhold.

Kannel, W. B., & Thom, T. J. (1984). Declining cardiovascular mortality. *Circulation, 70,* 331–336.

Kanner, A. D., Coyne, J. C., Schaefer, C., & Lazarus, R. S. (1981). Comparison of two modes of stress measurements: Daily hassles and uplifts versus major life events. *Journal of Behavioral Medicine, 4,* 1–39.

Kanter, R. M. (1976, May). Why bosses turn bitchy. *Psychology Today,* pp. 56–59.

Kaplan, M. (1983). The issue of sex bias in DSM III: Comments on articles by Spitzer, Williams, and Kass. *American Psychologist, 38,* 802–803.

Karacen, I., & Williams, R. L. (1983). Sleep disorders in the elderly. *American Family Physicians, 27,* 143–152.

Kastenbaum, R. (1975). Is death a life crisis? On the confrontation with death in theory and practice. In N. Datan & L. Ginsberg (Eds.), *Life-span developmental psychology: Normative life crises* (pp. 19–50). New York: Academic Press.

Kastenbaum, R., & Aisenberg, R. B. (1976). *The psychology of death* (rev. ed.). New York: Springer.

Kastenbaum, R., & Briscoe, L. (1975). The street corner: Laboratory for the study of life-threatening behavior. *Omega: Journal of Death and Dying, 6,* 33–44.

Katzman, R. (1987). Alzheimer's disease: Advances and opportunities. *Journal of the American Geriatrics Society, 35,* 69–73.

Kaufman, D. W., Rosenberg, L., Helmrich, S. P., & Shapiro, S. (1985). Alcohol beverages and myocardial infarction in young men. *American Journal of Epidemiology, 121,* 548–554.

Kausler, D. H. (1982). *Experimental psychology and human aging.* New York: Wiley.

Kausler, D. H. (1985). Episodic memory: Memorizing performance. In N. Charness (Ed.), *Aging and human performance* (pp. 101–141). Chichester, England: Wiley.

Kausler, D. H., & Hakami, M. K. (1983). Memory for activities: Adult age differences and intentionality. *Developmental Psychology, 19,* 889–894.

Kausler, D. H., Lichty, W., & Freund, J. (1985). Adult age differences in recognition memory and frequency judgments for planned activities. *Developmental Psychology, 21,* 647–654.

Kausler, D. H., Lichty, W., Hakami, M. K., & Freund, J. S. (1986). Activity duration and adult age differences for activity performance. *Psychology and Aging, 1,* 80–81.

Kegan, R. (1982). *The evolving self.* Cambridge, MA: Harvard University Press.

Keith, J. (1982). *Old people as people: Social and cultural influences on aging and old age.* Boston: Little, Brown.

Keith, P. M. (1979). Life changes and perceptions of life and death among older men and women. *Journal of Gerontology, 34,* 870–878.

Kekes, J. (1983). Wisdom. *American Philosophical Quarterly, 20,* 277–286.

Keller, J. W., Sherry, D., & Piotrowski, C. (1984). Perspectives on death: A developmental study. *Journal of Psychology, 116,* 137–142.

Kelley, C. M. (1986). Depressive mood effects on memory and attention. In l. W. Poon (Ed.), *Handbook for the clinical memory assessment of older adults* (pp. 238–243). Washington, DC: American Psychological Association.

Kelley, H. H. (1967). Attribution theory in social psychology. *Nebraska Symposium on Motivation, 15,* 192–241.

Kelly, J. B. (1982). Divorce: The adult perspective. In B. B. Wolman (Ed.), *Handbook of developmental psychology* (pp. 734–750). Englewood Cliffs, NJ: Prentice-Hall.

Kelly, J. R., & Steinkampl, M. W. (1986). Later life leisure: How they play in Peoria. *Gerontologist, 26,* 531–537.

Kendall, M. J., Woods, K. L., Wilkins, M. R., & Worthington, D. J. (1982). Responsiveness to B-adrenergic receptor stimulation: The effects of age are cardioselective. *British Journal of Clinical Pharmacology, 14,* 821–826.

Kenney, R. A. (1982). *Physiology of aging: A synopsis.* Chicago: Yearbook Medical.

Kenshalo, D. R. (1977). Age changes in touch, vibration, temperature, kinesthesis, and pain sensitivity. In J. E. Birren & K. W. Schaie (Eds.), *Handbook of the psychology of aging* (pp. 562–579). New York: Van Nostrand Reinhold.

Kenshalo, D. R. (1979). Changes in the vestibular and somasthetic systems as a function of age. In J. M.

Ordy & K. Brizzee (Eds.), *Aging: Vol. 10. Sensory systems and communication in the elderly* (pp. 269–282). New York: Raven.

Kertzer, D. I., & Madison, O. B. B. (1981). Women's age-set systems in Africa: The Latuka of southern Sudan. In C. L. Fry (Ed.), *Dimensions: Aging, culture, and health* (pp. 109–130). New York: Praeger.

Kiecolt-Glaser, J. K., Speicher, C. E., Holliday, J. E., & Glaser, R. (1984). Stress and the transformation of lymphocytes in Epstein-Barr virus. *Journal of Behavioral Medicine, 7*, 1–12.

Kiefer, C. W., Kim, S., Choi, K., Kim, L., Kim, B.–L., Shon, S., & Kim, T. (1985). Adjustment problems of Korean-American elderly. *Gerontologist, 25*, 477–482.

Kieffer, G. H. (1979). *Bioethics: A textbook of issues.* Reading, MA: Addison-Wesley.

Kieffer, J. A. (1986). The older volunteer resource. In Committee on an Aging Society (Ed.), *Productive roles in an older society* (pp. 51–72). Washington, DC: National Academy Press.

Kii, T. (1981). Status changes of the elderly in Japan's legal, family, and economic institutions. In C. Nusberg & M. M. Osako (Eds.), *The situation of the Asian/Pacific elderly.* Washington, DC: International Federation on Aging.

Kimmel, D. C. (1978). Adult development and aging: A gay perspective. *Journal of Social Issues, 34*, 113–130.

Kimmel, D. C., Price, K. F., & Walker, J. W. (1978). Retirement choice and retirement satisfaction. *Journal of Gerontology, 33*, 575–585.

King, P. M., Kitchener, K. S., Wood, P. K., & Davison, M. L. (1989). Relationships across developmental domains: A longitudinal study of intellectual, moral, and ego development. In M. L. Commons, J. D. Sinnott, F. A. Richards, & C. Armon (Eds.), *Adult development: Vol. 1. Comparisons and applications of adolescent and adult developmental models.* New York: Praeger.

Kingston, P. W., & Nock, S. L. (1987). Time together among dual-earner couples. *American Sociological Review, 52*, 391–400.

Kinney, J. M., & Stephens, M. A. P. (in press). Hassles and uplifts of giving care to a family member with dementia. *Psychology and Aging.*

Kirasic, K. C. (1980, November). *Spatial problem solving in elderly adults: A hometown advantage.* Paper presented at the meeting of the Gerontological Society of America, San Diego.

Kirasic, K. C. (1981, April). *Studying the "hometown advantage" in elderly adults' spatial cognition and spatial behavior.* Paper presented at the meeting of the Society for Research in Child Development, Boston.

Kirasic, K. C., & Allen, G. L. (1985). Aging, spatial performance, and spatial competence. In N. Charness (Ed.), *Aging and human performance* (pp. 191–223). Chichester, England: Wiley.

Kirkwood, T. B. L. (1985). Comparative and evolutionary aspects of longevity. In C. E. Finch & E. L. Schneider (Eds.), *Handbook of the biology of aging* (2nd ed.) (pp. 27–44). New York: Van Nostrand Reinhold.

Kitchener, K. S., & King, P. M. (1989). The reflective judgment model: Ten years of research. In M. L. Commons, J. D. Sinnott, F. A. Richards, & C. Armon (Eds.), *Adult development: Vol. 1. Comparisons and applications of adolescent and adult developmental models.* New York: Praeger.

Kitson, G. L., & Sussman, M. B. (1982). Marital complaints, demographic characteristics, and symptoms of mental distress in divorce. *Journal of Marriage and the Family, 44*, 87–101.

Kivnick, H. Q. (1982). *The meaning of grandparenthood.* Ann Arbor, MI: UMI Research.

Klatsky, A. L., Friedman, G. D., & Siegelaub, A. B. (1981). Alcohol and mortality: A ten-year Kaiser-Permanente experience. *Annals of Internal Medicine, 95*, 139–145.

Klatzky, R. L. (1984). *Memory and awareness.* San Francisco: W. H. Freeman.

Klerman, G. L. (1986, March). *Evidence for increases in rates of depression in North America and Western Europe in recent decades.* Paper presented at the Conference on New Research in Depression, Murnau, West Germany.

REFERENCES

Kline, D. W., & Schieber, F. (1985). Vision and aging. In J. E. Birren & K. W. Schaie (Eds.), *Handbook of the psychology of aging* (2nd ed.) (pp. 296–331). New York: Van Nostrand Reinhold.

Klingman, A. M., Grove, G. L., & Balin, A. K. (1985). Aging of human skin. In C. E. Finch & E. L. Schneider (Eds.), *Handbook of the biology of aging* (2nd ed.) (pp. 820–841). New York: Van Nostrand Reinhold.

Klingman, L. H., Aiken, F. J., & Klingman, A. M. (1982). Prevention of ultraviolet damage to the dermis of hairless mice by sunscreens. *Journal of Investigative Dermatology, 78,* 181–189.

Koestenbaum, P. (1976). *Is there an answer to death?* Englewood Cliffs, NJ: Prentice-Hall.

Koff, T. H. (1981). *Hospice: A caring community.* Cambridge, MA: Winthrop.

Koh, J. Y., & Bell, W. G. (1987). Korean elderly in the United States: Intergenerational relations and living arrangements. *Gerontologist, 27,* 66–71.

Kohn, M. L., & Schooler, C. (1978). The reciprocal effects of the substantive complexity of work and intellectual flexibility: A longitudinal assessment. *American Journal of Sociology, 84,* 24–52.

Kohn, M. L., & Schooler, C. (1982). Job conditions and personality: A longitudinal assessment of their reciprocal effects. *American Journal of Sociology, 87,* 1257–1286.

Kornhaber, A. (1985). Grandparenthood and the "new social contract." In V. L. Bengtson & J. F. Robertson (Eds.), *Grandparenthood* (pp. 159–172). Beverly Hills, CA: Sage Publications.

Kornhaber, A., & Woodward, K. L. (1981). *Grandparent/grandchildren: The vital connection.* Garden City, NJ: Anchor.

Kosnik, W., Winslow, L., Kline, D. W., Rasinski, K., & Sekular, R. (1988). Visual changes in everyday life throughout adulthood. *Journal of Gerontology, 43,* P63–P70.

Kotre, J. (1984). *Outliving the self: Generativity and the interpretation of lives.* Baltimore: Johns Hopkins University Press.

Kozma, A., & Stones, M. J. (1983). Predictors of happiness. *Journal of Gerontology, 38,* 626–628.

Kram, K. E. (1980). *Mentoring processes at work: Developmental relationships in managerial careers.* Unpublished doctoral dissertation, Yale University, New Haven, CT.

Kram, K. E. (1985). *Mentoring at work: Developmental relationships in organizational life.* Glenview, IL: Scott, Foresman.

Kram, K. E., & Isabella, L. (1985). Mentoring alternatives: The role of peer relationships in career development. *Academy of Management Journal, 21,* 110–132.

Kramer, D. A. (1983). Post-formal operations? A need for further conceptualization. *Human Development, 26,* 91–105.

Kramer, D. A. (1987). Cognition and aging: The emergence of a new tradition. In P. Silverman (Ed.), *The elderly as modern pioneers* (pp. 88–103). Bloomington: Indiana University Press.

Krieger, S., Epsting, F., & Leitner, L. M. (1974). Personal constructs, threat, and attitudes toward death. *Omega: Journal of Death and Dying, 5,* 289.

Krout, J. A. (1988a). Community size differences in service awareness among elderly adults. *Journal of Gerontology, 43,* 528–530.

Krout, J. A. (1988b). Rural versus urban differences in elderly parents' contacts with their children. *Gerontologist, 28,* 198–203.

Krympotic-Nemanic, J. (1969). Presbycusis, presbystasis, and presbyosmia as consequences of the analogous biological process. *Acta Otolaryngolica, 67,* 217–223.

Kübler-Ross, E. (1969). *On death and dying.* New York: Macmillan.

Kübler-Ross, E. (1974). *Questions and answers on death and dying.* New York: Macmillan.

Kuhn, D., & Angelev, J. (1976). An experimental study of the development of formal operational thought. *Child Development, 47,* 697–706.

Kuhn, D., Ho, V., & Adams, C. (1979). Formal reasoning among pre- and late adolescents. *Child Development, 50*, 1128–1135.

Kuhn, D., Langer, J., Kohlberg, L., & Haan, N. S. (1977). The development of formal operations in logical and moral judgment. *Genetic Psychology Monographs, 95*, 97–188.

Kurdek, L. A., & Schmitt, J. P. (1986). Early development of relationship quality in heterosexual married, heterosexual cohabiting, gay, and lesbian couples. *Developmental Psychology, 22*, 305–309.

Labouvie-Vief, G. (1977). Adult cognitive development: In search of alternative interpretations. *Merrill-Palmer Quarterly, 23*, 227–263.

Labouvie-Vief, G. (1980). Beyond formal operations: Uses and limits of pure logic in life-span development. *Human Development, 23*, 141–161.

Labouvie-Vief, G. (1981). Proactive and reactive aspects of constructivism: Growth and aging in life-span perspective. In R. M. Lerner & N. A. Busch-Rossnagel (Eds.), *Individuals as producers of their development* (pp. 197–230). New York: Academic Press.

Labouvie-Vief, G. (1984). Logic and self-regulation from youth to maturity: A model. In M. L. Commons, F. A. Richards, & C. Armon (Eds.), *Beyond formal operations: Late adolescent and adult cognitive development* (pp. 158–179). New York: Praeger.

Labouvie-Vief, G. (1985). Intelligence and cognition. In J. E. Birren & K. W. Schaie (Eds.), *Handbook of the psychology of aging* (pp. 500–530). New York: Van Nostrand Reinhold.

Labouvie-Vief, G., Adams, C., Hakim-Larson, J., Hayden, M., & Devoe, M. (1985). *Logical problem solving and meta-logical knowledge from preadolescence to adulthood.* Unpublished manuscript, Wayne State University, Detroit.

Labouvie-Vief, G., & Gonda, J. N. (1976). Cognitive strategy training and intellectual performances in the elderly. *Journal of Gerontology, 31*, 327–332.

Labouvie-Vief, G., Hakim-Larson, J., & Hobart, C. J. (1987). Age, ego level, and the life-span development of coping and defense processes. *Psychology and Aging, 2*, 286–293.

Labouvie-Vief, G., & Lawrence, R. (1985). Object knowledge, personal knowledge, and process of equilibration in adult cognition. *Human Development, 28*, 25–39.

Lachman, J. L., & Lachman, R. (1980). Age and the actualization of world knowledge. In L. W. Poon, J. L. Fozard, L. S. Cermak, D. Arenberg, & L. W. Thompson (Eds.), *New directions in memory and aging* (pp. 285–311). Hillsdale, NJ: Erlbaum.

Lachman, M. E. (1983). Perceptions of intellectual aging: Antecedent or consequence of intellectual functioning? *Developmental Psychology, 19*, 482–498.

Lachman, M. E. (1985). Personal efficacy in middle and old age: Differential and normative patterns of change. In G. H. Elder, Jr. (Ed.), *Life-course dynamics: Trajectories and transitions, 1968–1980.* Ithaca, NY: Cornell University Press.

Lachman, M. E. (1986). Locus of control in aging research: A case for multidimensional and domain-specific assessment. *Psychology and Aging, 1*, 34–40.

Lachman, R., Lachman, J. L., & Butterfield, E. C. (1979). *Cognitive psychology and information processing: An introduction.* Hillsdale, NJ: Erlbaum.

Lacks, P., Bertelson, A. D., Gans, L., & Kunkel, J. (1983). The effectiveness of three behavioral treatments for different degrees of sleep onset insomnia. *Behavior Therapy, 14*, 593–605.

Laird, D. A., & Breen, W. J. (1939). Sex and age alterations in taste preferences. *Journal of the American Dietetic Association, 15*, 549–550.

Lajer, M. (1982). Unemployment and hospitalization among bricklayers. *Scandinavian Journal of Social Medicine, 10*, 3–10.

Lakatta, E. G. (1985). Heart and circulation. In C. E. Finch & E. L. Schneider (Eds.), *Handbook of the biology of aging* (2nd ed.) (pp. 377–413). New York: Van Nostrand Reinhold.

Lakatta, E. G. (1988). Cardiovascular system aging. In B. Kent & R. Butler (Eds.), *Human aging research: Concepts and techniques* (pp. 199–220). New York: Raven.

Lakatta, E. G., Goldberg, A. P., Fleg, J. L., Fortney, S. M., & Drinkwater, D. T. (1988). Reduced cardiovascular and metabolic reserve in older persons: Disuse, disease, or aging? In R. Chernoff & D. A. Lipschitz (Eds.), *Health promotion and disease prevention in the elderly* (pp. 75–88). New York: Raven.

Lando, H. A. (1977). Successful treatment of smokers with a broad-spectrum behavioral approach. *Journal of Consulting and Clinical Psychology, 45,* 361–366.

Langer, E. J. (1985). Playing the middle against both ends: The usefulness of older adult cognitive activity as a model for cognitive activity in childhood and old age. In S. Yussen (Ed.), *The growth of reflection in children* (pp. 267–285). New York: Academic Press.

Langer, E. J., & Rodin, J. (1976). The effects of choice and enhanced personal responsibility for the aged: A field experiment in an institutional setting. *Journal of Personality and Social Psychology, 34,* 191–198.

Larson, R. (1978). Thirty years of research on the subjective well-being of older Americans. *Journal of Gerontology, 33,* 109–125.

Larson, R., Mannell, R., & Zuzanek, J. (1986). Daily well-being of older adults with friends and family. *Psychology and Aging, 1,* 117–126.

LaRue, A., Dessonville, C., & Jarvik, L. F. (1985). Aging and mental disorders. In J. E. Birren & K. W. Schaie (Eds.), *Handbook of the psychology of aging* (2nd ed.) (pp. 664–702). New York: Van Nostrand Reinhold.

Latack, J. C. (1984). Career transitions within organizations: An exploratory study of work, nonwork, and coping strategies. *Organizational Behavior and Human Performance, 34,* 296–322.

Laudenslager, M. L., Ryan, S. M., Drugan, R. C., Hyson, R. L., & Maier, S. F. (1983). Coping and immunosuppression: Inescapable but not escapable shock suppresses lymphocyte proliferation. *Science, 221,* 568–570.

Lavey, R. S., & Taylor, C. B. (1985). The nature of relaxation therapy. In S. R. Burchfield (Ed.), *Stress: Psychological and physiological interactions* (pp. 329–358). Washington, DC: Hemisphere.

Lawton, M. P. (1980). *Environment and aging.* Pacific Grove, CA: Brooks/Cole.

Lawton, M. P. (1982). Competence, environmental press, and the adaptation of old people. In M. P. Lawton, P. G. Windley, & T. O. Byerts (Eds.), *Aging and the environment: Theoretical approaches* (pp. 33–59). New York: Springer.

Lawton, M. P. (1985). Housing and living environments of older people. In R. H. Binstock & E. Shanas (Eds.), *Handbook of aging and the social sciences* (2nd ed.) (pp. 450–478). New York: Van Nostrand Reinhold.

Lawton, M. P., & Cohen, J. (1974). The generality of housing impact on the well-being of older people. *Journal of Gerontology, 29,* 194–204.

Lawton, M. P., Moss, M., & Moles, E. (1984). The supra-personal neighborhood context of older people: Age heterogeneity and well-being. *Environment and Behavior, 16,* 89–109.

Lawton, M. P., & Nahemow, L. (1973). Ecology of the aging process. In C. Eisdorfer & M. P. Lawton (Eds.), *The psychology of adult development and aging* (pp. 619–674). Washington, DC: American Psychological Association.

Lawton, M. P., & Nahemow, L. (1979). Social areas and the well-being of tenants in housing for the elderly. *Multivariate Behavior Research, 14,* 463–484.

Lawton, M. P., & Yaffe, S. (1980). Victimization and fear of crime in elderly public housing tenants. *Journal of Gerontology, 35,* 768–779.

Layde, P. M., Ory, H. W., & Schlesselman, J. J. (1982). The risk of myocardial infarction in former users of oral contraceptives. *Family Planning Perspectives, 14,* 78–80.

Lazarus, R. S. (1984). Puzzles in the study of daily hassles. *Journal of Behavioral Medicine, 7,* 375–389.

Lazarus, R. S., DeLongis, A., Folkman, S., & Gruen, R. (1985). Stress and adaptational outcomes. *American Psychologist, 40,* 770–779.

Lazarus, R. S., & Folkman, S. (1984). *Stress, appraisal, and coping.* New York: Springer.

Leacock, E. (1978). Women's status in egalitarian society: Implications for social evolution. *Current Anthropology, 19,* 247–275.

Leaf, P. J., Berkman, C. S., Weissman, M. M., Holzer, C. E., Tischler, G. L., & Myers, J. K. (1988). The epidemiology of late-life depression. In J. A. Brody & G. L. Maddox (Eds.), *Epidemiology and aging: An international perspective* (pp. 117–133). New York: Springer.

Lebowitz, M. D. (1988). Respiratory changes of aging. In B. Kent & R. Butler (Eds.), *Human aging research: Concepts and techniques* (pp. 263–276). New York: Raven.

Lee, G. R. (1985). Kinship and social support of the elderly: The case of the United States. *Aging and Society, 5,* 19–38.

Lee, G. R. (1988). Marital satisfaction in later life: The effects of nonmarital roles. *Journal of Marriage and the Family, 50,* 775–783.

Lee, G. R., & Ellithorpe, E. (1982). Intergenerational exchange and subjective well-being among the elderly. *Journal of Marriage and the Family, 44,* 217–224.

Lee, R. B. (1968). What hunters do for a living, or how to make out on scarce resources. In R. B. Lee and I. DeVore (Eds.), *Man the hunter.* Chicago: Aldine-Atherton.

Lehmann, H. E. (1981). Classification of depressive disorders. In T. A. Ban, R. Gonzalez, A. S. Jablensky, N. A. Sartorius, & F. E. Vartanian (Eds.), *Prevention and treatment of depression* (pp. 3–17). Baltimore: University Park Press.

Leibowitz, H. W., & Gwozdecki, J. (1967). The magnitude of the Poggendorff illusion as a function of age. *Child Development, 38,* 573–580.

Leibowitz, H. W., & Judisch, J. M. (1967). Size constancy in older persons: A function of distance. *American Journal of Psychology, 80,* 294–296.

Lemon, B. W., Bengtson, V. L., & Peterson, J. A. (1972). An exploration of the activity theory of aging: Activity types and life satisfactions among in-movers to a retirement community. *Journal of Gerontology, 27,* 511–523.

Lent, R. W., & Hackett, G. (1987). Career self-efficacy: Empirical status and future directions. *Journal of Vocational Behavior, 30,* 347–382.

Leon, G. R., Gillum, B., Gillum, R., & Gouze, M. (1979). Personality stability and change over a 30-year period: Middle to old age. *Journal of Consulting and Clinical Psychology, 47,* 517–524.

Leonard, J. A., & Newman, R. C. (1965). On the acquisition and maintenance of high speed and high accuracy on a keyboard task. *Ergonomics, 8,* 281–304.

Lepp, I. (1968). *Death and its mysteries.* New York: Macmillan.

Lerner, M. (1970). When, why, and where people die. In O. G. Brim, Jr., H. E. Freeman, S. Levine, & N. A. Scotch (Eds.), *The dying patient* (pp. 5–29). New York: Russell Sage Foundation.

Lerner, R. M. (1984). *On the nature of human plasticity.* New York: Cambridge University Press.

Lerner, R. M. (1986). *Concepts and theories of human development* (2nd ed.). New York: Random House.

Lerner, R. M., Skinner, E. A., & Sorrell, G. T. (1980). Methodological implications of contextual/dialectic theories of development. *Human Development, 23,* 225–235.

Le Shan, L. (1969). Psychotherapy and the dying patient. In L. Pearson (Ed.), *Death and dying.* Cleveland: Case Western Reserve University Press.

Lesser, J., Lazarus, L. W., Frankel, R., & Havasy, S. (1981). Reminiscence group therapy with psychotic geriatric inpatients. *Gerontologist, 21,* 291–296.

LeVine, R. (1978). Adulthood and aging in cross-cultural perspective. *Items, 31/32,* 1–5.

Levinson, D. J. (1979). Adult development — Or what? *Contemporary Psychology, 24,* 727.

Levinson, D. J., Darrow, C., Kline, E., Levinson, M., & McKee, B. (1978). *The seasons of a man's life.* New York: Knopf.

Lewin, K. (1936). *Principles of topological psychology.* New York: McGraw-Hill.

Lewinsohn, P. M. (1975). The behavioral study and treatment of depression. In M. Hersen, R. M. Eisler, & P. M. Miller (Eds.), *Progress in behavior modification: Vol. 1* (pp. 19–64). New York: Academic Press.

Lewinsohn, P. M., Steinmetz, J. L., Antonuccio, D. O., & Teri, L. (1984). *The coping with depression course*. Eugene, OR: Castalia.

Lewis, R. A. (1979). Macular degeneration in the aged. In S. S. Han & D. H. Coons (Eds.), *Special senses and aging*. Ann Arbor, MI: Institute of Gerontology, University of Michigan.

Lewontin, R. C. (1981). On constraints and adaptation. *Behavioral and Brain Sciences, 4*, 244–245.

Liang, J., & Warfel, B. L. (1983). Urbanism and life satisfaction among the aged. *Journal of Gerontology, 38*, 97–106.

Lieberman, A. (1974). Parkinson's disease: A clinical review. *American Journal of Medical Science, 267*, 66–80.

Lieberman, A., Dzietolowski, M., Kupersmith, M., Serby, M., Goodgold, A., Korein, J., & Goldstein, M. (1979). Dementia in Parkinson's disease. *Annals of Neurology, 6*, 255–259.

Light, L. L., & Anderson, P. A. (1975). Working-memory capacity, age, and memory for discourse. *Journal of Gerontology, 45*, 737–747.

Light, L. L., & Zelinski, E. M. (1983). Memory for spatial information in young and old adults. *Developmental Psychology, 19*, 901–906.

Light, L. L., Zelinski, E. M., & Moore, M. (1981). Adult age differences in reasoning from new information. *Journal of Experimental Psychology: Learning, Memory, and Cognition, 8*, 435–447.

Lincoln, Y. S., & Guba, E. G. (1985). *Naturalistic inquiry*. Beverly Hills, CA: Sage Publications.

Lindsay, P. H., & Norman, D. A. (1977). *Human information processing: An introduction*. New York: Academic Press.

Lipowski, Z. J. (1975). Physical illness, the patient and his environment: Psychosocial foundations of medicine. In M. Rieser (Ed.), *American handbook of psychiatry: Vol. 4* (pp. 1–42). New York: Basic Books.

Lipowski, Z. J. (1980). *Delirium*. Springfield, IL: Charles C Thomas.

Lishman, W. A. (1978). *Organic psychiatry: The psychological consequences of cerebral disorder*. Oxford, England: Blackwell Scientific.

List, N. (1987). Perspectives in career screening in the elderly. *Geriatric Clinic, 3*, 433–445.

List, N. D. (1988). Cancer screening in the elderly. In R. Chernoff & D. A. Lipschitz (Eds.), *Health promotion and disease prevention in the elderly* (pp. 113–129). New York: Raven.

Livson, F. B. (1981). Paths to psychological health in the middle years: Sex differences. In D. Eichorn, N. Haan, J. Clausen, M. Honzik, & P. Mussen (Eds.), *Past and present in middle life* (pp. 183–194). New York: Academic Press.

Locke, E. A. (1976). The natures and causes of job satisfaction. In M. Dunnette (Ed.), *Handbook of industrial/organizational psychology*. Chicago: Rand McNally.

Loevinger, J. (1976). *Ego development*. San Francisco: Jossey-Bass.

Logan, R. D. (1986). A reconceptualization of Erikson's theory: The repetition of existential and instrumental themes. *Human Development, 29*, 125–136.

Lombardo, N. E. (1988). ADRDA: Birth and evolution of a major voluntary health association. In M. K. Aronson (Ed.), *Understanding Alzheimer's disease* (pp. 323–326). New York: Scribner's.

Longino, C. F. (1982). American retirement communities and residential relocation. In M. A. Warnes (Ed.), *Geographical perspectives on the elderly* (pp. 239–262). London: Wiley.

Lopata, H. Z. (1973). *Widowhood in an American city*. Cambridge, MA: Schenkman.

Lopata, H. Z. (1975). Widowhood: Societal factors in life-span disruptions and alternatives. In N. Datan & L. H. Ginsberg (Eds.), *Life-span developmental psychology: Normative life crises* (pp. 217–234). New York: Academic Press.

Lorayne, H., & Lucas, J. (1974). *The memory book.* New York: Ballantine.

Lovejoy, C. O. (1981). The origin of man. *Science, 211,* 341–350.

Lovelace, E. A., Marsh, G. R., & Oster, O. J. (1982). *Prediction and evaluation of memory performance by young and old adults.* Paper presented at the meeting of the Gerontological Society of America, Boston.

Lowenthal, M. F. (1972). Some potentialities of a life-cycle approach to the study of retirement. In F. M. Carp (Ed.), *Retirement* (pp. 307–338). New York: Behavioral Publications.

Lowenthal, M. F., & Haven, C. (1968). Interaction and adaptation: Intimacy as a critical variable. *American Sociological Review, 33,* 20–30.

Lowenthal, M., Thurnher, M., & Chiriboga, D. (1975). *Four stages of life.* San Francisco: Jossey-Bass.

Luborsky, M., & Rubinstein, R. L. (1987). Ethnicity and lifetimes: Self-concepts and situational contexts of ethnic identity in late life. In D. E. Gelfand & C. M. Barresi (Eds.), *Ethnic dimensions of aging.* New York: Springer.

Ludeman, K. (1981). The sexuality of the older person: Review of the literature. *Gerontologist, 21,* 203–208.

Lund, D. A., Dimond, M. S., Caserta, M. F., Johnson, R. J., Poulton, J. L., & Connelly, J. R. (1985–86). Identifying elderly with coping difficulties after two years of bereavement. *Omega: Journal of Death and Dying, 16,* 213–224.

Lundgren, B. K., Steen, G. B., & Isaksson, B. (1987). Dietary habits in 70- and 75-year-old males and females: Longitudinal and cohort data from a population study. *Näringsforskning.*

Lundin, T. (1984). Morbidity following sudden and unexpected bereavement. *British Journal of Psychiatry, 144,* 84–88.

Maas, H. S. (1985). The development of adult development: Recollections and reflections. In J. M. A. Munnichs, P. Mussen, E. Olbrich, & P. G. Coleman (Eds.), *Life-span and change in a gerontological perspective* (pp. 161–175). New York: Academic Press.

Maas, H. S., & Kuypers, J. A. (1974). *From thirty to seventy.* San Francisco: Jossey-Bass.

Maas, J. W. (1978). Clinical and biochemical heterogeneity of depressive disorders. *Annals of Internal Medicine, 88,* 556–563.

Mace, N. L., & Rabins, P. V. (1981). *The 36-hour day.* Baltimore: Johns Hopkins University Press.

Macklin, E. D. (1978). Review of research on nonmarital cohabitation in the United States. In B. I. Murstein (Ed.), *Exploring intimate life styles* (pp. 197–243). New York: Springer.

Madden, D. J. (1982). Age differences and similarities in the improvement of controlled search. *Experimental Aging Research, 8,* 91–98.

Madden, D. J. (1986). Adult age differences in the attentional capacity demands of visual search. *Cognitive Development, 1,* 335–363.

Madden, D. J. (1987). Aging, attention, and the use of meaning during visual search. *Cognitive Development, 2,* 201–216.

Madden, D. J., & Nebes, R. D. (1980). Aging and the development of automaticity in visual search. *Developmental Psychology, 16,* 377–384.

Maddox, G. L., & Campbell, R. T. (1985). Scope, concepts, and methods in the study of aging. In R. H. Binstock & E. Shanas (Eds.), *Handbook of aging and the social sciences* (2nd ed.) (pp. 3–31). New York: Van Nostrand Reinhold.

Mahoney, M. J. (1980). *Abnormal psychology.* New York: Harper & Row.

Maier, D. E. (1988). Skeletal aging. In B. Kent & R. Butler (Eds.), *Human aging research: Concepts and techniques* (pp. 221–244). New York: Raven.

Maletta, G. J. (1984). Use of antipsychotic medication in the elderly. In C. Eisdorfer (Ed.), *Annual review of gerontology and geriatrics: Vol. 4* (pp. 174–220). New York: Springer.

Malinak, D. P., Hoyt, M. F., & Patterson, V. (1979). Adults' reactions to the death of a parent: A preliminary study. *American Journal of Psychiatry, 136,* 1152–1156.

Mandel, R. G., & Johnson, N. S. (1984). A developmental analysis of story recall and comprehension in adulthood. *Journal of Verbal Learning and Verbal Behavior, 23,* 643–659.

Margolin, L., & White, J. (1987). The continuing role of physical attractiveness in marriage. *Journal of Marriage and the Family, 49,* 21–27.

Markides, K. S., & Levin, J. S. (1987). The changing economy and the future of the minority aged. *Gerontologist, 27,* 273–280.

Marlatt, G. A., & Gordon, J. R. (1980). Determinants of relapse: Implication for the maintenance of behavior change. In P. O. Davidson & S. M. Davidson (Eds.), *Behavioral medicine: Changing health lifestyles* (pp. 410–452). New York: Brunner/Mazel.

Marshall, L. (1981). Auditory processing in aging listeners. *Journal of Speech and Hearing Disorders, 46,* 226–240.

Marshall, V. (1980). *Last chapters: A sociology of aging and dying.* Pacific Grove, CA: Brooks/Cole.

Martin, L. G. (1988). The aging of Asia. *Journal of Gerontology, 43,* S99–S113.

Martin, T. R., & Bracken, M. B. (1986). Association of low birth weight with passive smoke exposure in pregnancy. *American Journal of Epidemiology, 124,* 633–642.

Maslow, A. H. (1968). *Toward a psychology of being* (2nd ed.). New York: Van Nostrand Reinhold.

Mason, S. E. (1981, November). *Age group comparisons of memory ratings, predictions, and performance.* Paper presented at the meeting of the Gerontological Society of America, Toronto.

Masters, R. D. (1978). Jean-Jacques is alive and well: Rousseau and contemporary psychobiology. *Daedalus, 107,* 93–105.

Masters, W. H., & Johnson, V. E. (1966). *Human sexual response.* Boston: Little, Brown.

Materi, M. (1977). Assertiveness training: A catalyst for behavior change. *Alcohol Health and Research World, 1,* 23–26.

Matthews, R., & Matthews, A. M. (1986). Infertility and involuntary childlessness: The transition to nonparenthood. *Journal of Marriage and the Family, 48,* 641–649.

Mattis, S. (1976). Mental status examination for organic mental syndrome in the elderly patient. In L. Bellak & T. B. Karasu (Eds.), *Geriatric psychiatry: A handbook for psychiatrists and primary health care physicians* (pp. 79–121). New York: Grune & Stratton.

Maxwell, R. J., Silverman, P., & Maxwell, E. K. (1982). The motive for gerontocide. In J. Sokolovsky (Ed.), *Aging and the aged: Part 1* (pp. 67–84). Williamsburg, VA: Studies in Third World Societies (Public No. 22).

Maybury-Lewis, D. (1984). Age and kinship: A structural view. In D. I. Kertzer & J. Keith (Eds.), *Age and anthropological theory* (pp. 123–140). Ithaca, NY: Cornell University Press.

McAdoo, H. P. (1982). Levels of stress and family support in black families. In H. M. McCubbin, A. Cauble, & J. Patterson (Eds.), *Family stress, coping, and social support.* Springfield, IL: Charles C Thomas.

McAllister, T. W. (1981). Cognitive functioning in the affective disorders. *Comprehensive Psychiatry, 22,* 572–586.

McClearn, G., & Foch, T. T. (1985). Behavioral genetics. In J. E. Birren & K. W. Schaie (Eds.), *Handbook of the psychology of aging* (2nd ed.) (pp. 113–143). New York: Van Nostrand Reinhold.

McCrae, R. R., & Costa, P. T., Jr. (1983). Psychological maturity and subjective well-being: Toward new synthesis. *Developmental Psychology, 19,* 243–248.

McCrae, R. R., & Costa, P. T., Jr. (1984). *Emerging lives, enduring dispositions.* Boston: Little, Brown.

McCrae, R. R., & Costa, P. T., Jr. (1987). Validation of the five-factor model of personality across instruments and observers. *Journal of Personality and Social Psychology, 52,* 81–90.

McCrae, R. R., Costa, P. T., Jr., & Busch, C. M. (1986). Evaluating comprehensiveness in personality systems. *Journal of Personality, 54,* 430–446.

McDonald, R. S. (1986). Assessing treatment effects: Behavior rating scales. In L. W. Poon (Ed.), *Handbook for the clinical memory assessment of older adults* (pp. 129–138). Washington, DC: American Psychological Association.

McGeer, E., & McGeer, P. L. (1975). Age changes in the human for some enzymes associated with metabolism of catecholamines, GABA, and acetylcholine. In J. M. Ordy & K. R. Brizzee (Eds.), *Neurobiology of aging* (pp. 287–305). New York: Plenum.

McGeer, E., & McGeer, P. L. (1980). Aging and neurotransmitter systems. In M. Goldstein, D. B. Caine, A. Liegerman, & M. O. Thorner (Eds.), *Advances in biochemical psychopharmacology: Vol. 23. Ergot compounds and brain function: Neuroendocrine and neuropsychiatric aspects* (pp. 305–314). New York: Raven.

McGinnis, J. M. (1988). The Tithonus syndrome: Health and aging in America. In R. Chernoff & D. A. Lipschitz (Eds.), *Health promotion and disease prevention in the elderly* (pp. 1–16). New York: Raven.

McKellin, W. H. (1985). Passing away and loss of life: Aging and death among the Managalese of Papua New Guinea. In D. A. Counts & D. R. Counts (Eds.), *Aging and its transformations* (pp. 181–202). Lanham, MD: University Press of America.

McKhann, G., Drachman, D., Folstein, M., Katzman, R., Prince, D., & Stadlam, E. M. (1984). Clinical diagnosis of Alzheimer's disease: Report of the NINCDS–ADRDA Work Group under the auspices of the Department of Health and Human Services Task Force on Alzheimer's disease. *Neurology, 34*, 939–944.

Meacham, J. A. (1982). A note on remembering to execute planned actions. *Journal of Applied Developmental Psychology, 3*, 121–133.

Meacham, J. A. (1983). Wisdom: The context of knowledge: Knowing that one doesn't know. In D. Kuhn & J. A. Meacham (Eds.), *On the development of developmental psychology* (pp. 111–134). Basel: Karger.

Meichenbaum, D. (1985). *Stress inoculation training.* New York: Pergamon Press.

Meichenbaum, D., & Cameron, R. (1983). Stress inoculation training: Toward a general paradigm for training coping skills. In D. Meichenbaum & M. E. Jaremko (Eds.), *Stress reduction and prevention* (pp. 115–154). New York: Plenum.

Meier, D. E. (1988). Skeletal aging. In B. Kent & R. Butler (Eds.), *Human aging research: Concepts and techniques* (pp. 221–244). New York: Raven.

Mellinger, G. D., Balter, M. B., & Uhlenhuth, E. H. (1985). Insomnia and its treatment. *Archives of General Psychiatry, 42*, 225–232.

Menaghan, E. G., & Lieberman, M. A. (1986). Changes in depression following divorce: A panel study. *Journal of Marriage and the Family, 48*, 319–328.

Mendelson, M. (1982). Psychodynamics of depression. In E. S. Paykel (Ed.), *Handbook of affective disorders* (pp. 162–174). New York: Guilford.

Menken, J., Trussell, J., & Larsen, U. (1986). Age and fertility. *Science, 233*, 1389–1394.

Merriam, S. (1979). Middle age: A review of the research. *New Directions for Continuing Education, 2*, 7–15.

Messer, M. (1967). The possibility of an age-concentrated environment becoming a normative system. *Gerontologist, 7*, 247–251.

Messer, M. (1968). Age grouping and social status of the elderly. *Sociologist and Social Research, 52*, 271–279.

Meyer, B. J. F. (1983). Text structure and its use in studying comprehension across the adult life span. In B. A. Huston (Ed.), *Advances in reading/language research: Vol. 2* (pp. 9–54). Greenwich, CT: JAI.

Meyer, B. J. F. (1987). Reading comprehension and aging. In K. W. Schaie (Ed.), *Annual review of gerontology and geriatrics: Vol. 7* (pp. 93–115). New York: Springer.

Meyer, B. J. F., & Rice, G. E. (1981). Information recalled from prose by young, middle, and old adults. *Experimental Aging Research, 7*, 253–268.

Meyer, B. J. F., & Rice, G. E. (1983). Learning and memory from text across the adult life span. In J. Fine & R. O. Freedle (Eds.), *Developmental studies in discourse* (pp. 291–306). Norwood, NJ: Ablex.

Meyer, B. J. F., & Rice, G. E. (1989). Prose processing in adulthood: The text, the reader, and the task. In L. W. Poon, D. C. Rubin, & B. Wilson (Eds.), *Everyday cognition in adulthood and late life*. Cambridge: Cambridge University Press.

Meyer, B. J. F., Rice, G. E., Knight, C. C., & Jessen, J. L. (1979). *Effects of comparative and descriptive discourse types on the reading performance of young, middle, and old adults* (Prose Learning Series No. 7). Tempe, AZ: Department of Educational Psychology, Arizona State University Press.

Meyer, B. J. F., Young, C. J., & Bartlett, B. J. (1986, August). *A prose learning strategy: Effects on young and old adults*. Paper presented at the meeting of the American Psychological Association, Washington, DC.

Meyer, J. W. (1987). A regional scale temporal analysis of the net migration patterns of elderly persons over time. *Journal of Gerontology, 42,* 366–375.

Meyerhoff, B. (1978). *Number our days*. New York: Simon & Schuster.

Meyers, G. C. (1985). Aging and worldwide population change. In R. H. Binstock & E. Shanas (Eds.), *Handbook of aging and the social sciences* (2nd ed.) (pp. 173–198). New York: Van Nostrand Reinhold.

Miles, C. C., & Miles, W. R. (1932). The correlation of intelligence scores and chronological age from early to late maturity. *American Journal of Psychology, 44,* 44–78.

Miles, L. E., & Dement, W. C. (1980). Sleep and aging. *Sleep, 3,* 119–120.

Miller, I. J., Jr. (1988). Human taste bud density across adult age groups. *Journal of Gerontology, 43,* B26–B30.

Miller, P. H. (1983). *Theories of developmental psychology*. San Francisco: W. H. Freeman.

Miller, S. S., & Cavanaugh, J. C. (1987, August). *The meaning of grandparenthood and its relationship to demographic, relationship, and social participation variables*. Paper presented at the meeting of the American Psychological Association, New York.

Miller, W. R., & Hester, R. K. (1980). Treating the problem drinker: Modern approaches. In W. R. Miller (Ed.), *The addictive behaviors* (pp. 11–142). Oxford: Pergamon Press.

Minkler, M., & Pasick, R. J. (1986). Health promotion and the elderly: A critical perspective on the past and future. In K. Dychtwald (Ed.), *Wellness and health promotion for the elderly* (pp. 39–54). Rockville, MD: Aspen.

Mohs, R. C., Kim, Y., Johns, C. A., Dunn, D. D., & Davis, K. I. (1986). Assessing changes in Alzheimer's disease: Memory and language. In l. W. Poon (Ed.), *Handbook for the clinical memory assessment of older adults* (pp. 149–155). Washington, DC: American Psychological Association.

Moody, R. A. (1975). *Life after life*. Atlanta: Mockingbird.

Moody, R. A. (1977). *Reflections on life after life*. New York: Bantam Books.

Moore, L. M., Nielsen, C. R., & Minstretta, C. M. (1982). Sucrose taste thresholds: Age-related differences. *Journal of Gerontology, 37,* 64–69.

Moore, S. F. (1978). Old age in a life-term social arena: Some Chagga in Killimanjaro in 1974. In B. G. Meyerhoff & A. Simic (Eds.), *Life's career: Aging* (pp. 23–76). Beverly Hills, CA: Sage Publications.

Moos, R. H. (1980). Specialized living environments for older people: A conceptual framework. *Journal of Social Issues, 36,* 75–94.

Moos, R. H., & Lemke, S. (1984). *Multiphasic environmental assessment procedure: Manual*. Palo Alto, CA: Social Ecology Laboratory, Stanford University Press.

Moos, R. H., & Lemke, S. (1985). Specialized living environments for older people. In J. E. Birren & K. W. Schaie (Eds.), *Handbook of the psychology of aging* (2nd ed.) (pp. 864–889). New York: Van Nostrand Reinhold.

Moramarco, S. (1979, April 22). Long-distance marriage can work. *Parade Magazine*.

Moran, J. A., & Gatz, M. (1987). Group therapies for nursing home adults: An evaluation of two treatment approaches. *Gerontologist, 27,* 588–591.

Morewitz, J. (1988). Evaluation of excessive daytime sleepiness in the elderly. *Journal of the American Geriatrics Society, 36,* 324–330.

Morris, J. N. (1975). Changes in morale experienced by elderly institutional applicants along the institutional path. *Gerontologist, 15,* 345–349.

Morris, J. N., & Sherwood, S. (1984). Informal support resources for vulnerable elderly persons: Can they be counted on, why do they work? *International Journal of Aging and Human Development, 18,* 1–17.

Morris, P. E. (1979). Strategies for learning and recall. In M. M. Gruneberg & P. E. Morris (Eds.), *Applied problems in memory* (pp. 25–57). London: Academic Press.

Morrow, P. C. & McElroy, J. C. (1987). Work commitment and job satisfaction over three career stages. *Journal of Vocational Behavior, 30,* 330–346.

Mortimer, J. T. (1974). Patterns of intergenerational occupational movements: A smallest-space analysis. *American Journal of Sociology, 5,* 1278–1295.

Mortimer, J. T. (1976). Social class, work, and family: Some implications of the father's occupation for family relationships and son's career decisions. *Journal of Marriage and the Family, 38,* 241–256.

Mortimer, J. T., Finch, M. D., & Kumka, D. (1982). Persistence and change in development: The multidimensional self-concept. In P. B. Baltes & O. G. Brim, Jr. (Eds.), *Life-span development and behavior: Vol. 4* (pp. 263–313). New York: Academic Press.

Mortimer, J. T., & Kumka, D. (1982). A further examination of the occupational linkage hypothesis. *Sociological Quarterly, 23,* 241–256.

Morycz, R. K. (1985). Caregiving strain and the desire to institutionalize family members with Alzheimer's disease: Possible predictors and model development. *Research on Aging, 7,* 329–361.

Moscovitz, M. C. (1982). A neuropsychological approach to perception and memory in normal and pathological aging. In F. I. M. Craik & S. Trehub (Eds.), *Aging and cognitive processes* (pp. 55–78). New York: Plenum.

Mulrow, C. D., Feussner, J. R., Williams, B. C., & Vokaty, K. A. (1987). The value of clinical findings in the detection of normal pressure hydrocephalus. *Journal of Gerontology, 42,* 277–279.

Munn, K. (1981). Effects of exercise on the range of motion in elderly subjects. In E. Smith & R. Serfass (Eds.), *Exercise and aging: The scientific bases* (pp. 167–186). Hillsdale, NJ: Enslow.

Munro, H. N. (1981). Nutrition and aging. *British Medical Bulletin, 37,* 83–88.

Munro, H. N., & Young, V. R. (1978). New approaches to the assessment of protein status in man. In A. N. Howard & I. M. Baird (Eds.), *Recent advances in clinical nutrition* (pp. 33–41). London: Libby.

Murphy, C. (1985). Cognitive and chemosensory influences in age-related changes in the ability to identify blended foods. *Journal of Gerontology, 40,* 47–52.

Murphy, C. (1986). Taste and smell in the elderly. In H. L. Meiselman & R. S. Rivlin (Eds.), *Clinical measurement of taste and smell* (pp. 343–371). New York: Macmillan.

Murphy, C., & Withee, J. (1987). Age and biochemical status predict preference for casein hydrolysate. *Journal of Gerontology, 42,* 73–77.

Murphy, M. D., Sanders, R. E., Gabriesheski, A. S., & Schmitt, F. A. (1981). Metamemory in the aged. *Journal of Gerontology, 36,* 185–193.

Murphy, Y., & Murphy, R. F. (1974). *Women of the forest.* New York: Columbia University Press.

Murray, H. A. (1938). *Explorations in personality.* New York: Oxford University Press.

Murray, J. (1979). Subjective retirement. *Social Security Bulletin, 42,* 20–25, 43.

Murstein, B. I. (1982). Marital choice. In B. B. Wolman (Ed.), *Handbook of developmental psychology* (pp. 652–666). Englewood Cliffs, NJ: Prentice-Hall.

Mussen, P. (1985). Early adult antecedents of life satisfaction at age 70. In J. M. A. Munnichs, P. Mussen, E. Olbrich, & P. G. Coleman (Eds.), *Life-span and change in a gerontological perspective* (pp. 45–61). New York: Academic Press.

Myers, J. E., Wass, H., & Murphey, M. (1980). Ethnic differences in death anxiety among the elderly. *Death Education, 4*, 237–244.

Myers, T. (1983). Corroboration of self-reported alcohol consumption — A comparison of the accounts of a group of male prisoners and those of their wives/cohabitees. *Alcohol and Alcoholism, 18*, 67–74.

Nagel, J. E., & Adler, W. H. (1988). Immunology. In B. Kent & R. Butler (Eds.), *Human aging research: Concepts and techniques* (pp. 299–310). New York: Raven.

National Institute of Aging. (1980). Senility reconsidered. *JAMA, 244*, 259–263.

National Institute of Alcoholism and Alcohol Abuse (NIAAA). (1983). *Fifth special report to the U.S. Congress on alcohol and health.* (DHHS Publication No. ADM 84–1291). Washington, DC: U.S. Government Printing Office.

National Research Council. (1988). *The emerging population in the twenty-first century: Statistics for health policy.* Washington, DC: National Academy Press.

National Research Council, Food and Nutrition Board. (1980). *Recommended dietary allowances, revised.* Washington, DC: National Academy Press.

National Safety Council. (1981). *Accident facts.* Chicago: Author.

National Urban League. (1964). *Double-jeopardy — The older Negro in America today.* New York: Author.

Nehrke, M. F., Bellucci, G., & Gabriel, S. J. (1977). Death anxiety, locus of control, and life satisfaction in the elderly. *Omega: Journal of Death and Dying, 8*, 359–368.

Neimark, E. D. (1975). Longitudinal development of formal operational thought. *Genetic Psychology Monographs, 91*, 171–225.

Neisser, U. (1976). *Cognition and reality.* San Francisco: W. H. Freeman.

Neisser, U., & Winograd, E. (Eds.). (1988). *Remembering reconsidered.* New York: Cambridge University Press.

Nesselroade, J. R., & Labouvie, E. W. (1985). Experimental design in research on aging. In J. E. Birren & K. W. Schaie (Eds.), *Handbook of the psychology of aging* (2nd ed.) (pp. 35–60). New York: Van Nostrand Reinhold.

Neugarten, B. L. (1969). Continuities and discontinuities of psychological issues into adult life. *Human Development, 12*, 121–130.

Neugarten, B. L. (1973). Personality change in later life: A developmental perspective. In C. Eisdorfer & M. P. Lawton (Eds.), *The psychology of adult development and aging.* Washington, DC: American Psychological Association.

Neugarten, B. L. (1977). Personality and aging. In J. E. Birren & K. W. Schaie (Eds.), *Handbook of the psychology of aging* (pp. 626–649). New York: Van Nostrand Reinhold.

Neugarten, B. L., & Associates (Eds.). (1964). *Personality in middle and late life.* New York: Atherton.

Neugarten, B. L., & Datan, N. (1973). Sociological perspectives on the life cycle. In P. B. Baltes & K. W. Schaie (Eds.), *Life-span developmental psychology: Personality and socialization* (pp. 53–69). New York: Academic Press.

Neugarten, B. L., & Hagestad, G. O. (1976). Age and the life course. In R. H. Binstock & E. Shanas (Eds.), *Handbook of aging and the social sciences* (pp. 35–55). New York: Van Nostrand Reinhold.

Neugarten, B. L., Havighurst, R. J., & Tobin, S. S. (1968). Personality and pattern of aging. In B. L. Neugarten (Ed.), *Middle age and aging* (pp. 173–177). Chicago: University of Chicago Press.

Neugarten, B. L., & Weinstein, K. K. (1964). The changing American grandparent. *Journal of Marriage and the Family, 26*, 299–304.

Neulinger, J. (1974). *The psychology of leisure.* Springfield, IL: Charles C Thomas.

Newman, B. M. (1982). Mid-life development. In B. B. Wolman (Ed.), *Handbook of developmental psychology* (pp. 617–635). Englewood Cliffs, NJ: Prentice-Hall.

REFERENCES

Nock, S. L. (1981). Family life transitions: Longitudinal effects on family members. *Journal of Marriage and the Family, 43,* 703–714.

Nock, S. L. (1982). The life-cycle approach to family analysis. In B. B. Wolman (Ed.), *Handbook of developmental psychology* (pp. 636–651). Englewood Cliffs, NJ: Prentice-Hall.

Noe, R. A. (1987). *An exploratory investigation of the antecedents and consequences of mentoring.* Unpublished manuscript, University of Minnesota, Minneapolis.

Nolen-Hoeksema, S. (1988). Life-span views on depression. In P. B. Baltes & R. M. Lerner (Eds.), *Life-span development and behavior: Vol. 9* (pp. 203–241). Hillsdale, NJ: Erlbaum.

Norris, F. N., & Murrell, S. A. (1987). Older adult family stress and adaptation before and after bereavement. *Journal of Gerontology, 42,* 606–612.

Norris, M. L., & Cunningham, D. R. (1981). Social impact of hearing loss in the aged. *Journal of Gerontology, 36,* 727–729.

Norton, A. J., & Moorman, J. E. (1987). Current trends in marriage and divorce among American women. *Journal of Marriage and the Family, 49,* 3–14.

Nuttall, R. L. (1972). The strategy of functional age research. *International Journal of Aging and Human Development, 3,* 149–152.

Nydegger, C. N. (1986). Asymmetrical kin and the problematic son-in-law. In N. Datan, A. L. Greene, & H. W. Reese (Eds.), *Life-span developmental psychology: Intergenerational relations* (pp. 99–124). Hillsdale, NJ: Erlbaum.

Ochs, A. L., Newberry, J., Lenhardt, M. L., & Harkins, S. W. (1985). Neural and vestibular aging associated with falls. In J. E. Birren & K. W. Schaie (Eds.), *Handbook of the psychology and aging* (2nd ed.) (pp. 378–399). New York: Van Nostrand Reinhold.

O'Donohue, W. T. (1987). The sexual behavior and problems of the elderly. In L. L. Carstensen & B. A. Edelstein (Eds.), *Handbook of clinical gerontology* (pp. 66–75). New York: Pergamon Press.

Ohta, R. J. (1981). Spatial problem-solving: The response selection tendencies of young and elderly adults. *Experimental Aging Research, 7,* 81–84.

Ohta, R. J., & Kirasic, K. C. (1983). The investigation of environmental learning in the elderly. In G. Rowles & R. J. Ohta (Eds.), *Aging and milieu* (pp. 83–95). New York: Academic Press.

Ohta, R. J., Walsh, D. A., & Krauss, I. K. (1981). Spatial perspective-taking ability in young and elderly adults. *Experimental Aging Research, 7,* 45–63.

Olian, J. D., Carroll, S. J., Giannantonia, C. M., & Feren, D. B. (1988). What do proteges look for in a mentor? Results from three experimental studies. *Journal of Vocational Behavior, 33,* 15–37.

Olsho, L. W., Harkins, S. W., & Lenhardt, M. L. (1985). Aging and the auditory system. In J. E. Birren & K. W. Schaie (Eds.), *Handbook of the psychology of aging* (2nd ed.) (pp. 332–377). New York: Van Nostrand Reinhold.

Olson, D. H., & McCubbin, H. (1983). *Families: What makes them work.* Beverly Hills, CA: Sage Publications.

Ordy, J. M. (1981). Neurochemical aspects of aging in humans. In H. M. van Praag, M. H. Lader, O. J. Rafaelson, & E. J. Sacher (Eds.), *Handbook of biological psychiatry.* New York: Dekker.

Ortner, S. (1974). Is female to male as nature is to culture? In M. Z. Rosaldo & L. Lamphere (Eds.), *Women, culture, and society* (pp. 67–88). Stanford, CA: Stanford University Press.

Ortner, S. B. (1978). *Sherpas through their rituals.* New York: Cambridge University Press.

Osgood, N. J. (1985). *Suicide in the elderly.* Rockville, MD: Aspen.

Ostrow, A. C. (1980). Physical activity as it relates to the health of the aged. In N. Datan & N. Lohman (Eds.), *Transitions of aging* (pp. 41–56). New York: Academic Press.

Overstall, P. W., Johnson, A. L., & Exton-Smith, A. N. (1978). Instability and falls in the elderly. *Age and Ageing, 7* (Supplement 6), 92–96.

Paffenbarger, R. S., Hyde, R. T., Wing, A. L., & Hsieh, C. (1986). Physical activity, all cause mortality and longevity of college alumni. *New England Journal of Medicine, 314,* 605–613.

Palmer, G. J., Ziegler, M. G., & Lake, C. R. (1978). Response of norepinephrine and blood pressure to stress increases with age. *Journal of Gerontology, 33,* 482–487.

Palmore, E. (1975). *The honorable elders: A cross-cultural analysis of aging in Japan.* Durham, NC: Duke University Press.

Palmore, E., & Maeda, D. (1985). *The honorable elders revisited.* Durham, NC: Duke University Press.

Panek, P. E. (1982). Relationship between field-dependence/independence and personality in older adult females. *Perceptual and Motor Skills, 54,* 811–814.

Panek, P. E., Barrett, G. V., Sterns, H. L., & Alexander, R. A. (1977). A review of age changes in perceptual information processing ability with regard to driving. *Experimental Aging Research, 3,* 387–449.

Panek, P. E., & Reardon, J. R. (1986). *Age and gender effects on accident types for rural drivers.* Paper presented at the meeting of the Gerontological Society of America, Chicago.

Panek, P. E., & Sterns, H. L. (1985). Self-evaluation, actual performance, and preference across the life-span. *Experimental Aging Research, 11,* 221–223.

Papalia, D. E. (1972). The status of several conservation abilities across the life-span. *Human Development, 15,* 229–243.

Papalia, D. E., & Bielby, D. (1974). Cognitive functioning in middle and old age adults: A review of research based on Piaget's theory. *Human Development, 17,* 424–443.

Papalia, D. E., Salverson, S. M., & True, M. (1973). An evaluation of quantity conservation performance during old age. *International Journal of Aging and Human Development, 4,* 103–109.

Papalia-Finley, D. E., Blackburn, J., Davis, E., Dellmann, M., & Roberts, P. (1980). Training cognitive functioning in the elderly — Inability to replicate previous findings. *International Journal of Aging and Human Development, 12,* 111–117.

Parfitt, A. M., Gallagher, J. C., Heaney, R. P., Johnston, C. C., Neer, R., & Whedon, G. D. (1982).

Vitamin D and bone health in the elderly. *American Journal of Clinical Nutrition, 36,* 1014–1031.

Park, D. C., Puglisi, J. T., & Smith, A. D. (1986). Memory for pictures: Does an age-related decline exist? *Psychology and Aging, 1,* 11–17.

Park, D. C., Puglisi, J. T., & Sovacool, M. (1983). Memory for pictures, words, and spatial location in older adults: Evidence for pictorial superiority. *Journal of Gerontology, 38,* 582–588.

Park, D. C., Puglisi, J. T., & Sovacool, M. (1984). Picture memory in older adults: Effects of contextual detail at encoding and retrieval. *Journal of Gerontology, 39,* 213–215.

Park, D. C., Royal, D., Dudley, W., & Morrell, R. (1988). Forgetting of pictures over a long retention interval in young and older adults. *Psychology and Aging, 3,* 94–95.

Parkes, C. M. (1972). *Bereavement.* New York: International Universities Press.

Parkes, C. M. (1975). Determinants of outcome following bereavement. *Omega: Journal of Death and Dying, 6,* 303–323.

Parkinson, S. R., Lindholm, J. M., & Inman, V. W. (1982). An analysis of age differences in immediate recall. *Journal of Gerontology, 37,* 425–431.

Pascual-Leone, J. (1983). Growing into human maturity: Toward a metasubjective theory of adult stages. In P. B. Baltes & O. G. Brim, Jr. (Eds.), *Life-span development and behavior: Vol. 5* (pp. 115–156). New York: Academic Press.

Passuth, P. M. (1984). *Children's socialization to age hierarchies within the peer group and family.* Unpublished doctoral dissertation, Northwestern University, Evanston, IL.

Passuth, P. M., & Bengtson, V. L. (1988). Sociological theories of aging: Current perspectives and future directions. In J. E. Birren & V. L. Bengtson (Eds.), *Emergent theories of aging* (pp. 333–355). New York: Springer.

Pastalan, L. A. (1982). Research in environment and aging: An alternative to theory. In M. P. Lawton, P. G. Windley, & T. O. Byerts (Eds.), *Aging and the*

REFERENCES

environment: Theoretical approaches (pp. 122–131). New York: Springer.

Pattison, E. M. (1977a). The dying experience — Retrospective analysis. In E. M. Pattison (Ed.), *The experience of dying*. Englewood Cliffs, NJ: Prentice-Hall.

Pattison, E. M. (Ed.). (1977b). *The experience of dying*. Englewood Cliffs, NJ: Prentice-Hall.

Pearlin, L. I., & Johnson, J. (1977). Marital status, life strains, and depression. *American Sociological Review, 42*, 704–715.

Pearlman, J., Stotsky, B. A., & Dominick, J. R. (1969). Attitudes toward death among nursing home personnel. *Journal of Genetic Psychology, 114*, 63–75.

Peck, R. (1968). Psychological developments in the second half of life. In B. L. Neugarten (Ed.), *Middle age and aging* (pp. 88–92). Chicago: University of Chicago Press.

Peele, S. (1984). The cultural context of psychological approaches to alcoholism: Can we control the effects of alcohol? *American Psychologist, 39*, 1337–1351.

Peplau, L. (1981, March). What homosexuals want in relationships. *Psychology Today*, pp. 28–38.

Peplau, L., & Gordon, S. L. (1985). Women and men in love: Sex differences in close heterosexual relationships. In V. O'Leary, R. K. Unger, & B. S. Wallston (Eds.), *Women, gender, and social psychology* (pp. 257–292). Hillsdale, NJ: Erlbaum.

Pepper, S. C. (1942). *World hypotheses*. Berkeley, CA: University of California Press.

Pepper, S. C. (1967). *Concept and quality: A world hypothesis*. La Salle, IL: Open Court.

Perlmuter, L. C. (1989). Motivation. In L. W. Poon, D. C. Rubin, & B. Wilson (Eds.), *Everyday cognition in adulthood and late life*. Cambridge: Cambridge University Press.

Perlmutter, M. (1978). What is memory aging the aging of? *Developmental Psychology, 14*, 330–345.

Perlmutter, M., Adams, C., Berry, J., Kaplan, M., Person, D., & Verdonik, F. (1987). Aging and memory. In K. W. Schaie (Ed.), *Annual review of gerontology and geriatrics: Vol. 7* (pp. 57–92). New York: Springer.

Perlmutter, M., Metzger, R., Miller, R., & Nezworski, T. (1980). Memory for historical events. *Experimental Aging Research, 6*, 47–60.

Perlmutter, M., Metzger, R., Nezworski, T., & Miller, K. (1981). Spatial and temporal memory in 20- and 60-year-olds. *Journal of Gerontology, 36*, 59–64.

Perry, W. I. (1968). *Forms of intellectual and ethical development in the college years*. New York: Holt, Rinehart & Winston.

Pershagen, G., Hrubec, Z., & Svensson, C. (1987). Passive smoking and lung cancer in Swedish women. *American Journal of Epidemiology, 125*, 17–24.

Pezdek, K. (1983). Memory for items and their spatial locations by young and elderly adults. *Developmental Psychology, 19*, 895–900.

Pfeiffer, E., & Davis, G. C. (1974). Determinants of sexual behavior in middle and old age. In E. Palmore (Ed.), *Normal aging 2* (pp. 251–262). Durham, NC: Duke University Press.

Phillis, D. E., & Stein, P. J. (1983). Sink or swing? The lifestyles of single adults. In E. R. Allgeier & N. B. McCormick (Eds.), *Changing boundaries: Gender roles and sexual behavior* (pp. 202–225). Palo Alto, CA: Mayfield.

Piaget, J. (1970). Piaget's theory. In P. H. Mussen (Ed.), *Carmichael's manual of child psychology: Vol. 1* (3rd ed.) (pp. 703–732). New York: Wiley.

Piaget, J. (1972). Intellectual evolution from adolescence to adulthood. *Human Development, 15*, 1–12.

Pincus, L. (1976). *Death and the family: The importance of mourning*. New York: Pantheon.

Pino, C. J., Rosica, C. M., & Carter, T. J. (1978). The differential effects of relocation on nursing home patients. *Gerontologist, 18*, 167–172.

Plath, D. W. (1972). Japan: The after years. In D. O. Cowgill & L. D. Holmes (Eds.), *Aging and modernization*. New York: Appleton-Century-Crofts.

Plath, D. W. (1980). *Long engagements: Maturity in modern Japan.* Stanford, CA: Stanford University Press.

Plato, C. C., & Norris, A. H. (1979). Osteoarthritis of the hand: Age specific joint-digit and prevalence rates. *American Journal of Epidemiology, 109,* 169–180.

Pleck, J. H. (1983). Husbands' paid work and family roles: Current research issues. In H. Z. Lopata & J. H. Pleck (Eds.), *Research on the interweave of social roles: Vol. 3. Families and jobs* (pp. 251–333). Greenwich, CT: JAI.

Plude, D. J. (1987). Sensory, perceptual, and motor function in human aging. In P. Silverman (Ed.), *The elderly as modern pioneers* (pp. 73–87). Bloomington: Indiana University Press.

Plude, D. J., & Hoyer, W. J. (1981). Adult age differences in visual search as a function of stimulus mapping and processing level. *Journal of Gerontology, 36,* 598–604.

Plude, D. J., & Hoyer, W. J. (1985). Attention and performance: Identifying and localizing age deficits. In N. Charness (Ed.), *Aging and human performance* (pp. 47–99). Chichester, England: Wiley.

Plude, D. J., Kaye, D. B., Hoyer, W. J., Post, T. A., Saynisch, M. J., & Hahn, M. V. (1983). Adult age differences in visual search as a function of information load and target mapping. *Developmental Psychology, 19,* 508–512.

Pollack, R. H., & Atkeson, B. M. (1978). A life-span approach to perceptual development. In P. B. Baltes (Ed.), *Life-span development and behavior: Vol. 1* (pp. 85–109). New York: Academic Press.

Ponzio, F., Calderini, G., Lomuscio, G., Vantini, G., Toffano, G., & Algeri, S. (1982). Changes in monoamines and their metabolite levels in some brain regions of aged rats. *Neurobiology of Aging, 3,* 23–29.

Poon, L. W. (1985). Differences in human memory with aging: Nature, causes, and clinical implications. In J. E. Birren & K. W. Schaie (Eds.), *Handbook of the psychology of aging* (2nd ed.) (pp. 427–462). New York: Academic Press.

Poon, L. W. (Ed.). (1986). *Handbook for the clinical memory assessment of older adults.* Washington, DC: American Psychological Association.

Poon, L. W., & Fozard, J. L. (1980). Age and word frequency effects in continuous recognition memory. *Journal of Gerontology, 35,* 77–86.

Poon, L. W., Fozard, J. L., Paulshock, D. R., & Thomas, J. C. (1979). A questionnaire assessment of age differences in retention of recent and remote events. *Experimental Aging Research, 5,* 401–411.

Poon, L. W., Gurland, B. J., Eisdorfer, C., Crook, T., Thompson, L. W., Kaszniak, A. W., & Davis, K. L. (1986). Integration of experimental and clinical precepts in memory assessments: A tribute to George Talland. In L. W. Poon (Ed.), *Handbook for clinical memory assessment of older adults* (pp. 3–10). Washington, DC: American Psychological Association.

Poon, L. W., & Schaffer, G. (1982). *Prospective memory in young and elderly adults.* Paper presented at the meeting of the American Psychological Association, Washington, DC.

Popkin, S. J., Gallagher, D., Thompson, L. W., & Moore, M. (1982). Memory complaint and performance in normal and depressed older adults. *Experimental Aging Research, 8,* 141–145.

Post, F. (1987). Paranoid and schizophrenic disorders among the aging. In L. L. Carstensen & B. A. Edelstein (Eds.), *Handbook of clinical gerontology* (pp. 43–56). New York: Pergamon Press.

Potash, M., & Jones, B. (1977). Aging and decision criteria for the detection of tones in noise. *Journal of Gerontology, 32,* 436–440.

Powell, L. A., & Williamson, J. B. (1985). The mass media and the aged. *Social Policy, 16,* 38–49.

Power, T. G., & Parke, R. D. (1982). Play as a context for early learning: Lab and home analyses. In E. Siegel & L. M. Laosa (Eds.), *The family as a learning environment.* New York: Plenum.

Pratt, O. E. (1980). The fetal alcohol syndrome: Transport of nutrients and transfer of alcohol and acetaldehyde from mother to fetus. In M. Sandler

REFERENCES

(Ed.), *Psychopharmacology of alcohol* (pp. 229–258). New York: Raven.

Pratt, O. E. (1982). Alcohol and the developing fetus. *British Medical Bulletin, 38,* 48–52.

Price, D. L., Whitehouse, P. J., Struble, R. G., Clark, A. W., Coyle, J. T., DeLong, M. R., & Hedreen, J. C. (1982). Basal forebrain cholinergic systems in Alzheimer's disease and related dementias. *Neuroscience Commentaries, 1,* 84–92.

Prinz, P. N., & Raskind, M. (1978). Aging and sleep disorders. In R. Williams & I. Karacan (Eds.), *Sleep disorders: Diagnosis and treatment* (pp. 303–322). New York: Wiley.

Pritikin, N., & Cisney, N. (1986). Dietary recommendations for older Americans. In K. Dychtwald (Ed.), *Wellness and health promotion for the elderly* (pp. 179–200). Rockville, MD: Aspen.

Protinsky, H., & Hughston, G. (1978). Conservation in elderly males: An empirical investigation. *Developmental Psychology, 14,* 114.

Pruchno, R. A., & Resch, N. L. (1988). Intrainstitutional relocation: Mortality effects. *Gerontologist, 28,* 311–317.

Puder, R., Lacks, P., Bertelson, A. D., & Storandt, M. (1983). Short-term stimulus control treatment of insomnia in older adults. *Behavior Therapy, 14,* 424–429.

Quadagno, J. (1982). *Aging in early industrial society: Work, family and social policy in nineteenth century England.* New York: Academic Press.

Quayhagen, M. P., & Quayhagen, M. (1988). Alzheimer's stress: Coping with the caregiving role. *Gerontologist, 28,* 391–396.

Quigley, M. W. (1979, June 19). Executive corps: Free advice pays off for both sides. *Newsday,* p. 9.

Quilter, R. E., Giambra, L. M., & Benson, P. E. (1983). Longitudinal age changes in vigilance over an eighteen year interval. *Journal of Gerontology, 38,* 51–54.

Quinn, R. P., & Staines, G. L. (1979). *The 1977 quality of employment survey.* Ann Arbor: Institute for Social Research, University of Michigan.

Rabbitt, P. (1977). Changes in problem solving ability in old age. In J. E. Birren & K. W. Schaie (Eds.), *Handbook of the psychology of aging* (pp. 606–625). New York: Van Nostrand Reinhold.

Rabinowitz, J. C., Ackerman, B. P., Craik, F. I. M., & Hinchley, J. L. (1982). Aging and metamemory: The roles of relatedness and imagery. *Journal of Gerontology, 37,* 688–695.

Rackoff, N. S., & Mourant, R. R. (1979). Driving performance of the elderly. *Accident Analysis and Prevention, 11,* 247–253.

Radloff, L. S. (1977). The CES-D Scale: A self-report depression scale for research in the general population. *Applied Psychological Measurement, 1,* 385.

Ragland, O. R., & Brand, R. J. (1988). Type A behavior and mortality from coronary heart disease. *New England Journal of Medicine, 318,* 65–69.

Ramig, L. A., & Ringel, R. L. (1983). Effects of physiological aging on selected acoustic characteristics of voice. *Journal of Speech and Hearing Research, 26,* 22–30.

Raphael, B. (1983). *The anatomy of bereavement.* New York: Basic Books.

Rapoport, R., & Rapoport, R. N. (1975). *Leisure and the family life cycle.* London: Routledge and Kegan Paul.

Rapoport, R., & Rapoport, R. N. (1980). Three generations of dual-career family research. In F. Pepitone-Rockwell (Ed.), *Dual career couples.* Beverly Hills, CA: Sage Publications.

Reddan, W. G. (1981). Respiratory system and aging. In E. L. Smith & R. C. Serfass (Eds.), *Exercise and aging: The scientific basis* (pp. 89–107). Hillsdale, NJ: Erlbaum.

Redmore, C. D., & Loevinger, J. (1979). Ego development in adolescence: Longitudinal studies. *Journal of Youth and Adolescence, 8,* 129–134.

Reedy, M. N., Birren, J. E., & Schaie, K. W. (1981). Age and sex differences in satisfying love relationships across the adult life span. *Human Development, 24,* 52–66.

Reese, H. W., & Overton, W. F. (1970). Models of development and theories of development. In L. R. Goulet & P. B. Baltes (Eds.), *Life-span developmental psychology: Research and theory* (pp. 115–145). New York: Academic Press.

Reese, H. W., & Rodeheaver, D. (1985). Problem solving and complex decision making. In J. E. Birren & K. W. Schaie (Eds.), *Handbook of the psychology of aging* (2nd ed.) (pp. 474–499). New York: Van Nostrand Reinhold.

Register, J. C. (1981). Aging and race: A Black-White comparative analysis. *Gerontologist, 21,* 438–443.

Regnier, V. (1983). Urban neighborhood cognition: Relationships between functional and symbolic community elements. In G. D. Rowles & R. J. Ohta (Eds.), *Aging and milieu: Environmental perspectives on growing old* (pp. 63–82). New York: Academic Press.

Reinke, B. J., Holmes, D. S., & Harris, R. L. (1985). The timing of psychosocial change in women's lives: The years 25 to 45. *Journal of Personality and Social Psychology, 48,* 1353–1364.

Reisberg, B., Ferris, S. H., Anand, R., de Leon, M. J., Schneck, M. K., & Crook, T. (1985). Clinical assessment of cognitive decline in normal aging and primary degenerative dementia: Concordant ordinal measures. In P. Pinchot, P. Berner, R. Wolf, & K. Thau (Eds.), *Psychiatry: Vol. 5* (pp. 333–338). New York: Plenum.

Reisberg, B., Ferris, S. H., Borenstein, J., Sinaiko, E., de Leon, M. J., & Buttinger, C. (1986). Assessment of presenting symptoms. In L. W. Poon (Ed.), *Handbook for clinical memory assessment of older adults* (pp. 108–128). Washington, DC: American Psychological Association.

Reisberg, B., Ferris, S. H., de Leon, M. J., & Crook, T. (1982). The global deterioration scale for assessment of primary degenerative dementia. *American Journal of Psychiatry, 139,* 1136–1139.

Reynolds, C. F., Kupfer, D. J., Taska, L. S., Hoch, C. C., Sewitch, D. E., & Spiker, D. G. (1985). Sleep of healthy seniors: A revisit. *Sleep, 8,* 20–29.

Reynolds, D. K., & Kalish, R. A. (1974). Anticipation of futurity as a function of ethnicity and age. *Journal of Gerontology, 29,* 224–231.

Rhyne, D. (1981). Basis of marital satisfaction among men and women. *Journal of Marriage and the Family, 43,* 941–955.

Ribot, T. (1882). *Diseases of memory.* New York: Appleton.

Rice, G. E., & Meyer, B. J. F. (1985). Reading behavior and prose recall performance of young and older adults with high and average verbal ability. *Educational Gerontology, 11,* 57–72.

Richards, O. W. (1977). Effects of luminance and contrast on visual acuity, ages 16 to 90 years. *American Journal of Optometry and Physiological Optics, 54,* 178–184.

Ricklefs, R. (1988, May 19). Adult children of elderly parents hire "surrogates" to oversee care. *Wall Street Journal,* p. 29.

Riegel, K. F. (1973). Dialectical operations: The final period of cognitive development. *Human Development, 16,* 346–370.

Rikli, R., & Busch, S. (1986). Motor performance of women as a function of age and physical activity level. *Journal of Gerontology, 41,* 645–649.

Riley, M. W. (1971). Social gerontology and the age stratification of society. *Gerontologist, 11,* 79–87.

Riley, M. W. (1979). Introduction. In M. W. Riley (Ed.), *Aging from birth to death: Interdisciplinary perspectives* (pp. 3–14). Boulder, CO: Westview.

Riley, M. W. (1985). Age strata in social systems. In R. H. Binstock & E. Shanas (Eds.), *Handbook of aging and the social sciences* (2nd ed.) (pp. 369–411). New York: Van Nostrand Reinhold.

Riley, M. W. (1987). On the significance of age in sociology. *American Sociological Review, 52,* 1–14.

Riley, M. W., & Foner, A. (1968). *Aging and society: An inventory of research findings.* New York: Russell Sage Foundation.

Riley, M. W., Johnson, M., & Foner, A. (1972). *Aging and society: Vol. 3. A sociology of age stratification.* New York: Russell Sage Foundation.

Riley, V. (1981). Psychoneuroendocrine influences on immunocompetence and neoplasia. *Science, 212,* 1100–1109.

Ritzer, G. (1977). *Working: Conflict and change* (2nd ed.). Englewood Cliffs, NJ: Prentice-Hall.

Roberto, K. A., & Scott, J. P. (1986). Equity considerations in the friendships of older adults. *Journal of Gerontology, 41,* 241–247.

Roberts, P. (1983). Memory strategy instruction with the elderly: What should memory training be the training of? In M. Pressley & J. R. Levin (Eds.), *Cognitive strategy research: Psychological foundations* (pp. 75–100). New York: Springer-Verlag.

Roberts, P., & Newton, P. M. (1987). Levinsonian studies of women's adult development. *Psychology and Aging, 2,* 154–163.

Robertson, J. F. (1976). Significance of grandparents: Perceptions of young adult grandchildren. *Gerontologist, 16,* 137–140.

Robertson, J. F. (1977). Grandmotherhood: A study of role concepts. *Journal of Marriage and the Family, 39,* 165–174.

Robinson, B., & Thurnher, M. (1979). Taking care of aged parents: A family cycle transition. *Gerontologist, 19,* 586–593.

Robinson, D. S., Nies, A., Davis, J. N., Bunney, W. E., Davis, J. M., Colburn, R. W., Bourne, H. R., Shaw, D. M., & Coppern, A. J. (1972). Aging, monoamines and monoamine oxidase levels. *Lancet, 1,* 290–291.

Robinson, J. K. (1983). Skin problems of aging. *Geriatrics, 38,* 57–65.

Rockstein, M., & Sussman, M. (1979). *Biology of aging.* Belmont, CA: Wadsworth.

Rodeheaver, D., & Datan, N. (1988). The challenge of double jeopardy: Toward a mental health agenda for aging women. *American Psychologist, 43,* 648–654.

Rodeheaver, D., & Thomas, J. L. (1986). Family and community networks in Appalachia. In N. Datan, A. L. Greene, & H. W. Reese (Eds.), *Life-span developmental psychology: Intergenerational relations* (pp. 77–98). Hillsdale, NJ: Erlbaum.

Rodin, J., & Langer, E. J. (1977). Long-term effects of a control-relevant intervention with the institutionalized aged. *Journal of Personality and Social Psychology, 35,* 897–902.

Rodin, J., McAvay, G., & Timko, C. (1988). A longitudinal study of depressed mood and sleep disturbances in elderly adults. *Journal of Gerontology, 43,* P45–P53.

Rogers, C. S., & Levitin, P. M. (1987). Osteoarthritis. In C. S. Rogers, J. D. McCue, & P. Gal (Eds.), *Managing chronic disease* (pp. 299–305). Oradell, NJ: Medical Economics Press.

Rogers, J., & Bloom, F. E. (1985). Neurotransmitter metabolism and function in the aging central nervous system. In C. E. Finch & E. L. Schneider (Eds.), *Handbook of the biology of aging* (2nd ed.) (pp. 645–691). New York: Van Nostrand Reinhold.

Root, N. (1981). Injuries at work are fewer among older employees. *Monthly Labor Review, 104,* 30–34.

Roper Organization. (1980). *The 1980 Virginia Slims American women's opinion poll.* Storrs: Roper Center, University of Connecticut.

Rosenthal, M. J., & Goodwin, J. S. (1985). Cognitive effects of nutritional deficiency. In H. H. Draper (Ed.), *Advances in nutritional research: Vol. 7* (pp. 71–100). New York: Plenum.

Rosow, I. (1967). *Social integration of the aged.* New York: Free Press.

Rosow, I. (1985). Status and role change through the life cycle. In R. H. Binstock & E. Shanas (Eds.), *Handbook of aging and the social sciences* (2nd ed.) (pp. 62–93). New York: Van Nostrand Reinhold.

Rosnow, R. L., & Georgoudi, M. (1986). The spirit of contextualism. In R. L. Rosnow & M. Georgoudi (Eds.), *Contextualism and understanding in behavioral science: Implications for research and theory* (pp. 3–22). New York: Praeger.

Ross, J. K. (1977). *Old people, new lives.* Chicago: University of Chicago Press.

Rossi, A. S. (1980). Aging and parenthood in the middle years. In P. B. Baltes & O. G. Brim, Jr. (Eds.), *Life-span development and behavior: Vol. 3* (pp. 137–205). New York: Academic Press.

Rossi, A. S. (Ed.) (1985). *Gender and the life course.* New York: Aldine.

Rowles, G. D. (1980). Growing old "inside": Aging and attachment to place in an Appalachian community. In N. Datan & N. Lohman (Eds.), *Transitions of aging* (pp. 153–170). New York: Academic Press.

Rowles, G. D. (1983). Geographical dimensions of social support in rural Appalachia. In G. D. Rowles & R. J. Ohta (Eds.), *Aging and milieu: Environmental perspectives on growing old* (pp. 111–130). New York: Academic Press.

Rowles, G. D., & Ohta, R. J. (1983). Emergent themes and new directions: Reflections on aging and milieu research. In G. D. Rowles & R. J. Ohta (Eds.), *Aging and milieu: Environmental perspectives on growing old* (pp. 231–240). New York: Academic Press.

Royce, A. P. (1982). *Ethnic identity: Strategies of diversity.* Bloomington: Indiana University Press.

Rubinstein, R. L. (1987). Never-married elderly as a social type: Reevaluating some images. *Gerontologist, 27,* 108–113.

Rudzitis, G. (1984). Geographical research and gerontology: An overview. *Gerontologist, 24,* 536–542.

Ryan, C. (1982). Alcoholism and premature aging: A neuropsychological perspective. *Alcoholism: Clinical and Experimental Research, 6,* 22–30.

Ryan, C., & Butters, N. (1980). Learning and memory complaints in young and old alcoholics: Evidence for the premature aging hypothesis. *Alcoholism: Clinical and Experimental Research, 4,* 288–293.

Ryckman, R. M., & Malikioski, M. (1975). Relationship between locus of control and chronological age. *Psychological Reports, 36,* 655–658.

Ryff, C. (1984). Personality development from the inside: The subjective experience of change in adulthood and aging. In P. B. Baltes & O. G. Brim, Jr. (Eds.), *Life-span development and behavior: Vol. 6* (pp. 243–279). New York: Academic Press.

Ryff, C., & Baltes, P. B. (1976). Value transition and adult development in women: The instrumentality-terminality sequence hypothesis. *Developmental Psychology, 12,* 567–568.

Ryff, C., & Heincke, S. G. (1983). The subjective organization of personality in adulthood and aging. *Journal of Personality and Social Psychology, 44,* 807–816.

Rykken, D. E. (1987). Sex in the later years. In P. Silverman (Ed.), *The elderly as modern pioneers* (pp. 125–144). Bloomington: Indiana University Press.

Saar, N., & Gordon, R. D. (1979). Variability of plasma catecholamine levels: Age, duration of posture and time of day. *British Journal of Clinical Pharmacology, 8,* 353–358.

Safilios-Rothschild, C. (1977). *Love, sex, and sex roles.* Englewood Cliffs, NJ: Prentice-Hall.

Sainsbury, P. (1986). The epidemiology of suicide. In A. Roy (Ed.), *Suicide* (pp. 17–40). Baltimore: Williams & Wilkins.

Salthouse, T. A. (1984). Effects of age and skill in typing. *Journal of Experimental Psychology: General, 113,* 345–371.

Salthouse, T. A. (1985). Speed of behavior and its implications for cognition. In J. E. Birren & K. W. Schaie (Eds.), *Handbook of the psychology of aging* (2nd ed.) (pp. 400–426). New York: Van Nostrand Reinhold.

Salthouse, T. A. (1988). The role of processing resources in cognitive aging. In M. L. Howe & C. J. Brainerd (Eds.), *Cognitive development in adulthood* (pp. 185–239). New York: Springer-Verlag.

Salthouse, T. A., Kausler, D. H., & Saults, J. S. (1988). Utilization of path analytic procedures to investigate the role of processing resources in cognitive aging. *Psychology and Aging, 3,* 158–166.

Salthouse, T. A., & Somberg, B. L. (1982). Isolating the age deficit in speeded performance. *Journal of Gerontology, 37,* 59–63.

Salzman, C. (1975). Electroconvulsive therapy. In R. Shader (Ed.), *Manual of psychiatric therapeutics* (pp. 115–124). Boston: Little, Brown.

REFERENCES

Salzman, C. (1984). *Clinical geriatric psycho-pharmacology.* New York: McGraw-Hill.

Salzman, C., & Shader, R. I. (1979). Clinical evaluation of depression in the elderly. In A. Raskin & L. F. Jarvik (Eds.), *Psychiatric symptoms and cognitive loss in the elderly* (pp. 39–72). Washington, DC: Hemisphere.

Samet, J., Hunt, W., & Key, C. (1986). Choice of cancer therapy varies with age of patient. *JAMA, 255,* 3385–3390.

Sanders, C. M. (1980–1981). Comparison of younger and older spouses in bereavement outcome. *Omega: Journal of Death and Dying, 11,* 217–232.

Sandler, D. P., Everson, R. B., & Wilcox, A. J. (1985). Passive smoking in adulthood and cancer risk. *American Journal of Epidemiology, 121,* 37–48.

Sanjek, R. (1984). *Crowded out: Homelessness and the elderly poor in New York City.* New York: Coalition for the Homeless.

Sarason, I. G., Sarason, B. R., & Johnson, J. H. (1985). Stressful life events: Measurement, moderators, and adaptation. In S. R. Burchfield (Ed.), *Stress: Psychological and physiological interactions* (pp. 241–262). Washington, DC: Hemisphere.

Saunders, C. (1977). Dying they live: St. Christopher's Hospice. In H. Feifel (Ed.), *New meanings of death.* New York: McGraw-Hill.

Scarr, S., & McCartney, K. (1983). How people make their own environments: A theory of genotype→ environment effects. *Child Development, 54,* 424–435.

Schachter, S. (1982). Recidivism and self-cure of smoking and obesity. *American Psychologist, 37,* 436–444.

Schaie, K. W. (1965). A general model for the study of developmental change. *Psychological Bulletin, 64,* 92–107.

Schaie, K. W. (1977). Quasi-experimental designs in the psychology of aging. In J. E. Birren & K. W. Schaie (Eds.), *Handbook of the psychology of aging* (pp. 38–58). New York: Van Nostrand Reinhold.

Schaie, K. W. (1977–1978). Toward a stage theory of adult cognitive development. *International Journal of Aging and Human Development, 8,* 129–138.

Schaie, K. W. (1979). The primary mental abilities in adulthood: An exploration in the development of psychometric intelligence. In P. B. Baltes & O. G. Brim, Jr. (Eds.), *Life-span development and behavior: Vol. 2* (pp. 67–115). New York: Academic Press.

Schaie, K. W. (1983). The Seattle longitudinal study: A twenty-one year exploration of psychometric intelligence in adulthood. In K. W. Schaie (Ed.), *Longitudinal studies of adult psychological development* (pp. 64–155). New York: Guilford.

Schaie, K. W. (1984). Historical time and cohort effects. In K. A. McCluskey & H. W. Reese (Eds.), *Life-span developmental psychology: Historical and generational effects* (pp. 1–45). New York: Academic Press.

Schaie, K. W., & Baltes, P. B. (1975). On sequential strategies and developmental research. *Human Development, 18,* 384–390.

Schaie, K. W., & Hertzog, C. (1983). Fourteen-year cohort-sequential studies of adult intelligence. *Developmental Psychology, 19,* 531–543.

Schaie, K. W., & Hertzog, C. (1985). Measurement in the psychology of adulthood and aging. In J. E. Birren & K. W. Schaie (Eds.), *Handbook of the psychology of aging* (2nd ed.) (pp. 61–92). New York: Van Nostrand Reinhold.

Schaie, K. W., & Labouvie-Vief, G. (1974). Generational versus ontogenetic components of change in adult cognitive behavior: A fourteen-year cross-sequential study. *Developmental Psychology, 10,* 305–320.

Schaie, K. W., Orchowsky, S., & Parham, I. A. (1982). Measuring age and sociocultural change: The case of race and life satisfaction. In R. C. Manuel (Ed.), *Minority aging, sociological and social psychological issues* (pp. 223–230). Westport, CT: Greenwood.

Schaie, K. W., & Parham, I. A. (1977). Cohort-sequential analysis of adult intellectual development. *Developmental Psychology, 13,* 649–653.

Schaie, K. W., & Strother, C. R. (1968). A cross-sequential study of age changes in cognitive behavior. *Psychological Bulletin, 70,* 671–680.

Schaie, K. W., & Willis, S. L. (1986). Can decline in adult intellectual functioning be reversed? *Developmental Psychology, 22,* 223–232.

Scheibel, A. B. (1982). Age-related changes in the human forebrain. *Neurosciences Research Progress Bulletin, 20,* 577–583.

Scheidt, R. J., & Schaie, K. W. (1978). A situational taxonomy for the elderly: Generating situational criteria. *Journal of Gerontology, 33,* 848–857.

Scheidt, R. J., & Windley, P. G. (1985). The ecology of aging. In J. E. Birren & K. W. Schaie (Eds.), *Handbook of the psychology of aging* (2nd ed.) (pp. 245–258).

Schein, E. H. (1975). How career anchors hold executives to their career paths. *Personnel, 52,* 11–24.

Schermerhorn, R. A. (1970). *Comparative ethnic relations: A framework for theory and research.* Chicago: University of Chicago Press.

Schiffman, S. (1977). Food recognition by the elderly. *Journal of Gerontology, 32,* 586–592.

Schiffman, S., & Covey, E. (1984). Changes in taste and smell with age: Nutritional aspects. In J. M. Ordy, D. Harman, & R. B. Alfin-Slater (Eds.), *Aging: Vol. 26. Nutrition in gerontology* (pp. 43–64). New York: Raven.

Schiffman, S., & Pasternak, M. (1979). Decreased discrimination of food odors in the elderly. *Journal of Gerontology, 34,* 73–79.

Schmitt, F. A., Murphy, M. D., & Sanders, R. E. (1981). Training older adults free recall rehearsal strategies. *Journal of Gerontology, 36,* 329–337.

Schneider, E. L., & Reed, J. D. (1985). Modulations of aging processes. In C. E. Finch & E. L. Schneider (Eds.), *Handbook of the biology of aging* (2nd ed.) (pp. 45–76). New York: Van Nostrand Reinhold.

Schneirla, T. C. (1957). The concept of development in comparative psychology. In D. B. Harris (Ed.), *The concept of development* (pp. 78–108). Minneapolis: University of Minnesota Press.

Schooler, K. K. (1982). Response of the elderly to environment: A stress-theoretical perspective. In M. P. Lawton, P. G. Windley, & T. O. Byerts (Eds.), *Aging and the environment: Theoretical approaches* (pp. 80–96). New York: Springer.

Schow, R., Christensen, J., Hutchinson, J., & Nerbonne, M. (1978). *Communication disorders of the aged: A guide for health professionals.* Baltimore: University Park Press.

Schuknecht, H. (1974). *Pathology of the ear.* Cambridge, MA: Harvard University Press.

Schultz, N. W. (1980). A cognitive-developmental study of the grandchild-grandparent bond. *Child Study Journal, 10,* 7–26.

Schulz, R. (1978). *The psychology of death, dying and bereavement.* Reading, MA: Addison-Wesley.

Schulz, R. (1985). Emotion and affect. In J. E. Birren & K. W. Schaie (Eds.), *Handbook of the psychology of aging* (2nd ed.) (pp. 531–543). New York: Van Nostrand Reinhold.

Schulz, R., & Hanusa, B. H. (1978). Long-term effects of control and predictability enhancing interventions: Findings and ethical issues. *Journal of Personality and Social Psychology, 35,* 1194–1201.

Schulz, R., Tompkins, C. A., & Rau, M. T. (1988). A longitudinal study of the psychosocial impact of stroke on primary support persons. *Psychology and Aging, 3,* 131–141.

Schwab, D. P., & Heneman, H. G., III. (1977). Age and satisfaction with dimensions of work. *Journal of Vocational Behavior, 10,* 212–222.

Scialfa, C. T., Kline, D. W., & Lyman, G. J. (1987). Age differences in target identification as a function of retinal location and noise level: Examination of the useful field of view. *Psychology and Aging, 2,* 14–19.

Scott, R. B., & Mitchell, M. C. (1988). Aging, alcohol, and the liver. *Journal of the American Geriatrics Society, 36,* 255–265.

REFERENCES

Sears, P. S., & Barbee, A. H. (1978). Career and life satisfaction among Terman's gifted women. In J. C. Stanley, W. C. George, & C. H. Solano (Eds.), *The gifted and the creative: Fifty year perspective* (pp. 28–66). Baltimore: Johns Hopkins University Press.

Selye, H. (1956). *The stress of life.* New York: Macmillan.

Selye, H. (1979). *The stress of my life: A scientist's memoirs.* New York: Van Nostrand Reinhold.

Selye, H. (1982). History and present status of the stress concept. In L. Goldberger & S. Breznitz (Eds.), *Handbook of stress: Theoretical and clinical aspects* (pp. 7–17). New York: Free Press.

Sendbeuhler, J. M., & Goldstein, S. (1977). Attempted suicide among the aged. *Journal of the American Geriatrics Society, 25,* 245–248.

Shainess, N. (1984). *Sweet suffering: Woman as victim.* Indianapolis: Bobbs-Merrill.

Shanas, E. (1972). Adjustment to retirement. In F. M. Carp. (Ed.), *Retirement* (pp. 219–244). Berkeley, CA: Behavioral Publications.

Shanas, E. (1980). Older people and their families: The new pioneers. *Journal of Marriage and the Family, 42,* 9–15.

Shand, A. E. (1920). *The foundations of character.* London: Macmillan.

Shapiro, D. H. (1985). Meditation and behavioral medicine: Application of a self-regulation strategy to the clinical management of stress. In S. R. Burchfield (Ed.), *Stress: Psychological and physiological interactions* (pp. 307–328). Washington, DC: Hemisphere.

Sheehy, G. (1976). *Passages.* New York: Dutton.

Sheehy, G. (1981). *Pathfinders.* New York: Morrow.

Shekelle, R. B., Gale, M., & Norusis, M. (1985). Type A score (Jenkins Activity Survey) and risk of recurrent heart disease in the aspirin myocardial infarction study. *American Journal of Cardiology, 56,* 221–225.

Shephard, R. J. (1978). *Physical activity and aging.* Chicago: Yearbook Medical.

Shephard, R. J. (1981). Cardiovascular limitations in the aged. In E. L. Smith & R. C. Serfass (Eds.), *Exercise and aging: The scientific basis* (pp. 19–30). Hillsdale, NJ: Erlbaum.

Shephard, R. J. (1982). *Physiology and biochemistry of exercise.* New York: Praeger.

Sheppard, H. L. (1976). Work and retirement. In R. H. Binstock & E. Shanas (Eds.), *Handbook of aging and the social sciences* (2nd ed.) (pp. 286–309). New York: Van Nostrand Reinhold.

Shinar, D., McDowell, E. D., Rackoff, N. J., & Rockwell, T. H. (1978). Field dependence and driver visual search behavior. *Human Factors, 20,* 553–559.

Shirom, A., & Mazeh, T. (1988). Periodicity in seniority–job satisfaction relationship. *Journal of Vocational Behavior, 33,* 38–49.

Shneidman, E. S. (1973). *Deaths of man.* New York: Quadrangle/New York Times.

Shore, R. J., & Hayslip, B., Jr. (1988, August). *Variables affecting grandchildren's perceptions of grandparents.* Paper presented at the meeting of the American Psychological Association, Atlanta.

Siedler, H., & Malamud, N. (1963). Creutzfeld-Jakob disease: Clinicopathologic report of 15 cases and review of the literature. *Journal of Neuropathology and Experimental Neurology, 22,* 381–402.

Siegel, R. K. (1980). The psychology of life after death. *American Psychologist, 35,* 911–931.

Siegler, I. C., & Gatz, M. (1985). Age patterns in locus of control. In E. Palmore, E. Bossé, G. Maddox, J. Nowlin, & I. C. Siegler (Eds.), *Normal aging 3.* Durham, NC: Duke University Press.

Siegler, I. C., George, L. K., & Okun, M. A. (1979). A cross-sequential analysis of adult personality. *Developmental Psychology, 15,* 350–351.

Silverman, P. (1987). Community settings. In P. Silverman (Ed.), *The elderly as modern pioneers* (pp. 185–210). Bloomington: Indiana University Press.

Simmons, L. W. (1945). *Role of the aged in primitive society.* New Haven, CT: Yale University Press.

Simon, A. (1980). The neuroses, personality disorders, drug use and misuses, and crime in the aged. In J. E. Birren & R. B. Sloane (Eds.), *Handbook of mental health and aging* (pp. 653–670). Englewood Cliffs, NJ: Prentice-Hall.

Simons, A. D., McGowan, C. R., Epstein, L. H., Kupfer, D. J., & Robertson, R. J. (1985). Exercise as a treatment for depression: An update. *Clinical Psychology Review, 5,* 553–568.

Singleton, W. T. (1979). Safety and risk. In W. T. Singleton (Ed.), *The study of real skills: Vol. 2. Compliance and excellence* (pp. 137–156). Baltimore: University Park Press.

Sinnott, J. D. (1982). Correlates of sex roles of older adults. *Journal of Gerontology, 37,* 587–594.

Sinnott, J. D. (1984a). *Everyday memory and solution of everyday problems.* Paper presented at the meeting of the American Psychological Association, Toronto.

Sinnott, J. D. (1984b). Postformal reasoning: The relativistic stage. In M. L. Commons, F. A. Richards, & C. Armon (Eds.), *Beyond formal operations: Late adolescent and adult cognitive development* (pp. 298–325). New York: Praeger.

Siskind, F. (1982). Another look at the link between work injuries and job experience. *Monthly Labor Review, 105,* 38–40.

Sivak, M., & Olson, P. L. (1982). Nighttime legibility of traffic signs: Conditions eliminating the effects of driver age and disability glare. *Accident Analysis and Prevention, 14,* 87–93.

Sivak, M., Olson, P. L., & Pastalan, L. A. (1981). Effect of driver's age on nighttime legibility of highway signs. *Human Factors, 23,* 59–64.

Sjogren, T., Sjogren, H., & Lindgren, A. G. H. (1952). Morbus Alzheimer and morbus Pick. *Acta Psychiatrica Scandinavica, 82*(Suppl.), 68–108.

Skolnick, A. (1975). Family revisited: Themes in recent social science research. *Journal of Interdisciplinary History, 5,* 703–719.

Skolnick, A. (1981). Married lives: Longitudinal perspectives on marriage. In D. H. Eichorn, J. A. Clausen, N. Haan, M. J. Honzik, & P. H. Mussen (Eds.), *Present and past in middle life* (pp. 269–298). New York: Academic Press.

Smith, A. D. (1975). Aging and interference with memory. *Journal of Gerontology, 30,* 319–325.

Smith, A. D. (1977). Adult age differences in cued recall. *Developmental Psychology, 13,* 326–331.

Smith, D. S. (1981). Historical change in the household structure of the elderly in economically developed societies. In R. W. Fogel, E. Hatfield, S. B. Kiesler, & J. March (Eds.), *Aging: Stability and change in the family* (pp. 91–114). New York: Academic Press.

Smith, E. L. (1988). The role of exercise in the prevention of bone involution. In R. Chernoff & D. A. Lipschitz (Eds.), *Health promotion and disease prevention in the elderly* (pp. 89–96). New York: Raven.

Smith, E. L., & Serfass, R. C. (Eds.). (1981). *Exercise and aging: The scientific basis.* Hillsdale, NJ: Erlbaum.

Smith, M., Colligan, M., Horning, R. W., & Hurrell, J. (1978). *Occupational comparison of stress-related disease incidence.* Cincinnati: National Institute for Occupational Safety and Health.

Smith, S. W., Rebok, G. W., Smith, W. R., Hall, S. E., & Alvin, M. (1983). Adult age differences in the use of story structure in delayed free recall. *Experimental Aging Research, 9,* 191–195.

Snyder, C. J., & Barrett, G. V. (1988). The Age Discrimination in Employment Act: A review of court decisions. *Experimental Aging Research, 14,* 3–47.

Sokolovsky, J., & Cohen, C. (1983). The cultural meaning of being a "loner" among the inner-city elderly. In J. Sokolovsky (ed.), *Growing old in different societies* (pp. 189–201). Belmont, CA: Wadsworth.

Sokolovsky, J., & Sokolovsky, J. (1982). *Aging and the aged in the Third World (Part 2): Regional and ethnographic.* Williamsburg, VA: Studies in Third World Societies (Publication No. 23).

Soldatos, C. R., Kales, J. D., Scharf, M. B., Bixler, E. O., & Kales, A. (1980). Cigarette smoking associated with sleep difficulty. *Science, 207,* 551–553.

Solnick, R. L., & Corby, N. (1983). Human sexuality and aging. In D. S. Woodruff & J. E. Birren (Eds.),

Aging: Scientific perspectives and social issues (2nd ed.) (pp. 202–224). Pacific Grove, CA: Brooks/Cole.

Somers, A. R. (1987). Insurance for long-term care: Some definitions, problems, and guidelines for action. *New England Journal of Medicine, 317,* 23–29.

Sontag, S. (1972, September 23). The double standard of aging. *Saturday Review,* pp. 29–38.

Sowers, J. R., Rubenstein, L. Z., & Stern, N. (1973). Plasma norepinephrine responses to posture and isometric exercise increase with age in the absence of obesity. *Journal of Gerontology, 38,* 315–317.

Spasoff, R. A., Kraus, A. S., Beattie, E. J., Holden, D. E. W., Lawson, J. S., Rodenburg, M., & Woodcock, G. M. (1978). Longitudinal study of elderly residents of long-stay institutions 1: Early response to institutional care. *Gerontologist, 18,* 281–292.

Speare, A., Jr., & Meyer, J. W. (1988). Types of elderly residential mobility and their determinants. *Journal of Gerontology, 43,* S74–S81.

Spilich, G. J. (1983). Life-span components of text processing: Structural and procedural differences. *Journal of Verbal Learning and Verbal Behavior, 22,* 231–244.

Spilich, G. J. (1985). Discourse comprehension across the life span. In N. Charness (Ed.), *Aging and human performance* (pp. 143–190). Chichester, England: Wiley.

Spirduso, W. W. (1980). Physical fitness, aging, and psychomotor speed: A review. *Journal of Gerontology, 35,* 850–865.

Spitzer, M. E. (1988). Taste acuity in institutionalized and noninstitutionalized elderly men. *Journal of Gerontology, 43,* P71–P74.

Spitzer, R. L., Endicott, J., & Robins, E. (1978). Research Diagnostic Criteria: Rationale and reliability. *Archives of General Psychiatry, 35,* 773–782.

Spokane, A. R. (1985). A review of research on person-environment congruence in Holland's theory of careers. *Journal of Vocational Behavior, 26,* 306–343.

Sporakowski, M. J., & Axelson, L. J. (1984). Long-term marriages: A critical review. *Lifestyles: A Journal of Changing Patterns, 7*(2), 76–93.

Stack, C. (1972). *All our kin: Strategies for survival in a Black community.* New York: Harper & Row.

Stanford, E. P., & Lockery, S. A. (1984). Aging and social relations in the Black community. In W. H. Quinn & G. A. Hughston (Eds.), *Independent aging: Family and social systems perspectives* (pp. 164–181). Rockville, MD: Aspen.

Stearns, P. N. (1977). *Old age in European society.* London: Croom Helm.

Steen, B. (1987). Nutrition and the elderly. In M. Bergener (Ed.), *Psychogeriatrics* (pp. 349–361). New York: Springer.

Stein, P. (1978). The lifestyles and life changes and the never married. *Marriage and Family Review, 1,* 1–11.

Stenback, A. (1980). Depression and suicidal behavior in old age. In J. E. Birren & R. B. Sloane (Eds.), *Handbook of mental health and aging* (pp. 616–652). Englewood Cliffs, NJ: Prentice-Hall.

Stephens, J. (1976). *Loners, losers, and lovers.* Seattle: University of Washington Press.

Stephens, L. R. (Ed.). (1975). *Reality orientation* (rev. ed.). Washington, DC: American Psychiatric Association.

Stephens, M. A. P., Norris, V. K., Kinney, J. M., Ritchie, S. W., & Grotz, R. C. (1988). Stressful situations in caregiving: Relations between caregiver coping and well-being. *Psychology and Aging, 3,* 208–209.

Sternberg, R. J. (1980). Sketch of a componential sub-theory of human intelligence. *Behavioral and Brain Sciences, 3,* 573–584.

Sternberg, R. J. (1985). *Beyond IQ: A triarchic theory of human intelligence.* Cambridge: Cambridge University Press.

Sternberg, R. J. (1986). A triangular theory of love. *Psychological Review, 93,* 119–135.

Sternberg, R. J., Conway, B. E., Ketron, J. L., & Bernstein, M. (1981). People's conceptions of intelligence. *Journal of Personality and Social Psychology, 41,* 37–55.

Sterns, H. L., Barrett, G. V., & Alexander, R. A. (1985). Accidents and the aging individual. In J. E. Birren & K. W. Schaie (Eds.), *Handbook of the psychology of aging* (2nd ed.) (pp. 703–724). New York: Van Nostrand Reinhold.

Sterns, H. L., Barrett, G. V., Alexander, R. A., Valasek, D., Forbringer, L. R., & Avolio, B. J. (1978). *Training and evaluation of older adult skills critical for effective driving performance.* Final report prepared for the Andrus Foundation of the NRTA/AARP. Cited in Sterns et al. (1985).

Sterns, H. L., Barrett, G. V., Alexander, R. A., Valasek, D., & McIlvried, J. (1984). *Research to improve diagnostic testing and training of older drivers.* Interim report prepared for the Andrus Foundation of the NRTA/AARP. Cited in Sterns et al. (1985).

Sterns, H. L., & Sanders, R. E. (1980). Training and education of the elderly. In R. R. Turner & H. W. Reese (Eds.), *Life-span developmental psychology: Intervention* (pp. 307–330). New York: Academic Press.

Stevens, J. C., Bartoshuk, L. M., & Cain, W. S. (1984). Chemical senses and aging: Taste versus smell. *Chemical Senses, 9,* 167–179.

Stevens, J. C., & Cain, W. S. (1985). Age-related deficiency in the perceived strength of six odorants. *Chemical Senses, 10,* 517–529.

Stevens, J. C., & Cain, W. S. (1986). Smelling via the mouth: Effect of aging. *Perception and Psychophysics, 40,* 142–146.

Stevens, J. C., & Cain, W. S. (1987). Old-age deficits in the sense of smell as gauged by thresholds, magnitude matching, and odor identification. *Psychology of Aging, 2,* 36–42.

Stevens, J. C., Plantinga, A., & Cain, W. S. (1982). Reduction of odor and nasal pungency associated with aging. *Neurobiology of Aging, 3,* 125–132.

Stevens-Long, J. (1988). *Adult life* (3rd ed.). Mountain View, CA: Mayfield.

Stine, E. L., Wingfield, A., & Poon, L. W. (1986). How much and how fast: Rapid processing of spoken language in later adulthood. *Psychology and Aging, 1,* 303–311.

Stoller, E. (1983). Parental caregiving by adult children. *Journal of Marriage and the Family, 45,* 851–858.

Stoller, E., & Earl, E. L. (1983). Help with activities of everyday life: Sources of support for the noninstitutionalized elderly. *Gerontologist, 23,* 64–70.

Storandt, M., & Wittels, I. (1975). Maintenance of functioning in relocation of community-dwelling older adults. *Journal of Gerontology, 30,* 608–612.

Storandt, M., Wittels, I., & Botwinick, J. (1975). Predictors of a dimension of well-being in relocated healthy aged. *Journal of Gerontology, 30,* 97–102.

Storck, P. A., Looft, R., & Hooper, F. H. (1972). Interrelationships among Piagetian tasks and traditional measures of cognitive abilities in mature and aged adults. *Journal of Gerontology, 27,* 461–465.

Strauss, A. L., & Glaser, B. G. (1970). *Anguish.* Mill Valley, CA: Sociology Press.

Streib, G. F. (1985). Social stratification and aging. In R. H. Binstock & E. Shanas (Eds.), *Handbook of aging and the social sciences* (2nd ed.) (pp. 339–368). New York: Van Nostrand Reinhold.

Streib, G. F., & Bourg, C. J. (1984). Age stratification theory, inequality, and social change. *Comparative Social Research, 7,* 63–77.

Streib, G. F., & Schneider, C. J. (1971). *Retirement in American society.* Ithaca, NY: Cornell University Press.

Super, D. E. (1957). *The psychology of careers.* New York: Harper & Row.

Super, D. E. (1980). A life span, life space approach to career development. *Journal of Vocational Behavior, 16,* 282–298.

Surwillo, W. W. (1975). Reaction-time variability, periodicities in reaction-time distributions, and the EEG gating signal hypothesis. *Biological Psychology, 3,* 247–261.

REFERENCES

Surwillo, W. W., & Quilter, R. E. (1964). Vigilance, age, and response time. *American Journal of Psychology, 77*, 614–620.

Sweer, L., Martin, D. C., Ladd, R. A., Miller, J. K., & Karpf, M. (1988). The medical evaluation of elderly patients with major depression. *Journal of Gerontology, 43*, M53–M58.

Swenson, C. H., Eskew, R. W., & Kohlhepp, K. A. (1981). Stages of the family life cycle, ego development, and the marriage relationship. *Journal of Marriage and the Family, 43*, 841–853.

Swenson, C. H., & Trahaug, G. (1985). Commitment and the long-term marriage relationship. *Journal of Marriage and the Family, 47*, 939–945.

Taietz, P. (1975). Community complexity and knowledge of facilities. *Journal of Gerontology, 30*, 357–362.

Taietz, P., & Milton, S. (1979). Rural-urban differences in the structure of services for the elderly in upstate New York counties. *Journal of Gerontology, 34*, 429–437.

Talley, T., & Kaplan, J. (1956). The Negro aged. *Newsletter of the Gerontological Society, 6*(December).

Tanfer, K. (1987). Patterns of premarital cohabitation among never-married women in the United States. *Journal of Marriage and the Family, 49*, 483–497.

Taub, H. A. (1979). Comprehension and memory of prose materials by young and old adults. *Experimental Aging Research, 5*, 3–13.

Teaff, J. D., Lawton, M. P., Nahemow, L., & Carlson, D. (1978). Impact of age integration on well-being of elderly tenants in public housing. *Journal of Gerontology, 33*, 126–133.

Templer, D., Ruff, C., & Franks, C. (1971). Death anxiety: Age, sex, and parental resemblance in diverse populations. *Developmental Psychology, 4*, 108–114.

Templer, D. I. (1972). Death anxiety in religiously very involved persons. *Psychological Reports, 31*, 361–362.

Terkel, S. (1974). *Working*. New York: Pantheon.

Teski, M. (1981). *Living together: An ethnography of a retirement hotel*. Washington, DC: University Press of America.

Thal, L. J. (1988). Treatment strategies. In M. K. Aronson (Ed.), *Understanding Alzheimer's disease*. New York: Scribner's.

Thayer, H. S. (1968). *Meaning and action: A critical history of pragmatism*. New York: Bobbs-Merrill.

Thayer, H. S. (Ed.). (1982). *Pragmatism: The classic writings*. Indianapolis: Hackett.

Thomae, H. (1970). Cognitive theory of personality and theory of aging. *Human development, 13*, 1–10.

Thomae, H. (Ed.). (1976). *Patterns of aging*. Basel: Karger.

Thomae, H. (1980). Personality and adjustment to aging. In J. E. Birren & R. B. Sloane (Eds.), *Handbook of mental health and aging* (pp. 285–301). Englewood Cliffs, NJ: Prentice-Hall.

Thomas, G. S., & Rutledge, J. H. (1986). Fitness and exercise for the elderly. In K. Dychtwald (Ed.), *Wellness and health promotion for the elderly* (pp. 165–178). Rockville, MD: Aspen.

Thomas, J. C., Waugh, N. C., & Fozard, J. L. (1978). Age and familiarity in memory scanning. *Journal of Gerontology, 33*, 528–533.

Thomas, J. L. (1985). Visual memory: Adult age differences in map recall and learning strategies. *Experimental Aging Research, 11*, 93–95.

Thomas, J. L. (1986a). Age and sex differences in perceptions of grandparenthood. *Journal of Gerontology, 41*, 417–423.

Thomas, J. L. (1986b). Gender differences in satisfaction with grandparenting. *Psychology and Aging, 1*, 215–219.

Thomas, J. L. (1988). Predictors of satisfaction with children's help for younger and older elderly parents. *Journal of Gerontology, 43*, S9–S14.

Thomas, J. L., Bence, S. L., & Meyer, S. M. (1988, August). *Grandparenting satisfaction: The roles of relationship meaning and perceived responsibility*. Paper presented at the meeting of the American Psychological Association, Atlanta.

Thomas, P. D., Hunt, W. C., Garry, P. J., Hood, R. B., Goodwin, J. M., & Goodwin, J. S. (1983). Hearing acuity in a healthy elderly population: Effects on emotional, cognitive, and social status. *Journal of Gerontology, 38,* 321–325.

Thompson, A. D. (1978). Alcohol and nutrition. *Clinics in Endocrinology and Metabolism, 7,* 405–428.

Thompson, L. W., & Gallagher, D. (1986). Treatment of depression in elderly outpatients. In G. Maletta & F. J. Pirozzolo (Eds.), *Advances in neurogerontology: Vol. 4. Assessment and treatment of the elderly patient.* New York: Praeger.

Thurstone, L. L. (1938). *Primary mental abilities.* Chicago: University of Chicago Press.

Tobach, E. (1981). Evolutionary aspects of the activity of the organism and its development. In R. M. Lerner & N. A. Busch-Rossnagel (Eds.), *Individuals as producers of their development: A life-span perspective* (pp. 37–68). New York: Academic Press.

Tobin, J. J. (1987). The American idealization of old age in Japan. *Gerontologist, 27,* 53–58.

Tobin, S. S., & Lieberman, M. A. (1976). *Last home for the aged.* San Francisco: Jossey-Bass.

Toffler, A. (1970). *Future shock.* New York: Random House.

Tomlinson, B. E., Blessed, G., & Roth, M. (1970). Observations on the brains of demented old people. *Journal of the Neurological Sciences, 11,* 205–242.

Tomlinson-Keasey, C. (1972). Formal operations in females from eleven to fifty-four years of age. *Developmental Psychology, 6,* 364.

Tomporowski, P. D., & Ellis, N. R. (1986). Effects of exercise on cognitive processes: A review. *Psychological Bulletin, 99,* 338–346.

Torrey, B. B. (1985). Sharing increasing costs on declining income: The visible dilemma of the invisible aged. *Milbank Memorial Fund Quarterly Health and Society, 63,* 377–394.

Treat, N. J., Poon, L. W., & Fozard, J. L. (1981). Age, imagery and practice in paired associate learning. *Experimental Aging Research, 7,* 337–342.

Treat, N. J., Poon, L. W., Fozard. J. L., & Popkin, S. J. (1978). Toward applying cognitive skill training to memory problems. *Experimental Aging Research, 4,* 305–319.

Troll, L. E. (1971). The family of later life: A decade review. *Journal of Marriage and the Family, 33,* 263–290.

Troll, L. E. (1975). *Early and middle adulthood: The best is yet to be — Maybe.* Pacific Grove, CA: Brooks/Cole.

Troll, L. E., & Bengtson, V. (1982). Intergenerational relations throughout the life span. In B. B. Wolman (Ed.), *Handbook of developmental psychology* (pp. 890–911). Englewood Cliffs, NJ: Prentice-Hall.

Troll, L. E., Miller, S. J., & Atchley, R. C. (1977). *Families in later life.* Belmont, CA: Wadsworth.

Turner, B. F. (1982). Sex-related differences in aging. In B. B. Wolman (Ed.), *Handbook of developmental psychology* (pp. 912–936). Englewood Cliffs, NJ: Prentice-Hall.

Turner, B. F. (1987). Mental health and the older woman. In G. Lesnoff-Caravaglia (Ed.), *Handbook of applied gerontology* (pp. 201–230). New York: Human Sciences Press.

Turner, R. M., & Ascher, L. M. (1982). Therapist factor in the treatment of insomnia. *Behavior Research and Therapy, 17,* 107–112.

Udry, J. R. (1971). Marital alternatives and marital disruption. *Journal of Marriage and the Family, 43,* 889–897.

Uhlenberg, P. (1987). A demographic perspective on aging. In P. Silverman (Ed.), *The elderly as modern pioneers* (pp. 145–160). Bloomington: Indiana University Press.

Uhlenberg, P. (1988). Aging and the social significance of cohorts. In J. E. Birren & V. L. Bengtson (Eds.), *Emergent theories of aging* (pp. 405–425). New York: Springer.

Uhlenberg, P., & Chew, K. S. Y. (1986). Changing place of remarriage in the life course. In D. Kertzer (Ed.), *Family relations in life course perspective.* Greenwich, CT: JAI.

Unger, R. K. (1979). *Female and male*. New York: Harper & Row.

United States Bureau of the Census. (1988). *Statistical abstract of the United States*. Washington, DC: U.S. Government Printing Office.

United States Department of Health and Human Services. (1984). *The health consequences of smoking: Chronic obstructive lung disease* (DHHS Publication No. PHS-50205). Washington, DC: U.S. Government Printing Office.

United States Department of Health and Human Services. (1988). *Vital statistics of the United States, 1985: Vol. 2. Mortality (Part A)*. Hyattsville, MD: Author.

United States Department of Labor. (1988). *Bureau of Labor Statistics*. Washington, DC: U.S. Government Printing Office.

United States Office of Technology Assessment. (1984). *Technology and aging in America*. Washington, DC: U.S. Government Printing Office.

Upp, M. (1983). Relative importance of various income sources of the aged, 1980. *Social Security Bulletin, 46*(January), 3–10.

VandenBos, G. R., DeLeon, P. H., & Pallack, M. S. (1982). An alternative to traditional medical care for the terminally ill. *American Psychologist, 37*, 1245–1248.

van Geert, P. (1987). The structure of Erikson's model of eight stages: A generative approach. *Human Development, 30*, 236–254.

Van Hoose, W. H., & Worth, M. R. (1982). *Adulthood in the life cycle*. Dubuque, IA: William C. Brown.

Van Maanen, J., & Schein, E. H. (1977). Career development. In R. J. Hackman & J. L. Suttle (Eds.), *Improving life at work* (pp. 30–95). New York: Goodyear.

Veatch, R. M. (1976). *Death, dying, and the biological revolution*. New Haven, CT: Yale University Press.

Venerable, W. R. (1974). Parental influence in college and vocational decisions. *Journal of the National Association of College Admissions Counselors, 19*, 9–12.

Vernon, S. W., & Roberts, R. E. (1982). Use of the SADS–RDS in a tri-ethnic community survey. *Archives of General Psychiatry, 39*, 47–52.

Verrillo, R. T., & Verrillo, V. (1985). Sensory and perceptual performance. In N. Charness (Ed.), *Aging and human performance* (pp. 1–46). Chichester, England: Wiley.

Verwoerdt, A. (1980). Anxiety, dissociative and personality disorders in the elderly. In E. W. Busse & D. G. Blazer (Eds.), *Handbook of geriatric psychiatry* (pp. 368–380). New York: Van Nostrand Reinhold.

Verwoerdt, A. (1981). *Clinical geropsychiatry* (2nd ed.). Baltimore: Williams & Wilkins.

Vickio, C. J., & Cavanaugh, J. C. (1985). Relationships among death anxiety, attitudes toward aging, and experience with death in nursing home employees. *Journal of Gerontology, 40*, 347–349.

Vickio, C. J., Cavanaugh, J. C., & Attig, T. (in press). Perceptions of grief among university students. *Death Studies*.

Viney, L. L. (1987). A sociophenomenological approach to life-span development complementing Erikson's sociodynamic approach. *Human Development, 30*, 125–136.

von Bertalanffy, L. (1933). *Modern theories of development*. London: Oxford University Press.

Waddell, K. J., & Rogoff, B. (1981). Effect of contextual organization on spatial memory of middle-aged and older women. *Developmental Psychology, 17*, 878–885.

Walford, R. L. (1983). Supergenes histocompatibility: Immunologic and other parameters in aging. In W. Regelson (Ed.), *Intervention in the aging process: Basic research, pre-clinical screening and clinical programs* (pp. 53–68). New York: Liss.

Walker, J. I., & Brodie, H. K. H. (1980). Neuropharmacology of aging. In E. W. Busse & D. G. Blazer (Eds.), *Handbook of geriatric psychiatry* (pp. 102–124). New York: Van Nostrand Reinhold.

Wall, P. D. (1975). Signs of plasticity and reconnection in spinal cord damage. In R. Porter & D. W. Fitzsimons (Eds.), *Outcome of severe damage to the central nervous system* (pp. 35–54). Amsterdam: Elsevier.

Wallace, A. F. C. (1971). Handsome Lake and the decline of the Iroquois matriarchate. In F. L. K. Hsu (Ed.), *Kinship and culture* (pp. 367–376). Chicago: Aldine-Atherton.

Wallace, J. (1985). Behavior modification methods as adjuncts to psychotherapy. In S. Zimberg, J. Wallace, & S. B. Blume (Eds.), *Practical approaches to alcoholism psychotherapy* (2nd ed.) (pp. 109–130). New York: Plenum.

Wallack, S. S., & Cohen, M. A. (1988). Costs of long-term care: Distribution and responsibility. In D. Evered & J. Whelan (Eds.), *Symposium on research and the aging population* (pp. 235–245). Chichester, England: Wiley.

Wallerstein, J. S., & Kelly, J. B. (1980). *Surviving the breakup: How children and parents cope with divorce.* New York: Basic Books.

Walsh, D. A., Krauss, I. K., & Regnier, V. A. (1981). Spatial ability, environmental knowledge, and environmental use: The elderly. In L. S. Liben, A. H. Patterson, & N. Newcombe (Eds.), *Spatial representation and behavior across the lifespan* (pp. 321–357). New York: Academic Press.

Walsh, E. K., & Cavanaugh, J. C. (1984, November). *Does hospice meet the needs of dying clients?* Paper presented at the meeting of the Gerontological Society of America, San Antonio.

Wantz, M. S., & Gay, J. E. (1981). *The aging process: A health perspective.* Cambridge, MA: Winthrop.

Wapner, S., Werner, H., & Comalli, P. E. (1960). Perception of part-whole relationships in middle and old age. *Journal of Gerontology, 15,* 412–415.

Ward, R. A. (1984a). *The aging experience: An introduction to social gerontology* (2nd ed.). New York: Harper & Row.

Ward, R. A. (1984b). The marginality and salience of being old: When is age relevant? *Gerontologist, 24,* 227–232.

Ward, R. A., & Kilburn, H. (1983). Community access and life satisfaction: Racial differences in later life. *International Journal of Aging and Human Development, 16,* 209–219.

Warrington, E. K., & Sanders, H. I. (1971). The fate of old memories. *Quarterly Journal of Experimental Psychology, 23,* 432–444.

Wattis, J. P. (1983). Alcohol and old people. *British Journal of Psychiatry, 143,* 306–307.

Waugh, N. C., Thomas, J. C., & Fozard, J. L. (1978). Retrieval time from different memory stores. *Journal of Gerontology, 33,* 718–724.

Weale, R. A. (1982). Senile ocular changes, cell death, and vision. In K. Dismukes, R. Sekuler, & D. Kline (Eds.), *Aging and human visual function.* New York: Liss.

Webb, W. B. (1975). *Sleep: The gentle tyrant.* New York: Spectrum.

Webb, W. B. (1982). Sleep in older persons: Sleep structures of 50- to 60-year-old men and women. *Journal of Gerontology, 37,* 581–586.

Webb, W. B., & Campbell, S. S. (1980). Awakenings and the return to sleep in an older population. *Sleep, 3,* 41–46.

Webb, W. B., & Dreblow, L. M. (1982). A modified method for scoring slow wave sleep of older subjects. *Sleep, 5,* 195–199.

Webb, W. B., & Levy, C. M. (1982). Age, sleep deprivation and performance. *Psychophysiology, 19,* 272–276.

Webb, W. B., & Swinburne, H. (1971). An observational study of sleep in the aged. *Perceptual and Motor Skills, 32,* 895–898.

Wechsler, D. (1958). *The measurement and appraisal of adult intelligence* (4th ed.). Baltimore: Williams & Wilkins.

Weg, R. B. (1983). The physiological perspective. In R. B. Weg (Ed.), *Sexuality in the later years* (pp. 39–80). New York: Academic Press.

Weiffenbach, J. M., Baum, B. J., & Burghauser, R. (1982). Taste thresholds: Quality specific variation with human aging. *Journal of Gerontology, 37,* 372–377.

Weiner, M. B., Brok, A. J., & Snadowski, A. M. (1987). *Working with the aged* (2nd ed.). Norwalk, CT: Appleton-Century-Crofts.

Weiner, R. D. (1979). The psychiatric use of electrically induced seizures. *American Journal of Psychiatry, 136,* 1507–1517.

Weiner, R. D. (1983). EEG related to electroconvulsive therapy. In J. R. Hughes & W. P. Wilson (Eds.), *EEG and evoked potentials in psychiatry and behavioral neurology* (pp. 101–126). Woburn, MA: Butterworth.

Weingartner, H., Cohen, R. M., & Bunney, W. E. (1982). Memory-learning impairments in progressive dementia and depression. *American Journal of Psychiatry, 139,* 135–136.

Weingartner, H., & Silberman, E. (1982). Models of cognitive impairment: Cognitive changes in depression. *Psychopharmacology Bulletin, 18,* 27–42.

Weisfeldt, M. L. (1980). Left ventricular function. In M. L. Weisfeldt (Ed.), *Aging: Vol. 12. The aging heart: Its function and response to stress* (pp. 297–316). New York: Raven.

Weishaus, S., & Field, D. (1988). A half century of marriage: Continuity or change? *Journal of Marriage and the Family, 50,* 763–774.

Weisman, A. D. (1972). *On dying and denying.* New York: Behavioral Publications.

Weiss, R. S. (1975). *Marital separation.* New York: Basic Books.

Weitz, S. (1977). *Sex roles.* New York: Oxford University Press.

Weitzman, L. J. (1985). *The divorce revolution: The unexpected social and economic consequences for women and children in America.* New York: Free Press.

Welford, A. T. (1977). Motor performance. In J. E. Birren & K. W. Schaie (Eds.), *Handbook of the psychology of aging* (pp. 450–496). New York: Van Nostrand Reinhold.

Welford, A. T. (1980). Sensory, perceptual, and motor processes in older adults. In J. E. Birren & R. B. Sloane (Eds.), *Handbook of mental health and aging* (pp. 192–213). Englewood Cliffs, NJ: Prentice-Hall.

Wells, C. E. (1979). Pseudodementia. *American Journal of Psychiatry, 136,* 895–900.

Wells, L., & Macdonald, G. (1981). Interpersonal networks and post-relocation adjustment of the institutionalized elderly. *Gerontologist, 21,* 177–183.

Wentkowski, G. (1985). Older women's perceptions of great-grandparenthood: A research note. *Gerontologist, 25,* 593–596.

Wessler, R., Rubin, M., & Sollberger, A. (1976). Circadian rhythm of activity and sleep-wakefulness in elderly institutionalized patients. *Journal of Interdisciplinary Cycle Research, 7,* 333.

West, R. L. (1984, August). *An analysis of prospective everyday memory.* Paper presented at the meeting of the American Psychological Association, Toronto.

West, R. L. (1986a). Everyday memory and aging. *Developmental Neuropsychology, 2,* 323–344.

West, R. L. (1986b). *Memory fitness over 40.* Gainesville, FL: Triad.

West, R. L., & Walton, M. (1985, March). *Practical memory functioning in the elderly.* Paper presented at the National Forum on Research in Aging, Lincoln, NE.

Whitbourne, S. K. (1985). *The aging body.* New York: Springer.

Whitbourne, S. K. (1986). *The me I know: A study of adult identity.* New York: Springer-Verlag.

Whitbourne, S. K. (1987). Personality development in adulthood and old age: Relationships among identity style, health, and well-being. In K. W. Schaie (Ed.), *Annual review of gerontology and geriatrics: Vol. 7* (pp. 189–216). New York: Springer.

White, A. T., & Spector, P. E. (1987). An investigation of age-related factors in the age-job satisfaction relationship. *Psychology and Aging, 2,* 261–265.

White, L. K., & Booth, A. (1985). The quality and stability of remarriages: The role of stepchildren. *American Sociological Review, 50,* 689–698.

White, N., & Cunningham, W. (1984, November). *The relationships among memory complaint, memory performance, and depression in young and elderly adults.* Paper presented at the meeting of the Gerontological Society of America, San Antonio.

Whitehouse, P. J., Price, D. L., Struble, R. G., Clark, W. W., Coyle, J. T., & De Long, M. R. (1982). Alzheimer's disease and senile dementia: Loss of neurons in the basal forebrain. *Science, 215,* 1237–1239.

Whitlock, F. A. (1986). Suicide and physical illness. In A. Roy (Ed.), *Suicide* (pp. 151–170). Baltimore: Williams & Wilkins.

Wiener, J. M. (1988, Winter). Financing options for long-term care. *Living-at-Home,* pp. 1–3.

Wiener, Y., & Vaitenas, R. (1977). Personality and developmental correlates of voluntary and mid-career change in enterprising occupations. *Gerontologist, 17,* 132.

Wiens, A. N., & Menustik, C. E. (1983). Treatment outcome and patient characteristics in an aversion therapy program for alcoholism. *American Psychologist, 38,* 1089–1096.

Wilkie, F., & Eisdorfer, C. (1971). Intelligence and blood-pressure in the aged. *Science, 172,* 959.

Williams, J. H. (1977). *Psychology of women.* New York: Norton.

Williams, S. A., Denney, N. W., & Schadler, M. (1983). Elderly adults' perception of their own cognitive development during the adult years. *International Journal of Aging and Human Development, 16,* 147–158.

Willis, S. L. (1987). Cognitive training and everyday competence. In K. W. Schaie (Ed.), *Annual review of gerontology and geriatrics: Vol. 7* (pp. 159–188). New York: Springer.

Willis, S. L., Blieszner, R., & Baltes, P. B. (1981). Intellectual training research in aging: Modification of performance on the fluid ability of figural relations. *Journal of Educational Psychology, 73,* 41–50.

Willis, S. L., & Schaie, K. W. (1986). Training the elderly on the ability factors of spatial orientation and inductive reasoning. *Psychology and Aging, 1,* 239–247.

Willis, S. L., Schaie, K. W., & Lueers, N. (1983, April). *Fluid-crystallized ability correlates of real life tasks.* Paper presented at the meeting of the Society for Research in Child Development, Detroit.

Wilson, B., & Moffat, N. (Eds.). (1984). *Clinical management of memory problems.* Rockville, MD: Aspen.

Wiseman, R. F. (1981). Community environments for the elderly. In F. J. Berghorn, D. E. Schafer, and Associates (Eds.), *The dynamics of aging.* Boulder, CO: Westview.

Wiswell, R. A. (1980). Relaxation, exercise, and aging. In J. E. Birren & R. B. Sloane (Eds.), *Handbook of mental health and aging* (pp. 943–958). Englewood Cliffs, NJ: Prentice-Hall.

Wittels, I., & Botwinick, J. (1974). Survival in relocation. *Journal of Gerontology, 29,* 440–443.

Wittkowski, J. (1981). *Attitudes toward death and dying in older persons and their dependence on life satisfaction and death-related experiences.* Paper presented at the International Congress of Gerontology, Hamburg.

Wohlwill, J. F. (1973). *The study of behavioral development.* New York: Academic Press.

Wolf, E. (1960). Glare and age. *Archives of Ophthalmology, 60,* 502–514.

Wood, V., & Robertson, J. F. (1978). Friendship and kinship interaction: Differential effect on morale of the elderly. *Journal of Marriage and the Family, 40,* 367–375.

Woodruff, D. S. (1985). Arousal, sleep, and aging. In J. E. Birren & K. W. Schaie (Eds.), *Handbook of the psychology of aging* (2nd ed.) (pp. 261–295). New York: Van Nostrand Reinhold.

Woodruff-Pak, D. S. (1988). *Psychology and aging.* Englewood Cliffs, NJ: Prentice-Hall.

Woolf, A. D., & Dixon, A. St. J. (1988). *Osteoporosis: A clinical guide.* Philadelphia: Lippincott.

Wright, R. E. (1981). Aging, divided attention, and processing capacity. *Journal of Gerontology, 36,* 605–614.

Yankelovich, D. (1981). *New rules: Searching for self-fulfillment in a world turned upside down.* New York: Random House.

NAME INDEX

SUBJECT INDEX